Bosnia & Herzegovina

the Bradt Travel Guide

Tim Clancy

Updated by Maria Hetman

edition
5

www.bradtguides.com

Bradt Travel Guides Ltd, UK
The Globe Pequot Press Inc, USA

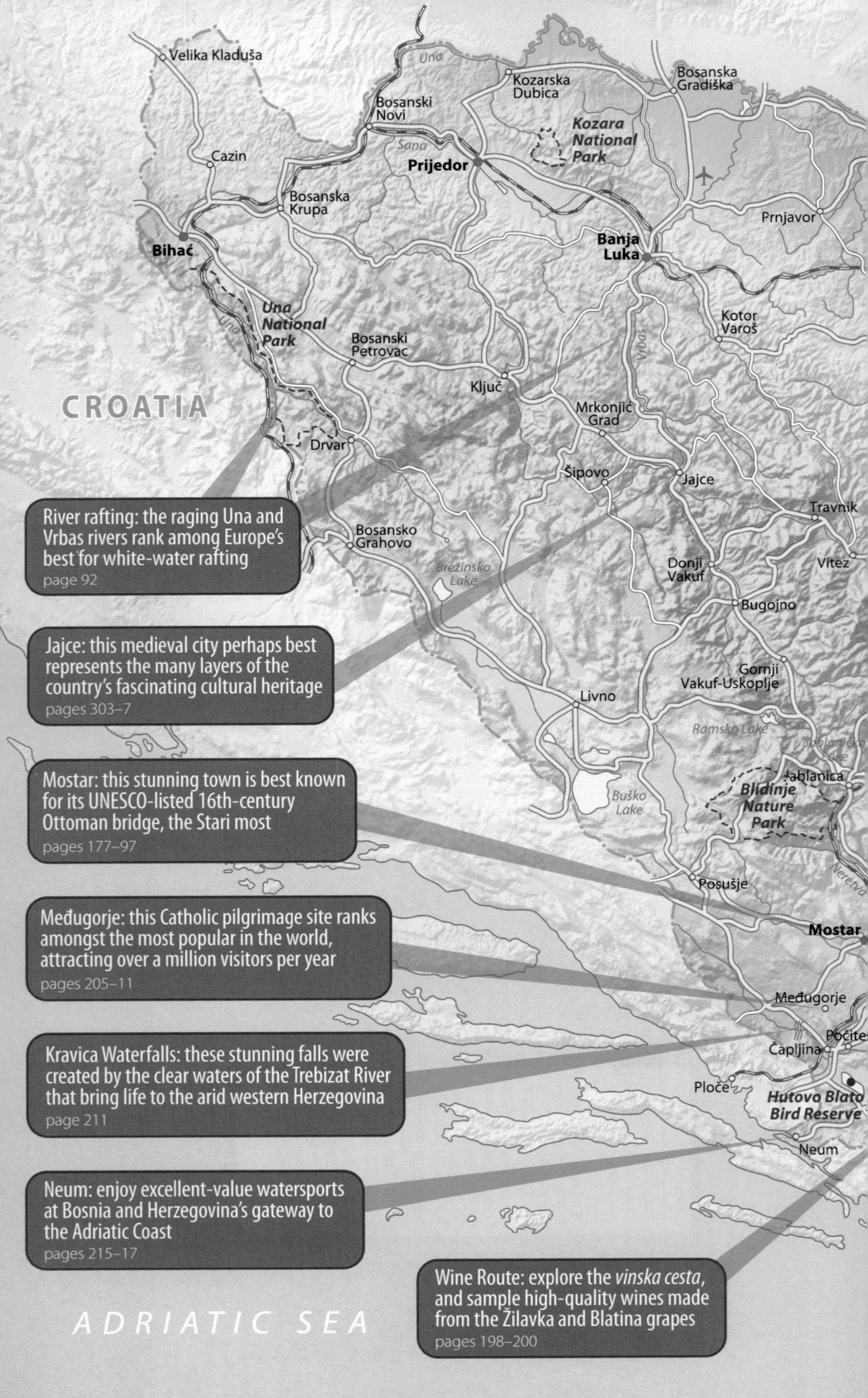
Velika Kladuša
Una
Kozarska Dubica
Bosanska Gradiška
Bosanski Novi
Kozara National Park
Cazin
Sana
Prijedor
Bosanska Krupa
Prnjavor
Bihać
Banja Luka
Una National Park
Una
Kotor Varoš
Vrbas
Bosanski Petrovac
Ključ
CROATIA
Mrkonjić Grad
Drvar
Šipovo
Jajce
Travnik
Bosansko Grahovo
Brežinsko Lake
Donji Vakuf
Vitez
Bugojno
Gornji Vakuf-Uskoplje
Livno
Ramsko Lake
Jablaničko Lake
Jablanica
Blidinje Nature Park
Buško Lake
Posušje
Neretva
Mostar
Međugorje
Počitelj
Čapljina
Ploče
Hutovo Blato Bird Reserve
Neum
ADRIATIC SEA
River rafting: the raging Una and Vrbas rivers rank among Europe's best for white-water rafting
page 92
Jajce: this medieval city perhaps best represents the many layers of the country's fascinating cultural heritage
pages 303–7
Mostar: this stunning town is best known for its UNESCO-listed 16th-century Ottoman bridge, the Stari most
pages 177–97
Međugorje: this Catholic pilgrimage site ranks amongst the most popular in the world, attracting over a million visitors per year
pages 205–11
Kravica Waterfalls: these stunning falls were created by the clear waters of the Trebizat River that bring life to the arid western Herzegovina
page 211
Neum: enjoy excellent-value watersports at Bosnia and Herzegovina's gateway to the Adriatic Coast
pages 215–17
Wine Route: explore the vinska cesta, and sample high-quality wines made from the Žilavka and Blatina grapes
pages 198–200

KEY
Capital city
Other city
Main town
Other town
Airport
Main road
Other road
Railway
National/nature park
International boundary
Slavonski Brod
Bosanski Brod
Bosanski Šamac
Županja
Derventa
Modriča
Gradačac
Brčko
Sava
Doboj
Bijeljina
Srebrenik
Tešanj
Tuzla
Maglaj
Lukavac
Lake Modrac
Živinice
Žepče
Zavidovići
Banovići
Zvornik
Zvorničko Reservoir
Tajan Nature Park
Zenica
Vareš
Vlasenica
Bratunac
Srebrenica
Drina
SERBIA
Visoko
Perućačko Reservoir
SARAJEVO
Ilidža
Hadžići
Pale
Višegrad
Lukomir
Goražde
Konjic
Neretva
Foča
Sutjeska National Park
Maglić 2386m
Stolac
MONTENEGRO
Bileća
Bilećko Lake
Trebinje
Dubrovnik
Tajan Nature Park: this beautiful little corner of Bosnia is a haven for nature lovers
pages 333–4
Sarajevo: one of Europe's most unique capitals, embracing the footprints left from both East and West
pages 105–44
Olympic ski resorts: top-notch skiing can still be had on the same slopes as when Sarajevo hosted the XIV Winter Olympic Games in 1984
pages 147–56
Lukomir: a rare window to old-world Europe where the traditional way of life is still the rule and not the exception
page 156
Sutjeska National Park: home to the Perućica Primeval Forest and Bosnia and Herzegovina's highest peak, Mt Maglic
pages 163–5
Blagaj: home to the mystical 16th-century Turkish Dervish Monastery, built into the high cliffs alongside the source of the River Buna
pages 200–3
0 50km
0 30 miles

Bosnia & Herzegovina Don't miss...

Medieval hilltop towns

With its stunning hilltop citadel, Ottoman-style homes and cascading waterfalls, the time warped town of Jajce is a must-see

(LK/A) pages 303–7

River rafting

River rafting on the gorgeous Una and Vrbas rivers is an unforgettable experience for novices and experts alike

(AT/S) page 92

Sutjeska National Park
Situated right up against the Montenegrin border, Sutjeska National Park boasts excellent hiking and astounding, untouched landscapes
(DT/S) pages 163–5

Sarajevo's old town
Walk through the *Baščaršija* in Sarajevo to experience the city's Ottoman past. Shopping, drinking Turkish coffee or just strolling through the craftsmen's quarters are pure delights
(F/S) pages 132–8

Međugorje
The second-largest Catholic pilgrimage site in the world, Međugorje is a popular day trip for the faithful and sceptics alike
(N/S) pages 205–11

Bosnia & Herzegovina in colour

left Situated in one of the most beautiful valleys of the Balkan peninsula, the cobbled, oriental town of Mostar is not to be missed (SS) pages 177–97

below Bosnia and Herzegovina is proud to have its own little slice of the Adriatic, even if it is only a 24km strip. Pictured, Neum seafront (A/S) pages 215–17

bottom Boasting 260 sunny days per year, a mild Mediterranean climate and the crystal-clear Trebišnjica River, Trebinje ranks among the most attractive towns in Herzegovina (LK/S) pages 220–28

above The unique Ottoman-era town of Počitelj was heavily damaged during the war but has been reconstructed to its former glory. Climb the steps to the fortress at the top of the town for stunning views (BN/S) page 203

below Banja Luka's 16th-century fortress has been home to every historical group moving through this strategically located town (LK/A) pages 278–91

above The Ethno Village Stanišić in Bijeljina has an array of facilities ranging from an open-air museum to a cocktail bar (NB/S) page 322

left It would be a shame not to make the 5km trip from Jajce to visit the wonderful medieval Pliva Watermills, some of which have been restored and are now functional (BS/S) pages 306–7

below At 1,469m above sea level, Lukomir is Bosnia and Herzegovina's highest and most isolated village, offering a charming glimpse of life in medieval Europe (TC) page 156

AUTHOR

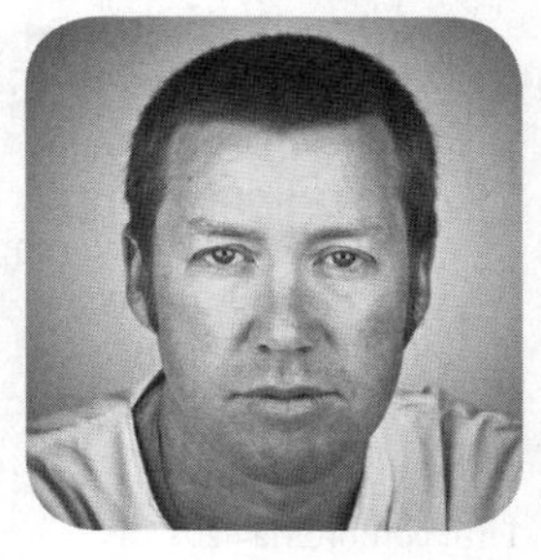

Tim Clancy was brought to the Balkans by a simple twist of fate in late 1992, when he hitched a ride from Germany to Croatia to join the grass-roots relief agency Suncokret (meaning 'sunflower'), which was involved in aid work in a refugee camp in western Herzegovina. His three-week stint turned into a two-decade commitment, and he now calls Bosnia home. Tim worked in refugee camps with women and children from all over Bosnia and Croatia and eventually saw out the end of the war as an active humanitarian in the besieged eastern quarters of Mostar. Driving aid convoys throughout the country had introduced him to its pristine nature and fabulous highlander traditions, a side of Bosnia and Herzegovina (BiH) that few people know of and one he thought worth helping to protect and preserve. After several years of development work in BiH, Montenegro, Albania and Kosovo following the war, Tim spent a year hiking through the mountains and learning more about the highland cultures. In 2000 he and some friends formed Green Visions, the first ecotourism and environment protection group in the country. Since then he has been dedicated to environmental activism, ecologically responsible development of BiH's cultural, historical and natural heritage, and changing the widespread negative image of Bosnia and Herzegovina as a tourism and environment consultant for the EU, UNDP and local governments. He recently co-founded an NGO called Terra Dinarica dedicated to the sustainable development of the Via Dinarica mega-trail that stretches from Albania to Slovenia.

UPDATER

Maria Hetman first came to Bosnia and Herzegovina on a one-way ticket in 2009 to work as a journalist for a summer, and immediately felt compelled to immerse herself in the local culture. The beautiful scenery, unspoiled nature, and warm hospitality of the region cast their spell on her, and she ended up staying much longer than planned. She lived in Sarajevo for six years, in Croatia for a year, and Montenegro for several months. She has travelled extensively in BiH and neighbouring countries. Maria has written numerous articles about tourism and environmental and social issues in BiH and Croatia, and has worked on projects with a number of local and international NGOs and media. She is fluent in Bosnian/Croatian/Serbian. Her strongest interests relate to working on policies and initiatives that protect the environment from exploitation, support sustainable agriculture, and enable local communities to thrive. She recommends hiking in the mind-blowing mountains of Herzegovina, trying local wine and food especially anything with wild plants like nettle, wild garlic or mushrooms, listening to people's stories, and river rafting.

PUBLISHER'S FOREWORD

Hilary Bradt

The launch party for the first edition of this guide was quite something: the ornate splendour of Lancaster House (built for a prince), hosted by Paddy Ashdown, and attended by a host of luminaries including author Tim Clancy, who has done as much as anyone to convince tourists that the country is not only safe but welcoming. They know that now. The tiny trickle of visitors that used Tim's book in the early days has become a regular stream, guided by his informed advice (carefully updated for this fifth edition by Maria Hetman). Bosnia and Herzegovina remains one of Europe's best-kept secrets. That's fine by us.

Fifth edition May 2017
First published 2004

Bradt Travel Guides Ltd
IDC House, The Vale, Chalfont St Peter, Bucks SL9 9RZ, England
www.bradtguides.com
Published in the USA by The Globe Pequot Press Inc,
PO Box 480, Guilford, Connecticut 06437-0480

Updated by Maria Hetman

Project managers: Claire Strange and Edward Alexander
Cover image research: Pepi Bluck

British Library Cataloguing in Publication Data
A catalogue record for this book is available from the British Library

ISBN: 978 1 78477 018 1 (print)
e-ISBN: 978 1 78477 163 8 (e-pub)
e-ISBN: 978 1 78477 263 5 (mobi)

Photographs Alamy: Ladi Kirn (LK/A); Dreamstime: Acgdzlxyq (A/DT), Marnel Tomic (MT/DT), Slavenko Vukasovic (SV/DT); FLPA: Biosphoto, Berndt Fischer (B/BF/FLPA), Jules Cox (JC/FLPA), Michael Callan (MC/FLPA), Winfried Wisniewski (WW/FLPA); Shutterstock: 369_photo (369/S), Adnan Vejzovic (AV/S), Aleksandar Todorovic (AT/S), asiastock (A/S), Berna Namoglu (BN/S), Boris Stroujko (BS/S), Dan Tautan (DT/S), evronphoto (E/S), Fotokon (F/S), Lena.Ko (LK/S), L Nagy (LN/S), Lucertolone (L/S), mariocigic (M/S), Nenad Basic (NB/S), Nightman1965 (N/S), Pe3k (P/S), Pim Leijen (PL/S), salajean (S/S); Superstock (SS); Tan Yilmaz (TY); Tim Clancy (TC); Tourism Association of Bosnia and Herzegovina (TABH)

Front cover Sebilj, Sarajevo (TY)
Back cover Ramsko Lake (LN/S)
Title page Stari most, Mostar (L/S); *Stećci* tombstones (TABH); Haystacks above Liplje Monastery (E/S)

Maps David McCutcheon FBCart.S; colour map relief base by Nick Rowland FRGS

Typeset by Ian Spick and Dataworks, India
Production managed by Jellyfish Print Solutions; printed in the UK
Digital conversion by dataworks.co.in

Acknowledgements

As I enter into the fifth edition of this guidebook I find a tremendous amount of people I would like to thank, including the countless young Bosnians and Herzegovinians who share the vision of an eco-friendly, sustainable Bosnia and Herzegovina. Since I wrote the first edition there has been so much progress in the tourism industry, and particularly with new local initiatives from young people who are enthused to show the world their little part of this magnificent country.

Where to start? I must certainly thank Mr John Bell. I'd always wanted to write a book about Bosnia and Herzegovina, but it was John who encouraged me to do it and then searched for a publisher for me.

Velika hvala to Alen Lepirica. (If you've never met a human encyclopaedia with a poetic touch, then you should meet Alen.) Thanks for all the little details that give the guide such richness, and for sharing with me so many parts of this beautiful country. Hana Curak, Maggie Cormack and Nejra Hodzic helped me swim through a sea of fact checks to make sure all the website and email addresses were correct and up to date.

Noel Malcolm's *Bosnia: A Short History* helped put a lot of the pieces together of a very complicated history and Ivan Lovrenović and his *Bosnia: A Cultural History* contributed significantly to my perspective on culture and history. Thanks to Jonathan Karkut for casting a careful eye over the history and politics sections, and to Iona Hill for her input on diving. Aleksandar Petkovic's journalism made me greatly appreciate a Yugoslavia I never saw or knew. I must thank Mark Wheeler for helping me to put all these ideas and opposing views of history in perspective. Bosnia and Herzegovina belongs to no-one … and yet to everyone.

The path I was led along brought me to a war zone and 20 years later I call it home. Thank you Bosnia and Herzegovina.

Tim Clancy

AUTHOR'S STORY *Tim Clancy*

Researching and writing *Bosnia & Herzegovina* has taken a lot of work. I've found that since writing the first edition in 2004 the number of tourism service providers has increased tenfold, with many welcome additions in terms of accommodation, tourist information and a plethora of activities for visitors, from rafting centres and upgraded skiing facilities to new hotels and traditional restaurants. Revisiting *Bosnia & Herzegovina* is always a challenge but a rewarding one indeed. It is an honour and a privilege to express my knowledge of – and passion for – the country and its people with the freedom many other writers can only dream of.

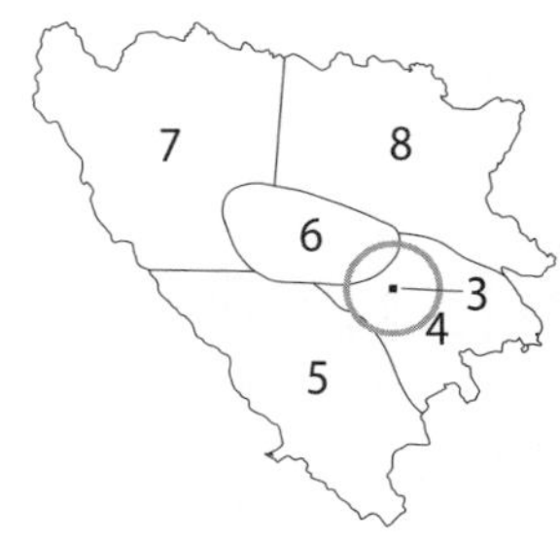

Contents

LIST OF MAPS

Introduction

I have spent a considerable amount of time recently reading all the reviews of my previous four editions of *Bosnia & Herzegovina*, and rereading all the emails and letters I received from thrilled and not-so-thrilled readers. Thank you all for your compliments and criticisms. They have helped in reshaping (and hopefully improving) this fifth edition.

I do hope that my passion for this place and its people does not blur my vision of what Bosnia and Herzegovina realistically has to offer for first-time visitors. If you've already been, you'll know well the charms and frustrations of this tiny central Balkan nation. I have taken considerable care to step back and reassess how easy and/or difficult it may be to navigate a country with tremendous tourism potential but also with limited infrastructure, information and travel services.

My enthusiasm for Bosnia and Herzegovina as a unique and dynamic tourism destination has not waned in the slightest. The country has made tremendous strides in the tourism sector since the first edition of this book in 2004. It continues its ardent attempt to recover from the devastation brought by the conflict of the 1990s. To be honest, it still has a long way to go to adequately address the many challenges of catering to foreign visitors but it is a raw, real and heck of a lot of fun place to visit.

Have no doubt that this country will dazzle you with its natural beauty. I make no exaggerations when it comes to praising the wonders of Mother Nature. This place is truly blessed with some of the most impressive scenery in southeast Europe. BiH will intrigue you with its melange of cultural heritage. Despite the conflict that ravaged the country in the early 1990s, you will find it to be a true crossroads between East and West.

Make no mistake, you will also get annoyed with the lack of road signs for certain destinations. Things like bus or train schedules will undoubtedly be changed, and it is near impossible to track them. Working hours of restaurants or attractions will not always be respected. A taxi driver just might overcharge you. Some of Bosnia and Herzegovina's best places to see are only reachable by rough gravel tracks where you can easily lose your way. It's just part of the trip.

That is Bosnia and Herzegovina. It is raw. It is beautiful. It is a place that requires you to adjust to it rather than it adjusting to tourists. To some that is frustrating, but to others it makes it a place of rare originality and authenticity.

Bosnia and Herzegovina continues to be wracked with political and economic turmoil, although this may be barely noticeable to travellers. Despite the long post-war transition, most will find BiH an attractive tourism destination with only the faint physical scars of war. Do not expect top-notch Western-style service and facilities everywhere you go, however, but do not be too surprised either if you are treated as an honoured guest in the most unexpected of places. The people of this country are warm and friendly. Your contribution as a visitor to Bosnia and Herzegovina is critical to its recovery – both economically and spiritually.

I warmly encourage you to seek out local products. Sleep in family-owned bed and breakfasts and small *pansions*. Find local tour operators and guides who will give you invaluable insight into Bosnia and Herzegovina. As a nature lover I also highly recommend that you bring your hiking boots; the walking and hiking here are truly spectacular. Enjoy your trip.

FEEDBACK REQUEST AND UPDATES WEBSITE

At Bradt Travel Guides we're aware that guidebooks start to go out of date on the day they're published – and that you, our readers, are out there in the field doing research of your own. You'll find out before us when a fine new family-run hotel opens or a favourite restaurant changes hands and goes downhill. So why not write and tell us about your experiences? Contact us on 01753 893444 or e info@bradtguides.com. We will forward emails to the author who may post updates on the Bradt website at www.bradtupdates.com/bosnia. Alternatively you can add a review of the book to www.bradtguides.com or Amazon.

HOW TO USE THIS GUIDE

MAPS

Keys and symbols Maps include alphabetical keys covering the locations of those places to stay, eat or drink that are featured in the book. Note that regional maps may not show all hotels and restaurants in the area: other establishments may be located in towns shown on the map.

Grids and grid references Several maps use gridlines to allow easy location of sites. Map grid references are listed in square brackets after the name of the place or site of interest in the text, with page number followed by grid number, eg: [103 C3].

ABBREVIATIONS Some of the more common abbreviations you might encounter on your travels in Bosnia and Herzegovina or within the pages of this guidebook are:

bb (*bez broja*) used in street addresses to indicate a house or other building with no number; sometimes used in small rural settlements

BiH Bosnia and Herzegovina

Ul (*ulica*) street

WEBSITES Although all third party websites were working at the time of going to print, some may cease to function during this edition's lifetime. If a website doesn't work, you might want to check back at another time as they often function intermittently. Alternatively, you can let us know of any website issues by emailing info@bradtguides.com.

LANGUAGE Grammatically, the Bosnian, Croatian and Serbian languages have cases. This means that the endings of nouns and adjectives alter depending upon their quantity and function within a sentence. You are most likely to encounter these differences in street names and on maps, but rest assured that it is not a huge reason for concern – Bosnians will not judge a visitor who stumbles over their language.

FOLLOW BRADT

For the latest news, special offers and competitions, subscribe to the Bradt newsletter via the website www.bradtguides.com and follow Bradt on:

BradtTravelGuides
@BradtGuides
@bradtguides
bradtguides

Part One

GENERAL INFORMATION

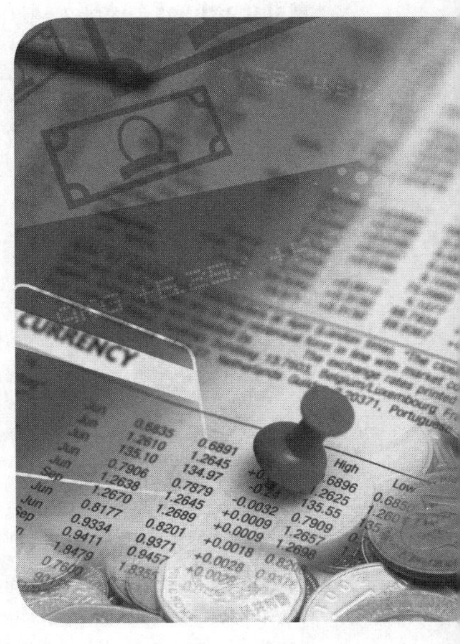

BOSNIA AND HERZEGOVINA AT A GLANCE

Country name Bosnia and Herzegovina
Location Southeast Europe; borders with Croatia (932km), Serbia (312km) and Montenegro (215km)
Land area 51,129km^2
Language Bosnian, Croatian, Serbian
Population Approximated at 4 million
Religion Muslim (44%), Orthodox Christian (32%), Roman Catholic (17%), others (7%)
Capital Sarajevo (estimated population 400,000)
Other major cities and towns Banja Luka, Tuzla, Zenica, Mostar, Bihać, Trebinje
Administrative division Two entities and one district: Federation of BiH (ten cantons) and Republika Srpska; Brcko district
Highest point Maglić Mountain 2,386m
National parks Three
Nature parks Four
Bird reserves Two
Time CET (GMT + 1 hour)
Currency KM (convertible mark) US$1 = 1.79KM, £1 = 2.31KM, €1= 1.95KM (fixed rate) (May 2017)
International telephone code +387
Climate Alpine continental in the north, Mediterranean in south
Economy Metal, agriculture, tourism, forestry, energy
Major airlines Austrian Airlines, Turkish Airlines, Croatia Airlines, Lufthansa
Principal airport Sarajevo
Voltage Standard European, 220v
Weights and measures Metric

SEND US YOUR SNAPS!

We'd love to follow your adventures using our *Bosnia* guide – why not send us your photos and stories via Twitter (@BradtGuides) and Instagram (@bradtguides) using the hashtag #bosnia. Alternatively, you can upload your photos directly to the gallery on the Bosnia destination page via our website (*www.bradtguides.com/bosnia*).

1

Background Information

FACTS AND FIGURES

Bosnia and Herzegovina (BiH) is the heart-shaped country in the middle of the former Yugoslavia. It is bordered by Croatia to the north and west, and by Serbia and Montenegro to the south and east. It is here that civilisations met, clashed and now unite East with West.

NAME The name Bosnia dates back to Roman times. There are several theories as to where the name came from but it is a common belief that Bosnia, from *bosana*, meaning 'water' (Bosnia's most plentiful resource), was named after its abundant freshwater rivers, streams and springs. Herzegovina was named after the last Duke of Hum, Herceg Stjepan, who was the last ruler from the Bosnian aristocratic Kosača family before the Ottomans invaded. Herzegovina literally means 'of the Duke' or 'belonging to the Duke'. Bosnia and Herzegovina is often shortened to BiH due to its rather long name. **In the text of this guide BiH will occasionally be used in place of Bosnia and Herzegovina.**

AREA The territory of BiH covers 51,129km², which is approximately the size of West Virginia. It has a small opening on the Adriatic Sea at the town of Neum. Its international waters mainly fall under Croatian territory.

LOCATION Bosnia and Herzegovina is not only the heart of the former Yugoslavia, but the heart of the Dinaric Alps as well. This southern extension of the Swiss Alps stretches deep into the Balkans and characterises much of BiH as well as its neighbours Croatia and Montenegro. It shares a 932km border with Croatia, a 312km border with Serbia and a 215km border with Montenegro. From BiH's northern borders Slovenia and Hungary are only a few hours' drive away and its southernmost point is a mere 10-minute drive from Dubrovnik, Croatia, on the southern Adriatic coast. Bosnia is the central and northern region of the country and Herzegovina comprises the entire southern region

POPULATION Today the total population of Bosnia and Herzegovina is estimated at around 4 million, although accurate statistics are difficult to come by as the results of the 2014 census have still to be published, for political reasons. There is a large diaspora scattered throughout Europe, North America and Australia, as well as in neighbouring Croatia, Serbia and Montenegro; it is believed that 1.2 million Bosnians live abroad.

Cities The capital city and the administrative, cultural, economic and academic centre of the country is Sarajevo, with an estimated population of 400,000. The wider region, including the predominantly Serbian East Sarajevo, brings the population closer to its pre-war figure of 600,000. A slow trickle of people are still returning to the city of their birth.

Banja Luka is the cultural, political and administrative centre of the Serb entity of BiH, Republika Srpska (RS). The city did once boast a rich multi-ethnic tradition but many of the non-Serbs have left or were driven out during the war. Banja Luka's population is 200,000.

Tuzla and Zenica are industrial towns representing two of the larger population centres. Tuzla's inhabitants number 170,000 and Zenica's 120,000. Mostar is the heart of Herzegovina and has always had one of the most ethnically mixed populations in the country. Unfortunately, the 100,000-plus residents of Mostar are still marred by an invisible dividing line – albeit a psychological one. The east bank and a small part of the west near the old town are largely Bosniak, and the west bank has mainly a Croatian population. Bosniak is the term used for the Bosnian Muslims. Their nationality is often referred to as Muslim, which is incorrect.

GEOGRAPHY AND CLIMATE

GEOGRAPHY It is rare to find a country that offers such diverse beauty and harmony of limestone mountains, lush valleys, centuries-old forests, crystal-clear rivers and green mountain lakes. It is from these pristine areas that Bosnia and Herzegovina's rich cultural heritage evolved. To understand Bosnia and Herzegovina one must have a sense of the immense geographical factors that have shaped this country since prehistoric times.

In a country that covers only just over 51,000km², it is no less than a phenomenon that it hosts so many dramatically varied landscapes. From rugged alpine peaks, dry and arid Mediterranean Herzegovina, the rolling green hills of central and northern Bosnia, to the vast flatlands of Semberija in the northeast along the River Sava, this tiny place offers a more fascinating array of climates, cultures, vegetation, watersheds and wildlife than any other country in southeast Europe.

Much of Bosnia and Herzegovina is covered by mountainous limestone terrain, creating the world's largest karst field. The long chain of the southern Alps – the Dinaric Alps – stretches from northwest Croatia through the heart of Bosnia and Herzegovina and into Montenegro, finishing in the Prokletija Mountains on the Albanian border. Herzegovina and eastern Bosnia host the highest and wildest part of this mountain range, which for centuries provided protection for the Illyrians from Roman invaders, slowed the Ottoman conquest of Bosnia and created a rugged self-reliant culture that still dominates in present-day Bosnia and Herzegovina.

Expanding from Bosnia and Herzegovina's western border with Croatia, the Dinaric chain cuts through the heart of central Herzegovina with the Prenj, Čabulja, Čvrsnica and Velež mountains – all above the 2,000m mark. This mountain range is the natural boundary of the Mediterranean and continental alpine climates. The warm Adriatic temperatures clash with the harsher alpine ones, producing one of the most diverse and unique ecosystems in all of Europe. More than 32 types of endemic flora and fauna can be found in the central Herzegovina mountains.

The valley of the Neretva River, which carries this emerald river into the Adriatic Sea, has been an area of human settlement since the Palaeolithic era. The Mediterranean climate offers ideal conditions for human settlement. The valley produces figs, mandarins and pomegranates, and has had a winemaking tradition since Roman times. The western valley is more arid and resembles the rocky terrain of the Dalmatian coast. The Neretva Valley is certainly one of the most interesting areas of BiH, and its cultural, historical and natural heritage has produced a wealth of tourist attractions.

From the high central ranges the Dinarics cut east towards the Visočica, Bjelašnica and Treskavica mountains. Deep canyons characterise this area and many highland settlements can be found dating back to medieval times. Moving even further east, bordering Montenegro, are Bosnia and Herzegovina's highest peaks. Protected in Sutjeska National Park, Maglić Mountain (2,386m) towers above the surrounding natural fortresses of Zelengora Mountain, Volujak, Lelija and the Mesozoic walls of Lebršnik Mountain. Sutjeska National Park hosts one of the two remaining primeval forests in Europe – Perućica. The old trees are the last remains of forests dating back 20,000 years. Through these peaks the Sutjeska, Tara and Piva rivers carve their way as three of the main tributaries of the Drina River. Throughout the entire chain are the prized ancient villages that preserve 'old world' Europe. In the open valleys between them sprawl the towns and cities of Mostar, Jablanica, Konjic, Sarajevo, Foča and countless smaller settlements. A rugged and creative mountain culture has emerged from this region, connecting humans and nature in ways rarely seen in modern times.

While most of Bosnia and Herzegovina's terrain is dominated by mountains, the northern areas, particularly the northeast, are part of the long plains that flow from

Hungary, through Slavonia in Croatia into the fertile fields of the Sava and Drina river valleys. These flatlands extend deep into neighbouring Serbia connecting to the Danube watershed. The northeast of Bosnia is one of the richest agricultural areas in the country.

The central belt of Bosnia is characterised by both mountains and green, rolling hills covered by lush conifer forests, and is lined with countless freshwater streams and rivers abundant in trout. These areas have always been rich in minerals and since Roman times have been mined for gold, silver, salt and copper, to name but a few. The Lašva Valley tucked deep below Vlašić, Komar and Kruščica mountains has long been a main trading route and served as a political and economic centre since the medieval Bosnia State.

The region known as the Krajina in the northwest of the country is a fascinating example of karst topography. Deep limestone caves line Livanjsko, Glamočko and Kupreško fields. Some of the largest caves in Europe can be found here. To the north the watershed of the Una River begins. The Una, Sana and Vrbas rivers are all tributaries of the mighty Sava and have long been frontiers for protecting against different invaders. These fertile valleys are holy to the local inhabitants, and guests will find these rivers spoken of as members of the family.

Bosnia and Herzegovina is also blessed with rich mineral deposits that have created 19 thermal mineral spas throughout the country. Mineral water is one of Bosnia's largest exports. It is estimated that over 35% of BiH is forested. Fed from its high mountain peaks Bosnia and Herzegovina is teeming with freshwater rivers that either flow south into the Neretva River and further to the Adriatic, or northeast via the Drina and Sava rivers that feed the Danube and eventually empty into the Black Sea.

Given that the country possesses so many wonders of nature it is rather disturbing that less than 0.6% of Bosnia and Herzegovina is protected. The European average for protected lands is 7%. Bosnia and Herzegovina is faced with the challenge of either preserving its rich natural wealth or risking the loss of much of its pristine wilderness and forests to uncontrolled development, clear-cutting and exploitation of its abundant fresh water supply. BiH possesses several major potable waterways, unheard of in today's polluted world, but plans for the construction of many hydro-electric dams (instead of investment in and modernisation of the existing and outdated infrastructure) will endanger most of these fabulous rivers. The Neretva River in the municipality of Konjic is under the most serious threat, with a series of four proposed dams that would forever destroy one of Europe's last and finest wilderness areas.

CLIMATE A number of factors influence the climate of BiH: its geographic position, its relief, which is predominantly mountainous, the proximity of the warm Mediterranean Sea, and the continental landmasses, mainly the Euro-Asian landmass. This transitional region where Mediterranean and alpine influences meet creates a mosaic of climate types within a relatively small area.

In layman's terms the south enjoys warm, sunny and dry weather, with very mild winters. In the more continental areas the weather is similar to that of central Europe – hot summers, cool springs and autumns, and cold winters with considerable snowfall. However, the mountains create a climate of their own and, where the Mediterranean and continental climates meet, some of the most unique ecosystems in Europe can be found.

The alpine climate rules the highest mountain terrains of the high Dinarics above 1,700m. The winters are extremely cold, with temperatures well below zero for more than six months of the year. Snow covers the terrain here until summer and the winds often reach hurricane strength. Bjelašnica Mountain (2,067m) is representative of this climate type, and it is there that the first weather observatory in the Balkans was built in 1894.

A note for those travelling to Sarajevo: being shielded by large mountains on all sides, Sarajevo's summer weather is often unpredictable. In 2006, both the coldest and hottest days were recorded for June. The blistering heat can quickly disappear with just a day of cloud cover and the temperatures can easily drop 10°C in a short time span. It's always wise to bring at least a fleece to Bosnia, even in July and August. It should also be noted that recent climate changes mean that weather patterns are harder to predict. The traditional heavy snowfalls that occurred regularly every winter are no longer a given. Mid-November through January in Sarajevo is often foggy and in recent years, smoggy. However, just above the Sarajevo valley in the mountains and hills, the air is always clean. Summers have also become drier with higher temperatures and less precipitation.

NATURAL HISTORY AND CONSERVATION

LAKES AND RIVERS *Dr Alen Lepirica*

The watercourses of BiH belong hydrographically to the Black Sea and the Adriatic Sea catchment areas. The main river of the Black Sea catchment is the Sava, which carves through the entire northern border of Bosnia with Croatia. Almost all the major rivers in Bosnia flow into the Sava, which is a large tributary of the Danube. The only direct tributary to the Adriatic Sea is the Neretva River in Herzegovina. There is also a massive region of karst fields (over 4,000km²) that do not directly feed into the Adriatic but create underground aquifer systems and surface as either springs and sources in the coastal area (such as Hutovo Blato) or submarine springs that exit in the sea itself.

Bosnia and Herzegovina has an amazing abundance of fresh water. Its high mountains feed the rivers that carve deep canyons and flow south. Towards the north, Bosnia and Herzegovina is rich in mineral water and thermal springs. Clean water must certainly be regarded as BiH's greatest natural resource. A special characteristic of Bosnia and Herzegovina's water systems is the plethora of waterfalls dotting the landscape. Among the most beautiful and most impressive are Strbački Cascade (24m), Martin Brod on the Una River, the Pliva Waterfall in Jajce (27m), and the Kravica and Kočuša waterfalls on the Trebižat River. The waterfalls with smaller flows are markedly higher: Skakavac (98m) near Sarajevo and another called Skakavac in Perućica Forest (75m). Among the highest waterfalls on the Balkan peninsula are the cascades of the Studeni stream which fall 400m into the deep canyon of Rakitnica – the least-explored canyon in southeast Europe.

BiH has few big natural lakes relative to its river flows. The largest lake is Boračko Lake in the eastern valley of Prenj, followed by Blidinje Lake between Vran and Čvrsnica mountains. At the southern end of the Neretva River, the Deransko and Svitavsko lakes create the wetlands of Hutovo Blato Bird Reserve. The mountain regions of Prenj, Čvrsnica, Satora, Vranica, Treskavica, Crvnja and Volujka have beautiful, clear, glacial lakes. The river lakes in BiH can be found on the Una, Pliva, Trebižat and Sanica rivers. Buško Lake, one of the largest artificial lakes in Europe with a surface area of 55km², was formed by regulating the waters of the Livanjsko and Duvanjsko valleys. The artificial lakes of Jablanica and Modrac, formed due to hydro-electric dams, are now popular tourist spots.

FLORA Two large floral regions intersect, as many things do, in Bosnia and Herzegovina. The Euro-Siberian and Mediterranean floral regions have created such a diverse biosystem that well over half the total number of flowering plants on the Balkan peninsula can be found here. Its richness is only comparable to that found in tropical and subtropical regions. Ancient species have been preserved due to especially favourable conditions, from the times of deluvial glaciations right up to the present. There are over 3,700 identified species of flowering plants in BiH and hundreds of endemic species. In spring the countryside is carpeted with wild flowers, many of them endemic to the Dinaric range. *Gentiana dinarica* (purplish-blue, trumpet-shaped flowers) can be found on Bjelašnica Mountain; you may see *Micromeria thymifolia*, a shrub-like plant with small flowers whose aroma will grab your attention in the Herzegovina highlands; the gentle violet and white flowers of *Euphrasia dinarica* dot the landscape around Konjic; and you can find the unique *Edraianthus niveus*, or Vranica's bell, on the hillsides near Prokoško Lake. Medicinal herbs have long been used here to cure illness, heal wounds and improve circulation, or to spice up a home-cooked meal.

Bosnia and Herzegovina is blessed with many wonders of nature. Perhaps one of its greatest gifts is the marvellous forests that cover slightly less than half the country. Although there has been significant deforestation due to unregulated clear-cutting, the countryside and mountainsides are still home to thick forests of beech, oak, chestnut, spruce and literally dozens of other types of trees.

The great variety of plant and tree types found in BiH is due to the unique climate of coastal and continental influences. Inland Bosnia and Herzegovina's forests are very similar to those found in northern and central Europe. Herzegovina and western Bosnia, which is covered by large areas of karst, is characterised by vegetation typical of the coastal and mountainous regions of the Mediterranean. Hidden below Bosnia and Herzegovina's highest peak, Maglić Mountain, lies the magical valley home of Perućica in Sutjeska National Park. Perhaps the most precious of all the forests, Perućica is one of the two remaining primeval forests in the whole of Europe. Massive beech trees are complemented by the high black pines on the rock faces that surround the valley. A hike through the heart of these woodlands is an unforgettable and awe-inspiring experience.

FAUNA The current status of the wildlife is largely unknown in post-war Bosnia and Herzegovina. It was once home to one of the largest bear populations in the world and had thriving wolf, deer, wild boar and chamois (*Divokoza*) communities. These populations have suffered severely from the war and unregulated hunting. Throughout the conflict many front lines were in the high mountain regions exposing Bosnia and Herzegovina's bear, wild goat, wild boar and wolf populations to heavy gun and artillery fire, and to being hunted for food by soldiers. Wild boar has, however, made a tremendous comeback. They are usually found in lush, conifer areas in the medium-sized mountain ranges but can be seen in Herzegovina as well. It is fair to say that the bear and the wild goat are both now endangered species in Bosnia and Herzegovina. The government has made no attempt to place hunting moratoriums on these animals or even investigate their plight. In BiH hunting is regulated by law but in practice there is little or no enforcement. Even if the opportunity presents itself you are advised not to hunt. Bring a camera and enjoy a photo hunt instead. Despite their diminished numbers it is not uncommon to see a bear, or occasionally a wolf in Sutjeska National Park in eastern Bosnia. Wild goats are mainly concentrated in Herzegovina's Neretva Valley but have a large safe haven found in Sutjeska National Park and on the southern slopes of Bjelašnica and Visočica mountains.

ATTENTION WILDLIFE ENTHUSIASTS

For more on wildlife in Bosnia and Herzegovina why not check out Bradt's *Central and Eastern European Wildlife*. Go to www.bradtguides.com and key in BOSWILD20 at the checkout for your 20% discount (while stocks last).

Fish and game are abundant in BiH. Most of the freshwater rivers are teeming with trout; carp, eel and bass are found throughout the country. The high mountains have always been home to eagles, hawks and falcons and it is not uncommon to see them on a walk or hike almost anywhere in the country. Driving on the main highway from Bihać towards Bosanski Petrovac you are almost guaranteed to spot a large hawk perched on one of the old electricity cables lining the road.

Hutovo Blato is the largest bird migration centre in southeast Europe. This marshy wetland in southern Herzegovina is home to 240 types of birds. Heron, Greek partridge, coot, owl, pheasant and wild duck make their permanent home in this tiny oasis. Bardača Reserve in the north of the country is also a haven for many types of birds. As a Ramsar Convention member it does enjoy protected status, although this is largely lip service.

With so much of Bosnia and Herzegovina's territory being untouched and wild, you can expect to see a wide range of little creatures: foxes, otters, pine martens, bobcats, deer, porcupines and many types of snakes (including two poisonous species; see *Mountain safety*, pages 90–1).

MOUNTAINS *Dr Alen Lepirica*

The geological structure of the terrain in present-day Bosnia and Herzegovina is the result of a long geological past in which various events created a variety of rock formations – magmatic, sedimentary, metamorphic and many ore deposits. Examples of Palaeozoic, Mesozoic and Cenozoic eras may be seen throughout the country. The intensive neo-tectonic processes have created a unique diversity of relief in BiH.

In the middle part of the country are the young mountains of the Dinaric system, which consist mostly of limestone. Their peaks are often higher than 2,000m. These high rock ranges consist of the following mountains: Vran (2,074m), Čvrsnica (2,228m), Čabulja (1,789m), Velež (1,969m), Prenj (2,155m), Bjelašnica (2,067m), Visočica (1,974m), Crvanj (1,921m), Treskavica (2,088m), Lelija (2,032m), Zelengora (2,015m), Ljubišna (2,242m), Volujak (2,297m) and the highest peak of the country, Maglić (2,386m). These mountain ranges are divided by 1,000m-deep canyon valleys: Neretva, Drina, the upper flow of the Bosna and its tributaries. The mountain ranges of Ivan (950m), Makljen (1,123m), Kupreška Vrata (1,324m), Čemerno (1,293m) and others present the natural connection between Herzegovina and Bosnia.

To the north, next to the Sava and the low basin of the Bosna River, is the flat valley of Posavina. This is surrounded by a long stretch of low Pannonian mountains; Majevica (916m), Motajnica (652m), Vučjak (368m), Prosara (363m) and Kozara (977m) appear like lonely islands rising out of the valley. The lowest part of the country is on the coast, next to Neum-Klek, together with the valleys of Humina. The low limestone valleys found here are also characteristic of this region, the largest being Popovo Valley towards Trebinje and Dubrovnik. All of these mentioned mountain ranges are now part of the new mega trail called the Via Dinarica that extends from northern Albania to southern Slovenia.

NATURE CONSERVATION

Hutovo Blato Bird Reserve In the south of Herzegovina not far from the ancient Roman settlement of Mogorjelo in Čapljina, and protected on all sides by arid hills and mountains, is the wetland bird reserve of Hutovo Blato. During the migratory season Deransko Lake is known to be filled with over 10,000 birds *en route* to southern Europe, destinations in north Africa and the Near East. UNESCO has placed Hutovo Blato Nature Park and Bird Reserve on Bosnia and Herzegovina's protected cultural and natural heritage list. It is a Ramsar-protected area. This area used to be open to hunters and fishermen but with its new status has become more a haven for tourists, birdwatchers and researchers. Boat rides on *barcos* (swamp canoe boats) are available with a professional guide, and the park is an ideal place for a picnic, walk or a bike ride. There are facilities at the park including a café, restaurant and motel. The high season for bird sightings is January and February but throughout the year dozens of domestic birds, fish and wildlife can be seen. It is located only 4km off of the M-17 highway from the Adriatic coast to Mostar, and is signposted (pages 214–15).

Sutjeska National Park Sutjeska is one of Bosnia and Herzegovina's oldest parks. It is famous for the Partisan victory over the Germans in World War II and there are large stone monuments commemorating the event. The park itself is 17,500ha of magnificent wilderness, including Perućica primeval forest. Beech trees tower over 55m high and endemic black pines grow from the rocky faces that protect the ancient forest. Skakavac Waterfall can be seen from the lookout point – this 75m waterfall is dwarfed by the massive blanket of green trees that covers the valley.

The Sutjeska River has carved a stunning valley through the middle of the park and divides Zelengora (Green Peaks) Mountain from Maglić and Volujak mountains. Bosnia and Herzegovina's highest peak at over 2,386m (7,400ft), Maglić is located in the park, directly on the border with Montenegro, and presents a challenging climb for experienced hikers. The park has a hotel in Tjentište (the flat valley along the Sutjeska River) and a café and restaurant. The hotel is socialist style and not particularly attractive but the nature within the park border competes with that found anywhere in Europe. Zelengora Mountain is great for hiking and walking and there are several newly renovated mountain huts on its slopes. Bear and wolf sightings are common. The park, although maintaining its pristine nature, is not as well organised as it should be. However, in terms of marked paths, good maps or visitor information there has been much improvement over the years. Since Sutjeska National Park is the main trail head for the new Via Dinarica trail, much of the hiking information can be found on **w** viadinarica.com. The park also has a new website **w** npsutjeska.info. Guides from the park can be hired for 50KM per day.

Kozara National Park Like Sutjeska, Kozara was also a former battleground during World War II. The Partisans' intimate knowledge of Bosnia and Herzegovina's rough terrain obviously gave them an advantage over the newly occupying Germans. Kozara National Park was named a national park by Tito in 1967. It is situated in the northwest Krajina region of Bosnia between the rivers Una, Sava, Sana and Vrbas. Its soft rolling hills and thick conifer forests make it a great spot for a day out in nature.

There is also a large hunting reservation of over 18,000ha within Kozara. Hunting is regulated by the local hunting association and a permit must be purchased. The remaining quarter of the park is designated for visitors, and for walking, hiking, biking, picnics, and herb and flower picking. The park offers lodging, restaurants and other facilities. Most information can be found at **w** npkozara.com. Kozara is situated close to the city of Prijedor and is just a few hours' drive from Bihać, the rafting centre of northern Bosnia (page 292).

Blidinje Nature Park Blidinje rests in a long valley between the Čvrsnica and Vran mountains. It is the natural divide of the Mediterranean and alpine climate zones, creating a fascinating array of flora and fauna. Like most conservation areas in BiH you'll be lucky to find a good map or a visitor information centre but the drive through the park is amazing in itself. There are several new mountain lodges being built near the Masna Luka Franciscan Monastery which will add a new element to Blidinje's overall offer. It is an important hub for the Via Dinarica and a main trail head for the central and western portions of the Via Dinarica White Trail (**w** *viadinarica.com*). Blidinje Lake rests in the middle of the park and one can see an occasional windsurfer. There is a well-run motel and restaurant by the ski-lifts further into the park. The entire road system through the park is gravel but is still easily negotiated by any car. Ancient *stećci*, intricately carved tombstones, are situated throughout the park as well as the traditional huts of Croatian shepherds, replete with straw roofs (pages 236–7).

Bjelašnica/Igman As part of the Dayton Peace Accords this region was foreseen as a potential new national park for BiH. Bjelašnica was home to the 1984 Winter Olympics, but much of the infrastructure was subsequently destroyed in the war. While the national park designation of Igman and Bjelašnica is only in the planning stages, this area still offers perhaps some of the most varied mountain tourism in the country.

Bjelašnica and Igman both have ski-lifts and offer **Olympic-style skiing**. Igman has a great traditional restaurant and mini-lifts for children. Bjelašnica is for more experienced skiers: from the peak (2,067m) to Babin Do (1,200m) is a fast 10-minute ride. Poor spatial planning and the construction of large apartment blocks have compromised the ski centres and indeed the wider area. It has been built in a rather intrusive manner and does not at all fit with the magnificent landscapes and natural environment.

As possibly the only one of its kind in southern Europe, the village of **Lukomir** on Bjelašnica is highly recommended for a visit. Lukomir is the highest and most isolated village in BiH, at 1,469m above sea level, and offers the visitor a glimpse of life in medieval Europe. The village is accessible by car for only about six months of the year – the other six you'll need some skis or a good pair of snowshoes. Other villages such as Umoljani and Sinanovići are also exceptional, with stunning mountain scenery, lodging and a handful of local eateries. Umoljani is an important hub for the Via Dinarica trail where one can travel south towards the Herzegovina Himalayas or east towards Sutjeska National Park.

The tourist information centre in downtown Sarajevo has all the information you will need on skiing in Bjelašnica/Igman. For biking, hiking or village tourism there is Green Visions (page 61). The roads to Bjelašnica/Igman are all well maintained and marked and it is about a 45-minute drive from the centre of Sarajevo (pages 152–3).

Prenj, Čvrsnica and Čabulja In the heart of the central Dinaric Alps lies the most imposing set of mountains in the country. Starting on the northern edge of the Mostar county line these ranges climb north all the way to Konjic in northern Herzegovina. Locally this chain is known as the Herzegovina Himalayas, especially Prenj for its sharp tooth-like peaks that seem never-ending. The lowlands, however, are very accessible and offer one of the most scenic drives in the whole country. This area is known for its numerous endemic species of wild flowers only found in this region of the world. It is home to dozens of sleepy Herzegovinian villages where one can find traditional cheese, meats and the local moonshine called *rakija* (from plums) or *loza* (from grapes). Honey and trout are also trademarks of this region and there are usually local villagers selling honey and apple vinegar along the main road (M-17).

Nearby, **Jablanica Lake** has great trout and carp fishing and there are a number of hotels, pensions and private rooms on the lake.

Unfortunately, this area has seen little in terms of ecotourism development, but these mountains offer the best and most challenging hiking in Herzegovina. Prenj Mountain hosts a wonderful glacier lake named Boračko near the town of Konjic. Not far from there is the Neretva Canyon where several white-water rafting operators offer an unforgettable adventure through this magical canyon (pages 228–9). There are also camping facilities, cafés and fishing.

Čvrsnica Mountain is the most accessible of the three mountains for hiking, and is only 9.5km south of Jablanica in the valley of Diva Grabovica. From here there are half a dozen hikes through some of the most magnificent terrain in Bosnia and Herzegovina. This area was largely spared during the war and the entire valley is mine free. The trails are marked but the trailheads are often very difficult to find. Starting at 200m above sea level some of the hikes take you to over 2,000m, through forests of massive beech trees and to the endemic black pines at the higher altitudes.

There are other equally beautiful and easier hikes. For those just looking for an easily accessible taste of nature the village of **Diva Grabovica** (pages 204–5) is a fascinating place for a gentle stroll. The valley itself is very self-contained, so by staying in the vicinity of the village it is nearly impossible to get lost. Hiking further, however, reveals true wilderness and an extensive system of trails, some made by wild goats, that may confuse even the most experienced hiker. A guide is highly recommended. Environmentalists have been trying for years, in vain, to get the obtrusive and illegal Prominvest Sand Quarry out of the valley. It has been working illegally (no permits) in the valley since 1996 and despite decisions by the High Court and repeated threats by the Ministry of the Environment, nothing has been done to remove the company. Once you get beyond this eyesore, the valley remains as magical as ever!

Just north of Mostar off the M-17 is the **Drežnica Valley**, with an 18km road winding through 12 breathtaking canyons. It is an ideal place for a slow drive to admire the view, or, for the more adventurous, to hop on a road bike or head up a mountain. The road is paved to the end of the valley where it tails off into a small dirt road. The Drežanka River carves the deep valley between Čvrsnica and Čabulja mountains and offers great swimming and fishing at the mouth where it feeds the Neretva River. There is a bed and breakfast place called Pansion Teatar (page 204) at the entrance of the valley which has a lovely terrace on the river for a nice meal or just a cool drink, and has a small beach nearby.

Due to the difficult post-war economic situation little attention has been paid to Bosnia and Herzegovina's natural wonders. Prior to the war, most parks and conservation areas offered prearranged guided walks but now that service has mostly fallen by the wayside. There are, however, several ecotourism operators that provide professional guided tours in these areas (pages 89–90). Until recently there had not been any effort to make the many trails and attractions on these spectacular mountains available. That all changed with the evolution of the long-distance Via

Dinarica walking trail. The new website (w *viadinarica.com*) has detailed trail maps with relevant GPS coordinates, points of interest like lodging and food, and a plethora of information so you can finally enjoy these amazing places with proper guidance.

HISTORY

The history of the region of the former Yugoslavia has, for many, been a bewildering subject. Bosnia and Herzegovina's place in this history has often been overlooked due to its geographical and, on many occasions, cultural isolation from mainstream Europe. BiH had a very distinct history from that of its eastern neighbours and therefore can be viewed in many senses as virgin ground for historians, particularly from the Illyrian period up to medieval Bosnia and Hum (Herzegovina), about which little is known from primary sources.

Perhaps the most important thing to keep in mind while trying to fit the pieces of the Bosnian puzzle into a coherent context is that the nationalist sentiments that were born at the end of the 19th century and which persist today do not reflect the life and sentiments of the tiny, isolated communities of this country from the 7th to the 13th centuries. The 'mental baggage' that is carried today by Serbs, Croats or Bosniaks (the term used for Bosnian Muslims, identifying nationality and not religion) simply cannot be applied to a population that previously held little or no affiliation to a national or ethnic identity. The Orthodox from eastern Herzegovina did not wave a Serbian flag, the Catholics from Srebrena Bosna did not have dreams of coming under Zagreb's rule, and the converted Muslim community had no aspirations to create a European Mecca in the heart of Bosnia. It is largely unknown whether the original Slav settlers, well into the Middle Ages, even referred to themselves at all as Serbs or Croats. All too often history is the story of kings and queens, conquerors and defenders, and provides little if any understanding of the life of the ordinary people. The early Slav tribes never engaged in bitter debates or wars over their Serbian or Croatian belonging; they lived in peace with each other, spoke the same language and worshipped the same God. Outside influences often divided communities, but the impetus for such divisions never came from within.

In the historical context of Bosnia and Herzegovina much is still argued over, both domestically and internationally. What no-one can debate, however, is today's rightful claim of all the peoples of Bosnia and Herzegovina to call this their home. Serbs, Croats and Bosniaks can confidently say that their homeland is Bosnia and Herzegovina and that they have been here for many, many generations. Claiming rightful ownership of one group over another from a historical perspective, with all its complexities, is simply an impossibility.

ANCIENT HISTORY The territory of Bosnia and Herzegovina is so profusely scattered with remnants of prehistoric life that much more space would be needed here to do it justice. Human life in BiH reaches far back, across an enormous span that stretches from the Palaeolithic period to the emergence of the Illyrian clan alliances.

Research into the **Stone Age** indicates that the northern parts of Bosnia and Herzegovina near the Bosna, Ukrina and Usora rivers were the most developed at that time. The leap from Neanderthal man in the middle Palaeolithic to the *Homo sapiens* of the late Palaeolithic is signified by the first cave drawing of that period found in Badanj Cave near Stolac in Herzegovina. This rare sample is dated at 12000BC and there have been similar finds in only three other locations: Spain, France and Italy. The end of the Palaeolithic era saw climatic changes so drastic that much of human life disappeared from this area until about 4000BC.

After this long, dark Mesolithic period, a rich **Neolithic culture** developed in the 3rd millennium BC. Conditions were ideal for the formation of settlements that developed a new kind of social organisation and enjoyed over a millennium of continuity. Many of the fine pottery and arts and crafts of this age are on display in the National Museum in Sarajevo. This highly skilled culture signified a golden age where spiritual life was matched by creative talent. The ancient settlement of Butmir, presently a suburb south of Sarajevo at the base of Igman Mountain, can alone testify to the craftsmanship achieved in that territory by Neolithic humans. This unique culture disappeared from Bosnia and Herzegovina without a trace at some point between the 3rd and 2nd millennia BC.

A great metamorphosis swept across the Balkans in a movement that began with the arrival of nomadic tribes from the Black Sea steppes. With their arrival to the Balkans came a new **Copper Age**. This Aeneolithic period saw a parallel development of stone and metal. The use of metal became increasingly valued for weapon making into the **Bronze Age** as well-armed tribes from west Pannonia expanded south and southeast towards the end of the 2nd millennium BC. Wars became more frequent, and Bosnia became very popular for the sanctuary it provided with its deep valleys, thick forests and rugged mountains.

ILLYRIANS The first few centuries of the 1st millennium BC in Bosnia and Herzegovina, as throughout the entire western Balkan peninsula, saw a process of the stabilisation of a broad ethnic and cultural foundation. From these tribes, belonging to the Iron Age culture, emerged an ethnic group that history has collectively named the Illyrians.

The Illyrian tribes settled across a large swathe of the western Balkans from the Adriatic coast in the west to the Morava River in the east, and from present-day Albania in the south to the Istrian Peninsula in what today is northwest Croatia. These loosely bound tribes began to form new territorial and economic ties in the middle of the 1st millennium BC. This process appears to have been most profound amongst the southern Illyrian tribes, including those of present-day Bosnia and Herzegovina.

The Celtic migration inland and the Greek colonies established on the Adriatic coast in the 4th century BC marked a new and painful chapter in Illyrian history. These events brought about significant cultural and spiritual change, but more importantly they increased the desire of the **Roman Empire** to expand and conquer these areas.

The Romans attacked in 229BC, first capturing the islands and crushing the Illyrian navy. In 168BC, the famous Illyrian king Gentius was defeated and this gave the Romans a stronghold on Illyrian soil. The inland tribes of Illyria, however, put up a ferocious fight and it took a century and a half of the Romans' best commanders and military forces to defeat the defiant clans. Finally, from 35–33BC, under the direct command of Emperor Octavian, the Roman army launched a major attack that, after the emperor himself was seriously wounded from a guerilla attack, forced the surrender of the Delmetae clan. The coastal clans were by and large conquered by the overwhelming size of the Roman army.

In the last 'battle royal' for the inland territories held by the Illyrian tribes in what is the heart of present-day Bosnia, the clan alliances staged what is known as the **Batonian Uprising**. Two large Illyrian tribes united to fend off the invaders. Panicked by the rumours that there were '800,000 insurgents, including 200,000 elite warriors and 9,000 horsemen', Emperor Augustus sent two of his top commanders, Tiberius and Germanicus, to subdue and conquer the fierce and stubborn Illyrians. The fighting went on for years, with both sides exchanging defeats and victories.

The last Illyrian stronghold to fall was the citadel at Vranduk near the central Bosnian city of Zenica. According to Roman records, when the Illyrian leader Bato surrendered, the Illyrian women, holding their children, threw themselves into the fire rather than be captured and enslaved. The Romans incorporated the two Illyrian provinces of Pannonia and Dalmatia into their empire. Some extremely isolated remnants of Illyrian tribes probably survived and eventually assimilated with the Slavs when they arrived in the 7th century.

There are still a few archaeological sites that mark the Illyrian civilisation in Bosnia and Herzegovina. Many of the Illyrian fortifications were expanded upon by the Romans and later by the Bosnian aristocracy and the Ottomans. New research, however, has uncovered a fascinating aspect of Illyria. At **Vranduk** in central Bosnia, **Blagaj** near the Buna River in Herzegovina and at the **Cyclopean walls at Osanići** near Stolac, finds have indicated that the culture of antiquity came long before the Romans, most likely in Hellenistic form. Osanići was home to the Daorsi tribe and recent archaeological findings point to a 3rd-century BC link to a northerly extension of the great **Hellenistic civilisation**.

Much of Illyrian culture will forever remain a mystery but one cannot deny the spiritual and cultural impact it has had, even almost two millennia after its disappearance.

ANCIENT ILLYRICUM With the fall of the Illyrian clan alliances to the Romans, present-day Bosnia and Herzegovina became part of the vast Roman Empire.

The early period of **Roman occupation** was peaceful and stable for the Illyrians. There were, of course, some tribes who rejected Roman rule but for the most part the efficient Romans quickly set aim at taming Illyricum to cater to the empire's needs. A Roman administration was established and the tasks of building roads, mining for iron, gold, lead and rock and mobilising a large labour force and military were the first priorities. The Illyrians were actively recruited into the Roman army.

The most populated areas continued to be the empire's regional centres. By the 3rd century Illyricum had flourished into a proper Roman province. Its people had equal standing within the empire and could even aspire to political office. Although Christianity was introduced and largely accepted, elements of Illyrian pagan beliefs were maintained and passed on.

With the disintegration of the Western Empire in the 5th century much of the Illyrian lands fell into the hands of the **Ostrogoths**. The Illyrians again enjoyed a period of relative peace and stability but by the mid-6th century the Eastern Empire was able to regain most of the Illyrian lands. As the Roman Empire declined, new attacks occurred on the northern frontiers, this time from the Avars and Slavs.

After several centuries of drastic social change in Europe a melange of cultures made their mark on what is now Bosnia and Herzegovina. Basilicas from the late Roman period can be found as their use was continued by the new settlements of Slavs. Remains can be found in Čapljina, Blagaj and Ljubuški in Herzegovina; Breza, Zenica, Travnik and Kiseljak in central Bosnia; and Banja Luka and Mrkonjić Grad in the northwest of the country.

THE SLAVS With the fall of the Western Empire the new era in Bosnia and Herzegovina was largely dominated by the Slavs. From the 6th century onwards sizeable Slav migrations came from the east. The Avars gradually retreated to Pannonia but the Slavs remained in their new homeland. It is this ethnic group that comprises most of present-day Bosnia and Herzegovina's ethnic make-up.

Historical evidence of the first century of **Slav settlements** in the area of Bosnia and Herzegovina is practically non-existent. The first recorded evidence of Bosnia and Herzegovina under the Slavs dates from the 10th century. Several centuries later a Byzantine writer stated that: 'Bosnia is not a vassal state but is independent; the people lead their own life and rule themselves.'

Assimilation of the Slavs with the indigenous peoples of Bosnia and Herzegovina came much quicker than in other areas, due largely to BiH's geographical isolation. As coastal areas were much better defended with fortified cities, Slavic culture spread at a much slower pace elsewhere. Ethnographers have still not completely explained the unique Slavic component in Bosnia and Herzegovina. Many of the rituals, folklore, dance and pagan beliefs found in the Slavic society were not typical Slav characteristics. This lends credibility to the theory that the inland Illyrians (with heavy Roman, Hellenistic and even Celtic influence) and the new settlements of Slavs had very intimate contact and both adopted each other's customs and traditions to form one of the most complex ethnic groups in Europe.

With the arrival of the Slavs this region once again – after tremendous Christian influence from the Roman and Frankish cultures of the west and Byzantium to the east – became a pagan nation. And, as before, forces from beyond began the immense undertaking of reconverting the new population. Granted, elements of Christianity already existed and conversion happened fairly quickly along the coast and in the more accessible areas, but conversion in Bosnia and Herzegovina came much slower. It wasn't until the 9th century that Bosnia and Herzegovina became exposed to open conversion movements from the missionaries **Cyril and Methodius**. It was during this time that Bosnian literacy was established and the use of both the Glagolitic and Cyrillic alphabets was introduced.

Graveyards have become the most accurate source for study of the culture of this time. Archaeological digs in older necropolises have unearthed locally made jewellery and weapons from the Slav period. A unique aspect of this time was the development of skilled work with stone. This art would later surface in what is seen today as a national trademark of Bosnia and Herzegovina – the *stećak* (plural *stećci*). These medieval tombstones were elaborately carved with drawings depicting Christian and pagan beliefs. *Stećci* date from the 11th to the 13th century and can be found today at dozens of locations all over Bosnia and Herzegovina. The tombstones are unique to this part of the world and mark early Slavic heritage in these parts.

MEDIEVAL BOSNIA 1180–1463 The early Middle Ages placed the southern Slavs in a very precarious position – wedged between the two great cultural bodies of eastern and western Christianity. Both Byzantium and Rome set out to influence the political and religious structure of this crossroads region. The geographical position of the southern Slavs became an important factor in the 11th-century split between the Orthodox and Catholic churches. Both churches asserted their influence and left a permanent mark on the region's cultural history.

The southern Slavs were hesitant to embrace any outside influences. They diligently evaded religious and cultural assimilation from both sides. The Slavs had their own script due to the missionary work of Cyril and Methodius in the 9th century, placing the Glagolitic and later Cyrillic alphabets on even ground with the holy languages of Latin, Hebrew and Greek.

The **spiritual culture** that developed in medieval Bosnia was very similar to that of its Illyrian predecessors. There was a large degree of cultural resistance and fierce independence that resulted in a creative mould of Christianity. In a relatively inaccessible and isolated area emerged what was to be one of the most unique forms of Christianity in medieval Europe – the **Bosnian Church**. Whilst still influenced by the great divide and spread of Orthodoxy and Catholicism the Bosnian Church,

along with its own alphabet – *Bosančica* (similar to both Glagolitic and Cyrillic) – flourished in the medieval Bosnian state. In an era that saw Europe dominated by religious exclusiveness, Bosnia was able to maintain a high level of secularism in all spheres of life. The followers of this unique church have often been called *Bogomils.* Until recently this theory has been the common belief among most people in Bosnia and Herzegovina. However, overwhelming evidence has contradicted it. Bogomils were found in Bulgaria, Macedonia and parts of southern Serbia and no evidence points to their belief system being practised here. Nevertheless, the Pope attempted to use purported Bogomil duality, a belief that the divine was of another world and that life on earth was unholy, as justification for an invasion and cleansing of what were viewed by the Catholic Church as heretics.

Medieval Bosnia is marked by three powerful rulers of Bosnian aristocracy. In the early Middle Ages Bosnia was first ruled by **Ban Kulin**, who reigned from 1180 to 1204 and was largely responsible for opening important trade routes to Ragusa (present-day Dubrovnik). He also encouraged Dalmatian merchants to exploit the rich Bosnian mines, especially in the area around Fojnica in central Bosnia. This was a major factor in the political and territorial stabilisation of Bosnia. Ban Kulin is fondly remembered in history books for securing a golden era for Bosnia during his 24 years in power. Although Bosnia enjoyed two decades of peace during this time, constant pressure was being asserted from beyond its borders. Hungary continued to press for control of Bosnia, even campaigning in Rome to bring Bosnia under the jurisdiction of the pro-Hungarian Archbishop of Split. After the death of Ban Kulin the papacy pressured the Hungarians to eliminate heresy from the Bosnian Church, which was believed to not abide by strict Catholic ritual and to maintain pagan rites. Some historians believe this was simply religious justification for Hungary's desire to acquire Bosnian lands. By 1238, the Hungarians had invaded and captured Vrhbosna in central Bosnia and had plans to install a Dominican order before they were forced to retreat north in 1241 to fend off an encroaching Mongol threat.

Ban Stjepan Kotromanić enjoyed over 30 years of power, from 1322–53. He replaced the noble Šubić family after they had ruled Bosnia for the first two decades of the 14th century. Kotromanić immediately began to expand the Bosnian state by uniting some of the old northern territories. He conquered several hundred kilometres of Dalmatian coast and in 1326 annexed the southern province of Hum (later named Herzegovina). This made Bosnia and Herzegovina, for the first time, a united political entity. Hum had previously led a rather distant existence under the rule of local noble families to the Bosnian state, and its religious heritage became largely Orthodox in comparison with the Bosnian Church, which strongly resembled the Catholic Church. Kotromanić nurtured strategic relations with many of Bosnia's larger neighbours. He signed treaties with Ragusa in 1334 and with Venice in 1335 and openly co-operated with the Hungarian king to assist with uprisings in Croatia. The large Serbian kingdom to the east, under the rule of King Dušan, was too busy expanding south into Macedonia, Albania and parts of Greece to occupy itself with the expanding Bosnian state.

Kotromanić not only accepted but supported the Bosnian Church. This put him on shaky ground with the Pope and in 1340, in an attempt to improve relations, he allowed the Franciscans to set up their first order in Bosna Srebrena. Although the Franciscans had visited as early as 1290, this gesture would forever open the doors to the Catholic Church and greatly influence the rising Bosnian state. While still maintaining many pagan and so-called 'heretic' practices, Bosnia became overwhelmingly Catholic. Kotromanić is said to have converted to Catholicism and at his death in 1353 he was buried in the Franciscan monastery at Visoko. He left behind an independent and prosperous Bosnian state.

King Tvrtko succeeded Kotromanić. At only 15 he inherited a country where his youth made it impossible to prove his political and military authority. The first 14 years of his 'rule' were troublesome times but with the help of the Hungarian king he was able to assert his leadership, and in 1367 Tvrtko expanded the kingdom, making Bosnia the most powerful state in the western Balkans at the end of the 14th century. By assisting the Serbian nobleman Lazar Hrebljanović carve out territory in Serbia, Tvrtko was rewarded with large swathes of land in Hum (Herzegovina), Zeta (Montenegro), southern Dalmatia (including the Bay of Kotor) and the Sandžak of Novi Pazar (present-day Serbia). His appetite did not lessen there as he later expanded his kingdom into parts of northern Croatia and Slavonia. King Tvrtko later named himself 'King of Croatia and Dalmatia' in addition to Bosnia.

By the end of Tvrtko's rule in 1391 the Franciscan Church had been well established in many parts of the Bosnian state, particularly along the coastal areas and in the central Bosnian province of Bosna Srebrena. The Venetians acted quickly upon Tvrtko's death and gained most of Dalmatia, except for Ragusa (now Dubrovnik). In the years following Tvrtko's death Bosnia began a prolonged period of weak rule. At this time a fourth religion began to take hold and assert its influence on medieval Bosnia.

Islam had been rapidly spreading in several other parts of the world, and by the end of the 1300s the **Ottoman Empire** turned its attentions north. In 1404, the Bosnian king Ostoja was driven out and replaced by a son of King Tvrtko (Tvrtko II). Ostoja returned with a Hungarian army in tow and managed to regain control of much of the country. In 1414, the balance of political and military power drastically changed. The Ottomans proclaimed the exiled Tvrtko II the rightful King of Bosnia and sent a large force into Bosnian lands. Some of the far eastern border towns of the Bosnian kingdom were conquered by the Turks in the early 15th century but they had lost several battles in the Neretva Valley in 1386 and at Bileća in 1388. Local nobleman Vlatko Vuković led these skirmishes which sparked a 140-year resistance to Ottoman takeover.

For decades Bosnia saw its kingdom's loyalties divided by two forces – the Hungarian army and the Ottoman Turks. Ostoja regained the throne only to lose it several years later to Tvrtko II again. Patterns of allegiances continually shifted and many regions of Bosnia changed hands several times. Tvrtko II then sought help from the Hungarians against the Turks. Inside rivalry and opposing loyalties divided Bosnia. Little by little the Ottomans strengthened their hold, often with the help of local nobles. There are many different accounts of how the Turks slowly conquered Bosnia – some recounting a brave and spirited resistance, others telling of betrayal and convenient alliances.

Towards the middle of the 15th century Turkish incursions continued and, with the death of Tvrtko II and the succession of Tomas in 1443, the attacks intensified. In an attempt to lobby for further papal assistance, King Tomas agreed to persecute the clergy of the Bosnian Church in 1459. Earlier attempts by the Franciscans to ease the worries of the Pope's accusations of doctrinal irregularities and heresy had failed. Most of the clergy opted for conversion while an estimated 40 of them fled to Herzegovina. Four years before the destruction of the kingdom, the Bosnian king ousted what was one of the most unique and self-reliant churches in medieval history.

When a large Turkish army marched on Bobovac Fortress in 1463, Tomas's successor Stjepan Tomašević fled to Jajce and then sought refuge in a fortress in Ključ in the northwest. The Turks soon besieged him there and on a promise of safety Tomašević surrendered. It is said that once the sultan took possession of the fortress he ordered King Tomašević and his court to be beheaded. Bosnia then ceased to be a feudal state and the kingdom's stronghold at Jajce changed hands several times before it finally fell in 1528, marking the end of the last remains of the Bosnian Kingdom.

Cultural development in medieval Bosnia Much of what history doesn't offer us in its account of medieval Bosnia relates to how the ordinary person lived, what lifestyle he/she enjoyed, and what cultural heritage developed during these times. What we do know is that many unique forms of language, art, literature and worship evolved in Bosnia during the Middle Ages. Keep in mind, however, that due to its geographical location the region remained rather isolated from 'mainstream' trends in Europe.

The key to Bosnia's wealth was its rich natural resources, particularly copper, silver, lead and gold. Copper and silver were mined at Kreševo and Fojnica in central Bosnia; lead was mined in Olovo to the northeast of Sarajevo; and gold, silver and lead were mined in Zvornik on the River Drina. The most significant and productive area in all of Bosnia and Herzegovina was the silver mine at Srebrenica.

During the Middle Ages Bosnia became a very important trading route. Merchants from both East and West moved and traded their goods through or in Bosnian territory. Trading towns and routes sprung up in Visoko, Jajce, Travnik, Goražde and Livno. Many locals became involved in trade, particularly with Ragusa (Dubrovnik). Bosnia and Dubrovnik today still share close cultural ties.

A unique **alphabet** evolved in medieval Bosnia. Cyrillic and Glagolitic had been introduced in the 10th century and a special form of Cyrillic developed during the

Middle Ages. Glagolitic and Cyrillic were used simultaneously for some time, both copying texts and manuscripts from each other. The use of these two alphabets slowly merged into one – Bosnian Cyrillic or *Bosančica* – and became the most commonly used alphabet in later medieval times. In Bosnia and Hum four different alphabets were in use at one time or another: Cyrillic, Glagolitic, Greek and Latin.

Whereas most **literature** and distinguishing marks of literacy in medieval Europe came from clergy and monasteries, Bosnian writings were remarkably secular. The most famous of these is the Kulin Charter of 1189, written to the people of Dubrovnik. This was the first official act written in the national language of the Slavic south. Many documents show that it was not only the nobility but also merchants and craftsmen who reached a relatively high level of literacy. There are, however, also many religious documents from this time. Examples include the Cyrillic Miroslav's Gospel (12th century), produced by the Duke of Hum; the Divos Tihoradic Gospel from the 14th century; and the Čajniče Gospel, which is the only medieval codex still in existence in Bosnia today. These manuscripts used a wealth of human and animal miniatures all drawn in a unique south Slav style. At the Franciscan monastery in Kraljeva Sutjeska are some of the earliest written works, and the first Bible, complete with the *Bosančica* alphabet, can be viewed at the museum and library in this small town in central Bosnia.

Art took many forms in medieval Bosnia. Silver, gold, bronze and copper were used, particularly in the 14th and 15th centuries, for jewellery-making, costumes, coins, bowls and other artefacts. Many of the designs resemble Romanesque-Gothic styles, some with an Eastern mystical flavour. The most important art of medieval Bosnia, however, was the stonework of the *stećci*. These gravestones from Bosnia and Hum are not found anywhere else in Europe.

The symbols found on *stećci* vary. There are several different styles portraying crosses, swords, symbols of purity, and anthropomorphic symbols (dance, traditional attire, sacred symbols, deer and horses). Bosnian Cyrillic script developed its most outstanding artistic characteristics on the *stećci*. But the most remarkable trait of the *stećci* is their poetic and philosophical power. They stand apart from any known conventional European burial rites. Mak Dizdar, the most famous of Bosnian poets, wrote frequently of the *stećci* and their meaning, especially in *Kameni Spavač* ('Stone Sleeper').

There are various interpretations of the origins of *stećci*. Their emergence has been traced back at least to the time of the rule of Ban Kulin. They may have been, and most likely were, art forms even before the age of Kulin. The blend of Romanised Illyrians and the incoming Slavs obviously created a unique mixture of ritual, belief and mythology. However, there are no reliable records for the almost half a millennium from when the Slavs first arrived to the time of Ban Kulin. These stone marvels are found mostly in BiH but there are also *stećci* in Dalmatia, the Croatian hinterland, western Serbia and Montenegro – all within the boundaries of the former Bosnian state. This art form continued into Ottoman times and well into the 16th century, with some of the later *stećci* including Islamic symbols.

Bosnia and Herzegovina is a living gallery of the **stone art** of the Middle Ages. Over 60,000 *stećci* tombstones are dotted throughout the country with the largest necropolis at Radimlja near the Herzegovinian town of Stolac. Whether or not the mystery of the *stećci* is ever solved, they remain a national symbol of Bosnia and Herzegovina.

OTTOMAN RULE In the summer of 1463 the Turkish army, after years of penetration into Bosnian territory, captured the Bosnian banate and the region around Sarajevo. These lands would be in firm Turkish control for the next four centuries. Many of the gains in the northern half of Bosnia, however, were reversed by King Mathias of Hungary. He established a northern banate under Hungarian rule and named the Bosnian '*ban*', King of Bosnia. The kingdom slowly dwindled as Turkish incursions wore down the resistance, and by the 1520s the kingdom's capital, Jajce, came under constant siege until it fell in 1528.

Herzegovina also succeeded in repelling the Turks for a time after 1463. Herceg Stjepan Vukčić held most of Herzegovina for the next two years, until another swarming **invasion** sent him into exile in Novi (later named Herceg Novi in his honour), Montenegro. His son Vlatko attempted to enlist the help of the Hungarians and Venetians but internal strife with local noblemen and neighbouring Ragusa enabled the Ottomans to take a strong hold by the 1470s, and in 1482 the last fortress in Herzegovina was overrun.

It is worth noting that the territories of Serbia, Kosovo and Macedonia fell to the Turks 80 years prior to the fall of Bosnia, and on several occasions Bosnia's army went to aid their neighbours against the Turks. The Ottoman invasion of Bosnia, however, was aided by many Slav janissaries then serving in the Turkish army.

The Ottomans conquered territories, particularly in the north towards Europe, not to convert the inhabitants, but for a country's wealth, for acquiring new conscripts for further Ottoman gains, and for the taxes the empire could impose to wage these wars. Besides conquering Bosnia and Herzegovina, Mehment II destroyed the Venetian army in Greece, began making incursions into Moldavia and Hungary, and was on the verge of launching a full-scale invasion of Italy when he died in 1481. His successor, Bayezit II, continued consolidating Ottoman gains. Suleyman the Magnificent's rule from 1520–66 managed to reduce Hungary to the status of a vassal territory and the Turks came literally inches away from capturing Vienna. The 1533 peace treaty with Austria established a long and static confrontation line between the Habsburg and Ottoman empires. Each side spent years building up its respective frontier zones, thus assuring that Bosnia's borders did not see heavy military activity until the sultan waged war on the Habsburgs in 1566. Military campaigns continued from 1593–1606. The Ottoman presence in Bosnia was a military enterprise from where major offensives against the Habsburgs were launched. The process of **Islamicisation** lasted for 150 years, dispelling any myths that the Ottoman Turks had a widespread intentional policy of forced conversions to Islam.

During the Ottoman reign, boys and young men from European villages would be collected and brought back to Istanbul for training as janissary troops, personal servants to the sultan, or as officials in the administrative state. The Ottoman army depended heavily on its recruitment of **janissaries**, and this system was widely practised in the 15th and 16th centuries. It is estimated that at least 200,000 boys from the Balkans passed through this system in just over two centuries of operation. Whilst many boys were taken against their and their families' will some were given freely due to the many advantages of sending sons to Istanbul. Many of the boys were permitted to later reunite with their Christian or Muslim families. Those who came from Christian families often converted to Islam. Janissaries received many privileges in the empire, enough so that there were even reported cases of families bribing officials to take their children. It is reported that, in 1515, Bosnian Muslims sent 1,000 of their children for training to the imperial palace.

The basic legal system of the Ottomans did not abide by Islamic holy law. Later there were elements of **Islamic law** placed on Ottoman territories, but when the Turks conquered Bosnia it was still possible, for example, for a Christian to become a *spahi* (cavalry soldier paid directly by the Ottoman government) and to be granted an estate without renouncing his Christian beliefs. Although Muslims enjoyed many advantages, the Christian peasantry were not always tied to the land as serfs and they were, at least for a time, reasonably taxed. In a last appeal for help against the Turks before the conquest King Tomašević wrote: 'The Turks … are showing a kindly disposition towards the peasants. They promise that all who desert to them shall be free and they welcome them graciously … The people will be easily induced by such tricks to desert me.' But this trickery had a ring of truth to it. The state policy was not directed towards converting subjects to Islam, but was aimed at keeping the country under its control and extracting taxes, riches and men for further conquests. The Christians and Jews within the Ottoman state were permitted to worship, albeit under certain restrictions.

As the main focus of Ottoman rule was on collecting men and money, and not on how local officials behaved, many local provincial governors, or pashas, had a relatively free hand and were often very corrupt and oppressive. So whilst it can be confidently said that in the first few centuries forced conversion was not a practice and that Islamic holy law was not imposed on its conquered subjects, it cannot be assumed that any 'rule of law' existed in the Ottoman Empire. Many Christians in present-day Bosnia and Herzegovina hold a great deal of resentment towards the Turks. No-one, of course, likes to be under occupation and have their cultural and religious beliefs exchanged for the occupier's. Christians most definitely received the short straw within the Ottoman Empire, particularly the Catholics, who were seen as allies to the enemy Austro-Hungarians. In a European context, however, the alternatives were brutal regimes that not only punished heretics but murdered, raped and pillaged in massive numbers. Historians generally view the Ottomans, who had large Jewish and Christian populations, as being exceptionally tolerant when compared with their European counterparts at that time in history.

The **Islamicisation of Bosnia** was a process that lasted as long as the Illyrian defence against Rome, and the Bosnian kingdom's century-and-a-half resistance against the Turks. This process, however, did not usually come through force or war. The Islamicisation of the Bosnian population is possibly the most distinctive and maybe the most important event in its history. There was, and still is, a lot of controversy surrounding this issue, with most arguments being based on myth and folklore. A rather vigorous investigation of Ottoman administrative records took place in the 1940s and dispelled many old myths. One will still find today, though, bitter 'memories' of 'forced' conversion. Perhaps the truth is somewhere in the middle.

By the late 1460s, Islam's strongest influence was in and around Sarajevo as the city had been exposed to Islam for at least 15 years before Bosnia fell to the Turks. Its influence was not markedly felt elsewhere in the country. Christians were an overwhelming majority, although the 'defters' (tax registration records) do not distinguish types of Christians. Bosnia was at this time mostly Catholic and Herzegovina largely Orthodox, with remnants of the old Bosnian Church in both regions. The number of Muslims increased steadily over the next few decades but defters also indicate a large exodus (relative to population size at the time) out of Bosnia. The registers point to a large number of villages being abandoned, presumably Catholics fleeing to Austro-Hungarian territories. Some Catholics feared persecution for siding with or aiding the Hungarian armies, others retreated to Catholic 'ground', and although there is no recorded evidence it seems logical that some communities that were suspected of co-operation with the enemy were forced to leave.

By 1520 the ratio of Muslims to Christians in Bosnia was almost 50:50, with the Christians having a slight majority over the growing Muslim population. This process was slower in Herzegovina, but by the turn of the 16th century church records indicate voluntary conversions to Islam. Islamicisation wouldn't take place in the northern and northeastern parts of the country until later when these areas were taken from the Hungarians. Records from a Dominican historian, Father Mandić, claim there was a deliberate campaign of conversion in the northeast from around 1516–24. There is much dispute over this claim but it is quite apparent that many Franciscan monasteries did cease operating in these areas. It seems likely that an Ottoman strategy of isolating communities from the Church would create smoother conversion. But the community of Srebrenica, mainly Ragusan and Catholic German, despite Ottoman influence in the town, remained largely Catholic until the mid-16th century.

While the evidence available does not prove that there was a policy of forced conversions, this is not to say that there was no persecution and oppression of Christians. The Orthodox Church, falling under the jurisdiction of the Ottoman Empire, was an accepted institution. The **Catholic Church**, the Church of the enemy Austrians, was treated with a heavier hand. In the geographical territory of Bosnia at the time of the Turkish conquest, there were few Orthodox communities. Herzegovina, on the other hand, had a large Serb and Vlach (eastern Orthodox) population. Before the invasion there were an estimated 35 Franciscan monasteries in Bosnia and Herzegovina; by the mid-1600s only ten remained. The **Orthodox Church**, however, actually grew in size during the Ottoman occupation.

A theory that is often held by many Bosniak (Bosnian Muslim) historians and intellectuals is that the Bosnian Church was directly linked to the Islamicisation of Bosnia. This theory asserts that the followers of the Bosnian Church, in defiance of the pressures from official Church authorities, readily converted to Islam and maintained many of their belief systems within their new Islamic faith. It is fairly well proven, however, that at the time of the collapse of the Bosnian kingdom, the Bosnian Church was weak and isolated. The Franciscans had been operative in Bosnia since 1340, and in the century leading up to the arrival of the Turks they exercised great influence on the heretic Christians of Bosnia. What must be recognised, though, is that no Church organisation was able to claim strong control over many regions of both Bosnia and Herzegovina. It cannot be argued that they were not Christians but it can be argued that little influence of the major powers from within the Orthodox and Catholic churches was felt by the small, isolated communities throughout the country. The idea that there were mass settlements of Muslims from Turkey into Bosnia can be firmly rejected, as evidenced by the defters. Some Turkish people did settle in the territory of Bosnia and Herzegovina, but their numbers were in no way significant enough to point to an Ottoman strategy of 'importing' Muslims.

The religious practices of both the Bosnian Christians and Muslims strongly point to a mystical convergence of the two faiths. Even today, Christians and Muslims share the same superstitions in the power of amulets, with many Muslims having them blessed by Franciscan monks. Many holy days and festivals were celebrated by both religious communities. 'Muslim' ceremonies were often conducted in Christian churches and Masses were held in front of the Virgin Mary to cure or ward off illness. There are records of Christians calling for Muslim dervishes to read verses from the Koran to cure or bless them. It is quite clear that a synthesis of diverging beliefs occurred in BiH, where 'all sects meet on a common basis of secular superstition'.

Little has been mentioned about the **Serbs** in Bosnia thus far. Before the arrival of the Ottomans the Orthodox Church was barely active in Bosnia. There are records of some Serbian noblemen settling in the region of Vrhbosna (present-day Sarajevo) and it is likely that the Orthodox from Herzegovina migrated north through the mountains. The first Orthodox church built in Sarajevo was completed in the mid 16th century. In Herzegovina, however, the Church had been well established and most of Hum, particularly the eastern parts adjacent to Serbia and Zeta (Montenegro), were populated by a mainly Orthodox community. It is also important to note that only in the last hundred years leading up to the Turkish occupation of Herzegovina did the Catholic Church significantly spread to Herzegovina – this topic, mind you, is the subject of heated debate.

Keeping in mind that Serbia fell to the Ottomans many years before Bosnia, and that many of the janissaries in the Turkish army were Serbian, it seems a natural and logical event that Slav subjects from a neighbouring Ottoman-occupied state would migrate to Bosnia. Although some of the Orthodox communities of the 16th and 17th centuries were a result of Catholic conversions, most of them were established by large migrations from other Orthodox lands. It seemed to be a deliberate policy of the Ottoman administration to repopulate lands that had been depleted by war, plague, or by Catholics abandoning their villages. There are also records of 'Christian herdsmen' being relocated to devastated eastern Herzegovina and central and northern Bosnia around Visoko and Maglaj. These herdsmen were identifiably **Vlachs**. The question of the origins of the Vlachs is complex but they are believed to be Thracian tribes that arrived well before Slav settlement in the 6th and 7th centuries. Vlachs were found all around the Balkans. The term 'Vlach' is generally understood to have referred in ancient times to a semi-nomadic herdsman. Vlachs were found in the Dalmatian hinterland, Herzegovina, Montenegro, Greece, Bulgaria, Serbia and Macedonia. Most of the Romanised and Latin-speaking peoples of this area, including the Illyrians, disappeared or assimilated with the invaders, particularly the Slavs. It is fair to say that the Vlachs blended with the new Slav settlers, most of whom, but certainly not all, assimilated with the Serbian tribes.

Migrations also occurred in great numbers along the frontier lands of northwestern Bosnia in the early 16th century, as Catholic communities fled to Habsburg lands. The Vlachs and Serbs, with a long tradition of being fierce fighters, were moved into these border regions and were one of the most feared elements of the Ottoman army. At the same time on the other side of the front line, Vlachs and Serbs that had fled the Ottoman advance in the 15th century were being organised by the Habsburgs. Many of the Vlachs and Serbs from the Ottoman side are said to have crossed the frontier borders to join the Habsburgs.

Most of Bosnia and Herzegovina's present cities and towns were created during the Ottoman period. A focus on building towns and constructing roads and bridges to connect these towns brought the whole country, for the first time, into an urbanised sphere. Never before had any central administration effectively embarked on a vision of building a country. Islamic art and culture added a remarkable aspect to life in Bosnia and Herzegovina. The Orthodox Church and the introduction of a new **Jewish community** enjoyed growth and prosperity within the empire, unlike the often brutal feudal systems seen elsewhere in Europe at that time.

A small community of Sephardic Jews who had been expelled from Spain in 1492 settled in several towns, namely Sarajevo, Travnik and Mostar, and was tolerated by the Ottomans. Jewish merchants quickly established themselves in the cloth and silk trades. This tradition would stand until the destruction of the Jewish community in World War II. Some were skilled metalworkers and it is believed that the Anatolian Jews greatly advanced Ottoman weaponry. For this gift it is said that the Jews were given their own *mahala* (quarters) in Sarajevo near the central market. One of the most priceless articles in the National Museum is the Hebrew codex Haggadah. Several synagogues and a *hram* were built. The Jews of Bosnia and Herzegovina from an early stage after their arrival played an important role in the cultural and religious life of the cities where they settled.

Ottoman characteristics began to predominate by the end of the 15th century in many of Bosnia's towns and cities. The cities of Sarajevo and Mostar were two of the most significant projects of Ottoman times. From the smallest settlements the Ottomans built two of the most striking cities in Bosnia and Herzegovina. In Sarajevo it was **Gazi Husrev Beg** who embarked on a mission to build a city. In his time as Governor of Sarajevo he built many mosques, primary schools, roads, bridges, inns, fountains and markets. **Sarajevo** blossomed from a tiny settlement in the Miljacka Valley to one of the most beautiful cities in the Balkans. Within the empire it was praised for its striking beauty, which was said to be comparable only to Damascus.

The finest examples of Ottoman religious architecture were Ferhadija Mosque in Banja Luka, which was destroyed in the most recent conflict, and the Gazi Husrev Begova Mosque in Sarajevo. The intricate details and creative design are certainly amongst the finest in Europe. **Mostar** stands out as one of the most magnificent Ottoman achievements of all time. The Stari most (Old Bridge), also destroyed during the recent conflict, was the national symbol of Bosnia and Herzegovina. **Travnik** and **Banja Luka** also became centres of Ottoman administration. Travnik was once hailed as the European Istanbul and was a major trading and political town during Turkish rule. Travnik's old town is one of the few remaining in Bosnia that have preserved a functional residential quarters in their original authenticity. Banja Luka too played a major role as the empire spread north. The city's size greatly increased during this period and several of Bosnia's most significant mosques were built here.

THE DECLINE OF THE OTTOMAN EMPIRE A major Turkish defeat at the hands of the Austrians in 1683 signalled a drastic decline in the empire. In 1697, **Eugene of Savoy** advanced on Bosnia and reached Sarajevo. Sarajevo was put to the torch and most of the town went up in flames. When he retreated many Catholics left with his army for fear of reprisals. This decimated the Catholic population and only three Franciscan monasteries remained open. The frontier lands in the Krajina were in constant conflict, and unrest in eastern Herzegovina along the Montenegrin border became commonplace.

For the first half of the 18th century the Turks were in retreat and losing ground to both the Austrians and the Venetians. Tax increases to regain lost territories in other regions were met with violent uprisings by both Christians and Muslims. Tax revolts broke out in Herzegovina from 1727 to 1732. In addition, the plague devastated Bosnia in the 1730s and an estimated 20,000 people died. Austrian gains in Bosnia would not come so easy though. A greatly skilled defence crushed the Austrian army at the **Battle of Banja Luka** in 1739. After the **Peace Treaty of Belgrade** was signed in 1739 Austria renounced all lands south of the Sava River, which marks Bosnia and Herzegovina's present-day boundaries. This treaty ensured almost 50 years of peace from the outside enemies of the Ottoman Empire. It did not, however, quell the tidal wave of revolts engulfing the country. Tax revolts became more frequent as the overstretched and underfunded empire consistently raised taxes and became more and more corrupt and lawless. In 1748, the new Governor of Bosnia, Mehmetpasha Kukavica, received a letter from the sultan stating that 'Bosnia must be conquered again.'

The next war with the Austrians had a new dimension added to it. Joseph II of Austria and Catherine the Great of Russia agreed to conquer the Balkans, and divide the peninsula between the two Christian empires. This was the basis of the geopolitical interests that would erupt into World War I after the fall of the empire. The political chess that followed became a pattern seen many times in the 19th century. Austria captured most of Bosnia in 1789, and in 1791 agreed to give it all back to the Ottomans. The sultan in return proclaimed the Austrians the official 'protectors' of the Christians under Ottoman rule.

At the turn of the 19th century **Napoleon** and France defeated Austria and took over Venetia, Istria and Dalmatia. Austria again declared war on France in 1809 and by 1813 Austria ruled those areas again. The biggest threat, however, was no longer the Austrians but the powerful rebellions to the east in Serbia. Large-scale revolts took place in which Slav Muslims were massacred. The Ottomans granted Serbia a greater amount of autonomy in 1815. By the end of the Napoleonic Wars it became clear to Istanbul that the empire was so weak it would collapse without aggressive reform. Now fighting battles on all fronts it was too difficult for the Turks to re-establish control of Bosnia. Bosnia's local governors and military leaders looked for more autonomy and began making demands to the Ottoman authorities. Many local militias offered the Ottomans military assistance but with strict demands on self-rule and that taxes levied by the empire be waived. Christians and Muslims alike were seeking sweeping reforms within the empire. A final blow was struck in a massive revolt that lasted three years from 1875–78, and which effectively ended Ottoman rule in Bosnia and Herzegovina. Russia had declared war on the Ottoman Empire in 1877, and the earlier plans of the Austrians and Russians would soon become reality. By 20 October 1878, the total occupation of Bosnia and Herzegovina was complete. A new era under Austro-Hungarian rule began.

BOSNIA AND HERZEGOVINA UNDER AUSTRO-HUNGARIAN RULE With not a moment's rest, the fate of Bosnia and Herzegovina transferred from one foreign occupier to the next. The Austro-Hungarians wasted no time in establishing their rule. The **Congress of Berlin** in 1878 redrew the map of the Balkans, already established by Russian interest in the San Stefano Treaty earlier that year, and approved the Austro-Hungarian occupation of Bosnia and Herzegovina.

By holding the territory of Bosnia and Herzegovina, Austria-Hungary acquired great economic and market potential. It also enabled them, maybe more importantly, to effectively establish an opposition to Russian influence in the Balkans. They were able to keep a close watch on Serbia and could begin 'experimenting' with an even greater ambition – expansion to the east. These factors shaped Austro-Hungarian policy in Bosnia and Herzegovina. Austro-Hungarian rule allowed the **feudal system**, however backward and outdated, to continue and govern everyday life. Meanwhile, progressive and modern measures in certain spheres of life were rapidly embarked upon.

The next 40 years, half of those spent as an occupied province and the latter half as an annexed state, saw one of the most profound transformations of internal politics in Bosnia and Herzegovina's history. When the occupation army arrived in BiH the struggle for national identity among the three groups – Orthodox (Serb), Catholic (Croat) and Muslim – had already begun. Having lived through and survived two millennia of historical drama, the peoples of Bosnia and Herzegovina – with a vast memory of negative experiences and a long tradition of resistance to outside forces – found that once again they were not in control of their own destiny. Austro-Hungarian politicians, with much expertise in this field, understood what conditions were necessary to secure the stability of the monarchy in such an environment. Having been under occupation for so long, Bosnia possessed little political and national maturity in an emerging 'new world'. The administration knew that the prevention of political and/or national development would further strengthen their hold on Bosnia and Herzegovina and establish more links to the territories of the southern Slavs. Henceforth the Austro-Hungarian administrator Benjamin Kallay attempted to isolate Bosnia and Herzegovina from nationalist political movements in Croatia and Serbia, and to promote the idea of **Bosnian nationhood** as a separate and unifying factor.

The most visible changes under Austro-Hungarian occupation occurred in everyday life where more European styles of architecture, cuisine, behaviour and dress were introduced. Lacking confidence in the native inhabitants, foreign officials, mainly Slav, assumed the administrative duties of governing the state. Large numbers of peasants from the empire's other territories were brought into BiH's already overwhelmingly peasant population. Muslims from Bosnia and Herzegovina emigrated south and east on a massive scale as the empire implemented a policy of rebalancing the country's religious make-up.

The Austro-Hungarians began to develop **modern industries** alongside the old, feudal agrarian traditions. Primary importance was given to the timber, mining and metallurgy industries. Great strides were made in the improvement of the infrastructure with road building and the construction of a railway. With these improvements an industrial working class appeared for the first time in Bosnia and Herzegovina, and the empire began to see spontaneous rebellions form into **organised strikes**. In 1906 in Sarajevo, the tobacco factory and brick-making workers went on general strike demanding a shorter working week and regular pay. This quickly spread to almost all towns in Bosnia. Large-scale military intervention was able to suppress the strikes but trade unions were soon organised thereafter, as was the first Social Democratic Party of Bosnia and Herzegovina. Thus, according to historian Ivan Lovrenović, 'in those regions, for the first time in history, political organisations were created on the basis of the class conception of association and common struggle against exploitation'.

Social problems persisted despite the empire's investment in Europeanising Bosnia and Herzegovina. The peasant class generally lived in dire conditions. The population ratio of rural to urban in 1910 was more than 6:1. The government announced the 'gradual voluntary purchasing of freedom by serfs' which required that a high cash payment be made by the serfs for the land they worked, and for their freedom. High interest rates imposed by the banks only worsened the situation for the peasantry. This resulted in yet more revolts. In eastern Herzegovina there were revolts against military law and recruitment in 1882, Muslims and Serbs set up rebel command and military units and *hajduk*, or rebel, banditry expanded on a massive scale that would give the empire's army and administration trouble for decades. In 1910, a **peasant rebellion** erupted in the Bosnian Krajina (the western wing of Bosnia) and spread to many other districts.

Rebellions erupted not only along class lines but along nationalist ones as well. The Bosnian Serb idea of nationhood had been a constant factor since the First Serbian Uprising under the Ottomans, which had later culminated in the uprising of 1875–78. This created a powerful and permanent consciousness of national integrity amongst the Serbs, which was manifested in the movement for religious and educational autonomy from 1893 to 1903. The Bosnian Croats shared a similar birth of national consciousness before the arrival of the Austro-Hungarians. They were reluctant, however, to abandon their long ties to the Franciscan Church and traditional home of Bosnia and Herzegovina. The Muslims had no say whatsoever in the Berlin Congress

THE BANOVINAS: 1929 AND 1939
KEY
International boundary
Banovinas boundary, 1929
Croatian Banovina boundary, 1939
Main city
0
200km
0
120 miles
N
Bradt
DRAVSKA
Ljubljana
Zagreb
SAVSKA
VRBASKA
Banja Luka
DUNAVSKA
Novi Sad
Prefecture of Belgrade
DRINSKA
Sarajevo
PRIMORSKA
Split
ZETSKA
Cetinje
MORAVSKA
Niš
VARDARSKA
Skopje
ADRIATIC SEA

when Turkey was forced to hand over Bosnia to the Austro-Hungarians, and they were reluctant to accept a fate in whose determination they did not participate. It took a force of 200,000 well-trained and well-equipped soldiers three months to subdue the Muslim (and others of the anti-occupation spirit) population.

During a time of significant social unrest during the rule of the Austro-Hungarian Empire, the cultural life of Bosnia and Herzegovina experienced positive changes. For the first time Bosnia and Herzegovina was in direct contact with European cultural currents. This first generation of European-educated intellectuals produced a large number of writers, scientists and experts in various fields. Cultural centres were established throughout the country. With a new image of the world offered by the wide horizons of European life, Bosnia and Herzegovina enjoyed a great addition to its rich cultural heritage. Perhaps the greatest strides came in literature and publications. Many newspapers and literary magazines were established for the first time in Sarajevo and Mostar. The most valuable cultural institution left by the occupying government was the **National Museum**. From this institution much scientific activity was spurred that developed through research and learned journals. In the fields of archaeology, anthropology, ethnography and natural history the museum established itself as one of the eminent scientific institutions in Europe.

Within the framework of a new colonial policy, widespread and rapid social change and national diversification occurred in Bosnia and Herzegovina. These changes fuelled national and political antagonisms so powerful that even the mighty Austro-Hungarian Empire could not keep them at bay. It was not so much an organised agenda of political affiliation but rather a spontaneous expression, largely by youth, of a revolutionary spirit. Nationalist agendas did arise in the beginning of the 20th century but the general resistance was more at a class level than a national one. In a place where drastic social conditions prevailed, combative acts of terrorism began when Bosnia and Herzegovina was officially annexed in 1908. In 1910, an assassination attempt on Emperor Franz Joseph was organised for his visit. In the same year the Governor of BiH, General Marijan Varešanin, was shot, and on 28 June 1914 a young Serbian nationalist by the name of Gavrilo Princip shot dead **Archduke Franz Ferdinand** and his pregnant wife on the streets of Sarajevo. This event not only sparked the end of Austro-Hungarian rule in Bosnia and Herzegovina, but also led to the large political fallouts between the great powers that preceded the first battles of **World War I**.

Austria-Hungary's declaration of war on Serbia on 28 July 1914 carved deep wounds and strengthened aged alliances amongst the world powers. Bosnians and Herzegovinians were sent to fight against the regime that repressed them.

THE KINGDOM OF SERBS, CROATS AND SLOVENES AND THE FIRST YUGOSLAVIA Towards the end of World War I the Austro-Hungarians attempted to 'rearrange' the status of Bosnia and Herzegovina. The Governor of BiH, Baron Sarkotić, suggested to the emperor that the country join with Croatia or be granted special autonomy under the Hungarian crown. As the war efforts continued to falter towards the end of 1918, the idea of Bosnia and Herzegovina remaining under Austro-Hungarian rule was completely abandoned and talks of the creation of a Yugoslav state began. The leader of the Bosnian Muslims, Mehmed Spaho, had the task of uniting the divided loyalties of the Muslim populations. Although some disparities still existed amongst the Muslims, he declared the Muslims of Bosnia and Herzegovina were in favour of a Yugoslav state. National Councils were formed, first in Zagreb and then in Bosnia and Herzegovina, renouncing the rule of the Habsburgs in countries formerly under Austro-Hungarian authority, clearly signifying the push for a united Yugoslav state. Days later, Croatia, Bosnia and Herzegovina and Slovenia joined with the Kingdom of Serbia to form the Kingdom of Serbs, Croats and Slovenes. The Kingdom of Serbia insisted on a centralist-style rule from Belgrade whereas Croatia sought more regional governance within the kingdom. The Bosnian Muslims were in favour of more autonomy for BiH, which placed them on the side of the Croats. The Bosnian Croats were also against Serbian centralism; the Bosnian Serbs were in favour of a centralised Yugoslav state.

Bosnia and Herzegovina entered the kingdom with a severely depleted population, a depressed social and economic atmosphere, and strained religious and ethnic relations after 40 years of Austro-Hungarian rule.

Massive **land reforms** took place in Bosnia and Herzegovina in 1919 and serfdom was abolished. Many Muslim landowners were stripped of their lands that were given to the peasantry after the sweeping reforms, reducing some to poverty. But the landowners were only a very small faction of the Muslim population, most being peasant smallholders. The battle between Zagreb and Belgrade continued in the 1920s. It was during these times of great political division that the Muslims began to identify themselves as Muslim Croats or Muslim Serbs. The trends of the Muslims to side with the Serbs against Vienna at the turn of the century had now shifted to siding with the Croats as natural allies against Belgrade's centralist schemes.

During a tense and difficult 11 years no conditions existed for the development or enrichment of cultural life in Bosnia and Herzegovina. By the late 1920s, the political atmosphere became dangerously explosive. In 1928, the Croat leader Stjepan Radić was suspended from parliament for slandering the minister of social policy. Some months later a Montenegrin deputy, angered by the constant interruptions to his speech, pulled out a gun and shot several deputies, including Radić. By 1929 the Serbian king Alexander suspended the constitution and renamed the kingdom 'Yugoslavia'. The new state, in all its attempts to thwart nationalist tendencies, was unable to placate any group. Banovinas were established in Bosnia to appease nationalist sentiment between Croatia and Serbia, which basically divided the country up into Croatian and Serbian subdivisions. The Croats were the least happy with this new reassignment of territories into banates, and saw it only as the realisation of the dream of a Serbian state. The most radical Croatian politician, **Ante Pavelić**, left the country and with the help of Mussolini began organising the **Ustasha movement** for Croatian independence.

The leader of the Croatian party, Vlatko Maček, issued a 'Resolution' in 1932 calling for a return to democracy and the end of Serbian hegemony. The Slovenian and Bosnian leaders followed suit with similar statements and all three were subsequently arrested. King Alexander was assassinated in 1934 and in 1935 Prince Paul, his successor, ordered new elections. Milan Stojadinović, a young Serbian politician, was appointed to form a government. This loose new alliance lasted a shaky four years and ended when a Serbian minister asserted to parliament in a speech that the 'Serb policies will always be the policies of this house and this government'. Later that evening five key ministers resigned, forcing Prince Paul to dismiss Stojadinović and appoint Serbian minister Dragiša Cvetković in his place.

Hitler had by now begun advancing on Czechoslovakia, and his devout admirer Ante Pavelić in Italy was pushing for the break-up of Yugoslavia. It was apparent that there was a desperate need to bring the Croats on board and to find a solution the Croats would accept. Cvetković and Maček met and began discussing the restructuring of the national territories, which would include giving Croatia some political power of its own. The new solution carved up significant parts of Bosnia, giving some to Croatia and leaving others to be devoured by Serbia. The Bosnian Muslim leader

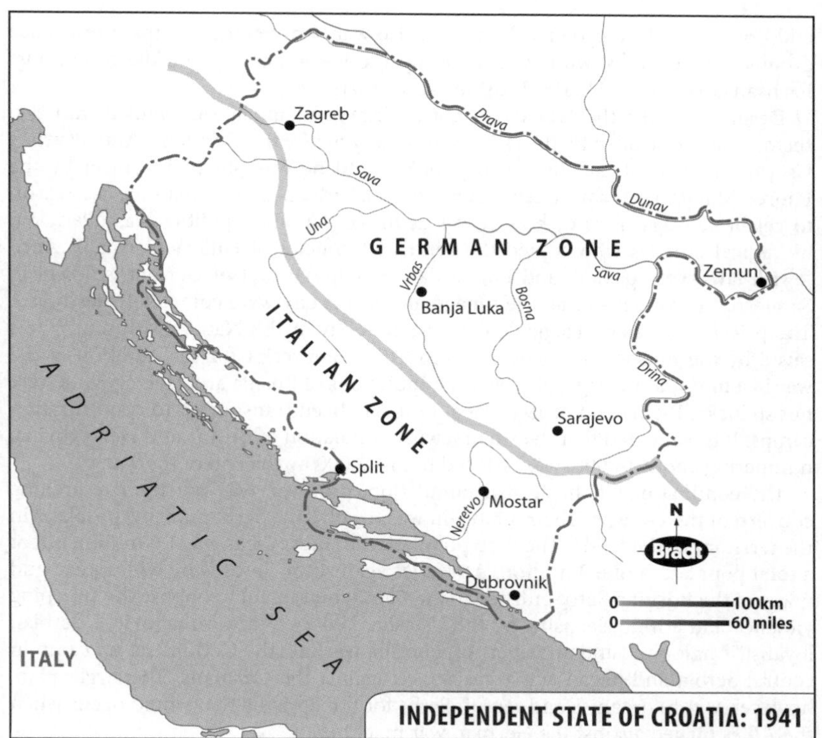

INDEPENDENT STATE OF CROATIA: 1941

Spaho died during these negotiations and his successor Džafer Kulenović sought the creation of a separate banate for Bosnia. His requests were ignored as many of the banates not absorbed into the new Croatia banates had a majority Serb population who wanted to maintain close ties with the remaining banates dominated by Serbia.

These debates continued until the pressure asserted from the German Reich became too much to bear for the Yugoslav government. With Hitler on their border and the Italians already in Greece, Prince Paul realised the impossibility of protection from Great Britain and signed the **Axis pact** in Vienna on 25 March 1941. When the Yugoslav delegation returned, the prince was ousted in a bloodless coup and a new government of national unity was formed. The new government tried to continue a conciliatory policy towards Germany but ten days later on 6 April massive bombing raids on Belgrade began, and Yugoslavia was invaded by German, Bulgarian, Hungarian and Italian forces. The 'resistance' lasted 11 days before the Yugoslav army surrendered to the German High Command.

WORLD WAR II Yugoslavia was literally dismembered and divided between the Axis powers after the defeat of the Yugoslav army. Its territories became important for communication and supplies of natural resources and labour to fight the Allied powers. The Axis powers were focused on defeating the Allied forces and were not prepared for the war against the Yugoslav resistance movements, and the two civil wars that ensued.

Before the end of the Blitzkrieg the Germans had proclaimed a new '**Independent State of Croatia**' (known as NDH), which also engulfed all of Bosnia and Herzegovina. Croatian extremists conducted a war largely against the Serb populations in Croatia and Bosnia and Herzegovina. There was also war between the two main resistance groups – the Četniks, who were Serbs loyal to the monarchy, and the communist Partisans that enlisted Serbs, Muslims and Croats.

Despite its title, the NDH was not so independent. It was divided into two sectors, one controlled by the Italians and the other by the Germans. Ante Pavelić's Ustasha movement had not been popular until he was placed in power by the Führer. Many Croats saw independence from a Serbian-dominated state as a reason to celebrate, regardless of how it was achieved. Croatian politics was overtaken by radical fanatics who copied the genocidal policies of Hitler's Germany. **Anti-Jewish laws** were passed, and only a day after the arrival of German soldiers in Sarajevo, the contents of all the synagogues in the city were completely destroyed. The priceless Sarajevo Haggadah (viewable today at the National Museum) was saved by the museum's director who hid the manuscript for the duration of the war in a mountain village. The Jewish populations of Bosnia and Herzegovina were not so lucky. By the end of 1941 most Jews had been transported to concentration camps. It is estimated that the small Jewish population of Bosnia and Herzegovina, numbering about 14,000, was reduced to just 2,000 by the end of the war.

The elimination of the Jewish population, however, was not the overarching concern of the Ustasha. Their main aim was to solve the Serb minority 'problem' in the territory of the NDH. The Serb population in these areas was 1.9 million out of a total population of 6.3 million. Atrocities against the Serbs were widespread and many of the Bosnian Serbs enlisted in the **Četnik movement** to oppose the sweeping violence and ethnic cleansing by the Ustasha. Led by Draža Mihailović, a Serbian loyalist, Anglophile and an expert on guerilla warfare, the Četniks set up camp in central Serbia and began active resistance against the Germans. The larger plan, however, was to organise and recruit Serbs for the uprising that would occur when the Allies turned against the German war machine.

The other resistance movement, the communist Partisans, had different aims. Under the leadership of Josip Broz, or **Tito**, the Partisans envisioned a communist victory over the Germans and a social revolution that would create a post-war communist state. Tito was a Stalin loyalist whose revolutionary ideology attracted a population that was weary and worn by nationalist agendas.

Two of the most crucial battles of World War II in Yugoslavia took place in Bosnia and Herzegovina. In the early months of 1943 the most epic battle for the Partisans began – the **Battle of the Neretva**. A surprise counter-offensive was launched by the Partisans in the direction of Herzegovina and Montenegro. In retreat from battles in the Krajina region the Partisans reached the Neretva River with 4,000 wounded and many more villagers who had joined them in fleeing from German attacks. With over 20,000 Četnik troops on one side and Axis forces on the other, Tito sabotaged the bridge at **Jablanica**, leading the enemy to believe the Partisans had changed course. He ordered the bridge to be destroyed and improvised a wooden footbridge. All the wounded were brought across and the footbridge destroyed, thus deceiving the German forces. The Partisans now faced the Četnik army, and in a fierce battle the Četniks were wiped out. Tito and the Partisans were able to secure a safe passage to Montenegro. The remains of the bridge can still be seen today in Jablanica and there is a full account of the battle at the museum.

By May the Germans had begun preparations for the largest campaign of the war. Over 100,000 troops, backed by air power, surrounded the outnumbered Partisans in the mountainous region near the River Sutjeska in eastern Bosnia. The Partisans attempted to break through to the eastern border with Montenegro and over 7,000 of them lost their lives. Today Sutjeska is a national park that pays tribute to them.

POST-1945 YUGOSLAVIA: SIX REPUBLICS

With the surrender of the Italians in late 1943 large quantities of their equipment fell into Partisan hands. The latter gained much momentum at this stage and in November 1943 the Anti-Fascist Council for the People's Liberation of Yugoslavia (AVNOJ) meetings in Jajce and Mrkonjić Grad declared Bosnia and Herzegovina as a multi-ethnic communist state. Mihailović's Četniks, after years of support from the Italians, began directly collaborating with the Germans for the first time. By 1944 Allied support of the Partisans had significantly increased and mass desertions of Muslims and Croats from the Ustasha ranks bolstered Tito's fighting force. In the summer of 1944 the Germans began to withdraw from Yugoslavia and the Allied powers managed to persuade the Serbian king Peter to appeal to Yugoslavs to back Tito. Soviet forces would occupy one-third of the country by the year's end and **communist victory** in Yugoslavia was basically secured.

The NDH vanished as quickly as it was formed – overnight. Tito and the Partisans had set the stage for the formation of the Socialist Federal Republic of Yugoslavia.

TITO'S YUGOSLAVIA Depending on whom you talk to, Tito was either a monstrous communist dictator or a peacekeeping socialist visionary. Both viewpoints could arguably be correct but the truth probably lies somewhere in the middle. At the end of World War II, Yugoslavia, like much of Europe, was a mess. Tito quickly introduced Stalinist methodology in running his new communist republic. His logic was that in order to plant the seeds of socialist ideology, nationalist sentiments must be uprooted and weeded out at all costs. This resulted in the death of what some estimate to be 250,000 anti-communists, opponents and collaborators. The Department for the Protection of the People, Tito's **secret police**, arrested and often severely punished anyone who opposed 'brotherhood and unity', and in fact anyone they *thought* might threaten the new fragile state. The Croats were especially targeted, some having supported the Ustasha and been followers of Ante Pavelić. The Franciscan clergy in Herzegovina were also singled out, having been suspected of supporting the Ustasha against the Partisans. Many churches were destroyed and monasteries shut down. Serbian Četniks were also seriously persecuted and many either left the country or retreated to isolated mountain areas. The Muslims were also served harsh punishments; executions of the Muslim intellectual elite were commonplace in the early years after the war. The courts of Islamic sacred law were suppressed, teaching of children in mosques became a criminal offence, women were forbidden to wear the veil and many Muslim cultural societies were forced to close.

In 1948, Stalin expelled Yugoslavia from the Cominform, the union of communist states formed after World War II. This time Tito quickly changed his platform from being a stark Stalinist to being more an open-minded, independent and liberal socialist. By the mid-1950s, religious life in Yugoslavia had improved, with new laws that allowed freedom of religion, although the state was mandated with directing and controlling these institutions.

Unresolved issues from the first Yugoslavia resurfaced in the early years of Tito's reign. Many felt the negotiations for the banates that were agreed upon by Croatia and Serbia at the dawn of World War II should remain. This would leave Bosnia and Herzegovina with no nationhood and no clear position for its majority Muslim population. Party leaders, however, remained true to the principles outlined at the anti-fascist meetings held in Mrkonjić Grad and Jajce during World War II. The question of Muslim nationhood took time to resolve and was often met with fierce opposition, particularly from the Serbs. In 1948, the Communist Party conducted a census giving the Muslims three options in terms of their national identity: Muslim Serb, Muslim Croat or Muslim undeclared. Out of a total of 875,000 Muslims, 778,000 registered as undeclared. The party, however, wanted to promote 'Yugoslavism' and later removed the Muslim option from the census but still allowed people to register as 'Yugoslav, nationally undeclared'. Almost a million people in Bosnia and Herzegovina did so. **Muslim nationhood** would eventually be established in the late 1960s.

It wasn't until the 1960s that Yugoslavia began to change its policies. It is from this point on that people speak of the glorious days of Tito – when everyone had a job, a free education, there were no homeless, one was free to travel around the world (thanks to Yugoslavia's position as a founding member of the non-aligned movement), and one 'could sleep in a park' and no-one would bother you. Whereas the first half of the new Yugoslavia was built around establishing authority, rebuilding, and weeding out opposition, this new era brought about a kind of **national renaissance.**

Massive changes to the infrastructure, particularly road systems, opened impenetrable Bosnia and Herzegovina for the first time. The **National Roads Launch** of 1968 aimed at connecting every town in the country with asphalt roads. Almost a thousand schools and libraries were built. The **library programme** was largely funded by Nobel laureate Ivo Andrić. He donated half of his prize money to this project. Schools in rural areas and small villages were established as were small medical clinics or 'ambulanta'. The **university system** was expanded from Sarajevo to Banja Luka, Tuzla, Mostar, Zenica and other major cities in BiH.

New incentives by the Communist Party for 'self-management' within the republics gave the population a sense of pride and independence, but the decentralising measures of the 1960s and 1970s damaged the economy. Tito established and maintained good relations with both the United States and the Soviet Union, and Yugoslavia received financial aid from both of them in a typical Cold War tug-of-war. But for the average person in Bosnia and Herzegovina, life was good. People had jobs, relatively comfortable lifestyles and were free to travel and work abroad.

There were some revivals of nationalist sentiment in the 1970s. These revivals followed the ousting in 1966 of Serb 'centralist' Alexsander Ranković, who had dominated the Ministry of the Interior and the secret police. His strategies had led to the suppression of expressions of ethnicity; hence when he left there was a reactionary movement towards nationalism. Croats complained that high-ranking officials, judges, directors, mayors and police chiefs were all Serbs. Although the Croats represented 20% of the population they felt they were not equally well represented in the Bosnian communist establishment. Both Croatian and Serbian nationalists again began to speak of carving up Bosnia and Herzegovina and integrating the pieces into Croatia or Serbia. Serbian nationalism grew at a more destructive pace. Even though the central government was based in Belgrade and the party and armed forces were overwhelmingly Serb, there was still strong resentment of any territorial rewards. Macedonia had been given republic status under the new Yugoslavia but many Serbs viewed this region as 'Southern Serbia' after it had been conquered in 1912. The northern region of Serbia, Vojvodina, had a large Hungarian and Croat population and was given autonomous status as a province under Tito. The southern region of Kosovo, also conquered in 1912, had a large Albanian majority and was also declared an autonomous region by Tito in the 1946 constitution.

AFTER TITO After the death of Tito in 1980, Bosnia and Herzegovina continued to enjoy relative prosperity. The deepening crisis in Kosovo in the early 1980s, however, gave further fuel to the Serbian nationalist cause. Dobrica Ćosić, a Serbian nationalist communist, complained that 'one could witness even among the Serbian people a re-ignition of the old historic goal and national idea – the unification of the Serbian people into a single state'. This statement led to him being expelled from the Central Committee. Ćosić also fiercely opposed the granting of national status to the Bosnian Muslims. Anti-Muslim, and for nationalist propaganda purposes, anti-Islamic sentiment was fuel for the fire of **Serbian nationalism**. It should be noted that the Serbs in Yugoslavia were a significant majority. The Muslims throughout the former Yugoslavia were a significant minority and did not hold tremendous political power, posing no real threat to the Serbs, unlike the Turks during Ottoman rule.

By the mid 1980s, the economic situation in Yugoslavia had begun to deteriorate. Without the strong leadership of Tito, poor economic times gave further rise to nationalism. In 1987, inflation rose to 120% and by the next year that rate had doubled. In the last few years of the 1980s strikes and protests became commonplace. In 1989, strikes against the local party leaders in Vojvodina and Montenegro set the stage for the new leader of the Serbian communists – **Slobodan Milošević**.

PERSPECTIVES

One key aspect of the history of the war was perspective. Just as the American and British publics were duped into believing the farce of weapons of mass destruction in Iraq, all the local populations here fell under the spell of one propaganda machine or another. In this war there were no winners. Everyone lost and most people in BiH feel their respective ethnic group is the victim. So what follows is three perspectives – regardless of their historical or factual integrity, people react to what they see, hear and feel (or what they think they see, hear and feel). This is not about wrongs and rights, but rather viewpoints from different sides of the 'playing field'.

In the case of the **Bosnian Serbs** they saw the Croatian model as a sign of what was to come should Bosnia become an independent state. The Serbs, still dealing with unhealed wounds from World War II and concentration camp crimes such as those in Jasenovac, made them uneasy and as a result they favoured Yugoslavia remaining intact. Most of them were born in Yugoslavia and it was the only country they (and others) knew. The Bosnian Serbs did not see Yugoslavia as being Serbian-dominated as other ethnic groups did. They saw it as a multi-ethnic state composed of six republics, all of which had fair and equal representation. To them, and fairly so, it was logical to support and 'defend' the country they were born in. They saw the rise of Croatian nationalism and the rise of the Muslim SDA party as a direct threat to them. When the Yugoslav People's Army (JNA) supported the Serbs, it was seen as the legitimate government of Yugoslavia defending its citizens and its territory. To many of them it was very much as if Texas had declared independence and the federal government sent the troops to quell the rebellion. Therefore, they saw all military operations by the JNA and Bosnian Serb forces as defensive in nature.

The **Bosnian Croat** point of view greatly differed, obviously. The Croats, who had once had significant numbers throughout BiH, had seen their numbers drastically reduced throughout history – from the Ottoman to Partisan eras. Some fled to Canada, Australia and other parts of the world whilst others migrated to Croatia proper. The Croats, many of whom aligned themselves with Hitler in World War II, suffered greatly in defeat. They viewed the early years of Tito's regime as brutal and murderous. Many Croatian areas, viewed by the Partisans as being loyal to the Ustasha and the fascist state, were heavily persecuted and were denied many of the development programmes that Tito's Yugoslavia implemented.

Milošević clearly had an agenda of transformation in Serbia and he quickly set about replacing party leaders with his own supporters. In March 1989, at Milošević's request, the Serbian Assembly passed a constitutional amendment that abolished the autonomy of Kosovo and Vojvodina. This was met by massive strikes in **Kosovo** that were violently dealt with by the Serbian security forces. With a general atmosphere of discontent among the masses due to the worsening economic times, political finger-pointing stirred a nationalist fury that few could have imagined. The Serbs could now either dominate Yugoslavia or break it up. Even at this point, however, few Bosnians saw the rise of nationalism or the deepening economic woes as a sign of war or disintegration. Life, for the most part, carried on as normal.

THE BREAK-UP OF YUGOSLAVIA The symbolic turning point in the collapse of Yugoslavia came in the summer of 1989 at Kosovo Polje. Hundreds of thousands of Serbs gathered at this ancient battlefield to pay respects to Prince Lazar, who had been slain at this place in 1389 in battle against the Turks. In the weeks leading up

This sentiment was (and is) quite heavy in western Herzegovina. The Croats strongly felt they were underrepresented in business, government, police and the military and that the Serbs were overrepresented. When Croatia proper voted for independence, it was only natural for them to do the same. When Tuđman's policy developed from an independent BiH to expanding Croatia's borders into Bosnia, this seemed very attractive to many Bosnian Croats. The Croats were a small minority in Bosnia, comprising only 17% of the population. As the war progressed, the Serbs soon controlled 70% of the territory of BiH. This put the Croats and Muslims in a rather precarious position: 65% of the population was now either sent fleeing or crammed into 30% of the country's territory. The Croats now became an even smaller minority and began to feel threatened by the overwhelmingly larger Muslim population. They viewed Herceg-Bosna, an autonomous Croatian state, as a way to protect their identity and join with Croatia and fit into the majority.

The **Bosnian Muslims** were caught in the middle of these two nationalist sentiments. The Bosnian Muslims (Bosniaks) were and are largely a secular Muslim community. They are mostly Slavs, sharing the same language and similar identity with their Croatian and Serbian neighbours. They, however, did not have a 'reserve' country. Bosnia and Herzegovina was and is the homeland. Whereas much sentiment of the Bosnian Serbs bends towards Belgrade and the Bosnian Croats towards Zagreb, the Bosniaks knew that Sarajevo was their capital and BiH their only country. The Bosnian Muslims were literally stuck in the middle of a violent tug-of-war. They knew that for BiH to survive it would have to be consistent with its historical multi-ethnic context but not be dominated by its larger neighbours. Most Bosniaks always viewed themselves as Bosnians, and defended the multi-ethnic principles as such. The first so-called Muslim government had Serb and Croat generals and an equally represented cabinet of Croat, Serb and Muslim ministers and figureheads. Their vision was not an ethnically pure one like those that soon developed from both the east and west. BiH was a republic before the war and its independence was recognised by the UN and the entire international community. They saw themselves as part of the legitimate new multi-ethnic government of a sovereign state.

to the ceremony the bones of the prince toured Serbia, stirring the pot of unsettled scores in the minds of many Serbs. Milošević addressed those assembled with these words: 'We are again engaged in battles and quarrels. They are not yet armed battles, but this cannot be ruled out yet.' His words clearly struck a resounding chord and were met with thundering applause. Through carefully implemented communist methodology and nationalist rhetoric Milošević secured half of the eight votes in the federal government. He controlled Serbia, Montenegro, Kosovo and Vojvodina. In his eyes that left only the challenge of getting Macedonia on board to gain a majority and further implement constitutional change in favour of Serbian dominance.

With the fall of the Berlin Wall came the unification of East and West Germany and the almost overnight collapse of the Soviet Union. Faced now with a struggling economy and the shift from a planned to a market economy, there were demands by the republics for more freedom and sovereignty from the federal government. The Serbian government attempted to block any movement towards the break-up of Yugoslavia. Talk of independence increased in Slovenia and Croatia in 1990, and at the 14th Congress of the League of Communists of Yugoslavia, President Slobodan Milošević, backed by the Yugoslav People's Army (JNA), issued a warning that republics seeking independence would face border changes on the assumption that anywhere a Serb lived was part of Serbia. This only fuelled Croatian nationalism, which had become more radical in the late 1980s. The 'dream' of an independent Croatia was becoming deeply rooted in the psyche of the people as Milošević's power base expanded. For many Serbian nationalists, Yugoslavia had always represented a type of Greater Serbia and was often viewed as territorial reward for its victory and suffering in World War II. For many ordinary Serbs, though, Yugoslavia was simply the only country and homeland they'd ever known.

Croatia The elections held in Croatia in 1990 were won by the Croatian Democratic Union (HDZ), headed by nationalist **Franjo Tuđman**. Meanwhile, the Serbs in the Croatian Krajina formed the Serbian Democratic Party (SDS). Tuđman's strong anti-Yugoslav rhetoric had scared many Serbs who envisioned a revival of the Ustasha state. Local Serbian nationalists manipulated this sentiment by publicising false media reports of the planned slaughter of Serbs. By January 1991 the SDS in Croatia was taken over by an extremist loyal to Milošević, who soon declared the 'Serb Autonomous Region of the Krajina', with its own parliament.

The propaganda machine of the Serbian-run state television intended to radicalise the Serb population in response to Tuđman's bid for secession. Milošević instilled fear into the local population and every act of Tuđman was branded a Ustasha act. The Croatian government, for its part, did little to ease the worries of its Serb population and widespread distrust gripped both populations. With two rather fierce nationalist agendas on the table the war in Croatia would soon turn very ugly. Another method the Serbs effectively utilised was what Noel Malcolm in *Bosnia: A Short History* has called '**compromising the villages**'. This technique involves staging an incident – for example, shooting a carload of Croatian policemen outside a particular village – to invite a crackdown or reprisal, and then distributing arms to the villagers, telling them that the police are planning to attack them. When the armed police do arrive it is easy to spark a gun battle, and suddenly a whole village, previously uncommitted, is now on the side of the insurgents.

Bosnia and Herzegovina In Bosnia and Herzegovina the situation was still relatively calm. The Communist Party had almost vanished and the country was governed by three parties: the Muslim Social Democratic Party (SDA); the Serb Democratic Party (SDS), led by the later indicted war criminal Radovan Karadžić; and the Croatian Democratic Union (HDZ) which was a branch of Franjo Tuđman's Croatia Proper Party.

In BiH the Serbian propaganda machine shifted its focus from the Ustasha hordes to the Islamic fundamentalist threat. Bosnia's Muslim population, especially after almost 50 years of socialism, was mainly secular and very pro-Europe. Holding a 44% majority in the country they feared that both Serbian and Croatian lust to take Bosnia and Herzegovina would leave them nationless. For years they were sandwiched between the power struggles of Croatia and Slovenia on the one hand and Serbia on the other. Major towns in Bosnia had been peacefully occupied by the army since the fall of 1991. Mostly unknown to the city dwellers below, heavy artillery and tanks, mainly in the mountains and hills above, had surrounded Sarajevo and several other cities.

As was done in Slovenia and Croatia, a **referendum for independence** was held in February 1992. The Bosnian Croats and Muslims were among the 65% of Bosnia's population who voted in favour, whilst a majority of the Serbian population boycotted the vote. Despite Serbian threats, Bosnia and Herzegovina declared independence. The day the results were announced Serb paramilitary forces set up barricades and sniper posts near the parliament building in Sarajevo. On 6 April 1992 the European Union and the United Nations recognised Bosnia and Herzegovina as an independent state. On the same day the JNA and Serbian paramilitaries attacked Sarajevo. Tens of thousands of Sarajevans of all nationalities took to the streets to protest in front of the barricades. As they peacefully marched towards the barricade a sniper from the hill fired into the crowd, killing a Serbian woman from Sarajevo and a Muslim girl from Dubrovnik. This sparked the beginning of what would be a long and brutal campaign against Bosnia's non-Serb populations.

In less than a year Yugoslavia saw three of its six republics secede. Macedonia followed suit and a UN preventative force was sent to interrupt any pending ambitions Serbia had on Macedonia. Serbia and Montenegro, together with the provinces of Vojvodina and Kosovo, were now all that remained of Yugoslavia.

INDEPENDENCE AND WAR 'Freedom' for Bosnia and Herzegovina was greeted with atrocities not seen on European soil since the attempted extermination of the Jews in World War II. The well-planned tactics of Milošević and his regime were designed to encompass all lands where Serbs lived into one Greater Serbia. These territories included large swathes of the Krajina and Slavonia in Croatia and all of Bosnia and Herzegovina.

The events that followed confused an increasingly bewildered Western public. Was it civil war? Ancient ethnic hatreds? Wasn't it just always like this with 'these people'? As Western politicians scrambled to make head or tail of the Bosnian conflict, Serbian paramilitaries (grouped under the banner of the 'Serb Volunteer Guard') had already moved into northeastern Bosnia. Led by Željko Ražnatovic (aka **Arkan**) and his Tigers of Serbia, they began to systematically terrorise, loot and slaughter non-Serbs. This same unit was responsible for many of the earlier crimes against humanity in Vukovar, and it was now preparing to let loose on the Bosnian population. Vukovar had been strategically important for the Serbs, as their next move was to conquer territories to the west towards Banja Luka and the Bosnian Krajina which would then link them to the breakaway Serb region in Croatia and extend south all along the border with Serbia thus securing supply lines. By the end of April 1992 several main towns in eastern Bosnia had seen their Muslim populations cleansed from the area.

The use of terror by the paramilitaries proved effective and it is estimated that 95% of the Muslims fled the towns of Višegrad, Foča and Zvornik.

The psychology of convincing the local Serb population that they were under threat was a decisive factor in turning the Bosnian Serbs against their neighbours. Months of television reports warned Serbs of Croatian fascists and an impending Muslim jihad. The fighting in Croatia was often portrayed by the Belgrade-run Radio Television as a repeat slaughter by the Ustasha regime that had killed so many Serbs in World War II. It was easy to manipulate and scare the largely peasant Serb population of eastern Bosnia. In an interview with a Reuters journalist one Serbian woman stated: 'Do you see that field? The jihad was supposed to begin there. Foča was going to be the new Mecca. There was a list of Serbs who were marked for death.' These kinds of fears amongst the peasantry were more than enough to turn them against their neighbours.

Reports of the existence of **concentration camps** began to surface in the summer of 1992. It was later confirmed that mass rapes and killings were taking place, especially in the area around Banja Luka and Prijedor. The war the West had labelled as a civil war had no front lines and no opposing armies. It became clear who was implementing a policy of **ethnic cleansing**. By the end of 1992 over 70% of Bosnia and Herzegovina was occupied by Serbian forces and over a million Bosnian Muslims and Croats had fled the country. The Serbs had linked up with their brothers-in-arms in the Croatian Krajina and the Slavonia region in eastern Croatia, and the realisation of a Greater Serbia was in sight. Now that Milošević had gained much of what he and Serbs saw as Serbian land, his tactics changed to political manoeuvring to secure his new-found Serbian state.

The role of the **UN** in the Bosnian conflict continues to stir much debate and has been viewed by many as at best ineffective, and at worst negligent and bordering on criminal. After President Mitterrand of France visited Sarajevo most Bosnians, including Bosnian President Alija Izetbegović, believed that the West would not allow this horror to continue. They were mistaken. Instead of any action designed to stop the slaughter of innocent civilians, the French president recommended that a large **United Nations Protection Force (UNPROFOR)** be sent to Bosnia. The UN was mandated to secure humanitarian routes, and as peacekeepers they were denied the right to defend themselves. As a consequence, a total of 320 UNPROFOR were killed while on duty. They were sent to 'keep peace' with no peace to keep. British and French policies towards the conflict were driven by political concerns at home and in the European Union.

UNPROFOR was mandated to protect and, as an agency of the UN, to uphold fundamental elements of international law and most importantly to abide by 'neutrality'. This neutrality was often seen as moral indifference between aggressor and victim, between a concept of multi-ethnic principles and that of ethnic purity and separation. In 1992, the peacekeepers were welcomed as saviours by the Bosnians, but people soon painfully realised that this force was not a protection one. In the safe zones established at Srebrenica and Žepa, UNPROFOR disarmed the Bosnian defence forces (at the insistence of the Serbs) yet failed to protect them. Over 8,000 people were eventually massacred at Srebrenica in 1995, under the 'protection' of UN forces, which the international war crimes tribunal legally categorised as genocide. In Omarska, Trnoplje, Manjača and other concentration camps in Serb-held territory, through which an estimated 100,000–200,000 civilians were processed as part of a systematic plan of ethnic cleansing, UNPROFOR simply never arrived. The vast majority of those camps were organised by the Serbs, though the Croats and Bosniaks did operate some smaller ones.

It became apparent in early 1993 that the Bosnian Croats were firmly under the control and influence of Franjo Tuđman in Zagreb. After the **Vance Owen Plan (VOP)** was put on the table at the beginning of 1993, it became clear that any peace drawn up by the international community was going to somehow reward Serbian aggression. The VOP called for a redrawing of Bosnia and Herzegovina into ten cantons, and gave the Croats much more territory than even they had planned for. The VOP failed, and instead set the stage for an armed conflict between the Croat and Muslim forces. Tuđman now had territorial ambitions in Bosnia and drew up plans to carve out a chunk of Bosnia and Herzegovina for Croatia. This would mean forcibly displacing large numbers of Bosnian Croats and moving them to the areas planned to come under Croatia's rule, mainly in western Herzegovina. It would also mean fighting against their former allies – the Bosnian Muslims. Under the leadership of Mate Boban, a Herzegovinian Croat, the **Croatian Defence Council (HVO)** began making plans with Tuđman to implement the final destruction of Bosnia. In a secret meeting, Tuđman and Milošević apparently agreed on splitting the Bosnian state between them. The two sat and bargained town by town, region by region until both were satisfied with the new maps. These plans, however, did not include the Bosnian Muslims. The Muslims would be deported, expelled or killed, or would live as minorities in Greater Serbia or Greater Croatia.

The arms embargo imposed on the countries of the former Yugoslavia in 1991 was highly advantageous to the Serbs. The Yugoslav army, the JNA, was the fourth-largest standing army in Europe, and had enough weapons and ammunition to wage war for another ten years. The Croats had already been building up their stocks for some time and with a 1,125km-long coastline it would be impossible to stop all arms shipments. The Bosnian Muslims, however, did not have an army or proper weaponry. This placed them in a double jeopardy – as victims of genocide who the international community said were not allowed to defend themselves. So although the UN recognised Bosnia as a sovereign, independent member state, they continued to apply the embargo – illegally and against international law. The Bosnian Muslims had two tanks and two armoured personnel carriers (APCs) at the onset while the Serb army in Bosnia alone had 300 tanks, 200 APCs, 800 artillery pieces and 40 aircraft.

Even though in June 1992 President Tuđman and President Izetbegović had signed a formal military alliance with each other, the Croats were getting ready to betray their allies. Angered by Izetbegović's unwillingness to form a confederation of Bosnia and Croatia, the Bosnian Croats formed an autonomous 'Croat Community of Herceg Bosna'. By early spring 1993 the Bosnian Croats had finalised their plans and with the help of the Croatian army they attacked the Muslims in Prozor and the surrounding villages. On 9 May 1993 at 05.00, the HVO launched a major offensive in the capital city of Herzegovina, Mostar. It was to be the new capital of the 'Croat Community of Herceg Bosna' and its Muslim allies would either have to leave or come under Croatia's wing. In less than a 24-hour span 12,000 projectiles were fired at the east bank to where the Muslims were being pushed by the HVO. Thousands of Muslims were expelled from their homes and hundreds killed. Mostar would remain under siege for over 11 months until the Washington Agreement was signed in March 1994, which ended the Croat–Muslim conflict. A former British Royal Navy admiral, Jerry Hume, was the head of UNHCR for Herzegovina during the siege of the city. Largely due to his tireless efforts and bold acts, international attention was focused on the fate of Mostar. Many believe that without his influence the conflict would have continued longer than it did.

When the **Croat–Muslim conflict** ended many aid routes were opened towards central and northeast Bosnia. Encircled and starving populations were finally enabled to receive aid. Sarajevo, however, remained in its valley prison – still under siege by the Serbs. Foodstuffs, ammunition and supplies were brought to Sarajevo by its only self-sustaining lifeline – a **700m tunnel** that ran under the UN-controlled airport. Sarajevo's population was forced to live with little food and water, no electricity and under constant sniper and artillery fire for over 1,200 days. Some 10,000 civilians including 1,500 children were killed in Sarajevo alone, while it was under UN protection. The fate of populations in the other 'safe zones' was no better. UN convoys reached these enclaves only at the whim of the Serbs.

With increasing pressure from the media, and a bewildered public, the image the UN had managed to build in its public relations campaign began to falter. UN troops were increasingly in danger. The 'blue helmets' were being regularly targeted by the defiant Serbs, and the UN mandate gave them little means to protect themselves. There has been much criticism of the UN soldiers on the ground, but it was the policymakers within the UN, in particular Boutros Boutros Ghali and Yasushi Akashi, who managed the conflict and made the decisions. It was not until a large rift divided NATO and the UN that decisive action was taken.

After years of failed diplomacy attempts by the Europeans, America began to assert more pressure to end the conflict. After pinpoint NATO air strikes severely damaged Serbian communication networks and supply routes, the Bosnian and Croat armies were able to retake large swathes of land in the Bosnian Krajina. They marched almost to the entrance of Banja Luka, the largest Serb-held city, before the Americans called all three parties to Dayton air force base in Ohio. After weeks of exhausting negotiations, a peace deal was struck. The **Dayton Peace Accords** gave 49% of the territory of BiH to the Bosnian Serbs and 51% to the Croat–Muslim Federation. Many saw this as appeasing Serbian aggression and genocide, but it did stop the slaughter and suffering of millions of Bosnian civilians. The Dayton agreement is the framework under which Bosnia and Herzegovina is governed today.

What one rarely learns or reads about of conflicts such as this one is the 'other side of the coin'. A **spirit of resistance and survival** thrived during these times. Communities mobilised to help one another. An untapped strength and creativity was expressed through the war theatre in Sarajevo that put on plays for the duration of the siege. The newspaper *Oslobođenje*, meaning 'Freedom', did not miss a single day of print despite the shortage of paper and supplies. Cultural life did not die during these times; it flourished in the most defiant form of non-violent resistance. Bosnians walked through the hail of gunfire to have coffee with a friend and held a Miss Sarajevo beauty pageant in a basement during one of the worst periods of the war. The attempts to erase all material traces of Bosnia's Muslim and Islamic culture may have partially succeeded in the torching of libraries and razing of mosques, but the spirit of a multi-ethnic community never died. Over 100,000 Bosnians – Muslim, Serb and Croat – lost their lives, some in the most horrific ways imaginable. And although in some circles the madness of ethnic purity still exists you will find that in most places in Bosnia today people are determined to live a normal life again, and to live together as they always did.

POST-WAR BOSNIA AND HERZEGOVINA Difficult times and a long rehabilitation process followed the signing of the Dayton Peace Accords. Although progress and reform have come slowly in the eyes of the local inhabitants, great strides have been made in the normalisation of life in Bosnia and Herzegovina. In the early years after Dayton the peace was monitored and enforced by a large NATO presence. Sarajevo became the headquarters of the multinational peacekeeping force and the British, Americans and French looked after their respective jurisdictions in the rest of the country with representations from other NATO countries under their command. More importantly, electricity, food and water were returned to the beleaguered population. Shops were once again filled with European products and a massive reconstruction programme began on a scale not seen since the Marshall Plan.

Freedom of movement between the entities was improved with the introduction of standardised car licence plates. Registration plates after the war clearly stated the entity a person was from, which often led to harassment and/or random violence. The return of refugees was a slower process and one that is still ongoing in Bosnia and Herzegovina. Large numbers of refugees and displaced persons have returned to their rightful homes, but many remain in other countries or internally displaced within BiH.

Government reform was and still is a painful process. The nationalist parties that led the country into war still ruled in the immediate years after Dayton. The new constitution stipulates the full equal rights and representation of all three peoples of Bosnia and Herzegovina, giving even minority groups an unprecedented voice in government. The presidency is not a one-man position but rather a three-man consortium with rotating powers to the Serb, Croat and Bosniak delegates. The circus of establishing an equally balanced government was no less than a poorly constructed jigsaw puzzle. Ministry positions were given to political parties regardless of the background or competency of that individual. Appointees stuck hard to party lines instead of nation building. Corruption was rampant and became an inherent part of the system, and has proved very difficult to uproot. This did little to improve the power of a centralised government or help begin the process of reconciliation.

Bosnia and Herzegovina was assigned a UN-mandated governing body to oversee the rebuilding process, called the Office of the High Representative (OHR). Most Bosnians viewed the NATO forces as peaceful and necessary occupiers and have a similar opinion of the OHR. The powers of the OHR are broad and sweeping, so much so that in essence they play an ad hoc protectorate role. **Free and fair elections** were implemented by the Office for Security and Cooperation in Europe (OSCE). The elections in 2002 were the first elections to be fully implemented by the local government. Previously elected officials were only able to serve two-year terms that were often counter-productive to time-consuming reform. The elections of 2002 were the first four-year term mandates in post-Dayton Bosnia and Herzegovina. The OHR has embarked on an aggressive campaign to eliminate corruption and bureaucratic overspending. Steps to attract foreign investment have finally been implemented and a centralised military has opened the doors for Bosnia and Herzegovina to become a NATO 'Partner for Peace'. As of 2017 BiH is still not a NATO member, but most NATO experts agree that BiH's NATO acceptance will happen long before it is accepted as an EU member. European standards are being pushed on taxes, environment and transparency. Bosnia and Herzegovina has begun on the long path towards European integration, and EU membership is now a crucial political aim.

New attempts on **constitutional reform** failed in 2006 and the independence vote in Montenegro and the succession talks of Kosovo have again flared heated debates about Bosnia's status. This political stalemate has halted most political progress since then. The key elections in October 2010 finally broke the nationalist stronghold but created an even deeper political crisis because of the disparity between right and left. The OHR had plans to dismantle itself in 2007 but the Peace Implementation Committee (PIC) continue to rule into 2017, albeit with less influence and a more watchdog approach due to the fact that the country is still not ready for the OHR and the powers it possesses to close its doors. This may mean yet another uphill battle for political stability, but the responsibility for this country's progress (or demise) will ultimately land in the hands of its elected representatives.

What this means for the ordinary person here is hope for a stable future. The short-term reality however is a rather corrupt system that lacks a coherent vision of building a united country. Great strides have been made but life in Bosnia and Herzegovina still faces tough economic times, with war criminals still not brought to justice, and many people left to deal on a daily basis with the scars of war.

MAIN HISTORICAL DATES IN BiH

949	Bosnia is mentioned for the first time as being a regnum (kingdom)
1189	29 August: the Kulina Bana Charter trade agreement signed between Bosnia and Dubrovnik
1203	Papal representatives and Ban Kulin meet in Bosnia and agree on execution of Bosnian heretics
1377	Bosnia becomes a kingdom under King Tvrtko I
1448	Herceg Stjepan Vukčić founded 'pokrajina' Herzegovina
1463	The Ottomans conquer Bosnia
1482	The Ottomans conquer Herzegovina
1878	The Austro-Hungarian occupation of Bosnia and Herzegovina begins
1908	5 October: Austria-Hungary annexes BiH
1914	28 June: Franz Ferdinand assassinated by Gavrilo Princip sparking World War I
1918	1 December: BiH becomes part of Kingdom of Serbs, Croats and Slovenes
1929	3 October: Kingdom of Serbs, Croats and Slovenes renamed Yugoslavia
1939	26 August: BiH is divided by Croatian/Serbian agreement of Cvetković–Maček
1941	6 April: Germany attacks and conquers Yugoslavia
1941	20 April: BiH becomes a part of NDH (Independent State of Croatia)
1943	25 November: BiH sovereignty restored at AVNOJ
1945	29 November: Bosnia and Herzegovina becomes part of the new Yugoslavia
1980	4 May: Tito dies
1990	18 November: first free elections in the country
1992	29 February: referendum for the independence of BiH
1992	6 April: Bosnia and Herzegovina recognised as an independent country. BiH attacked by Yugoslav army
1995	21 November: Dayton Peace Accords signed by Croatia, Bosnia and Herzegovina and Serbia/Montenegro.
2006	April: failed set of American-led constitutional reforms politically paralyses BiH
2009	October: Butmir Process of a new EU-American led negotiations for constitutional reforms fails.
2014	February: Major unrest and riots throughout BiH due to lack of workers' rights, high unemployment and corruption
2016	15 February: BiH submits its application for accession into the EU

Even as talks proceed for European Union and NATO integration, the political roller-coaster is still the favourite ride of most Bosnian (and unfortunately international) politicians. In 2009 a renewed effort by the Americans and Europeans to negotiate a set of constitutional reforms that would put BiH back on track to becoming a member of the EU failed miserably. The prime minister of the Republika Srpska (see *Politics*, below), Milorad Dodik, openly dismissed and disregarded any attempt by 'foreign powers' to push a solution on the Serbs. Bosniak President Bakir Izetbegović continues the tradition of his predecessor of having unreal aspirations of a fully united and centralised state. The Bosnian Croats are still looking for a third entity that would inevitably create even more tensions and further disintegrate the state. The capture of two of Europe's most wanted war criminals, Radovan Karadžić and General Ratko Mladić, again brought BiH and the Yugoslav war back to the headlines. Karadžić's trial lasted for years, but in March 2016 he was found guilty on 11 counts, including genocide, war crimes, and crimes against humanity. He was sentenced to 40 years' imprisonment. Mladić's trial has lasted for several years but is anticipated to provide justice. The years 2011–12 were especially difficult politically. A government was not formed for over 15 months and when it finally happened in late 2012, it subsequently fell apart again at both the Federation entity and state level. Even with the entry of the more liberal SDP (Social Democrat Party), animosities soared, creating the worst political environment since the failure of the 2006 April 'packet' of constitutional reforms. In-fighting at the Federation level caused the Federation parliament to collapse, the Sarajevo Canton government to collapse and the inability of the city of Mostar to form a government.

The political strife and stalemate may not seem so evident to the visitor. The resilience for a normal life has in many places created a lively atmosphere. Cafés are always full of smiling faces, people walk the streets wearing the finest of European fashions, and the warm hospitality you're sure to find everywhere will certainly make you ask 'Why did this happen here? This is really a great place.' Bosnians ask themselves this question every day. The bright side is that Bosnia and Herzegovina, after experiencing social unrest and riots in 2014, submitted their application for accession to the European Union in February 2016. Many hope this will lead to more political and economic stability.

POLITICS

Just this simple word makes most people from the former Yugoslavia cringe. Politics in this region are, at best, horrendous. Some may say that it's like that wherever you go, but most here will argue that the situation is not only dire, but offers little hope of politics and politicians changing anytime soon. The Dayton Peace Accords signed by the leaders of Croatia, Serbia and Bosnia and Herzegovina created a new constitution for BiH that is still in effect today. The country has two entities: the **Federation** (mainly Bosniaks and Croats) and the **Republika Srpska** (predominantly Serb). Although the constitution and the Dayton agreement specify human rights and the right to return, there are still great strides to be made in those fields. The country teeters on the border of democratic society although many remnants from its socialist period can be found. The three major peoples, the Croats, Bosniaks and Serbs, were not even able to agree on the design of a new national flag and a designer in the European Parliament from Brussels apparently presented the flag after several deadlines to come up with a new flag were not met by the local politicians. Even the simplest of tasks are politicised in BiH and the enormous numbers of ministries, deputies, entity governments, canton governments and municipal governments are sure to confuse even the sharpest of political analysts.

To make it simple I'll break it down into a few comprehensible pieces: the Federation has **ten regional cantons**. Each canton has its own government and is largely responsible for taxes, education, public works, policing, etc. There is also a **Federation government** responsible at the entity level for implementing Dayton, and for entity-level institutions such as trade, health, military, communications, etc. The Federation has its own parliament in a first-order administrative role. The Republika Srpska entity does not have cantons and governs itself on a municipal and entity level. First-order administration falls under the parliament of the Republika Srpska. On the state level there are several ministries, including the Ministry of Foreign Affairs and Commerce and Foreign Trade. The **Executive Office** rotates policy of each nationality. In each election a Bosniak, a Serb and a Croat delegate are chosen by popular vote to share a rotating four-year presidential term. The state-level Council of Ministers acts as a pseudo-national parliament whose powers are increasing due to reforms introduced by the international community. The activities of the OHR are largely dedicated to strengthening state institutions.

There are over 50 political parties in Bosnia and Herzegovina. The main parties are the SDA (Party of Democratic Action – largely Bosniak), the HDZ (Croatian Democratic Union – exclusively Croat) and the SDS (Serbian Democratic Party – exclusively Serb). Other major parties include the Social Democrats (SDP), the Party For BiH (Stranka za BiH), the Party of Democratic Progress (PDP), the Party of Independent Social Democrats (SNDS), the New Croatian Incentive (NHI), the Liberal Party and the Bosnian Party (BOSS).

ECONOMY

Bosnia and Herzegovina's independence in 1992 incited a war that devastated its economy and infrastructure. Since the Dayton Peace Accords were signed at the end of 1995, BiH has embarked on a long, slow and painful process of stabilising the nation's economy. The reform process has been slow due mostly to the corrupt nationalist governments that are more efficient at obstructing than endorsing reform. In the former Yugoslavia, Bosnia and Herzegovina was a base for natural resources – exploiting its forests, hydro-electric power, mining and agriculture for its economic structure. Production fell by 80% from 1990 to 1995 and unemployment plagued the country. The unemployment rate is still high and hovers at around 40%. The GDP still remains far below the pre-war levels and output growth continues at a snail's pace.

The international community, namely here the World Bank, IMF and the OHR, along with the government, have aggressively embarked on strategic reforms aimed at reducing governmental administration costs, attracting foreign investors, speeding up the privatisation process, overhauling the tax system and weeding out the overwhelming corruption and incompetence that continue to cripple the country.

The currency (convertible mark – KM), introduced in 1998, has gained wide acceptance and the Central Bank of Bosnia and Herzegovina has dramatically increased its reserve holdings. Privatisation has in many instances failed but recent attempts at implementation have seen marked improvements. The country still relies on much foreign aid, particularly on humanitarian assistance in the reconstruction effort. This aid has been declining steadily for some years and Bosnia and Herzegovina is now obliged to begin payments on its World Bank debts, which will surely have a negative impact on the national economy.

Bosnia and Herzegovina's main industries are logging, agriculture, steel, coal, iron ore and salt mining, services, textiles, tobacco products and building materials. The logging industry is particularly corrupt and BiH has lost an estimated 35% of its forests to unregulated clear-cutting since the end of the war. This poorly regulated industry is supported by its EU neighbours who are able to purchase cheap, high-quality wood. Italy is the primary purchaser of Bosnian cut timber.

Imports to Bosnia and Herzegovina are at least six times higher than exports, severely limiting local production growth. The country has ideal potential for significant growth in agriculture (with a comparative advantage in organic farming), ecotourism, hydro-electric power (many of the large dams function at only a quarter of their full potential), wood processing, small services and vehicle assembly (Volkswagen had a large factory in Sarajevo before the war).

The government is still struggling with its national strategic development plan that intends to introduce European Union standards into the economic reform platform. Admittance to the EU is not expected before 2018. The OHR utilised a Bulldozer Committee to allow the private sector to suggest changes in laws that would stimulate the economy and ease the burdens of heavy taxation. This has had limited effects.

Amidst a rather gloomy economic outlook, some local industries have seen great progress: BH Telecom has recorded profits for several years and Bosnia's richest natural resource – water (still and mineral) – has been successfully introduced to international markets. What this means for the economic situation of most people in the country is a different question.

The monthly average national income is less than US$550. Food prices remain relatively low but utilities, transport and commodities prices are high relative to the standard of living. The capital Sarajevo enjoys the most wealth, while many people in rural areas continue to live in poor economic conditions.

The 'economic crisis' that stung most of the world continues to plague BiH and indeed the entire region. Even with frighteningly high unemployment rates job losses continued into 2016 and many expect the economic situation to deteriorate even further. Many Bosnians joke though that since the war ended they have never really come out of an economic crisis, so the new international wave of economic collapse affects them less … or at least they're used to it!

TOURISM Tourism in Bosnia and Herzegovina has had the rather daunting challenge of changing the image of a war-torn country to a warm, hospitable and friendly destination. In terms of a national strategy for developing this industry, the proverbial ball has just started to roll. Many of the visitors to BiH in the years after the war were businessmen, diplomats and aid workers. With rather loose budgets this drove up the prices of accommodation, particularly in Sarajevo.

Since the first Bradt travel guide to BiH was written there have been dramatic strides made in tourism offers, particularly in terms of accommodation. Prices have fallen in most areas and even in Sarajevo one can find good-quality but affordable accommodation. Road signs have also greatly improved, particularly in Herzegovina, as have the road conditions themselves. The official site of BiH tourism is **w** bhtourism.ba. Although it provides decent basic information, there are many more dynamic sites that offer more and better information, such as: **w** visitmycountry.net/bosnia_herzegovina/en/ or **w** sarajevo.travel/.

The past few years have witnessed a considerable rise in tourists visiting BiH. Bosnia and Herzegovina is a transit country for many tourists travelling to the Croatian coast. Excursions from the Croatian coast into BiH have also greatly increased, the majority of them being to Međugorje and Mostar in Herzegovina.

Međugorje is the backbone of tourism in BiH, attracting over a million guests per year to one of the top Catholic pilgrimage sites in the world. Mostar and Sarajevo also attract a large number of guests. Although tourism information services are far from perfect, more and more tourist information centres are opening up that can accurately point the traveller in the right direction. Road signs in both Cyrillic and Latin letters have been installed throughout most of the country making it easier for travellers to read maps and road signs. Tourism has been placed as a top priority in the strategic development plan for Bosnia and Herzegovina but few resources have been allocated for this purpose. Despite this, Bosnia and Herzegovina is still one of the top ten growing tourism destinations in the world, with a 28% increase in arrivals in 2015. With a renewed sense of importance and the current tourist boom in neighbouring Croatia, both the public and private sectors have just begun to take the prospect of incoming tourism seriously. There are a steadily increasing number of local tour operators throughout the country, and combination tours with Croatia have become popular with foreign guests.

One can expect that in the near future much more information will be readily available and more international tour operators will have Bosnia and Herzegovina on their list of destinations. Sarajevo was named by Lonely Planet as one of the top ten cities to visit in 2010 and *National Geographic* named BiH in the top ten mountain-bike destinations in the world in 2012. In 2014, *Outside Magazine* named the Via Dinarica the best new trail in the world, giving a boost to the advantages of adventure tourism in BiH. By visiting now you will, at the very least, get an authentic taste of the real Bosnia and Herzegovina.

PEOPLE

According to the population census of 1991 there were 4,354,911 inhabitants in Bosnia and Herzegovina. By the end of the war that number had sunk to less than four million. It is estimated that over one million Bosnians of all ethnic groups now live abroad. However, although Bosnia and Herzegovina experienced a mass exodus as a result of the war, its in-country population is a steadily growing one, and has risen to its former levels. The ethnic composition (unofficially) remains similar to the pre-war percentages: Bosniaks (Muslims) 45%+, Serbs (Christian Orthodox) 30%, Croats (Catholics) 15% and 'others' the remaining. Others include Yugoslavs (mixed marriages), Albanians, Gypsies, Jews and several other minority groups. Although the Bosniak population saw a mass migration due to expulsion and ethnic cleansing, its population has been the fastest growing in post-war BiH. The Serbs have the lowest birth rate and have seen the slowest rate of growth of all the peoples of BiH.

Despite the most difficult moments of existence, Bosnia and Herzegovina has survived for over five centuries as a multi-cultural, multi-national and multi-confessional community.

LANGUAGE

There are three 'official' languages spoken in Bosnia and Herzegovina: Bosnian, Croatian and Serbian. For the local people there is a great importance attached to the name of the language. For practical purposes, they are one and the same. The differences are similar to those between American and British English. The pre-war language of the former Yugoslavia was Serbo-Croat. This term is virtually extinct

SIGN LANGUAGE

Although isolated by a rather large range of mountains, Bosnia and Herzegovina still possesses many Mediterranean characteristics – body and hand language being one of them. If you're having trouble communicating with a non-English-speaking Bosnian, be prepared for him/her to give it their best go at getting the message across. They don't behave like the British or Americans and just speak louder – they move.

- If a Bosnian makes a waving motion (sort of like 'come here') in the vicinity of his/her mouth – that means 'Eat' or 'Would you like to eat?'
- If a local takes a hitchhiker's thumb and bobs it towards his/her mouth – that means 'Do you want a drink?'
- If one pinches the index finger and thumb together, with the pinky finger out and gently bobs the hand – that means 'Let's go for a coffee'.
- If the right arm shoots up above the shoulder it means one of two things – either 'Forget it' or 'Screw you' … your call.
- If the right arm sweeps across the front of the chest like hitting a ball or something, that probably means 'Don't worry about it' or 'So what?'
- A thumbs-up does not mean you are great or that things are OK – it means one, the number one.
- If the neck disappears into the shoulders and both hands are shrugged in front it means 'It wasn't me' or 'How do I know?'
- Two fingers, namely the index and middle fingers, tapped against the lips means 'Can you spare a cigarette?'

now. Bosnian/Croatian/Serbian is a Slavic language. Many words are similar in Czech or Slovakian, even Polish and Ukrainian. It is in the same family as Russian but is distinctly different.

In the Republika Srpska entity of Bosnia and Herzegovina many signs will be in Cyrillic, including road signs, which may make it difficult to know exactly where you are. In the Federation only the Latin alphabet is used. In the cities it is very common to find English-speaking people; the heavy presence of the international community has almost made it a second language here. Most young people will have at least some knowledge of English almost anywhere you go. Because of the large refugee and immigrant population that lived in Germany during the war there are many German speakers as well. In the rural areas it will be hard to find English-speaking adults, but don't be surprised to find children able to 'small chat' with you in English. Some useful words and phrases can be found in *Appendix 1*.

RELIGION

This topic has to a large extent been addressed in the *History* section above. If there is any place on earth that symbolises the crossroads of Eastern and Western civilisations then it would have to be Bosnia and Herzegovina. The only European city able to boast having a Jewish synagogue, an Orthodox church, a Catholic church and a mosque, all in the same square, is Sarajevo. It is hard to find a town in Bosnia and Herzegovina that doesn't have both churches and mosques. It is this rich religious heritage that has created such a diverse society.

This ancient crossroads has survived many trying times from invaders from beyond its borders but Bosnia and Herzegovina has enjoyed centuries of living as multi-cultural communities.

The uniqueness of the medieval **Bosnian Church** is most likely the key factor in Bosnia and Herzegovina's vast religious diversity. Inheriting the fierce self-reliant attitude from the indigenous Illyrian clans, the newly arrived Slavic tribes adopted their own form of Christianity. While most of Europe and the Balkans were under the influence of the two major church organisations, geographically isolated Bosnia and Herzegovina celebrated a Christian God with many elements of paganism and without the structure and hierarchy of the organised churches. For centuries both churches vied for power in the region, but the Bosnian Church was able to maintain its unique belief system for some time. It is fair to say that to the far east of Hum (Herzegovina) Orthodoxy had the strongest influence in the centuries before the arrival of the Ottoman Empire. **Catholicism** reached parts of western Herzegovina and Dalmatia after the split between Constantinople and Rome. The Bosnian Church flourished in the territories of Bosnia before the 'heretics' were converted to Catholicism. The Franciscan Church established its first order in 1340, only 125 years before falling under Ottoman control. Most of Bosnia became Catholic in this time frame; its Christian roots before that lie undeniably with the Bosnian Church.

The arrival of the Turks had the most significant religious influence on the history of Bosnia and Herzegovina for many reasons. **Islam** was introduced for the first time in the mid-15th century, and over the next 150 years Bosnia saw a large proportion of its population convert to Islam. The Ottomans, however, were very tolerant of the Orthodox Church whose entire jurisdiction fell within the empire. With the arrival of the Turks in Bosnia and Herzegovina, the Orthodox population significantly increased in size whereas the Catholics, seen more as brothers to the enemy Austrians, experienced a severe depletion of their population due to conversions to Islam or Orthodoxy and several large exoduses to Austro-Hungarian-controlled territories. In the 16th century a fourth component was added when the Sephardic Jews, expelled from Spain in 1492, were resettled by the Ottomans in Sarajevo, Mostar, Travnik and other major Bosnian cities.

In Tito's Yugoslavia most people strayed from their religious beliefs. Although there was a certain degree of religious freedom, secularism was encouraged and the religious leaders were chosen and approved by the Communist Party. Since the fall of communism there has been a significant rise in the sense of national and religious belonging – and much of that can be attributed to nationalist agendas that often used religion to rally national fervour. The marked increase in church- and mosque-goers reflects the ongoing struggle for national identity in such a mixed region but also symbolises the peaceful coexistence that has more often than not reflected community life in Bosnia.

It is here in Bosnia and Herzegovina that one can still feel, see and taste the styles and influences of the Byzantines, Venetians, Romans and Ottomans – representing Eastern and Western forms of Christianity and Islam from the Orient. Today's religious make-up can be seen as a reflection of the clashes of civilisations but even more so as a magical blend of these forces.

EDUCATION

Bosnia and Herzegovina, like most republics of the former Yugoslavia, had an education system to brag about. The war brought that excellence to an abrupt end. A large number of the highly educated class were killed, driven out or left. The war also brought about a total collapse of the system, including education. In many places in BiH, there are now three educational systems all following a certain nationalist agenda. BiH is the only country in Europe to still experience apartheid in some schools. In some Croatian-controlled areas the Croatian and Bosniak children are kept separate, often use different facilities and follow totally different curricula. UNICEF has done comprehensive research on the state of education in BiH. The main problems identified were largely administrative and political. There are 14 ministries of education all with separate programmes. Politics plays a major role in education, severely obstructing what are basically a good teaching staff and decent facilities. The two schools under one roof phenomenon is an openly discriminating practice that has either been supported or ignored by the political structures. Nonetheless, Bosnian schools still manage to produce competitive students. The universities are also fragmented but to a lesser extent, especially since the system is being integrated into the Bologna process, a framework for higher education that is common across Europe. The Sarajevo School of Science and Technology (SSST) is perhaps the best example of a successful private university; SSST is an affiliate of Buckingham University in the UK, founded by Margaret Thatcher. The institution follows a UK programme, taught in English (**w** *ssst.edu.ba*)

CULTURE

Until contemporary times Bosnia and Herzegovina usually fell outside the realm of European artistic movements. Creative forms, however, have a long and fascinating history dating back to Neolithic times. The museums and galleries in Bosnia and Herzegovina are not filled with Renaissance or Romantic paintings but rather with the living forms that represented everyday life. Contemporary art has been a key influence in the cultural revolution that took place in the second half of the 20th century. Culture in the centuries leading up to this revolution can be visited today as a living museum through the architecture, traditional dress, stone carvings, pottery and jewellery, and sacral places. The culture of Bosnia and Herzegovina will not be found hanging on the walls of a museum but can be seen in the intricate paintings of the mosques, the beautiful woodwork of traditional furniture, or the magnificent stitch of the highlander's attire. It is this mix of old and new creative forms that sets Bosnia and Herzegovina apart from its European neighbours.

ART Art forms have been traced back into the Palaeolithic period, with the oldest discovered engravings in the Balkans at Badanj Caves near the southern town of Stolac in Herzegovina. These works are dated to 12000BC and are amongst only a handful of such art forms found in all of continental Europe. The older Neolithic period is characterised by artistically sculpted figures of human bodies made of baked earth, and pottery decorated with intricate hand carving. Many of these pieces are now on display at the National Museum in Sarajevo. Remnants of the Classical Greek era are best represented by the rich tradition of the Daorsi tribes and the Hellenistic influence in southern Herzegovina at Osanići. Moulds from jewellers' workshops indicate the casting of miniature metal figures for jewellery and coins. The Roman-Illyrian period is characterised by the ruins of old settlements and castles, like the Mogorjelo settlement in the Neretva Valley near Čapljina. Perhaps the most inspiring form of art was left in the countryside. The ancient tombstones, *stećci* in Bosnian, have left a permanent reminder of the creative spirit of the early Slavs. This natural gallery of human creativity is stylised with both pagan and Christian symbols of earth, moon, family, animals, dance and crosses.

Along the lines of Classical art, many mosaics and basilicas from this period that used universal symbols of early Christianity have been found throughout the country. Medieval times marked a new era for art forms in Bosnia and Herzegovina. From ancient cities such as Ključ, Jajce, Dabar, Sokol and Bobovac emerged the new scripts of Hvalov, Zbornik, Hrvoj's Missal and Miroslav's Gospel. But oriental culture, during four centuries of Ottoman rule, had a huge impact on this region. During this period many monuments were constructed, including the bridges at Višegrad, Mostar, and the Arslanagića bridge in Trebinje; Alipašina and Gazi-Husrevbegova mosques in Sarajevo; Karađoz-begova mosque in Mostar; the coloured mosque in Travnik; Ferhad-pašina in Banja Luka; and bezistan markets, hans, religious dervish convents and libraries, all representing the highest of oriental art forms.

Frescoes and icons were popular art forms at the end of the 16th century and the finest examples can be seen in such monasteries as Paprača, Lomnica, Dobričevo, Žitomislice and Trijebanj. Georgije Mitrofanović was one of the greatest Serbian painters of late-16th-century frescoes. In addition, almost every Catholic monastery dating from this time (Kraljeva Sutjeska, Fojnica, Kreševo, Olovo, Gorica, Tolisa) possesses a large collection of paintings. It is this influx and infiltration of so many cultural influences that has shaped the artistic identity of contemporary art in Bosnia and Herzegovina. Copper-, gold-, silver- and leathersmiths still practise their trade of beautifully crafted objects.

Modern painters such as Gabriel Jurkić and Karlo Mijić and the abstract work of Affan Ramić depict the vast natural wonders of the Bosnian landscape, demonstrating the intimate ties between humans and nature. Safet Zec is famous for his delicate paintings of the oriental feel of a European Bosnia, and Mersad Berber portrays Muslim life in works such as *Chronicle about Sarajevo*. Newer forms of art from the younger generations have appeared in the post-war period and display expressions of resistance, hope and peace. Sculpture, paintings, graffiti and graphic design all portray the new generation's struggle to heal the wounds of the past and rid the collective consciousness of the lunacy of the war.

LITERATURE Perhaps of all art forms the greatest strides have been made in literature. During Turkish times true literary forms began to appear. They appeared in many forms and languages: Turkish, Persian and Arabic and the *Bosančica* alphabet used by the Franciscans and Cyrillic as the Serbian writer's script. The earliest writers were mainly theologians, all of whom expressed a strong sense of patriotism. Bosnian Muslims achieved high rank in the Ottoman political and military structures, and many were included among the intellectual elite. Most of the literature from that time is theological in nature. The best of Islamic scholarly thought came from writers such as Mustafa Ejubović and Ahmed Sudi. Classic poetry from the Muslims was written in Turkish, Arabic or Persian and received acclaim throughout the Ottoman world. Fevzi Mostarac wrote the famous *Bulbulistan* in 18th-century Persian and Mula Mustafa Bašeskija wrote a diary of life in Sarajevo in the second half of the 18th century in the unique Turkish dialect that was spoken only in Sarajevo. What most writings of this period depicted, however, was the spirit of self-reliance and the moral issues of political and social abuses suffered by all three peoples. Hasan Kaimija was a poet who gained popularity as a defender of common folk. Fra Matija Divković wrote the first published book in *Bosančica* from Bosnia and Herzegovina in 1611 (printed in Venice). The Franciscans became the most important link with the medieval Bosnian state and served as the only continuous institution from the pre-Ottoman invasion. Divković wrote many books, including his most famous, *Christian Teachings for Slav People*.

Brother Filip Lastrić was the best-known historian of the Bosna Srebrena province and wrote many books preserving the heritage of the old Bosnian state. Serbian priests and monks in the 19th century made profound contributions to literature. Nicifor Dučić, an Orthodox monk, published nine volumes of historical works. Joanikije Pamučina portrayed folklore and history in the story *Glorious Martyrdom of the Virgin Hristina Rajković*.

The self-taught writer Gavro Vučković Krajišnik had two books banned by the Turkish government, *Slavery in Freedom or Mirror of Justice in Bosnia* and *The Bloody Book of Brother Ante Knežević*. The greatest of the 19th-century Bosnian Serb writers was Vaso Pelagić, who stood out not only for his literary skill but also as one of the sharpest thinkers and political figures of his time. Ivan Franjo Jukić, a Franciscan from Banja Luka, personified the freedom struggle and wrote great works in many genres reflecting the emancipation movement that dominated 19th-century life in Bosnia and Herzegovina.

The first half of the 20th century saw a great emergence of nationalist literature. The struggle for national identity after more than four centuries of Turkish and Austrian rule was portrayed in the literature of the early 1900s. It was this struggle that had polarising effects on the future of Bosnia: on the one hand it paved the way for the union of the southern Slavs and on the other it created ethnic rifts amongst the Slavs through the intensity of the nationalist voices that emerged. Many newspapers were established at this time and for the first time Bosnian writers were fully exposed to the main currents of European influence. Nobel Prize winner Ivo Andrić from Travnik began his writing career in this era, and from the 1920s became a figurehead of Bosnian literature. Alongside the nationalist fervour was the liberal movement of writers mentioned in *The Comrades Book*. This left-wing-oriented movement, with a passion for the social issues of the time, produced famous writers such as Novak Šimić, Hasan Kikić and later Mak Dizdar, who is one of the greatest poets to emerge from Bosnia and Herzegovina. This was a catalyst to the cultural revolution that would greatly define itself in the second half of the 20th century. The greatest writers in Bosnia's history emerged in post-World War II socialist Yugoslavia. Ivo Andrić continued his literary domination with the *Bridge over the Drina*, *Travnik Chronicles* and *The Damned Yard*. In 1961, he was awarded the Nobel Prize in literature. Mak Dizdar and Meša Selimović soon after published two of Bosnia's most famous pieces, *Stone Sleeper* and *Death and the Derviš*. In the late 1960s yet more masterpieces were published: Nedžad Ibrišimović's *Urgusuz*, Vitomir Lukić's *Album*, Skender Kulenović's first book of sonnets *Stojanka majka Knezopoljka*, and Branko Ćopić's book of stories *The Blue Mallow Garden*. Philosopher and writer Ivan Lovrenović offers one of the most insightful and objective viewpoints in Bosnian intellectual circles, particularly in his book *Bosnia: A Cultural History*. Modern Bosnia and Herzegovina has seen many of its intellectuals scattered across the globe, yet the themes and inspiration for their work remain close to home.

Nostalgia is a powerful literary tool and is perhaps best exemplified in the war stories of Miljenko Jergović's *Sarajevo Marlboro* and Zlata Maglajlić's *Zlata's Diary*, which is reminiscent of Anne Frank's famous war account. Alexander Hemon, Nenad Veličković, Faruk Šehić, Dario Džamonja, Dževad Karahasan and Marko Vešović are the leading literary thinkers in post-war Bosnia. Most of these writers have been published in English as well; see page 339 for these and other suggestions.

MUSIC In former Yugoslavia, Sarajevo was always best known for its great *ćevapi* (grilled sausages), humour and its incredible ability to produce music hits from all genres. Most of the folk music that is still very much alive today traces its origins to Turkish times in the lyrical songs of *sevdalinka.* Although this genre possesses oriental elements in style and form, it has embodied the whole folk heritage of Bosnia and Herzegovina. Most of these songs are of love and/or tragedy and grip the most turbulent of times with passion and perseverance. Song here has so permeated the collective consciousness that the sound of a *sevdalinka* will almost always spark a spontaneous sing along. The power of nostalgia cannot be underestimated when it comes to the old songs of the 'glory days' before the war. Safet Isović is the godfather of Bosnian *sevdalinka*. The best contemporary interpretations of *sevdah* are by Damir Imamović, Amira Medunjanin and Divanhana.

The sounds of the highlanders are also a fascinating aspect of Bosnia's musical tradition. The music of the Dinaric shepherds has for centuries echoed through mountain valleys. This type of mountain yodel is called *ojkanje* and is a mixed melody of male and female 'oi' sounds. Highlanders have always celebrated in open fields with the *gluho kolo* or the deaf dance. Here the young bachelors and girls from the villages would gather for a large circle dance accompanied by song. This ceremony would continue through the night and was often the setting for courting amongst the highlanders.

The *ganga* is a deep, non-instrumental chant-like music most often sung by men. This tradition is strongest in Herzegovina amongst the Croats. The Serbian *gusle* (traditional type of guitar) is accompanied by stories that are centuries old. Similar traditions exist in the northwest of the country and are played with *sargija* instruments, whilst in the cities the Persian *saz* is most often heard accompanying traditional music.

The best side of contemporary music here is definitely rock and roll. The famous bands from the old Yugoslavia are still held in high regard and the songs still crowd the airwaves. Bands like Bijelo Dugme, Zabranjeno Pušenje, Index and Crvena Jabuka represent the climax of Yugoslav rock in the 1980s. There are often favourite cover songs for today's bands and they carry a magical Yugo-nostalgia that is still loved in every republic of the former Yugoslavia. The most famous pop stars of yesterday and today are Halid Bešlić, Dino Merlin and Kemal Monteno. Although their musical styles are very different, they all enjoy huge popularity with both young and old. Halid Bešlić tends to have a following of all peoples of the former Yugoslavia aged 1–99; Dino Merlin has produced several new albums, *Sredinom* being the most popular. The modern music scene in Bosnia and Herzegovina is concentrated in Sarajevo. Jazz bands and clubs have become more popular and Sarajevo hosts a great International Jazz Festival every year in November. The tradition of rock and alternative music never dies though – groups like Letu Stuke, Dubioza Kolektiv and Skroz carry on that tradition along with a new wave of alternative and rap music from Laka, Edo Maajka and Frenki that have rocked the music scene with great new sounds and lyrics.

FILM Despite being a small provincial capital Sarajevo has produced some of the finest films to come out of the former Yugoslavia. Even many of the great film-makers in Serbia, like Emir Kusturica, were born and raised in Sarajevo. The modern film scene has taken off in recent years producing BiH's first Oscar winner for best foreign film with Danis Tanović's *No Man's Land* (Ničija Zemlja). The tragicomedy depicts several opposing soldiers stuck in an abandoned trench between the front lines and the very human elements of men forced into a war and the international community's attempts to 'keep peace' where no peace was to be found. His new films *An Episode in the Life of an Iron Picker* (2013), *Tigers* (2014) and *Death in Sarajevo* (2016) have received excellent reviews. *An Episode* *in the Life of an Iron Picker* won the Jury Grand Prix at the Berlin Film Festival in 2013 and *Death in Sarajevo,* about the 100-year anniversary of Gavrilo Princip's assassination of Franz Ferdinand, premiered at the Berlinale and won the 2016 Silver Bear award.

Other striking films, mostly based on war themes, include *Perfect Circle* (*Savršeni Krug*) by Ademir Kenović, *Fuse* (*Gori Vatra*) by Pjer Žalica, *Re-Make* by Dino Mustafić, and the 2004 winner of the Rotterdam Film Festival Tiger Award *Summer in the Golden Valley* (*Ljeto u Zlatnoj Dolini*). Author Namik Kabil's *At Uncle Idriz's* (directed by Pjer Žalica) is a wonderful depiction of a Muslim family from Sarajevo. The quaint details and slow pace offer great insight into many of the traditions and mindsets of Sarajevans and Bosnians alike.

The creative forces that have emerged after many years of being silenced, underfunded, or just plain ignored have been a driving force in reshaping the cultural and artistic flavour that now defines both Sarajevo and the country as a whole. Namik's film *Night Watchers* (Cuvari Noci) is a slow but ingenious story of man's battle with himself and his demons. Perhaps BiH's most popular director and activist, Jasmila Žbanić's *Grbavica* won the Golden Bear award at the Berlin Film Festival. This is a gripping story of women who were raped and impregnated during the war and how they are dealing with the scars and the plight of raising a child whose father is a rapist. The film was so successful that it helped push through new protective laws for civilian war victims shortly after its premiere. Her 2010 film *Na putu* touches on the cultural and emotional sensitivities between a secular and religious Muslim couple from Sarajevo struggling to make their love work despite their different world views. The 2008 film *Snow* marks the emergence of yet another key female film-maker in Bosnia. Aida Begic's film won the Cannes Critic Week Grand Prize and was the Bosnian Oscar nominee in 2012 for her film *Djeca*.

BOSNIA ONLINE

For additional online content, articles, photos and more on Bosnia and Herzegovina, why not visit www.bradtguides.com/bosnia.

2

Practical Information

WHEN TO VISIT

Having the advantage of two types of climate, there are several 'good' seasons to visit Bosnia and Herzegovina. **Summers** throughout the whole country are hot and dry. Bosnia enjoys cool evenings in the mountainous regions whereas Herzegovina has an arid Mediterranean climate that makes summer sunny and hot with temperatures averaging over 30°C – (90°F). Prices for accommodation are generally higher in the summer season (July–August). From June to mid-September the weather in Bosnia is warm. In Herzegovina the warm weather starts earlier, in May, and lasts easily into the end of September. Spring and autumn are lovely months to visit. In May the countryside is teeming with wild flowers, the days are pleasantly warm with cool, refreshing evenings and people come out in crowds after the cold winter months. October and November are good months to avoid the crowds and enjoy the barrage of orange, red and yellow leaves that paint the forests. These months do experience some rain but there is an equal number of cool, sunny days – particularly in Herzegovina.

The best time for a **winter** visit is the snow months, particularly if you are a skier. Herzegovina experiences little snow and has mild winters. Bosnia and the mountainous regions have very cold winters and high snow precipitation. Olympic skiing on mounts Bjelašnica, Igman and Jahorina is ideal in January through to March. February, however, is the coldest month of the year with frequent temperatures below zero. Bear in mind that due to global warming trends snowfall in Bosnia is not as consistent as in the past. The roads in winter are decent but not great. The winter road clearance teams are getting better but the roads are nowhere near as safe as European or North American ones during or after heavy snowfalls. Any extensive winter travelling in Bosnia should be accompanied by snow chains. It is also worth mentioning that fog and sometimes very bad smog in Sarajevo can be intense during the winter, especially in December and January. However, just 15 minutes outside the Sarajevo valley and into the hills and mountains, the air is always much fresher. When it is grey in Sarajevo in the winter, it is often sunnier in the mountains.

It's safe to say that May through to October is a great time to visit Bosnia. Herzegovina enjoys a long period of pleasant weather from April well into November.

HIGHLIGHTS

Bosnia and Herzegovina is an ideal place for the active visitor. There isn't a lot of lying around on sandy beaches or in luxurious resorts, but for the adventure seeker or nature lover BiH is a wonderland of pristine wilderness. Culture and history buffs will have a field day. Despite the lack of modern museums most visitors usually find 'real-life' Bosnia and Herzegovina to be a living museum. City visitors will be delighted with Sarajevo and Mostar and all the nightlife, festivals, architecture and beauty that are available. For those on a spiritual journey, Međugorje attracts the faithful from every corner of the globe to this sleepy mountain-top Herzegovinian village. Western travellers not accustomed to Eastern and oriental faiths will find the mysticism of Christian Orthodox monasteries and Ottoman mosques an enchanting experience.

Below are my highlights when visiting Bosnia and Herzegovina.

MOSTAR Some say I favour Herzegovina. It's true, I do. Being the heart of Herzegovina, Mostar is definitely a place not to be missed. The oriental old town, the old bridge, mosques and churches, and the emerald Neretva River will mesmerise you. (See pages 177–97.)

SUTJESKA NATIONAL PARK Although there is still a considerable amount to be done organisation-wise, Sutjeska is home to the last primeval forest in Europe. Here you will find a true wilderness adventure with bears, wolves and other wild things in this nature oasis. (See pages 163–5.)

SARAJEVO OLD TOWN Sarajevo in general has a magnetic effect on visitors. It's amazing how quickly one feels at home and begins to think of ways to prolong the stay. The *baščaršija* (old town) in Sarajevo is a walk through its ancient Ottoman past. Shopping, drinking Turkish coffee or just strolling through the craftsmen's quarters are pure delights. (See pages 132–7.)

MEĐUGORJE A quarter of a century ago six teenagers walking in the hills surrounding the small village of Međugorje had an apparition of the Mother Mary. Despite scepticism from 'official' circles, the visions continued. Međugorje has grown to be the second-largest Catholic pilgrimage site in the world. Millions of the faithful, curious and even sceptics have visited Međugorje. It is said that miracles occur here on a regular basis. Believe or not, this holy site is something to experience. (See pages 205–11.)

BLAGAJ This is one of the best examples of the interconnectedness of Herzegovina's cultural and natural heritage. Atop the mountain in Blagaj are the ruins of an ancient Illyrian fortification. The Romans added to the original structure, and by the Middle Ages it had become the castle of the ruling noble family of Hum. The Ottomans added even more to the large fort and the ruins stand witness to four civilisations that have at one time or another made Herzegovina their home. The *tekija* dervish house built at the base of a 200m rock face at the source of the Buna River is a magical place, blessed with the powers of both humans and nature. (See pages 200–1.)

RIVER RAFTING The residents of the Krajina treat the Una and Vrbas rivers like members of the family. They are the best-cared-for rivers in the country and many of the regional traditions revolve around (and on) these gorgeous rivers. Rafting or kayaking on the Una and Vrbas is an unforgettable experience and if you tackle the falls at Strbački Buk, you've conquered some of the toughest in Europe! The Neretva and Tara are just as thrilling but Strbački's 24m waterfall is tops! (See page 92.)

OLYMPIC MOUNTAINS Jahorina and Bjelašnica mountains were hosts to the 1984 Winter Olympic Games. They both offer the country's best skiing and are a short and convenient drive from the capital Sarajevo. The highlanders in these areas are extremely friendly and usually make foreign guests rethink their whole idea of hospitality. Hiking and walking here are some of the best in the country. (See pages 147–50 and 152–3.)

KRAVICA WATERFALLS Bosnia and Herzegovina is a country of mountains and water. Kravica is a remarkable waterfall on the Trebižat River. It's a great spot for a picnic and a swim and is only a hop-skip-and-a-jump from Međugorje, Ljubuški and Čapljina. If that's not enough you can go on a canoe safari on the Trebižat just a few kilometres down the road. (See page 211.)

LUKOMIR The medieval highland village of Lukomir is the highest (1,469m) and most isolated permanent settlement in the country. Here is a last-chance peek at old Europe and the way things 'used to be'. It's an amazingly beautiful spot on the ridge of Rakitnica Canyon, and a visit here is like travelling to a place time has forgotten. (See page 156.)

JAJCE The hilltop settlement perhaps best sums up the vast layers of history that have crossed through this central Balkan state. From the ancient Illyrians and Romans, through the medieval Bosnian Kingdom and the four centuries of Ottoman rule, this is a precious element of BiH's cultural heritage. (See pages 303–7.)

TREBINJE Some say this town just has it all and I'd have to agree. Located just a 30-minute drive from the world-famous city of Dubrovnik, Trebinje is perched on the highland valley just to the northeast of Croatia's largest tourist destination. Dubrovnik's influence is obvious in Trebinje, with a clear Adriatic spatial influence and remarkable architecture. Trebinje has great wine, monasteries, high mountains, beautiful buildings, good restaurants, caves, and more history than one could process in just one trip. (See pages 220–2.)

VIA DINARICA Last, but certainly not least, is the new long-distance trail that connects the mountains, rivers, valleys and highland villages of the Dinaric Alps mountain chain all the way from northern Albania to Slovenia. It has a little bit of something for everyone, from world-class hiking, highland-village stays, rafting, caving and mountain biking through some of the most pristine terrain in all of Europe. (See pages 88–9.)

There are literally dozens more. But those are my top 12.

SUGGESTED ITINERARIES

FOUR-DAY EXCURSION FROM THE COAST

Day 1 If you are up for an easy, soft adventure, a canoe safari on the Trebižat River is a wonderful trip. The drive to Mostar is only 30 minutes.

Day 2 Take a whole day and stroll the streets of Mostar. A walking tour is recommended in the Mostar section of Herzegovina (see pages 192–5).

Day 3 The drive to Sarajevo will take a little over 2 hours. The drive through the Neretva Canyon is an unforgettable one. A day tour of Sarajevo, coupled with café-hopping and shopping, is the order of the day. If you get the chance, try to find your way to the top of some of the hills surrounding Sarajevo – the views are magnificent. Restaurants Park Prinčeva and Kibe Mahala offer the best views in town.

Day 4 Heading back towards the coast take the Sarajevo–Foča–Trebinje route and enjoy a half day in Sutjeska National Park and one of the last primeval forests in Europe. Bring a camera! Dinner in Trebinje old town (only 30 minutes from Dubrovnik) is recommended.

ONE WEEK BY BUS OR CAR

Day 1 Mostar old town.
Day 2 Visit medieval cities of Blagaj and Počitelj (30 minutes from Mostar).
Day 3 Sarajevo old town and central district (2 hours from Mostar).
Day 4 Kraljeva Sutjeska Franciscan Monastery and Bobovac Fortress (1½ hours from Sarajevo) then overnight in Travnik.
Day 5 Explore Travnik – the European Istanbul and the seat of the last Bosnian kingdom at Jajce (1–2 hours from Kraljeva Sutjeska) – and head to Bihać.
Day 6 Rafting on the Una River near Bihać.
Day 7 Day trip to Banja Luka (2 hours from Bihać) – visit the old town, the Orthodox churches, the museum and Kastel.

TWO WEEKS BY BUS

Day 1 Sarajevo old town and National Museum.
Day 2 Bear Caves near Pale (30 minutes from Sarajevo) then Jahorina Olympic Mountain (walks, restaurants, cafés, fresh air – just 45 minutes from Sarajevo).
Day 3 Kraljeva Sutjeska Franciscan Monastery and Bobovac Fortress.
Day 4 Visit Travnik old town, coloured mosque, Blue Water Springs (Plava Voda).
Day 5 Rama Lake and the Franciscan monastery. Then to Jablanica to visit the museum, take a train ride through the mountains (2 hours) and dinner at the famous grilled lamb restaurants of Jablanica.
Day 6 Mostar old town. Evening dinner on Podveležje Plateau at Motel Sunce.
Day 7 Blagaj and Počitelj medieval cities.
Day 8 Stolac – Radimlja necropolis, Osanići Illyrian settlement then a half-hour trip to Hutovo Blato for *barco* ride through bird reserve.
Day 9 Holy pilgrimage site at Međugorje.
Day 10 Visit Kravica Waterfalls and Humac Museum in Ljubuški.
Day 11 Northward trek through Livno Fields, visit Tito's Cave in Drvar and drive on to Bihać.
Day 12 White-water rafting or kayaking on the Una River.
Day 13 Visit Banja Luka old town, churches and mosques, fortress on Vrbas River.
Day 14 Return to Sarajevo.

TWO WEEKS BY CAR

Day 1 Bihać, rafting on the Una River.
Day 2 Visit Jajce and Travnik, overnight on Mount Vlašić.
Day 3 Visit Kraljeva Sutjeska Monastery and museum, overnight in Sarajevo.
Day 4 Sarajevo old town.
Day 5 Bjelašnica highland villages.
Day 6 Sutjeska National Park.
Day 7 Trebinje, overnight in Dubrovnik.
Day 8 Dubrovnik.
Day 9 Drive to Neum, overnight in Neum.
Day 10 Kravica Waterfalls and Trebižat canoe safari, overnight in Mostar.

Day 11 Mostar old town, overnight on Podveležje.
Day 12 Visit Blagaj, Počitelj and Stolac, overnight on Podveležje Plateau.
Day 13 Visit Jablanica and Ramsko Lake.
Day 14 Rafting on Neretva.

REGIONAL ITINERARIES – BY CAR OR WITH A TOUR OPERATOR

Slovenia, Croatia, BiH, Montenegro

Day 1 Low-cost flight to Ljubljana, Slovenia. Visit Ljubljana city centre.
Day 2 Plitvica National Park, Croatia.
Day 3 Rafting on the Una River, Bihać.
Day 4 Jajce medieval town, Pliva River/Lake.
Day 5 Travnik, the European Istanbul.
Day 6 Kraljeva Sutjeska, Royal Residency.
Day 7 Sarajevo – old town.
Day 8 Sarajevo – Lukomir medieval village.
Day 9 Sutjeska National Park.
Day 10 Rafting on Tara River.
Day 11 Visit Durmitor National Park, Montenegro.
Day 12 Montenegrin coast – Budva, Bar or Sveti Stefan.
Day 13 Dubrovnik, Croatia.
Day 14 Low-cost flight from Dubrovnik.

Croatia, BiH, Montenegro

Day 1 Low-cost flight to Dubrovnik. Visit Dubrovnik.
Day 2 Mljet Island, Croatia – arrive via Dubrovnik, depart via Pelješac.
Day 3 Visit Mostar, overnight Mostar.
Day 4 Blagaj Dervish Monastery, Počitelj Turkish town, Kravica Waterfalls, overnight Mostar.
Day 5 Canoe safari, Trebižat River, overnight in Mostar.
Day 6 Visit Sarajevo.
Day 7 Sarajevo.
Day 8 Bjelašnica Olympic Mountain.
Day 9 Višegrad Kamengrad and Bridge on the Drina.
Day 10 Mokra Gora Ethno-Village, Serbia.
Day 11 Durmitor National Park, Montenegro.
Day 12 Durmitor National Park, Montenegro.
Day 13 Rafting on Tara River.
Day 14 Sutjeska National Park (Perućica primeval forest).
Day 15 Dubrovnik – departure.

TOUR OPERATORS

There has yet to be a Bosnian tourist office established in any country. The Bosnian embassies have little or no information regarding tour operators or tourist information and, with the exception of Međugorje, Bosnia and Herzegovina has only begun to seriously promote tourism in the last decade. Many of the large tour operators from Croatia and Slovenia have now begun organised tours to Bosnia and Herzegovina. Through their partners in western Europe and the US, groups are brought into the country. If you are looking for an organised trip it is best to see if a travel agent in your area co-operates with one of the tour operators listed below.

There are relatively few tour operators who work throughout Bosnia and Herzegovina, although at the present time the best way to organise a trip is from agencies within the country. For short excursions from the coast there are several Croatian agencies that organise regular trips to Herzegovina.

IN THE UK

Exodus Grange Mills, Weir Rd, London SW12 0NE; +44 (0)870 240 5550 or (0)20 8675 5550; **e** info@exodus.co.uk; **w** exodus.co.uk

Intrepid Travel UK 76 Upper St, London N1 0NU; +44 (0)1420 593096 **e** info@intrepidtravel.com; **w** intrepidtravel.com. Intrepid brochure request service: **w** intrepidtravel.com/brochures.

Regent Holidays Colston Tower, 6th Floor, Colston Street, Bristol BS1 4XE; 0207 666 1244; **e** regent@regentholidays.co.uk; **w** regent-holidays.co.uk. Provides individual itineraries throughout BiH & also the possibility to combine a tour there with one to the neighbouring republics. Short-break tours are also offered to Sarajevo.

IN EUROPE

Akaoka Haneau de la Combe 30440, St Laurent le Minier, France; + 33 01 83 62 19 68; **e** akaoka@akaoka.com; **w** akaoka.com

Eastern Trekker Kuehbergstrasse 20A, 5023 Salzburg, Austria; + 44 (0)8450 267 567 UK sales; **e** office@easterntrekker.com; www.easterntrekker.com

IN NORTH AMERICA

G Adventures 19 Charlotte St, Toronto, Ontario M5V 2H5; +1 416 260 0999 **e** travel@gadventures.com; **w** gadventures.com

Mir Corporation 85 South Washington St, Suite 210, Seattle, WA 98104; +1 206 624 7289; **e** info@mircorp.com; **w** mircorp.com. Cultural adventures for groups & independent travellers to Russia, the Baltic, the Balkans, central Asia, Iran, the Caucasus, Mongolia, China, Tibet & central/east Europe since 1986.

Mountain Trek Sobek 1266 66th St, Emeryville, CA 94608; +1 1 888 831 7526; **e** info@mtsobek.com; **w** mtsobek.com. One of North America's leading adventure-travel groups with hiking treks to BiH.

IN CROATIA

Maestral Travel Split; +385 21 470 944; **e** info@maestral.hr; **w** maestral.hr. Maestral is one of the more recent agencies to add BiH to its itinerary list. They organise coach trips from Croatia to Bihać, Travnik, Sarajevo, Mostar, Međugorje & Neum.

Atlas Travel Vukovarska 19, Dubrovnik; +385 12 415 619; **w** atlas.hr. The region's largest & most active tour operator, Atlas runs regular trips to Bosnia from its Croatian bases.

IN BOSNIA & HERZEGOVINA

Fortuna Tours Kujundžiluk br 2, Mostar; +387 36 552 197; **e** headoffice@fortuna.ba; **w** fortuna.ba. Fortuna Tours has been in the travel business for over 20 years. This is arguably the best tour operator in BiH; they organise coach tours around the country, accommodation, Mostar & Herzegovina guides & car hire. They are very flexible & speak all major European languages.

Globtour Međugorje; +387 36 651 393/593; **e** globtour@medjugorje.com; **w** globtour.com. Globtour organise trips & accommodation mainly in Međugorje but also to areas in Herzegovina & the Dalmatian coast.

Green Visions Trg Barcelone, Sarajevo; +387 33 717 290; **e** sarajevo@greenvisions.ba; **w** greenvisions.ba. Green Visions is BiH's only ecotourism group. They promote the cultural & natural heritage of BiH & specialise in hiking, rafting, mountain biking, village tourism & tour skiing throughout the country.

Guideline Agency Cerska 54, 78000 Banja Luka; +387 66 714 170; **e** info@guidelinebl.com, **w** guidelinebl.com. Guideline is a tourist agency offering adventure tourism in their rafting centre, near Banja Luka, on the River Vrbas. In addition to great rafting trips, Guideline provides many other adventure activities like canyoning, hiking, hydrospeed, kayaking, canoeing, paintballing, mountain biking, free climbing, etc. They also offer night rafting (floodlit) in the Tijesno Canyon, plus transport, hotel accommodation & camping in the pleasant village of Krupa na Vrbasu, near Banja Luka.

Lasta Travel Kralja Petra Krešimira IV 1, Mostar; +387 36 332 011; **e** travel@lasta.ba; **w** lasta.ba. Lasta Travel specialise in unique & authentic tours of Herzegovina for both groups & independent travellers. They offer superb service, excellent guiding & some of the more original trips being offered in Herzegovina. One can visit little-known medieval graveyards, small vineyards in sleepy villages, as well as seeing & experiencing the more popular highlights of Herzegovina. See ad, page 239.

Paddy Travel Glavna ulica bb, 88266 Međugorje; ☎ +387 36 650 482; e paddy@tel.net.ba; w paddy-travel.info.com. Paddy is an Irish/Herzegovinian-run travel agency. They specialise in Međugorje & organise trips from Ireland & the UK.

Zepter Passport Banja Luka Veselina Masleše 8/I, Banja Luka; ☎ +387 051 213 394; e info@zepterpassport.com; w zepterpassport.com. One of the best travel agencies that organise tours & guides in the Krajina & in other areas of BiH. They also arrange hunting & fishing trips. Zepter can arrange permits, gear/gun rental & customs papers if the hunters would like to take their spoils with them.

RED TAPE

Border control in Bosnia and Herzegovina resembles border control in European countries. Customs and border crossing, particularly for EU and American citizens, are very easy and painless. At Sarajevo airport immigration is relatively quick. Land border crossings can sometimes be delayed for 30 minutes or they might simply wave you through and not even check your passport. Customs are quite lax, especially on border crossings from Croatia. Limits on cigarettes and alcohol are standard at 200 cigarettes and two litres of alcohol but, again, they are not very strict on that. Cigarettes are very inexpensive in BiH, as are local wines and spirits. Brand-name alcohol is quite expensive and is certainly cheaper at duty-free shops.

VISAS All EU members are exempt from visa requirements and may enter BiH at any time. American and Canadian citizens are not required to have visas for entry to the country either. Bosnia and Herzegovina can only be entered with a valid passport. The country's border authorities do not accept any other type of personal identification.

Entry visa requirements Visas are issued by BiH's diplomatic missions. Visas for private travel require an application form and a certified letter of intent of a BiH citizen. This can normally be arranged through a tour operator. Business visas require an application form, an invitation from a BiH business partner and a certified letter of intent from the BiH trade office.

For certain countries, visa applicants should also submit evidence of possession of cash assets, as well as HIV test results.

Foreigners are required by law to register with the local police within 48 hours of arrival. However, in practice, this law appears not to be enforced very often.Visitors who stay in hotels may be registered automatically by the hotel, but it is best to ask at check-in. Not registering could have the consequence of problems at the border, but this appears to happen rarely.

For a full list of BiH embassies and consulates overseas and a list of foreign embassies and consulate within BiH, go to w embassypages.com/bosnia.

TOURIST INFORMATION

Tourism in post-war Bosnia and Herzegovina has been a bit slow getting off the ground, though it is steadily increasing especially in Sarajevo and Herzegovina. One will not find tourist information centres in most towns, at least not easily identifiable ones. With the exception of Sarajevo and Mostar, promotional material is often in poor English and lacks key information. At the main tourist destinations, however, there are decent information centres. These offer mainly information and cannot book hotels or hire cars. They do, however, offer guide services from the centres themselves in most places. No border crossings offer tourist information and Sarajevo airport has limited information.

The main tourist information offices are:

Tourism Association of Sarajevo Sarači 58; 033 580 999; e tourinfo@bih.net.ba; w sarajevo-tourism.com; summer 09.00–21.00 Mon–Fri; other times of year 09.00–17.00 Mon–Fri. The tourism office is located in the centre of the old town. The crew here are sharp & helpful & speak a number of languages. Visitors should stop in here first for information about tours, accommodation, restaurants, travel & sightseeing.

Herzegovina-Neretva Canton Tourist Board Dr Ante Starčevića bb, Mostar; 036 355 090; e hercegovina@hercegovina.ba; w hercegovina.ba; summer 08.00–20.00

Banja Luka Tourism Association Kralja Petra I Karadordevica 87; 051 490 308; e tobl@teol.net; w banjaluka-tourism.com; summer 08.00–21.00

Trebinje Preobraženska St bb; 059 273 410; e tourist_trebinje@yahoo.com; w trebinjeturizam.com; 08.00–20.00 Mon–Fri, 09.00–15.00 Sat. Conveniently located in the town centre near the Platani Hotel, this tourist information centre has a wide range of information & can organise guided tours to Trebinje & the surrounding area. There is an interactive, electronic map outside the building that can be used at all times.

In each chapter that is region-specific there are contacts for all tourism information centres found throughout BiH. These are not nationally operated offices and each has its own office hours. Check out the interactive websites (w *bhtourism.ba or* w *visit-bosniaherzegovina.com*). The former is the **official website of BiH** and has quite a lot of useful information, including maps with destination locations.

MAPS There are good road maps available for Bosnia and Herzegovina in most travel shops, bookstores and in airports around Europe. Buying maps locally can be more of a challenge. They are easily found at petrol stations and most maps of Croatia include all of BiH due to Croatia's odd shape and the large amount of transit traffic going through BiH to Croatia. Studio FMB from Italy offers the best available road map of Bosnia and Herzegovina. It can be frustrating without a good navigator at your side though: the two-sided map is very detailed at 1:300,000 and enormous. Nonetheless, it will get you where you need to go. All updated European maps include Bosnia and Herzegovina and its main communication arteries. The Freytag and Berndt maps of Bosnia and Herzegovina and Europe are excellent and cost around 12KM. Maps online can be found at w mapabih.com, w mapquest.com and perhaps the best are on Google and w openstreetmap.org. As for hiking and outdoor activity maps, the best can be found on w viadinarica.com and w outdooractive.com.

GETTING THERE AND AWAY

During the siege of 1992–95 only UN flights could land at Sarajevo airport, and even that was questionable. Almost all border crossings were closed and no-one, with the exception of humanitarian and UN workers, dared venture into the territory of Bosnia and Herzegovina. Since then, BiH's borders have long been reopened and the new border and customs unit ensures professional and expeditious access to Bosnia and Herzegovina. Bosnia and Herzegovina is also a transit country for the sun worshippers flocking to the Croatian coast. This factor has greatly reduced delays in both the north and southwest crossings. Sarajevo airport has direct daily flights to several major European and Middle Eastern cities and connecting flights to many other destinations.

BY PLANE As Bosnia and Herzegovina is neither a main destination nor a major hub, the extra connection to Sarajevo will jack up the price of your ticket by US$100–200. A return ticket from London to Sarajevo will cost between £200 and £400 depending on the season. Flights from New York and most major east coast airports will run to US$800+ in the off-season and over US$1,200 in season. The best place to contact most airlines is **Sarajevo International Airport** (*Kurta Schorka 36, 71000 Sarajevo;* ☎ *033 289 100;* w *sarajevo-airport.ba*), just 15–20 minutes from town. The airport was reconstructed after the war and is one of the smallest and most laid back in the region. You may ask your ticketing agent to include the tax when you purchase the ticket. Airline tickets to Sarajevo tend to be a bit more expensive than the other major cities in the region due to its low traffic rate.

The following cities have regular direct flights to Sarajevo: Belgrade (five times a week), Copenhagen (once a week), Düsseldorf (once a week), Istanbul (three times a week), Ljubljana (daily), Munich (daily), Vienna (daily), Zagreb (daily) and Bonn (twice per week).

The best connections from the US are via London, Vienna, and Munich, and other European destinations can be most cheaply reached with a connection through Zagreb or Ljubljana.

The following are among the airlines flying to Sarajevo:

✈ **Adria Airlines** 23 Ferhadija, 71000 Sarajevo; w adria.si

✈ **Air Serbia** Terminal B, Kurta Schorka 36, 71210 Sarajevo; ☎ 033 289 265; w airserbia.com/en-BA

✈ **Austrian Airlines** Kurta Schorka 36, 71000 Sarajevo; e airport.sjj@austrian.com; w austrian.com

✈ **Croatia Airlines** Kurta Schorka 36, 71000 Sarajevo; e sjjto@croatiaairlines.hr; w croatiaairlines.hr

✈ **Germanwings** Kurta Schorka 36, 71000 Sarajevo; w germanwings.com

✈ **Lufthansa** Kurta Schorka 36, 71000 Sarajevo; e office.sjj@austrian.com; w lufthansa.com. Lufthansa is represented by Austrian Airlines in BiH.

✈ **Pegasus Airlines** Kurta Schorka 36, 71210 Sarajevo; 033 289 267, w flypgs.com/en

✈ **Turkish Airlines** Branilaca Sarajeva 3, 71000 Sarajevo; ☎ 033 565 750; e sarajevo@thy.com; w turkishairlines.com or w thy.com

During high season it can be rather expensive to fly into Sarajevo, and it may be cheaper to fly to neighbouring **Croatia** with a low-cost airline. Both Dubrovnik and Split are popular destinations for most major airlines, including the cheap-flight giants Ryanair (w *ryanair.com*), easyJet (w *easyjet.com*) and Germanwings (w *germanwings.com*). Dubrovnik is a 2-hour car ride from Mostar or 4–5 hours to Sarajevo. From Split it is some 3 hours by car to Mostar and just over 5 hours to Sarajevo. There are regular buses from both places and various firms also offer car rental, but be sure to double check with the car-hire agency that the insurance covers BiH.

Airports Sarajevo is the only major international airport in BiH with daily flights. See pages 110–11 for airport transfer from Sarajevo airport. Mostar airport does have weekly flights to Zagreb and has charter flights for groups coming to Međugorje (usually from Ireland, Italy, and the UK). Banja Luka also has several weekly flights to Belgrade and Vienna. It is usually more expensive, less convenient and less reliable to fly out of Mostar and Banja Luka airports. Wizz Air flies to Tuzla from Scandinavia and other places in Europe, depending on the season.

BY FERRY As Bosnia and Herzegovina has only about 24km of coast, at Neum, there are no ferries that dock in BiH. The ports of Split and Dubrovnik, however, are very popular and provide an efficient means of transport from Italy (Ancona and Bari). The bus station in Split is located at the port, making the transfer an easy and hassle-free one. Ferries from Ancona to Split and Bari to Dubrovnik can be found on the websites of these companies: SEM (**w** *sem-marina.hr*), Jadrolinija (**w** *jadrolinija.hr*) and Adriatica Navigazione (*www.adriatica.it*).

Dubrovnik's bus station is also located near the port. It does not have the same volume of traffic as Split, but nonetheless has several weekly ferries from Bari on the southeastern coast of Italy. The ferry schedules vary depending on the season.

BY TRAIN Bosnia and Herzegovina's rail system was badly damaged during the war and in the past 20 years has gone through phases of being better and worse. It is very difficult to find reliable, up-to-date information about train schedules and ticket prices online. It is best to go to the train station in person and enquire. Currently, only a few train lines are active: Sarajevo–Zagreb; Sarajevo–Doboj; and Sarajevo-Čapljina (that line has been under construction for some time and currently only runs between Konjic and Sarajevo, though that appears to be somewhat irregular at this point in time). In 2005, Bosnia and Herzegovina was added to the Eurail system, making travel much easier by train than in the past. The trains are generally slow but offer a great way of seeing the countryside. In 2006, the railway bought seven trains from the UK, albeit older ones, but certainly a step up from the old German and Swedish carriages that date back to the 1970s and 1980s. Recently, an even more contemporary train was put into service. The Sarajevo–Ploče line on the Croatian coast was recently cut, though may be put in service again.

Travelling from Zagreb to Sarajevo via Banja Luka is a long ride (9 to 10 hours) compared to the bus journey, which is usually between 6 and 9 hours, although it is a bit more cramped.

The following schedule shows daily trains to Sarajevo:

From	Via	Departure	Cost sgl/rtn (KM)	Duration
Konjic		15.30/19.21	6.9/11.0	1hr 40min
Zagreb	Banja Luka	10.21	60/98	9hrs

BY BUS The main bus operator in BiH is called Centrotrans (**w** *centrotrans.com*) and almost every bus connection can be made through them. They are operating together with the main European bus operators including Eurolines. Bus schedules, online reservations and main European office addresses can be found on the website.

Direct connections from Europe to BiH by bus are mainly from Germany (Berlin, Dortmund, Düsseldorf, Duisburg, Essen, Frankfurt, Hildesheim, Ingolstadt, Nuremberg, Mannheim, Munich, Stuttgart and Ulm) and Croatia (Dubrovnik, Makarska, Pula, Rijeka, Split and Zagreb), as well as from Antwerp, Rotterdam, Vienna, Ljubljana (Slovenia) and Skopje (Macedonia). Ticket prices vary from 30–250KM depending on the distance. Ticket reservations can be made at Eurolines offices abroad, at bus stations in BiH, or at the Centrotrans office in the centre of Sarajevo (*Ferhadija 1;* ☎ *033 407 407;* 🕘 *08.00–20.00 Mon–Fri, 09.00–16.00 Sat*).

At the time of writing, the Centrotrans schedule to Sarajevo (stopping in many cities within BiH along its respective routes) is as follows:

From	Days	Single (KM/Euros)	Return (KM/Euros)
Amsterdam	Tue, Thu, Sat	189/94.5	272/136
Antwerp	Tue, Sat	189/79	272/136
Berlin	Tue, Sat	176/88	298/149
Dortmund	every day	266/133	390/195
Dubrovnik	every day	45/22.5	67/33.5
Hamburg	Fri	240/120	340/170
Ljubljana	Mon, Wed, Fri	88/44	141/70.5
Makarska	every day	48.50/24.25	68/34
Munich	every day	136/68	186/93
Paris	Sun	260/133	390/199
Pula	Fri, Sat	97/50	155/79
Rotterdam	Tue, Thu, Sat	189/94.5	272/136
Stuttgart	every day	184/92	282/141
Split	every day	52.50/26.25	74/37
Vienna	every day	88/44	137/68.5
Zagreb	every day	50/25.50	80/41

BY CAR The drive from the UK to Bosnia and Herzegovina is exceptionally long. Fuel and tolls in Europe are not cheap either. Although it is always an advantage to have your own vehicle in Bosnia and Herzegovina it may be easier to fly, bus it, or take a train to BiH and then hire a car (see opposite). From London to Sarajevo the trip is over 2,000km and could prove rather exhausting. If you have the time and the will, however, you can certainly pack in much more of the country than you would without your own personal transport.

Traffic in Bosnia and Herzegovina, even during the busiest season, is heaviest on the roads towards the coast, particularly at the M-17 crossing at Metković. The northern border crossing at Brod is also one of the busiest crossings year round. New border controls have expedited border crossings but delays can still be expected. Owing to the dual-carriageway 'highway' system, traffic can at times move slowly but it is nothing compared with the traffic jams on the Croatian coast in the high season. Most people travelling to Bosnia and Herzegovina create a combination trip and rarely miss the opportunity to see the beautiful Adriatic coast. Alternative routes to avoid some of the crazy traffic to and from the coast are the Trebinje–Dubrovnik route, Kamensko crossing by Livno and the Imotski–Posušje route in the Croatian hinterlands. All of these routes are off the beaten track and offer the beautiful scenery of the back country in BiH and Croatia.

If you decide to drive and are looking to avoid the long trek through Germany, Austria or the northern strip of Italy there are regular ferries from Ancona and Bari that dock at Split and Dubrovnik. It's a great way to miss the traffic along the entire length of the Croatian coast. See *By ferry* above for website details.

HEALTH *with Dr Felicity Nicholson*

Although there are no legal requirements for vaccinations when travelling to Bosnia and Herzegovina, visitors are advised to be immunised with hepatitis A vaccine (eg: Avaxim, Havrix Monodose). One shot gives protection for a year and a second booster shot (6–12 months after the first) extends the protection for at least 25 years. The vaccine should ideally be taken at least two weeks before travel, but can still be effective even if given the day before.

QUICK TICK REMOVAL

European ticks are not the prolific disease transmitters they are in the Americas, but they may spread Lyme disease, tick-borne encephalitis and a few other rarities

Travellers planning to go rambling or trekking in the countryside during the spring–autumn period are at risk of tick-borne encephalitis. The ticks that transmit this potentially fatal disease live in long grass and overhanging tree branches. Precautions include wearing long trousers tucked into boots and a hat. Using tick repellents and checking for ticks at the end of the day can also help. If you do find ticks, remove them as soon as possible (see below) and go to a doctor for treatment. Pre-exposure vaccine is available in the UK, and is worth considering. Two doses of vaccine should ideally be given a month apart but can be given with only a two-week gap if time is short. However, it's still important to seek medical help in the event of a tick bite. In rare cases, this disease can also be spread by consuming unpasteurised milk products so those are best avoided, too.

The best way to remove ticks is to use special tick tweezers, which should be available from reliable travel clinics. Failing that, manoeuvre your finger and thumb so that you can pinch the tick's mouthparts, as close to your skin as possible, and slowly and steadily pull away at right angles to your skin. This often hurts. Jerking or twisting will increase the chances of disease transmission, as well as leaving the mouthparts behind. Once the tick is off, dowse the little wound with alcohol (local spirit, whisky or similar are excellent) or iodine. An area of spreading redness around the bite site, or a rash or fever coming on a few days or more after the bite, should stimulate a trip to the doctor.

It is also sensible to be up to date with tetanus, diphtheria and polio (all ten-yearly).

For those who are intending to work in a medical setting or with children, or who are at risk through lifestyle, immunisation against hepatitis B is advised. Ideally, three doses of vaccine should be taken. There is a variety of schedules – the shortest being over 21 days for those aged 16 or over. Similarly, you should consider rabies vaccine for trips of a month or more. This too is a course of three doses over a minimum of 21 days (see below). BiH is considered to be a high-risk rabies country so all travellers should consider vaccination, particularly if you are going to be away from medical help, and definitely if you are working with animals.

To ensure a healthy trip, visit your doctor or a travel clinic at least six weeks before travel.

RABIES Bosnia and Herzegovina is considered high risk for rabies so any bite, scratch or saliva on skin from any warm-blooded mammal should be considered a risk. Wash the wound with soap and in running water for a good 15 minutes, then apply antiseptic and go for medical help. There is very specific treatment for rabies which is not always easily available. Having three pre-exposure doses of rabies vaccine before you go (over three to four weeks) simplifies treatment and makes treatment more likely to be available in BiH. Always seek expert medical advice.

TUBERCULOSIS TB is common in BiH (there were 42 cases per 100,000 population, according to 2014 WHO statistics) and can be spread by respiratory droplets and through unpasteurised dairy products. Consider vaccination if you are under 16 and are spending 3 months or more living with the local population. Those under 35 should also consider vaccination if they are occupationally at risk. It may be necessary to perform a Mantoux test prior to vaccination, so allow at least 6 weeks before travel.

MEDICAL FACILITIES Going to a public health clinic in Bosnia and Herzegovina can be a frightening experience. The 'system' of medical care from the socialist era is very much alive in BiH. Many Westerners would be shocked at the standard procedures (or lack of them) and type of treatment given at public hospitals and health centres in many areas. With that said, Bosnians tend to give extra care to visitors and major centres like Sarajevo, Banja Luka, Mostar and Tuzla can offer decent quality medical care. First contact your embassy for emergencies. There are some very good local doctors, mostly in the private sector.

For a list of emergency health phrases, see *Appendix 1*.

TRAVEL CLINICS AND HEALTH INFORMATION A full list of current travel clinic websites worldwide is available on **w** istm.org. For other journey preparation information, consult **w** travelhealthpro.org.uk (UK) or **w** wwwnc.cdc.gov/travel/ (US). Information about various medications may be found on **w** netdoctor.co.uk/ travel. All advice found online should be used in conjunction with expert advice received prior to or during travel.

SAFETY AND SECURITY

Despite the image of Bosnia and Herzegovina's violent past it is actually one of the safest places in Europe. There is a very low rate of violent crime and most cases of violence are domestic. Walking the streets of any town or city at any time of day or night is a relatively safe bet, although take the usual precautions in the late evening as you would in any capital city. Driving in Bosnia and Herzegovina is a new experience for those used to the wide and well-paved roads of the West. Most of Bosnia and Herzegovina's roads are only double lane and quite curvy due to the mountainous terrain. Road maintenance is getting better but don't let a pot-hole surprise you. The locals tend to drive fast and have little fear of overtaking on a solid line.

The main concerns for travellers to Bosnia and Herzegovina are pickpockets on the main Ferhadija promenade and the tramways in Sarajevo and in Mostar, car thieves and landmines. The pickpockets and car thieves can be avoided by simple precautions and awareness. On trams in Sarajevo keep your purse close and your wallet in your front pocket. These people are quick and talented and you won't even know that you've been had until later. Always lock your car door and if you have an alarm, engage it.

If you are looking for a taxi it is best to find the taxi stands – that way you know the drivers are official. There are usually several taxi stands in most towns and cities.

LANDMINES There is definitely a threat and danger of landmines in BiH, but it does not mean that you cannot step off the asphalt. Highly populated areas are clear of mines and are perfectly safe to visit. The most significant danger is in the countryside where the former lines of confrontation were. These are not easily known by travellers so the best policy is – if you don't know, don't go. Many mountain ranges are also mined. There is plenty of safe hiking, walking, wandering and exploring to be done in Bosnia and Herzegovina – it's simply not wise to do it alone. Take a guide or a local who knows the terrain. There are mountain associations and ecotourism organisations that are your best bet for a safe mountain adventure. Bosnia and Herzegovina receives millions of guests per year and there has (touch wood) never been a mine incident with a tourist. Their job is to make sure you are aware of any possible safety hazards.

Here are some hints for mine safety:

- If you are in the countryside look for signs that the area is frequented by people – cut grass, tyre tracks, footprints, rubbish. These are usually indications of safe areas.
- If you see taped areas, either in yellow or red – even if they appear to be old markers – stay clear.
- Abandoned villages may seem fun to explore but they may pose a threat – stay away from abandoned areas.
- Concentrate your activities where there is obvious human 'traffic'. National parks and conservation areas are safe places to visit. If you see people walking, jogging, barbecuing, etc, then it is generally safe to assume the area is clear.
- As a general rule (it does not apply to every case) populated areas and major routes are safe. Isolated areas in the mountains or countryside that were mined have not all been cleared. Use your best judgement and be smart.
- The Mine Action Centre (MAC) offers short 'courses' on mine safety in Sarajevo. You can check the website (**w** *bhmac.org*) for more information.

See also *Mountain safety*, pages 90–1.

WOMEN TRAVELLERS

Bosnia and Herzegovina is considered a friendly place for women travellers, for whom it is safe to walk at night, even late at night on your own. That does not mean there aren't potential dangers; you should always take precautions when travelling. Avoid travelling alone if possible, and it is always best to walk in lit areas and with a friend. Take precautions when choosing taxis as well by using official taxi services and finding a cab at an official taxi stand. Be cautious of night trains and make sure your personal belongings are in a safe place. Don't accept seemingly kind offers of drinks or coffee from strangers on trains.

LGBTQ TRAVELLERS

The Balkans, although having made significant strides in the acceptance of LGBTQ people, is still rather conservative, so you should take a low-key approach to travelling. If with a partner, it's best to act as friends and present yourself as such unless in comfortable and trusted company. Be careful of public shows of affection in clubs. Reactions to LGBTQ people can unfortunately be provocative and there have been a few cases of violence.

TRAVELLING WITH A DISABILITY

Although the war has created literally thousands of disabled people, access to buildings, sidewalks, street crossings and public transport pay little or no attention to the needs of the disabled. The same goes for a lot of hotels and restaurants. There will usually be a kind person to assist you but don't count on there being disability-friendly infrastructure. It can be a frustrating experience trying to get around BiH.

WHAT TO TAKE

The contents of your luggage depend largely on what type of tourist you are. The basics, however, apply to everyone. Don't forget your passport, driver's licence (international driver's licence if travelling from North America or Australia), money, credit cards (even if just for emergencies) and any health insurance cards or forms you need as required from your insurance company. The other necessities I'll leave up to you.

For women travellers, tampons and pads are easy to find here and are not expensive. Any toiletries that you may have forgotten can also be found here, especially at the big supermarkets. Sunglasses and sunscreen are a must whether you've come to hike or to hang out on Neum's beaches. Summers are hot and sunny, spring and autumn have plenty of sunny days, and the beam of the sun off the snow in winter is blinding.

The beaches at Neum mainly consist of rocks and pebbles so proper footwear is necessary, especially for those with wimpy feet (like me). If you get into the local groove of walking – walking a lot – then make sure you bring comfortable walking shoes. Most places in Bosnia and Herzegovina are fairly casual, even the ritzy ones. If you plan on staying with some Bosnians or in private accommodation it is recommended that you bring a light pair of slippers. Most homes have extra slippers, called *papuče*, but I always find it nice to have my own. It is a custom in many Bosnian homes to remove shoes at the doorstep.

Backpackers should bring a water bottle with them. Those of you who are the adventurous types probably already know what you need but I recommend a sleeping bag if you plan on hopping from town to town or camping in the mountains.

Even on the hottest days in the summer, evenings can be cool and require a jumper. Herzegovina is an exception to that rule, but Sarajevo and the mountainous areas of Bosnia can be chilly at night. Spring and autumn are similar in that many days are warm and sunny and evenings are quite chilly. Bring layers. The air is very refreshing, but not if you're dressed inadequately. Winter can be seriously cold. Herzegovina is much milder but when the *bura* winds get kicking they chill you to the bone.

Good winter gear is a must for Bosnia: thermal underwear, gloves, hat, scarf and rain gear are recommended, as are good shoes, preferably hiking or walking boots. Snow clearing in the winter leaves something to be desired and many pavements will be covered with ice and dirty, cold slush. Nice dress shoes will do you no good then.

I've covered this in the *Eating and drinking* section on pages 79–84 but for dedicated tea drinkers, 'proper' tea is a must (ie: bring a box of PG Tips or similar with you). Electricity in Bosnia and Herzegovina is standard European size and shape (220V and 50Hz) with twin round-pin plugs. Adapters for UK or American plugs cannot be found here. Bring your own if you anticipate needing one.

WALKING AND HIKING GEAR We will go season by season for what to take if you're coming on an outdoor activity holiday to Bosnia and Herzegovina. The **summers** offer hot, central European temperatures in Bosnia, and an even hotter Mediterranean climate in Herzegovina. Bring a hat to protect your head from the sun, especially if you'll be taking some high mountain hikes. Boots are a must, as many of the trails are not well maintained and loose rocks or roots could mean a serious ankle injury. If you plan on camping be sure to bring a light sleeping bag, watch or alarm clock, warm fleece, light rain gear, walking sticks if you use them, and a comfortable pack.

NOTES FOR TRAVELLERS WITH A DISABILITY

Accessibility in Bosnia and Herzegovina is not as well organised as it is in other European countries. However, the local people are very helpful and do understand the situation regarding disability because many in the country were affected during the war from 1992–95.

PLANNING AND BOOKING There are few specialist travel agencies running trips to Bosnia and Herzegovina. Companies such as Fibula Travel (*www.wheelchairholiday.com*) have locations in BiH available for those wishing to travel there.

GETTING THERE The airport in Sarajevo is fully accessible, with all necessary facilities on offer for people with disabilities (assistance services, disabled toilets, etc) and this is the same for the other airports in the country.

SIGHTSEEING As Bosnia has many landmarks and old buildings in their original form, it is not that easy for anyone to get around in a wheelchair. However, reconstruction has taken place on a large scale since the internal struggles ended in 1995, and many of the newer establishments now have full access for those in wheelchairs.

Public transportation does not have good accessibility but does have a few seats available for disabled people.

ACCOMMODATION A number of hotels in Bosnia have wheelchair access, eg:

Courtyard Marriott Sarajevo; w marriott.com (page 116)
Hotel Bristol Sarajevo; w bristolsarajevo.com (page 116)
Hotel Central Sarajevo; w hotelcentral.ba; (page 116)
Hotel Europe Sarajevo; w hoteleurope.ba (page 116)
Hotel Villa Regina Međugorje; 036 651 808; e info@hotel-villaregina.com; w hotel-villaregina.com
Hotel Almira Rade Bitange bb, Mostar; 036 554 310; e info@almira-hotel.ba; w almira-hotel.ba

TRAVEL INSURANCE There are a few specialised companies that deal with travel to Bosnia and Herzegovina. A number of operators deal with pre-existing medical conditions, eg: **Orbis Plus** (*+44 (0) 845 338 1638; w orbisplus.co.uk*) and **Medici Travel** (*+44 (0) 845 082 1265; w medicitravel.com*).

FURTHER INFORMATION Health facilities can accommodate wheelchair patients in most places. Further information is available from the **Tourist Association of Sarajevo** (*033 250 200; w sarajevo-tourism.com*) and the **Bosnia and Herzegovina Department of Tourism** (*033 252 928; e media@tourism.ba; w bhtourism.ba*).

Spring and autumn experience more rain so good waterproof gear is recommended. Gaiters, poncho and waterproof trousers are always a good idea, just in case. Putting a protective coating on your shoes, even if they are already waterproof, is good for them and even better for your feet!

Winter hiking is an amazing experience in BiH. Don't bother to embark on any challenging hikes, though, if you haven't brought good-quality gear with you or rented it from a local ecotourism outfit (pages 89–90). You can avoid the big snow hiking in some parts of Herzegovina but be prepared for more than a metre of snow above the 1,000m mark during the coldest months. Whatever waterproof gear you have, bring it. Warm fleeces and thermals are a must. If you plan to hike above 2,000m (there are over a dozen peaks in this range) boots that can be worn with crampons are best.

Green Visions (page 89) offers hikes and walks all year round for both hard-core hikers and nature lovers looking for a day in the wild. They provide gear rental.

MONEY AND BUDGETING

Bosnia and Herzegovina was fortunate enough to have its currency, the convertible mark (KM or, on international currency exchange, BAM), directly pegged to the German mark. With the introduction of the euro, the KM maintained a steady value and has experienced little or no inflation. The war days saw three or four different currencies, some of which could experience inflation rates in the thousands overnight. The Central Bank of Bosnia and Herzegovina has recorded a steady growth rate of 5% and there is no indication that the value of the KM will change in the near future.

The local currency comes in .10, .20, .50, 1 and 2 mark coins. Banknotes are printed in 10, 20, 50, 100, 200 and 500 mark bills. The fixed rate to the euro is €1 = 1.95KM and has been at this rate for some time. At the time of going to press, the sterling rate was £1 = 2.31KM.

It is not uncommon to use euros in very touristic areas of BiH, however it is becoming less common and you should count on using the local currency. Most places now have exchange offices and every bank will convert your currency for you. US dollars and British pounds, however, need to be changed at a bank, post office or bureau de change. In western Herzegovina, and in fact on the west side of Mostar, the Croatian kuna is often accepted if you have leftovers from your visit to Croatia, although many shops and cafés in BiH will not be happy about giving change for large banknotes.

Cashing travellers' cheques is possible but the rates are often poorer than for cash. There are enough ATMs in big cities to take out cash if you need to. Sarajevo is the best-equipped city for using credit and debit cards, whether for purchases or taking out cash. You will find, however, that many shops and restaurants still don't take Visa, MasterCard, American Express or any other major credit card (even though they may advertise that they do). Many hotels do but some don't so make sure you check with the hotel if they accept credit cards when making your reservation. Be sure to take out the cash you need for travelling in the country while you are in a major city.

BUDGETING Budgeting a trip is largely dependent on your travel style and, of course, how much money you have to part with. Bosnia and Herzegovina is inexpensive in comparison with European and North American prices.

Food prices are extremely low and probably the best bargain around. Most food here is natural and often organic. You can stuff yourself on *burek* for 2–3KM or enjoy a three-course meal in a good restaurant for less than 30KM. Wine is also relatively inexpensive; in restaurants you shouldn't pay more than

25KM for a bottle of decent domestic wine and double that for a bottle of high-quality wine. Even eating out twice a day at a mid-priced restaurant will cost around 30KM (€15). Markets sell food products that are often half the standard European prices.

Accommodation will certainly be the main expense when visiting BiH. Hotel prices range from 75–250KM per night; pensions and motels will cost 50–80KM per night. There has been a recent explosion of good-quality, good-value hostels in many of the tourist towns like Mostar, Sarajevo, Banja Luka and Trebinje. Most places do, however, offer significant discounts for two persons in a double bedroom. For longer stays almost all hotels give discounts – don't be afraid to ask. Private accommodation will run between 25KM and 40KM.

Public transport is also very inexpensive. Buses and trams cost 1.80KM for a one-way trip. A day pass for public transport in Sarajevo can be bought for 5.30KM and you can travel all you like on either the buses or the trams. Intercity travel is very reasonable too. Mostar to Sarajevo will cost 20KM one way. Sarajevo to Bihać in the far northwest of the country costs around 40KM one way. All cities and towns are linked by bus routes that operate daily.

As a **budget** traveller you can comfortably live on a daily budget of 30–50KM if you are diligent enough in finding cheap accommodation. The travellers staying in **pensions** can easily get by on 75KM per day. Those who want to stay in **mid-range** accommodation can expect to spend 150–250KM per day. Most of that will be spent on accommodation. Travellers who want to stay in **luxury** (although there is not a luxurious catering culture in Bosnia and Herzegovina) will find it hard to spend 500KM per day, even including some shopping.

For **hikers and adventure seekers** a weekend trip with food, guide, transport and accommodation can cost 150–300KM, depending on the accommodation. Week-long trips in the mountains with everything included run from 700–1,500KM. Accommodation is often simple: camping, mountain lodges, villagers' homes or mountain motels. Nonetheless, it is significantly cheaper than the pricey accommodation in most cities and one gets to enjoy the great taste of nature.

Museums are often free and if there is an entrance fee it won't be more than 6KM. **Attractions** are also frequently free or very cheap; admission to the Kajtaz Turkish House in Mostar, for example, is only 4KM. Going to the cinema is never more than 10KM and plays, festivals or concerts range from 5KM to 25KM.

If you can find reasonable accommodation, you're looking at an unforgettable trip with great food, culture and nature for a fraction of the cost of most European countries.

Petrol prices varies between 1.70–2.60KM (€0.90–€1.30) per litre. Diesel fuel is slightly more expensive. A postcard will cost you 1KM in most places and the price for a T-shirt ranges from 10–20KM in the old town souvenir shops.

See also *Tipping* on page 100.

OPENING TIMES

As the concept of time is a bit different in the Balkans, it becomes a question of relativism and opening times can vary. Businesses and institutions usually start work at 08.00 or 09.00. Depending on their status, whether public or private, their closing times can range from 15.00 to 18.00. **Cafés, restaurants and bars** stay open until much later, usually until 22.00 or midnight, or when the last customer leaves.

Museums, galleries and historical sites open at varying times in the morning but most open between 08.00 and 10.00 and close rather early, ranging from 13.00 to 17.00.

Supermarkets are open all week from 09.00 to 22.00 but on Sundays they close earlier. **Pharmacies** are open late in bigger cities, many until 22.00, and some operate 24 hours. In the smaller towns, however, almost everything closes by 18.00, with the exception of cafés, bars, restaurants and some small convenience shops. Many restaurants, shops and pharmacies are closed on Sundays.

The lack of a well-developed tourist industry leaves opening times up in the air, so to speak. Sarajevo, Mostar and western Herzegovina are used to catering for tourists and have certain services available, and with accurate operating hours. Most places, though, do not. It's best to check ahead before just showing up at a place. (See also *Business/time*, pages 98–9.)

GETTING AROUND

However limited the ways and means of getting around Bosnia and Herzegovina are, moving around the country is fairly easy and always attractive. Whether by car, rail, bus, bike or hitching, travel in Bosnia and Herzegovina is rather inexpensive, reliable but slow. The curvy mountain roads offer better countryside scenery than you'd imagine. Tito's road engineers did an amazing job of connecting all of the mountainous regions. Even though highways are currently being built, taking it slowly through the valleys and over the mountains makes the experience that much more interesting.

BY TRAIN Before the war the rail network connected most Bosnian cities. This has drastically changed. Two routes currently originate in Sarajevo: the Sarajevo–Zenica–Banja Luka–Zagreb route takes about 10 hours from start to finish; the southern route towards the Adriatic coast currently goes to Konjic. It used to, and hopefully will again, extend to Jablanica, Mostar, Čapljina and Ploče (Ploče is in Croatia).

BiH is covered by the InterRail and Eurail schemes, which offer international rail passes. Booking is best done in person at the train station (*željeznička stanica*). As you enter the station, the ticket booths are to the far right. During the high season buy your tickets a day in advance, but there are no online reservations available and staff do not speak English.

Getting around by train is slow but enjoyable and offers some terrific scenery. It is also a comfortable alternative for those who may be nervous travelling by bus on the curvy roads. Bus and train prices are about the same. Buses run more frequently but you can't get up and walk around on a bus and the possibilities of motion sickness are considerably less on a straight-travelling train.

The train ride from Sarajevo to Mostar, if the line is reinstated in the near future, offers stunning scenery through the Neretva Canyon and is more than worth the trip. Expect delays at border crossings but they are nothing out of the ordinary for eastern Europe. Do not expect new, high-tech carriages for your train journeys as most of them were destroyed or rusted away during the war. Many of the carriages are gifts of old rolling stock from western European countries, namely Germany, or bought in from the UK. There is, however, one new train running. Trains are usually quite punctual, which is an oddity in a place where time takes on a new meaning.

BY BUS The public and private bus system in Bosnia and Herzegovina is the best available transportation option next to having your own car. Literally every town and most villages are connected one way or another by very reliable bus routes.

Every city and town will have a bus station and the daily departure and arrival times should be posted on the wall of the station. If not, ask the person behind the counter. They are not likely to speak English but will point you in the right direction. Asking a person who is standing around waiting is also a good idea, to double check that you are getting on the right bus. People are very willing to help. Centrotrans is the main intercity bus line but there are many bus companies operating throughout the country. Be sure to check out the bus before you get on. Most buses are comfortable and clean but there is the occasional private bus company that has run-down buses with broken seats, windows that don't open, no air conditioning and a driver who smokes the entire length of the journey.

Between major routes there are several daily buses. It is important to note that buses between the Republika Srpska entity and the Federation entity are less frequent, especially from smaller towns. As inconvenient as it may be, it is easier to get a bus from East Sarajevo to Banja Luka than from the main bus station in Sarajevo. Sarajevo, Mostar, Tuzla, Zenica, Travnik and Bihać are the main transit centres within the Federation. In the Republika Srpska the main stations are Banja Luka, Doboj, Bjeljina and East Sarajevo.

Bus travel is very reasonably priced and the furthest destination in BiH will cost around 50KM one way. Tickets at the main bus stations must be bought at the ticket booth whereas at most other stations you have to pay when you get on the bus. There is usually an extra charge for luggage of 2KM per bag.

Bus drivers have special deals with certain restaurants on their routes. This means that breaks will be longer (they'll say 15 minutes but often this really means half an hour) to encourage you to eat and drink. Breaks may occur more often than normal, which is quite the norm for a population so addicted to nicotine. At every break the entire bus will empty out and 90% of the people will have a cigarette lit seconds after they step off the bus. Bussing it is also a great way to see some fantastic countryside. For useful travel terms see *Appendix 1*.

BY CAR Travelling by car is by far the easiest way of seeing the country the way you would like and at your own pace. The roads are in decent condition and short sections of motorway have been completed recently, with more sections planned. Most of the roads are curvy and wind through river valleys and up and over mountains. Bosnia and Herzegovina does enjoy a well-connected road system though, thanks to Tito's road improvement launch in the late 1960s and early 1970s. This project connected every city and town with asphalt roads. It wasn't too long ago that BiH was a very isolated province in the heart of the Dinaric Alps. Fuel stations are plentiful; there are probably too many, so there are few worries of running out of fuel in the middle of nowhere. Note though that purchasing fuel in the Federation is the safer bet; some stations in the Republika Srpska have a reputation for mixing other substances in the fuel, namely water.

There are toll roads on the new motorways between Zenica and Sarajevo and from Sarajevo south towards Konjic. The Zenica–Sarajevo motorway costs 6KM. The C-5 corridor is planned to connect Sarajevo to the Croatian coast by a main highway and towards Slavonia to the north. This will create quick and easy access to and from Bosnia. Approximately 90km of motorway has been built linking Sarajevo to Zenica, and 20km of motorway has opened, running towards the southern exit from Sarajevo towards Mostar. There is also a toll-free new motorway between Banja Luka and Gradiska.

It is important to travel with a good **map** (page 63). Road signs in some areas are frequent and accurate but all of a sudden there may not be a sign in sight to indicate anything at all. Travelling through the Republika Srpska can also be a challenging

THE JOYS OF DRIVING IN BiH

No-one can argue that the southern Europeans have a different approach to driving from most. Bosnia and Herzegovina is no exception. Whereas the madness of driving in Rome, for example, may have some sort of Zen energy to it, driving in Bosnia does not. Here are a few tips on what to expect.

- Bosnians love to overtake on solid white lines. It's a common practice, especially on curves – don't fret too much over it; they're good at it.
- If a Bosnian driver sees a friend, whether walking or in a car, he will stop and chat – in the middle of the road – until he is done. Don't bother honking; he'll either curse you or simply ignore you. You just have to wait.
- At intersections where you feel you have the right of way, approach with caution. Local drivers will often pull halfway out into the intersection, blocking one half and aggressively nudge into your lane. Sometimes they'll respect the right of way, sometimes not. Defensive driving is the key phrase.
- Pedestrians, especially at zebra crossings, have no right of way whatsoever. Bosnian drivers may even speed up so be careful walking and if you do stop at a pedestrian crossing don't be confused by the dazed look of the pedestrian staring at you for being the first car to stop at these crossings in his/her lifetime.
- Even though there may be 3m of open pavement, Bosnians love to walk in the road. Don't ask me why, that's just the way it is. You will find this defiance in smaller towns that experience less traffic but don't be too shocked if in the middle of Sarajevo or Mostar someone is walking in the middle of the street completely unconcerned with the fact that you are behind them…waiting.
- Bosnian men are particularly fond of their cars but are less so of Bosnia's beautiful nature. If you see large bags of rubbish being hauled out of a car window, that is simply the driver keeping his car clean. God forbid he should have a dirty car.
- Most of Bosnia's roads are only double lane. When stuck behind a lorry climbing a hill, close the windows – the diesel fumes can kill. Most drivers stuck behind will attempt daredevil overtaking of the lorry – use your best judgement.
- Last warning – along any road in Bosnia and Herzegovina you might see a policeman on the side of the road holding a little lollipop like a stop sign. He may convincingly hold it out and stop you or may just nonchalantly wave it. Stop anyway and don't let the policeman talk you into paying a fine, unless of course you were speeding like the rest of them. Play the dumb foreigner and try to get out of it. Most policemen are either just looking for coffee money or to give you a hard time, simply because they can. Even if they appear serious or mean, policemen can always be spoken to here (unlike the Florida Highway Patrol that approaches you with hand on gun for speeding).

experience as the road signs are mainly in Cyrillic. The good news is that all major roads are now required to have road signs in both Cyrillic and Latin letters. There is a Cyrillic alphabet section in *Appendix 1*.

For repairs and flat tyres there are plenty of garages. An auto-repair shop is *auto mehaničar* and a garage that can fix a flat is a *vulkanizer.* They are usually cheap and will do the job right away. Spare parts for British-made cars will be difficult to come by but German cars are most popular and spare parts for them can be easily found. If you are travelling with your own vehicle it is always wise to carry extra fuel, air and oil filters; they are often the cause of car troubles and are easily fixed – if you have the parts. It is the law to always carry a spare tyre, jack, extra headlight bulb, first-aid kit, tow rope and hazard triangle. During a routine check by the police they will often ask if you have all the necessary gear. In the winter months it is a must to have snow chains in the car and there's a good chance you may need to use them. In the first edition I dedicated an entire section to the deadly black tunnels of BiH, but every major tunnel in BiH now has lighting and these horrible black holes with massive pot-holes are a thing of the past. Always use caution when entering tunnels though, as you will still find some pot-holes in some of the less-developed regions. Most of the main roads, however, are now in pretty good shape tunnel-wise.

Renting a car is very easy and with the small boom in tourism has become less expensive due to increased competition. The normal daily rate for car hire runs from 75–150KM. There is a discount for longer hires. All major cities have car-hire companies. If you arrive at Sarajevo airport there are several rental places there and many have airport pick-up. **City Car Rental** (*Kranjčevićeva 39;* ☏ *033 555 255;* **e** *info@citycarrental.ba;* **w** *citycarrental.ba*) do airport pick-ups and offer some of the best rates in town. **Avis** (☏ *033 469 933*), **Budget** (☏ *033 766 670*), **Europcar** (☏ *033 771 899;* **e** *reservation@europcar.ba*) and **Hertz** (☏ *033 668 186*) all have desks at the airport. In the summer season, it is wise to look for a car rental at least a week in advance, though it is possible to get lucky and find something on the spot. Many of the major car-hire companies' local information can be found via links from the international websites and international toll-free phone numbers. Budget and Hyundai (also located at the airport) offer automatic transmission cars.

BY BICYCLE Road biking for the exceptionally fit is certainly a challenging adventure in Bosnia and Herzegovina. The roads throughout the region are usually rather narrow with little or no hard shoulders. **Road biking** is not popular in BiH and therefore there is not much of a bike culture, though that is slowly changing with the addition of bike lanes to several streets in Sarajevo and a bike-sharing service that covers most of Sarajevo's city centre (page 113); drivers are known for their fast and risky driving. Certain areas of the country, however, are made for cycling. One can travel for hours on end without experiencing much traffic at all in Popovo Polje from Stolac towards Trebinje; and the large, picturesque valleys of Livanjsko and Glamočka fields in western Bosnia are perfect for challenging road biking.

Mountain biking is another story altogether. Hundreds of highland villages are connected by good gravel roads almost everywhere in the country. Igman–Bjelašnica–Visočica in the Sarajevo area offers days of mountain-biking trails in breathtaking mountain landscapes.

Bikers should follow the same safety precautions as hikers and stick to the roads and marked paths. Don't wander if you don't know where you're going. Roads have been cleared of mines, even the isolated gravel ones, but in some faraway places a mine could be just 10m off the side of the road. If you don't know, don't go. There are bicycle repair shops in most major towns, and several to choose from in Sarajevo.

HITCHHIKING Hitchhiking is still a common practice in Bosnia and Herzegovina, especially in the rural areas. In small towns and villages everyone seems to know everyone anyway so picking up a hitcher is nothing new. In and around the bigger cities it is less common. For women hitchers it is always wise not to travel alone and to check out who you are getting in the car with. If you're not sure, it's probably your gut talking to you – listen to it!

Hitching is often like playing cards: sometimes you get lucky and sometimes you don't.

WALKING AND HIKING Hiking is a highly popular activity in Bosnia and Herzegovina and can also be a useful way of getting around. See *Hiking* on pages 88–92 for more information.

ACCOMMODATION

There is no lack of good accommodation in Bosnia and Herzegovina. Although the war destroyed much of the infrastructure, including hotels, there have been many new ones built, with modern facilities. There are, however, still many hotels from the old Yugoslavia that are run-down and out of date.

Hotels and motels can be found in all towns and cities. Private rooms and apartments are also common throughout the country. A few proper hostels have opened in BiH, namely in Sarajevo, Banja Luka, Trebinje and Mostar. There are many pensions and bed and breakfasts that are priced similarly to a western European hostel. I have added a lot of budget places to stay in each region. Prices for small hotels outside of the main cities are very affordable, and it is not unheard of to bargain if you are on a tight budget. Lodges dotted every mountain before the war. Many of them were destroyed or are now run-down. However, the Via Dinarica project has managed to revitalise many of the mountain huts. They can be found on **w** viadinarica.com.

HOTELS Like most places, hotels in BiH are overpriced relative to the standard of living. When compared with Western prices, however, hotels are certainly affordable. It is definitely wise to check out the hotel before booking in. There are many very nice new hotels and small motels. Many hotels built during the socialist period are not very pleasant, a tad uncomfortable, and although they claim to have hot water they often don't. A simple stroll through the lobby is usually enough to assess the situation.

Sarajevo, Mostar, Banja Luka and Međugorje have the best large hotels. When travelling elsewhere, take a look at the smaller hotels or motels. Booking.com and

ACCOMMODATION PRICE CODES

Peak summer price ranges:

$$$$	Luxury	Above 250KM
$$$	Upmarket	140–250KM
$$	Mid range	60–140KM
$	Budget	20–60KM

These categories absorb the small numbers of luxury and shoestring establishments, where they exist. **$$$$** denotes where the prices in an establishment extend beyond the **$$$** range shown above.

Airbnb have significantly more listings than just a few years ago. Tripadvisor also has a plethora of neutral ratings on the quality and amenities of hotels. They are usually family owned, affordable and well kept, and most include breakfast in the price. Breakfast can be continental in the larger hotels but you are more likely to be served white coffee, juice, rolls, jam, butter, cheese and maybe a hard-boiled egg. Don't count on the hard-boiled egg though. There is a 2KM accommodation tax that is not usually included in the price. Hotels usually offer *polupansion* or a *pun pansion*, which mean half board (breakfast and dinner) and full board (breakfast, lunch and dinner). Dining in BiH is so inexpensive that it may be wiser and more enjoyable to try out some of the restaurants in town.

PRIVATE ROOMS/APARTMENTS Private accommodation is not as well organised as in neighbouring Croatia but many travel agencies in towns throughout BiH do offer accommodation in apartments and private homes. Međugorje is the exception to almost every rule in Bosnia and Herzegovina; here there is a well-developed system for private accommodation, plenty of information, and travel agents that can do direct booking for you. In **Mostar**, Fortuna Tours has a great network of pensions, apartments and private rooms throughout Herzegovina. Lasta Travel can also arrange accommodation throughout **Herzegovina**; Ljubičica and Sartour in the old town of **Sarajevo** has the best offers ranging from pensions in the centre of town to low-budget rooms on the outskirts; Unis Tours and Zepter Passport can also organise accommodation for you in **Banja Luka**. Much effort has gone into upgrading existing private accommodation and opening new facilities according to best practice standards. There is a lot of good private accommodation in Bihać, Šipovo and many other areas, which can also be booked through the local tour operators listed in *Tour operators*, pages 60–2.

Anywhere you see the sign *sobe/Zimmer/rooms/camere* feel free to knock on the door. Prices range from 20KM to 50KM in private homes and are ideal for independent travellers. Most are clean and friendly but the host may not always speak English. A few German words are usually helpful. Adventurous types who would like to wander into the countryside will be unlikely to find a room sign or anywhere offering private accommodation, but the locals are extremely friendly. If you hit it off with someone and would like to spend the night, it is not offensive to ask. They will probably refuse money but leaving a gift or 10KM for coffee and cigarettes is a welcomed gesture. For solo women travellers it is always advisable to make sure there is a woman around if you plan to stay in private accommodation. If not, maybe it's best to find somewhere else. Better safe than sorry.

CAMPING Despite the tremendous potential for ecotourism there are few proper camping facilities in Bosnia and Herzegovina. Pitching a tent on your own is certainly possible but it could be risky if you are not fully confident that you are in a mine-free area (see *Landmines*, pages 68–9). The best and safest camping opportunities are found through the rafting operators on the Tara, Neretva and Una rivers. Boračko Lake near Konjic also has camping areas but don't expect too much. Jajce on the Pliva Lake has a great facility and the Oasis campsite in Ilidža near Sarajevo is also quite good. My advice is to contact any of the rafting groups or national parks for camping information. Don't risk camping if you're not sure or you don't have a guide.

EATING AND DRINKING

EATING Breakfast is hard to find except in hotels and pensions that offer some sort of buffet breakfast; certain restaurants and cafes will offer scrambled eggs, omelettes, or pancakes but typical English, Australian or American breakfasts will be few and far between. In places like Međugorje where they are used to having ham and eggs, it is possible to find a filling brekkie. In the larger cities there will be an occasional restaurant that serves 'English breakfast'. For budget travellers the large supermarkets carry fruit, yoghurt, muesli and juices and the open markets are always filled with fresh fruit. Bakeries open early and sell hot rolls, croissants, brown bread and apple and cherry strudels, which you can take to a café and enjoy with a morning cappuccino.

While ideal for budget travellers, all travellers should enter a *buregdženica* (savory pie shop) and try the famous traditional pitta dishes of *burek*, *zeljanica*, *sirnica* and *krompiruša*. They are all made from scratch and have been a traditional meal since Ottoman times. *Burek* is a meat pie wrapped in filo-dough; the *zeljanica* is made from spinach and cheese; *sirnica* is made from a fresh, homemade cheese; and *krompirusa* is diced potatoes with spices. Usually one portion (*porcija*) is enough to fill you and will cost around 2–3KM. You may be asked if you'd like *pavlaka* spread on top. This is a fresh cream that tastes wonderful with the pita. Thin yoghurt is also a popular drink alongside your pita.

Cooking methods include the use of the *ispod saća* – similar to a Dutch oven. A metal dish is placed on hot coals, the food is placed in the dish and covered by a lid which is then completely covered in hot coals and left to bake.

Be forewarned that smoking is permitted in most restaurants in BiH. If you are a non-smoker and are particularly bothered by cigarette smoke, check out how the ventilation system works. Many restaurants don't have ventilation systems and locals will light up right next to you in the middle of your meal, and think nothing of it.

Meats Now to the long list of meat specialities. Most meats here, whether chicken, beef, lamb or pork, are fresh from the mountainside. It is common practice to raise all animals free range, and with no added hormones or chemicals. Most people say they can taste the difference. Here is a list of the most popular traditional dishes.

Ćevapi Small meat sausages of lamb and beef mix. They are usually served with fresh onions and pitta bread on the side. *Ćevapi* usually come in index-finger-sized sausages and are offered as five or ten pieces.

Teletina Veal, usually served in cutlets. Veal in BiH is not produced by locking calves in a crate to ensure softer meat.

Pršut The equivalent to Italian prosciutto and a speciality with the Bosnian Christians. It is more difficult to find in Sarajevo but readily available in most places in Herzegovina and the Republika Srpska.

RESTAURANT PRICE CODES

Average price of a main course

$$$$	Luxury	More than 132KM
$$$	Above average	26–132KM
$$	Mid range	13–26KM
$	Cheap and cheerful	2–13KM

Jagnjetina	Lamb grilled over an open fire.
Begova čorba	The most popular soup, made of veal and vegetables.
Musaka	A meat 'pie' made of minced beef, very similar to cottage pie.
Filovane paprike	Fried peppers stuffed with minced meat and spices.
Bosanski lonac	Meat stew cooked over an open fire.
Sudžuk	Beef sausages with a similar form to pepperoni.
Suho meso	Dried meat, either beef or pork.
Sogandolma	Fried onions stuffed with minced meat.
Bamija	Okra with veal.
Sarme	Meat and rice rolled in cabbage or grape leaves.

Cheeses

Travnički	A white, feta-like cheese from the Travnik district in central Bosnia. It is a bit salty and very popular with *meza*, which is the tradition of slow drinking and eating throughout the course of a whole day.
Vlašićki	Similar to *travnički* cheese. It is a highland cheese from the villages on Vlašić Mountain in central Bosnia.
Livanjski	More similar to the dry, yellow cheeses of Dalmatia. It is very tasty and usually more expensive than others. It originates from the west Bosnian town of Livno.
Mladi sir	Literally means young cheese. There isn't an equivalent in English. It has a soft texture and is unsalted. Often it is served with a cream sauce on top.
Kajmak	The most difficult of all cheeses to translate. It is the top layer skimmed from milk, creamy and extremely tasty. *Kajmak* and *uštipak* (doughnut-type roll) is a wonderful appetiser.
Iz mjeha	Sheep's milk poured into a specially sewn sheepskin 'bag'. After a time the dry cheese is taken out of the skin container and the result is a strong, dry cheese that resembles real Parmesan.

Sweets For those with a sweet tooth, look out for a *slastičarnica*: a bakery or dessert shop, which focuses on sweets such as cakes, strudel, cookies and chocolates. Sometimes they serve ice cream. Some *slastičarnice* offer treats made in-house, others serve a selection from industrial bakeries.

Tufahija	Stewed apples stuffed with a walnut filling.
Baklava	Cake made with pastry sheets, nuts and sugar syrup.
Ružica	Similar to *baklava* but baked with raisins in a small roll.
Hurmašica	Date-shaped pastry soaked in a very sweet syrup sauce.
Rahatlokum	Turkish delight, a jelly-like candy covered in powdered sugar and often served with Turkish coffee.

DRINKING I've had many suspicious eyes cast upon me while walking through the mountains and drinking from every spring and **water** spout. By far Bosnia and Herzegovina's greatest natural resource is the overwhelming quantity of the highest-quality drinking water, both fresh and mineral. Almost every town will have public fountains, particularly in front of mosques. This water is perfectly fine for drinking. Many roadside fountains were built even before Tito's time, for foot or horse travellers. These are all underground aquifer-fed fountains – the water is deliciously cold. Mineral water is also in great abundance. Local slang for mineral water is *kisela voda*, after the town of Kiseljak near Sarajevo. Kiseljak has public fountains of mineral water direct from the source! Definitely buy local mineral water during your stay; it most certainly tops Perrier or any other top brand names. Look for Ilidžanski Dijamant, Sarajevo Kisela, Tešanjski Dijamant or Oaza. There are plenty more and my only advice is to avoid Olimpija – it is artificially carbonated and simply doesn't taste good.

The **local beer** is extremely cheap: a half-litre bottle is only 1KM in a shop and 2–4KM in a bar. The best local mass-produced beers are Sarajevsko, Nektar, Premium and Hercegovacko. Ožujsko is a good Croatian beer that is also produced locally. Draught beer is about a third of the standard European price. Imports are reasonably priced and are available in most bars, restaurants and cafés. If you are looking for a Guinness 'meal' I'm afraid you might be disappointed with the draught Guinness here; for some reason it just isn't the same. Local craft brews and micro brews are slowly becoming popular among the young, hip crowd and are available in a few pubs in Sarajevo, Mostar, and elsewhere (see, for example, pages 127 and 191). Some are excellent. Old Bridž brewery from Herzegovina produces a reliably delicious beer. **Soft drinks** and juices are also plentiful and easily available. It's always good to support local business and industry so look for Vegafruit or Vitaminka juices.

Wines and spirits Herzegovina has not yet become a world-renowned name in wine, but don't be surprised if in a few years that great glass of Žilavka or Blatina that you drank while visiting is listed as one of the top new 'third world' wines. The winemaking traditions of Herzegovina date back to Roman times. Sharing a similar climate and topsoil as Dalmatia, the savoury reds and dry whites of Herzegovina can easily compare to some of Croatia's finest. Ask for domestic wines like Blatina, Vranac and Žilavka from the towns of Mostar, Čitluk, Ljubuški, Stolac, Međugorje and Trebinje. The best of the best are from Gentille Winery, Nuić, Brkić, Tvrdoš Monastery wines, and Vukoje Winery.

In the shops local wines cost anywhere from 8–28KM and in restaurants from 30–60KM. Ask for *bijelo vino* (white wine) or *crno vino* (red wine). There are now several cellars that receive guests for wine tasting throughout Herzegovina, for example Vukoje and Tvrdoš in Trebinje, Nuić in Ljubuški, and Brkić in Čitluk.

Made from plums, pears, grapes, or other fruits the **local spirit *rakija*** will put hair on your chest. It is very strong, usually with a 45% alcohol content, and is drunk at all times of the day and at all times of the year. *Šljivovica* (plum) or *kruška* (pear) are found more in Bosnia while *loza*, made of grapes, is more a speciality of Herzegovina and Dalmatia. It is easy to find them on the shelf of any shop but it's well worth the effort to try and find some homemade spirits. The men take great pride in the careful process of making homemade spirits and if you get a good batch you can really taste the difference. Some of the slightly lighter and tastier spirits are *višnjevača* (cherry), *dunjevača* (quince) and *kasijevača* (apricot). It is even possible to find spirits from *rogač* (carob) or *nar* (pomegranate). *Travarica* (herbal) helps with digestion.

The Croats in Herzegovina have mastered the art of making wine and *loza* whereas the Serbs are the experts in *šljivovica* and *kruška*. You'll be offered one or the other almost as much as coffee. Just remember the smooth spirits tend to sneak up on you, and only after a few will you realise that walking is going to be the greatest challenge of the moment. Drink slowly and do what the locals do – *meza*. *Meza* is drinking slowly and accompanying the drinking with cheese, meat and bread. Sessions can often last all day and night. Taking fast 'shots' of *rakija* as one might do with vodka is not the norm.

As in many Slavic cultures, is considered rude not to toast someone before taking the first sip of alcohol, and it is important to look your co-drinkers in the eye while saying 'cheers' (*živjeli*).

Coffee and tea Think of Britain and the rituals and traditions built around a cup of tea with some milk and a lump or two of sugar. Think of being an American and the dedication to jumbo Coca-Cola with lots of ice. Or better yet, think of London without Big Ben or New York without the Statue of Liberty. Only that could compare to thinking of Bosnia without coffee. And you think I'm kidding. Bosnia and Herzegovina may be the only place on earth where the largest profit margin from any product sold in a country comes from coffee sales – and they don't grow it here. Coffee is the backbone of social life in Bosnia and Herzegovina. Its significance cannot be overestimated. Cafés serve espresso drinks, whereas 'Bosnian' coffee (also known as *domaća kafa)* is similar to Turkish-style coffee and is made at home or served in very traditional establishments. It is almost impossible to find American-style filter coffee in a café or restaurant.

At the end of the war the international community sponsored a 'tolerance' programme to encourage the different ethnic groups to come together and talk. The billboard campaign around the country showed only five words: 'Tolerance. Let's have a coffee.' The picture was of a pot of coffee and steaming cups filled with the magical potion that heals ethnic strife. When a man wants to test the water with a potential new girlfriend – he asks her out for a coffee. When you haven't seen a friend in ages – you go and have a coffee. When you go to anyone's house, at any time of day or night – you are served coffee. When you want to strike a business deal – you go for a coffee.

It comes in only a few forms though – straight coffee (no million flavours from Starbucks), espresso, cappuccino, Turkish coffee, and for those who simply can't stomach a good, strong cup there is always Nescafé. The standard price for a coffee

THE CULTURE OF COFFEE

On so many occasions I've watched confused visitors make a mess of the ritual of drinking a good Bosnian coffee, Turkish style. So here are the ABCs.

Turkish coffee comes in a small metal *džezva* (pronounced 'jezva') coupled with a small round cup called a *fildžan* ('filjohn'). With the tiny spoon you gently stir the top layer of coffee in the *džezva*. When the top turns a cream colour you are ready to pour. The *džezva* is usually filled with a little more coffee than the *fildžan* can hold. Be aware that at the bottom of *džezva* are the coffee grounds that will feel like a mouthful of sand if you pour all the way to the bottom. Leave a tiny layer on the bottom of the *džezva* just to be sure. Traditionally the sugar cubes are dipped into the *fildžan* and eaten. Feel free to plump them into the coffee and stir. Always hold the *fildžan* from the outer rim and never by the body, for it will more than likely be hot. If the *fildžan* is served in a copper holder that is meant to hold the heat in, don't pick up the copper holder to drink your coffee – that stays on the table. In some places a jelly-like candy called *rahatlokum* is served. It will be coated with powdered sugar and have a toothpick sticking out from it. It seems obvious what is next but I've seen people trying to dip the *rahatlokum* into the coffee. Please don't do that. Bend towards the table (the powdered sugar tends to go everywhere) and enjoy your Turkish delight.

is 1–2KM, and a cappuccino will cost you about 2–4KM, which is only a small fraction of the cost in any Western nation.

The locals just can't seem to grasp the English love of tea. English tea, referred to in Bosnia and Herzegovina as black tea, is a bit hard to come by and will usually not suffice for the finicky tea-drinker. Three tea bags in a mug seems to create a slight resemblance to PG Tips. Bring your own box of tea if you can't live without a decent cup for more than a day or two. Other teas available in Bosnia and Herzegovina can be rather remarkable if you avoid the mass-produced brands. *Šipak* (rosehip) and *menta* (peppermint) are popular. Most types of fruit teas can be found in any café, restaurant or bar. In rural places or in the mountains, one can often find homemade, organic herbal teas.

PUBLIC HOLIDAYS AND FESTIVALS

NATIONAL HOLIDAYS (see also *When to visit*, page 56)

Gregorian New Year	1 January
Orthodox Christmas	7 January
Orthodox New Year	14 January
Independence Day	1 March
Labour Day	1 May
Catholic Christmas	25 December
Bajram (Muslim Holy Day)	This date is related to moon cycles and is not the same every year.

FESTIVALS

'Sarajevan Winter' (February/March) Every winter Sarajevo hosts a regional theatre festival of friends and colleagues from former Yugoslavia. Contact Ibrahim Spahić, director (*M Tita 9a;* ☎ *033 266 620;* e *ibrahim.spahic1@gmail.com*).

Celebration of the Apparition (24 June in Međugorje) This event usually attracts over 100,000 faithful each year from every corner of the globe. It celebrates the day when a group of young teenagers saw the apparition of the Mother Mary on a stony hill in western Herzegovina.

'Baščaršijske Nights' (July in Sarajevo) For the entire month of July the old town in Sarajevo (*baščaršija*) hosts cultural events from whirling dervishes to Viennese philharmonic and Celtic concerts. Each night has something special and most events are free of charge. It's the longest and one of the best events in the whole country. Contact Halid Kuburovic, JU Sarajevo Art (*Dalmatinska 2/1;* ☎ *033 207 921/929;* e *koncagsa@bih.net.ba*).

International Folklore Festival (July in Sarajevo) Whereas folklore events in most countries aim to pay homage and preserve the old traditions that once existed in their homeland, folklore here is still very much alive and part of both rural and urban life. The great folk traditions of the Croats, Bosniaks and Serbs invite dozens of other folk groups from around the world to offer a 'peek into our past … how we dressed, danced, played music, sang and lived'. Contact JU Sarajevo Art/Sarajevo Arts Agency (*Dalmatinska 2/I;* ☎ *033 207 921/929;* e *koncagsa@bih.net.ba*).

Mostar Summer Festival (July) Mostar is slowly creeping back into the cultural scene. To match its stunning architecture and beautiful surroundings, Mostar's summer festival hosts a great range of local productions in drama, music, art and film as well as international events in music and drama. It takes place for several weeks in July in venues all over the city. One of the main venues is the Croatian Cultural Centre near the Rondo.

Demofest (late July in Banja Luka) A three-day music festival, centring around 30 young local bands, including a few from other countries. It takes place in the unique atmosphere of the Roman-built castle in Banja Luka. In addition to good music, visitors can enjoy a number of workshops, musicians and talks, and some very interesting after-party events (see **w** demofest.org).

Una International Regatta (late July in Bihać) The Una Regatta celebrated its 30th anniversary not too long ago. This rafting event is unmatched in the region as more and more enthusiasts gather to kayak, raft and have fun on Bosnia's most beautiful river.

Summer on the Vrbas (end of July in Banja Luka) This Banja Luka tradition is a good time to visit this northern city. The cool Vrbas is a great attraction in itself, and the perfect setting for this festival of events and concerts.

Sarajevo Film Festival (August in Sarajevo) The rebellious and artistic soul of Sarajevo flared during the war years. Amidst the death and destruction of the city, several Sarajevan artists decided to host an international film festival. It has gone from an improvised vision to one of the best film festivals in Europe. It's a great place to meet and mingle with actors, producers and the stars. Unlike Venice and Cannes, Sarajevo's film festival has no barriers between the viewing public and the artists themselves. It's a fun, laid-back occasion and an opportunity to check out great regional films, short films and documentaries from some of the world's greatest. Contact Mirsad Purivatra, director (*Obala Art Centar, Hamdije Kreševljakovića 13;* ☎ *033 209 411 or 263 380;* **e** *info-sff@sff.ba;* **w** *sff.ba*).

Teatar Fest (September in Sarajevo) This theatre fest highlights young actors and actresses from around Europe and North America. The festival is free of charge and brings a wide array of excellent university theatre and dance groups.

MESS (October in Sarajevo) MESS international theatre festival has been a tradition in Sarajevo for over a century. Some of the finest theatre groups in Europe regularly take part in this annual gathering. MESS also highlights the event with alternative and modern dance. Alongside the well-known names are also the best regional performers from southern Europe. Tickets are sometimes hard to come by but can be purchased online in advance. Check out the website. Contact Dion Mustafi, director (*M Tita 54/1;* ☎ *033 200 392;* **e** *mess@mess.ba;* **w** *mess.ba*).

Jazz festival (November 2017 and 2018, in Sarajevo) More and more of the big names in jazz are starting to buzz around the annual jazz fest in Sarajevo. The venues are usually small and intimate and there are always free jam sessions in jazz clubs around town after the show. Tickets can be purchased over the internet and there is good information about all the acts. Unfortunately, Jazz Fest will only exist for two more years. The venue will be closing after its 22nd and final edition in 2018. Contact Edin Zubčević (☎ *033 668 975;* **e** *info@jazzfest.ba;* **w** *jazzfest.ba*).

Other festivals include **European Literary Encounters** (*Institut Francais; Mula Mustafe Bašeskija 8, Sarajevo;* ☎ *033 582 277;* e *info@institutfrancais.ba*) and Sarajevo's days of poetry in September.

SHOPPING

There are many opportunities for shopping in cities like Sarajevo, Mostar and Banja Luka. Western shops and capitalism have slowly penetrated Bosnian society, but the Western brand names will most likely be cheaper wherever you came from. Many of the locally owned and operated shops have great value items though including handicrafts, all types of jewellery, leather goods, art and clothes. The wide array of handicrafts is well worth dedicating an afternoon to. Art galleries also have excellent collections of local artists' works that are a great buy for the money. Framing is also very cheap here, so if you've bought an unframed picture it may be worth getting it done while you're in town. Antiques and neat little knick-knacks from the socialist days can be found in the open markets or in souvenir shops in old town quarters.

In Bosnia and Herzegovina you will still find small corner shops just about everywhere. They may not have a large selection of luxury goods but the basics can always be found there, including bread, alcohol, sweets and usually fruits and vegetables. For a larger selection there are a number of larger food chains throughout the country, namely Bingo and Konzum.

HANDMADE GOODS The art of handmade goods, called *stari zanati*, has a long tradition that mainly took form during Ottoman times. *Stari zanati* developed with the arrival of the Turks in the mid-15th century. As Sarajevo expanded into the administrative centre of Ottoman rule in Bosnia so did its volume of trading with faraway lands. Many crafts were brought by the Turks to keep the soldiers in good footwear, make swords, and design and create more modern weaponry for the military. By the early 15th century the Ottoman defters (administrative records) registered more than 19 new crafts including coppersmithing, locksmithing, slipper-making and carpentry.

Craftsmanship continued to develop during the first half of the hundred-year occupation. Tailoring, clock-making and quilt-making became famous trades by the end of the 17th century. By the end of Ottoman rule over 70 *zanati* trades are mentioned in historical records, as Sarajevo developed into the largest trading town in all of Bosnia and Herzegovina.

Jewellery, gold, copper and bronze tea and coffee sets, and metal plates with oriental design can be found in most *čaršijas* (old Turkish quarters) throughout the country. Handmade oriental-style rugs are also a good bargain. You are most likely to find these authentic objects in Sarajevo, Mostar, Travnik and Banja Luka as well as in some smaller trading towns like Visoko, Konjic and Jajce. Traditional-style hand-carved wooden coffee tables, chairs and boxes are unique to Bosnia. You can buy these items for a reasonable price in Sarajevo and Mostar old towns or you can visit the woodworkers themselves in Konjic where a long tradition of woodcarving has been passed on from father to son (page 228). Intricately designed woollen socks, jumpers and hats are a great bargain and your purchases will more often than not support poor villagers who sell their wares in town markets or to vendors in tourist areas. Go to any open market and you'll find the colourful socks, which make great winter slippers for around the house and are ideal for hiking. The going price is 10–25KM a pair. To fetch more they need to be extra special. Feel free to bargain with people, especially in the shops in the old towns of Sarajevo and Mostar. They tend to charge up for the tourists but can almost always be talked down a bit.

There have been many initiatives throughout the country, mainly funded by the EU, to revitalise the ancient handicraft trades. Smaller communities such as Visoko, Kraljeva Sutjeska, Jajce, Vranduk and Prusac have effectively revived much of the old craftsmanship of woodwork, leather and beautiful carpet weaving. All of these initiatives are aimed at cultural heritage preservation and offering new incomes to women and people from the rural areas. Take home an authentic, homemade souvenir rather than a cheaply produced factory one!

BOOKS Finding English books is not easy outside of Sarajevo, Mostar or Banja Luka. You will find some small selections in Herzegovina and they are usually religious/historical books about the Catholics of BiH. If you're looking for some local writers that have been translated into English your best bets are Buybook, and Šahinpašić in Sarajevo (page 129) and the Cambridge Centre Bookstore or Knjizara Kultura in Banja Luka.

MUSIC If you're into local music, all the larger towns and cities have music shops. The chances are you won't find Bosnian and Herzegovinian pop or traditional music in the Western markets so it is advisable to purchase them here. The traditional music of the Croats, Serbs and Muslims is both vocally and instrumentally entrancing – have a listen before you buy a CD though, as some are better than others. The turbo folks scene, however popular, can be quite an earache. See pages 53–4.

ARTS AND ENTERTAINMENT

The heart and soul of Bosnia and Herzegovina's **theatre** lies in Sarajevo. Although there are good theatres in Mostar, Banja Luka, Tuzla and Zenica, the theatre tradition in Sarajevo is head and shoulders above the rest. Alongside the century-old tradition of the international theatre fest, MESS, there are fantastic year-round performances in several theatres in Sarajevo. Sarajevo has been a magnet for great actors and musicians since Yugoslavian times.

The Sarajevo War Theatre performed throughout the entire war in basements or in the safe areas of the National Theatre. This spirit of resistance, the triumph of the human spirit and the tragedy of war are often the themes of local productions. The mainstream theatre here has an underground spin to it that gives it such a powerful role in society. The new generation of young actors perform year round at the many theatres in Sarajevo, with the main productions showing at Kamerni Theatre, East West Centre and the National Theatre. Most plays are in the local language but even so most are certainly worth a visit for the atmosphere and experience. MESS Festival takes place in autumn, as does the relatively young Ballet Fest. Tickets can be purchased on the day of the production but due to the very low prices they are often sold out fairly quickly. Plays cost anywhere from 5KM to 15KM.

During the holidays, both Christian and Islamic, there are often plays, concerts and other events that epitomise the multi-ethnic soul of Bosnia and Herzegovina. The Ramadan concerts at Zetra Stadium and the National Theatre are particularly interesting for their mystical oriental flavour and dervish traditions.

American and British films are shown regularly at the cinemas here and they almost always have Bosnian subtitles so you don't have to deal with bad dubbing. Be warned that many cinemas are old and haven't been renovated since the 1980s. They are uncomfortable and it can be painful to sit through a whole film. In Sarajevo,

Meeting Point and Cinema City are the most comfy places to enjoy a film and not have a backache afterwards.

Most cities in Bosnia and Herzegovina have a **museum** or a **gallery**, and often both. Outside the main centres, however, most museums are poorly funded. The Franciscans have a long tradition of keeping fascinating small museums in monasteries throughout the country. Among the many small-town monasteries that have collected and preserved most of the remains of the medieval Bosnian state from the 12th century onwards, Kraljeva Sutjeska near Kakanj Fojnica, Humac near Ljubuški, Livno and Prozor are the best. The finest Orthodox museums are in Sarajevo's Old Church near *baščaršija*, and in Banja Luka. The most interesting part of any museum is the representative timeline of invasions that have occurred over two millennia. The Illyrians, Romans, early Slavs, Catholics, Byzantines, Ottomans, Austro-Hungarians, Venetians and even the Avars and Goths have at one time or another bid for this gateway to the East and West.

ACTIVITIES

HIKING One thing people seem to notice and appreciate in Bosnia and Herzegovina is the will to walk. Leisure time with friends or family is often spent taking a long stroll through town or in the park. The streets are usually filled with people walking. The bad habit of getting into a car for the shortest, or even some longer, errands has yet to catch on here. In most towns there are designated areas only for pedestrians.

VIA DINARICA (W VIADINARICA.COM)

The Via Dinarica is a network of trails which cut through the mountains, linking all the countries which comprise the area: Bosnia and Herzegovina, Albania, Croatia, Kosovo, Montenegro, Serbia, and Slovenia. Each country brings its unique contribution to the medley of cultures and landscapes along the Via Dinarica. Each trail – which together cover thousands of kilometres – offers something for everyone, including diverse challenges for a variety of fitness and knowledge levels. But what all the trails share in common is their offer of a vast range of adrenaline-fuelled or relaxing activities on land and water. In BiH specifically, hiking and trekking is a popular activity in the national parks, and whitewater rafting is a well-developed adventure sport. Rural tourism and enjoying the traditional lifestyles and cuisine of the highlands is not to be missed, even if it requires a little extra effort to navigate. There are more and more B&Bs and small guest houses being established in mountain villages that offer accommodation, food, and light outdoor activities. Hikers will no doubt be delighted by the little-explored, world-class hiking inside some of the most stunning natural scenery on the European continent.

Via Dinarica is not only the name of a trail: it is also a platform that serves to promote and develop the local communities and small businesses along the trail in the fields of hospitality, service and tourism, as well as agriculture and cultural heritage. The purpose of the trail and platform is to connect the countries and communities of Dinaric Alps by creating a unique and diversified tourist offer. This multi-country, multi-stakeholder effort promotes tourism for the purpose of the badly needed economic development of the region, while preserving the precious environment and respecting the sociocultural diversity and authenticity of local communities.

The overarching aim of Via Dinarica is to make connections between cities and rural communities in the region, raise awareness of good business practices and

This is a great way to mix and mingle with the locals or do a bit of window shopping. Walking from town to town is less convenient. Pavements are confined to city centres for the most part and road hard shoulders often don't exist. Drivers have little respect for pedestrians here and, as you'll see, the feeling is mutual.

The Western Balkan region is positioned deep in the heart of one of Europe's most unexplored and wildest mountain ranges – the central Dinaric Alps – and a new long-distance hiking trail, the Via Dinarica, has been developed to allow visitors to explore the landscape (see box, opposite). The region is a paradise for adventurers, nature lovers, and those seeking an experience that is at once thrilling, extraordinarily beautiful, and affordable.

As will be repeated many times throughout this book: even for the most experienced hiker it is recommended to opt for the sure bet and go with a guide. There are literally hundreds of safe trails to trek and hike. But best not to go it alone. The following companies offer guides:

Encijan Ul Kralja Petra, 73300 Foča; ☎ 058 211 150; **e** encijan@zona.ba; **w** pkencijan.com. Encijan run rafting & hiking tours in the highlands of eastern Bosnia, the Tara Canyon & Sutjeska NP.

Fikret's Hiking Adventures **m** 061 379 915; **e** fikret_kahrovic@yahoo.com; **f** FikretsHikingAdventures. Fikret is an independent guide who conducts hiking & city tours for those who have their own transport.

Green Visions Trg Barcelona 3, 71000 Sarajevo; ☎ 033 717 290; **e** sarajevo@greenvisions.ba; **w** greenvisions.ba. Responsible ecotour operator that runs various hiking, rafting, biking & other programmes all over the country.

environmental protection, create a tourist offer which highlights natural treasures, traditional products and unique cultural heritage, as well as to link stakeholders in the region for the purpose of jump starting sustainable economic development.

TRAILS

The **White Trail** is the main trail and travels along the entire length of the Via Dinarica, according to its natural flow, all the way to the highest peaks in each country. Although there are countless diverse activities and attractions along this route, such as mountain biking, rafting, and good food, its number one aspect is its excellence as a spectacular mountain trail in itself.

The **Blue Trail** got its name for a reason: it leads to the coastline and the crystal clear waters of the Adriatic Sea. Though the mountains along this trail are smaller than the ones on the White Trail, they are no less attractive and challenging. The fresh smell of medicinal herbs and the breeze of the Mediterranean will accompany hikers through some of the best coastal and hinterland hiking in all of Europe.

The **Green Trail**, as one might guess, has something to do with its landscape: a green carpet of conifer forests that zigzag through the lower mountains of the Dinaric Alps. The Green Trail has hundreds of kilometres of well-maintained bike trails, and is ideal for those who want to explore the region on two wheels. Hikers and walkers will also have endless beauties to discover, especially the rich wildlife of this eastern area. The Green Trail offers more soft adventures than its Blue and White counterparts.

Highlander Mojkovačka bb, 73300 Foča; m 065 475 201; e highlandertim@hotmail.com; w highlandertim.com. Rafting operator on the Tara, & also offers hiking trips to Sutjeska NP.

Limit Dzanica Mahala 7, 77000 Bihać; m 061 144 248; e lipa3@bih.net.ba; w limit.co.ba. Hiking & mountain-biking tours in the northwest town of Bihać near Una NP.

Scorpio Smetovski put bb, 72000 Zenica; m 061 608 130; e info@scorpio.ba; w scorpio.ba. Extreme Sports Club Scorpio has a nice sports centre on Smetovi for hiking, paragliding, alpine climbing & mountain biking.

Mountain lodges It's surprising how little attention people pay to one of the most beautiful mountain chains in southern Europe. This chain is dotted with countless mountain huts and lodges that have been used for decades by mountaineers, tourists, scouts, students and nature lovers. Unfortunately, as noted, many of these mountain lodges were destroyed during the war, but some survived and even more have been restored, so you can enjoy a most magical Bosnian mountain adventure.

In the former Yugoslavia, the highest concentrations of mountain huts were found along the *transversals*. The Neretva Valley with Prenj and Čvrsnica mountains had many huts along the entire range. Bjelašnica and Igman still preserve a long history of mountain huts and the associations that operate them. Towards Sutjeska National Park some of the huts have been rebuilt, such as the Zelengora Donje Bare hut. Vlašić and Vranica mountain huts still offer shelter and accommodation for hikers all year round. Konjuh has three mountain huts in its lush forests. Kruščica Mountain has four huts from Busovača to Novi Travnik.

Šefko Hadžialić's book on the history of mountaineering and mountain huts, *Planinarstvo i planinarski objekti u Bosni i Hercegovini 1892–2002 g*, clearly illustrates the well-organised and well-planned construction of mountain huts all over BiH. The author offers a short description of accessibility and services available at almost all the mountain huts in the country.

What is desperately needed, however, is a strong focus on the complete overhaul of the mountain huts and the trails that lead to and from them. The Mountain Association of BiH has done what it can to rebuild and renovate the destroyed and/or damaged huts. For years they have sought donations and remained active in their respective areas, but it is time for the public sector to understand the value of these facilities and what they represent. BiH will never be a massive tourist destination. It will, however, be a destination for those fascinated by the amazing nature that lies at the crossroads of East and West.

If you are interested in more information on mountain huts in BiH contact the **Mountain Association of BiH** (*Ferhadija 9, 71000 Sarajevo; 033 217 515*). A region wide website with all mountain huts can be found at w mountain-huts.net. The Via Dinarica site, w viadinarica.com, has a full list of mountain huts/lodges that offer accommodation.

Mountain safety The mine situation is addressed in the *Safety* section of this chapter on pages 68–9. General mountain safety should include a first-aid kit, maps and extra-warm gear. A guide is highly recommended. The high-altitude mountain ranges can experience **drastic temperature changes**. When a storm or fog rolls in, the temperature can easily drop 10–15°C in a matter of hours. Bosnia and Herzegovina is a mountainous land and each valley and range has its own unique system. A rainy day in Sarajevo could mean a sunny afternoon on Bjelašnica. A scorching hot day in Mostar could mean freezing winds on Velež peak overlooking the city.

Most **water sources** are perfectly safe for drinking. If a source is clogged with moss and algae then obviously stay away. Mountain water, on the other hand, is almost always a safe bet. Water-storage reservoirs were also built at many mountain huts where there are no sources. If you come across a metal lid near a hut it is probably a rain-collection tank. Check it first, but the water in them is usually fine to drink.

Mountain rescue services (Gorska Služba za Spašavanje – GSS; *121;* **m** *062 654 456 or 061 299 443;* **e** *gss@gss-sarajevo.com or* **e** *info@gss.ba;* **w** *gss-sarajevo.com or* **w** *gss.ba*), have made great strides in recent years with rescue units in every region of BiH. They often do not have access to helicopter assistance and it may take some time to reach you in an emergency, but rest assured, an SOS call will be answered. It is good practice to let someone know if you plan to hike solo. If you are going with a guide, make sure that safety precautions are taken.

Club Spasavalaca 2000 (**m** *061 345 701,* **e** *klubspasavalaca2000.sarajevo@gmail.com*) is an independent rescue team from Sarajevo, which is better equipped than the state-sponsored teams.

There are two types of **poisonous snakes** in Bosnia and Herzegovina. It is rare for bites to be fatal but it has occurred. In the summer months, snakes can be found in clear-water rivers and streams. They will also gather on the south side of the mountain where there is the most sunshine. Be careful around rocky areas with cracks and holes; these are favourite hiding spots for them. In the early autumn they tend to linger on tree limbs. The colder air keeps them rather lethargic and they are less of a threat than during the hot season. Poisonous snakes inject venom only 25% of the time. If you are bitten it is best to stay calm: the faster your blood circulates the faster the poison carries through your system. Prevention, of course, is always the best protection. Be aware of where you are stepping and don't forget that snakes are more afraid of you than you are of them. They are just as anxious to get out of your way.

Sunscreen in the mountains is a must, even for the darkest of skins; a minimum sunscreen protection of 15 is recommended. The high mountain **sun exposure** can be dangerous in the summer and sunstroke is not fun when you are hours away from help. During the summer bring a hat with you to cover your head – the face and back of the neck are important to keep protected to avoid sunstroke.

Bringing a few extras with you on longer hikes may be heavier but it may save your life in case of an emergency. It is always good to have some extra high-energy food items. Even outside of the summer months you should always carry a hat with you. A warm fleece and an extra shirt and socks could help prevent you from getting chilled to the core and becoming ill as a result.

Lightning strikes occur frequently on high ridges during a storm, particularly above river canyons. These highly exposed ridges are magnets for lightning strikes. If you see lightning while you are trekking a ridge get out of there quick. There are often signs (ie: struck-down black pines) that indicate dangerous areas.

As many trails are not maintained as they were before the war, it is best to wear good boots that give you adequate **ankle support**. Loose rocks, fallen tree limbs or erosion can be enough to twist an ankle and abruptly end your hike.

Trail markings The former Yugoslavia had one of the best-developed systems of mountain trails in Europe. *Transversala* connected the Slovenian Alps all the way to southern Macedonia and most of these trails went through the whole length of Bosnia and Herzegovina. Owing to the war many trails disappeared through overgrowth or lack of use but now most of them have been revitalised. Mountain associations are active on most mountains in BiH. Marked trails have a red circle with a white dot in the middle. This at least means that it is leading you somewhere. You may find them marked on trees or large stones along the trail. The best-marked mountain with trail maps is Bjelašnica. The mountain association here sells maps and has done an excellent job of keeping the trails clearly marked.

As the threat of landmines is real, it is important to pay attention to where you are. It is not advisable to walk or hike without first checking the mine situation. If you are on a trail that has obviously not been trekked in some time or has faded trail markings you may not want to be there. Fresh trail markings mean that the mountain association has had the area checked and that they trek it themselves. It is wise to bring a map, compass and GPS if you have one. The Via Dinarica White Trail is fully marked with almost 500 km of paths. You can find examples of the trail markers on **w** viadinarica.com.

BIKING The sport of mountain biking has exploded in recent years since National Geographic named BiH as one of the world's top ten mountain-bike destinations. Mountain biking is possible in the Bjelašnica, Igman and Visočica mountains and Kiro Rafting from Bihać also offer mountain biking in the beautiful and wild northwest of the country. There is also a full set of mountain biking trails throughout Bosnia and Herzegovina that can be found on both **w** viadinarica.com and the mountain-biking association website, **w** mtb.ba. The narrow roads are not ideal for cycling but places like Livno, Kupres and Glamočki Fields in west Bosnia have magnificent terrain for long valley biking with relatively little traffic.

RAFTING BiH is well known for its white-water rafting adventures and it is by far the best-developed outdoor activity. Bosnia has four raging rivers that offer professionally guided rafting tours. The Neretva, Vrbas, Una and Tara rivers rank among Europe's best and you'll be pleasantly surprised by the pristine wilderness that accompanies the ride. The World Rafting Championship 2009 was held on the Vrbas and Tara rivers, with teams from 35 countries competing.

SAILING You can probably catch enough wind on Buško or Blidinje lakes near Livno, but the best sailing is definitely on the Adriatic Sea at Neum. This beautiful inlet creates perfect winds at the mouth of the bay towards the open sea. Neum and the Croatian coast are easily comparable to the Greek coast and isles, and are more accessible and often less expensive.

DIVING *with Iona Hill*

Bosnia and Herzegovina is almost landlocked, save for a small 24km stretch of Adriatic coastline, on which the largest town is Neum. Rumour has it that it is possible to scuba dive around Neum, though it's difficult to find any dive operators. In time, dive outfits will undoubtedly become more popular, as they are already in Croatia. There are some freshwater springs inland leading to some amazing underwater cave systems that can also be dived (experienced divers only).

Dive operators should be affiliated with a professional dive association that sets standards for training, insurance cover, conduct and safety standards. PADI, CMAS, NAUI and BSAC are among the best-known reputable dive organisations. Look for their logos in the offices of dive shops, and think twice about using an operator that does not belong to one of these associations.

To book a trip, you will need your C-card (certification card) and preferably log book – without the former, no reputable dive operator should take you out. If you are renting dive gear, arrive a little early so that you can ensure that the

SNORKELLING TIPS *Iona Hill*

STAY WITHIN YOUR LIMITS If you are a relatively inexperienced snorkeller, then it's wise to wear a vest-like buoyancy device. You can usually ask for one at the place from which you hired your snorkelling gear. If you are a strong swimmer and an experienced snorkeller, you may wish to go without this, but do take advice on local currents and tides; anyone can get carried away by strong currents. If you don't feel comfortable snorkelling out of your depth, then don't – always stay within your comfort zones. There is nothing macho about swimming too far out and being towed back to shore.

PROTECT YOURSELF FROM THE SUN The sun is strong on the coast and it is very easy to get burned. Wear a T-shirt and lightweight shorts, and make sure you apply sun block to the back of your neck, arms and legs.

MAKE SURE YOUR MASK FITS This is very easy to do. Take the mask and, without putting the strap around your head, press it to your face, over the eyes and nose, with the strap on the outside of the eye pieces. Then take a breath in through your nose and count to five. If the mask stays fixed to your face, it's a good fit. If it falls off, try other masks until you get a good fit.

WEAR THE RIGHT FINS There are two choices of footwear for snorkelling: closed-heel fins and open-heel fins with booties. I would go for the latter every time, even if it means hiring booties that may have been worn by hundreds before you. If you have a stony beach to walk across to get to the sea, you can do this in booties and put the open-heel fins on once you are in the water. If you have closed-heel fins, walking backwards over a pebbly beach is neither easy nor fun – plus it makes you feel and look pretty silly.

HYDRATE Drink plenty of fluids, preferably water, to keep yourself well hydrated. This is important, as you will probably get a lot of exposure to the sun.

RESPONSIBLE SNORKELLING Do not leave litter on the beach – that includes orange peel or banana skins that can be mistaken by fish for food and in some cases can poison them. Look, but do not touch. The sea and its creatures are increasingly fragile ecosystems, so please respect this.

hired equipment fits properly; remember that buoyancy control devices (BCDs) get looser in the water and don't forget you will need weights. Six divers to one guide is the normal ratio, and be aware that if you only hold basic qualifications, you are usually not qualified to dive deeper than 18m. As a bare minimum, the dive boat should have a working radio, life jackets, a first-aid kit and oxygen in case of emergencies, and a boat handler should always remain on board.

The best recommendations are those from people who have just returned from a dive – ask around in the place you are staying for advice.

SKIING There are no five-star ski resorts or high-tech lifts in the skiing areas of BiH but you will be treated to the best skiing in southern Europe. Jahorina, Bjelašnica and Igman mountains were the venue for the 1984 Winter

Olympics. (See *Ski centres* in *Chapter 4*, pages 147–56.) Smaller centres in central and west Bosnia such as Vlašić, Kupres and Blidinje are also fun holiday spots for families.

OFF-ROAD EXPLORING Owing to the war and a large highland population, BiH is covered with great gravel roads that wind through hidden mountain valleys. For 4x4 lovers it is truly a unique way to explore the untouched outback of Bosnia. Many roads are not marked on maps.

FISHING You'd have to be a pretty poor angler not to hook at least a few freshwater fish while fishing in Bosnia and Herzegovina. The rivers and lakes are teeming with trout, carp, bass and many other types of fish, and good fishing can be found in most parts of the country. Some of the best fishing rivers are the Pliva near Šipovo and Jajce; Ribnik, where the European Flyfishing Championships took place in summer 2010; the Upper Drina; and the Neretva River. There are some fishing shops but the gear is hard to come by. It's best to bring your own if you're a serious angler and plan on a solo trip. However, organised fishing groups will more than likely provide the poles and gear for you (pages 60–2).

PHOTO SAFARI For those who like to capture the timeless beauty of nature there are many opportunities for photographing the wildlife in BiH. Hutovo Blato in Herzegovina is an ideal place for exotic bird photography and places like Sutjeska National Park host a plethora of large game that can be seen with a little luck.

CANOEING AND KAYAKING If Bosnia and Herzegovina has anything, it has water – pure, crystal-clear water. Canoeing and kayaking are popular on the three main rafting rivers but also on many other lakes and rivers throughout BiH. Both the Neretva and Vrbas rivers offer regular kayaking trips. The Trebižat River offers a great canoe safari, and the lake systems of Rama, Jablanica, Pliva and Buško are ideal spots for canoeing and fishing.

PILGRIMAGE It is quite humbling to think that such a tiny country is home to the second-largest Catholic pilgrimage site in the world, at Međugorje, and the largest Islamic pilgrimage site in Europe at Prusac in central Bosnia. The religious heritage in Bosnia and Herzegovina is a fascinating component of its history, and certainly tells of the strong spiritual influences of East and West.

VILLAGE TOURISM There isn't quite a culture of 'tourism' in many of the villages in BiH but there is a long tradition of providing any visitor with an incredibly warm welcome. A taste of Old World Europe – old farming methods, handmade tools and machinery, organic food, and a traditional lifestyle that has long since died out in the rest of Europe – all await the visitor. There are a few organisations that arrange such activities or if you choose to explore alone, you will certainly be warmly welcomed.

PHOTOGRAPHY

There are countless first-class photo opportunities in Bosnia and Herzegovina. The mountains and valleys keep the air circulating well and few places will have smog. Nature shots are easy to come by in this mountain land, especially with its abundance of beautiful waterfalls. The destruction from the war has largely been repaired, but you can still find disturbing scenes, particularly in Mostar. Feel free to photograph these sights and imagine being in the building when the damage was done to it. It's quite humbling. Wildlife photography is a bit tougher unless you are a patient professional. Owing to the war much of the wildlife has fled or been killed and the remaining bears, wolves, deer, wild goats and others largely remain out of human sight. Eagles and hawks can be seen in many places, though, even along main roads – especially by Bosanski Petrovac towards Bihać. Wildlife photography is best at Hutovo Blato Bird Reserve in Herzegovina and the Sutjeska National Park near Foča in eastern Bosnia. Sutjeska is still home to significant bear and wolf populations.

Most locals are very used to people taking photos. The numerous war photographers made them almost immune to having their pain and suffering captured on film. Nowadays, with the streets teeming with the young and old, and the war years behind them, taking photographs of people is fine. It is always courteous to ask, of course. Using sign language by pointing to the person and then to your camera is more than enough to get your point across. In the rural areas you'll find two extremes. The villagers will either vehemently oppose you taking photos or gather the whole family for a portrait. Men working the land seem to enjoy being photographed whereas women may tend to shy away. Muslims are not offended by or opposed to photography. Just be polite and ask.

Although digital photography has largely replaced film, there are a number of photo shops that still sell film, but it is more expensive here than in Western Europe or the US. It is advised that you wait till you get home to develop your film. If you want to see your photographs right away all the cities have decent one-hour photo-developing labs. For digital cameras make sure you bring your battery charger. Special batteries, including lithium batteries, may not be easy to find, especially outside of Sarajevo. Accessories for digital cameras are also very difficult to locate, but purchasing memory cards in any major town should not be a problem.

You may come across road signs with a 1920s camera-like symbol. During Tito's regime it was illegal to photograph dams, military installations, embassies or police stations. Don't photograph local military installations – soldiers don't seem to mind being photographed, but don't take pictures of the bases. Certain embassies are a bit paranoid about photography, the American embassy in Sarajevo being one of them. You're likely to be approached by a heavily armed guard if you are seen taking a photograph of the embassy compound. There isn't much to see from the outside anyway; it's just a large, thick wall that would probably repel an atom bomb.

MEDIA AND COMMUNICATIONS

The media from the old regime was used to create suspicion and paranoia amongst the local population, and the local population and people remain very wary of the media in general, even though vast improvements have been made in separating it from the stranglehold of the state and/or political entities. As elsewhere in the world, television stations, newspapers and magazines have political and other loyalties that are often a source of their funding. The individuals in the media are often quite outstanding, whilst the system in which they work is mostly unprofessional and inefficient.

Although there are a few shining stars in the media business it doesn't have the best reputation for being 'free and open'. The BBC has done a significant amount of training for local journalists, and reforms by the Office of the High Representative (OHR) have been introduced to avoid a repeat of the state-run media that helped drive the country into war. There is a long way to go in this field and with such poor economic conditions it is difficult for struggling independent media sources to turn down funding offers from interest groups. However, there are a number of online news portals that publish more independent and alternative information in the local language.

There are three main **television** stations. Federation Television (FTV) and its Republika Srpska counterpart (RTRS) are two stations formed from the Dayton Peace Accords. BH1 is a state-level television station that broadcasts to both entities and is supposed to act as a common voice for all of BiH. It airs films, news, documentaries, music specials and soaps. The best independent stations are Aljazeera Balkans, TV1 and N1. They are on the air 24 hours a day and carry many American and English films and television series, local news, talk shows and documentaries from all over the world. N1 is the CNN representative in BiH and offers satellite viewing for the large diaspora in Europe and North America. In Mostar and throughout most of Herzegovina the Croats have a private station but most watch Croatian HRT (Croatia proper) television.

The main **newspapers** in the country are *Oslobođenje* (meaning 'freedom'), *Dnevni Avaz, Nezavisni Novine* and *Jutarnji List.*

POST Some old habits die hard here, and the postal system is one of them. Letters and postcards to Europe and the US take anywhere from two weeks to two months. Miracles do happen but more often in Međugorje than at the post office. Don't expect the desk officer at the post office to be too helpful; he or she will probably act annoyed that you've even dared to walk into the building. If their chair is a few metres from his/her station and they are drinking a coffee and smoking a cigarette they will slowly finish both, remaining completely uninterested in the queue that is out the door. I apologise to all the kind and polite tellers; I wish there were more of you! The discretion line means absolutely nothing and most people will hover next to you while you are trying to send your postcard. Don't be surprised if people also cut ahead of you in the queue, especially pensioners!

Letters and postcards are fairly cheap to send, ranging from 1.20–2.50KM to Europe and the US.

Sending a package is quite expensive and there is zero respect for privacy. Don't bother wrapping or sealing the box; as a matter of fact most post offices require that you buy their box. They will look at everything without asking you, and get annoyed with you if you dare to ask what they might be doing. Receiving a package is even worse. You will receive a yellow slip at the place where you are staying. The slip will tell you at which post office to pick up your package. When the teller finds your package he/she will ask for your ID. Then he/she will fill out a form and give it to you. No package yet. With that form you go to the cashier's desk. The form will clearly state what the cost is, for example 8KM. The cashier will then take 9KM from you without telling you why. The 1KM is a service charge for using the cashier. He/she will then give you yet another form, or receipt, that you take back to the person holding your package hostage. You are then free to go but don't be too angry to find that your package has been opened and rummaged through by a behind-the-scenes customs official. Privacy is not the strongest trait of the postal system in Bosnia and Herzegovina. It is not uncommon for a package of goods sent or received at the post office to go 'missing' or for an item to be missing from a package.

TELEPHONE In the early 1990s it was easier to reach the lost city of Atlantis than a phone in downtown Sarajevo. Since then great strides have been made in telecommunications in Bosnia and Herzegovina. Most places here are now on a par with Western standards. Interestingly enough there are three phone companies in the country, BH Telecom being the main one. HPT is found more in the Croat-controlled areas, and the Serbs, too, have their own telecom company – Telecom RS. Rates do differ between the three but the methods are all the same. International calls from BiH start with the standard 00 followed by the code of the country you are dialling (+44 for the UK; +353 for Ireland; +1 for the US and Canada; +61 for Australia; and +64 for New Zealand, for instance).

The international dialling code for Bosnia and Herzegovina is +387. When calling from outside BiH the 0 from the area code of the region calling is dropped. For example, if calling Sarajevo from abroad you dial +387 33 + six-digit number. When dialling from within Bosnia and Herzegovina the prefix for Sarajevo is then 033 + six-digit number. Within the Federation the prefixes all begin with 3. In the Republika Srpska area codes begin with 5.

Calls from hotels are, like in most places, ridiculously overpriced. Avoid hotel calls if at all possible; even local calls can be expensive. Another tip is that if you are calling Serbia or Montenegro from the BH Telecom or HPT areas (meaning the Federation) it is more expensive than calling the US. Make it a quick call.

There are several GSM servers and there are relatively good signals throughout the country. American or Canadian mobile phones may not have roaming in BiH – check with your service provider before you set off. European GSM mobiles have a roaming agreement with Bosnia and Herzegovina. Roaming prices are high. If you plan to use the phone a considerable amount during your stay it may be wisest to buy a local SIM card. The first purchase of a local SIM ultra card costs 5KM. You can purchase these cards at the post office or kiosks, and refill minutes at any time for any price. There are three main GSM servers in BiH (BiH Telecom – 061/062; Eronet – 063; and Mobi – 065) and the signal from any one is valid in the others, unlike the phonecard systems. Signals will be bad in the mountains, most canyons or deep river valleys, and in isolated villages.

Useful telephone numbers

Emergencies

Emergency 124
Police 122
Fire 123
Roadside service 1282/1288

General

Local operator 1182/1185/1186/1188
International operator 1201
Time 1401/1400
Express delivery 1417
Telegram service 1202
Taxi 1515

Airport information

Sarajevo 033 289 100
Banja Luka 051 212 802
Mostar 036 350 212
Tuzla 035 814 640

INTERNET In the past few years, most young people in Bosnia have acquired a smartphone and like elsewhere in the world, people spend all day surfing the web and social media on their devices. The use of free mobile applications like Viber and WhatsApp are very popular. Most restaurants, cafés, bars, and hotels have free Wi-Fi (you may need to ask for a password), and internet speeds in Bosnia are generally extremely fast and the connections are reliable. There is Wi-Fi at the Sarajevo airport (the first several minutes are free, then you can purchase more surfing time for a very reasonable price). However, there is no Wi-Fi at bus or train stations, and most intercity and international buses do not have Wi-Fi, in contrast with the rest of Europe.

More and more businesses, including hotels and tourist attractions, have websites and many of them even have email. Whether or not they answer the email is another question altogether. The existence of an email address doesn't necessarily mean someone will respond to your enquiries. You will find more and more Wi-Fi zones in all urban areas around BiH.

BUSINESS/TIME

Time is an interesting concept the further south in Europe one travels. Bosnia and Herzegovinians generally take life a bit slower than the Western world. I'm certain that is one of the main reasons why people who visit BiH love it so much and people who stay a bit longer get frustrated by it. Working hours for most institutions are from 09.00 to 16.00, Monday to Friday. Shops often don't open until 10.00 and usually close later in the evening, depending on where you are and what season it is. There isn't a general urgency placed on timeliness. There is always time for a coffee and if one is doing business then there is even more time for 'small talk' and a few shots of the local firewater (*rakija* or *loza*). Bosnia and Herzegovina is on Central

European Time (CET) – meaning it's 1 hour ahead of the UK, 6 hours ahead of the US east coast, 9 hours ahead of the west coast, and 8 hours behind eastern Australia. If you are planning a trip and need to call to make arrangements, it is worth keeping this in mind. See also *Opening times*, pages 73–4.

BUYING PROPERTY

Unlike in neighbouring Croatia, buying property by foreign nationals is not an easy undertaking in BiH. If you do plan on buying land or real estate, make sure you have an excellent lawyer with a lot of experience in this field. Laws and procedures are complicated, the bureaucracy is intimidating and ownership structures can make one's head spin. Be sure, too, that the ownership issues have been resolved. Very often there will be many owners of the same property. Inheritance laws automatically pass ownership to next of kin and with each generation the number of owners only seems to grow. If going through a real estate agent, be sure to play hardball. They often ask exorbitant fees whilst pretending to be your best friend and be looking out for your best interests. Try to get an English copy of land ownership laws and get second opinions on any decision you make. Municipalities are responsible for providing deeds and titles to land and the registry will clearly show the ownership structure. Many people, even locals, have been cheated by dodgy real estate sales. Be careful.

CULTURAL ETIQUETTE

ECOLOGY The habits of some of the local people aren't always the best example of how to care for Bosnia and Herzegovina's precious nature. Please don't follow suit. There is a shortage of bins in some areas but if you look just a bit harder you'll find one, however, as there's no recycling in Bosnia you won't find a recycling bin. In summertime, nature in Herzegovina is dealt a similar fate to that in neighbouring Croatia, with a large number of forest fires. They are easily sparked from cigarette butts tossed to the side of the road or from untended campfires. Do be careful about fire in the summer. Wherever you travel it is good practice to follow the 'leave no trace' policy, whether in town or in the mountains.

DRESS Depending on where you are in the country you'll find different types of dress, particularly amongst the women. The majority of men and women in Bosnia and Herzegovina dress in Western European styles. For most urban young people, looking fashionable, neat, and contemporary is considered important, and at first glance, it might look like everyone in the cities is dressed to impress. Bosnian Muslims are, for the most part, very secular and do not have a singular way of dressing, though there is currently somewhat of a religious revival happening, partly due to post-war identity politics. Nevertheless, how individuals interpret their religion, especially in terms of dress code, varies widely. In the rural areas you'll find that many women – Christian and Muslim – cover their head with a scarf. For some, this has more to do with old European or Slavic traditions than it does with religion. For others, it is a religious practice connected to Islam. On rare occasions you might see local women wearing the type of attire found in certain Middle Eastern or North African countries, where the women are covered from head to toe. It is not common practice to do that in Bosnia and Herzegovina, but there are small groups who have a stricter interpretation of the Koran. There are increasing numbers of tourists from the Gulf States and elsewhere who wear full length dresses and face veils. Regardless of what you wear, generally in Bosnia it is safe to assume that your personal attire will be perceived as just that, your personal attire. No-one will be offended by what you do or don't wear. However, it is common practice for women to wear at least long trousers and a 'decent' top when entering a church or a mosque. Many Orthodox monasteries will not allow visitors wearing shorts to enter. When entering a mosque, you should remove your shoes. It is also Islamic custom that women enter mosques with their heads covered (a simple scarf will do). Many mosques that receive guests have scarves available at the entrance. The mosque open for tourists in Mostar does not require women to cover their heads.

There is no naturist beach on the coast at Neum. If you plan to bathe nude, as many do, it is best to get off the beaten track a bit. Natural sunbathing in large crowds could attract a policeman who will ask you to put your clothes on or at the very worst give you a ticket. For the most part, however, it is tolerated. You won't find many (or any) locals with a naturist approach to sunning themselves, so sitting on the terrace or walking around naked or topless will surely offend.

TIPPING Waiters earn horrendously low salaries in Bosnia and Herzegovina. Gratuity is never included in the bill. Food prices are so low that a 10% tip won't leave much of a hole in your wallet or purse. Some of the waiters who behave as if you've bothered them for entering the premises should rightfully be exempt from your generosity. Taxi drivers will usually round the fares themselves without asking, but that, too, amounts to little. (See *Budgeting*, pages 72–3.)

INTERACTING WITH LOCAL PEOPLE

Even though there hasn't been a tourist boom since the end of the conflict, the locals are more than familiar with guests from every country in Europe and North America. The international influx in Bosnia and Herzegovina since the war began in 1992 has brought tens if not hundreds of thousands of people here as aid workers, soldiers, curious visitors, peace activists, diplomats, businessmen and pilgrims paying homage to the Virgin Mary in Međugorje. The point is that anywhere you go in Bosnia and Herzegovina, big city or small village, you will be no surprise to the locals. In the rural areas they may stare a bit at first but that seems to be a tradition in any small town or village in any other country that I've visited. You'll hardly be noticed in places like Sarajevo, Mostar or Banja Luka, where there is a significant international presence.

Local people will almost always be very friendly. This is common to the region but Bosnian hospitality is something special. A Bosnian will go out of their way to assist you in finding something and it is common for them to invite someone home for a coffee. Once you enter someone's home as a guest, expect the red carpet treatment. Rich or poor, your host will most certainly serve you coffee, followed by an offer of cigarettes. The unwritten rule is never light up without offering the people around you a cigarette. More than likely the host will bring out sweets (biscuits or chocolate) and if the energy is right, out come the local spirits and food. Visiting from the West, you might see it as going a bit overboard, but the tradition of treating guests like one of their own is taken seriously. My advice is to sit back and enjoy it, and if you're in a rush – too bad. The best way to turn down the ninth or tenth coffee, or a chunk of meat (for vegetarians – many villagers don't understand the concept) is to say '*Ne mogu*', which means 'I can't'. Saying 'No, thank you' simply does not work. If you find yourself shaking from the strong Turkish

THE YAYS AND NAYS IN BOSNIA AND HERZEGOVINA

- Although in the West we think that visiting an unknown person is uncomfortable or that we shouldn't impose – Bosnians think the exact opposite. Bosnians and Herzegovinians treat their guests as if they're tired, cold and hungry. Even if you've never seen these people in your lives it is a tradition for them to ask you in and at least give you coffee. Don't be surprised if sweets, cigarettes and alcohol are pulled out next. It's the best hospitality around – because they really mean it and they really enjoy it.
- Do treat yourself to a bottle, or two, of Blatina red or Žilavka white wine. They've been making it for ages on the hillsides of Međugorje – and it's a heavenly taste!
- It's mostly a Muslim practice but many Christians also do it in Bosnia: removing one's shoes before entering a house has been a custom for centuries – whether you're in a village or a city apartment, do remove yours as well, even if the host says you are not obliged to.
- Bosnians will usually go very far out of their way to help you. Don't get the wrong impression if someone seems too helpful. Of course, conmen exist anywhere you go, but for the most part you're probably safe.
- Drinking coffee is a national pastime. If you meet a group of Bosnians and go for a coffee or drink they will probably pay the whole bill. It is common practice not to divide up bills. What goes around comes around, so do pick up the next round.
- If you are engaged in a political or historical conversation be aware of who you are talking to. People here have very different opinions on most things regarding history and politics – and some take it personally. Do be a good listener unless you feel you are in a comfortable position to speak your mind.
- Bosnians tend to speak rather loudly to each other when they converse – whether about art, politics, sport … it doesn't really matter. There may even be strong body language or strange faces, but it's normal, so don't be alarmed – they're unlikely to be arguing.
- While in Herzegovina don't refer to Bosnia and Herzegovina as just Bosnia. They get offended if left out.
- Do go to Željo's (page 125) for a *ćevapi*. If you go to Sarajevo and don't eat at Željo's then you haven't visited Sarajevo.

coffees and just want the host to stop filling your cup, then leave a bit of coffee in it. Otherwise, as soon as you finish, the host will ask if you would like some more and quickly give you a refill.

Most young people will speak English, as it is taught in all the schools from an early age. American movies are popular here and many people have learned English from watching films. In western Herzegovina and northern Bosnia many people speak German. Over 300,000 refugees lived in Germany during the war and many more lived and worked in Germany before the conflict began. For the most part, young people here don't want to speak about the war or politics. They would rather hear about new music, cool films, good books or just shoot the breeze with you.

The older generation often brings the war and politics into conversation. Many find it therapeutic so lending an ear may be the best service you can offer someone.

Comments aren't even necessary. Everyone here bears a burden from the war and often they cannot handle dealing with someone else's despair. Being a good listener can have a greater effect than you could imagine. It's nice to exchange addresses, emails and phone numbers with people. An email when you get home is always much appreciated. Most will find that the younger generations don't necessarily want to talk about the war at all and have moved on.

TRAVELLING POSITIVELY

Bosnia and Herzegovina is still in many ways reliant on aid. There are dozens of local and international aid agencies still operational there. Although much focus is aimed at the physical and economic reconstruction of the country many organisations are dedicated to psychosocial work, working with youth, and aiding widowed mothers. Remember that only 20 or so years ago tens of thousands of homes were destroyed, and hundreds of thousands were killed. The effects of the war still linger in the hearts of many. As most international organisations usually have good funding sources I recommend donating to local agencies which, in the long run, will continue to heal the wounds and deal with rebuilding the country – both physically and spiritually.

CHARITIES There are literally hundreds of both local and international charities that are dedicated to making Bosnia and Herzegovina a better place. I could list dozens of them that are professional, compassionate and committed to the improvement of life, be it in psychosocial assistance, environmental protection or peace and reconciliation. Tremendous progress has been made in BiH but there is a long way to go to emotionally and physically rebuild from the horrors of war.

Local charities

Budi Moj Prijatelj (Be my friend) Patriotske Lige 24, Sarajevo 71000; ☎ 033 668 660; e bmf@bih.net.ba. This group works with Roma (Gypsy) children & integrates them into the education system. Roma children are particularly vulnerable in this part of the world & more often than not suffer from abuse, lack of education, health problems & discrimination.

Centre for Self-Reliance ☎ 033 766 260 e scsr@bih.net.ba. w scsr.com.ba/pridruziteSeENG.htm A group dedicated to empowering & employing disabled people.

Pomozi/Help Dr Fetaha Bećirbegovića br 8, 71000 Sarajevo; m 062 839 000; e pomozi@pomozi.ba; w pomozi.ba. Pomozi.ba are very active in helping with emergencies such as the devastating floods of 2014 and assisting the Syrian refugees fleeing war along the Balkan Route. They are continually active in BiH helping the poor with a strong focus on impoverished families with children.

International NGOs

Healing Hands Network Bank Hse, Stoke Bliss, Tenbury Wells, Worcs WR15 8QH, UK; m +44 (0)7815 628372; e healinghandsnetwork@gmail.com; w healinghandsnetwork.org.uk. The big charities get most of the publicity & funds to carry out international aid programmes. This unique group of healers come to BiH to work with former prisoners of war or people with serious war injuries. Healing Hands offers physical therapy, massage & any kind of alternative healing methods to deal with war wounds, physical & emotional. They are a wonderful group of individuals!

Part Two

THE GUIDE

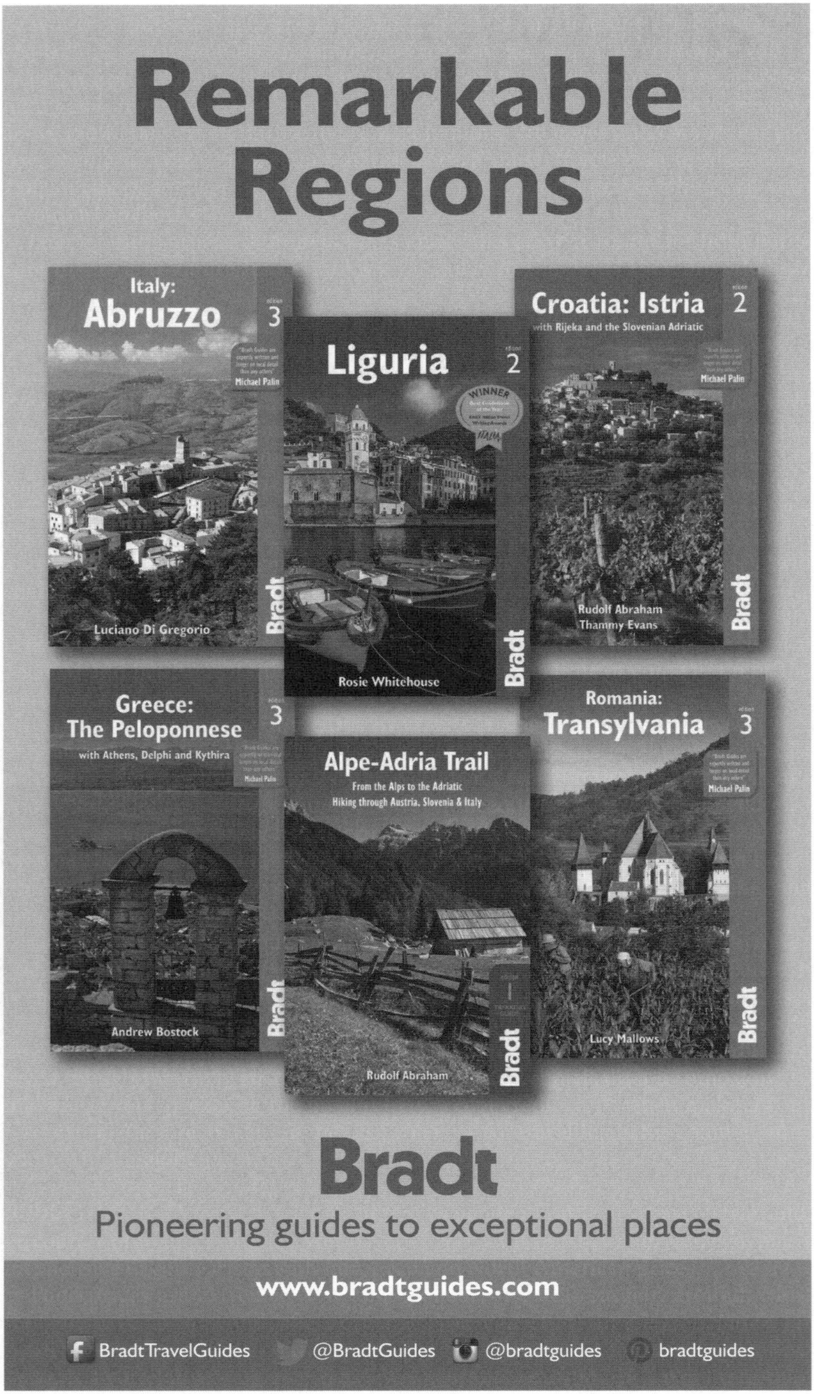
Remarkable Regions
Italy: Abruzzo
3
Michael Palin
Luciano Di Gregorio
Bradt
Liguria
2
WINNER
Rosie Whitehouse
Bradt
Croatia: Istria
2
with Rijeka and the Slovenian Adriatic
Michael Palin
Rudolf Abraham
Thammy Evans
Bradt
Greece: The Peloponnese
3
with Athens, Delphi and Kythira
Michael Palin
Andrew Bostock
Bradt
Alpe-Adria Trail
From the Alps to the Adriatic
Hiking through Austria, Slovenia & Italy
Rudolf Abraham
Bradt
Romania: Transylvania
3
Michael Palin
Lucy Mallows
Bradt
Bradt
Pioneering guides to exceptional places
www.bradtguides.com
BradtTravelGuides
@BradtGuides
@bradtguides
bradtguides

3

Sarajevo

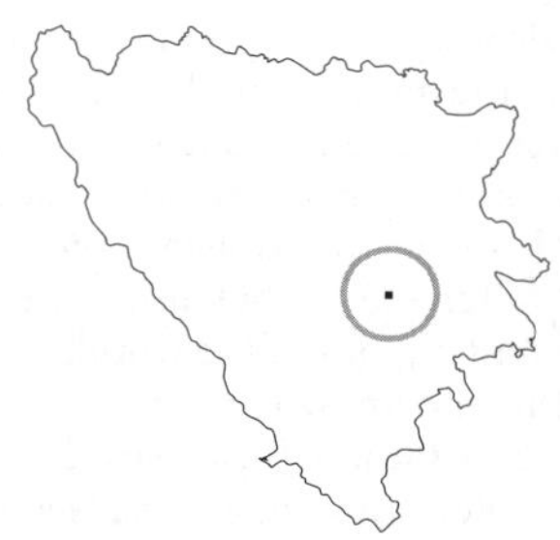

If there is one place in continental Europe that symbolises the crossroads between East and West, Sarajevo would have to be it. It is here that the Byzantine and Ottoman empires to the east and the empires of Rome, Venice and Vienna to the west brought their culture, traditions and religions. Only a few spots on earth can boast of hosting an Orthodox and a Catholic church, a mosque and a synagogue, all in the same square. This city, in particular, epitomises the centuries-old struggle against outside forces and the ability to assimilate all of these influences into one of the most diverse indigenous cultures in Europe. Whereas other parts of Bosnia and Herzegovina may still be burdened with ethnic strife, this city's long-standing tradition of multi-ethnicity enables it to thrive in its diversity. A walk through Sarajevo is a walk through the past.

From the oriental Ottoman-style quarters lined with sweet shops, cafés and handicraft workshops, to the administrative and cultural centre of Austro-Hungarian times, to the socialist-era housing blocks with their everyday neighbourhood feel, playgrounds and small businesses, Sarajevo encompasses a variety of worlds in one small valley. In Sarajevo people have time for family and friends. It is often said that a person's wealth is not measured in their material belongings but rather in their friendships, and here they invest the time to nurture them.

Sarajevo is a city that feels like home. You won't be overwhelmed by its size or massive buildings; rather you will be mesmerised by its quaint beauty, cafés teeming day and night with young and old, and the hospitality of a perfect stranger who invites you for a drink. The hills and mountains surrounding Sarajevo have always in a sense isolated the city, creating a whole world unto itself but which also kept its doors open to the rest of the world. Although Sarajevo is a capital city busy with the routines of everyday life and is becoming an increasingly popular tourist destination, there is a special energy here that gets into one's soul.

HISTORY

Sarajevo has had a long and rich history. It has always been an important crossroads for many different cultures, from both East and West. Owing to its unique location in the heart of the Balkan peninsula, Sarajevo has acted as a gateway for the peoples of Greece and Asia Minor migrating towards mid-western Europe and vice versa, since ancient times.

Sarajevo is also situated on the crossroads of two major water basins along the valleys of the Bosna and Neretva rivers that connect northern Europe with the Mediterranean Sea. Sarajevo's geographical position once divided the struggling powers of East and West but now unites these great civilisations.

The **first inhabitants** of this area were the Illyrians, followed by the major cultures from east and west: Hellenism in the prehistoric period, Mithraism in the late classical age, the Byzantine culture and the Ottoman Islamic culture beginning from the middle of the 15th century, the great Roman classical era, and the powerful Venetian and Austro-Hungarian influences. The topography of the city reveals an interesting coincidence: surrounded by sloping mountains from both the north and south, Sarajevo spreads east and west as if to open not only to the winds and watercourses, but also to the influences of the variety of cultures flowing from different regions of the world.

The first known human settlements found in this valley date back almost 5,000 years. At **Butmir** (near Sarajevo International Airport) the remains of one of the most interesting and richest Neolithic findings in the Balkans were discovered. More than 90 urban settlements and a great number of weapons, tools and finely chiselled domestic utensils were uncovered. As a result of this 19th-century archaeological discovery, the Neolithic culture of this area was called Butmir culture and is dated from 2400 to 2000BC.

The **Illyrians** lived on this territory at the end of the Bronze Age; remains of their settlements have been located in many areas around Sarajevo, at Debelo brdo, Zlatište, and at Soukbunar. When the **Romans** conquered the Illyrians in the 1st century AD, they established their headquarters near the thermal springs of what is today known as Ilidža. The remains of Roman villas, baths, mosaics and sculptures can still be seen there. When the Slavic tribes from the north arrived in the 7th century, Slav culture and state models began to dominate. In the 12th century Bosnia gradually established itself as a regional power, with its territorial expansion culminating in the 14th century. A major centre of the Bosnian state was established in the area of present-day Sarajevo, where the Vrhbosna region – with the fortified cities of Hodidjed, Kotorac and Vrhbosna as well as Trgovište – was situated.

The timeline of human settlements in the area of Sarajevo is preserved in the rich collections displayed in the **National Museum of Bosnia and Herzegovina**, one of the oldest scientific and cultural establishments in Sarajevo. The existence of tens of thousands of tombstones (*stećci*) erected by Bosnian Church followers bears evidence of medieval, heretic Bosnia and its unique artistic expression. Some of the finest examples of this magnificent stone art can be seen in the National Museum gardens.

In the middle of the 15th century Sarajevo was annexed by the **Ottoman Empire**. The Turks asserted much influence in Sarajevo decades before Bosnia was officially conquered. In the early years after the Ottoman invasion the city of 'Saraj-ovasi' (*Saraj* meaning castle or palace and *ovas* meaning field) is mentioned for the first time. The Slavs then adapted this name to their own language and pronunciation. Sarajevo became the first Turkish administrative military base in Bosnia, and soon afterwards the centre of the Bosnian *sandžak* (largest territorial subdivision in the Ottoman Empire). In this newly founded city emerged the first craftsmen in leather, blacksmiths, saddlers, millers and bakers. Life in the city, from both economic and cultural points of view, developed at an increasingly rapid pace during the 16th century. Many bridges were built over the Miljacka River that runs through the heart of the city; the Kozja ćuprija, Šeherija and Latinska bridges attest to the magnificence of oriental architecture. On the right bank of the river flourished the *baščaršija* quarter which became the social, economic and cultural centre of the young oriental city and the largest commercial centre in the central part of the Balkans. The streets in Baščaršija have been named after the crafts that were practised there for centuries.

The caravans arriving from Venice, Vienna, central Europe, the Mediterranean and the East were accommodated in one of the 50 inns of Sarajevo, called *hans*. The most famous was **Morića Han** [117 E2], which was built at the end of the 16th century. Today it is a tourist attraction that offers an authentic peek into Sarajevo's past, but in those days it offered facilities such as guest rooms, a café on the first floor, a courtyard with a porch for loading and unloading goods, warehouses and horse stables.

By the 16th century the city had regular contacts with other European cities and began to resemble a true metropolis. The first wooden-pipe waterworks were built to supply both private and public dwellings, and water fountains (*šadrvani*) were built in mosque courtyards and other public areas. The Turkish baths, called *hammams*, were constructed in authentic Ottoman-oriental style. There were seven Turkish baths in the city, the most important of which was **Gazi Husrev Begova** [117 D2], part of the mosque complex of the same name.

The vision of building a city expanded with Ottoman rule and many new buildings were erected: mosques, Islamic places of worship (*mesdžidi*), elementary and secondary school buildings (*mektebi* and *medrese*) and centres of mystic philosophy (*tekija*). One of the most impressive mosques in Sarajevo is Gazi Husrev Begova. It was built in 1531 and is named after the Governor of Bosnia who systematically embarked on creating a city that was often compared to Damascus.

One of the distinctive features of Ottoman rule was its tolerance of other religious creeds, particularly compared with the wretched record of religious persecution by most European powers of that time. The Orthodox, the Catholics and the Sephardic Jews (expelled from Spain in 1492 and resettled in Sarajevo) lived and worked together in relative harmony in the Čaršija quarter. This tradition thus laid the foundations for the cultural pluralism by which the city distinguishes itself today.

The old **Orthodox church** [117 E1] was built at the beginning of Ottoman rule and the school founded next to it was mentioned for the first time only two years after the first Muslim secondary school was established in Sarajevo. The church museum still hosts a great number of icons dating back to the 14th and 15th centuries. The new Orthodox Serbian church [117 A3] erected at the end of Ottoman rule demonstrates how Baroque and Russian Orthodox trends became popular within the same cultural framework.

The old **Roman Catholic church**, which had probably existed in Latinluk since the Middle Ages, was destroyed in 1697 when Prince Eugene of Savoy swept through the Bosna river valley and burned Sarajevo to the ground. It was later rebuilt and eventually replaced by the Catholic churches erected after the Austro-Hungarian occupation of Bosnia and Herzegovina in 1878. A large number of Sarajevo's Catholic population left in fear of reprisals after the Austro-Hungarians razed the city, but the Catholic merchants' influence has never left Sarajevo.

Sarajevo is one of the few European cities that has had a water supply system for more than 400 years. In the 17th century a Turkish travel writer named Evlija Čelebija pointed out in his journal the existence of 110 drinking water fountains.

Sarajevo for the first time experienced the full currents of European culture during the 40 years of Austro-Hungarian administration. New schools and European-structured scientific institutes were opened and Sarajevo's young intellectuals were educated in major cities around Europe. The city also enjoyed strong economic, cultural and political development; the first modern industries appeared: a furniture factory in 1869, a tobacco factory in 1880, a carpet-weaving factory in 1888 and a soap factory in 1894, in addition to the power plants, and textile and food industries. The first railway was also officially opened, although this was mainly used to exploit Bosnia's rich natural resources. Alongside these developments, there was also growing resistance to yet another occupying power in Sarajevo. The rebellions in the last years of Turkish dominion in Bosnia and

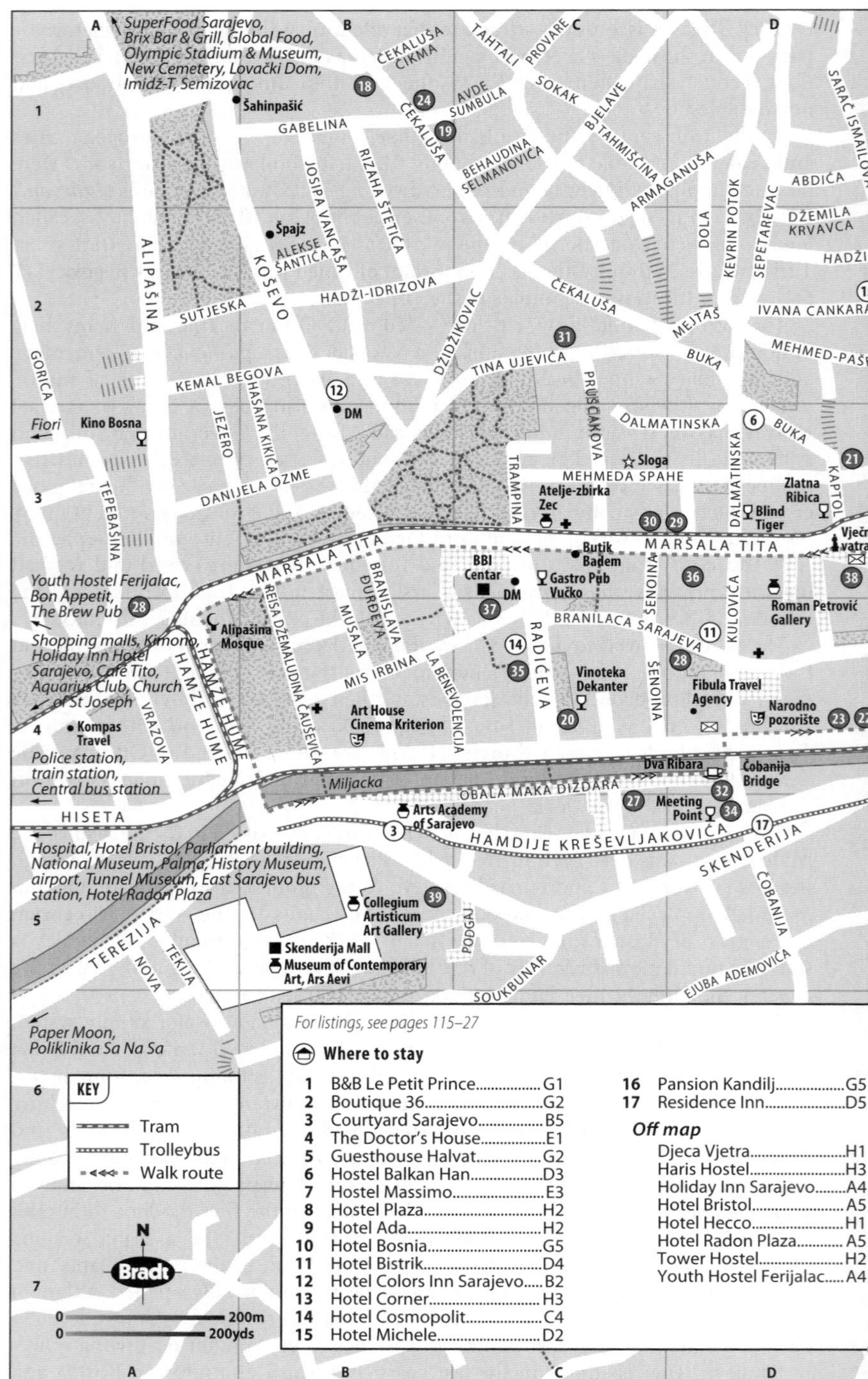
SuperFood Sarajevo, Brix Bar & Grill, Global Food, Olympic Stadium & Museum, New Cemetery, Lovački Dom, Imidž-T, Semizovac
Šahinpašić
Špajz
DM
Kino Bosna
Fiori
Sloga
Atelje-zbirka Zec
Zlatna Ribica
Blind Tiger
Vječna vatra
Butik Badem
BBI Centar
DM
Gastro Pub Vučko
Roman Petrović Gallery
Youth Hostel Ferijalac, Bon Appetit, The Brew Pub
Alipašina Mosque
Shopping malls, Kimono, Holiday Inn Hotel Sarajevo, Café Tito, Aquarius Club, Church of St Joseph
Kompas Travel
Art House Cinema Kriterion
Vinoteka Dekanter
Fibula Travel Agency
Narodno pozorište
Police station, train station, Central bus station
Dva Ribara
Čobanija Bridge
Miljacka
Arts Academy of Sarajevo
Meeting Point
Hospital, Hotel Bristol, Parliament building, National Museum, Palma, History Museum, airport, Tunnel Museum, East Sarajevo bus station, Hotel Radon Plaza
Collegium Artisticum Art Gallery
Skenderija Mall
Museum of Contemporary Art, Ars Aevi
Paper Moon, Poliklinika Sa Na Sa
ALIPAŠINA
KOŠEVO
GABELINA
JOSIPA VANCAŠA
RIZAHA ŠTETIĆA
ČEKALUŠA ČIKMA
ČEKALUŠA
AVDE SUMBULA
TAHTALI SOKAK
PROVARE
BJELAVE
TAHMIŠČINA
BEHAUDINA SELMANOVIĆA
ARMAGANUŠA
DOLA
KEVRIN POTOK
SEPETAREVAC
ABDIĆA
DŽEMILA KRVAVCA
HADŽI
SARAČ ISMAILOVA
IVANA CANKARA
MEJTAŠ
BUKA
MEHMED-PAŠE
ALEKSE ŠANTIĆA
HADŽI-IDRIZOVA
SUTJESKA
DŽIDŽIKOVAC
TINA UJEVIĆA
GORICA
KEMAL BEGOVA
HASANA KIKIĆA
JEZERO
PRUŠČAKOVA
DALMATINSKA
TRAMPINA
MEHMEDA SPAHE
KAPTOL
TEPEBAŠINA
DANIJELA OZME
MARŠALA TITA
BRANISLAVA ĐURĐEVA
REISA DŽEMALUDINA ČAUŠEVIĆA
MUSALA
ŠENOINA
KULOVIĆA
BRANILACA SARAJEVA
RADIĆEVA
MIS IRBINA
LA BENEVOLENCIJA
HAMZE HUME
VRAZOVA
OBALA MAKA DIZDARA
HISETA
HAMDIJE KREŠEVLJAKOVIĆA
SKENDERIJA
ČOBANIJA
TEREZIJA
NOVA
TEKIJA
PODGAJ
SOUKBUNAR
EJUBA ADEMOVIĆA
KEY
Tram
Trolleybus
Walk route
N
Bradt
0 200m
0 200yds
For listings, see pages 115–27
Where to stay
1 B&B Le Petit Prince.....G1
2 Boutique 36.....G2
3 Courtyard Sarajevo.....B5
4 The Doctor's House.....E1
5 Guesthouse Halvat.....G2
6 Hostel Balkan Han.....D3
7 Hostel Massimo.....E3
8 Hostel Plaza.....H2
9 Hotel Ada.....H2
10 Hotel Bosnia.....G5
11 Hotel Bistrik.....D4
12 Hotel Colors Inn Sarajevo.....B2
13 Hotel Corner.....H3
14 Hotel Cosmopolit.....C4
15 Hotel Michele.....D2
16 Pansion Kandilj.....G5
17 Residence Inn.....D5
Off map
Djeca Vjetra.....H1
Haris Hostel.....H3
Holiday Inn Sarajevo.....A4
Hotel Bristol.....A5
Hotel Hecco.....H1
Hotel Radon Plaza.....A5
Tower Hostel.....H2
Youth Hostel Ferijalac.....A4

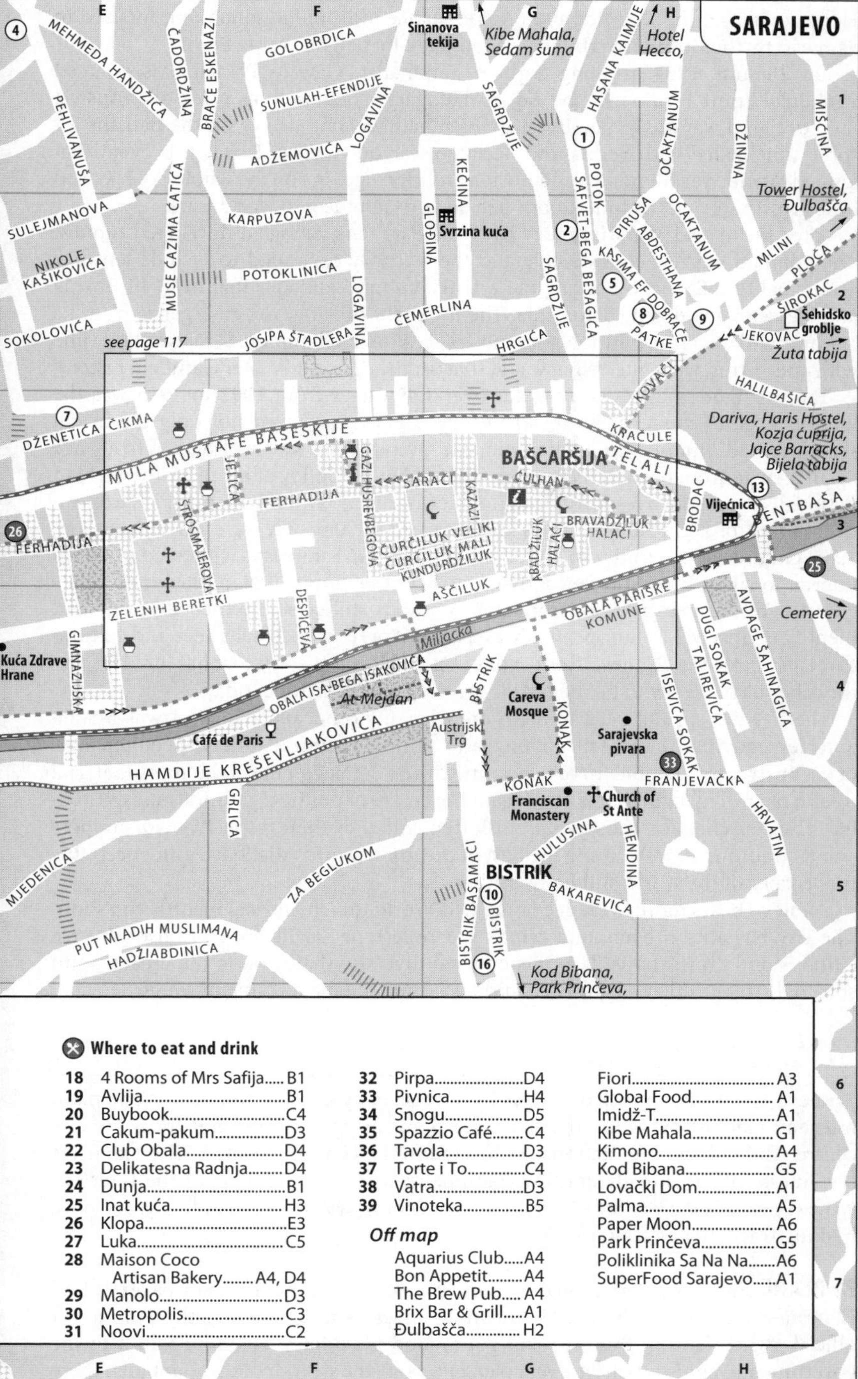
SARAJEVO
E
F
G
H
1
2
3
4
5
6
7
Sinanova tekija
Kibe Mahala, Sedam šuma
Hotel Hecco,
Tower Hostel, Đulbašča
Svrzina kuća
Šehidsko groblje
Žuta tabija
Dariva, Haris Hostel, Kozja ćuprija, Jajce Barracks, Bijela tabija
BAŠČARŠIJA
Vijećnica
Cemetery
Kuća Zdrave Hrane
Careva Mosque
At-Mejdan
Austrijski Trg
Café de Paris
Sarajevska pivara
Franciscan Monastery
Church of St Ante
BISTRIK
Kod Bibana, Park Prinčeva,
see page 117
MEHMEDA HANDŽIĆA
ČADORDŽINA
BRAĆE EŠKENAZI
GOLOBRDICA
SUNULAH-EFENDIJE
LOGAVINA
ADŽEMOVIĆA
SAGRDŽIJE
HASANA KAIMIJE
POTOK
SAFVET-BEGA BEŠAGIĆA
OČAKTANUM
DŽININA
MIŠČINA
PEHLIVANUŠA
SULEJMANOVA
NIKOLE KAŠIKOVIĆA
MUSE ĆAZIMA ĆATIĆA
KARPUZOVA
POTOKLINICA
KEČINA
GLOĐINA
PIRUŠA
ABDESTHANA
KASIMA EF DOBRAČE
MLINI
PLOČA
ŠIROKAC
JEKOVAC
PATKE
SOKOLOVIĆA
JOSIPA ŠTADLERA
ČEMERLINA
HRGIĆA
KOVAČI
HALILBAŠIĆA
DŽENETIĆA ČIKMA
MULA MUSTAFE BAŠESKIJE
JELIĆA
FERHADIJA
GAZI HUSREVBEGOVA
SARAČI
KAZAZI
ČULHAN
KRAČULE
TELALI
BRODAC
BENTBAŠA
ŠTROSMAJEROVA
ČURČILUK VELIKI
ČURČILUK MALI
KUNDURDŽILUK
ABADŽILUK
HALAČI
BRAVADŽILUK
AŠČILUK
ZELENIH BERETKI
DESPIĆEVA
Miljacka
OBALA KULINA BANA
OBALA ISA-BEGA ISAKOVIĆA
OBALA PARIŠKE KOMUNE
GIMNAZIJSKA
HAMDIJE KREŠEVLJAKOVIĆA
GRLICA
BISTRIK
KONAK
AVDAGE ŠAHINAGIĆA
DUGI SOKAK
TALIREVIĆA
ISEVIĆA SOKAK
FRANJEVAČKA
HRVATIN
HULUSINA
HENDINA
BAKAREVIĆA
BISTRIK BASAMACI
MJEDENICA
ZA BEGLUKOM
PUT MLADIH MUSLIMANA
HADŽIABDINICA
Where to eat and drink
18 4 Rooms of Mrs Safija.....B1
19 Avlija.....B1
20 Buybook.....C4
21 Cakum-pakum.....D3
22 Club Obala.....D4
23 Delikatesna Radnja.....D4
24 Dunja.....B1
25 Inat kuća.....H3
26 Klopa.....E3
27 Luka.....C5
28 Maison Coco Artisan Bakery.....A4, D4
29 Manolo.....D3
30 Metropolis.....C3
31 Noovi.....C2
32 Pirpa.....D4
33 Pivnica.....H4
34 Snogu.....D5
35 Spazzio Café.....C4
36 Tavola.....D3
37 Torte i To.....C4
38 Vatra.....D3
39 Vinoteka.....B5
Off map
Aquarius Club.....A4
Bon Appetit.....A4
The Brew Pub.....A4
Brix Bar & Grill.....A1
Đulbašča.....H2
Fiori.....A3
Global Food.....A1
Imidž-T.....A1
Kibe Mahala.....G1
Kimono.....A4
Kod Bibana.....G5
Lovački Dom.....A1
Palma.....A5
Paper Moon.....A6
Park Prinčeva.....G5
Poliklinika Sa Na Na.....A6
SuperFood Sarajevo.....A1

Herzegovina set the stage for a strong resistance movement, much of it focused in Sarajevo by the Bosnian Serbs and encouraged by neighbouring Serbia.

On 28 June 1914 a young Serbian nationalist, Gavrilo Princip, assassinated Archduke Franz Ferdinand, the Austro-Hungarian heir, and his wife Sofia. Austria then declared war on Serbia. Russia, which had also had its eye on the Balkans for some time, sided with Serbia and declared war on Austria. It was this event that ignited World War I. Sarajevo and Bosnia and Herzegovina on the whole experienced little growth during the tumultuous period between the two world wars.

After the World War II victory by Tito's Partisans, Sarajevo developed rapidly. The population grew considerably and the territory expanded to include ten new municipalities. Sarajevo became the artistic, cultural and spiritual heart of Bosnia and Herzegovina during Tito's rule. The highlight of Sarajevo's emergence from its cultural and social revolution was the 1984 Winter Olympics. Sarajevo, this time with open arms, welcomed what was at that time the largest Winter Games in history.

The war that ravaged Sarajevo for over 1,400 days from 1992 to 1995 was the longest siege in modern European history. The city survived not only the brutal slaughter and humiliation of the innocent, but also the waves of hatred that once again blew in from beyond its borders. The calculated policy of terror by the Serbian nationalists, and the irresponsible diplomacy of Bosnia and Herzegovina's European neighbours, brought Sarajevo to its knees. Over 11,000 people were killed, including 1,500 children, while under so-called UN 'protection'. Sarajevans witnessed a neutral international military presence that watched the premeditated slaughter of its citizens. Yet Sarajevans of all ethnic backgrounds still celebrate their diversity and identify themselves as European. It was the spirit of resistance, tolerance and cultural diversity that saved Sarajevo from extinction and it is this spirit that has lifted it from the ashes of yesterday to be the fastest-growing city in Europe today.

The city has sprung back to life more than any other place in post-war Bosnia and Herzegovina. Many of its national and cultural monuments have been repaired or reconstructed. Despite hard economic times, Sarajevo enjoys the most material wealth of any city in BiH. It is once again the centre of political, cultural and spiritual life. The churches and mosques are still frequented by their respective worshippers and its tradition of welcoming the best of the many worlds that have influenced this tiny corner of the world still holds strong.

Sarajevo bears more evidence of the Old World than historical records can show. The city has always been, and remains, a milestone for its absorption of diverse cultures and civilisations. It is this cultural diversity that powers the creative and spiritual strength that has resisted and overcome the most trying of times.

GETTING THERE AND AWAY

Sarajevo is a well-connected city, easily accessible by air, bus, rail or car. The main international airport is located in Sarajevo and is only 20 minutes from the city centre. The rail and bus stations are located in the centre, the latter with extensive bus lines, both regionally and internationally. BiH has been part of the InterRail (*www.interrailnet.com*) and Eurail (**w** *eurail.com*) systems for several years now, making travelling by train easier.

BY PLANE Sarajevo International Airport (**w** *sarajevo-airport.ba*) [map, pages 148–9] is located at the base of Igman Mountain. My guess is that some wealthy communist official owned land in this area and got a good price for it when he sold it to the government. The airport itself is very pleasant, as are the surrounding mountains. There is always a 'but' though, and this 'but' is a big one. During the winter the entire area is usually covered with heavy fog until late morning or mid-afternoon. Early-morning flights are regularly cancelled during the winter, making it a good bet that you'll miss your connecting flight in Zagreb or Budapest. During the other three seasons flights come and go without problems, and are for the most part uninterrupted.

The airport is only 12km from the centre of town. A private bus service runs from the airport to the city centre. Its schedule roughly follows flight arrivals and departures, from early morning to late in the evening. A one-way ticket is 5KM and a round trip ticket is 8KM. Detailed information about the bus in English is not yet available online, though a schedule can be found at w centrotrans.com by clicking on the Bosnian language link for 'aerodrom-baščaršija'. The bus stops in front of City Hall (Viječnica) in the old town and at the entrance to the airport. Taxis waiting outside the airport will take you to town, usually for a non-metered, inflated rate of 20–30KM or more to the city centre, depending on the driver. Ask the price before you get in the car and feel free to bargain for the fixed rate. The actual rate for a taxi ride from the airport to the city centre is closer to 12–15KM. Calling one of the taxi companies listed on page 112 is a better bet for finding an honest fare. The major hotels, and even some of the smaller ones, offer airport pick-up and drop-off. Fees vary.

You can change money in the airport at the one exchange desk. If you intend to hire a car, most car-hire companies are located in the airport (page 77).

BY BUS

Central bus station [108 A5] Put života 8; ☎ 033 213 100

East Sarajevo bus station [108 A5] Srpskih vladara 2; ☎ 057 317 377

From morning till night buses from abroad and from local destinations arrive at and depart from Sarajevo. The Central bus station is the country's largest. There are some buses travelling to Sarajevo from northwest Europe but most direct lines come from Germany and Austria. Centrotrans is now a Eurolines member and runs regular buses from many European destinations to Sarajevo: see pages 65–6 and check w centrotrans.com or w sarajevo-tourism.com for timetables, prices and tickets.

Zagreb has other bus lines to Sarajevo and is a good connection point to this part of the world. Zagreb–Sarajevo usually takes 6–8 hours Buses regularly arrive from Split (7–9 hours) and Dubrovnik (5 hours) on the Dalmatian coast and from Belgrade to the east (5 hours). Mostar can be reached in 2½–3 hours by bus. There are an equivalent number of buses leaving Sarajevo to the major regional and international destinations. The bus station doesn't have information posted in English but the information desk, although painfully slow, can usually help in English. There are no lockers or temporary luggage storage. It is best to check the timetables online (good sites to check are w autobusni-kolodvor.com or w getbybus.com), and then call the bus station or go in person to confirm. It would be impossible to list all of the buses coming in and out of Sarajevo's central bus station (not to mention the other bus station in East Sarajevo that offers more lines to and from towns in Republika Srpska and Serbia, some of which can only be reached from this station), but here are some important ones (although do confirm that the timetable hasn't changed when planning your trip):

Sarajevo–Mostar (via Konjic & Jablanica) 06.00, 09.00, 11.30, 12.30, 15.30, 18.00, 19.55 daily (20KM/30KM)
Sarajevo–Banja Luka 05.00, 06.30, 12.30, 16.30, 22.00 daily (30KM/50KM)
Sarajevo–Zagreb 6.30, 9.30, 12.30, 22.00 daily (48KM/64KM)
Sarajevo–Belgrade 06.15, 11.00, 15.00, 22.00 daily (48KM/64KM)

Sarajevo–Dubrovnik 07.15, 10.00 daily, with additional summer routes (40KM/60KM)
Sarajevo–Split (via Mostar) 06.00, 16.30 daily, with additional summer routes (42KM/68KM)
Mostar–Sarajevo (via Konjic & Jablanica) 06.00, 06.30, 09.45, 11.35, 13.35, 17.35, 18.50, 20.50 daily (20KM/30KM)
Banja Luka–Sarajevo 05.00, 06.30, 14.30, 17.00 daily (30KM/50KM)
Zagreb–Sarajevo 06.30, 12.30, 16.45, 18.50, 22.00 daily (48KM/64KM)
Belgrade–Sarajevo 06.15, 07.00, 10.00, 13.15, 16.00, 22.30 daily (48KM/64KM)
Dubrovnik–Sarajevo 16.00 daily, with additional summer routes (40KM/60KM)
Split–Sarajevo 07.00, 14.30 daily, with additional summer routes (42KM/68KM)

BY CAR Travelling to Sarajevo by car becomes a different experience when you cross the border from Croatia. If you are used to the massive motorways of Europe you'll find that Bosnia and Herzegovina has only a few four-lane roads, and a highway which is still only partially built. Most roads are one lane. This will certainly slow you down but it won't stop you from reaching Sarajevo eventually. If you are crossing the border at Metković/Doljani in southern Dalmatia, it will take another 3 hours plus to reach Sarajevo. From the northern frontiers, the quickest route to and from Sarajevo is from Slavonski Brod and Bosanski Brod. From the Split area the best roads for crossing are Kamensko to Livno then Bugojno–Travnik–Sarajevo.

BY TRAIN

Train Station [108 A5] Put života 2; ☎ 033 655 330

The rail system in BiH is modest at best. Most of the rolling stock is slow and old. The system has seen some recent improvements, like a new train on the Sarajevo–Doboj line, but also some lines have been decommissioned. Sarajevo is the hub of the few trains which move in and out of the country, currently just to Zagreb, Croatia, and possibly in the future to Ploče, Croatia, where it used to go daily. As I said in the *Getting there and away* section in *Chapter 2* (page 65), it can be a great way to see the countryside if you're not in a hurry. See Chapter 2 also for train schedules to and from Sarajevo. I have heard of several incidents of robbery in both Croatia and Bosnia. If you take the overnight train, be sure to strap your valuables to your person. One Swiss diplomat was offered coffee once, kindly accepted, and woke up hours later with his wallet stolen. Although these are isolated incidents, it is always good to keep your guard up.

GETTING AROUND

Taxis are fairly inexpensive in Sarajevo. The starting fare is pre-set at 1.5KM and is 1KM per each additional kilometre. With few exceptions a taxi ride to anywhere in Sarajevo shouldn't cost more than 12–15KM. Taxi stands are located all over town and operate 24 hours a day. It is also easy to flag one down on main streets, although some of the cabs on the street are fake. When possible, it is better to call one of the taxi companies listed below, as hailing a taxi or catching one at a taxi stand may result in a higher rate, especially for foreigners. That doesn't mean you will necessarily be overcharged, but if you want to avoid it, call Crveni Taxi (Red Taxi) (☎ *033 760 600*) or Samir & Emir (☎ *033 1516*). Tipping is not necessary but always welcome. Taxi drivers tend to round up fares without asking.

Walking in Sarajevo is a local pastime. The compact city centre and old town make it easy and enjoyable to do most moving around by foot. Ferhadija and Sarači are famous pedestrian promenades that go through the heart of town and are always filled, day and night, with walkers of all ages. The Vilsonovo Šetalište or 'Wilson's Walkway' is closed to vehicles after 17.00 and is a popular spot for lovers taking up a whole park bench, rollerbladers cruising up and down, and people walking their pets. Pedestrians anywhere in Sarajevo need to be alert – zebra crossings or a green signal for pedestrians do not at all mean it is safe to cross the street.

For **cyclists** there is even less tolerance. It is fun to cruise the old town on a mountain bike but there are lots of pedestrians and the narrow roads and rude drivers don't make for the safest biking. However, there are long trails along the Miljacka River starting from the Grbavica area, and a new bike lane is being built on the city's main thoroughfare, though currently it does not extend all the way to the old town. For 20KM a year, you can rent a bike for up to 30 minutes a day through Nextbike (**w** *nextbike.ba*), a bike sharing system with hubs in several central locations including at BBI and Alta shopping centres. Every additional 60 minutes is 1.50KM. Wherever you go, I highly recommend wearing a helmet and to think safety when riding in Sarajevo.

The **local bus** system is run down, but is the best in the country. Run by GRAS it may, in fact, be the most efficiently operated state-owned enterprise and will get you to even the most isolated villages on Bjelašnica. The 31e bus runs the entire length of the city every half-hour and costs 1.80KM, whether you are going one stop or all the way to the end. Starting by the National Archives and finishing in Dobrinja by the airport it is the quickest, cleanest and easiest bus route in town. The 31e buses are yellow with a Japanese flag. Strange, I know, but they were donated to the city by the government of Japan. Much of the public transport will have donor signs on it, as most of the buses and tramways in Sarajevo were completely destroyed in the war. You can purchase tickets for the 31e on board the bus, but for all other routes you should buy tickets from the small news-stands located near most stops.

Trams and trolleybuses are also reliable means of transportation. Trams constantly run up and down the main east–west road, Zmaja od Bosne. There is also a tram station at the main bus/rail station that goes to/from the centre. The tram lines extend all the way to Ilidža, a suburb to the west of Sarajevo, and for budget travellers are a great way to check out the Bosne River Springs and the park in Ilidža. Trolleybuses run to and from Austrijskitrg in the centre and Dobrinja, through the leafy Grbavica neighbourhood, via Zagrebačka. Depending on the line and the time of year, trams run everyday from approximately 05.00 to midnight, and trolleybuses run daily from approximately 05.45 to 23.30. Check the exact schedules of all public transport services in the city (GRAS) on the official GRAS website at **w** gras.ba. Although the site is in the local language, one can still find a way to navigate it by clicking on *redovivožnje* (schedules) on the right-hand menu and then choosing the type of transport from the list (tram = *tramvaj*; trolleybus = *trolejbus*; bus = *autobus*; minibus = *minibus*).

Tram and trolleybus tickets cost only 1.60KM one way. Unfortunately, little or no information is available for tourists using public transport, although signage has improved in the last year. Tram or trolleybus ticket inspections can be somewhat intimidating: you should be sure to buy your ticket before you get on, and then to 'clock in' using the machines on the tram. Be aware that some inspectors will try to slap on a hefty fee for not having a ticket or failing to stamp it. Tickets can be bought at the kiosks along main roads (locally called a *trafika*) or, for 1.80KM, direct from the driver. At the kiosks, two-journey tickets are 3KM, five-journey tickets are 7.10KM and ten-journey tickets are 12.80KM.

Driving around town is always fun. Sarajevo is not very big and the main road (Zmaja od Bosne) running east–west in the valley should help you keep your bearings. Traffic can be a bit maddening in the mornings between 08.00 and 10.00, and in the afternoons between 15.00 and 17.00. Don't be alarmed at cars running red lights or people inconsiderately blocking the intersection; it all comes with the territory. Parking is often problematic in town; there are now three times more cars in Sarajevo than before the war. With public transport being relatively good and the centre of town compact enough to walk almost anywhere, it is easier and wiser to find a parking space close to the centre. Skenderija Street has several parking areas, and behind the Holiday Inn on Zmaja od Bosne there is also a large public car park. It is not impossible to find a place downtown if you are really not prepared for the walk or if you're carrying some heavy souvenirs. It is better to pay 1–3KM per hour for parking than to risk being towed away by the feared *pauk*. The *pauk*, which literally translates as 'spider', is on regular patrol and will tow your car away without letting you know. It will cost 120KM to free your vehicle.

Cars with foreign registration have become more of a target for thieves in Sarajevo. You're more apt to get a broken window and your CD player nicked than for the car to be stolen, but an unpleasant hassle nonetheless. Practical precautions should be followed anywhere when travelling.

TOURIST INFORMATION

Good information is a bit hard to come by anywhere in BiH, and in Sarajevo there is only one main **tourist information centre** [117 F2] (☎ *033 580 999;* **e** *tourinfo@bih.net.ba;* **w** *sarajevo-tourism.com;* ⏱ *09.00–16.00 Mon–Fri, 10.00–14.00 Sat–Sun)* located on Sarači in the old town, the pedestrianised promenade that joins with Ferhadija. Information for hotels, museums, excursions, city tours and other activities can be found here. The staff speak English, German and French and will go out of their way to help. There is also a *Don't Miss Sarajevo* guide as well as an *In Your Pocket* guide. There is a helpful site promoting tourism in and around Sarajevo: **w** sarajevo.travel/en. It offers an online reservation system and tours.

A useful programme around town is the **Sarajevo Navigator** (**w** *navigator.ba*). It now has information points all around town with maps marked with important locations. They also produce Navigator, a monthly guide to cultural events, highlighting concerts, museums, galleries, festivals, films and much more. It's a great source of up-to-date information and can be found in the tourist information centre as well as in hotels and certain travel agencies.

A website on topical events in the city can be found at **w** Sarajevo.travel.

TOUR OPERATORS

Explore Bosnia Čurčiluk veliki bb; **m** 061 558 621; **e** info@explorebosnia.ba; **w** explorebosnia.ba; ⏱ hours vary. This operator has an excellent website & a very competitive online reservation system. They can organise tours in & around Sarajevo as well as throughout the country.

Green Visions Trg Barcelone 3; ☎ 033 717 290; **m** 061 213 278; **e** sarajevo@greenvisions.ba; **w** greenvisions.ba; ⏱ 09.00–17.00 Mon–Fri. Green Visions is the only ecotourism agency operating throughout the country. They specialise in hiking, biking, village tourism, rafting, mountain-hut rental & educational/cultural tours as well as a full range of tourism services.

Insider [117 D4] Zelenih Beretki 30; ☎ 033 534 353; **m** 061 190 591 **e** info@sarajevoinsider.com; **w** sarajevoinsider.com; ⏱ 09.00–18.00 Mon–Fri. Insider has perhaps the most competent collection of guides for the city of Sarajevo & beyond. They speak a heap of languages, offer interesting tours of all kinds & basically know their stuff.

Kompas Travel [108 A4] Maršala Tita 8; ☎ 033 565 600; **e** info@kompas.ba; **w** kompas.ba; ⏱ 09.00–17.00 Mon–Fri. Kompas specialises in youth travel & is a good place for ISIC (International Student Identity Card) travellers to check out. They have all the info on what places offer discounts for ISIC holders. They also offer guided tours to villages, farms & dairies.

Kuk Travel Željeznička 11–13; 033 639 449; m 063 929 303; e kuktravel@gmail.com; w kuk.ba; 09.00–17.00 Mon–Fri, 09.00–noon Sat. Kuk Travel has initiated a programme for tour operators coming to BiH. Although they mainly focus on groups they do offer excursions, & hotel reservations in Sarajevo for independent travellers as well.

Relax Tours [117 B4] Zelenih Beretki 22; 033 263 330; e relaxtours@relaxtours.com; w relaxtours.com; 08.30–20.00 Mon–Fri, 09.00–17.00 Sat. Although they are largely focused on outgoing tourism they have expanded their local itineraries & offer city tours & special excursions to destinations around Sarajevo.

Sarajevo Discovery Main tourist info centre [117 F2], Kundurdžiluk 1 [117 D3] & Mudželeti veliki 2; 033 238 423; summer: 09.00–19.00 daily, winter: 10.00–17.00 Mon–Sat. This group of young guides offers only one service, but they do it well. They are the largest group of certified guides that give 3-hr city tours for individuals or groups. Very reasonably priced.

WHERE TO STAY

Hotels in Sarajevo are generally mid-range in price. *Pansions*, or smaller guesthouses/bed and breakfasts, dominate the accommodation market in Sarajevo, particularly in the old town. The number of affordable, high-quality private apartments available for booking online is steadily increasing. There are a handful of hostels that also offer private accommodation in flats around town. The best experience in Sarajevo is certainly the smaller *pansions* or guesthouses. Service in both first and tourist class is good. Don't expect, however, the same 'bend-over-backwards' service found in the UK and the US. Most of the first-class hotels offer an airport transfer service. They all have the standard satellite television, air conditioning, minibar, phone and internet connection. All prices include breakfast unless otherwise specified.

There are other hotels outside of town in the suburb of Ilidža (page 145).

UPMARKET

Holiday Inn Hotel Sarajevo [108 A4] (206 rooms) Zmaj od Bosne 4; 033 288 200; e reception@hotelholiday.ba; w hotelholiday.ba. The hotel was built for the Olympics in the early 1980s. The rooms are the standard Holiday Inn type. The national restaurant has decent food & the café at the back of the hotel is quite fancy & a good place to do business. It is a major hub for businessmen who come to town but certainly not a place to write home about. If you're a tourist & are looking to save cash, there are plenty of other less expensive hotels with the same comforts. **$$$$**

Hotel Art [117 C3] (40 rooms) Vladislava Skarića 3; 033 475 410; e reception@hotelart.ba; w hotelart.ba. Centrally located & completely renovated, Hotel Art is a tiny but chic hotel. The rooms are cosy with tasteful décor & its location provides peace & quiet from traffic. It is just behind the Ferhadija walkway, which is busy but never too loud. All rooms have sat TV, minibar & AC. **$$$$**

Hotel Astra [117 B3] (15 rooms) Zelenih beretki 9; 033 252 100/200; w hotel-astra.com.ba. The décor at the Astra is quite classy. They managed, however, to build a hotel in a somewhat small area &, for some, it seems a bit cramped. The rooms are great as is the service & its location is one of the most convenient around. If you don't mind smaller spaces it's well worth a look. **$$$$**

Hotel Astra Garni [117 E3] (30 rooms) Kundurdžiluk 2; 033 475 100; e reception@hotelastragarni.ba; w hotelastragarni.ba. Owned by the same gentleman who runs the Hotel Astra. This location has a greater capacity & is locally categorised as a 3-star hotel. **$$$$**

Hotel Bosnia [109 G5] (80 rooms) Kulovića 9; 033 567 010; e bosniahotel@bih.net.ba; w bosniahotels.com. For those of you who might have visited Sarajevo before the war this is the former Hotel Beograd. Although the name has changed not much else has. The hotel is centrally located, which makes getting around by foot very easy. That's what you are paying for. The rooms are nice with the standard facilities. The hotel has a restaurant & café. The restaurant serves good food, particularly the traditional Bosnian dishes. Rates for foreigners are higher than for locals. **$$$$**

Hotel Bristol [108 A5] (120 rooms) Fra Filipa Lastrica 2; 033 705 000; e info@bristolsarajevo.com; w bristolsarajevo.com. Bristol was & is a major landmark of the city of Sarajevo. Although it's a dry establishment, it has a modern restaurant & an international feel. The quality of service is impeccable. It has a café/patisserie along the river with a non-smoking section inside. The rooms are all equipped with the best amenities. The hotel also has a small swimming pool & fitness centre in the basement. Parking is free for all guests. **$$$$**

Hotel Europe [117 C3] (125 rooms) Vladislava Skarića 5; 033 580 580; e reception@hoteleurope.ba; w hoteleurope.ba. Sarajevo's oldest hotel was completely destroyed during the war. It has come back in fine fashion & can once again boast to be one of the city's best hotels. This 5-star hotel is centrally located in the old town. It has a swimming pool, spa centre & excellent restaurant. **$$$$**

Hotel Radon Plaza [108 A5] (120 rooms) Dzemal Bijedica 185; 033 752 906; w radonplazahotel.ba. Situated at the far western end of town, closer to the airport, in a rather charmless section of town, the Radon is one of a handful of 5-star hotels in Sarajevo. It is more of a business hotel than a leisure one. The pool & spa centre is a favourite with guests. The revolving restaurant on the top floor offers great views of the city as well. **$$$$**

Courtyard Sarajevo [108 B5] (130 rooms) Skenderija 1; 033 954 500; e welcome@courtyardsarajevo.com; w marriott.com. Sarajevo has seen many new additions to its accommodation facilities. Marriott is the first major hotel chain to set up shop in Sarajevo. Whether travelling for business or pleasure, Courtyard by Marriott Sarajevo provides what it provides all over the world – high-speed internet access, excellent breakfast, nice dining facilities, a well-equipped fitness centre, & spacious rooms in the heart of the city. The Marriott caters to all kinds of guests but it is a favourite with visitors from the Gulf States during the hot summer months. **$$$**

Hotel Central [117 B4] (16 rooms) Ćumurija 8; 033 561 800; e info@hotelcentral.ba; w hotelcentral.ba. As central as it gets. This non-smoking hotel was bought & renovated by the Irish group Westwood. They have a good fitness centre & an excellent spa & wellness centre. The rooms are spacey & comfortable & its location makes just about everything in town walkable. **$$$**

Hotel Michele [108 D2] (25 rooms) Ivana Cankara 27; 033 560 310; e contact@hotelmichele.ba; w hotelmichele.ba. Hotel Michele is where many of the stars tend to stay. During the Sarajevo Film Festival (& for other major events), superstars like Richard Gere, Kevin Spacey & Michael Moore all made Michele their home for the week. The hotel has quite a pizzazz, with a funky interior design &, obviously, all the creature comforts one needs for a most remarkable stay in Sarajevo. **$$$**

SARAJEVO *Baščaršija*

For listings, see pages 115–27

Where to stay

1	Hostel City Centre	C3
2	Hostel Inn Luxury Sarajevo	B2
3	Hostel Srce Sarajevo	C3
4	Hostel Story	C3
5	Hostel Vagabond	B2
6	Hotel Art	C3
7	Hotel Astra	B3
8	Hotel Astra Garni	E3
9	Hotel Central	B4
10	Hotel Europe	C3
11	Hotel Latinski Most	E4
12	Hotel Old Town	D3
13	Hotel Opal Home Sarajevo	C4
14	Hotel President	E3
15	Hotel Villa Orient	G2
16	Hotel VIP	C1
17	Identiko	F3
18	Isa Begov Hamam	E4
19	Lion Hostel	G3
20	Ljubičica	F1
21	Pansion Stari Grad	F1
22	Samm Šeher	G2

Where to eat and drink

23	Aščinica ASDž	D3
24	Baklava Shop Sarajevo	F3
25	Barhana	E2
	Bečka Kafana	(see 9)
26	Buregdžinica Bosna	F3
27	Buregdžinica Sač	F3
28	Ćulhan	F2
29	Dveri	F2
30	Egipat	C2
31	Halvat	F2
32	Karuzo	A1
33	Libertas	D1
34	Nanina Kuhinja	F3
35	Planeta	G3
36	Pod Lipom	F2
37	Rahatlook	D2
38	Ramis	D2
39	Sevdah House	F3
40	Slatko Ćoše	D2
41	Stari Grad	E2
42	To be	E3
43	Željo	E3

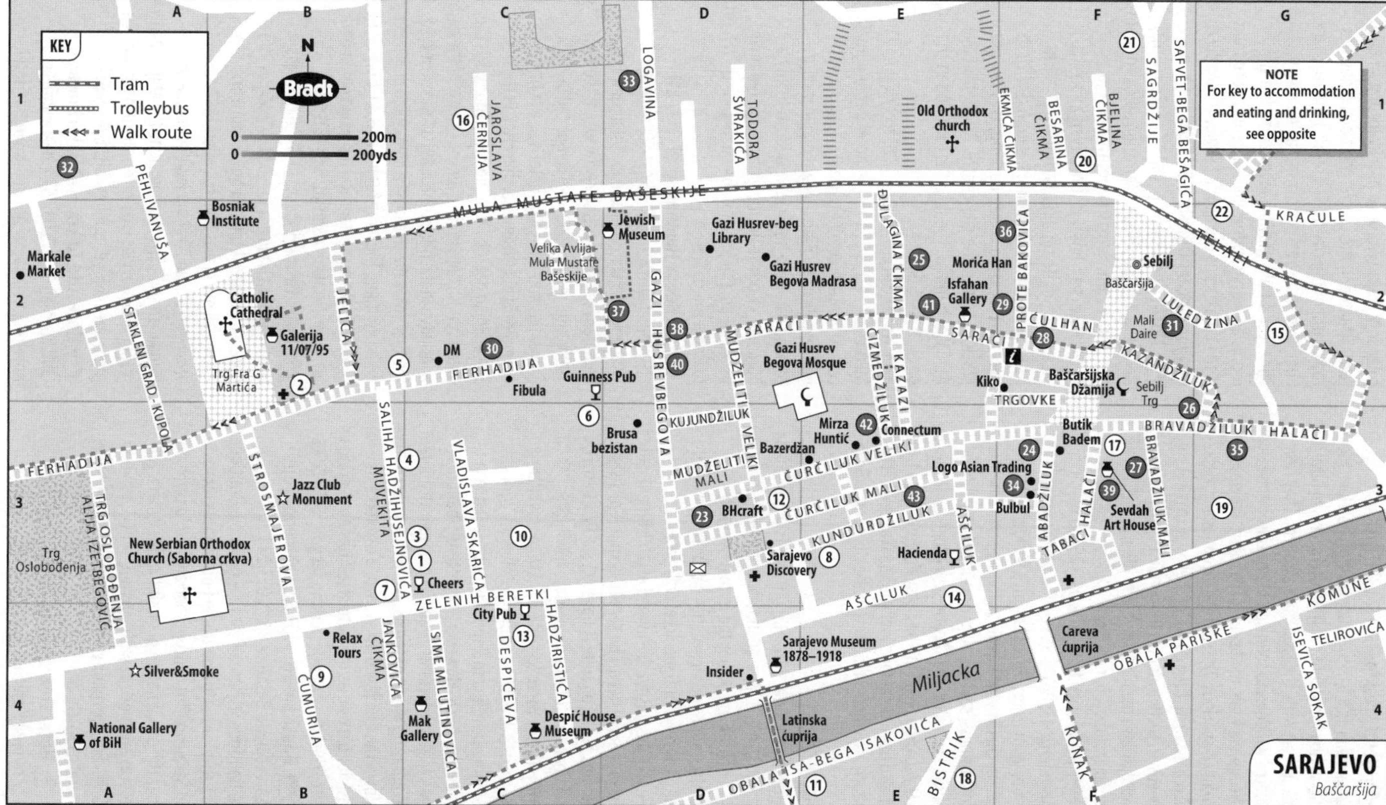
SARAJEVO
Baščaršija
NOTE
For key to accommodation and eating and drinking, see opposite
KEY
Tram
Trolleybus
Walk route
N
Bradt
0 200m
0 200yds
Markale Market
Bosniak Institute
PEHLIVANUŠA
STAKLENI GRAD - KUPOLA
Catholic Cathedral
Galerija 11/07/95
Trg Fra G Martića
JELIĆA
FERHADIJA
JAROSLAVA ČERNIJA
LOGAVINA
TODORA ŠVRAKIĆA
MULA MUSTAFE BAŠESKIJE
Jewish Museum
Velika Avlija-Mula Mustafe Bašeskije
Gazi Husrev-beg Library
Gazi Husrev Begova Madrasa
GAZI HUSREVBEGOVA
ĐULAGINA ČIKMA
Old Orthodox church
EKMIĆA ČIKMA
BESARINA ČIKMA
BJELINA ČIKMA
SAGRDŽIJE
SAFVET-BEGA BEŠAGIĆA
KRAČULE
TELALI
Sebilj
Baščaršija
LULEDŽINA
Mali Daire
Morića Han
Isfahan Gallery
PROTE BAKOVIĆA
ČULHAN
SARAČI
KAZANDŽILUK
Baščaršijska Džamija
Sebilj Trg
Kiko
TRGOVKE
DM
Fibula
Guinness Pub
Brusa bezistan
Gazi Husrev Begova Mosque
ČIZMEDŽILUK
KAZAZI
KUJUNDŽILUK
MUDŽELITI VELIKI
MUDŽELITI MALI
Mirza Huntić
Connectum
Bazerdžan
ČURČILUK VELIKI
ČURČILUK MALI
KUNDURDŽILUK
Logo Asian Trading
Bulbul
Butik Badem
BRAVADŽILUK HALAČI
BRAVADŽILUK MALI
ABADŽILUK
HALAČI
TABAČI
Sevdah Art House
BHcraft
Sarajevo Discovery
Hacienda
AŠČILUK
Jazz Club Monument
ŠTROSMAJEROVA
SALIHA HADŽIHUSEJNOVIĆA MUVEKITA
VLADISLAVA SKARIĆA
Cheers
ZELENIH BERETKI
City Pub
HADŽIRISTIĆA
DESPIĆEVA
SIME MILUTINOVIĆA
JANKOVIĆA ČIKMA
Relax Tours
ČUMURIJA
Trg Oslobođenja
TRG OSLOBOĐENJA ALIJA IZETBEGOVIĆ
New Serbian Orthodox Church (Saborna crkva)
Silver&Smoke
National Gallery of BiH
Mak Gallery
Despić House Museum
Sarajevo Museum 1878–1918
Insider
Miljacka
Latinska ćuprija
OBALA ISA-BEGA ISAKOVIĆA
BISTRIK
KONAK
Careva ćuprija
OBALA PARIŠKE KOMUNE
TELIROVIĆA
ISEVIĆA SOKAK

Hotel President [117 E3] (72 rooms) Bazardžani 1; 033 575 000; e: info@hotelpresident.ba; w hotelpresident.ba. This hotel seems to have it all. To start with, the location is excellent. They have special windows to sound proof any traffic noise from the tram or main road below. The rooms are classy, comfy & spacious. The staff are exceptionally friendly & professional. They go out of their way to meet your needs. Hotel President is surrounded by the unique cultural sites the old town has to offer, as well as the popular clubs & bars. **$$$**

Residence Inn [108 D5] (75 rooms) Skenderija 43; 033 563 600; e welcome@sjjri.com; w marriott.com. Marriott's Residence Inn serves clients who intend on longer stays whether for business, sabbatical, or consultants staying for short-term gigs. The service is excellent, apartments very spacious with all the classy amenities you need. It also has a great location: you can walk to pretty much anywhere of interest in the city centre. **$$$**

MID RANGE

Hotel Ada [109 H2] (10 rooms) Abdesthana 8; 033 475 870; e adahotel@adahotel.ba; w adahotel.ba. Ada is the former Swedish ambassador's residence that has been converted into a lovely boutique hotel only 5mins from Baščaršija. This family-owned establishment caters to your every need. The service is kind & pleasant. Rooms are all en suite & have AC, sat TV, internet, minibar. The b/fast is the best in town. **$$**

Hotel Bistrik [108 D4] (16 rooms) Bistrik 34; 033 475 475; e info@hotelbistrik.com; w hotelbistrik.com. From the outside it doesn't look like much. However, this recently built hotel has very comfortable rooms, a pleasant restaurant & amazing views of the old town that is just 100m down the hill. If you arrive with a car make sure to ask for parking as the hotel itself has no parking on site. They can arrange parking for you. **$$–$$$**

Boutique 36 [109 G2] (12 rooms, 1 apt) Safvet-bega Bašagića 36; 033 233 309; e boutique36@gmail.com; w hb36.ba. Boutique 36 epitomises the boutique hotels now emerging in Sarajevo. This concept took a while to catch on but the combination of quaint & chic is here. All rooms are modern with internet, sat TV, minibar & AC. For the quality & location it is a great-value hotel. **$$–$$$**

Hotel Colors Inn Sarajevo [108 B2] (37 rooms) Koševo 8; 033 276 600; e info@colorsinnsarajevo.com; w hotelcolorsinnsarajevo.com. Situated in the centre, this hotel embodies the charm of the city itself. From all the feedback I get, this place gets consistent raving reviews. The foyer & halls may be a bit narrow but the rooms are very comfortable, tastefully decorated & the breakfast is top notch. Service is friendly & everyone speaks English. **$$–$$$**

Hotel Cosmopolit [108 C4] (16 rooms) Radićeva 15; 033 251 100; e hotel.cosmopolit.sa@gmail.com; w cosmopolithotel.com. This very urban hotel just received a facelift after years of being a fairly dull hotel. With its upgraded look & comfort, coupled with its excellent location & free parking, this is a great place to stay in the city centre. All rooms have AC, TV & minibar. Breakfast is included in the price. **$$–$$$**

Hotel Hecco [109 H1] (20 rooms, 2 apts) Medrese 1; 033 273 730; e hotel.hecco@gmail.com; w hotel-hecco.net. Hotel Hecco is a hotel with excellent facilities, including jacuzzis, a parking garage & internet. It is located only a 10min walk north-northeast from the old town. Book ahead, the price for the quality makes it hard to find a room. **$$–$$$**

Isa Begov Hamam Hotel [117 E4] (19 rooms) Bistrik 1; 033 570 050; e info@isabegovhotel.com; w isabegovhotel.com. This hammam stood in ruins since the war of the early 1990s until renovations were completed in 2015, & now this boutique-style hotel is one of finest examples of old Ottoman architecture in the city. The building dates back to the 15th century & is the oldest Turkish bath in the country. The use of the bath is included in the prices. The hotel is located next to the Czar's Mosque so expect a loud call to prayer early in the morning. The room furnishings are truly unique & special with many hand-carved wood ornamental furniture. No alcohol served. **$$–$$$**

Hotel Latinski Most [117 E4] (8 rooms) Obala Isa Bega Isakovića 1; 033 572 660; e info@hotel-latinskimost.com; w hotel-latinskimost.com. This small motel was built between 1881–83. It was renovated in 2011 but kept its original Austro-Hungarian style. The location along the Miljacka River is superb & provides easy access to the old town. The rooms are basic yet comfortable. **$$–$$$**

Hotel Old Town [117 D3] (12 rooms) Čurčiluk mali 11a; 033 574 200; e info@hoteloldtown.ba; w hoteloldtown.ba. Hotel

Old Town is a welcome addition to Baščaršija's accommodation repertoire. The location is in the epicentre of the old town making access to the fun literally at your doorstep. The rooms are modern, all are en suite & have internet. **$$–$$$**

Hotel Opal Home Sarajevo [117 C4] (12 rooms) Despića 4; 033 445 445; **e** info@opalhome.ba; **w** opalhome.ba. In addition to the central location & proximity of the old town, the hotel offers organised tours around the country with professional drivers & guides. The hotel itself is rather tiny, which certainly has its advantages. Customer service is excellent & with only 12 rooms it is easy to get quick & undivided attention. The rooms are very comfortable & tastefully decorated. Sarajevo's narrow streets don't always allow natural light to penetrate directly so ask for the room with the most natural light. The restaurant is quite good with daily lunch specials that are very good value. **$$–$$$**

Hotel VIP [117 C1] (9 rooms) Jaroslava Černija 3; **m** 061 434 383; **e** hotelvipsarajevo@gmail.com; **w** hotelvip.info. This small hotel tries its best to give VIP service. The rooms are spacious & immaculately designed. They offer a free shuttle service to & from the airport. The service is top notch & breakfast is excellent. **$$–$$$**

Djeca Vjetra B&B [109 H1] (4 apts) Donje Biosko 9; **m** 062 877 877; **e** djeca-vjetra@live.com; **w** airbnb.com/rooms/1453686. The Children of the Wind horse farm is a charming & rustic B&B establishment 5km from the centre of Sarajevo in the rolling hills to the northeast of town. They have 8 Arabian horses for riding & can provide riding lessons. Accommodation comprises 3 comfortable & tastefully decorated apartments located in traditional-style houses. The hosts are exceptionally friendly & professional. **$$**

Guesthouse Halvat [109 G2] (10 rooms) Kasima ef Dobrace 5; 033 237 714/5; **e** halvat@bih.net.ba; **w** halvat.com.ba. This is a popular spot with young & 30-something travellers, although not exclusively for them. The Halvat House is near the old town & offers small but comfortable accommodation. There is quite a friendly atmosphere about the place & previous guests always seem to come back. **$$**

Hotel Corner [109 H3] (11 rooms) Telali 19; 033 842 355; **e** mail@hotelcorner.ba; **w** hotelcorner.ba; Situated in the very heart of Baščaršija, Hotel Corner is close to many of the main cultural & historical locations. The name of the hotel may be odd, but the service, amenities, parking & staff are certainly not. The rooms are a bit small but it's hard to beat the location. **$$**

Hotel Villa Orient [117 G2] (20 rooms) Oprkanj; 033 232 754 **e** info@hotelvillaorient.com; **f** hotelvillaorient. If you are looking to get away from the traditional hotel look & feel, then this 'villa' is it. Orient is located in the heart of the old town. Its structure is more like a downtown house than a hotel yet it offers all of the comforts you'd find in other places. The rooms are nicely decorated & the whole building has a classy feel to it. **$$**

Pansion Kandilj [109 G5] (10 rooms) Bistrik (potok) 12a; 033 572 510; **e** info@kandilj.com; **w** kandilj.com. Located on a quiet side street in the Bistrik quarters of the old town, this small but charming B&B has excellent service, cosy rooms & a lovely Ottoman sitting room. **$$**

Samm Šeher Hotel [117 G2] (13 rooms) Savfet-bega Bašagića 34; 033 446 126; **e** stay@sammseherhotel.com; **w** sammseherhotel.com. The old town is booming with new B&Bs. This guesthouse is literally a stone's throw from the centre of the old town. The 300-year-old structure was renovated in 2010 with a classic stone & wood décor. The rooms are basic & a bit small. Be sure to ask for a room not on the main road as it tends to be a bit noisy during the season. **$$**

BUDGET

B&B Le Petit Prince [109 G1] (6 rooms) Safvet-bega Bašagića 55a; 061 868 616; **e** info@lepetitprince.ba; **f** lepetitprincesarajevo. Le Petit Prince offers the feeling of a warm home with comfortable & well-equipped rooms. They even have free parking & special apartments with fireplaces & private balconies. It's no ordinary B&B. They truly have gone out of their way to make it like home but unique & special as well. Book early. **$$**

Hostel City Centre [117 C3] (9 rooms) S H Muvekita 2/3; 033 203 213; **e w** hcc.ba. This comfortable, clean & affordable hostel is located exactly where its name says it is – dead centre. Perfect for budget travellers & those looking to soak up the atmosphere of the younger side of the city. The staff are exceptionally friendly & helpful. They have sgl, dbl & trpl rooms. **$–$$**

Hostel Inn Luxury [117 B2] (3 rooms) Trg Fra Grge Martića 2; 033 841 748; **e** info.hostelinnluxury@gmail.com;

w hostelinnluxury.com. Situated just next to the cathedral on the main promenade in downtown Sarajevo, it's hard to beat a location like this. They have 6- & 8-bed dorms but only 3 bathrooms. The rooms & beds are clean & comfortable with a locker for your things. **$–$$**

Hostel Massimo [109 E3] (7 rooms) Dženetića Čikma 8; 033 953 486; e info@hostel.massimo.ba; w hostel.massimo.ba. Located just behind the Markale market in downtown this pleasant hostel is very good at the customer service side of things. They can organise pretty much anything you like, from tours to laundry services. The rooms are comfortable & clean with modern designs. **$–$$**

Hostel Plaza [109 H2] (8 rooms) Patke bb; m 062 520 000; e hostelplazasarajevo@gmail.com; w hostelplazasarajevo.com. Hostel Plaza offers en-suite private rooms & dormitories with shared bathrooms. Although it may not look entirely inviting from the outside, the facilities are reasonable & definitely clean. There is a summer garden with a terrace. They have a private car park that requires reservations prior to arrival. **$–$$**

Hostel Srce Sarajevo [117 C3] (8 rooms) S H Muvekita 2; 033 442 887; e hostelsrcesarajeva@gmail.com; w hostelsrcesarajeva.freshcreator.com. Located literally next door to the Hostel City Centre & Cheers bar; this street is becoming the place to be for travellers. Srce Sarajevo has a cool interior, Wi-Fi in all rooms, & all the amenities for a comfortable budget travel stay. This hostel certainly ranks amongst the better ones in town. **$–$$**

Hostel Story [117 C3] (12 rooms) Muvekita 4; 033 551 555; e recepcija@hostel-story.com; w story-hotel.com. Comfortable accommodation for individuals & groups located near the major attractions of the city. **$–$$**

Hostel Vagabond [117 B2] (7 rooms) Ferhadija 21; 033 238 811; m 061 794 141; e hostel@vagabond.ba; w vagabond.ba. Vagabond is at the very epicentre of all activities in the central pedestrian zone of Ferhadija St. This is a less than a 50-step walking distance from the old town area. They somehow managed to put a hostel dead smack in the middle of it all & yet offer a quiet & calm refuge from the street noise. Their target group is urban nomads. They are a young, extended family with loads of experience in the hospitality industry, which shows pretty much everywhere, from the spacious, airy rooms to the new bathrooms & fun common area. Good value all the way around. **$–$$**

The Doctor's House [109 E1] (5 rooms) Pehlivanuša 67; m 061 222 914; e doc@thedoctorshousehostel.com; w thedoctorshousehostel.com. This hostel is consistently rated number 1 on TripAdvisor. It is a vibrant place, located just a short walk uphill from the main cathedral in the old town. Modern, simple design is offset by traditional motifs. The hostel is committed to supporting other local businesses. Guests can buy hand-made souvenirs, locally produced domestic products & local, seasonal produce. Both private & dorm rooms have hand-made furniture. The staff are helpful & social. **$**

Hostel Balkan Han [108 D3] (6 rooms) Dalmatinska 6; m 061 538 331; e info@balkanhan.com; w balkanhan.com. It would be fair to say that this is one of the better party hostels in the country. With a beautiful green garden for BBQs, an open air-cinema, & a colourful bar it's a great place to meet locals & travellers alike. The rooms are clean & comfortable (with good mattresses) & the staff are the friendly, artsy type. **$**

Haris Hostel [109 H3] (6 rooms) Vratnik Mejdan 29; m 061 518 825; e info@hyh.ba; w hyh.ba. This hostel, located on Vratnik in the residential area of the old town, has quickly established itself as a favourite amongst backpackers. The family-owned & operated hostel has a small capacity (15 beds) but keeps its guests happy with exceptional hospitality. The hostel is clean & safe & the owners go out of their way to make one's stay a pleasant one. **$**

Identiko [117 F3] (8 rooms) Halači 3; 033 233 310; e identiko@gmail.com; w identiko.blogspot.ba. This is a tiny & inexpensive hostel right in the centre of the old town. The rooms are simple but clean; perfect for young or budget travellers. **$**

Lion Hostel [117 G3] (11 rooms) Bravadžiluk 30; 033 236 137; e lionsarajevo@gmail.com; w lion.co.ba. This hostel is ideally located in the old town. The rooms are quite nice & the owners friendly. There is no b/fast at the hostel. **$**

Ljubičica [117 F1] Mula Mustafe Bašeskije 65; 033 535 829; e taljubic@bih.net.ba; w hostelljubicica.com. One of Sarajevo's earliest established hostels, Ljubićica offers a wide range of services geared for backpackers & low-budget travellers. The hostel is basic with mainly dormitory-style accommodation. They can also place you in a private family home. **$**

Pansion Stari Grad [117 F1] (8 rooms) Bjelina Cikma 4 (Baščaršija); 033 239 898; **e** pansion_starigrad@hotmail.com; **w** sgpansion.co.ba. It may not seem like much from the outside but once you've entered you'll find a home-like atmosphere with pleasant en-suite rooms. There is parking, laundry services & internet. The pansion is tucked away just enough to avoid all the noise of the busy old quarters. **$**

Tower Hostel [109 G2] (12 rooms) Hadžišabanoviča 15; **m** 061 800 263; **e** tower.sarajevo@gmail.com; **w** sartour-hostel-sarajevo.ba. Offers perfect hostel accommodation for backpackers & low-budget travellers. Rooms come in dbl, trpl & dormitory capacity. They are very basic but clean. The hostel also has accommodation in private homes. **$**

Youth Hostel Ferijalac [108 A4] (25 rooms) Omera Stupca 19; 033 207 616; **e** info.ferijalac@gmail.com; **w** fss.ba. This Yugoslav-era youth hostel has received much-needed renovations. All rooms have private showers & free Wi-Fi. It is located just behind the Twin Towers in the city centre, making it an easy walk to the main road & about a 20-min walk to the old town. Rooms are basic but clean. **$**

WHERE TO EAT AND DRINK

Eating in Sarajevo has always been a tasty and affordable experience. For the most part, Sarajevo has a strong selection of mid-range dining with a heavy slant on national cuisine. The national cuisine is a mix of Turkish, central European and southern Slavic. Meat is the centrepiece of eating in Sarajevo, with very few choices for vegetarians or for those who prefer a lighter menu. Increasingly, however, larger restaurants in the centre and in shopping centres offer at least one vegetarian option. Vegan options are not impossible to find, but rare. In general, the cuisine is not super sophisticated but it is exceptionally tasty. In terms of international food on offer, there are a handful of Italian restaurants, and a few others in the above-average category, that serve superb food. Most people seem to find the Sarajevo dining experience good value and its food to be a unique combination of East and West.

For the budget traveller or lover of street food, there is an abundance of cheap, local fast-food places serving hearty portions; many will deliver. Very few international chain restaurants and cafés have made it to Sarajevo, which makes the selection of unique places to choose from vast. Most restaurants serve alcohol, but there are an increasing number of dry establishments. Smoking in bars is allowed, and this is particularly noticeable in the winter when ventilation is not ideal. Many restaurants also allow smoking. There are only a handful of 100% smoke-free places in the city.

Drinking coffee is an important Bosnian pastime, and most cafés are packed day and night. You will rarely see people working alone on their laptops as is the norm in many other cities in Europe. Rather you will witness people there to chat with one another for hours. In fact, when a local person wants to get to know you or catch up, they will usually ask you to go for a coffee, which just means they want to meet up. The actual type of beverage one orders is not important. It is perfectly acceptable to stay as long as you like in any café: for Bosnians, taking one's time with a coffee is almost sacred.

It is important to note that many restaurants are closed on Sundays. Otherwise, opening hours vary. You can count on most restaurants opening their doors for lunch by noon, and staying open until late in the evening. Only a few fast food outlets, bakeries, and pizza places stay open 24/7, including one establishment next to the central bus station.

It is wise to make reservations for popular restaurants in advance. It is also possible to reserve tables at most bars and cafés, and many people do. Many bars and smaller restaurants may be cash only.

Free Wi-Fi is available in just about every restaurant, bar, and café in the city. If the network is not open, ask for the password.

RESTAURANTS

Above average

4 Rooms of Mrs Safija [108 B1] Čekaluša 61; 033 202 745; 10.00–midnight; e info@4sgs.net; w restoransarajevo.com. Quite possibly the finest restaurant in Sarajevo, Mrs Sophie has fantastic, diverse food & superior service. The marinated sea bass with citrus fillets, rocket, purple onion, orange & parsley cream is highly unusual for a Bosnian menu & absolutely delectable. They have an impressive wine cellar, with a nice selection of Italian wines – particularly Barolo & Brunelo reds. $$–$$$

Delikatesna Radnja [108 D4] Obala Kulina bana 10; 033 208 855; e @delikatesnaradnja.ba; w delikatesnaradnja.ba; 08.00–midnight Mon–Sat, 10.30–23.00 Sun. Best to make reservations during the summer or at the w/end for this place. Delikatesna has consistently been one of the best restaurants in Sarajevo. The owner, Mladen, demands the same high-quality cuisine for his customers that he enjoys for himself. The man knows & enjoys his food – so will you. There are 2 buildings next to one another: one is a bar with high-quality snacks, the other is a sit-down restaurant. $$ –$$$

Fiori [108 A3] Antuna Hangija 67; 033 217 265; e fiorisarajevo@gmail.com; 11.00–23.00 Mon–Sat. A bit off the beaten track but easily reached by taxi, this excellent restaurant has great Italian-inspired dishes with fresh ingredients & an excellent offer of Italian wines. The chef cares about the quality & presentation of what is on the plate, & it shows. They often have fresh fish from the Croatian coast. $$–$$$

Karuzo [117 A1] Ulica Dženetića Čimka bb; 033 444 647; e info@karuzorestaurant.com; w restaurantkaruzo.com noon–15.00 and 18.00–23.00 Mon–Fri, 18.00–23.00 Sat. Near the Catholic cathedral & just behind the open fruit & veg market. It's not a fancy place, but the food is always fresh & well prepared. The chef, Sasha, is excellent & very friendly. It's a vegetarian & vegan restaurant, but they serve fish & sushi. As all food is prepared fresh in a small kitchen & the only server is the chef himself, expect to wait longer than usual. $$–$$$

Kimono [108 A4] Vrbanja 1; 033 733 165; e info@kimono.ba; 10.00–22.00 daily. This is one of the few Japanese restaurants in town, located in the Sarajevo City Centre mall downtown. There's a rich menu, including sushi, with a selection of Japanese meals for all budgets. It's on the 3rd floor in the food court. $$–$$$

Libertas [117 D1] Logavina 9; 033 447 830; 08.00–23.00 daily. If it's good seafood you're searching for, look no further. Coined as the Diplomatic Corps restaurant because of frequent visits from ambassadors, Libertas ranks amongst the best restaurants in the country. They have an exceptional wine list, fresh fish arrives daily from the Adriatic coast, & the service is top notch. $$–$$$

Luka [108 C5] Obala Maka Dizdara 8; 033 209 303; e luka.sarajevo@yahoo.com; 10.00–23.00 Mon–Sat. This restaurant is located in the central part of the city along a promenade that follows the Miljacka River. Situated in a funky Austro-Hungarian-era basement, they specialise in fresh fish & seafood. Expect a higher bill if you choose the fish menu as the prices can be rather dear. They also have an equally fine selection of Italian & international dishes. It is neither regular nor unusual to have tambourine players warming up the atmosphere around the tables. $$–$$$

Paper Moon [108 A6] Hamdije Čemerlića 45, Sarajevo; 033 956 939; e info@papermoon.ba; w papermoon.ba; 08.00–23.00 Mon–Sat. One of Sarajevo's newest editions of good restaurants with nice décor and lots of natural light. Opened by a former local football star, Paper Moon is a favourite lunch & dinner spot for both the local & international community in Sarajevo. Try the courgette with mozzarella appetizer. $$–$$$

Tavola [108 D3] Maršala Tita 50; 033 222 207; 08.00–22.00 Mon–Sat. This busy Italian restaurant is located in the heart of the city centre. The food & service are excellent. The pasta dishes are most popular for the business-lunch crowds with luscious meat dishes taking the crown on the dinner menu. It may be a bit hard to find because it's off in a seemingly small alleyway. Be diligent, it'll be worth your while. $$ –$$$

Vinoteka [108 B5] Skenderija 12; 033 214 996; w vinoteka.ba; 11.00–23.00 Mon–Sat, noon–22.00. This spot near the Skenderija Mall serves excellent food with 1st-class service & a special touch of class. It has a largely Italian menu using fresh ingredients. In the basement is a wine bar with the finest selection of wines in town. $$–$$$

Mid range

Bon Appetit [108 A4] Kranjčevićeva 11; m 061 287 618; e: bonappetitsarajevo@gmail.com; w bonappetitsarajevo.weebly.com; noon–22.00 Mon–Sat. Combining the best of European cuisine & Bosnian hospitality, he managed to create one of Sarajevo's best restaurants with professional & friendly service. Most seem happy with pretty much anything they order but the steaks & the burger get rave reviews. It is recommended to reserve a table during the winter period. $$

Brix Bar & Grill [108 A1] Husrefa Redžića 14; 033 211 854; 07.00–23.00 Mon–Thu, 07.00–midnight Fri–Sat, 11.00–21.00 Sun. The owner of this restaurant spent 25 years in the US gathering his culinary experience. When he came back to Sarajevo, he opened this place with the intent to do something different. Most will say he succeeded in his endeavour. Try the pizza with mozzarella, gorgonzola, pears & hazelnuts or try the unique squid calamari here. Prices are also good value. $$

Đulbašča [109 H2] Streljačka bb; 033 241 770; 10.00–23.00 Mon–Sun. If it's peace & quiet you're looking for, to accompany a tasty, good-value meal, you've found it. This family-owned & operated restaurant (mother does the cooking) has great views of the mountains to the east. The local dishes like *klepe* (Bosnian ravioli), *sitni ćevap* (chopped veal) & basically all of their meat dishes are superb. They have a small garden & playground, ideal for bringing the family for a long lunch. $$

Dunja [108 B1] Avde Sumbula 3; 033 214 318; 08.00–23.00 Mon–Sat, noon–23.00 Sun. Tucked away on a quiet street in a central residential neighbourhood, this restaurant offers a gorgeous summer garden with tables under a canopy of trees. The charming interior has an airy feeling. The food is affordable & well-prepared, & there is a wide selection of beverages. $$

Noovi [108 C2] Tina Ujevića 13; 033 222 242; e info@noovi.ba; w noovi.ba; 11.00–23.00 Mon–Sat. It's hard to decipher which is better at Noovi, the wine selection or the food. Most people come for both. Noovi's pizza claims to be amongst the best in town & the salmon dishes are fresh & wonderfully tasty. It's a perfect lunch or dinner spot, located behind the big park across from the BBI Centre. $$

SuperFood Sarajevo [108 A1] Husrefa Redžića 14, Sarajevo; 033 977 797; e tickyg@gmail.com; 11.00–22.00 Tue–Sat, noon–18.00 Sun. It may be difficult to find but it is a very short ride from the main street in Sarajevo. Superfood has an excellent menu & good service. They claim to have one of the most original & diverse menus in town. It is more of a casual lunch or dinner spot, with a summer terrace open May–Oct. The Moroccan lamb burger is truly amazing. $$

Dveri [111 F2] Prote Bakovića 12; 033 537 020; e info@dveri.co.ba; w dveri.co.ba; 08.00–23.00 daily. To enter this restaurant, turn off Sarači (the main promenade in Baščaršija) & walk through a small passage. Dveri is tiny but consistently full, & for good reason. They serve excellent cuisine, with great soups, homemade breads, & probably the only place in the old town that serves pork. The polenta with smoked beef is also a house speciality. It's a cosy atmosphere for a dinner with friends. There is no outside seating. $–$$

Global Food [108 A1] Braće Begić 6 (Koševsko brdo); m 061 274 955; e bizafood@gmail.com; 17.00–23.00 Mon–Fri. The name speaks for itself. It's one of several places in Sarajevo serving falafel & Middle Eastern cuisine, as well the chef's own unique recipes. It's got great atmosphere, earthy décor & the service is good. $–$$

Imidž-T [108 A1] Semizovac bb, Semizovac; 08.00–23.00 daily. A bit out of the way but certainly worth the drive. Located near the town of Semizovac in natural surroundings this is certainly one of the finest traditional restaurants around. It's a 20–30min drive northwest from the centre of town on the main road towards Olovo. $–$$

Inat kuća [109 H3] Veliki Alifakovac 1 (old town); 033 447 867; e kenan.niksic@gmail.com; w inatkuca.ba; 11.00–23.00 daily. This is a place most people visit while in Sarajevo. The food is good but feedback from guests reports the service is consistently so-so. Do try the *begova corba* (beg's soup); it is said to be the best in town. It's truly a great taste of local foods in an authentically Bosnian ambience. $–$$

✕ **Kibe Mahala** [109 G1] Vrbanjusa 164; ☏ 033 441 936; **w** kibemahala.ba; ⌚ 11.00–23.00 Mon–Sat. This is one of those 'do not miss' restaurants. If you come to Sarajevo, you have to dine at Kibe's once. The local food is tremendous – served in a light atmosphere with spectacular views & live music. The lamb dishes are excellent as are most of the traditional Bosnian dishes. **$–$$**

✕ **Klopa** [109 E3] Ferhadija 5, Sarajevo; ☏ 033 223 633; ⌚ 08.00–23.00 Mon–Sat, 08.00–20.00 Sun. One of the most cheerful restaurants in the city, it is described as the 'eternal spring' by locals. It is green, funky, comfy, well-lit & t-a-s-t-y. It was opened by a famous Sarajevo architect & is run by his children. The food is a mix of traditional Bosnian with a modern twist & new age. The service is quick & staff are very friendly. In short, it's a great place for a laid-back lunch or light dinner. A definite plus is the affordable prices. **$–$$**

✕ **Lovački Dom** [108 A1] Nahorevo 10 (in the hills near Sarajevo); ☏ 033 670 819; **w** lovackidom.com; ⌚ 11.00–21.00, daily. This traditional restaurant has set the standard for homemade cooking. Located in the gorgeous Naherevo Valley, surrounded by mountains only a 15min drive north from the city centre. The grilled lamb, trout, beignets & young cheese are the house specialities. **$–$$**

✕ **Park Prinčeva** [109 G5] Iza Hrida 7; **m** 061 222 708; **e** info@parkprinceva.ba; **w** parkprinceva.ba; ⌚ 09.00–23.00, daily. This place will dazzle you with not only the best view in town but with great food & live traditional music. The service is 1st class with a good wine selection & great traditional meals. **$–$$**

✕ **Pivnica** [109 H4] Franjevačka 15 (old town); **m** 062 318 624; **e** info@pivnica-sarajevo.ba; **w** pivnica-sarajevo.ba; ⌚ 08.00–02.00 daily. The old Sarajevo brewery in the Bistrik neighbourhood near the Franciscan Monastery of St Ante has a cozy, central European ambiance. They have built a great brewery restaurant with good food, great beer (try the unfiltered Sarajevsko) & a fun atmosphere. It is visited by both locals & foreigners alike & is a favourite place to be for long eating & drinking sessions. **$–$$**

✕ **To be** [117 E3] Čizmedžiluk 5; ☏ 033 233 265; ⌚ 11.00–23.00 daily. One of Sarajevo's best-kept secrets. This tiny eatery, on a quiet side street, has a superb ambience for a romantic dinner downtown. The menu is created from the owners' collection of recipes from around Europe. They offer several hearty vegetarian meals & the fantastic soups are made from scratch. **$–$$**

Cheap & cheerful

✕ **Avlija** [108 B1] Avde Sumbula 2; ☏ 033 444 483; **e**; **w** avlija.ba; ⌚ 08.00–23.00, Mon–Sat. Avlija means garden. Great little place for inexpensive food & drink. They serve mainly sandwiches & burger-type meals with a few salads to choose from. The atmosphere is always comfy & laid back; both locals & expats frequent the place. **$–$$**

✕ **Barhana** [117 E2] Đulagina Čikma 8; ☏ 033 447 727; **w** barhana.ba; ⌚ 10.00–midnight Mon–Sat, noon– midnight Sun. Hidden in a courtyard off the main walkway in Baščaršija, Barhana – a restaurant & bar – is a local institution. Perhaps better known for their many flavours of homemade *rakija* (brandy) & late-night fun, Barhana is an excellent spot for lunch. The sandwiches & pizzas are great & it's a lovely atmosphere in the summer garden. **$–$$**

✕ **Pod Lipom** [117 F2] Prote Bakovića 4; ☏ 033 440 700; **e** info@podlipom.ba; **w** podlipom.ba; ⌚ 08.00–23.00 Mon–Sat. A must-do dining experience when in Sarajevo. This good-value traditional restaurant serves all the classic Bosnian dishes at remarkable prices. Try the *solgan dolma* (stuffed onions), *sitni cevap* (diced veal stew) or *bamija* (okra) **$–$$**

✕ **Aquarius Club** [108 A4] Vilsonovo Šetalište; **m** 061 210 788; **e** aquariussarajevo@gmail.com; **w** aquariusvils.com; ⌚ 08.00–midday Mon–Wed & Sun, 08.00–02.00 Thu–Sat. Although not primarily a restaurant, there is a decent offer of sandwiches & light meals on the menu during the day. In the evening it reinvents itself into one of Sarajevo's most popular bars with frequent good music gigs. You might want to reserve a place. Located on a tree-lined avenue along the river, near the Importanne Centar mall. **$**

✕ **Aščinica ASDž** [117 D3] Čurčiluk mali 3; ☏ 033 238 500; ⌚ 08.00–19.00 daily. The concept of the *aščinica* is ideal for someone looking to try a large sampling of traditional Bosnian-home cooking for low prices. *Aščinicas* serve a wide selection of ready-made classical dishes, usually with a menu that varies slightly from day to day. It is sort of like a high-quality cafeteria, where you can eye the day's offerings & choose your portions. ASDž is always good & its central location on one of the little streets behind Hotel Europe makes it one of the most popular *aščinicas*. There is usually a vegetarian option. No alcohol served. $

Buregdžinica Bosna [117 F3] Bravadžiluk bb; 033 538 426 (old town); 08.00–22.00 Mon–Sat. The traditional pitta dish can be found all over Bosnia & Herzegovina & particularly in Sarajevo's old town. Migrant Albanians from Macedonia & Kosovo are famous for their bakeries & pitta places – Bosna is amongst the best around. A portion of pitta with homemade yoghurt costs from 3KM – it's good eating. $

Buregdžinica Sač [117 F3] Just off Bravadžiluk in the old town; 08.00–22.00. *Ispod sača* means 'dutch oven' & here they prepare the traditional pitta under hot coals. It's absolutely delicious. $

Cakum-pakum [108 D3] Kaptol 10; 033 838 690; m 061 955 310; e: cakumpakum777@gmail.com; 11.00–23.00 daily. Another great addition to the city's funky places to hang out & dine. They are becoming famous for 2 very different reasons – sweet & savoury crêpes & their pasta dishes. Good value! $

Club Obala [108 D4] Obala Kulina bana 11; m 061 575 556; clubobala; 08.00–midnight, Mon–Sat. A cult locale for the young artist types in Sarajevo, recently renovated & situated in the Academy of Performing Arts building. They have a large menu with reasonable prices. More popular as a lunch or evening drinking spot, the kitchen is open till around 20.00, so get there early if you want dinner. $

Kod Bibana [109 G5] Hošin brijeg 95; 033 232 026; e; kodbibana; 09.00–22.00. If you're looking for a beautiful view, simple & inexpensive traditional food then take the taxi ride up to Bibana in Hrid. $–$$

Metropolis [108 C3] Maršala Tita 21; 033 203 315; e info@metropolis.ba; w metropolis.ba; 08.00–23.00 daily. Metropolis is one of Sarajevo's most popular downtown eateries, offering b/fast, great salads, choose-your-own-sauce dishes & mouth-watering cakes & ice cream. You should visit here at least once during your stay. $

Nanina Kuhinja [117 F3] Kundurdžiluk 35; 033 533 333; 08.00–23.00 daily. Grandma's kitchen is the perfect good-value lunch spot in the Baščaršija part of the old town. Serving well-prepared & affordable meals, Grandma won't disappoint you. The green bean & meat dish is excellent as are most of Nanina Kuhinja's traditional meals. $

Pirpa [108 D4] Čobanija 2; 033 208 183, 033 223 552; 24hrs Mon–Sat. Some would argue that Pirpa has the best doner in the city. The kebabs and falafel are definitely tasty. It's one of the few all-night venues to keep the hungry late-nighters happy. It's the Sarajevan equivalent to a midnight fish & chip shop. Cheap & tasty. $

Snogu [108 D5] Čobanija 4; m 062 501 378; 07.00–midnight daily. As the name itself indicates – 'while standing' – this is a great street wok bar for grabbing a bite on the go when you have no time to enjoy a long meal. There's a surprisingly rich wok offer which makes this fast food stand out from its competition. $

Željo [117 E3] Kundurdžiluk 19; 10.00–21.00. Most locals will say you haven't visited Sarajevo until you've tried Željo's famous *ćevapi* (lamb & beef sausages). They are so popular that they've opened up 2 restaurants right next to each other. $

CAFÉS

Bečka Kafana [117 C3] Vladislava Skarića 5; 033 580 400; 08.00–23.30 daily. An old Sarajevo institution. Located in the Hotel Europe, Sarajevo's first hotel built during Austro-Hungarian rule at the beginning of the 20th century, this café was always a favourite spot for the intellectual elite to chat, read newspapers or simply just be. Today it's a melange of locals & foreigners, often meeting for business or to sit & surf on the free Wi-Fi.

Buybook [108 C4] Radićeva 4 (centre); 033 550 495; e info@buybook.ba; w buybook.ba; 09.00–20.00 Mon–Fri, 10.00–18.00 Sat. This café, book & music store is where many of the local writers & artists hang out. It is a very laid-back place & you're more than welcome to grab a book & read while drinking your coffee. The music selection is always a step ahead of the rest.

Ćulhan [117 F2] Ćulhan bb (old town). The 'for everyone' café in Baščaršija. Situated in the heart of the old town it's a great outdoor café for the spring & summer months. It's closed when the cold weather comes.

Halvat [117 F2] Male Daire Sq, Luledžina 6; ⌚ 08.00–23.00 daily. This is one of Sarajevo's best-kept secrets. It's hidden in a narrow alley directly east of the Sebilj Fountain in Baščaršija. Here you can enjoy a lovely Ottoman atmosphere with oriental teas & coffees, *shisha* water pipes, Ottoman décor & fresh juices. It's a favourite hangout for university students as well as those looking to just chill out & get away from the bustle of the *čaršija*.

Manolo [108 D3] Maršala Tita 23; ☎ 033 205 058; ⌚ 08.00–23.00. Located right in the middle of one of Sarajevo's main thoroughfares, this café has a chic, young vibe with a very large assortment of non-alcoholic beverages, plus food & sweets. The enormous summer garden in the backyard has a chill, funky set up.

Rahatlook [117 D2] Ferhadija 41; ☎ 033 921 461; f rahatlook.sarajevo; ⌚ 09.00–22.00 daily. Located just behind the Jewish *hram* in the old town, Rahatlook is the perfect place for a quiet healthy drink & a snack with friends. They serve a wide array of teas, coffees & fresh juices coupled with their secret recipes for great cakes & snacks.

Sevdah House [117 F3] Halači 5, Velike Daire; ☎ 033 239 943; e info@artkucasevdaha.ba; ⌚ 10.00–18.00 Tue–Sun. If you've never heard traditional Bosnian music & would like a small taste, accompanied by some fresh rose or elderflower juice, make the time to check out Sevdah kuća. The café doubles as a museum of the great *sevdah* legends of the last century. The Bosnian coffee here is very good & is always served with *rahatlokum* (Turkish delight). There is occasional live music, ask the waiter for the week's schedule.

Spazzio Café [108 C4] Radićeva 11; ☎ 033 209 226; ⌚ 07.00–23.00 Mon–Sat, 09.00–22.00 Sun. Coffee only the Italians can do. Spazzio is on the infamous Radićeva street amongst at least 10 other cafés. Why go here then? Like I said, the coffee is *bellisimo*. Sandwiches & snacks are not only tasty but good value as well & there are gluten-free, lactose-free, and vegan options. It's a very comfortable & relaxing place for a morning or afternoon coffee.

Vatra [108 D3] Ferhadija 4; ☎ 033 222 244; e info@vatra.ba; w vatra.ba; ⌚ 08.00–midnight Mon–Sat, 09.00–23.00 Sun. Whether you're looking for a quiet & relaxing coffee in the back garden or to people-watch along the busiest streets in Sarajevo – Vatra's got both. It is well known for its super tasty cakes & sweets, but the savoury side of the kitchen is pretty impressive as well. It's an ideal place for a lunch snack or a sweet fix, & as for the people-watching – probably not a better place in town.

SLASTIČARNICE (CAKE SHOPS)

Baklava Shop Sarajevo [117 F3] Čurčiluk veliki 56; m 061 267 428; ⌚ 08.30–22.30. Lovers of baklava won't be disappointed. This place has a diverse selection of the mouth-watering, expertly crafted pastries. The pistachio triangles seem to disappear pretty fast. Tea, coffee, & indoor/outdoor seating areas make this a great place to people – watch while gaining weight.

Egipat [117 B2] Ferhadija (old town). Legendary for its ice cream. Some Italians were so impressed by the vanilla ice cream that they offered to pay big money for the recipe. The owners refused, leaving Egipat with the magic potion that keeps the Sarajevans in long queues over the summer.

Maison Coco Artisan Bakery [108 A4] Kranjčevićeva 4A, & Branilaca Sarajeva 10 [108 D4]; ☎ 033 668 558; e maisoncocosarajevo@gmail.com; f francuskapekara; ⌚ 07.00–20.00 Mon–Sat. The only truly French bakery in Sarajevo, this also happens to serve likely the best bread in town. A wide variety of artisanal loafs & an array of beautiful, seasonal pastries may result in repeat visits. The Kranjčevićeva location is larger, with more variety. Take a machine-made coffee to go or sit at a small table outdoors. Gluten-free bread can be ordered a day in advance.

Palma [108 A5] Palma Porodice Ribara 5 (Grbavica); ☎ 033 714 700; e info@palma.ba; w palma.ba; ⌚ 08.00–23.00 Mon–Sat. Old traditions never die in Sarajevo. Palma is one of Sarajevo's most prestigious & well-known cafés/sweet shops. Amidst the shrapnel-riddled buildings of Grbavica the beautiful fountain in Palma's summer garden stands out like spring blossom. You may think it's just a café but Palma is really so much more.

Planeta [117 G3] Bravadžiluk bb (old town); ⌚ 08.00–22.00 Mon–Sat. Not only a great place for sweets & strong espresso, but also a perfect place for people-watching.

Ramis [117 D2] Sarači (old town); ⌚ 08.00–22.00 Mon–Sat. Along the main Ferhadija walkway, at the point it changes to

Sarači, Ramis is probably one of the most famous of all the sweet shops in town. The amount of traffic that goes through there amazes me. The cakes & sweets are mostly traditional & are a bargain for the low price of 1–2KM per cake.

Slatko ćoše [117 D2] Sarači; 08.00–22.00 Mon–Sat. Located across from Ramis (opposite), the two are not at all in competition with each other, & both places are usually full. Slatko ćoše tends to be a bit more smoky than Ramis, but the sweets are good & it has a better outside seating arrangement.

Stari Grad [117 E2] Sarači (old town); 08.00–22.00 Mon–Sat. Near the end of the promenade towards Sebilj. May be second in the running against Egipat (opposite).

Torte i to [108 C4] BBI Centre, Gazi-Husrev Begova 61; 033 717 176; **e** info@torte-i-to.ba; **w** torte-i-to.ba; 08.00–23.00 Mon–Sat, noon–22.00 Sun. The cheesecake is so good they even claim it's better than New York's. As a New Yorker, I might tend to agree with them. For proper cappuccinos, proper service & an overall proper time, Torte i to is very good at paying attention to the details. Service is great, the cake to die for, coffee is always good & it has a non-smoking & child-friendly sitting area. Don't miss the views from the terrace.

ENTERTAINMENT AND NIGHTLIFE

BARS

Baghdad [117 E3] Čurčiluk veliki by Željo; 10.00–midnight, daily. Resembling the brighter side of the real Baghdad, the Arabic-style bar is a bit more upscale. They serve good cocktails as well as *shisha* (flavoured tobacco water pipes). Open late & DJs in the summer party months.

Blind Tiger [108 D3] Dalmatinska 2; 033 849 522; 07.00–01.00 daily. This 2-level bar has a fantastic list of cocktails & various types of burgers, including veggie. If your cocktail of choice is not on their list, the bartenders will do their best to whip it up for you. Please be patient: certain ingredients are hard to come by in this town. If you're aiming for a drink with an unusual ingredient that has to be imported, you might not be able to obtain the exact mix you are looking for.

The Brew Pub [108 A3] Kranjčevićeva 18; **m** 061 709 565; 16.00–23.45 daily. This is possibly the first independent craft brewery to open in Sarajevo. Serving homemade & other craft brews, & savoury things to chomp on, this place has the vibe of a modern American pub, with minimalist-style furnishings & high ceilings. It's a 5-min walk from the main bus station.

Cafe Tito [108 A4] Behind National Museum & Revolution Museum (Marijin Dvor), Zmaja od Bosne 5; **m** 061 208 881; 07.00 until guests leave, daily. A great local hangout. It's a bit out of the centre, which pretty much guarantees an exclusively local crowd. It's named after the late Josip Broz Tito & pays tribute to the 'good ol' days' of Yugoslavia. Local folks, local prices, good atmosphere (very smoky). Great family-friendly summer garden with a small play area.

Cheers [117 C3] Mukevita 4; 08.00–05.00 daily. According to most, Cheers ranks high in the best-bar category for Sarajevans. With live music at w/ends & a great location on a small side street in the heart of the city centre, it's the perfect place for the afternoon or evening pint.

City Pub [117 C4] Despiceva bb; 033 209 789; **e** kontakt@citypub.ba; 08.00–05.00 daily. Perhaps the most happening place in town. It was converted from a Lebanese restaurant to a hopping city bar. It's a great lunch spot during the day & at night is quite packed with a good mix of foreign & local hipsters. Live music most w/ends.

Gastro Pub Vučko [108 C3] Radićeva 10; 033 208 028; 08.00–midnight daily. Opened in summer 2016, this place is already becoming one of Sarajevo's most talked about bars. It's the first place in Sarajevo dedicated exclusively to serving the increasingly wide range of craft brews from the ex-Yugoslav region & beyond. There are over 60 brews to choose from, along with other drinks. Tucked behind a building across the street from BBI shopping centre, it is easy to miss – but that would be a mistake. There's a semi-open air space for warm nights. The waiting staff are excellent.

Guinness Pub [117 C2] Old town; 10.00–02.00 daily. No town would be complete without an Irish pub. Located just off the Ferhadija walkway it serves many foreign beers & has Guinness, naturally, on draught.

Hacienda [117 E3] Bazardžani 3; 10.00–03.00 daily. This place doubles as a hopping bar by late night & decent Mexican restaurant by day & early evening. Upstairs is a comfy & laid-back restaurant sitting area. Come evening time, Hacienda is one of the most popular (& crowded) bars in town.

Kino Bosna [108 A3] Alipašina 19; kinobosna; m 061 866 946; 17.30–midnight Mon–Sat. I figured I owed it to the alternative crowd to add a few local 'dives' & this is certainly one of them. It's a smoky place with no ventilation that often has the aroma of a crowded English pub on a Fri night. It's almost always packed with hip locals & the beer is amongst the cheapest in town. Mondays are most popular & crowded, with a crew of local guys playing old-time folk songs starting around 20.00.

Meeting Point [108 D5] Hamdije Kreševljakovića 13 (centre); 033 668 186; e info@kinomeetingpoint.ba; w kinomeetingpoint.ba; 08.00–23.00 Mon–Sat, 15.00–23.00 Sun. The main location during the Sarajevo Film Festival. It's a great local hangout, usually for the 20–30-year-old range. It also doubles as a cinema & cultural space.

Vinoteka Dekanter [108 C4] Radićeva 4; 033 263 815; 10.00–midnight Mon–Sat, 18.00–midnight Sun. If you're seeking the widest selection of regional & international wines to try by the glass or by the bottle, look no further. This is the most extensive wine bar in Sarajevo. They have outdoor tables facing the tree-lined street & a swanky, cosy interior for chilly evenings. If you like to nibble something while savouring a glass of wine, you can order cheeses, smoked & dried meats, bruschetta & other cold appetisers.

Zlatna ribica [108 D3] Kaptol 5; zlatnaribica.goldfish; 09.00–23.00 daily. This small hideaway has a fantastic atmosphere. The music is a great mix of blues, jazz & occasional soul. You'll usually get a surprise snack with your drink. I've yet to meet someone who didn't dig the décor.

NIGHTCLUBS

☆ **Jazz Club Monument** [117 B3] Štrosmajerova 3; 033 209 660; w clubmonument.ba; 08.00–02.00 daily. For lovers of jazz, fusion & other creative music, this is the place to be. Located deep in a basement near the central cathedral, this cosy place boasts an impressive & lively line-up several nights a week. Reservations are recommended if you want a seat. There is usually a modest cover charge.

☆ **Silver&Smoke** [117 A4] Zelenih beretki 12. With superb DJs & a reputation to match, Silver&Smoke is the late-night destination in Sarajevo. Starting somewhere around midnight, the party goes till the fat lady sings. Great music, great crowd, good times.

☆ **Sloga** [108 C3] Mehmeda Spahe 20 (centre); 033 218 811; 18.00–05.00 daily. The 'Mecca' of old-school Sarajevo bars & clubs. With 3 floors it has a more folk & acoustic touch to the 1st floor. On the 2nd floor is the concert hall & bar where local & foreign bands play every week. The 3rd floor is dedicated to the Yugo-nostalgics. Cheap beer & simple service are what you'll get – an authentic taste of a pre-war bar in Sarajevo.

SHOPPING

Aside from the plethora of handmade souvenirs in the old part of town, Sarajevo has an ancient tradition of handicrafts in leather, metal, wood, textiles, shoes, gold, carpets and rugs … and just about any practical thing you can think of. Many of these trades were brought here from Persia and Turkey during the Ottoman period, as well as from Dubrovnik, or ancient Ragusa. It wasn't too long ago that Sarajevans made almost everything they needed in life, from the basic necessities to luxury items for the more fortunate. This tradition has been passed down through many generations, from father to son and mother to daughter. Unfortunately, as tourism has increased in Sarajevo, so have the number of shops selling imported goods that merely resemble the craft and quality of an original. Still, for the discerning eye, it is possible to find many authentic goods.

The more modern styles in clothes and shoes are mainly from western Europe and are usually the kind of things you can buy at home. However, you may find some high-quality Italian shoes at much cheaper prices than you'd find elsewhere. The true value of shopping in Sarajevo though is in the old crafts known as *stari zanati* in Bosnian. These were introduced by the Turks in the mid 15th century. As the trade centre in the old town developed, certain streets became 'blacksmith' streets and others 'goldsmith' streets. In time each craft was located in a particular part of town as is seen today. You'll find Kazazi Street named after the silk tailors, Kazandžiluk named after the coppersmiths and Mudželeti named after the bookbinders. Each craft was headed by a master craftsman or *cehaja* and they formed official bodies, representing their crafts to the local government.

Baščaršija is filled with shops of the *stari zanati*. Prices for handmade goods are very reasonable and local vendors are usually willing to bargain with you. When compared with prices at home for handmade goods, the craft shops in Sarajevo are a steal. Take advantage of it! Bezistan, on the main Ferhadija walkway, is a small Ottoman-style market space slightly below street level with many shops selling knock-off goods and inexpensive souvenirs. The entire area around Sebilj is lined with shops.

If you're looking for **oriental spices** and some amazing **sweets and nuts** then pay a visit to Butik Badem [117 F3] on Abadžiluk 12 and on Maršala Tita 12 [108 C3]. The Turkish delights and candied almonds are something you've got to try. I promise you'll find something you fancy there.

For those of you on a mission to find oriental or Bosnian **rugs and carpets** there are many shops in the old town that specialise in *čilims* (hand-woven rugs). Bulbul [109 F3] on Abadžiluk 13a are very knowledgeable and have a variety of old and new rugs from Bosnia and around the Balkans. Isfahan Gallery [117 E2] on Sarači 57 and 77, one located inside Morića Han, is run by an art historian. He's an enthusiastic gentleman with loads of information on the origins of Persian art and rugs. Kiko [117 F2] on Trgovke 19 in Baščaršija has a nice selection of new and used rugs. They are local specialists and also have a repair service.

Gift and souvenir shops are in abundance in the old town. Some of the best handmade gift shops are run by women's clubs or refugee consortiums. The BHcrafts, Fair Trade knitwear shop [117 D3], on Čurčiluk veliki 8, sells handmade sweaters, gloves, scarves and toys made by Bosnian women. Logo Asian Trading Co [109 F2] on Abadziluk is run by a member of the International Women's Club and deals in neat lamps, mirrors, dishes and jewellery. An unemployed **art** teacher named Vahida Ključa creates lovely pictures of old town settings made out of corn stalks and dried flowers. She doesn't have a shop but you can email her (**e** *vahida@yahoo.com*) or phone (**✆** *033 457 526*) to view her work. I came across her art at a Christmas bazaar run by the women's club and bought presents for my whole family from her. Mirza Huntić has an art workshop [117 E3] (**✆** *033 537 165*) on Čurčiluk veliki 37 in the old town. He does excellent framing and has a unique collection of local paintings for sale. He speaks fluent English as well. Some new shops have opened selling trendier handmade crafts, accessories and garments made by Bosnian artists. One shining example with high-quality, trendy local designs (copper and silver jewellery, clothing, linens, cutting boards with geometric shapes hand-crafted from reclaimed wood by local artisans at Waga Wood, and more) is Bazerdžan (*Čurčiluk veliki 12;* **m** *061 227 192*).

There are three English-language **bookshops** in town: Buybook [108 C4] on Radićeva 4; Šahinpašić [108 A1] on Koševo 44; and Connectum (Klub Knjige) [117 E3] on Čurčiluk veliki 27. Buybook has a decent collection of English books about the war, and local authors translated into English.

The BBI Centar [108 C3], Alta, Importanne Centar and Sarajevo City Center are Sarajevo's best and most modern **shopping centre** attractions. Alta, Importance and City Centre malls are all located just off the map on pages 108–9 to the west. BBI is located in the centre of town near the Presidency building on Maršala Tita Street. The eight-storey building offers five floors of modern shopping and eateries. Although there are many Western brand shops and boutiques, BBI is also home to several locally owned boutiques and gift shops and a lovely café on the roof, with a view of the city and the surrounding hills. It's well worth the visit if it's shopping you're looking for. Alta is located just across the street from the Parliament building and next to the Holiday Inn. This American shopping centre is an almost exclusively Western brand mall with many high-street names and Vapiano, the Italian-style chain restaurant. Sarajevo City Center, offering even more name-brand stores, is right across the street. It is one of the most conspicuous new buildings in town, with an enormous flashing screen as a façade, showing commercials through the day and night. The blinding lights from the screen can be seen even from some surrounding hills, not to mention from the living rooms of the poor souls residing across the street. Importanne is on Zmaja od Bosne, just next door to the National Museum and across the road from the American Embassy. Working hours vary, but most stores are open until 22.00.

There are a few fabulous **little shop**s around town that sell all-natural or organic local products like liqueurs, honey, jams, cheese, yoghurt, fresh produce, pasta, herbal tea, etc. One is Špajz (meaning 'pantry') [108 B2] on Koševo 28, about a 5-minute walk from BBI Shopping Centre (☎ *033 941 403]; ⌚ 09.00–18.00 Mon–Fri, 09.00–14.00 Sat*). It is a really cute place that is fun just to browse. Kuća Zdrave Hrane [109 E4] (House of Healthy Food; ☎ *033 208 428; ⌚ 08.00–20.00 daily*) is another. Located at Branilaca Sarajevo 30, it is quite near the centre of town. The German chain store DM (⌚ *varies depending on the location, but usually from 09.00–21.00 Mon–Sat*) is all over town. Although it is a primarily for cosmetics and household goods, it is a great place to buy gluten-free, organic, and health foods, mainly dry goods. For affordable, delicious Bosnian craft chocolates (try the pralines!) made Belgian-style, visit Mak Zara on the ground floor of the Alta shopping centre or the second floor of BBI shopping centre.

WHAT WE DON'T KNOW IN THE WEST

During the war I visited a family living in the mainly Muslim quarter of Bistrik. Their house was very close to the front line and we had to sit in the dark (there was no electricity anyway) so the snipers could not see us. An old man stared at me from across the room and I could see he had something to say to me. He eventually made his way across the room and spoke softly: 'Son, just down there in Baščaršija is a shoemaker who has a wife and two children. One morning a customer walks into his shop and wants to buy a pair of shoes. The shop owner replied: "Thank you for your business, sir, but my neighbour also makes good shoes and he too has a wife and two children. I have already sold a pair of shoes this morning; please buy from him so that he may take care of his family."' The old man paused and then unaccusingly continued: 'That, son, you don't know in the West. That is the way we grew up and that is how things need to be.' The sense of community in the *čaršija* is quite remarkable. It carries a piece of the past that reminds us of what it means to take care of each other and look out for our neighbours. This rule may not hold true for everyone in Baščaršija, but it is this type of tradition that makes the Sarajevo experience such a special one.

OTHER PRACTICALITIES

Sarajevo is like most capital cities in eastern and southeastern Europe. There are a plethora of banks and ATMs throughout the city. There are several in and around BBI shopping centre for example, and countless on the main streets of the city, particularly along Ferhadija and Maršala Tita. Credit and debit cards are accepted in many places but not in all, so it's always good to check beforehand. If you purchase something in a shop, be aware that it will most likely be impossible to return it for a refund, however, most larger stores allow you to exchange items within seven days for something of equal or lesser value. Any of the basic and regular amenities one needs, from banks to medical care to access to information, is readily available in Sarajevo. If one has a serious condition that requires medication, it is advised to bring your supply with you: while pharmacies in Sarajevo are probably reliable, counterfeit medicine has been known to be sold. Although Sarajevo is generally rather safe, it is like any city and it is important to be cautious. There are notorious pick-pockets on the trams. Wherever you go, but especially on isolated streets, it is wise not to unnecessarily expose expensive electronic equipment. Car robberies are the most common crime. Never leave anything of importance in a parked car, and it is advisable to remove your radio and make sure there is nothing out on the seat to tempt a thief. The recreational areas and parking areas on Mount Trebević to the northeast of the city are a hotspot for car thefts. Stray dogs are a problem in Sarajevo. Some are harmless and just looking for a friend, but others may become aggressive. Local people are generally helpful and friendly, and for some people it is a cultural point of pride to help others. Free Wi-Fi is available in many establishments. You can purchase a local SIM card at a kiosk for 5KM, including some free minutes. To add additional minutes, ask the kiosk vendor.

CLINICS & PHARMACIES

Accident & emergency ('Hitna pomoć') Kolodvorska 14; 033 611 111/124; e hitnabih@yahoo.com; w hitnasa.com

Poliklinika Sa Na Sa Grbavička 74; 033 661 840; e poliklinikasanasa@smartnet.ba; w poliklinikasanasa.com

Sarajevo Pharmacy Saliha Hadžihuseinovića Muvekita 11; 033 722 660; e centrala@apoteke-sarajevo.ba; w apoteke-sarajevo.ba. There is at least one pharmacy in every municipality open 24 hours.

POLICE

Police station [108 A4] Augusta Brauna 5; 033 226-676; 24 hours

POST OFFICE

Central post office [117 D3] Obala Kulina bana 8; 033 252 834; 07.00–20.00 Mon–Sat

TRAVEL AGENT

Fibula Travel Agency [108 D4] Ferhadija 24; 033 570 700; 09.00–20.00 Mon–Fri, 09.00–15.00 Sat

WHAT TO SEE AND DO

Although Sarajevo, simply by default, is a fascinating place to visit, the city has done a good job in recent years of improving its facilities and providing more information to tourists on what to do and see. One of the first things to do in Sarajevo is to get one's bearings. There's no better way than the walking tour followed by the bus tour of the city.

CITY-CENTRE WALKING TOURS (This route is marked on the Sarajevo maps, pages 108–9 and 117) Sarajevo city centre continues its 20-year face-lift and the city has come on in leaps and bounds. There are walkways throughout the entire city centre that used to be jammed with vehicles and festooned with horrendous pot-holes. Have no fear though, there are still plenty of pot-holes and illegally parked vehicles blocking pedestrians. New façades in the centre have brought back the old charm to the Austro-Hungarian-era walkway on Ferhadija. The main roads have also been repaved, making driving a much more pleasant experience than it used to be. More time, energy and resources have been invested in parks and green areas. When strolling through Sarajevo, try to imagine a city that basically didn't have a single intact window, was marred with shrapnel holes in every building, and had cut down most of its trees to heat and cook with. Thank goodness, those days are over.

Most of a walking tour through Sarajevo centres around the old town, Baščaršija, and Marijin Dvor – all of which lies in the flat valley of the Miljacka River. There are a few sites, however, that require a considerable uphill walk. The old narrow streets above Baščaršija are well worth the wander, but for those not up for the steep trek to places like **Jajce Barracks** [109 H3] (Eugene of Savoy Castle) and the ruins of the medieval town, there are local buses and car tours. The views of the whole city from this area are spectacular. Otherwise a walking tour of the main sites can be done in about 3 hours depending on your pace and number of café stops. There are several city guides but the best of the certified ones can be found via the tourist information centre on Zelenih Beretki 22a.

The full-loop walk through the central area covers about 4–5km at most. The downtown area is all flat and easy to navigate. If you include the Vratnik area and decide to walk up to the top of the hill for the spectacular views, then add on a few more hours.

It's probably wiser to start in the hilly area above the old town if you opt to see **Jajce Barracks** and the ruins of the medieval city. Local bus 51 to Vratnik leaves hourly from the main taxi, bus and tram station in Baščaršija near Sebilj (fountain square, also known locally as 'pigeon square'). You know you've arrived at the medieval fort when you reach the second large, arched gate. This is the last stop where the bus turns around. Get out there and head right before the archway. After that it's all downhill and a very nice walk through the backstreets of Sarajevo's oldest quarters, Vratnik and Jekovac.

From the heart of the old town If you prefer to start from the heart of the old town, as many do, the best starting place is **Sebilj square** (also known as 'the pigeon square') [117 F2]. Baščaršija, as the old town is called, is the far east corner of Sarajevo and is the part of town that displays its oriental flavour. This was the centre of life during Ottoman rule from the 1440s until the empire collapsed here in 1878. It is famous for the craftsmen of every kind who still hammer away at making authentic handmade goods as their forefathers did centuries ago. Sebilj square is where the main public fountain is located in the old town. It has been refurbished after falling into disrepair during and after the war. The Bosnian governor under the Ottomans, Hadži-Mehmed-Pasha Kukavica, built the *sebilj* in 1753 on Baščaršija. The original fountain was relocated in 1891 by the architect Vitek. He modelled the *sebilj* in pseudo-Moorish style, copied from the stone *sebilj* in Constantinople. The city of Sarajevo gave a copy of that *sebilj* as a gift to the city of Belgrade, in 1989. The square is always filled with pigeons and for 1KM you can buy a cup of corn, which will be completely covered by the little flying creatures in seconds. The coffee and sweet shops near Sebilj all serve Turkish coffee with *rahatlokum* (Turkish delight).

Just outside the square is **Kazandžiluk Street**, the famous coppersmith trading place on the west side of Baščaršija. Here you'll find great antiques, hand-beaten copper dishes and oriental décor. It may seem strange to find shell cartridges left over from the war on sale, but Sarajevo was hit with enough artillery and anti-aircraft fire that if you stacked them they'd reach the moon. Over one million projectiles pounded the city over its 1,400-day siege. So what did they do with all the leftover cartridges? They carved beautiful designs on them and now sell them to tourists! Make sure to bargain with the friendly vendors and ask specifically if the item of interest is handmade by the craftsman or imported from Turkey; they sell both. Next to Kazandžiluk Street is **Baščaršijska džamija** [117 F2] or the marketplace mosque. Its official name is Džamija Havadže Duraka (Havadja Durak's Mosque) and it was built in the 1530s. This mosque often has the imam (local Muslim priest) singing the call to prayer from the minaret. Its mystical sounds resonate throughout the *čaršija* (old Turkish quarter).

Ferhadija Ferhadija walkway is perhaps the most charming part of town. It stretches from Sebilj in the heart of Baščaršija all the way to the eternal flame in the city centre. The lower part of Ferhadija is officially called Sarači, but it is the same walkway that changes name near the Austro-Hungarian part of town. Ferhadija is almost always filled with locals strolling through town, window shopping, chatting or just enjoying the pleasant energy of walking up and down. Along the Ferhadija is **Morića Han** [117 E2]. It was known as a caravanserai, meaning 'castle of the caravans'. The function of the *han* (inn) was to provide warehouse space, stables and accommodation for traders coming from near and far. It was built by the Gazi Husrevbegova fund and got its name much later from the inn operator Mustafa Morić. In the 1970s it was renovated and restored as a tourist attraction. It now has several restaurants and cafés, an oriental rug shop, and office spaces on the first floor where the inn rooms used to be. It's a lovely place to sit and have a drink in the courtyard and imagine how it used to be. There is a great Persian carpet shop there with very knowledgeable salesmen. Most of the carpets are handmade in Iran and are good value compared with high-street costs in the West.

Only a few hundred metres following the one-way system on Mula Mustafe Bašeskije Street is the **old Orthodox church (Stara pravoslavna crkva)** [117 E1], often referred to as simply the old church. It is estimated that the church was built in 1539–40. The Orthodox Church grew considerably in Bosnia from this point on. The church caught fire several times. The turret by the church had a dome until the first half of the 20th century. Following the reconstruction designed by architect Dušan Smiljanić, the turret became the simple form it is today. The museum (*admission free*) has many icons and frescoes from that era, and even earlier relics brought to Sarajevo from other Orthodox lands. The museum was arranged by Jeftan Despić, the sexton of the old church. Be sure there isn't a Mass in session before entering.

Gazi Husrev Begova Mosque [117 E2] (🕘 *to visitors at certain times of the day; admission through side entrance; women should be covered before entering*) on Ferhadija is the most significant Islamic building in Bosnia and Herzegovina. It is perhaps the finest example of Ottoman Islamic architecture on the Balkan peninsula. The Persian architect Adžem Esir Ali was the leading architect of his time within the empire and his mosque design favours the early Istanbul style. The original structure was built in 1530 but was largely destroyed when Eugene of Savoy plundered Sarajevo in 1697. It was fully restored by 1762 but was destroyed again in 1879. The last reconstruction of Gazi Husrev Begova Mosque was in 1886. Although it was damaged during the last conflict most of its precious original oriental design survived unscathed. It is important to stay to the side during prayer time as it is the main mosque in the city and is usually filled by local worshippers. No need for shyness, they are used to visitors and simply expect them to be courteous and follow the rules. Directly across the stone walkway is the **Gazi Husrev Beg Madrasa** [117 D2] (*Sarači; admission free*). A madrasa is an Islamic educational institution and this one was founded on 8 January 1537; it is now often the location for Islamic art exhibitions.

Near the old town, in walking distance of Sebilj, are many of the Islamic institutions built by or dedicated to Gazi Husrev-beg. Heading up Gazi Husrev-begova street in the direction of Ferhadija Street, just past the Madrasa is the **Gazi Husrev-beg Library** [117 D2] (*08.00–18.00 Mon–Sat*), the most important institution of its kind in the Balkans. It was founded in 1537 by the eponymous Bosnian governor and benefactor and now contains over 100,000 volumes of manuscripts and books in Arabic, Persian, Bosnian and other languages. The collection includes works on Islamic sciences, oriental languages, literature, philosophy, logics, history, medicine, veterinary science, mathematics, astronomy and other sciences. The library is open to the public.

At the end of the marble-like walkway in the old quarter is the **Brusa bezistan** [117 D3]. This beautiful oriental department store, with a long corridor topped by six domes, was the main trade centre for silk from Bursa in Asia Minor. Masons from Dubrovnik helped build the structure designed by Grand Vizier Rustem pasa in 1551. After being heavily damaged during the bombing of Sarajevo, Bezistan is once again a trade centre lined with tiny boutiques and souvenir shops, though most of the goods sold there these days are knock-offs or imported. It's definitely worth a browse, at least to see the architecture or find a bargain. This spot is known as the crossroads of East and West. You will notice the change in the architecture and even the street pavement.

Jewish quarter Through a small passageway between Ferhadija and Baševskija streets is the **Velika Avlija** (Grand Yard) [117 D2], also known as the Jewish quarter. The **City Museum** (*033 535 586; 10.00–16.00 Mon–Fri, 10.00–13.00 Sun*) and **Jewish Museum** [117 D2] (*033 535 688; 10.00–16.00 Mon–Fri, 10.00–13.00 Sun*) are located here. The Sephardic Jews that settled in Sarajevo quickly established themselves as tradesmen within the Ottoman Empire and the first temple to be built was the **Stari Hram** in 1581, less than a century after the Jews were expelled from Spain. The old synagogue, or Il Kal Grandi, was also destroyed in 1697 and again in 1788. As the Jewish community increased, there were growing calls to build a larger place of worship and the old temple was expanded in 1821. The upper floors were used by the women and the ground floor by men – the same tradition is practised by Muslims. You can arrange a tour of the old Jewish synagogue by calling **Despić House Museum** [117 C4] (*Despićeva 2; 033 215 531; 10.00–18.00 Mon–Fri, 10.00–15.00 Sat; admission* 3 KM), a Serbian tradesman's house from Ottoman times that is preserved in its original form. It's an interesting look at how a Christian craftsman may have lived during Turkish rule. A short walk out of the Turkish quarter and you'll find yourself in the part of Ferhadija that resembles the centre of Vienna instead of Istanbul.

Christian and Muslim quarters Religious harmony has always been the backbone of Sarajevo's multi-ethnic community. The **Catholic cathedral** [117 B2] was completed in 1889 when the Austrians had gained full control of the city. It is the seat of the Vrh-Bosna archbishop and is dedicated to the Most Holy Heart of Jesus. The cathedral was designed by the architect Noble Josip Vancaš in neo-Gothic style, with some elements of Romanesque. It is very similar to Notre Dame Cathedral in Dijon. The Pope led Mass here during his visit in 1997. Don't be surprised to find Sarajevo's youth gathering on the steps of the cathedral; it has always been a popular (and central) place to hang out or wait for a friend. The cathedral is also open to visitors free of charge when there is no Mass taking place.

GALERIJA 11/07/95

Sarajevan photographer Tarik Samarah spent most of the mid-1990s trying to uncover the truth of massacres that occurred in Srebrenica in 1995. He followed exhumation teams, stayed with women who had lost their sons, husbands and brothers and systematically recorded the eerie and sad process of the aftermath of the Srebrenica genocide. This award-winning photographer knew there had to be another step in his mission, their mission, to pay homage to the victims. With a lot of patience and love, he managed just that.

Gallery 11/07/95 is not only Bosnia and Herzegovina's most professionally curated gallery but is one that will humble you for its moving and thoughtful content. With a multitude of media, the gallery depicts the horrifying events that led up to the 11 July 1995 genocide in Srebrenica and, just as important, its aftermath. With its vivid photos, videos, interviews with survivors, and the wall of death (that names each of the more than 8,000 victims), this is an experience you shouldn't pass up. Sarajevo is a fun and vibrant city. This gallery is not meant to be a downer to anyone's good time, but a solemn reminder of the depths of human suffering that occurred in this country not long ago.

It is located just next to the cathedral on the Ferhadija promenade [117 B2] (*Trg Fra Grge Martića 2/III;* ☎ *033 953 170;* **e** *info@galerija110795.ba;* **w** *galerija110795.ba;* 🕘 *10.00–18.00 daily*).

Behind the cathedral near the music school is one of the newer museums in town, the **Bosniak Institute** [117 A2] (*Mula Mustafa Baseskije 21;* ☎ *033 279 800;* 🕘 *08.00–16.00 Mon–Tue & Thu–Sat, 08.00–19.00 Wed*). The institute is dedicated to the history of the Bosnian Muslims, or Bosniaks. It's an interesting place to see old documents and read about famous Muslim writers and historians, and it offers a fascinating insight into the national identity of the Bosnian Muslims.

Back on to Ferhadija, continuing west to **Trg Oslobođenja** [117 A3], or Liberation Square, you come to the **New Orthodox Serbian Church** [117 A3]. This is the largest Orthodox church in Sarajevo, and is dedicated to the Most Holy Mother of God. Its builder and architect was Andrija Damjanov and it's an example of a mixture of Baroque and Byzantine-Serb style. Construction lasted several years, and it was completed in 1872 and consecrated that year on St Elijah's Day, 2 August. The construction of the church was supported by the Turkish sultan Abdul Aziz and the Russian tsar's family. The great icon on the north wall was painted by Paja Jovanović. The church is open to visitors every day, from 08.00 to 17.30, and there may be an admission fee of 2KM. Trg Oslobođenja itself is another popular gathering spot, and vendors will often be selling paintings in the square. Pensioners gather year round to play chess with life-size pieces on the far end of the square. During the summer and early autumn months there is a book fair and honey festival.

Across the street from the Orthodox church, at Zelenih beretki 8, is the **National Gallery of BiH** [117 A4] (☎ *033 266 550;* **w** *ugbih.ba;* 🕘 *10.00–20.00 Mon–Sat; admission 5KM*). In this art gallery the works of the best-known artists of Bosnia and Herzegovina, past and present, are displayed. In the main hall is the 1568 work of the famous 'icon painter', Tudor Vuković Desisalić, as well as most of the great artists from BiH.

Jumping back on to Ferhadija and continuing west takes you to the end of this charming walkway. You may see several holes in the pavement filled with red candle-wax-like material. These commemorate massacre sites from the siege and are dubbed 'Sarajevo roses'. There will usually be plaques nearby describing the incidents. The victims were always civilians waiting in line for bread or water. As Ferhadija meets Maršala Tita Street the **Vječna Vatra** (eternal flame) [108 D3] burns in memory of the Serbs, Croats, Muslims and other partisans who gave their lives in liberating Sarajevo from the fascists during World War II.

It is well worth exploring all the little side streets off Ferhadija as it will be hard not to find something that grabs your interest. There are plenty of other sights to see and with the small tourist maps distributed for free at the tourist information centre they should be easy to find.

Ferhadija meets Maršala Tita Once Ferhadija meets Maršala Tita (also known as Titova) things get a bit busier: there are plenty of cafés and boutiques on either side of the street. A few hundred metres from the Vječna Vatra (Eternal Flame), heading west, is one of Sarajevo's largest shopping malls. Once a socialist-era department store, the **BBI Centre** [108 C3] has transformed itself into Sarajevo's most modern shopping centre. With five floors of shops, a good food court and the best no-smoking café in town (Torte i to on the fifth floor, page 127), it's an excellent place to wander and, of course, have another coffee. Further west, **Alipašina Mosque** [108 A4] (*cnr Tito St & Alipašina St*), was one of the most dangerous spots during the war. Hastily made blinds of sheets, bombed-out buses and whatever was available were placed near the mosque to block the snipers' view. The Alipašina endowment was built in 1560–61 by the Bosnian governor Ali-Pasha and it is renowned as the most harmonious mosque in Sarajevo. The architect was a scholar of Sinan, a master builder within the empire. Alipašina Mosque is located along the Koševski stream, very close to the Sarajevo town hall building. The *turbeh* tombstones on the corner of the property are the graves of Avdo Sumbul and Behdžet Mutavelić, fighters against the Austro-Hungarian army.

Turning left after the mosque, heading south towards the Miljacka River is the **Skenderija Mall** [108 B5]. This was built as the media centre for the 1984 Olympics and is often used as a concert hall for large performances. On the bottom floor of Skenderija is the **Museum of Contemporary Art, Ars Aevi** [108 B5] (☎ *033 216 927;* 🕘 *09.00–16.00 Mon–Fri; admission 4KM*), which stages frequent exhibitions of international and local artists. Next to the museum is the **Collegium Artisticum Art Gallery** [108 B5] (*Terezije bb;* ☎ *030 270 750;* 🕘 *10.00–18.00 Mon–Sat*). It's more of a place where the older intellectual corps gathers. There is always a small exhibition on the walls and you can find out information on cultural events inside.

The pedestrian path on the south side of the Miljacka leads to what was once the only Evangelist church in Bosnia and Herzegovina; it was built in the last years of the 19th century. The structure, however, is no longer a church. The building was donated to the city and made into the **Arts Academy of Sarajevo** [108 B5]. Feel free to have a wander. The end of the pedestrian pavement takes you to **Čobanija Bridge** [108 D4]. You'll know you're there once you've reached another Sarajevo landmark – Dva Ribara café/restaurant, better known for its cold beer than its food, but a favourite spot for locals. Crossing back over the river you'll find the main post office. This Viennese structure is one of the finest examples of Austrian architecture in town. The inside has been completely renovated and is well worth a peek if you're into architecture. Next to the post office is the **Narodno pozorište** or National Theatre [108 D4] (*Obala Kulina bana 9;* 🕘 *09.00–noon & 16.00–19.30 Mon–Sat*), built by the same architect as the Evangelist church and representing the neo-Renaissance style. Construction was finished in 1899 and the first professional theatre group was founded in Sarajevo in 1923. The Sarajevo Opera was established within the National Theatre in 1946 and a few years later a ballet ensemble was formed. The institution of the International Festival of Small and Experimental Scenes (MESS) has played a great role in the development of the performing arts. The National Theatre has plays and operas all summer long, and even though most events are in the local language, productions there are often top notch and tickets are extremely affordable.

East from the National Theatre If you double back to the river and head east from the theatre along the Miljacka you'll come across many bridges built during Ottoman times, the most famous being the **Latinska ćuprija** (Princip's bridge) [117 D4]. It was here that Archduke Franz Ferdinand and his pregnant wife were travelling when the Serbian nationalist Gavrilo Princip shot and killed them both on St Vitus's Day, 28 June 1914. The assassination sparked Austria to declare war on Serbia. Russia immediately sided with the Serbs and the world plummeted into World War I. Despite being remembered mostly for this tragic event, the bridge itself is quite a remarkable example of Ottoman bridge building. It was built in 1798 as a legacy for the merchant and benefactor from Sarajevo, Hadži Abdullah-agha Brigo. In Turkish times its official name was Frenkluk ćuprija, after the neighbouring Catholic quarter in Bistrik. A monument to Archduke Franz Ferdinand and Sofia Hotek was built in 1917 near the bridge only to be demolished in 1918. The name 'Princip's bridge' was unofficially introduced after 1918 in memory of Gavrilo Princip. In 1993, the bridge was renamed Latinska ćuprija. Sarajevo has the unfortunate label of being the instigator of World War I. On the opposite side of the street from the bridge is Sarajevo Museum 1878–1918 [108 D4] (🕘 *10.00–16.00 Mon–Sat*), dedicated to that day and the assassination of the archduke and his wife. Although it's a small exhibition, it is well worth the 2KM admission fee.

By crossing south across the Latin Bridge you enter the **Bistrik** district of the old town. The park along the river to the right is a favourite gathering spot during the summer; its tree-covered green space provides a cool and pleasant break on hot summer days. It's called **At-Mejdan** [109 F4]. The pavilion in the centre has a lovely café and in the summertime there are small train rides and bumper cars for children. It's a pleasant spot for a break, especially if you have nippers. Heading back east upriver is the **Careva Mosque** [109 G4]. The original mosque was built in 1457 as a gift for Sultan Mehmed II by Isa-beg Ishaković, who also built the famous Castle Saraj, from which Sarajevo was named. The present-day mosque was built in 1566 by order of Suleyman the Great. Past Careva Mosque to the right up Konak Street are the **Franciscan Monastery** and **Church of St Ante** [109 G5], in the old Catholic quarter of Bistrik. The monastery and church were built during the Austro-Hungarian period in 1894 and 1912, the church now holding many ancient artefacts and documents in the old Bosanćica script. The church is open to visitors and on Sundays they have English-language masses. There is also a small gift shop in front of the monastery. Just across the street is the **Sarajevska pivara** (brewery) [109 G4]. It is not accessible to guests but the brewery played a great role in the survival of the city during the siege. It is built on top of one of the largest freshwater springs in the city and, with all water cut off, this became the only source of clean drinking water for thousands of Sarajevans. It's no wonder that Sarajevo beer is by far the favourite! If the brewery itself isn't open for viewing at least the attached pub is. It is one of the nicest pubs in town and most certainly the largest one. The Pivnica, as it is called (page 124), is one of the few places in town to serve both Sarajevsko dark beer and unfiltered beer. The locals rave about the spicy sausages as well. Take a wander through some of the side streets before heading back down towards the river. You should come out near **Inat Kuća** (page 123), which is one of the finest traditional restaurants in town and a landmark in the city.

From Inat kuća Passing Inat Kuća to the right is Alifakovac Street. **Alifakovac** is the eastern quarter of old Sarajevo. Its original name was believed to have been chosen after Ali Ufak ('Alija the Short'), a legendary sheikh, who was buried at the Alifakovac graveyard. In fact, the origin of this name is in honour of Ali Fakit, a scientist from Sarajevo from the first half of the 15th century and who was mentioned in Gazi Husrev-beg's foundation from 1462. The Alifakovac graveyard is a final resting place for Muslim foreigners who died and were buried in Sarajevo. The cemetery is interesting not only from a historical perspective but for the great view of the old town from up on the hill.

Double back towards Inat Kuća and cross the Cehaja Bridge to reach **Vijećnica** (National Library/City Hall) [109 H3], which was phosphorous bombed during the last war, incinerating almost a thousand years of history and millions of books. This is the most significant architectural monument in Sarajevo. The reconstruction was recently completed, and it is worth visiting. There is a 2KM entrance fee which allows full access to the building and all the time you want to admire the pseudo-Moorish and other architectural styles. There is a permanent exhibition in the basement, and there are sometimes other special exhibitions or concerts. You now have several directions to choose. To the east side of the library, still along the river is the **Bentbaša** canyon area. A bit further on is a long footpath used by joggers, walkers and bikers. It is closed to vehicles and is a wonderful place to take a peaceful walk along the river (which cleans up considerably after leaving the old town). Along the footpath is also an open-air climbing area called **Dariva**, a favourite local spot with pre-marked paths for both free climbing and bouldering.

A longer walking tour If you're up for an even longer walk, further east in the canyon is the **Kozja ćuprija** or Goat Bridge, an elegant stone bridge (over 10m high). According to the travel journals of Katrin Zen, the bridge existed before 1550. Bosnian viziers were welcomed at Kozja ćuprija and it is here that the pilgrims to Mecca began their long journey east. One can walk the 4km circuit or take a *fijaka* (horse and carriage) ride to the bridge and back.

West from the National Library/City Hall If you choose to head west from the National Library just let your nose lead you. Bravadžiluk Street is famous for its *ćevapi* and *burek*. The smell of fresh meat and homemade pitta is hard to resist. You can't go wrong no matter where you sit on this street. As you re-enter the main square of the Baščaršija don't miss **Sevdah House** [117 F3] (*Halači 5;* 🕘 *summer 10.00–18.00 daily*) to the left on Bravadžiluk Street. Sevdah kuća is a museum/café of BiH's most favourite form of entertainment – *sevdah* music. The traditional love songs of *sevhah* are loved by most; it is a unique music form to Bosnia and Herzegovina. The museum has a great assortment of traditional music. On the north side of the old town, behind Sebilj, are many of the Islamic institutions built by or dedicated to Gazi Husrev-beg. Heading up Sagrdzije Street is **Sinanova tekija** (Dervish House) [109 G1] of the Kaderija dervish order. Here the mystical order chant prayers intended to move them into a trance. It seems that the *tekija* was constructed by Hadži-Sinan-agha, a rich merchant from Sarajevo. Otherwise, it is possible that his son Mustafa-pasha Silahdar built the *tekija* in honour of his father. It is not open to visitors.

To get a look at an authentic Turkish house from the 18th century pay a visit to the **Svrzina kuća** (Svrzo's House) [109 G2] (*Gložina 8 St, parallel with Logavina St; ⏲ 10.00–15.00 Mon–Sat; admission 2km*). This house/museum is a great example of a wealthy beg's house from that period. The high walls around the garden mark the intimate and secret life of the wealthier begs. The balconies are made of intricately carved wood and the large sitting rooms are typical of Turkish-style homes created to receive a large extended family. The house has been well restored and guided tours around the house are possible throughout the week.

Doubling back to Mula Mustafe Baseskija Street, where the tramway runs westward, is the **Markale Market** [117 A2]. It was bombed by the Bosnian Serbs in 1995, killing over 60 civilians. Although today it is a bustling place the memorial to the back of the market is a stark reminder of the massacre that led the Clinton administration to push for air strikes. Within months of the Markale massacre all parties were at the peace table and the Dayton Peace Accords were signed soon after.

West on Maršala Tita By now you've zigzagged a good part of the city. If you haven't had enough, keep travelling west on Maršala Tita street where it turns into Zmaja od Bosne in the centre of the Marijin Dvor quarter. This area of the city is off the western edge of the map on pages 108–9. It is marked by the Parliament building and the Sarajevo Twin Towers (a very mini version of the former New York skyscrapers). At the intersection near the twin towers is the **Church of St Joseph**. This Catholic building is the work of Karl Parzika. The large blue building across the street is the **Parliament building**. It was in this square in early 1992 that tens of thousands of Sarajevans of all ethnicities took to the streets to say no to war. A peaceful march headed south behind the building towards Serbian-laid barricades on the Vrbanj Bridge. A sniper opened fire on the crowd killing the first victim of the war, Suada Dilberović, a young woman from Dubrovnik. The bridge is now named after her. The **National Museum** (Zemaljski Muzej) (*Zmaja od Bosne 3; w zemaljskimuzej.ba; ☎ 033 668 027; ⏲ 10.00–19.00 Tue–Fri, 10.00–14.00 Sat–Sun; admission 6KM*) is a few blocks west of the Parliament building. It is a fascinating place to see the many pieces of Bosnia and Herzegovina's long history. There is a botanical garden with many of the endemic flowers and plants found throughout the country and beyond. Some of the greatest stone carvings of the medieval *stećci* (tombstones) are housed in the museum. The halls dedicated to the traditional attire and décor of the Serbs, Bosniaks and Croats are interesting to see for both the similarities and differences in style. The Haggadah, a holy ancient Jewish codex brought in the 15th century when the Sephardic Jews fled Spain, has a special room dedicated to it, the oldest Jewish codex in the Balkans. Archaeological findings from the Neolithic era and the Butmir culture are evidence of a long continuous line of human settlements in this region. Roman and Illyrian pottery, jewellery, tools and mosaics can also be viewed. The building itself dates from 1885 and was the first institution dedicated to scientific research and to preserving the cultural and natural heritage of BiH. Don't expect the New York Museum of Natural History. The museum was damaged during the war, with reparation work on the façade finishing in 2008. Although they are desperately underfunded and aren't able to fully restore and expand on the existing exhibitions, the museum is more than worth the entry fee; do go and see it. Just to the right of the National Museum is the **History Museum of Bosnia-Herzegovina** (*⏲ 09.00–19.00 daily; admission 5KM*). They have an excellent and moving permanent exhibition of the siege of Sarajevo, with a lot of personal touches.

There is also a souvenir shop with some artsy gifts like reprinted posters from Yugoslavia and tote bags. The building itself is an exhibit of sorts – it is a unique cube-form design from the socialist period, in the vein of Mies van der Rohe, but is now badly damaged and in need of repair.

Off the beaten path The tours and places mentioned above are certainly the most significant aspects of the city's cultural heritage. Walking/wandering is by far the best way to get to most of these places and get a good feel for the city. By no means are they the only thing to do in Sarajevo, though.

Mali Daire [117 F2] is a small square hidden just to the east of Sebilj. You'll find it through a little alleyway next to the pharmacy. Mali Daire is a favourite daytime hangout spot for young Sarajevans. There are two shisha cafés, both comfortably shaded by a large oak tree. It's a relaxing place for a Turkish tea, Bosnian coffee or to smoke flavoured tobacco from a water pipe. There is also a small gallery where the famous writer Mak Dizdar wrote *Kameni Spavač* ('Stone Sleeper'). At certain times of the year it hosts open art exhibitions.

Another favourite spot is closer to the river in the old town on the corner of **Veliki Čurčiluk** next to Željo restaurant (page 125). This collection of cafés and bars is amongst the city's most popular nightspots. Hacienda (page 128) and Baghdad (page 127) are at the centre of it all. On Strossmayer Street, just opposite the cathedral [117 B3], is the 'see and be seen' café scene.

No visit to Sarajevo is complete without a **panoramic view**. There are three great spots to find one. The first is Žuta tabija, which is a fairly easy walk from the old town. From the **Sehidsko groblje** (Martyrs' Cemetery) [109 H2] at Kovači there is a small side street to the far right called Jekovac. Follow that street straight up to the top to a walled green area. The entrance is to the rear side of the stone enclosure. Number two is **Bijela tabija** [109 H3]. This is at the top of Vratnik. It will take a good half-hour to walk up to the summit from the old town but a taxi from the stand just behind Sebilj will cost only 3–4KM. Bijela tabija is the large fortress with great views to both east and west. The best view, however, is from **Sedam šuma** – Vidikovac [109 G1]. Just in front of the old barracks is Sarajevo's best scenic viewpoint. The café there is a perfect place to sit for a long drink and soak up the spectacular view of this ancient city. Be sure not to forget your camera!

OTHER SITES AND SIGHTS

Art House Cinema Kriterion [108 B4] (*Obala Kulina bana 2;* ☎ *033 203 113;* **w** *kriterion.ba;* **e** *kriterion.info@gmail.com;* 🕒 *09.00–23.00 Mon–Sat, 11.00–23.00 Sun*) One of Sarajevo's best art houses, Kriterion has many personalities. It's a café/bar all the time and serves breakfast all week. There are films, concerts, exhibitions, discussion groups and anything artsy pretty much every night of the week.

Atelje-zbirka Zec [108 C3] (*Maršala Tita 31/2;* ☎ *033 205 343;* 🕒 *10.00–18.00 Mon–Fri, 10.00–14.00 Sat; admission free*) Safet Zec ranks amongst the country's most renowned artists. The fact that he is one of the rare painters from the region to have a gallery of their creations before they have passed on also means one gets a taste of the artist's newest works displayed and sold at his personal gallery on the main drag, Maršala Tito.

Baščaršija [117 F2] Despite popular belief, this area of town is not necessarily the 'old town' as it is often referred as. Baščaršija was an intentionally built market and trading square in the flat valley on the north side of the Miljacka River. The 'old town' is actually more up the hill towards Kovači and Vratnik, which was the residential area developed before the marketplace. This was the official market and trading quarters in Ottoman Bosnia. The creation of the market area began sometime in 1462. Baščaršija is the main magnet for the city's visitors, hosting a plethora of street food, souvenir shops, cafés, mosques, churches and a synagogue. It is also the headquarters of the specialised handicraftsmen/women whose families have been making and selling their wares for centuries. The Sebilj fountain is the main landmark and often a meeting point if looking to hook up with friends. It is often referred to as 'pigeon square'.

Bijela tabija [109 H3] Perched on a hilltop to the east of the old town, Bijela Tabija is well worth the trek up for magnificent views of the city and the eastern Miljacka river canyon. The ancient fortress, recently restored due to war damage, doesn't offer much in terms of information but for a wander and photograph, make time to see it.

Ferhadija and Sarači [117 C2 and 117 D2] Walking is a national pastime in Sarajevo. Why not do it where one can see and be seen? Sarači and Ferhadija – more or less the same pedestrianised street (Sarači is the Ottoman-era side of the street whereas Ferhadija is the Austro-Hungarian-era part) – is where most of the shopping and coffee sipping takes place in Sarajevo. When in Rome …

Kozja ćuprija [109 H3] From the Bentbaša area of the Baščaršija – just east of Vjecnica – is Sarajevo's longest walkway. Following the Miljacka River, it meanders to the ancient meeting point for journeys to Mecca. Kozja ćuprija, meaning Goat Bridge, is a gorgeous Ottoman-era bridge that spans the Miljacka River about a 30-minute casual walk from Bentbaša. It's worth the walk.

Latinska ćuprija [117 D4] The Latin Bridge is most famous because it is the location of the 1914 assassination of Franz Ferdinand and his pregnant wife Sofia. Many historians attribute this single act as the spark that started World War I. Any way you look at it – it is an important historical site. The museum just across the street has an interesting collection of photos and a timeline of the events of that fateful day. Be careful of pickpockets in front of the museum.

Morića Han [117 E2] (*Sarači 77;* ☎ *033 236 119,* 🕘 *08.00 – midnight*) Although not being anything like its glory days, Morića Han is nonetheless a must-see spot in Sarajevo. The Persian carpets make the small detour more than worthwhile. There are a handful of cafés and a restaurant inside and none serve alcohol. The *han* was where traders would come and be housed (for free) and stalls for their horses would be provided. It was a smart tactic by the Ottomans to get traders to bring their wares to Sarajevo.

Olympic Stadium and Museum [108 A1] (*Alipašina bb;* ☎ *033 226 414;* **e** *info@okbih.ba;* **w** *okbih.ba;* 🕘 *09.00–15.00 Mon–Fri; entrance free*) By no means is it the most modern or awe-inspiring museum in the world, though it is interesting and very Yugoslavian. It hosts a fascinating collage of Olympic paraphernalia coupled with modern art paintings and sculptures that are somewhat irrelevant to anything Olympic.

Roman Petrović Gallery [108 D3] (*Maršala Tita 54;* ☎ *033 668 009;* **e** *ulubih@smartnet.ba;* **w** *ulubih.ba;* 🕘 *10.00–19.00 Mon–Sat; admission free*) This pre-war

THE DREARY TUNNEL CROSSING

I sometimes forget a few things about crossing through the tunnel during the height of the war. After visiting the museum, I realised that it's difficult to get a real feel for what it was like to disappear into the earth in order to reach the besieged city. The tunnel was closed to internationals during the war and very few non-Bosnians ever crossed through it. I did three times but not because I was someone special. VIPs were allowed to cross the airport with a UN tank escort. Working for a small (but effective) NGO I wasn't high on the UN's priority list. Luckily the work we did meant a lot more to the Bosnians, and thanks to their trust and help I can now tell you one story amongst thousands of the 'Sarajevo Tunnel Crossing'.

Arriving at the tunnel after creeping down Mount Igman on a dark night with no lights was an unforgettable experience. The sound of the hundreds of people waiting to pass through the tunnel was like the desperate murmur of some back alley filled with the homeless and junkies. Garbage was strewn everywhere. Thin and pale people stood over small fires waiting for word that the tunnel crossing was open. Besides moving the human cargo that could carry a week's worth of food on its back, the tunnel was the only means by which ammunition could reach the town. Small trolleys were built on rail bars to move ammunition and humanitarian aid back and forth. Artillery and small arms fire peppered the night and every few minutes a round would land in the vicinity. I was the only one startled by the close calls. Waiting in circumstances like these gives a new meaning to the concept of time. The shaken but determined energy of the masses waiting to cross gave me a sort of silent courage and aroused my instincts of survival.

Badly wounded civilians and soldiers were sometimes carted through the 1m x 1m passageway. We would often wait hours for the long queue from the other side to file out like moles. I crossed the tunnel only at night due to the

gallery has been hosting local artists' work since 1980. It is one of the better galleries in town and exhibitions are usually visited by swarms of creative, heavy-smoking, arty crowds. It is a good spot to check out local art and even purchase a piece if you fancy.

Sedam Šuma/Seven Forests [109 H2] Sarajevo is a mountainous town. The city sprawls up the hillside in every direction and Sedam Šuma is perhaps the best spot to witness the beauty of the city from above. After a short taxi ride to the top, there is a comfortable café called Vidikovac, where one can sit and soak in the sun and the amazing views of the entire city.

Vijećnica [109 H3] (*☎ 033 292 800; ⏱ 10.00–17.00 Mon–Sun; admission 5 KM)* This structure has been many things. It started off as a town hall when first constructed during the Austro-Hungarian period. It was later converted to the National Library and Archives until it was phosphorous bombed in 1992. After years and years of delays, the façade was finally completed in 2012. The grand opening took place in summer 2014.

Žuta tabija [109 H2] Great views, great walk up, bring lunch. Just a 15-minute walk from Baščaršija, this seemingly tiny outcrop above the cemetery is a wonderful place to sit and gaze out at the beautiful views. Many couples visit here for a snuggle, or young people to have a drink with a view. Either way, it's a place you'll appreciate visiting. Bring a camera.

treacherous road down Igman that constantly came under fire regardless of who or what you were. Amongst the many killed on this road were an American peace negotiator and a British humanitarian aid driver. The chaos and buzzing energy that would grip the entire group when our side of the tunnel opened was intense to say the least. I always had to go with a military escort and I was forbidden to travel with a camera or any electrical devices. If I'm not mistaken, we entered the tunnel through what resembled a kitchen. The maze of walls and trenches seemed to be intentionally designed to confuse. Once we entered, the air changed, the smell changed, as did our state of consciousness from the very first steps. The walls hugged our elbows and we literally had to bend in half to walk, or more like waddle, through the 700m corridor. The iron reinforcements above dripped with moisture and the muddied floors were covered with wooden planks. We all banged our heads at least once.

A woman carrying a sack of potatoes, that appeared to weigh more than me, collapsed from exhaustion. My friend and colleague Skye Corbett, also an American aid worker, didn't hesitate to sling the sack on his back and carry it the rest of the way for the old woman. Sweat dripped from our foreheads and the muscles in our backs began to reject our unnatural position.

Exiting was as chaotic as entering. An even deeper maze of trenches wound its way through a field and into a flat in the suburbs of Dobrinja. Walls, sweat, sniper fire, dirt, mud, babies crying, men arguing, everyone chain smoking were just some of the thousands of pictures my senses registered in those few minutes of clambering to safety. One journey was over and now the challenge of reaching town through the deadly sniper alleys was next on our agenda. In a nutshell, it went a little something like that.

Out of town There are more things to see and do which are rather too far from the centre for a walking tour. On the other side of the airport in Butmir is the **Tunnel Museum also known as the 'Tunel spasa'** [108 A5] (*033 778 672;* e *suad@tunelspasa.ba;* w *tunelspasa.ba* ⌚ *Apr–Oct 09.00–7.00; daily, Nov–Mar 09.00–16.00 daily; admission 10KM)*. The tunnel ran 700m under Sarajevo airport and during the siege was the only self-sustaining lifeline for the city of 400,000 people. The tunnel was dug from the garage of someone's house and exited on the other side in the suburb of Dobrinja. It became the symbol of resistance and survival for the besieged city (see box, opposite). Finding the museum can be a bit tricky. Ask about guided tours at the tourist information centre in the middle of town, or take a taxi (a one-way trip should cost around 15KM and take about 20 minutes, depending on traffic). The tunnel is accessible by public transport: from the city centre, take tram 3 to the last station in Ilidža. At the adjacent bus terminal, take bus 32 (in the direction of Kotorac). Get off at the last stop, walk across the bridge, then turn left down Tuneli Street and continue for 500m or so. It is not possible to go through the entire tunnel; only about 20m is open for public viewing. You can bet that just the little bit you are able to see will leave a lasting impression on you. There are now plans to reopen the entire tunnel under the airport. In the coming years it will certainly be one of the city's most remarkable tourist attractions.

If by chance you find yourself in the north end of town by the **Olympic Stadium** (page 141) with the copper roof, notice the endless rows of new white tombstones. The **New Cemetery** [108 A1] on both sides of Patriotske Liga street holds the graves of victims of the longest siege in modern European history. It's a startling reminder of the immense number of people killed there, all while under UN 'protection'.

EXCURSIONS FROM SARAJEVO

SKAKAVAC WATERFALL Skakavac means 'grasshopper'. This is the largest constantly flowing waterfall in Bosnia and Herzegovina (98m). The stream that creates the waterfall originates from four sources at the base of **Bukovik Mountain** to the north of Sarajevo. This is a popular picnic spot for locals. It has been placed under protection as a 'green belt' and has many hiking, biking and walking trails. The entire region is safe from mines and is one of the closest places to Sarajevo for a nature excursion. Don't be intimidated by the burnt-out mountain lodge that still sits in ruins near the falls. When the Dayton Peace Accords were signed, the Serbs abandoned many of the areas they had held and often set fire to what was left behind. Nonetheless this doesn't detract from the beautiful pine and beech forests, miles and miles of great mountain-biking or walking trails, and a beautiful view of the waterfall.

If driving you would head north out of town towards the Olympic Stadium on Patriotske Liga street. Staying to the right of the zoo, the road turns into Nahorevska Ulica (street) and continues to climb through the hills for about 3km. Although the road is curvy, it is one road all the way to the falls. Once you reach the village of Nahorevo, and the local shop or *granap*, you have three options: down to the right towards a small stream, back up to the left or straight on a single-lane road. Go straight on and after about 1km the asphalt road will end. Continue climbing and stay on the main road. There will be an option to go down to the right; just stay straight and after 9km you'll reach the waterfall area. It is only a 10-minute walk from the parking area to the falls, and there are signs and maps on location for the entire area. There are no facilities at the waterfall.

If you're up for a pleasant 2-hour walk then take the 69 bus from in front of 2nd Gimnazija on Sutjeska street. It goes all the way to the last stop at the village of Nahorevo. From there head north up the valley which is fairly well marked all the way to the waterfall. It should take about 2 hours at medium pace. The closest eatery to the town is the **Lovački Dom Restaurant** (page 124). This traditional restaurant is set in a lovely valley below eagle peaks and serves fantastic local dishes. There is also great terrain for walking, a pony ride for the kids, and quite a few exotic animals running around. Try the young cheese (*mladi sir*) and pastries (*uštipak*) for starters. They also have a playground for children. Further up the hill, in the direction of Skakavac, is a rustic mountain eatery run by a man named Dragan. Homemade food, usually seasonal stews and other mountain fare, is available alongside homemade *rakija* (sometimes they have one infused with pine needles, *borove igle*), coffee, and tea made with mixed mountain herbs from the surrounding area. In the summer, there are picnic tables outdoors, and in the winter there is a fireplace indoors where hikers can warm up and dry their socks.

ILIDŽA Situated 12km southwest of Sarajevo, Ilidža has long been a close retreat for city dwellers to enjoy the thermal springs, recreation centre and the lovely park at the source of the River Bosna called **Vrelo Bosne**. The park has acres of lush green fields, gushing fresh waters that spring from the surrounding mountains, a park for children to play in and a tasty traditional restaurant near one of the largest cascades in the park. I definitely recommend weekday visits during the summer; weekends are super-crowded and this tends to take away from the tranquil ambience of the park. The springs are accessible by car, foot, bike or horse and carriage. The long tree-lined *aleja* (lane) is closed to vehicle traffic and is perfect for a jog, walk or bike ride. From the top of the avenue it is possible to take a horse-and-carriage ride in an old carriage from the Austro-Hungarian period. This is one of the few places in Bosnia and Herzegovina that still practises this tradition. The Austrian nobility were particularly fond of this area and many luxurious houses were built in the area around the sources during that period.

Not far from the source is the **Roman bridge**. Although it resembles a Roman bridge it is of Ottoman design. Ilidža is known for its ancient Roman settlements, particularly near the source and the thermal spas. The bridge was named after the ancient settlers of this region.

The **Terme Ilidža** (*Butmirska cesta 18 Ilidža;* ☎ *033 771 000;* e *info@terme-ilidza.ba;* w *terme-ilidza.ba;* ⏱ *09.00–22.00 daily*) is a new swimming-pool complex – it's great for families with children. There are indoor and outdoor pools as well as jacuzzis and saunas. The restaurant and tropical garden café are open for an additional 30 minutes before and after the pool. Entrance fees for the day range from 11–13KM for adults and 6–10KM for kids. The pool complex is open all year round and is a perfect place to either beat the heat or enjoy a warm swim after skiing.

Where to stay and eat If you are looking for less expensive accommodation than is found in the centre of town, Ilidža has many good hotels and can be up to 20% cheaper. Ilidža is connected to Sarajevo by regular buses and the tramway that travels all day to the city centre and back. There are **camping** facilities in the tourist settlement of Oaza (see below). It is the only place to park your camper van and has suitable plug-ins and facilities.

Hotel Hercegovina Ilidža; ☎ 033 772 000; e info@hoteliilidza.ba; w hoteliilidza.ba. The Hercegovina is part of the Ilidža spa complex. Situated in a lovely Austro-Hungarian-era garden it's an excellent place for peace & quiet. The renovated rooms are of high calibre as is the service. All guests have access to the thermal spas. **$$$**

Hotel Hungaria Banjska bb Ilidža; ☎ 033 772 000; e info@hoteliilidza.ba; w hoteliilidza.ba. With renovations completed in 2009 the shine of the Austro-Hungarian era in BiH is starting to return. Located by the popular walking area & Vrelo Bosne Park, Hungaria offers very good accommodation. **$$$**

Hotel Terme Banjska bb Ilidža; ☎ 033 772 000; e info@hoteliilidza.ba; w hoteliilidza.ba. This thermal spa has great accommodation, indoor pools & spas, jacuzzis & the works. During the winter months they organise transport to & from the ski centres. It's an ideal & quiet place to stay very close to both Sarajevo & the Olympic Mountains. **$$–$$$**

Hotel Hollywood Dr Pintola 23, Ilidža; ☎ 033 773 100; e info@hotel-hollywood.ba; w hotel-hollywood.ba. Reasonably priced spot in the centre of Ilidža. **$$**

Oaza Četvrte viteske brigade 3, Ilidža; ☎ 033 636 140; e info@hoteliilidza.ba; w hoteliilidza.ba. This hotel complex is 15km from Sarajevo & has the only camping facilities in the area. Besides the hotel there are small bungalows. **$$**

OTHER EXCURSIONS FROM SARAJEVO

Bijambara Caves Travel 400m deep into the belly of Cemerska Mountain or enjoy a day out at the mountain lodge set in a pristine pine forest (page 268).

Bjelašnica/Igman Olympic skiing or magnificent hiking and biking through the chain of ancient highland villages (pages 152–6).

Jahorina The largest ski centre in the country. High-quality skiing for a fraction of the price and no long queues (pages 147–52).

Kraljeva Sutjeska One of the most important pieces of Bosnia and Herzegovina's cultural heritage. The Franciscan monastery, its museum and library, attest to the Bosnian state and its noble families (pages 249–57).

Orlovača Cave The oldest known cave bear skull, 16,000 years old, was uncovered in the limestone den of this hidden cave just east of Sarajevo (page 161).

Rafting on the Neretva Awaiting the adventure seekers are the white-water rapids of the Neretva (page 177).

Visoko Only a short drive from Sarajevo this busy trading town has a unique old quarter with a 500-year-old tradition in leather making and a tourism industry which has grown up around what some claimed to be the first European pyramids (pages 257–63).

4

Around Sarajevo

Just the title 'Around Sarajevo' may leave the reader unclear as to what exactly that means. 'Around Sarajevo' will focus mainly on the territories east and immediately southeast of Sarajevo, including the Olympic Mountains of Jahorina, Bjelašnica and Igman. Many parts of northern Herzegovina and central Bosnia are very close to Sarajevo but have been addressed elsewhere in the guide. All destinations to the north of Sarajevo have also been covered in other chapters.

SKI CENTRES

For some, Sarajevo not only reminds them of its grim recent past, but also of its glorious debut as Winter Olympic Games host in 1984. Twenty-four hours away from the opening ceremonies, Sarajevo and the surrounding mountains had very little snow – all the competition venues were ready but organisers feared even a slight temperature increase. Many thought it would end or even begin in disaster. The Sarajevo miracle occurred on the eve of the XIV Winter Olympics – it snowed all night and then for the first couple of days, so that no artificial snow was needed after all.

The glory days have passed for now, but the Olympic-style skiing most certainly has not. While there was considerable damage to Bjelašnica and Igman mountain ski centres, Jahorina went largely untouched – and all three centres offer great skiing and snowboarding for a mere fraction of the cost of ski resorts in the West. The lifts are not high tech and there aren't many posh alpine villas, but no-one can dispute the quality of the slopes, snow and fun to be had skiing on these Olympic mountains.

One of the beauties of skiing in Sarajevo is the proximity of the mountains to the city centre. If you prefer to stay on the mountains, by all means do so, there is a growing selection of excellent accommodation facilities, on Jahorina Mountain in particular. But if you'd like to combine your ski holiday with a Sarajevo getaway, all three ski centres are no more than a 45-minute drive from the city. As the sun sets at between 16.00–17.00 in winter, it's a great opportunity to get the best of both worlds and pop into the city for dinner, a film or a play, or just bar hop before hitting the slopes the next morning.

JAHORINA Jahorina is the mountain range to the southeast of Sarajevo. Its ideal geographical position more or less guarantees four months of good ski snow. Its highest peak reaches 1,910m. The ski-lifts climb to 1,894m with fabulous views towards Sarajevo. The slopes of Jahorina are covered in tall pines and spruce up to the tree line at 1,500m. It is the country's most popular ski destination, so book ahead if you are thinking of going for a ski holiday.

The north face of the mountain was home to many of the competitions of the 1984 Winter Olympic Games, and has been the venue for many regional, national and

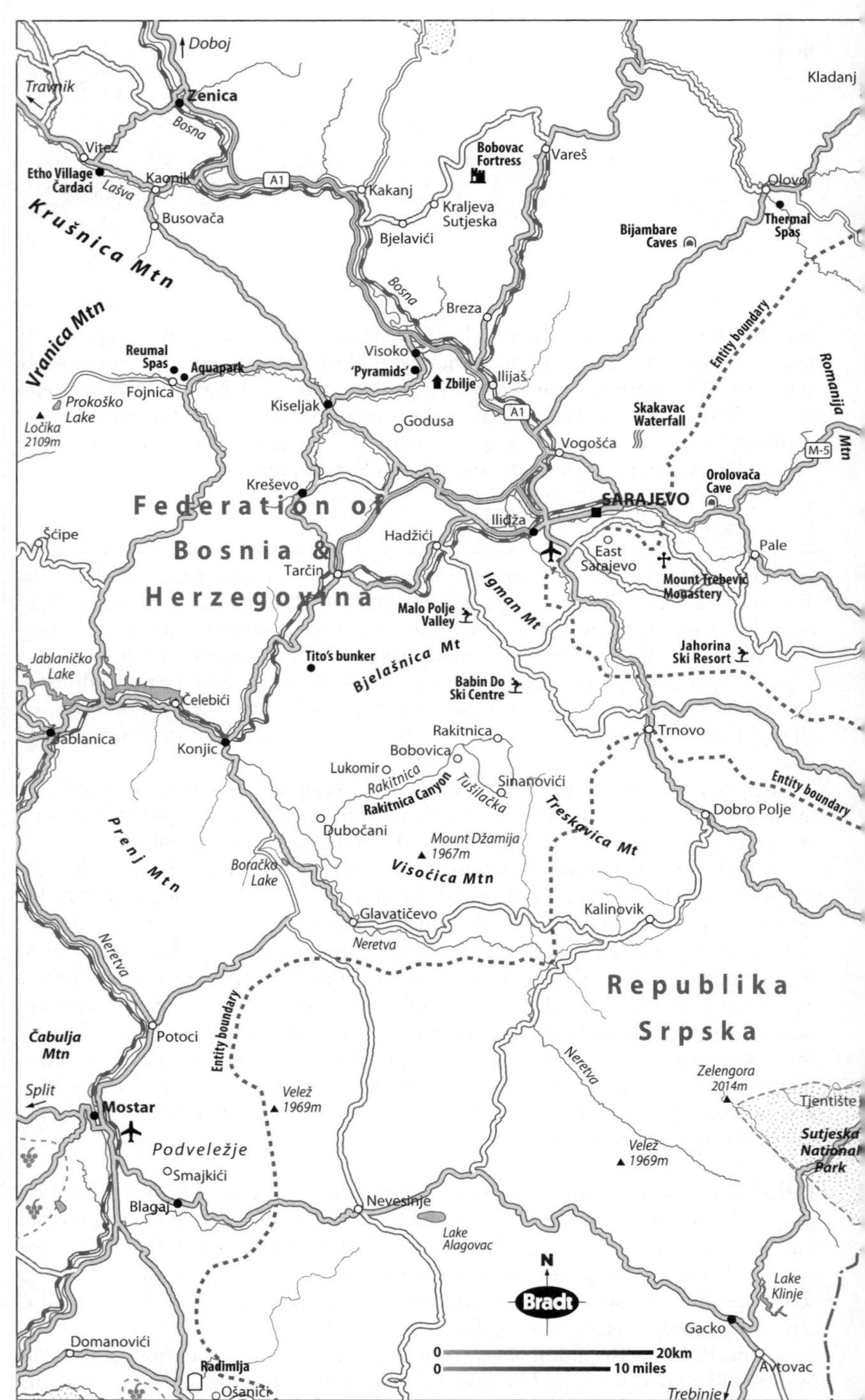
Doboj
Travnik
Zenica
Bosna
Vitez
Etho Village Čardaci
Kaonik
Lašva
A1
Kakanj
Kraljeva Sutjeska
Bjelavići
Bobovac Fortress
Vareš
Kladanj
Olovo
Thermal Spas
Bijambare Caves
Busovača
Krušnica Mtn
Vranica Mtn
Bosna
Breza
Reumal Spas
Aquapark
Fojnica
Prokoško Lake
Ločika 2109m
Visoko
'Pyramids'
Zbilje
Ilijaš
Kiseljak
Godusa
A1
Vogošća
Entity boundary
Skakavac Waterfall
Romanija Mtn
M-5
Orolovača Cave
Kreševo
SARAJEVO
Federation of Bosnia & Herzegovina
Ilidža
Hadžići
Šćipe
Tarčin
East Sarajevo
Mount Trebević Monastery
Pale
Igman Mt
Malo Polje Valley
Tito's bunker
Bjelašnica Mt
Jahorina Ski Resort
Babin Do Ski Centre
Jablaničko Lake
Čelebići
Jablanica
Konjic
Trnovo
Rakitnica
Bobovica
Lukomir
Rakitnica
Rakitnica Canyon
Tušilačka
Sinanovići
Entity boundary
Treskavica Mt
Dobro Polje
Prenj Mtn
Dubočani
Mount Džamija 1967m
Boračko Lake
Visočica Mtn
Glavatičevo
Kalinovik
Neretva
Neretva
Republika Srpska
Entity boundary
Potoci
Čabulja Mtn
Neretva
Split
Mostar
Velež 1969m
Zelengora 2014m
Tjentište
Sutjeska National Park
Podveležje
Velež 1969m
Smajkići
Blagaj
Nevesinje
Lake Alagovac
N
Bradt
Lake Klinje
Gacko
Domanovići
0 20km
0 10 miles
Avtovac
Radimlja
Ošanići
Trebinje

AROUND SARAJEVO
Tuzla
Tišća
Konjevići
Mihaljevići
Bratunac
SERBIA
Vlasenica
Milići
Potočari
Memorial Centre
Srebrenica
Han-Pijesak
Užice
Skelani
Bajina Bašta
Drina
Republika
Srpska
Barakovići
Sokolac
Perućačko
Reservoir
Bogovići
Rogatica
Višegrad
Dobrun
Monastery
Prača
1
Ustiprača
Stećci
Goražde
Novo
Goražde
Lim
Rudo
Drina
Rafting
Priboj
Ustikolina
Čajniče
Metaljka
Foča
SERBIA
Ćeotina
Prijepolje
Pljevlja
Tara
Drina
Skakavac
Waterfall
Šćepan
Polje
Tara Canyon
rafting
Maglić
2386m
MONTENEGRO
Trnovačko
Lake
Trsa
For listings, see page 168
Where to stay and eat
1 Bijele Vode
Plužine
Žabljak
Durmitor
National
Park
Nikšić
Nikšić

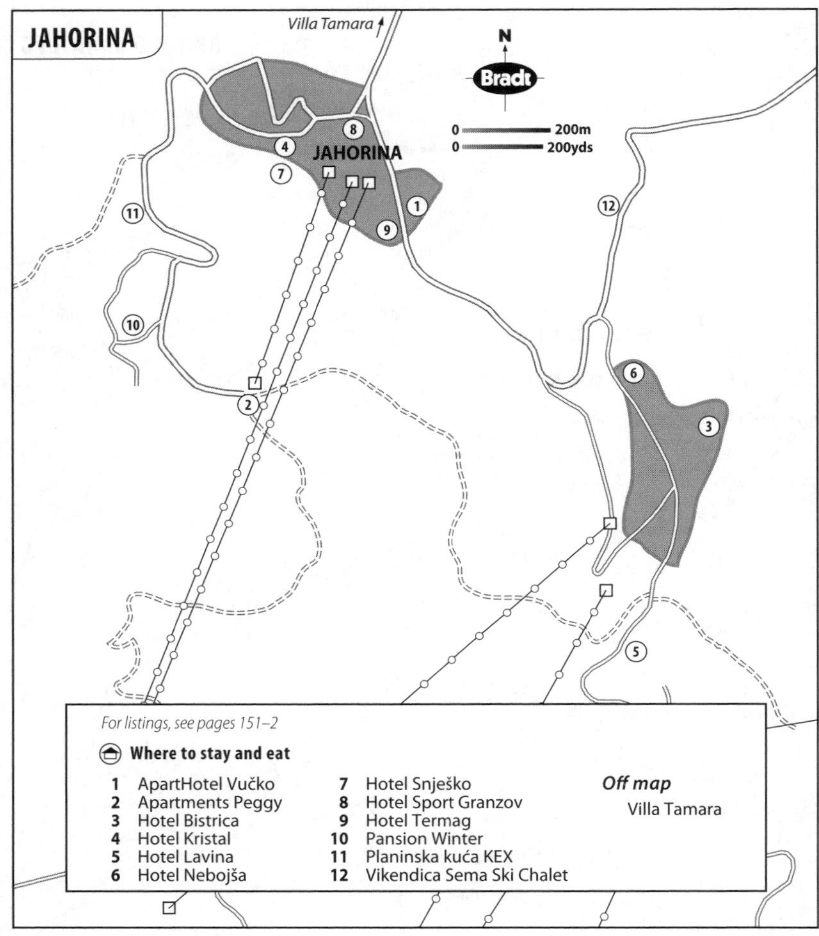

European competitions and races before and since. The resorts and infrastructure escaped the ravages of war and several new hotels and pensions have been erected in the past few years. Jahorina is the largest ski centre in the country. It has 12 lifts all over the mountain that offer Olympic-style professional trails and novice trails for children and beginners, with two six-seater lifts opened in early 2010. A day pass costs 34KM on weekdays and 39KM at the weekend. The high season on Jahorina is mid-December to late January, and then middle to late February. Around the New Year it is near impossible to get accommodation without advance reservations. An alternative for last-minute travellers is to book a hotel in Sarajevo, then drive to Jahorina. On the mountain you will find a full range of facilities including an indoor swimming pool, medical centre, information centres, ski rentals, restaurants and cafés, skiing instruction in English and internet access.

Getting there Jahorina is easily accessible from Sarajevo. The Sarajevo–Pale road is a 20-minute drive and from Pale the ride to the top takes only another 20 minutes or so. From the far east side of the city, near the old town, the M-5 road is an 18km direct drive to Pale. During the winter, Centrotrans operates a daily bus connecting Sarajevo to the Jahorina Ski Centre from the National Museum (Zemaljska Muzej) and the Town Hall (Vjećnica) at 09.00 and returning from Jahorina at 16.00. Return tickets are 7KM (5KM for children) and can be bought on the bus. It is wise to arrive early to be sure of a seat. The best way to locate the bus stop in Sarajevo is to ask someone near the departure area.

Where to stay and eat *Map, page 150*

In addition to the facilities listed below, Jahorina has a selection of small chalets – stone and wood, traditional A-framed cottages – offering rooms or self-catering apartments. Several good websites promote all types of accommodation on Jahorina, including **w** hoteljahorina.com, **w** jahorina.org and **w** jahorinaonline.com.

There are a number of **restaurants** not tied to the hotels at the bottom of the ski trails. The food is, by and large, traditional and finding a seat is usually a challenge.

ApartHotel Vučko (23 rooms, 21 apts) Olimpijska1; 057 206 300; **e** rezervacije@aparthotelvucko.com; **w** aparthotelvucko.com. Vučko is one of the best mountain hotels in the country. They offer the full spectrum of services & have excellent wining & dining facilities. Vučko has attractive apts with fireplace & kitchen as well as standard hotel rooms. They offer ski lessons, rentals & a wide range of summer & winter sports activities. **$$$**

Hotel Nebojša (26 rooms, 4 apts) Olimpijska 25; 057 270 500; **e** hotelnebojsa@yahoo.com; **w** hotel-nebojsa.com. Another of Jahorina's nice hotels. This hotel sleeps 80 & has a great location near the top of the mountain. The rooms are nice & they have a large 'ski garden' where many skiers gather to have a coffee or lunch. Hotel Nebojša has its own 'baby lift', a 300m lift & run for children & beginners. Ski rental & lessons are available through the hotel. **$$–$$$**

Hotel Termag (18 rooms, 13 apts) Poljice bb; 057 272 100, 057 270 422 or 057 272 072; **w** termaghotel.com. This hotel is the best on the mountain &, in fact, among one of the best in the country. The architecture, interior, restaurant & rooms are all done in the finest fashion & it has an indoor swimming pool & wellness centre. There is also a conference centre, bowling alley & several child-friendly facilities. Termag is located near the lower ski-lifts on Jahorina & is a steal for the price. The restaurant is one of the most popular spots for a break between intense skiing sessions. They have a year-round offer, with excellent deals over the summer for great hiking, spa holidays, mountain biking or just breathing in the fresh air. The food is excellent. Try the local pura (corn-meal) dish. **$$–$$$**

Pansion Winter Jahorinski put bb; 057 270 449; **e** pansionwinter@yahoo.com; **w** pansionwinter.com. This is a pleasant small pension of stone & wood construction. The rooms are simple but very clean & cosy. **$$–$$$**

Apartments Peggy (8 apts) Jahorina bb, Sarajevo; **m** 065 545 211; **e** peggy-jahorina@teol.net; **w** peggy-jahorina.ba. A slightly higher-end complex of rental flats, this wood & stone structure has 8 luxury apts equipped with TVs, DVD players, free Wi-Fi, jacuzzis, hydro massage tubs & sauna. Not a bad place to spoil oneself. **$$**

Hotel Bistrica (152 room, 8 apts) Jahorina bb; 057 270 020; **f** BistricaHotel. This is the largest hotel built specifically for the Olympics & is located 1,620m above sea level. Bistrica's interior still embraces the socialist style, particularly the rooms. They are comfortable enough but nowhere near Western standards. The restaurant/bar serves good traditional food & it offers by far the best view on the mountain. It is 1 of only 2 hotels on Jahorina with an indoor swimming pool (the other being Termag). The hotel also owns a small pension called Poljice, named after the valley in which it is located. It, too, is very near the ski-lifts & is a smaller alternative to the large, state-run Bistrica. **$$**

Hotel Lavina (22 rooms, 23 apts) Olimpijska 44; **m** 066 010 723; 057 272 310; **e** reservations@lavina.ba; **w** hotel-lavina.com. The excellent Lavina is ideally located between Ogorijelica & Prača ski pistes. It is the newest hotel on Jahorina, built in 2013. The rooms & apts are fully equipped with modern décor & all the creature comforts you need for a ski trip. There is a lavish spa & wellness centre, & the restaurant/

club has excellent cuisine. The chocolate lava cake, served with blueberry sauce & vanilla ice cream, is insanely good. **$$**

Planinska kuća Kex (4 rooms) Jahorina bb; m 066 167 370; e kex@visitjahorina.info; w kex.visitjahorina.info. Mountain house Kex is a small cottage built for 6–8 people & located near the ski slopes. A kitchen, bathroom & dining room are located on the ground floor, with 3 bedrooms upstairs. The chalet is heated by a wood stove & there is a large fireplace in the living room with 2 beds. If you're looking for a private chalet to rent with friends or family, this is a good choice. **$$**

Hotel Kristal (23 rooms, 4 apts) Jahorina bb; 057 270 430; e info@jahorinakristal.com; w jahorinakristal.com. This is built in an alpine-mountain style. The rooms are excellent with good food to match. Rooms have sat TV, minibar & bath. The hotel also has a bar, restaurant, sauna & ski rental (& service). It is one of the few places on Jahorina where guests have garage facilities, which are great for the really cold days. It is wise to make reservations a few months ahead. **$–$$**

Hotel Snješko (25 rooms) Jahorina bb, Sarajevo; m 063 718 648; e info@hotelsnjesko.ba; w hotelsnjesko.ba. This owner's put a lot of effort into this hotel's interior: it is decked out with natural materials & authentic ethno details. They have free Wi-Fi, parking & organised transport to & from the bus station or airport. There is a common hall with a fireplace where guests gather to drink & spend their evenings. **$–$$**

Hotel Sport Granzov Jahorina bb; 057 270 444; w sport-granzov-jahorina.com/en. Located in the Poljice Valley on Jahorina, the Pension Sport prides itself on the national dishes it serves in its restaurant Ognijiste (meaning 'hearth'). It is a medium-sized pension with basic rooms (no TVs). There is a TV room, ski & snowboard rental & professional instructors. It overlooks the start of the lower ski-lifts nearby. **$–$$**

Vikendika Sema Ski Chalet Jahorina bb; m 061 276 128; e info@ski-jahorina.ba; w ski-jahorina.ba. This is one for hardcore skiers. It is a no-frills accommodation facility that attracts many young ski enthusiasts. Simple but clean. **$–$$**

Villa Tamara (4 rooms, 10 apts) 057 270 015; e vilatamara@mogul.ba. As you're driving up to Jahorina, you will see a sign pointing to the right towards Villa Tamara. Follow the gravel road & you'll see a tiny hotel. It is located 3km from the slopes, so the accommodation is a bit cheaper. On the positive side, Tamara is in the quiet & serene part of Jahorina. There is a restaurant, which serves a wide range of local dishes. **$–$$**

BJELAŠNICA AND IGMAN SKI CENTRES These two names are also synonymous with the 1984 Winter Olympic Games. Bjelašnica hosted the men's alpine competitions, while Igman was the hub for all the Nordic disciplines (ski jumping, cross country, etc). Most of the infrastructure in this region was destroyed during the war, as were many of the traditional highland villages.

Considerable reconstruction has been completed and constant improvements are introduced every year. Bjelašnica's ski runs have been revived to almost pre-war level; all but two of the drag lifts have been reopened. Accommodation facilities now include two hotels and many apartments for hire.

A total of nine lifts are operational on these mountains. Bjelašnica has the better infrastructure and more challenging slopes, while Igman is a bit easier and also has a children's lift with soft hills to practise on. Bjelašnica has the steepest of all ski slopes in the country – it's quite a rush – and with small or no queues or waiting.

The skiing area on Bjelašnica has been rebuilt and is the most challenging of Bosnia's ski mountains. Bjelašnica has one blue run (Kolijevka), while all the other runs are red or black. Lift tickets are extremely cheap. One-day passes cost 30KM on weekdays and 35KM at weekends. Provided there are no ridiculous queues (most likely at weekends), you can easily get in a dozen runs in a day. There are medical and toilet facilities on site as well as a mountain rescue team.

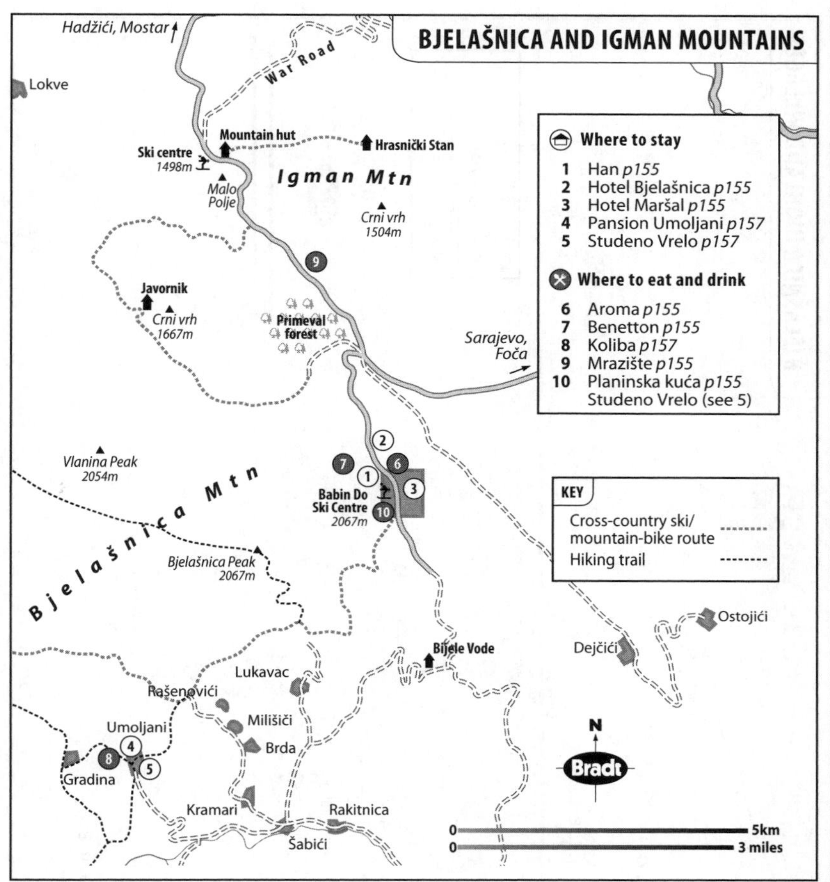

A few kilometres from the slopes of Bjelašnica are the ski runs on Igman Mountain, the north face of Bjelašnica. Igman is ideal for families and even has horse-drawn carriage rides through the snow. There are ski rentals here as well (for as little as 18KM per day), and the ski-lift passes are the same price as on Bjelašnica.

Getting there From Sarajevo via East Sarajevo, there are signs marked for Hotel Maršal about 6km east of the airport. There is only one right turn to be made at the large quarry, and that road leads directly to the ski centre and the hotel. From the centre of town the drive takes approximately 45 minutes. From the south, the best access route is again from Hadžići (20km south of Sarajevo centre). In the middle of Hadžići is a single road that leads directly to Igman. There is only one road, so it is nearly impossible to get lost once you're on the right route. The distance from Hadžići to Bjelašnica is 24km. Year-round, the public transport company GRAS services Igman and Bjelašnica from the suburb of Ilidža (see *Chapter 3*, pages 144–5) – minibuses travel twice daily to Igman–Bjelašnica–Sinanovići, via Hadžići. The cost is a mere 2KM. However, taking a direct bus (offered in winter only) is less complex. In the winter (usually January–March), Centrotrans offers a direct daily bus from Sarajevo to Bjelašnica. The bus leaves from Vijećnica at 08.30 and

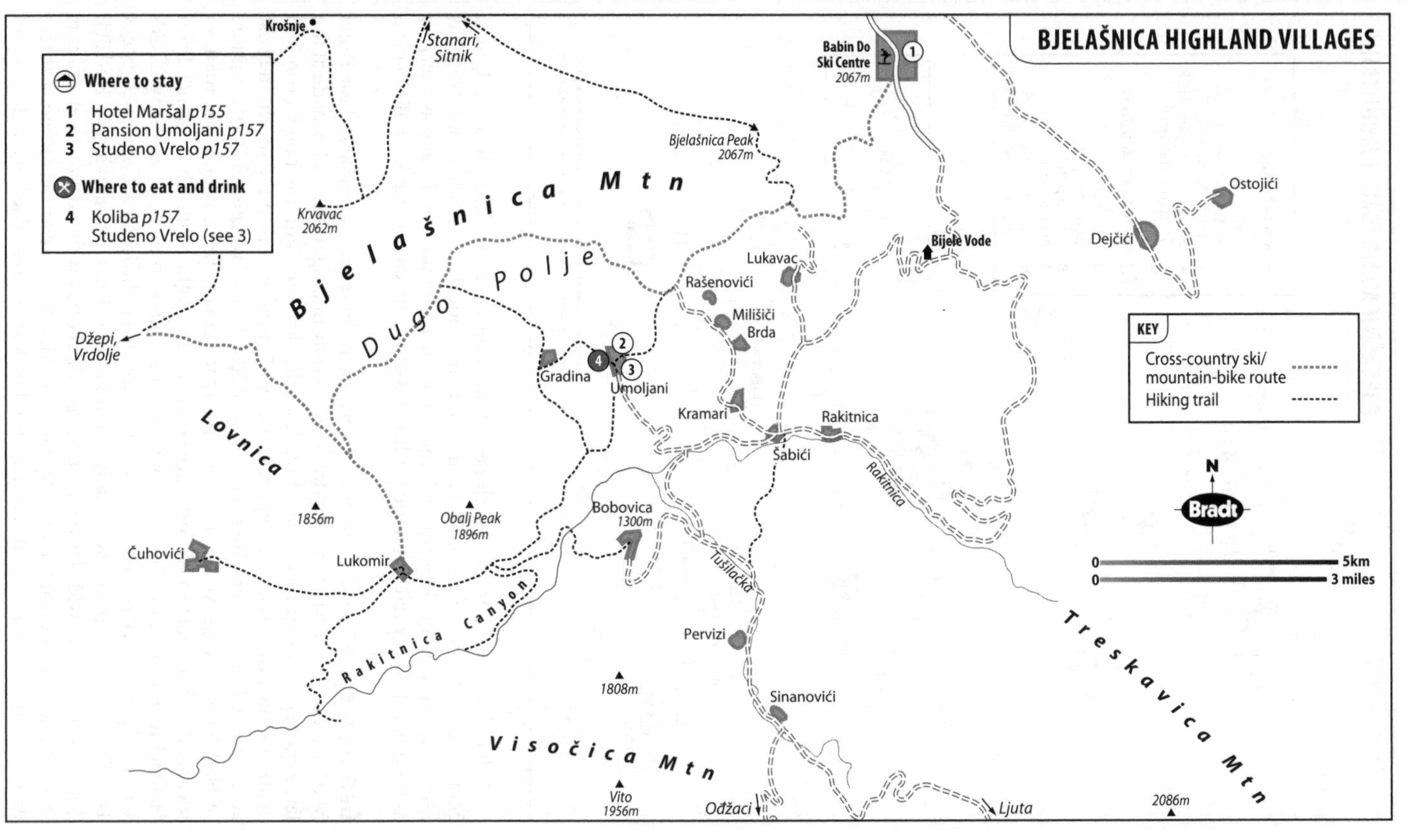

BJELAŠNICA HIGHLAND VILLAGES
KEY
Cross-country ski/ mountain-bike route
Hiking trail
N
Bradt
0 5km
0 3 miles
Where to stay
1 Hotel Maršal p155
2 Pansion Umoljani p157
3 Studeno Vrelo p157
Where to eat and drink
4 Koliba p157
Studeno Vrelo (see 3)
Babin Do Ski Centre 2067m
Bijele Vode
Ostojići
Dejčići
Lukavac
Rakitnica
Šabići
Rakitnica
Treskavica Mtn
2086m
Ljuta
Sinanovići
Odžaci
Pervizi
Tušilačka
Vito 1956m
1808m
Visočica Mtn
Bobovica 1300m
Kramari
Brda
Milišići
Rašenovići
Umoljani
Gradina
Bjelašnica Peak 2067m
Bjelašnica Mtn
Dugo polje
Obalj Peak 1896m
Rakitnica Canyon
Lukomir
Stanari, Sitnik
Krvavac 2062m
Krošnje
1856m
Lovnica
Čuhovići
Džepi, Vrdolje

departs from the mountain at 16.00. A ticket costs 7KM for the round trip (5KM for kids). Just like the bus for Jahorina, the best way to locate the bus in Sarajevo is to ask someone near the departure area. The timetable (**w** *bjelasnica.ba/local-transportation-en*) varies. A return ticket is 7.40KM (5.30KM for children). In both cases, you can buy tickets on the bus. It is wise to arrive early to get a seat.

Where to stay *Map, page 153*

In addition to the accommodation listed below, Bjelašnica offers self-catering apartments for rent. More information can be found at **w** bjelasnica.ba. Construction of new accommodation facilities continues at a steady pace, and the provision of bed and breakfast options in the surrounding villages is in the development stage.

Han (20 rooms) Babin do bb; 033 584 150; **e** info@hotelhan.ba; **w** hotelhan.ba. Han has improved the overall accommodation offer of Bjelašnica quite significantly. Perfectly located near the foot of the slopes, Han offers year-round activities from skiing to quad rides through the mountains. The rooms & design are modern & cosy. The restaurant serves excellent food but is a non-alcoholic establishment. However, one can go across the road to another hotel bar or to a café to have a drink. **$$–$$$**

Hotel Maršal (57 rooms, 13 apts) Babin do bb; 033 584 100, 033 584 200; **e** information@hotel-marsal.ba; **w** hotel-marsal.ba. Until recently the only hotel on Bjelašnica Mountain, it is located at the base of the ski-lifts, has space for about 70 guests & is a bargain for those accustomed to the outrageous prices of ski resorts in the West. All the rooms have sat TV & phone. They have a restaurant/bar that serves international & traditional foods. There is also a fast-food bar, disco & billiards room. The best fun is outside, however. The ski-lifts are 3mins away. Ski rentals are available in the hotel, and there are also lessons for beginners (in English). **$$–$$$**

Hotel Bjelašnica (63 rooms) Babin do bb; 033 976 921; **e** info@hotelbjelasnica.ba; **w** hotelbjelasnica.ba. This is the largest & perhaps most luxurious hotel on the mountain. The rooms, suites & apts are fitted out with the most contemporary & comfortable furnishings, & there is a posh restaurant with a panoramic view of the mountain. The hotel offers a fully equipped bar, plus a spa & wellness centre with a wide array of options for relaxation & fitness. **$–$$**

Where to eat and drink *Map, page 153*

As well as the three restaurants at the base of the Bjelašnica ski runs listed here, there are many other small cafés around the Bjelašnica ski lifts, but be forewarned that indoors you will inhale several packs of cigarettes just from the quantity of second-hand smoke. There are also a few fast-food stands scattered around, serving cheap, hearty food and warm drinks, such as mulled wine.

Bjelašnica

Planinska kuća Babin Do Ski Centre; 08.00–22.00 daily. This option serves authentic highland dishes & has a great traditional atmosphere. The homemade *pitta* (spinach or cheese pie) is the house speciality and is absolutely delicious. **$–$$**

Aroma Next to Hotel Maršal, Ski centre Bjelašnica. Serves traditional food of very good quality and with very low prices. Don't expect many veggies, as meat & stew are the order of the day in most mountain places. Aroma's international menu is head & shoulders above the rest. **$**

Benetton Babin Do Ski Centre; 08.00–16.00, 18.00–21.00 daily. Run by the ski centre, Benetton is open during the season only & serves fast food and drinks in a large, hangar-like building. **$**

Igman Mountain

Mrazište At the ski centre on Igman Mountain. The menu is a typically traditional one, and most of the fare is from the surrounding mountain villages. The food is excellent, especially after a few runs. There's often live light music. **$–$$**

What to see and do Bjelašnica is home to a large network of highland villages. There are fascinating medieval-like villages in the most stunning natural surroundings just a few minutes from the ski slopes. They are popular for one- or multi-day outings all year round; in winter it makes for great snow-shoeing trips, while the summer months offer spectacular hiking and mountain biking routes.

HIGHLAND VILLAGES

The highland villages of Bjelašnica and neighbouring Visočica Mountain have long been famous for their folklore, organic food, traditional architecture and lifestyles. Many of these villages were destroyed during the war but have been rebuilt, albeit not always in their traditional form. The villages are a last peek into Old World Europe and the traditional ways of life that have long since died out in the West.

LUKOMIR The village of **Lukomir** is perhaps the finest example of a highland village; it is the highest and most isolated permanent settlement in the country at 1,469m (4,500ft). The village, with its traditional architecture, has been deemed by the Historical Architecture Society of the United Kingdom as one of the longest continually inhabited villages in all of Europe. The stone homes with cherry-wood roof shingles mark a practice that can no longer be found elsewhere on Bjelašnica. The villagers are mainly shepherds who live off the sale of sheep products. Lukomir is known for its traditional attire as well, and the women still wear hand-knitted costume styles that have been worn for centuries. Electricity was introduced to the village and running water installation was completed in 2002. Access to the village is impossible between the first snows in December and late April, and sometimes even later, except by skis or on foot. Getting to Lukomir is complicated; you need an off-road vehicle to get close to it. There are no buses. It is best to visit the village as part of an organised tour, for example with Green Visions (page 89). However, if you decide to go on your own, you can drive from Sarajevo to Umoljani (pages 157–8) and hike (*approx 6½ hrs return*) the remainder of the way. This is mountainous terrain, so you should go prepared with hiking boots and other necessities. One way to hike is to go northwest on the road leading to the village of Gradina. Right before a place named 'Crveni Klanac' turn left (west). This is a marked trail leading to Obalj ridge. Following the edge of the ridge to the top, you can then descend to Lukomir. From Lukomir, you can continue on longer and even more scenic hikes, including Rakitnica. These hikes, too, are best organised with a tour guide, but if you are an experienced hiker and want to venture out on your own, visit **w** trailviadinarica.com and search for 'Lukomir' or 'Rakitnica' for directions and more information. There are easier or more difficult options to try, depending on fitness levels. If you have access to an off-road vehicle, you can drive to Umoljani and ask for driving directions from there. From Umoljani onwards, the road is not paved and accessible only during the warmer months.

There is magnificent hiking in the area along the ridge of the **Rakitnica Canyon**, which drops 800m below. This is the least-explored canyon in southern Europe. It stretches 26km and feeds the Neretva River in Herzegovina near Konjic.

Rakitnica is a natural wonderland. Hundreds of thousands of years of tectonic shifts have created the steep limestone walls of Visočica and Bjelašnica mountains. The crystal-clear river below is fed by the melting snows and the hundreds of underground aquifer systems, making Rakitnica River water potable for the entire length of the canyon. Thirty-two endemic species of plants, flowers and trees can be found in this tiny region of the Dinaric Alps.

UMOLJANI This village is more easily accessible than Lukomir. Although Umoljani was destroyed during the war, much of it has been rebuilt. The natural beauty of its surroundings, though, is still among the most striking in the area. The south side is a typical karst landscape that is dry and rather barren; the north side is lush with thick forest and green pastures and is ideal for hiking, walking or a picnic. The tombstones of ancient settlers can be found scattered around the village, with many medieval tombstones perched on high ridges.

There is no public transport to Umoljani. By car, it is a little over an hour's drive from Sarajevo. The easiest route is to go from Hadžići, a small town (practically a suburb) 20km southwest of the city, and close to Ilidža. At the entrance to Hadžići from Sarajevo, don't go towards the centre but straight towards Igman/Bjelašnica. Stay on the main road until Igman, and then at the intersection 'G Grkarica' where there is a police station, continue towards the Bjelašnica ski area, and then Šabići village. From here, it is about 16km to Umoljani. When you get to the village of Šabići, turn right towards Umoljani. If you get confused, you can ask for directions from someone in the Bjelašnica ski area.

There are several *pansions* now in Umoljani, with the best being Pansion Umoljani [map, page 153] (*30 beds;* **m** *061 228 142;* **e** *umoljani@gmail.com;* **w** *umoljani.com.ba;* **$**). There are also two **restaurants** in the village: Studeno Vrelo [map, page 153] (**m** *062 337 877;* **f** *StudenoVrelo;* **$**) situated in a log cabin close to the centre of the village, and Koliba [map, page 153] (**m** *061 511 323;* **f** *kolibaumoljani;* **$**), just past the main graveyard on the road to the summer settlement of Gradina. Both offer magnificent views and excellent food. Studeno Vrelo also has very nice accommodation.

THE LEGEND OF UMOLJANI VILLAGE

During Ottoman times a small village in the Bjelašnica highlands had to face its own demons. There were rumours of a dragon-like creature roaming the foothills of Obalj Mountain. Some shepherds swore they saw it, others claimed to have lost sheep to the creature. The villagers were panic-stricken. The local Muslim priest (*hodža*) decided to go and find this dragon. He expected to find nothing but asked the villagers to pray for him while he was gone. For days there was no sign of the *hodža* and the scared villagers diligently prayed. Then, as the tale goes, the *hodža* met the beast just above the shepherds' summer huts. He, too, used prayer as his main weapon, and in an instant the dragon was frozen in stone on top of the mountain. The *hodža* returned with news that he had defeated the dragon. He gave credit to the faith and prayers of the villagers for his impossible victory and named the village Umoljani, meaning 'Of the prayers'. On a peak just above the village of Umoljani is a rock formation that very much resembles a dragon.

During the last war the entire village was destroyed with the exception of the mosque. The story goes that before the war a Serbian commander's son was sick and none of the doctors could heal him or even diagnose the problem. He heard of a powerful *hodža* in the village of Umoljani and brought his son there. The *hodža* miraculously healed the ailing boy in the mosque. Several years later, when the Serbian military burnt down the village, the commander was the father of the healed boy – and out of superstition, guilt or who knows what, the mosque was spared and is the only remaining mosque of that type on Bjelašnica Mountain.

The seven old watermills that fell into disrepair during the war have been reconstructed and are a great place to visit on a hike. They can be seen on the left-hand (south) side on the approach to the village. There are now several homes open offering **bed and breakfast** services.

The valley of Studeno Polje is a magical little place, tucked behind the summer shepherd village of Gradina near Umoljani, and there have been several initiatives to start ecotourism in this area – Green Visions (page 89) is a regular visitor and several local villagers have set up establishments of their own. In between Umoljani and the summer settlement of Gradina is a small mountain hut run by a villager named Emin. You can have lunch, coffee and even spend the night there (**$**; $).

ŠABIĆI AND RAKITNICA These two villages are located only 15 minutes from Hotel Maršal (page 155). In Šabići the local community has attempted to preserve the *stećci* (page 20) and have created a necropolis in the centre of the village. Šabići is 1,160m above sea level and rests in the upper valley of the Rakitnica River. It acts as a centre for the other highland villages and is the only village with a school and medical clinic. There is also a hunting lodge. **Rakitnica** was the most beautiful representative of the Bjelašnica highland settlements. Its archaic architecture was of wood construction and many of the homes were over 150 years old. Unfortunately, the village was totally destroyed by Serbian forces during the war. The reconstruction of the village is complete but with modern design.

BOBOVICA The village of Bobovica sits high on the ridge above the Rakitnica Canyon, on the north slopes of Visočica Mountain. The village has stunning panoramic views of Bjelašnica, Visočica and Treskavica mountains, and there are well-maintained trails that travel deep into the steep canyon as well as to the high, sharp peaks of Visočica. **Sinanovići** is in the near vicinity of Bobovica and has several places to eat and overnight in traditional bed and breakfasts. It is situated in the valley of Tušilačka River, which is a tributary of the Rakitnica River. The area around the village is famous for its beautiful meadows, covered with wild flowers in the spring. Much of the village has been restored in traditional style. The Vrela mountain lodge is run by the Treskavica Mountain Association (*033 239 031*), and offers meals and accommodation. It is best to travel with a guide in this region as trails are not well marked and within 5km of the village are mined areas. There is a public bus line that travels along the main mountain routes from Ilidža via Maršal, Šabići, Umoljani (in the near vicinity), Bobovica and Sinanovići.

FARTHER AFIELD **Ostojići** and **Dejčići** villages are located further down off the main road from Sarajevo, towards the Bjelašnica ski centre. There are well-marked routes and a paved road that leads to both villages. These villages are set on the northeast side of Bjelašnica Mountain and are home to the largest medieval graveyards in Sarajevo Canton. These relics from Bosnia's heretic Christians mark the significance of highland life, dating back to the earliest Slavic settlers who assimilated with the indigenous Illyrian tribes as far back as the 7th century. There is a youth centre in Dejčići and accommodation is available in the homes of the villagers. This area too has mines on the upper slopes a few kilometres from the village and, although access to the village is perfectly safe, it is recommended to always travel with a guide.

TO THE EAST AND SOUTH OF SARAJEVO

EAST SARAJEVO At times it's hard to tell if East Sarajevo is a city, a town or an entire region. Geographically speaking, it only includes Pale to the east, and the suburbs of Lukavica and parts of Dobrinja to the south.

When the Dayton Peace Accords were signed, the Bosnian Serbs left Sarajevo city in droves. Whether in fear of retaliation for the siege of Sarajevo, or under pressure from the Serbian nationalist parties (SDS and the Radical Party) to form a unified Serbian Sarajevo, a large portion of the original Serbian population of Sarajevo now live on the eastern outskirts of the city and call it East Sarajevo.

Getting there and around There are regular public transport buses that run from the city (Federation) to East Sarajevo (Republika Srpska). The Centrotrans 'komercijala' bus route that starts in Sarajevo's old town (Vijećnica/City Hall) goes all the way to Dobrinja (🕘 *Buses run every 10mins 06.30–midnight Mon–Fri, 06.30–23.00 Sat, and every 30mins 08.30–23.00 Sun; one-way ticket costs 1.80KM*). From the last bus stop in Dobrinja, it is a mere 5-minute walk to the main centre of East Sarajevo, where a large international bus station is located. Trolleybus #103, which runs from Trg Austrije in the city centre, through Grbavica and all the way to Dobrinja, also gets close to East Sarajevo. From the last trolleybus stop in Dobrinja, it is a 5–10-minute walk to the main bus station in East Sarajevo, which services countless routes to other areas of the Republika Srpska (eg Trebinje and Banja Luka), Serbia, Montenegro, and more. Local transport around East Sarajevo is a bit more tricky. It's easier to take a taxi or walk.

Where to stay and eat Being that East Sarajevo was mainly built to house the many Serbs who left Sarajevo after the war in 1995, it is mainly a residential area with a small amount of businesses. There aren't really any tourist attractions to speak of. However, there is a handful of good restaurants and hotels that are generally less expensive than in Sarajevo and are conveniently close to the airport.

Hotel Espana (40 rooms) Ive Andrića bb; 057 961 200; **e** info@hotel-espana.net; **w** hotel-espana.net. This is the newest accommodation in East Sarajevo. The owner returned from living in Spain to start a restaurant & a small car wash. Those businesses went well, so he built a 4-storey hotel on top of the restaurant. Hotel Espana is the nicest hotel in East Sarajevo with modern amenities & all the creature comforts you could ask for. The mattresses are particularly comfortable. All rooms are en suite & have Wi-Fi, mini-bar, cable TV & AC. **$$**

Hotel Beograd (44 rooms) Vojvode Radomira Putnika 8; 057 316 877; **e** info@hotel-beograd.com; www.hotel-beograd.com. This hotel is conveniently located a 5-min drive from the airport. It offers decent accommodation, with a restaurant & bar. The rooms are basic but clean. All rooms are en suite & have sat TV, Wi-Fi, AC & a mini-bar. **$–$$**

Ribnjak Toplik Vuka Karadžića 250; 057 321 455; **e** restoran@ribnjaktoplik.ba; **w** ribnjaktoplik.ba; 🕘 09.00–23.00 daily. Toplik is one of the better restaurants in the wider Sarajevo region. Tucked into the countryside just beyond the Elektro-Techo Faculty, this place serves the best trout in town. The menu is impressive, with a wide selection of international & local cuisine. They serve excellent pork dishes, which are harder to find in Sarajevo city. **$–$$**

Knez Restaurant Đ D Mihajlovića 4; 057 320 220/221; **e** info@dak-is.com; 🕘 08.00–midnight daily. Knez is a bit hidden from sight & may be difficult to find; it is just east of Stadion Slavija, a small sports stadium. The restaurant serves a solid assortment of local & international cuisine. They have an excellent summer garden with a playground for children. **$**

Soho Lounge Bar Nikole Tesle 53A; **m** 065 436 029; **w** soholoungebar.ba; 🕘 07.00–23.00

daily. Soho used to be just a café/bar that served the best coffee in town. They have expanded their horizons & converted the café into a restaurant. They serve excellent soup, pasta & meat dishes. Soho generally attracts younger crowds & it is a popular place for socialising over afternoon coffee, or drinks in the evening. The food just seems to be an added bonus. $

Aroma Spasovdanska bb; 057 344 283; 08.00–23.00 daily. Across the street from Moja Radnja (see below) is Aroma, a charming & trendy café/bar with a wooden terrace. A generously sized glass of good Herzegovinian wine will cost you as little as 5KM, & in the summer, you can order a pitcher of sparkling Austrian-style spritzer: white wine, mineral water, lemon, & ice.

Shopping If you're looking to purchase high quality spirits (*rakija*) made from plum, wild pear, apple, apricot and more, there is a new shop in East Sarajevo called **Moja Radnja** (*Spasovdanska 27a; 057 344 288;* **w** *mojarakija.ba*), which sells locally produced *rakija* made with fruit grown in the owner's orchards, along with other local speciality foods and wine. The *rakijas* are expertly crafted and beautifully presented in stylish bottles. You can purchase small, souvenir-sized bottles with gold, silver or copper detailing.

Other Practicalities

Police

Police station Stefana Nemanje 13; 057 340 003

Bank

$ **UniCredit Bank** Vojvode Radomira Putnika 38; 24 hours. ATM.

Taxi

Radio Taxi East Sarajevo 057 340 200

Bus station

Bus station Srpskih vladara 2; 057 317 377

PALE AND ENVIRONS The mountain town of Pale is tucked in between Jahorina and Romanija Mountain. It was a small mountain town before the war, but has now blossomed into a significant centre. Aside from the universities and several administrative institutions of Republika Srpska being located here, its main economic activities are logging and tourism. Pale is close to Jahorina Olympic Mountain, in terms of geography and culture. It has been a ski centre since the 1984 Winter Olympics. Pale town itself doesn't have much to offer in terms of tourism, but the surrounding area has a tremendous wealth of natural resources, the most obvious being the dense, dark-green conifer forests that dominate the view in every direction.

Getting there and around The M-5 highway heads out of Sarajevo to Pale, 18km east. This is the only road out of Sarajevo to the east, via Bentbaša, near the old town. Just 12km along on the M-5 is the first main intersection to the left, and this leads up Romanija Mountain to Sokolac, Rogatica and the Prača River. The road eventually meets up with the Drina Valley and connects with Goražde to the west and Višegrad to the east. If you carry straight on at the first intersection, the road will take you to Pale, and from Pale there is only one mountain road to Jahorina ski centre. Centrotrans runs three buses daily from the bus station in East Sarajevo (page 111) to Pale, leaving at 06.00, 09.15 and 10.10, except for Sundays when only the 09.15 and 10.10 buses run. The buses returning from Pale to East Sarajevo depart at 14.00, 15.15, and 19.30 daily. The journey takes a little under an hour (single 4KM, return 8KM). This line is part of a longer route going to/from Montenegro, Bijelina, or elsewhere.

What to see and do The **Orthodox Ethno Gallery Ognjište** in Pale (*Trifka Grabeza bb; 057 225 779;* **e** *ognjiste@pakol.nel; 09.00–17.00*) not only exhibits Orthodox art and handicrafts, but is a gift shop with traditional musical instruments, pottery, clothes, literature and music.

To the east, Romanija Mountain dominates East Sarajevo. This lush, pine-covered mountain holds important historical significance for the Serbs. It is in these dense forests and scattered caves that Serbian *hajduks* (or rebels) hid from the Turkish armies. The most famous hiding spot is **Novak's Cave**. There is an excellent hiking trail to the cave with a wonderful view of **Jahorina Mountain**. The last 50m or so of the trail does require a bit of climbing, but climbing gear is not necessary. The *hajduks* co-ordinated raids from their hideouts in the heart of the mountain, and never gave in to Ottoman rule. Going even further back in time, on the **Glošina Plateau** between **Kopita** and **Romanija mountains**, are the remains of 2,000 gravestones believed to date to before Christ. In the same area a large field of *stećci* (medieval tombstones) implies the existence of the Bosnian Church (page 16). Nonetheless, this area is marked with traces of human settlements, going back thousands of years.

There are many caves worth exploring in this region. The most significant archaeological finds were in the **Orlovača Cave**, which is perhaps the most fascinating of all the accessible caves in Bosnia. The remains of cave bears (*Ursus spelaeus*) found are estimated to be more than 16,000 years old, and one of the largest bear skulls found in Europe has been excavated. The number, variety and size of the bones discovered make it one of the most significant palaeontological findings in the Balkans. The cave is also a habitat of the most endangered group of mammals in Europe – bats. There are professionally guided tours by students and professors from the **University of East Sarajevo** in Pale (**e** *univerzitet@u-es.com;* **w** *ues.rs.ba; guided tours 10.00–17.00 daily in the local language & English*). The cave itself, located on the limestone massif of Orlovača Mountain, is estimated to be over 2.5km long, and lit trails have been completed 610m deep into it. Digs in the vicinity of the cave suggest that there was a major prehistoric civilisation dating from the late Bronze Age that flourished here. Even remnants from the early Neolithic period have been found in nearby caves. The entire area is ideal for picnics along the river that flows through the cave, or for a wander in the surrounding hills. The region is safe from landmines. The entire area is now a base for scientific research and the funds raised from tourist visits are used to continue with further excavations and educational activities. Green Visions (page 89) also offers organised tours and hikes to the cave and the surrounding region.

There are also caves in **Bogovići** and **Litovac**, and the **Lednjača Cave** is named after the ice that can be found inside on a hot summer day. Orlovača Cave is the only cave that is marked and easily found. A guide is necessary for exploring the underworld of the others.

Monasteries or churches worth seeing are the **St George Church** from 1886 in Trnovo, and **St Luke's Monastery** on **Mount Trebević**, which is perhaps the most interesting church in the area. It is built in the old highland style with a wooden steeple and roof. Visitors are welcome and there are road signs off the main Trebević road to Jahorina from Sarajevo. Many of the churches in the region were built in the 1990s and although they are aesthetically attractive they are not a historical representation of the old Orthodox churches of Bosnia and Herzegovina. Speaking of Mount Trebević, I highly recommend walkers to trek to the top of Trebević through the beautiful pine forest. The views of Sarajevo and the large panorama of mountains to the south are stunning. Trebević is mined in the parts closer to town. If you are travelling from Trebević towards Jahorina, the right side of the road is safe but, as always, I recommend a guide in any areas that might pose a threat.

Treskavica Mountain I wasn't sure whether to write about this mountain or not. Treskavica changed hands half a dozen times during the war, and was heavily mined. However, it is remembered as the most beautiful mountain in the region, especially its four glacier lakes and dozens of smaller mountain lakes. It is said that there are more than 300 water sources throughout the entire range. Its highest peak, Pakliješ or Čaba Peak (Čaba meaning 'Mecca' from the Arabic word 'Kaba') at 2,086m, is one of the most remarkable tooth-shaped peaks in the country. Hikers and mountaineers do travel on Treskavica but **do not explore on your own**. If you must see it, like I did, then find an experienced guide who knows the mountain well. Stick to the trails. There are so many other beautiful mountains in the country; it is probably wisest to skip this one.

UPPER DRINA RIVER VALLEY The area of the Upper Drina has a long and rich cultural heritage. Marked by stunning mountains and canyon lands this is perhaps the most rugged part of the country, yet endowed with so much beauty. Nobel Prize winner Ivo Andrić's famous novel *The Bridge on the Drina* is set in the town of Višegrad. One can still walk across this magnificent bridge built to Ottoman design in the 16th century. It was in this region that Mehmed Paša Soković – statesman and perhaps the greatest personality ever to come out of Bosnia and Herzegovina – was born. He came from a small village near the town of Rudo along the Lim River.

Centuries later, Tito and the Partisans formed the first brigade in Rudo and fought one of the most decisive battles of World War II in Sutjeska, now the heart of the national park. It is an area as rich in history as it is in natural wonder. Ancient mosques and orthodox monasteries line the hilly countryside.

The **Drina River towns** of Foča, Višegrad and Goražde are the cultural and touristic centres of the region. Foča is home to both Sutjeska National Park (which hosts BiH's highest peak, Mount Maglić at 2,386m) and the crystal-clear Tara River. There is no better natural attraction in southeast Europe. Višegrad also has the only stretch of the Austro-Hungarian railway still functional. It runs from Mokra Gora in Serbia, home to film-maker Emir Kusturica's Ethno Village. Goražde is the largest city in the region as well as its geographical centre. From here it is easy to reach Foča to the southwest, or Višegrad and Rudo to the east and southeast. Although this region is not fully developed for tourism, the vast untapped potential makes it an ideal place for the wanderer, the independent or adventure traveller and fly fishers.

Getting there The road from Sarajevo east towards Pale turns off towards Sokolac and Rogatica; after Rogatica the E761 heads into the Prača river canyon before exiting at Ustiprača and the Drina River. From here Goražde and Foča are to the right and Višegrad and Rudo carry straight on. Travelling from Sarajevo to the southeast near the airport is the only other main route towards the Upper Drina region. This is the road that leads to Foča and travels through Trnovo and Dobro Polje. Near Foča the road again forks east and south. East leads to Goražde and south leads to Sutjeska National Park and eventually to Trebinje and Dubrovnik. Be aware that there are not many main routes in eastern Republika Srpska. The main arteries are all connected in a rather simple manner. It's just a matter of connecting the dots. A road map indicates all this quite clearly.

FOČA Foča is quite a nice little town on the edge of the mighty **Drina River** only 75km southeast of Sarajevo. The Ćehotina River flows through the town and feeds the Drina. The surrounding mountains are wild and beautiful. Hunting and fishing are popular sports in this region. Wildlife teems in the dense forest towards the border with Montenegro. Foča is also the gathering point for rafting on the Tara. There is nothing out of the ordinary about Foča except its proximity to two of the most beautiful places in Bosnia and Herzegovina: the Tara River Canyon and Sutjeska National Park. For nature lovers or adventurers, these are places you simply cannot allow yourself to miss.

For local advice visit the **tourist information centre** (*Tourism Organisation of Foča; Ul Šantićeva 16, 73300 Foča;* ☎ *058 212-416;* **e** *to.foca@yahoo.com;* **w** *focaravajuce.org;* 🕘 *08.00–15.00 Mon–Fri*).

Getting there There are a few buses every day running to and from Foča, most from the bus station in East Sarajevo, but a couple from the central bus station in the city of Sarajevo, too. The journey takes around 2 hours. It is best to call the stations in advance or to go in person to check the timetable and buy tickets.

Where to stay

Hotel Zelengora (25 rooms) Nemanjina 4, Foča; ☎ 058 210 013, 058 210 233; **e** info@hotel-zelengora.com. This hotel is a relic from Yugoslav times & is in fair condition. **$**

Motel Brioni (6 rooms) Solunskih dobrovoljaca 2, Foča; ☎ 058 210 646. This small motel is situated on the Cehotina River. Although it is not the ideal location for adventures on the Tara River or in Sutjeska NP, it is a very pleasant place for a meal on the riverbank. Rooms are simple but clean & nice. **$**

Where to eat and drink

Konoba Zlatna Dunja Njegoševa bb, Foča; ☎ 058 210 270; **f** Konoba-Zlatna-Dunja-509702312435130; 🕘 08.00–23.00 daily. Two brothers from Foča decided to open this tavern in 2015 feeling nostalgic about the lack of traditional places for gathering & eating. Zlatnja Dunja serves a true representation of the cuisine of eastern Bosnia, made the 'old way.' **$$$**

Monte Cristo Pizzeria Njegoseva bb, Foča; ☎ 058 210 555; **e**: montecristo.foca@gmail.com; 🕘 07.00–midnight daily. A truly refreshing change for Foča. This is a good value option, serving a range of food, not just pizza. The atmosphere is comfortable & simplistic. There is live music on some weekend evenings. Try the beefsteak, too. **$**

SUTJESKA NATIONAL PARK Although the park has been mentioned in the *Nature conservation* section of *Chapter 1*, page 10, it is worth mentioning again here. When a friend of mine travelled to Sutjeska for the first time he was struck by two things: the most amazing, untouched nature he'd ever seen, and the complete lack of information, road signs or even any sign of a person. What I aim to do here is help you do the visit yourself if you are travelling by car. If you are with a guide or an ecotourism group then just sit back and enjoy the ride.

Getting there Travelling from Sarajevo, take the **Sarajevo–Trnovo** road almost to **Foča** before turning right (roads are marked) for the **Trebinje–Dubrovnik** road. Once you turn right expect the road to become a bit narrower as you climb; the curvy bends barely give you enough room to stay on your side of the continuous road marking. Once you reach the top of the mountain (you'll know when you're there!) the massive faces of **Zelengora** and **Maglić** dominate the view. It's all downhill from there. Beware of the unconcerned cows in the road; they really could not care less that you are trying to get by, or that they are standing on what is purported to be a main road. After the fuel station (currently closed) you'll be in **Tjentište**. Thanks

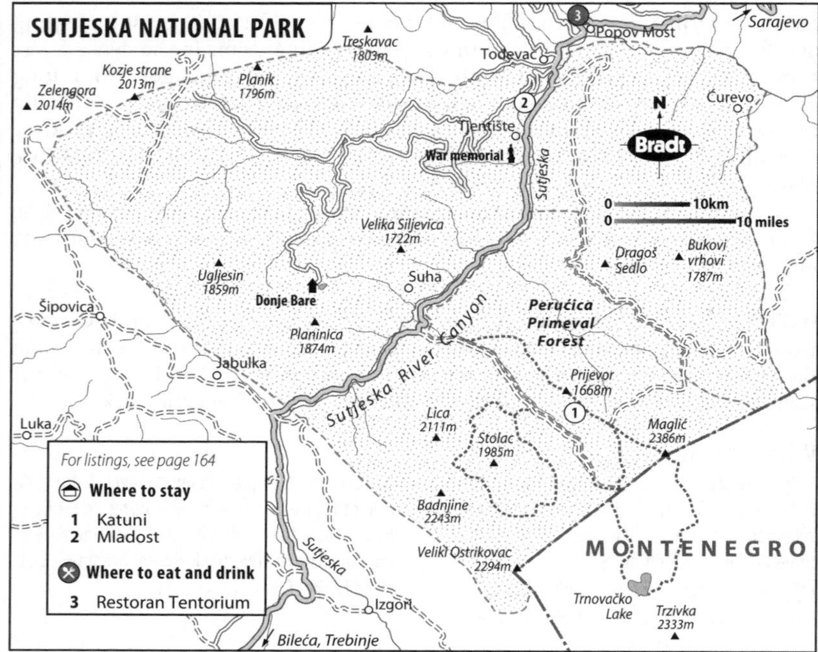

to an EU-funded project, signage within the park has drastically improved. There is even an information centre (that actually works) just next to Hotel Mladost.

Where to stay and eat *Map, above.*

Hotel Mladost (40+ rooms) Sutjeska National Pk, Tjentište bb; 73311; 058 233 118; e info@npsutjeska.net; w npsutjeska.net. This is the only accommodation in the park with facilities. It's nothing special, but the nature in the park makes up for the mediocre rooms & service. Be sure to ask for one of the 16 renovated rooms. The other rooms are stuck in the late 1980s & are not as comfortable or clean. The park can arrange for mountain-hut accommodation that is quite good, but without facilities (ie: electricity, running water). They now have English-speaking staff at reception & the information centre. $

Katuni (18 beds) Tjentište, Foča; 058 233 130; e info@npsutjeska.net; w npsutjeska.net. Katuni is located at the base of Maglić Mountain at an elevation of 1,700m. These traditional summer huts (*katuni*) have been recently restored to accommodate hikers. They are located inside the Sutjeska National Park & are open seasonally. Although they are just huts with bunkbeds, toilet & basic shower, the location & views are stupendous & are worth sacrificing small material luxuries to see. The closest shop is quite a way down the mountain so be sure to stock up. The road from Tjentište Valley to Katuni is gravel most of the way & not always in the best of shape. It is possible to pre-order meals at good prices. $

Restoran Tentorium Tjentište bb; m 065 414 465; e restoran.tentorium@yahoo.com; 07.00–23.00 daily. Cards not accepted. Tentorium is located in the Tjentište Valley, just outside of Sutjeska National Park. It is hands down the best restaurant in the region. The service is quick & friendly. They have an impressive selection of international & national dishes. The pork chops, soups & veal cutlets come highly recommended. $$

Shopping In May 2016, a lovely shop called **Bio Špajz** (Bio Pantry) was opened in Sutjeska. The shop sells original, handmade souvenirs and organic and healthy local foods and drinks, such as cheeses from the surrounding area and Trebinje, honey and wines from Herzegovina, and jams from Foča. Bio Špajz is located next to Hotel Mladost, near the main road between Foča and Gacko. Shopping here supports local communities and sustainable tourism.

What to see and do At Tjentište are the enormous monuments built in remembrance of the Battle of Sutjeska, which took place during World War II and was one of the key battles fought by the Partisans in defending the free territories. The sheer enormity of it makes it worth a look. From Tjentište you will need approximately 30 minutes to reach the scenic-view area of **Perućica Primeval Forest**. The road is now well marked and half way up the mountain there is a small ranger station, where you need to pay 5KM per person to enter the Perućica area of the park. There are information boards in English, with maps pointing out the various things to see in the immediate area. The walk out to the ridge takes only about 10 minutes and it gives an utterly amazing view. Bring a camera. The second stop is only 100m away at **Dragoš Sedlo**. Off to the left is a small hill, literally 20m away. From there you get a magnificent view of **Maglić Mountain**, the highest point in Bosnia and Herzegovina, at 2,386m above sea level. Down to the right of the road is a natural fountain of potable water (trust me) and the beginning of the marked trails that lead through Perućica. The trails are marked – they are not always highly visible, however – and lead deep into the last primeval forest in Europe. It's not a super-hard hike but you should be wearing good shoes, and if you're not in the best of shape maybe it would be better to drive up to the next spot, **Prijevor**.

From Dragoš Sedle, you'll travel another 4–5km before coming to a right turn. It's the first and only turn-off and the one you want to take. Another 3–4km and you'll reach **Prijevor** at 1,668m. Park here. The long, bald ridge in front of you is great for a picnic, stroll or a good hour-long walk. There are some *katuni* huts located here; they are available for rent during the summer season. The trail east leads you to **Trnovačko Lake** (we're on foot now). The trail is obvious for most of the way and then you'll have to use your trekking senses if you'd like to make it all the way to the lake. Trail markers appearing as a red circle with white interior markings lead to the lake. Bring your passports with you; you have just crossed into **Montenegro**. There may be a park ranger who will check your passports.

Back at Tjentište, if you'd like to travel to the other side of the park to **Zelengora** (green heights) Mountain, then you should turn left out of the hotel car park and left again after the fuel station. The drive to **Donje Bare** hut is only 15km to the northeast but it will take a good hour to get there. The road is gravel and you will climb 1,000m before you reach the six-berth mountain hut. There is usually a ranger at the hut, but here you are free to roam wherever you like. Open meadows and beech forests surround this tranquil lake. Walking further on, you stand the chance of spotting a bear; although wolves are in the area, sightings are rare.

If you travel south on the main road (past the cows) towards **Gacko–Trebinje–Dubrovnik,** you'll enter the rugged canyon of the river for which the park is named. The **Sutjeska River** has carved out this deep canyon lined with endemic Munika black pines. There are several places along the river to stop for a picnic or to simply stand in awe.

TARA RIVER

Getting there The Tara River runs along the border with Montenegro and is best approached from Foča with a guide. The small dirt tracks along the Tara on the Bosnian side are not clearly marked and it is easy to get lost. The easiest approach is from Durmitor National Park in Montenegro, but that requires border crossings and more directions. Stick with the guide when searching out the Tara River. Foča is accessible from the south via Trebinje–Gacko–Sutjeska National Park if you are coming from the coast or Herzegovina. From Sarajevo, the main southeast route via Trnovo and Dobro Polje leads directly to Foča.

Where to stay and eat

Rafting Centar Drina-Tara (70 bungalows) Bastasi bb, Foča; **m** 065 906 188; **e** office@raftingtara.com; **w** raftingtara.com. This centre is an excellent location for anyone planning a rafting trip on the Tara & Drina rivers. It is located on the banks of the Drina River. The camp has comfortable & clean rooms. Free parking & Wi-Fi are available. Traditional meals are made of organic, locally grown ingredients. At weekends it is the norm to have live music. Most of the guides & skippers are trained professionals. **$–$$**

Camp Hum (85 beds) Bastasi bb, Foča; **m** 066 006 990; **e** rezervacije@rafting-tarom.com. This is a sister camp of an older Camp Tara 87 & is located right next to it. You can choose between dbl- & multiple-bed rooms. An excellent restaurant serves local cuisine with an additional vegetarian menu. The camp also offers a sauna for relaxation after an exciting day of rafting. **$**

What to see and do Coined the 'jewel of Europe' (by the locals of course), this wild, turquoise-blue river is a raging mass of water fed by the towering mountains of **Durmitor National Park** in Montenegro. The Tara River traverses the border of Bosnia and Montenegro, with 30km of it in Bosnia and the rest belonging to the national park in Montenegro. It rises from the mountain ranges in the northern part of Montenegro and flows 140km until meeting with the **Piva River** and forming the **Drina River**, one of the longest and largest rivers in the Balkans.

For eons the powerful flow of the Tara River has hollowed out a soft limestone surface, creating the sculpted form of gorges and chasms that we see today. Age-old earth erosion has created the 82km-long canyon, the second largest in the world after the Colorado. At its deepest, the canyon soars 1,300m.

Along the river's banks the vegetation is very dense: black pine, eastern hornbeam, black ash, elm and linden, and in higher areas can be seen cork oaks, more hornbeams, maples and beech. In the areas above the 1,000m mark, there are fir and spruce forests. The black pine forests are of special interest. *Crni pod*, or the black floor, is home to unusually tall trees. Some reach as high as 50m and are more than 400 years old.

Aside from nature lovers and fishermen, the river also attracts a large number of adrenaline junkies. Rated at level 3–5, the river offers some of the most intense and challenging rafting in Europe. A ride on one of the 'real' rafts, wood logs tied together and guided by a massive wooden rudder, is quite an experience. There are, of course, rafting outfits that provide sturdy and safe rubber rafts with all the necessary gear. Most groups operate out of Foča (see below; there are also several rafting agencies in Montenegro) and offer breakfast, lunch and overnight camping in their rafting packages.

Rafting operators

Highlander Mojkovačka bb, Foča; **m** 065 475 201; **e** highlandertim@hotmail.com; **w** highlandertim.com

Rafting Club Drina-Tara Bastasi; 058 220 212; **m** 065 906 188; **e** office@raftingtara.com; **w** raftingtara.com

Rafting Club Encijan Kralja Petra bb, Foča; 058 211 150/220; **m** 065 626 588; **e** encijan@teol.net; **w** pkencijan.com; 09.00–17.00

Rafting Club Montings Karadjordjeva 61, Foča; 058 210 698; **m** 065 584 754; **e** info@tararafting.net; **w** tararafting.net

A MAGICAL MOUNTAIN ADVENTURE

For many locals, Sutjeska National Park is more of a cultural monument to a Partisan defeat of the Germans during World War II. But the true value of this gem is its old-growth forests, bear and wolf populations, and hundreds of square kilometres of pristine wilderness. If you are visiting BiH, this is certainly a 'can't miss' trip. I highly recommend at least two days in this natural oasis.

Day 1 would start in Sutjeska National Park, where you'll venture into Perućica Primeval Forest. This trip, however, does something out of the ordinary. You can trek down below the 98m Skakavac Waterfall that jumps out of the forest. It's a sight you'll never forget: trees that tower 60m into the skyline fighting for a piece of light and then the massive rock faces that the stream has carved right through the middle of the forest. The water pounds so hard into the pools below that anyone within a 30m radius will be drenched. It's not an easy trek, but a stunning 5- or 6-hour hike that I promise you won't be able to find anywhere else in Europe. At day's end you take about an hour's drive through more marvellous terrain to the campgrounds on the Tara. Here you'll have the comfort of wooden bungalows, magnificent local food and the turquoise-blue Tara flowing just a few metres from camp. Bonfire, guitars, good food and booze are on the menu all evening.

Day 2 is a slow start. After a long night you can sleep in and wake up to birds dancing on the tree lines. Breakfast is served around 09.00 and one has time to wander the many trails around the Tara before the next adventure begins. Around noon, when the sun is at its highest, you hit the water. Rafting the Tara for 3 hours will rejuvenate the soul like you've never known. Waterfalls, one of the deepest canyons in Europe at 1,300m, adrenaline, tons of fun and untouched nature are the only things on the agenda for today. The journey ends in Scepan Polje on the border with Montenegro where you'll be transported back to Foča so you can return to Sarajevo, Mostar or Dubrovnik.

This is a truly remarkable trip. Once you arrive in Foča on the first day, your worries are all over. You don't have to drive, cook or even think. Just enjoy. I've travelled this country through and through and must say this mystical mountain adventure was one I will never forget.

Encijan and Highlander are locally based clubs who organise these trips. They have internationally certified skippers and run the campgrounds on the Tara along with hiking, biking, wildlife observation and rafting trips. They are well organised, professional and fun. For reservations contact **Encijan Mountain Association** (*73300 Foča;* ☎ *058 211 150;* **m** *065 626 588;* **e** *encijan@teol.net;* **w** *pkencijan.com*) or **Highlander** (page 90).

Rafting Club Tara 87 Foča; **m** 065 719 195; **e** info@kamptara87.com; **w** kamptara87.com; ⏲ from April 15

Tara-raft Bastasi bb; **m** 065 782 014; **e** info@tara-raft.com; **w** tara-raft.com

GORAŽDE AND NOVO GORAŽDE Goražde is the largest east Bosnian town in the **Drina Valley**. Before the 1992–95 war it served as the industrial centre for the entire region. During the war, it was an isolated enclave and heavily bombed for three years. Today's Goražde is considerably changed and quite a bit brighter, although there aren't any don't-miss attractions for visitors.

With a dusting of economic activity, the town's industry has made a comeback of late that has improved conditions in Goražde. The Drina is a favourite spot for swimming and rafting and the cafés and restaurants along its banks are always full. **Novo Goražde** was home to the first printing press in Bosnia and Herzegovina in the early 1600s, which is now the location of St George's Church. It has long been a stopover along the trading routes from Serbia and Montenegro to Sarajevo. To the south of Goražde is one of the largest medieval graveyards in the country. It is estimated that around 600 *stećci* are in one hillside cemetery. Some of the old *mahalas* from Turkish times remain in decent condition, and the old-style homes can be seen in the centre of town. The mosques have been restored and the call to prayer can again be heard echoing through the valley. Alongside its Islamic culture, Goražde has a significant Orthodox history, as is evident from the Orthodox church here, built in 1446.

The Drina River is the largest tourist attraction in Goražde. There is excellent fishing in several spots from Ustiprača to Novo Goražde. From the centre of Goražde east to Novo Goražde there is a 12km walking path along the Drina. It's a fantastic place for a morning or evening stroll. There is also a fun wooden-rafting adventure on the slower waters of the Drina from Ustikolina to Goražde. It's an all-day trip with several stops for swimming and lunch along the way. At the starting point is a nice **motel and restaurant** called Pansion-Restoran Baša (*Omladinska bb, Ustikolina;* **m** *062 408 509;* **e** *kontakt@basa.ba;* **w** *basa.ba;* ⌚ *07.00–23.00 daily;* **$–$$**; **$–$$**), in Ustikolina.

At the end of the journey is the **restaurant** Ćukija. This is the last leg of the river before it turns into the artificial lake from the dam in Višegrad. Ćukija is a great place for a rest and an excellent lunch in the shade right next to the Drina with a wide range of home-cooked meals. Ustiprača – which literally means mouth of the Prača – is the nearby intersection from Goražde to Višegrad where the Prača River empties into the Drina. If you are in transit between Bosnia and Serbia and Montenegro a smart **motel** can be found on the main road.

There is a landmine problem in several mountains around Goražde, so you are not advised to walk or hike on your own. A local businessman, however, has created a mountain oasis near Goražde. About a half-hour drive towards the western mountain ranges of Goražde is an area called Bijele Vode. Bijele Vode means white waters and here a small water-bottling company has opened. The same company has built a **restaurant** and **lodge** that may well be one of the loveliest in the country. Entirely done in wood and stone construction, Bijele Vode [map, pages 148–9] (📞 *038 245 050)* truly integrates into its natural surroundings. The restaurant has excellent food with a traditional and international menu. The wooden bungalows all have small but cosy living rooms and a loft bedroom for two people. The bathroom facilities are all modern and there is always hot water. Bijele Vode also 'owns' 35km of forest in the mountains surrounding it. A hunting range has been created here but because it is private any walks and wildlife observation can be arranged by the management. They have guides and translators (English and German) and although they are new at this type of thing, customer service and organisation are very good.

The area has traditionally been a fruit-growing area, and Goražde is becoming known for its excellent apples. Each autumn the town hosts an Apple Fair celebrating the apple harvest, the fruit-growing tradition and the fruit itself – including all the local produce made from apples.

Where to stay

Drinska Bašta (4 apts) Omladinska 41; 📞038 221 543. Drinska Bašta is mostly known as a great restaurant (see opposite) but it also has 4 apts upstairs. All the apts have French beds, phones, TVs & internet access. Some have views of the Drina. Drinska Bašta is located on

above left **The Jahorina ski resort offers excellent, Olympic-quality runs and snow for four months of the year** (E/S) pages 147–52

above right **A network of stunning trails, including the Via Dinarica, runs through the Dinaric Alps** (MT/DT) pages 88–9

below **A kayaker watches one of the locals jump from the reconstructed Stari most in Mostar** (P/S) page 193

left Pensioners gather in Trg Oslobođenja in Sarajevo year-round to play chess with life-size pieces (SS) page 135

below Traditional craftsmen can still be found working in their shops (S/S) page 129

bottom Folk music and dance are still very much alive today in Bosnia and Herzegovina. Here, dancers at the Lukavac International Folklore Festival (A/DT)

above **The Srebrenica-Potočari Memorial Centre & Cemetery in Srebrenica was opened in 2003** (AV/S) page 324

below **In the remotest villages of the Bjelašnica Highlands traditional practices still live on. Here, men from Lukomir making scythes** (TC)

above The *tekija* dervish house in Blagaj is a magical place, built at the base of a 200m rock face at the source of the Bosna River (DT/S) page 201

left Religious harmony has always been the backbone of Sarajevo's multi-ethnic community. Here, the neo-Gothic Catholic cathedral (SS) page 134

below A range of *stećci* (medieval tombstones) across the country were inscribed by UNESCO in 2016 (TABH) pages 219–20

above The Tvrdoš Orthodox Monastery near Trebinje dates from the 15th century and is now famous for the wine and honey made by its monks (SV/DT) page 228

right For those willing to bear the dizzy spiral staircase to the top, the minaret of Mostar's Koski Mehmed-Pasha Mosque is open for public access. The view speaks for itself (SS) page 193

below Višegrad's magnificent Ottoman bridge features in Ivo Andrić's novel *The Bridge on the Drina* and came to fame when the author was awarded the 1961 Nobel Prize for Literature (369/S) page 169

above **The Hutovo Blato wetland centre is home to 240 types of birds: the largest bird migration centre in southeast Europe** (M/S) pages 214–15

left **At 2,386m, Maglić Mountain is Bosnia's highest peak and a challenging ascent even for experienced climbers** (SS) page 162

below **Ramsko Lake was created when the Rama River was dammed in 1968** (LN/S) page 234

above **The 25m Kravica Waterfalls are the most impressive in Herzegovina and a popular swimming spot for locals** (TC) page 211

left & below left **Although their numbers dropped during the 1990s, bears and wolves are not uncommon in Sutjeska National Park** (JC/FLPA, MC/FLPA) pages 163–5

below right & bottom right **Hutovo Blato Bird Reserve is home to a vast array of species, including ruff and great crested grebe** (WW/FLPA, PL/S) pages 214–15

bottom left **Chamois inhabit the pristine landscape of Vranica Mountain** (B/BF/FLPA) pages 266–7

the riverbank & only minutes from downtown Goražde. **$$$**

Behar (18 rooms, 6 apts) Trg Branilaca bb; 038 227 997; **e** hotel.behar@yahoo.com; **w** behar.co.ba. Cards not accepted. For years, Goražde was handicapped because it didn't have a hotel. In 2008, things finally changed. Behar was built where the Hotel Drina stood before the war. The rooms are clean, comfortable & nicely furnished. The outdoor terrace overlooks the river. Behar is known for one other thing: this is where Angelina Jolie & Brad Pitt stayed in 2010. Their room is now the 'Angelina & Brad' suite. There are photos of them all over the hotel. **$$**

Casablanca (2 apts plus rooms). See restaurant listing, below. **$–$$**

Motel Jagodić (9 rooms) Ustiprača bb; **m** 065 234 442. Jagodić is located in Ustiprača, on the way to Goražde from Sarajevo. This tiny motel has clean & comfortable rooms. All have phone & TV. There is a traditional restaurant. Jagodić also has its own floating deck – anchored on the Drina, of course – just several metres from the motel. In the summer, you can enjoy your meal there. **$**

Odmor na selu Alije Hodžića 60; 065 770 860; **m** 061 156 002; **e** odmornaselugd@gmail.com; **w** agroturizam.ba. A one-stop shop for those looking for an authentic rural experience. This cluster of rural homes offers an impressive selection of activities, whether it be simple country dining or picking herbs with the locals. Guests are treated as one of the family – which also means carrying one's own load. They can also organise rafting or biking excursions throughout the rural areas of the Drina Valley. Each home has the capacity to accommodate 8–10 people. **$**

Where to eat and drink

Drinska Bašta Omladinska 41; 038 221 543; 08.00–22.00 daily. Drinska Bašta, or Drina garden, is located on the right bank of the Drina River. As it implies, they have a beautiful, spacious garden, where you can enjoy their mouth-watering veal under the *sač*. If you're hungry, order the Diplomatic plate. This assortment of meat can easily feed 2 people with healthy appetites. But, don't leave without trying their *begova čorba* (bey's stew). Many say it's better than anywhere in Sarajevo. It costs only 3KM. Finish with apple pie – it's homemade & always fresh. **$$**

Casablanca Mravinjac bb; 038 822 000; 07.00–23.00 daily. One of Goražde's best-kept secrets. Casablanca – in the direction of Foča & 5km from Goražde – is widely regarded to be the best restaurant in the area. The owner-chef, Hamed, spent 15 years sailing around the world & learning about international cuisine. He cooks everything himself & everything is extraordinary. The menu contains Mediterranean, French, German & African dishes. The Hawaii steak with pineapple is a speciality. The fish is top-flight. For those less adventurous, go for the Casablanca plate (cordon bleu veal fillet, beef steak, chips, croquettes & vegetables). Also, all the ingredients are homegrown & organic. Hamed is a Slow Food Association representative for BiH. People travel from Sarajevo to eat here. Casablanca also offers 2 luxurious apts & several rooms. The best thing: Hamed makes your b/fast in the morning. **$–$$**

Pizzeria Gallery Prvi maj 1; **m** 061 206 596; 08.00–midnight daily. Located on the Lower Bridge (closer to the city stadium). It is one of the more elegant restaurants in town. Ćiro, the owner, has been in this business for more than 30 years. The interior is wonderfully decorated with wooden furniture, which is contrasted by soothing blue walls & drapes. Beautiful paintings cover the walls. If you are looking for an intimate atmosphere with unobtrusive soothing music & excellent pizza, this is your best option. **$–$$**

VIŠEGRAD This town, too, has seen better days, yet Višegrad is still a strikingly beautiful settlement along the Drina River, almost on the border with Serbia. The town is famous for the **Ćuprija na Drini** (Bridge on the Drina) which is a magnificent Ottoman bridge spanning the wide river. It gained its fame from the Nobel Prize winner Ivo Andrić's novel, *The Bridge on the Drina*. The **Mehmed paša Sokolović bridge**, a UNESCO World Heritage Site, was first built in 1577.

The old part of town, once a charming example of old Ottoman architecture, is in dire need of maintenance and the area around Višegrad is wild and untamed. In the remote hills towards the border you can hear the howl of wolves at night.

Dobrun Monastery, built in 1343, is one of the oldest monasteries in the country. It is open to visitors and is clearly visible on the main road from the border crossing to and from Serbia. The monastery has a very interesting museum and gallery, which is free (you are encouraged to leave a donation). It was funded under the royal Karadzordzevic family, whose living members now split their time between the UK and Serbia. The hills and caves around the monastery are close and offer ideal spots for photography. To the west the deep gorge of the **Lim River** plunges into the Drina from **Rudo**. The Lim originates in the Prokletija Mountains (the end of the Dinaric chain) in the small Montenegrin town of Plav. Hunting is quite popular and the Drina always seems to be willing to sacrifice some of its biggest fish to anglers. There are no organised tourist activities or even a sign to tell you where you are.

You can visit the **Gradska Galerija** (town gallery) on Užičkog korpusa 14 and the **People's Library Ivo Andrić** on the same street. For the wandering soul it's an interesting place to sit on the bridge and soak up the energy of the Drina racing below. The villagers may look at you with a bit of suspicion at first but after the first *rakija* you'll have made some new friends. Kamengrad, also known as Andrićgrad (**w** *andricgrad.com*), is a striking, albeit controversial, 'town within a town' built by the film director Emir Kusturica. It is a replica of old Ottoman, Austro-Hungarian and traditional Bosnian architecture built in honour of Nobel laureate Ivo Andrić. It is 23,000m^2 and cost approximately 30 million KM (€15 million) to build. With the up-and-coming addition of the narrow-gauge tourist train from Serbia (actually a reconstruction of a historical train route), Višegrad is certain to become one of eastern Bosnia's most attractive tourism destinations.

Getting there

By plane

Sarajevo airport (*Kurta Schorka 36, Sarajevo;* ☎ *033 289 100;* **w** *sarajevo-airport.ba*) Sarajevo airport is 120km from Višegrad. From Sarajevo there are regular buses to Višegrad from the main bus terminal. There are daily buses from the East Sarajevo bus terminal near the airport as well.

Belgrade airport (*11180 Beograd 59, Republic of Serbia;* ☎ *+381 11 209 4444;* **w** *beg.aero*) The closest major airport to Višegrad is in neighbouring Serbia. There are buses from Belgrade city centre that run to the southwest of Serbia where you can catch a bus to Višegrad. By car it is about a 3-hour drive.

By train The closest main international train station to Višegrad is in Sarajevo; however, no trains run between Sarajevo and Višegrad.

By bus From Sarajevo, there are regular buses to Višegrad from both the city of Sarajevo and the East Sarajevo bus station. There are several departures per day from both locations. It is best to call the bus stations or go in person to find the most up-to-date timetable and purchase a ticket.

Višegrad Bus Station Trg palih boraca bb; ☎ 058 620 873. There are daily buses to & from Višegrad from Sarajevo, Trebinje, Banja Luka & many other destinations within BiH. There are also daily buses from Serbia arriving from Belgrade, Novi Sad & Čačak.

By car The M-5 road is the main route between the central part of eastern Bosnia and Serbia. Višegrad is easily accessible from Belgrade (280km), via Užice, and Sarajevo (120km), via Rogatica and Ustiprača.

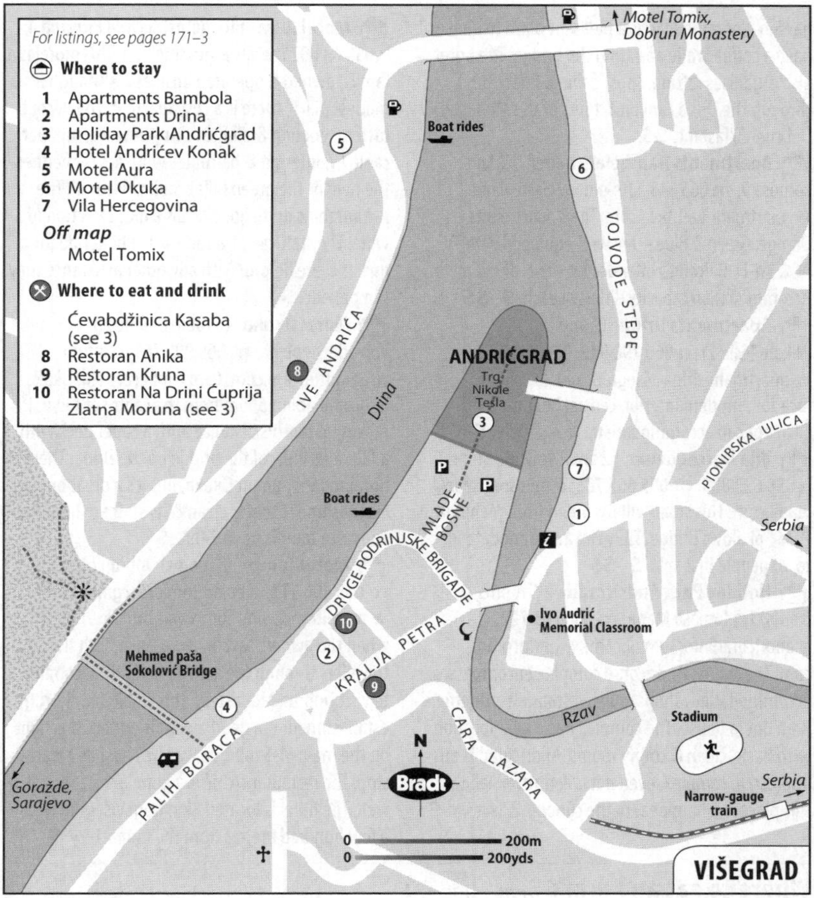

VIŠEGRAD

For listings, see pages 171–3

Where to stay

1 Apartments Bambola
2 Apartments Drina
3 Holiday Park Andrićgrad
4 Hotel Andrićev Konak
5 Motel Aura
6 Motel Okuka
7 Vila Hercegovina

Off map

Motel Tomix

Where to eat and drink

Ćevabdžinica Kasaba (see 3)
8 Restoran Anika
9 Restoran Kruna
10 Restoran Na Drini Ćuprija
Zlatna Moruna (see 3)

Motel Tomix, Dobrun Monastery · Boat rides · Vojvode Stepe · Ive Andrića · Drina · Andrićgrad · Trg Nikole Tesla · Pionirska ulica · Mlade Bosne · Druge Podrinjske Brigade · Serbia · Ivo Audrić Memorial Classroom · Kralja Petra · Mehmed paša Sokolović Bridge · Rzav · Stadium · Cara Lazara · Palih Boraca · Goražde, Sarajevo · Narrow-gauge train · 0 200m · 0 200yds

Tourist information

Tourism Organisation of Višegrad
Užičkog korpusa bb; 058 620 950; e info@visegradtourism.com, info@visegradturizam.com; w visegradtourism.com. The organisation has made considerable strides in the past few years in improving its website, information centre & gathering information on a wide range of tourism services. An information centre is located just near the Mehmed Paša Sokolović bridge, where all types of tourist information can be found.

Where to stay *Map, above.*

Višegrad is a small town that can be covered on foot comfortably. It has a number of decent hotels and other places to stay, all located within walking distance from one another. Višegrad had a difficult history during the war, and in some ways this is still palpable to the observant visitor.

Hotel Andrićev Konak (18 rooms, 5 apts) Trg palih boraca 6; 058 620 710; w hotelandricevkonak.com. Andrićev Konak is located in the centre of the Old Town, on the bank of the Drina River. Rooms have AC, TV, Wi-Fi, & a view of the Drina River & Mehmed Paša Sokolović bridge. The best aspect of the hotel is the location. The rooms are comfortable enough & the summer garden along the river is a pleasant place to dine or have a coffee while admiring the bridge. The hotel also organises rafting, sport fishing, boat rides through the Drina canyon & tours of the Monastery Dobrun. B/fast inc. **$$**

Apartments Bambola (3 apts) Užičkog korpusa 9; **m** 065 143 430; **e** dora95@teol.net; **w** apartmani-bambola.com. The 3 apartments – Orange, Green & Blue – are well-equipped with TV, AC & Wi-Fi. Balconies offer decent views of the town. Accommodation capacity differs in each. **$–$$**

Apartments Drina (2 apts) Nikole Tesle 2; **m** 066 190 049, 066 788 832; **w** apartmani-drina-visegrad.com. Excellent location, modern interior, central heating & AC. Each apt can accommodate up to 4 people. **$–$$**

Vila Hercegovina (2 apts) Vojvode Stepe 1; 058 622 888; **m** 065 665 785; **e** milosninkovic@ymail.com. This small 'villa' is 500m from Mehmed Paša Sokolović bridge. They can accommodate up to 10 people in 2 apts. **$–$$**

Holiday Park Andrićgrad (65 rooms, 8 apts) Trg Tomasa Mana; **m** 066 703 722; **e** andricgradinfo@gmail.com; **w** andricgrad.com. The tourist Andrićgrad complex encompasses accommodation, shops, pubs, restaurants, cinema & an opera house. The complex has a neat location with basic, clean & comfy rooms. Andrićgrad is an impressive complex, even if it is controversial, so this place might appeal to the curious. B/fast inc. **$**

Motel Aura (10 rooms) Gavrila Principa 4; 058 631 021; **e** auravgd@teol.net. This motel is a family-owned & operated business. Although it's a modest place, there is a cosy feel to it. The décor is tasteful enough & all the rooms have AC, minibar, cable TV, internet & balconies with views of either the river or the green hills around Višegrad. The restaurant is quite good & has a nice selection of wine. The staff can arrange a Drina boat ride for guests & are helpful with any other assistance they can provide. **$**

Motel Okuka (6 rooms/19 beds) Vojvode Stepe bb; **m** 065 998 761; **e** info@visegradturizam.com. Cards not accepted. Okuka is located about 500m from the centre of town. It makes up for this distance with a super deck with a fabulous view of the bridge on the Drina. There is nothing fancy about Okuka, but it's a great budget establishment that is clean & its staff are friendly. The restaurant is open 24hrs. **$**

Motel Tomix (8 rooms) Dobrun bb; **m** 065 406 111; **e** bojan.tomic79@gmail.com; **w** moteltomix.com. Tomix was built in 2009, when the owners saw an increase in both transit travellers through the area & the faithful coming to visit Dobrun Monastery. This small, family-run establishment is a good, no-frills option. It is right on the main M-5 road, so it serves best as a transit stop. The restaurant/café is a popular rest spot as well. The hotel is located 8km from Višegrad & just a few hundred metres from the monastery. **$**

Where to eat and drink *Map, page 171.*

Zlatna Moruna Mlade Bosne bb; **m** 065 445 674; **w** andricgrad.com – and search for 'Zlatna Moruna'; 09.00–23.00 daily. Brand new restaurant opened as a part of Andrićgrad, situated in the main entrance tower. The creator of Andrićgrad, a movie director, Emir Kusturica, says that the restaurant was named after famous Belgrade restaurant Zlatna Moruna, where members of the 'Mlada Bosna' (a pre-World War I revolutionary movement led by students) gathered & as such symbolises resistance. The walls of the restaurant are painted with frescoes by famous artist Bisenija Tereščenko. Offers a mix of traditional & international cuisine. **$–$$$**

Restoran Kruna Kralja Petra I 13; 058 620 352; **w** kruna.co.ba; 07.00–23.00 daily. Kruna, meaning crown, certainly deserves the crown when it comes to Višegrad dining. This is the town's best eatery. The restaurant is decked out in a tasteful combination of modern rustic & ethno style. They serve both national & international dishes. The wine selection is also quite good, with a range of excellent local wine. The beefsteak with grilled mushrooms is a house speciality, as is the grilled meat platter 'Kruna'. **$$**

Restoran Anika Ive Andrića 36; **m** 065 263 758; **e** kafanaanika@gmail.com; **w** apartmani-anika.com; 07.00–23.00 daily. This restaurant is locally known as the Višegradska Kafana. There is a massive red sign on the main road next to the river advertising this establishment. The interior décor is tasteful & comfy. The food is excellent & à la carte – in a semi-cafeteria style. Being that it's a *kafana* as well, expect good coffee & strong local spirits. **$–$$**

Restoran Na Drini ćuprija Nikole Pašića 3; 058 620 534; 07.00–22.00 daily. This restaurant, named for the famous bridge on the Drina, is not exactly located where its name might suggest. It is situated about 150m from the bridge. They have a slightly quirky, slightly funky garden terrace that seats around 40. The interior walls are a nice brick-&-wood combination. Serves a wide range of traditional national dishes, including tasty pork cutlets & several types of veal. $–$$

Ćevabdžinica Kasaba Mlade Bosne bb; m 066 802 512; e kasaba.ag@gmail.com; w kasaba.strikingly.com; 09.00–23.00 daily. Also located in Andrićtown. Serves *ćevapi* according to the Sarajevo recipe (there are several recipes depending on the area of the country you're in). $

What to see and do

Dobrun Monastery (*Dobrun bb, between Višegrad & the eastern border with Serbia; 058 620 950;* w *visegradturizam.com/english/dobrun-monastery*). This mid-14th-century Orthodox monastery (1343) is situated in the picturesque valley of the River Rzav. It is dedicated to the Annunciation of the Blessed Virgin Mary and was later expanded by one of Dobrun's monks in 1383. It was then that the rich collection of frescoes was added to the monastery's interior. The monastery was destroyed several times – first by the invading Ottomans just before the end of the 14th century and later reconstructed by the despot Stefan Lazarević. The Germans also razed the monastery during their retreat in 1945. Most of the frescoes were irreversibly damaged by the German mining of the church. Of the frescoes that did survive, the most famous are of the Zupanom Pribilom and his son, and of the Serbian Czar Dusan, with his wife Jelena and son Uros. The monastery has certainly seen the light of day. Today, it is a fully functioning monastery with an art gallery, museum of the first Serbian uprising, and an exhibition of the Dabro Bosnian Diocese. Dobrun is mainly visited by local tourists, stopping by in transit or as part of a religious trip or pilgrimage.

Dobrun Old Town The ruins of medieval Dobrun are located in the hills just above the Dobrun Monastery in Rzav river valley. The fortress was typical for the era – protecting parts of medieval Slavic kingdoms from various invaders. It was likely a strategic lookout settlement and resting place for traders from Dubrovnik *en route* to southern Serbia and Kosovo. It is believed the fortress was constructed in the 15th century, although many sources confirm a much earlier existence of a settlement in the hills of Dobrun. Today, only the ruins of towers remain as well as some small sections of the ancient walls. It is accessible by a walking path from the Dobrun Monastery.

Drina Boat Rides (m *Zelenika 065 363 049, Sonja 065 142 742*) This is perhaps the most popular and effective tourism product in eastern Bosnia. Drina Boat Rides began again in 2006 mainly to serve tourists visiting from Zlatibor, Serbia. The cruises usually depart between 10.00 and 11.00 and return in the evening. The excursions take visitors downriver towards Bajna Bašta through impressive canyons. Lunch is usually served on the boat. It is this attraction alone that brings in the greatest number of guests and offers them tangible tourism content.

Ivo Andrić Memorial Classroom (*Užičkog korpusa 12; 058 620 271; 09.00–15.00*) This school was opened in 1892, just a few years after the fall of the Ottoman Empire in Bosnia and Herzegovina. It was here that BiH's only Nobel laureate in literature, Ivo Andrić, learned his first letters and, in 2008, the municipality of Višegrad opened this memorial classroom. It attempts to replicate a classroom at the beginning of the 20th century and exhibits photographs of Andrić in Višegrad. The display is part of the Dom Kulture, which is the culture house of Višegrad.

Mehmed Paša Sokolović bridge *(Bridge on the Drina)* According to UNESCO, the Mehmed Paša Sokolović bridge of Višegrad (a World Heritage Site), which spans the Drina River, was built during 1571–77. Its architect, Kodža Mimar Sinan, was acting on the orders of Grand Vizier Mehmed Paša Sokolović. Characteristic of the apogee of Ottoman monumental architecture and civil engineering, the bridge has 11 masonry arches with spans of 11–15m, and an access ramp at right angles with four arches on the left bank of the river. The 179.5m-long bridge is a representative masterpiece of Sinan, one of the greatest architects and engineers of the classical Ottoman period and a contemporary of the Italian Renaissance, to which his work may be compared. The unique elegance of proportion and monumental nobility of the whole site bear witness to the greatness of this style of architecture.

Narrow-gauge train (w *visegradturizam.com/english/narrow-gauge-railway-visegrad-vardiste*) The Austro-Hungarian-built, narrow-gauge Višegrad–Vardište railway was a part of the once-famous Eastern railway that linked eastern Bosnia to Sarajevo. At the time of its construction (1903–06), it was the most expensive railroad in the world. It had great strategic importance for the Austro-Hungarians because of its frontier with Serbia. It is said that 1km of railway cost 1kg of gold. After World War I, the railway was utilised as a vital trade and transit link between Sarajevo and Serbia. In 1974, the Višegrad–Serbia line was put out of service. Four years later, the Sarajevo–Višegrad rail was permanently shut down after the construction of the Višegrad hydro-electric dam that flooded the Drina Valley east towards Ustiprača. The Mokra Gora–Višegrad line was recently reinstated as a tourist line, although for the moment it runs only at special times. Large charter reservations can be arranged in advance. There are plans to make it more regular soon, so check their website for updates – this revitalisation project will drastically change the face of tourism in Višegrad.

Special Višegrad tour The tour begins in Višegrad with a tour of the town and its attractions. Towards the end of the day, the tour continues with a 52km boat ride on the Drina to Perucca in Serbia. From there the tour continues – by land – to Tara National Park, where the tour group will overnight. There is a sightseeing tour of Tara Mountain before departing to Kremana. From Kremana, a small-gauge train ride on the popular *Ciro* goes through the Sargan 8 train route and ends in famous film-maker Emir Kusturica's Ethno Village in Mokra Gora. The trip returns towards Višegrad with a stopover at Dobrun Monastery and old town on the BiH side. Guests will overnight in Višegrad before departure the next day. The tour is organised by the Tourism Organisation of Višegrad (page 171).

5

Herzegovina

Bosnia and Herzegovina are two regions geographically divided by the towering Dinaric Alps, where a mild Mediterranean climate clashes with a harsher continental one. Herzegovina has always had a unique cultural history, distinct from Bosnia's, although there are also great similarities in language, ethnicity, culture and identity.

In pre-Yugoslavia days, Herzegovina was known for being poorer than other regions, particularly in the villages. By poverty, I mean the lack of material wealth that was the norm or standard for Bosnia or neighbouring Croatia. The tough life of rural Herzegovina has had a profound effect on the inhabitants, and can be seen today in the strong, self-reliant attitude of the people. They are generally regarded as hard workers, both on the land and in business. The natural surroundings, too, have a great influence over how traditions, rituals and mentalities evolved.

Most Bosnians would characterise Herzegovina as an arid moonscape. Although some areas of Herzegovina are indeed dry, it also possesses some of the greatest resources of freshwater springs, crystal-clear rivers and dozens of endemic types of flora and fauna. The limestone karst fields of BiH are the largest in the world, creating amazing water sources and underground aquifer systems and caves. The areas around **Jablanica**, **Prozor** and **Konjic** have dense green forests and beautiful serene lakes. The **Trebižat River** has created a wonderful green belt along its banks in western Herzegovina, as has the Bregava River from the southeast.

A warm Mediterranean climate dominates most of Herzegovina, creating a very different biosystem from that of Bosnia's central and northern regions. Figs, pomegranates, grapes, kiwi fruits, rose-hips and mandarins all grow in this sunny climate. According to the Decanter World Wine Awards, some of southern Europe's most outstanding wines are produced in the many small vineyards in western and southern Herzegovina.

This region has been settled for over 12,000 years and each civilisation has left its mark on Herzegovina. The natural and cultural heritage of Herzegovina and all its peoples can confidently be touted as the richest and most attractive region for tourism in Bosnia and Herzegovina. Many of the 'attractions' in Herzegovina are the simple but beautiful villages dotting the hillside and the people that work this precious land. While post-war reconstruction of properties has made great progress, unfortunately it is still possible to come across war ruins. Buildings without façades are even more common, as some property owners are still rebuilding, bit by bit. However, those reminders of the tragic past are offset by the region's cultural and physical beauty. Regardless of what you do or where you go, I'm more than willing to bet that Herzegovina will leave a lasting positive impression of your visit to Bosnia and Herzegovina.

The demographic picture of Herzegovina slightly differs from Bosnia. The west of Herzegovina is predominantly Croatian Catholic and was so even before the war. The east has an overwhelming majority of Serb Orthodox whilst the central and

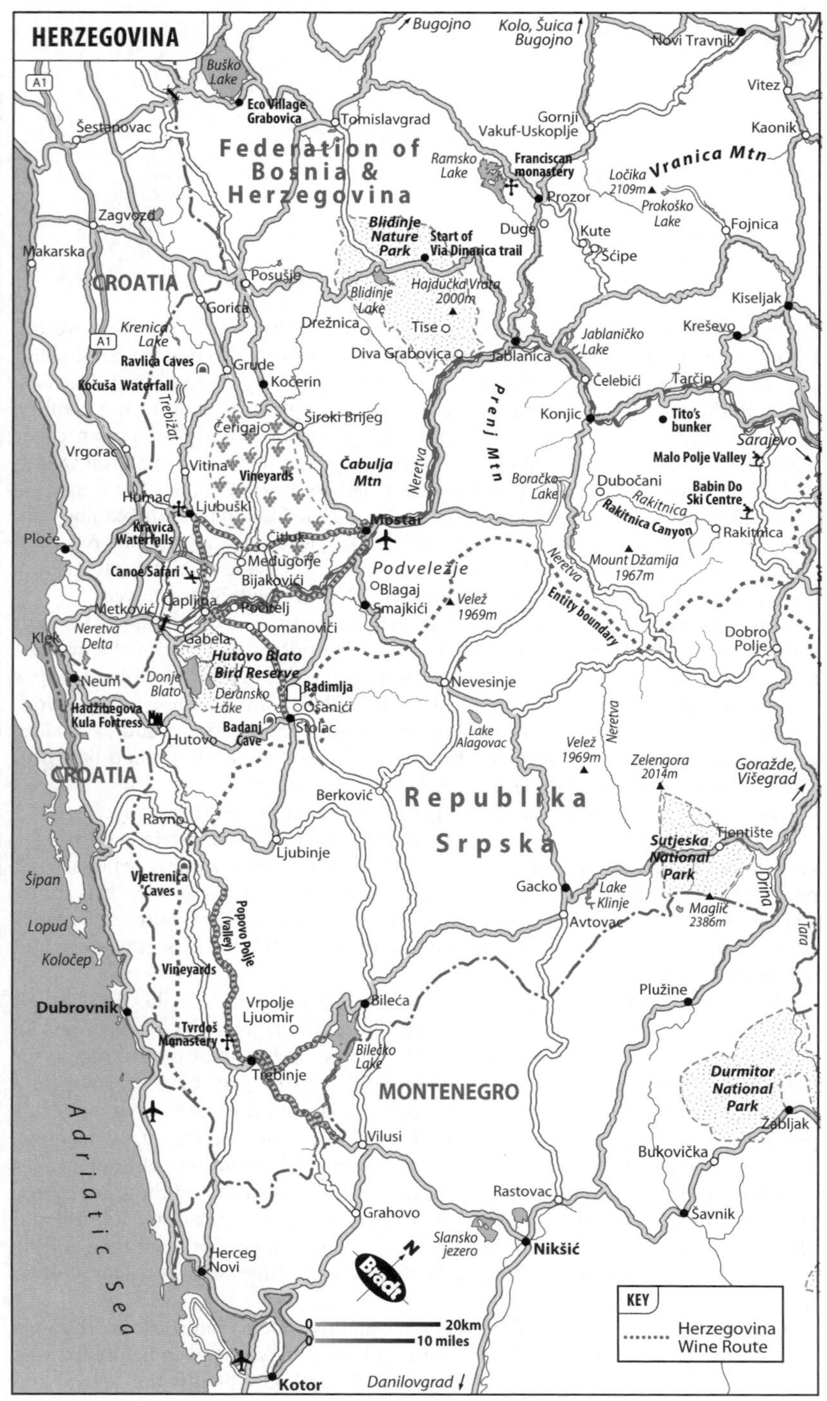

HERZEGOVINA
Federation of Bosnia & Herzegovina
Republika Srpska
CROATIA
MONTENEGRO
Adriatic Sea
Bugojno
Kolo, Šuica
Bugojno
Novi Travnik
Vitez
Kaonik
Buško Lake
Eco Village Grabovica
Tomislavgrad
Gornji Vakuf-Uskoplje
Šestanovac
Ramsko Lake
Franciscan monastery
Prozor
Vranica Mtn
Ločika 2109m
Prokoško Lake
Fojnica
Zagvozd
Blidinje Nature Park
Start of Via Dinarica trail
Duge
Kute
Šćipe
Makarska
Posušje
Blidinje Lake
Hajdučka Vrata 2000m
Kiseljak
Gorica
Drežnica
Tise
Kreševo
Krenica Lake
Jablaničko Lake
Ravlića Caves
Grude
Diva Grabovica
Jablanica
Kočerin
Čelebići
Tarčin
Kočuša Waterfall
Trebižat
Prenj Mtn
Čerigaj
Široki Brijeg
Konjic
Tito's bunker
Sarajevo
Vrgorac
Malo Polje Valley
Čabulja Mtn
Vitina
Vineyards
Neretva
Boračko Lake
Dubočani
Babin Do Ski Centre
Humac
Ljubuški
Rakitnica
Kravica Waterfalls
Mostar
Rakitnica Canyon
Rakitnica
Ploče
Čitluk
Međugorje
Mount Džamija 1967m
Canoe Safari
Bijakovići
Podveležje
Čapljina
Blagaj
Velež 1969m
Metković
Počitelj
Smajkići
Entity boundary
Neretva Delta
Domanovići
Dobro Polje
Klek
Gabela
Hutovo Blato Bird Reserve
Neum
Donje Blato
Radimlja
Nevesinje
Deransko Lake
Ošanići
Hadžibegova Kula Fortress
Badanj Cave
Stolac
Lake Alagovac
Hutovo
Velež 1969m
Zelengora 2014m
Goražde, Višegrad
Berković
Ravno
Tjentište
Ljubinje
Sutjeska National Park
Šipan
Vjetrenica Caves
Gacko
Lake Klinje
Drina
Lopud
Popovo Polje (valley)
Avtovac
Maglić 2386m
Tara
Koločep
Vineyards
Pližine
Bileća
Dubrovnik
Vrpolje Ljuomir
Tvrdoš Monastery
Bilećko Lake
Trebinje
Durmitor National Park
Žabljak
Vilusi
Bukovička
Rastovac
Grahovo
Šavnik
Slansko jezero
Nikšić
Herceg Novi
Bradt
N
KEY
Herzegovina Wine Route
0 20km
0 10 miles
Kotor
Danilovgrad
A1

northern parts of BiH's southern region are largely Bosnian Muslim (or Bosniak). Only the regional capital Mostar has a mix of the three ethnic groups and this relationship remains strained from the aftermath of the previous war. For the outsider, there are few differences in comparison with the similarities of culture, physique, tradition, language and cuisine. Ask a local and they may argue otherwise.

NERETVA RIVER

When talking about Herzegovina it would be impossible not to mention the river that most life in Herzegovina is built upon. The Neretva is the gem that has created fertile valleys from Glavetičevo to Doljani. Since ancient times this precious water source has allowed the prosperity and growth of human communities. To leave the Neretva out of any account of Herzegovina would be like writing about London and not mentioning the Thames.

The Neretva River has its beginnings in Zelengora Mountain in the Borač region. Like all rivers in Bosnia and Herzegovina it flows towards the north, or more precisely the northwest. In this upper section, the river forces its way between the massifs of the Visočica and the Bjelašnica mountains in the north, and between the massifs of the Crvanj and the Prenj mountains in the south. It flows through numerous canyons and a smaller number of fertile valleys.

Unlike the other Bosnian rivers, the Neretva River does not succeed in forcing its way further north. Passing to the north of the Prenj massif, the river turns south somewhere near the mouth of the Rama tributary. It then forces its way through the canyons between the Prenj and Čvrsnica mountains, until it reaches the Mostar Valley, where it loses the character of a rapid mountain river. This emerald beauty is in grave danger. Bosnia and Herzegovina's political elite have often been accused of being ecologically illiterate – and the Neretva is unfortunately suffering because of it. Although the Upper Neretva River is a vast resource of fresh and potable water, the energy lobbies are pushing to build several hydro-electric dams that would forever ruin its unique characteristics and wildlife. Environmental groups have been met with threats and obstruction, but continue to fight to preserve one of Europe's richest ecosystems.

MOSTAR

HISTORY In medieval times Mostar was no more than a tiny settlement along the banks of the mighty Neretva River. Fifteen kilometres to the south is the ancient settlement of Blagaj, which from Illyrian times up until the Ottoman invasion remained the centre of political power. It is said that before Herzegovina fell to the Turks, the settlement of Mostar had only 19 houses with a small suspension bridge that united both banks. With the arrival of the Turks came relative peace and stability, which meant the mountain-top fortresses used since Illyrian times, particularly by the Bosnian aristocracy in the centuries before Herzegovina fell, lost a great amount of their significance. The fertile but exposed valley where Mostar is now located proved an ideal place to build a city – and that's exactly what the Ottomans did.

Herzegovina officially came under **Turkish rule** in 1482 and Mostar as a town is first mentioned in 1474. The men that guarded the suspension bridge over the Neretva were called *mostari* (or bridge keepers) and it is presumed that the town is named after them. It didn't take long for Mostar to become the centre of Ottoman administrative and military rule in Herzegovina. The old town (*čaršija*) developed around the new stone bridge, now called Stari most (translated as the 'Old Bridge'), that by Ottoman design and Dalmatian local hands was completed in 1566. This oriental part of the city still preserves its old tradition of highly skilled handicrafts in engraving, painting and rug-making. A visit here is truly a walk through Mostar's ancient past.

With the Old Bridge at the centre, new *mahalas* (quarters) began to spring up on both sides of the Neretva. Mosques and *madrasas* (Islamic schools) were constructed as Islam spread in the growing town. In the late 16th and early 17th centuries, many of Mostar's most beautiful and significant Islamic structures were built. Cejvan-ćehaj Mosque was constructed in 1552 and is the oldest surviving monument of Ottoman rule in Herzegovina. Arguably, the most famous oriental object in Mostar is the Kara ozbegora Mosque that was built in 1557. In 1558, eight years before the construction of the Stari most, the Kriva ćuprija bridge was built over the Radobolje stream that feeds into the Neretva.

During Ottoman times Mostar quickly became a key **trading partner** with Dubrovnik and other coastal cities. Caravan routes led directly to Mostar, carrying Dalmatian goods such as olive oil, fish and linens. Cargoes of wool, meat, honey and oats were shipped from Mostar towards the seaside cities. Marketplace trade flourished in these times and one can still walk the streets of Kujundžiluk and find craftsmen and artisans of all sorts selling their wares.

After the third failure of the Ottomans in the battle for Vienna in 1683, the empire began its decline. Uprisings were more frequent in the 18th century, and in order to appease many of the internal opposing forces, both Muslim and Christian, the Ottomans granted certain freedoms. The old Orthodox church was renovated in 1833 and a Catholic church was constructed in 1864.

Despite occasional social unrest, Mostar continued to enjoy a long, peaceful period of cultural, political and economic growth. All three religious communities lived in harmony. Muslims obviously enjoyed more freedoms and tax breaks but the survival and growth of the Christian communities indicates that the Turks had a fairly high level of tolerance towards the Christian population, particularly in the first two centuries of rule. However, the second half of the Ottomans' four centuries of rule was strife-ridden and rebellions became commonplace.

The end of the 19th century marked the final decline of the Ottomans, and after a three-year uprising throughout the country from 1875–78, the empire collapsed. The opportunistic **Austro-Hungarians** jumped right in, and from 1878 included Bosnia and Herzegovina in their administrative region. A railway was immediately constructed, adding a European flavour to the oriental town. During the short reign of the Austro-Hungarians, a public bath was built, many newspapers and periodicals were established, more schools and bridges were erected and the city expanded its road system. All along the outskirts of the old town you can see the Viennese-style architecture from this period.

With the assassination of Archduke Franz Ferdinand in Sarajevo, Austro-Hungarian rule ended. In between the two world wars, much of Bosnia and Herzegovina experienced harsh economic and political struggles. With the end of World War II and the victory of Tito's Partisans came a challenging but peaceful time. Mostar became one of the major socialist strongholds in Yugoslavia. It had the highest rate of mixed marriages and continued to be the dominant city of Herzegovina. The city enjoyed great prosperity in the years leading up to the disintegration of Yugoslavia. It had a large aluminium industry that became one of the economic backbones of the city. That all changed when the Yugoslav People's Army (JNA), backed by paramilitary groups from Serbia and Montenegro, stormed Mostar. This was followed by a split in the Muslim–Croat forces, when the Croatian army turned on its former allies. Mostar experienced more destruction and damage in the recent war than in any other war in its history.

The 1992–95 conflict and beyond When the JNA attacked Mostar with units from Serbia and Montenegro, the city was heavily damaged. Although civilian casualties were relatively low, most of the public buildings, particularly on the east bank of the Neretva, were phosphorous bombed. After a short stalemate, the UN brokered an agreement for the JNA and Bosnian Serb forces to pull back to the east of Mostar. The defence of the city was left to the Bosniak and Croat armies. The Muslims and Croats had been long-time allies and shared the responsibility of defending Mostar. It should be noted that many of the Serbs from Mostar left or were forced to leave, and one of the greatest cultural and religious monuments in the city, the Serbian Orthodox church, was reduced to rubble. Mostar remained under frequent fire from the distant hills until fighting broke out between the allied Croat and Muslim forces.

Mostar became a divided city, militarily, when on 9 May 1993 the HVO (Bosnian Croat Defence Council) attacked its former allies loyal to the Bosnian government. Muslims were deported, expelled or killed in droves over the next few months, and front lines developed between the east and west banks of the Neretva River that divides the city. All the bridges connecting the two sides were destroyed and a brutal 11-month siege was brought upon the mainly Muslim community of east Mostar.

Up until 1993 the national symbol of Bosnia and Herzegovina spanned the raging Neretva River in the town of Mostar. The Old Bridge (Stari most) was the most magnificent relic left from Ottoman times. Since Turkish rule, Mostar has been the political, cultural and economic backbone of Herzegovina. Its ancient Babylon-like walls, connected by the beloved bridge, have been an inspiration to artists and travelers alike. Pre-war Mostar hosted one of the most balanced and multi-ethnic populations in the whole of the former Yugoslavia. The people here identified themselves with the town, and not with their national or ethnic background – they were *mostarci* or Mostarians.

Today, the town still preserves the remnants of its pre-war glory, but the war brought much devastation. Of all the cities you may visit in BiH, the scenes left over from the brutal conflict in Mostar might still startle the visitor, However, the centre of the town has largely been completely renovated, and little by little the rest of Mostar has been patched up. What can be most shocking is the sheer beauty that sits side by side with reminders of a time of utter destruction.

In March 1994, the Washington Agreement brokered a peace deal between the Muslim and Croatian forces, forming a loose alliance, which now represents the Federation entity of Bosnia and Herzegovina. The west bank was, by and large, untouched during the 11-month battle, while the east bank was almost completely destroyed. The east bank and the areas of Donje Mahala and Cernica on the west bank were held by Bosnian forces and, despite being overwhelmingly outgunned, they managed to defend the city (or what was left of it) until the international community was finally able to produce a workable peace agreement. The entire old town (Stari grad) was heavily damaged by ceaseless bombing. On a cool autumn day in November 1993, the bridge that had united Mostar for over 400 years was destroyed by dozens of tank rounds from the Croatian side.

Reconstruction of the bridge was completed in early 2004, paving the way for a new chapter for Mostar. Once again visitors and Mostarians alike can stroll through the old town and cross the Old Bridge as so many have done for centuries before them.

Mostar is now officially a 'united' city but it still remains divided along ethnic lines. To the visitor the ethnic division may not be evident, but nationalist parties on both sides have redrawn Mostar's municipal boundaries to suit their demographic dominance. The Croats see it as the capital of their self-declared state, and the ruling nationalist parties support its partition. The Bosniaks view Mostar more as a united town, but the nationalist parties still try to maintain their stronghold on the predominantly Muslim east bank. These corrupt and outdated policies continue to rob the local residents of a normal, stable life and hopes of a better future.

There are two bus stations, two hospitals, two school systems … two of almost everything. There has been much reconstruction since the war ended, but scenes of almost complete destruction can still be seen along the former confrontation line on the main boulevard. Many true Mostarians are now refugees in Europe and America, discouraged from returning to a divided city. There is a strong focus by the international community to unite Mostar, but the wounds will take a long time to heal.

GETTING THERE AND AROUND

By plane

Mostar airport [185 G8] (*Ortiješ bb;* ☎ *036 350 212;* **e** *info@mostar-airport.ba;* **w** *mostar-airport.ba*) The airport was in no-man's-land during the conflict and was heavily damaged, but it has been renovated. The airport is very small and offers only scheduled flights to a few destinations, which tend to vary depending on the year and the season. Currently, the only direct flights offered are to the Italian cities of Naples and Bergamo.

There is no bus service from the airport to the town. However, there is a taxi service to/from the city centre, which is only 3–4km away. A taxi ride to the centre ranges from 10–15KM depending on which hotel, the amount of luggage, and the

THE OPENING OF THE NEW BRIDGE

When the Stari most, or Old Bridge, collapsed from tank shelling in 1993, it was like the heart had been ripped out of most Mostar natives. Even mentioning the bridge for years afterwards could invoke tears, as it symbolised not only the city, but even the country, as a whole. The year 2004 proved to be quite a significant one for the city of Mostar. Its fragmented city administration was united and the beautiful stone structure that had spanned the Neretva River for over four centuries once again arched across its raging waters. The opening ceremony was rather spectacular – with almost every major television station in Europe and North America covering the lively event.

Reconstruction of the bridge took well over a year and the costs are estimated at more than US$17 million. The ceremony was attended by many world leaders, and Prince Charles was also present. The music, the fireworks and the traditional diving from the crest of the 21m-high bridge were witnessed by tens of thousands of people from around the country as well as tourists and dignitaries from across the world. Although it was portrayed as a symbol of bridging the Muslim east and Croat west sides of the city, the Stari most actually did nothing of the sort. The bridge is in what was 'Muslim-controlled territory' but, as most Mostar natives would say, the bridge belongs to all of them, and its reconstruction means that they feel even more that life is slowly but surely returning to normal in what many describe as the most beautiful city in Bosnia and Herzegovina.

honesty of your driver. Definitely do not pay more than 20KM (with your luggage) to any hotel in Mostar. If travelling to Mostar from abroad, it is far easier to find flights into Split or Dubrovnik in neighbouring Croatia, or to fly into the capital Sarajevo. Sarajevo International Airport is located just over 2 hours by car from Mostar. Renting a car at Sarajevo airport is an option, though it's wise to make a reservation in advance (page 77). It is also possible to take a taxi from Sarajevo airport to the central bus station in Sarajevo, and travel by bus from there. The bus ride takes 2–3 hours (page 111).

Split airport (*Cesta dr. Franje Tuđmana 1270;* ☎ *+385 21 203 555;* **w** *split-airport.hr*) Split is a good 3-hour drive from Mostar and a bit longer by bus. You can get a flight to Split (via Zagreb) from any major city in Europe, and during the summer, directly from several European capitals such as Stockholm, Olso, Berlin, Glasgow, Frankfurt, Rome, Zagreb, London, and others. Check the schedule of departures on the airport website to see what is available during different seasons, as the offering tends to change and new flights seem to be added every year.

There is a regular shuttle service that runs about every 30 minutes (30 kuna) from the airport to Split bus station, from where bus services run at least five times per day to Mostar. The bus station is conveniently located at the Split port (Luka Split), where ferries run to the islands and to Italy. Bus service is paid in the local currency which can be changed at the airport. There is a post office in the airport and they usually offer the best exchange rates. Several banks have currency-exchange offices in Split airport.

Dubrovnik airport (*Ćilipi-Konavle bb;* ☎ *+385 20 773 100;* **e** *info@airport-dubrovnik.hr;* **w** *airport-dubrovnik.hr*) Dubrovnik airport has also seen a dramatic increase in air traffic over the past decade. Many of the cheap-fare airlines like German Wings, easyJet and TUIfly, fly into Dubrovnik from many European capitals such as Amsterdam, London, Stockholm, Copenhagen and others. Many visitors book cheap flights to Dubrovnik and rent a car to drive to Mostar or Sarajevo. There are car-rental offices in Dubrovnik airport, but some companies don't insure travel into BiH. Make sure you ask before hiring. A regular shuttle from the airport to the bus station in Dubrovnik is available for 40 kuna. Bus lines are available from Dubrovnik bus station, which requires you to take a shuttle-bus transfer to town from the airport. Mostar is about a 2½–3-hour drive from Dubrovnik, and bus travel doesn't take significantly longer.

By car Herzegovina is easily navigable by car. Though there are currently no major highways to speak of, the roads are decent if a bit winding. Recently, a 10km stretch of highway was built, connecting the shrine town of Međugorje with the Croatian highway. A highway from Sarajevo to the Croatian coast via Herzegovina is under construction, but it is making very slow progress. To date, only 23km have been completed and the remainder will not be finished anytime in the near future. From Sarajevo, the M-17 road is the main access route to Mostar via Konjic and Jablanica, and it continues west after Mostar towards the Croatian coast, through Počitelj and Čapljina. Road signs are frequent, but rarely indicate the distance to the next destination. The road is in good condition and offers spectacular scenery, but the section from Sarajevo to Mostar is winding, and cautious driving is advised. Petrol stations are plentiful in central and western Herzegovina, although they are a bit scarcer to the east in the Ljubinje, Bileća, Nevesinje and Gacko areas.

By bus Like in most of Bosnia and Herzegovina, the bus system here is fairly well organised and, at the very least, consistent. Travelling by bus can be a cheap, fun way to see the region, but be sure to ask about the bus before buying your ticket. Some bus companies have modern vehicles with air conditioning, whilst others still drive relics from the Yugoslav era. In these buses the windows don't open, there is no air conditioning and the driver usually smokes.

Bus schedules do change seasonally, and sometimes more routes or varied routes are added at the beginning of the summer, so be sure to check at the bus station itself before organising your departure. Websites are not always updated

BUS TIMETABLE

IN BiH, MONTENEGRO AND CROATIA There are two bus stations in Mostar: one on the eastern side of the town (*Maršala Tita bb;* ☎ *036 552 025*) and one on the western side (*Vukovarska bb;* ☎ *036 348 680*). Most buses go to/from the eastern station. The timetable below refers to buses which will depart from or arrive from the eastern station, unless otherwise indicated (see also *Local buses*, opposite).

Mostar–Konjic–Sarajevo	06.00; 06.30; 07.00; 09.00; 11.00; 15.00; 16.00; 18.15
Sarajevo–Konjic–Mostar	06.00; 08.15; 09.00; 11.30; 12.30; 15.30; 16.00; 18.00; 19.55
Čapljina–Zagreb	06.15; noon; 19.30; 22.30
Zagreb–Čapljina	08.00; 13.55; 16.00; 21.30; 22.30
Mostar–Zagreb	06.55; 13.00; 20.15, 20.45, 21.40
Zagreb–Mostar	08.00; 13.55; 16.00; 22.30
Mostar–Split (West)	06.55; 11.10; 12.50
Split–Mostar (West)	10.55; 17.30; 22.10
Mostar–Međugorje	06.55; 16.00; 18.50; 20.15; 21.40
Međugorje–Mostar	05.45; 06.10; 09.15; 12.20; 14.10; 20.20; 21.40; 23.00
Mostar–Herceg Novi	07.00
Herceg Novi-Mostar	15.40
Mostar–Dubrovnik	07.00; 12:30
Dubrovnik–Mostar–Sarajevo	16.00; 17.15
Mostar–Trebinje	17.30
Trebinje–Mostar	10.00
Mostar–Neum	07.00; 12.30; 22.35
Neum–Mostar	05.15; 17.15; 18.30
Mostar–Banja Luka	13.00; 20.15
Banja Luka–Mostar	01.15; 11.00; 13.00; 17.00
Mostar–Tuzla	06.30; 16.00
Tuzla–Mostar	05.00; 12.30

OTHER INTERNATIONAL LINES

Mostar–Dortmund	06.45 (daily)
Dortmund–Mostar	05.00 (daily)
Mostar–Stockholm	06.55 (Sat)
Stockholm–Mostar	21.30 (Thu)

and may be unreliable. The main bus companies from the eastern bus station in Mostar are Centrotrans (**w** *centrotrans.com*), Autoprevoz (**w** *autoprevoz.ba*), Globtour (**w** *globtour.com*), and Čazmatrans (**w** *cazmatrans.hr*). In the summer, buses tend to fill up quickly, so it is advised to buy a ticket in advance and to arrive at the bus station at least 15 minutes before departure time, since having a ticket might not guarantee a seat. Unfortunately, the last bus from Mostar to Sarajevo leaves at 18.15. If one misses that bus, it is possible to wait for an international bus on its way to Sarajevo through Mostar from Croatia, but one has to purchase a ticket from the bus driver directly. There is also a chance that these buses will have no space during the summer season.

Local buses Local transport is excellent in and around Mostar. **Mostar Bus**, located at the main bus and rail station, covers the town and most of the surrounding areas with daily routes that run all day long. There is a Mostar Bus office in the main bus station with current schedules. Bus fares within the city are usually 1KM for a one-way trip within the city limits, regardless of how far the destination (see box, opposite).

By train Travelling by rail in Herzegovina is also a good and affordable option when the trains are running normally. There is a train from Ploče (on the Adriatic coast in Croatia) to Sarajevo, with stops in Čapljina, Mostar, Jablanica and Konjic *en route* to Sarajevo (and vice versa, of course), but it has not been running in full service for some time and it is not clear when it will resume full service. Currently, there is only one train per day travelling between Sarajevo and Konjic and back – the other stops on the route listed above have been cancelled until further notice, but will hopefully be reinstated soon. Schedules here change seasonally and regular updates on the internet are not always reliable. It's best to ask about exact details at a travel agency or directly at the station itself before departure. When in service trains are not much faster than the bus – it takes a little over 4 hours to get from Sarajevo to Ploče; a little over an hour from Sarajevo to Konijc; 2 hours to Jablanica; and about 2½ hours from Sarajevo to Mostar. While there are some spectacular views from the train, some are obscured by the frequent tunnels. A one-way ticket from Sarajevo to Ploče costs around 24KM, though this may change when the train lines reopen. Purchase tickets in person at the station.

Taxis As in all cities in BiH, there is no shortage of taxis in Mostar. There are taxi stands on both sides of town that operate independently from each other – as most things do in the city, unfortunately. The rates are the standard 2KM to start and 1KM for each additional kilometre. Tucked neatly into a valley, Mostar is fairly compact and easy to get around on foot. If you take a taxi anywhere around town it shouldn't cost more than 10KM.

TOURIST INFORMATION Although one can find a number of leaflets, booklets and web portals, a comprehensive, updated guide for Mostar is hard to come by. Much of the material you will find contains pre-war material and photographs. The best available short guide is *Mostar and its Surroundings,* which you can find in the tourist information centre on the west bank of the old town (page 186) and at Fortuna Tours (page 186) on Kujundžiluk on the east bank. This guide offers a short summary of the history, culture, art and things to see and do and has many outstanding photographs. It also has a colour tourist map complete with information centres, banks, post offices, police station, telephones, parking and taxi stands. It is not, however, detailed on hotels and restaurants or any inside local news.

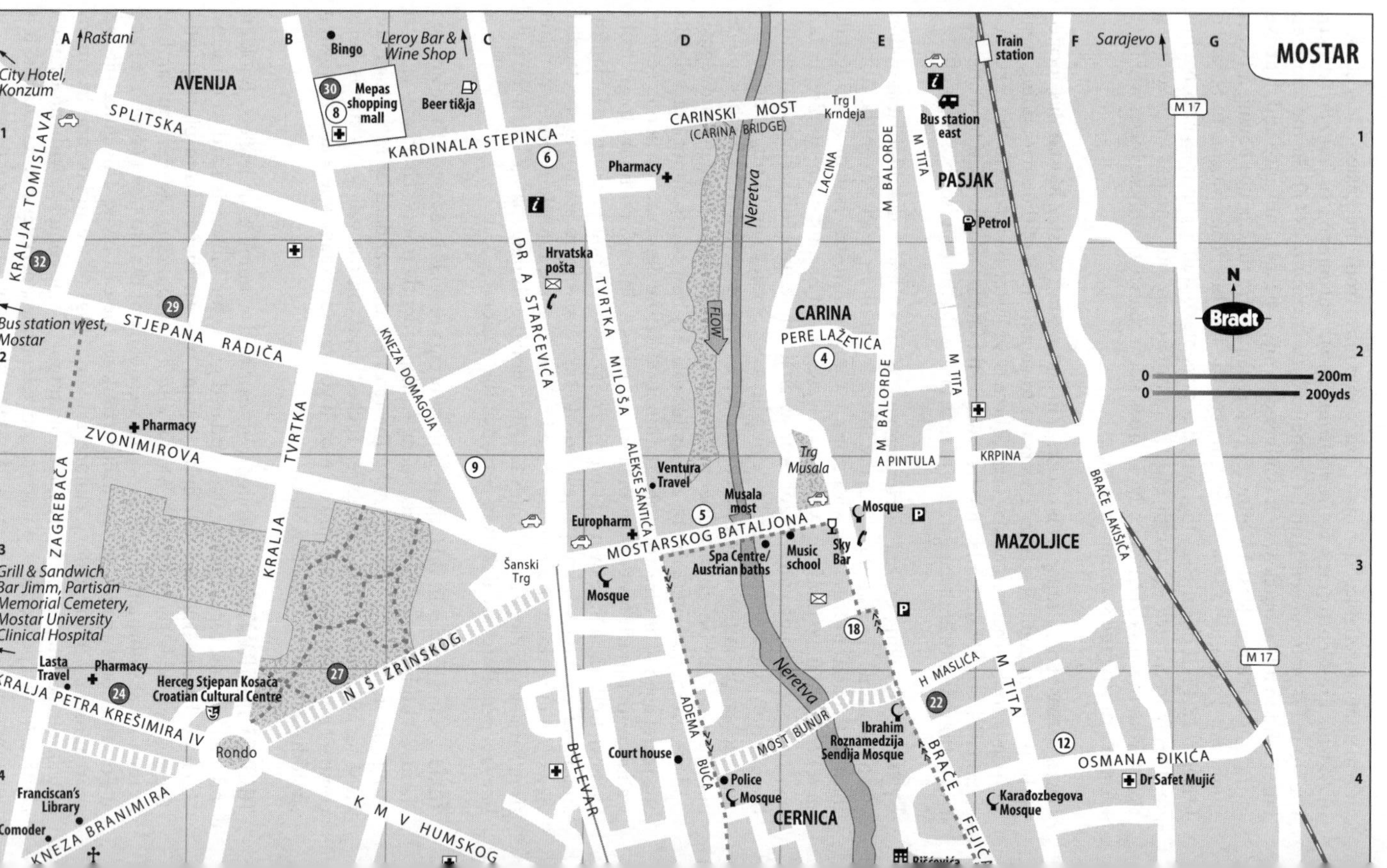
MOSTAR
Raštani
City Hotel, Konzum
AVENIJA
Bingo
Leroy Bar & Wine Shop
Mepas shopping mall
Beer ti&ja
SPLITSKA
KRALJA TOMISLAVA
KARDINALA STEPINCA
CARINSKI MOST (CARINA BRIDGE)
Trg I Krndeja
Train station
Sarajevo
Bus station east
PASJAK
Petrol
M17
Pharmacy
Neretva
LACINA
M BALORDE
M TITA
Hrvatska pošta
DR A STARČEVIĆA
TVRTKA MILOŠA
FLOW
CARINA
PERE LAŽETIĆA
N
Bradt
0 200m
0 200yds
Bus station west, Mostar
STJEPANA RADIĆA
KNEZA DOMAGOJA
ZVONIMIROVA
TVRTKA
A PINTULA
KRPINA
BRAĆE LAKIŠIĆA
Ventura Travel
ALEKSE ŠANTIĆA
Musala most
Trg Musala
Mosque
Europharm
MOSTARSKOG BATALJONA
Spa Centre/ Austrian baths
Music school
Sky Bar
MAZOLJICE
ZAGREBAČA
KRALJA
Šanski Trg
Grill & Sandwich Bar Jimm, Partisan Memorial Cemetery, Mostar University Clinical Hospital
N Š ZRINSKOG
Lasta Travel
KRALJA PETRA KREŠIMIRA IV
Herceg Stjepan Kosača Croatian Cultural Centre
Rondo
ADEMA BUĆA
Court house
BULEVAR
MOST BUNUR
Ibrahim Roznamedzija Sendija Mosque
H MASLIĆA
BRAĆE FEJIĆA
OSMANA ĐIKIĆA
Dr Safet Mujić
Karađozbegova Mosque
Police
CERNICA
Franciscan's Library
Comoder
KNEZA BRANIMIRA
K M V HUMSKOG

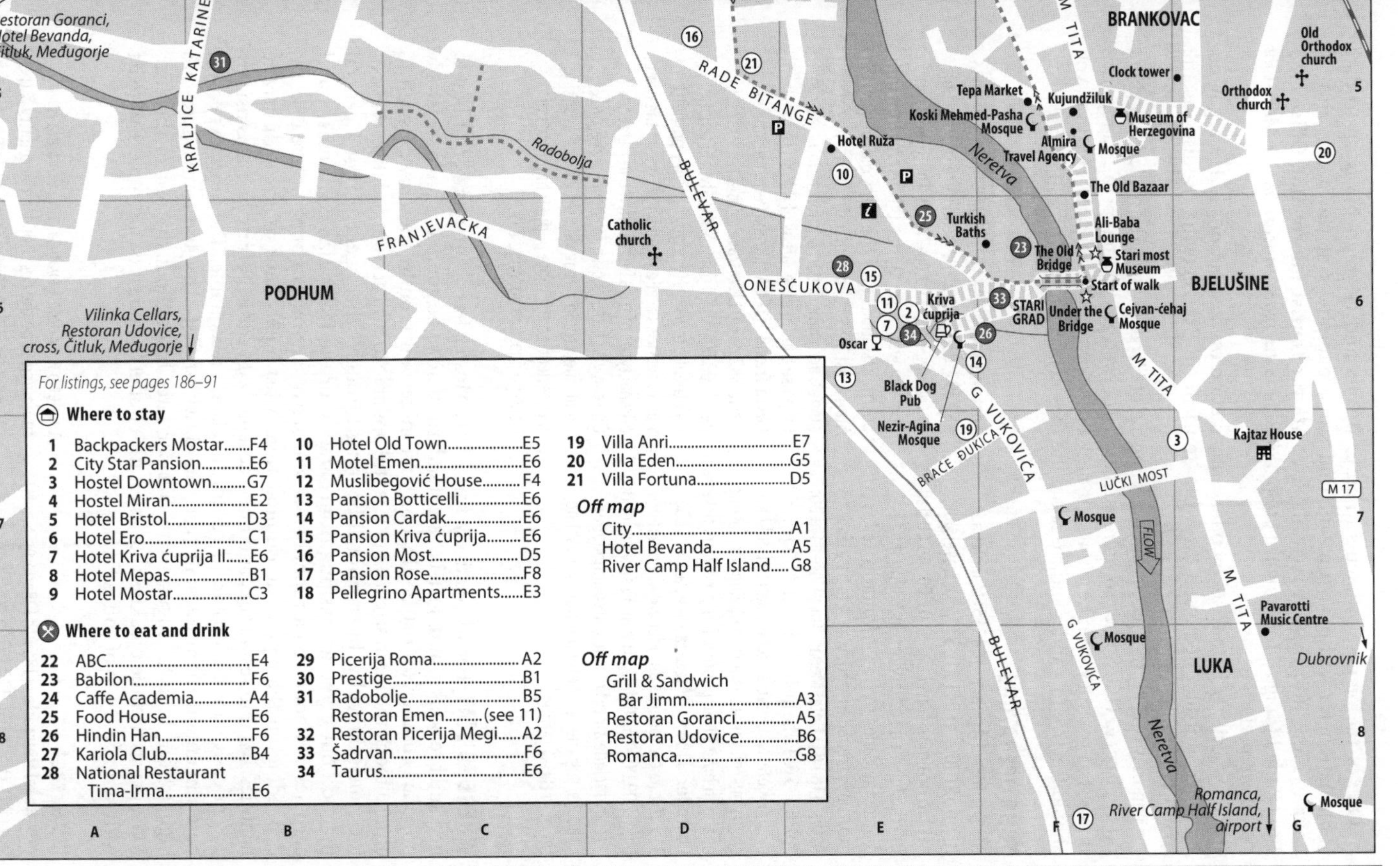
Restoran Goranci, Hotel Bevanda, Čitluk, Međugorje
KRALJICE KATARINE
RADE BITANGE
BULEVAR
Radobolja
FRANJEVAČKA
Catholic church
PODHUM
Vilinka Cellars, Restoran Udovice, cross, Čitluk, Međugorje
ONEŠĆUKOVA
Hotel Ruža
Neretva
Turkish Baths
BRANKOVAC
M TITA
Clock tower
Tepa Market
Kujundžiluk
Koski Mehmed-Pasha Mosque
Museum of Herzegovina
Almira Travel Agency
Mosque
The Old Bazaar
Ali-Baba Lounge
The Old Bridge
Stari most Museum
Start of walk
Under the Bridge
Cejvan-ćehaj Mosque
STARI GRAD
Kriva ćuprija
Oscar
Black Dog Pub
Nezir-Agina Mosque
G VUKOVIĆA
BRAĆE ĐUKICA
BJELUŠINE
Old Orthodox church
Orthodox church
Kajtaz House
LUČKI MOST
M 17
FLOW
Pavarotti Music Centre
Dubrovnik
LUKA
Romanca, River Camp Half Island, airport
For listings, see pages 186–91
Where to stay
1 Backpackers Mostar......F4
2 City Star Pansion......E6
3 Hostel Downtown......G7
4 Hostel Miran......E2
5 Hotel Bristol......D3
6 Hotel Ero......C1
7 Hotel Kriva ćuprija II......E6
8 Hotel Mepas......B1
9 Hotel Mostar......C3
10 Hotel Old Town......E5
11 Motel Emen......E6
12 Muslibegović House......F4
13 Pansion Botticelli......E6
14 Pansion Cardak......E6
15 Pansion Kriva ćuprija......E6
16 Pansion Most......D5
17 Pansion Rose......F8
18 Pellegrino Apartments......E3
19 Villa Anri......E7
20 Villa Eden......G5
21 Villa Fortuna......D5
Off map
City......A1
Hotel Bevanda......A5
River Camp Half Island......G8
Where to eat and drink
22 ABC......E4
23 Babilon......F6
24 Caffe Academia......A4
25 Food House......E6
26 Hindin Han......F6
27 Kariola Club......B4
28 National Restaurant Tima-Irma......E6
29 Picerija Roma......A2
30 Prestige......B1
31 Radobolje......B5
Restoran Emen......(see 11)
32 Restoran Picerija Megi......A2
33 Šadrvan......F6
34 Taurus......E6
Off map
Grill & Sandwich Bar Jimm......A3
Restoran Goranci......A5
Restoran Udovice......B6
Romanca......G8

One of the biggest problems in all of Bosnia and Herzegovina is up-to-date information for visitors. You will find some pamphlets at the hotels and, of course, more information is available at **Mostar Tourist Information Office** [185 E6] (*Rade Bitange 5 (old town);* ☎ *036 580 275;* **w** *turizam.mostar.ba;* ⌚ *May–Oct 09.00–noon daily*).

The website **w bhtourism.ba** offers information on destinations in Herzegovina. Another website dedicated to wine tourism in Herzegovina is also useful: **w** vinskacesta.ba/en.

You may find certain propaganda coming out of Herzegovina to be misleading about other places to visit. Some promotional material or even guides attempt to exclude areas in Mostar; you may even hear that it is not safe to travel to 'those' parts. However, you should feel free to wander and check out the sites all over Mostar (pages 192–5).

TOUR OPERATORS

Almira Travel Agency [185 F5] Mala Tepa 9; ☎ 036 551 406; **m** 061 212 570; **e** a.travel@bih.net.ba; **w** almira-travel.ba; ⌚ 09.00–16.00 daily. Offers a full range of services, including guide & accommodation services in Mostar as well as excursions around Herzegovina & to Sarajevo.

Atlas [184 B1] Hotel Mepas, Kneza Višeslava bb; ☎ 036 326 631. The main services of this agency include hotel & private accommodation bookings, excursions, pilgrimage tours to Međugorje, rafting on the Trebižat River, photo safari, air & ferry tickets.

Comoder [184 A4] Kneza Branimira 12; ☎ 036 319 201; **e** comoder@comoder.ba; **w** comoder.ba; ⌚ 09.00–16.00 daily. The main services of this agency include air ticket sales, accommodation, holidays, summer & winter programmes, skiing, travel in BiH & rafting.

Fortuna Tours [184 F1] Rade Bitange 34; ☎ 036 552 197; 036 551 888; **e** headoffice@fortuna.ba; **w** fortuna.ba; ⌚ 09.00–16.00. The largest tour operator working in Mostar. Offices are at the main bus/train station [184 F1] & in the old town by the Stari most [185 F6] on Kujundžiluk St. They offer guides, accommodation & information, and can organise trips in other areas of BiH & Croatia.

Lasta Travel [184 A4] Kralja Petra Krešimira IV 1; ☎ 036 332 011/012; **e** travel@lasta.ba; **w** lasta.ba; ⌚ 08.00–18.00 daily. Specialises in unique & authentic tours of Herzegovina. They provide superb service, excellent guiding & one of the more original types of trips being offered in Herzegovina. One can visit little-known medieval graveyards, small vineyards in sleepy villages, as well as seeing & experiencing the more popular highlights of Herzegovina. See ad, page 239.

WHERE TO STAY For its relatively small size, Mostar has a fair number of hotels, bed and breakfasts, and hostels. The standards tend to be good. It is an increasingly popular summer tourist destination and in certain months the crowds swell to almost block the main streets, but it is still possible to find accommodation without too much difficulty. International booking through other agents is not a general practice, but if you are visiting from Sarajevo or the Dalmatian coast most travel agencies can book you a room before you arrive, or you can book online directly, depending on the type of accommodation. Most hotels have rooms with private facilities, bar and restaurant, and many accept credit cards. Private *pansions* usually accept cash only. In Mostar, prices for hotels are reasonable. The more expensive hotels maintain room rates all year round, whilst first-class and tourist rates are higher from June to August, with cheaper rates throughout the rest of the year. Most prices include breakfast but ask if it's a buffet breakfast or just a piece of toast with jam and a cup of coffee.

Upmarket

Hotel Bevanda [185 A5] (28 rooms, 5 apts) Stara Ilička bb; ☎ 036 332 332; **e** hotel.bevanda@tel.net.ba; **w** hotelbevanda.com. Bevanda is rumoured to be the best hotel in the country & the service is second to none. Rooms are large with chic, arty décor, AC, phone, sat TV & minibar; suites come with a large jacuzzi in the bathroom. The building itself is spacious & decked out in a soothing red. The restaurant offers a wide range of European dishes & local specialities, as well as a wine menu that is not exclusively local. There is also a private parking garage below the hotel. **$$$$**

Hotel Old Town [185 E5] (9 rooms, 1 apt) Rade Bitange 9a, Onešćukova 30; 036 558 877; e oldtown@oldtown.ba; w hoteloldtownmostar.com. For a truly authentic & unique Ottoman Mostar experience, the old town is most certainly your pick. This modern facility has replicated the best of Ottoman architecture in the heart of Mostar's old town. The service is friendly & helpful, the rooms have all the comfort & extras one could ask for & the location is perfect. **$$$$**

Hotel Bristol [184 D3] (47 rooms, 1 apt) Mostarskog bataljona bb; 036 500 100; e info@bristol.ba; w bristol.ba. The Bristol was destroyed during the war & renovated some years ago. It is a 10-min walk to the old town. The rooms, restaurant & service are all excellent, & it definitely offers a comfortable atmosphere. Rooms have AC, minibar, phone & sat TV. The terrace overlooking the lovely Neretva River is a popular spot for locals. **$$$**

Hotel Ero [184 C1] (165 rooms, 8 apts) Dr Ante Starčevića; 036 386 777; e hotel.ero@tel.net.ba. Ero is sort of the hotel institution in Mostar. It was the first major hotel to open its doors after the war & remains one of the city's best hotels. Comfy rooms with sat TV, minibar, phone & AC. The restaurant serves excellent food & the reception is very helpful in assisting you with whatever you may need. **$$–$$$**

Hotel Mepas [184 B1] (72 rooms, 15 apts) Kneza Višeslava bb; 036 382 000; e info@mepas-hotel.ba; w mepas-hotel.ba. Mepas offers a step up from any other accommodation facility in Mostar. It is an elegant 5-star hotel that offers free access to its spa & wellness centre. The staff is professional, friendly & helpful. The rooms are spacious with massive bathrooms. It is located in the Mepas Mall & free parking is provided. The restaurant is also top notch with a wide selection of international & local cuisine. **$$–$$$**

Mid range

Hotel Kriva ćuprija II [185 E6] (12 rooms) Kriva ćuprija 2; m 061 135 286; e info@hotel-mostar.ba; w hotel-mostar.ba This branch of the Pansion Kriva ćuprija offers upscale accommodation just across the Luka Bridge on the east side of the Neretva. The rooms are modern & comfortable with AC, internet, TV, safes & minibar. They also have 2 outdoor jacuzzis on the terraces overlooking the Neretva & the Old Bridge. **$$–$$$**

Muslibegović House [184 F4] (10 rooms) Osmana Đikića 41; 036 551 379; e muslibegovichouse@gmail.com; w muslibegovichouse.com. This national monument (page 196) also doubles as what is perhaps one of the most unique & beautiful accommodation locations in the whole country. Enjoy an authentic Ottoman room with all the right modern tweaks for a perfect stay. The hospitality is exceptional, the accommodation original & comfortable. Being an easy walk to most destinations in Mostar, it's well worth the price. **$$–$$$**

Pellegrino Apartments [184 E3] (7 apts) Faladžića 1; m 062 969 000; e info@pellegrino.ba; w pellegrino.ba/en. AC studio apts with kitchen & modern décor. It's just off the main road in Fejića down a dead-end alley near the main post office on the east bank. They are really lovely flats & fairly priced. **$$–$$$**

Villa Anri [185 E7] (8 rooms) Braće Đukica 4; 036 578 477; m 062 432 098; e villa.anri@gmail.com; f air.ramke. Situated only a few hundred metres from the Old Bridge in Mostar's old town. This B&B has a great rooftop terrace with amazing views of the Stari most. The rooms are modern with the full range of services including AC, sat TV, minibar & internet. They also offer free parking. Room 301 has the best view of the Old Bridge. **$$–$$$**

Villa Fortuna [185 D5] (5 rooms) Rade Bitange 34 1; 036 552 197; e fortuna_headoffice@bih.net.ba. Fortuna is one of the premier travel agencies in Mostar & indeed Herzegovina. This small B&B is only a few mins' walk to the Old Bridge. This guesthouse is well equipped with just about everything, including parking, sat TV, AC, minibar & high-speed internet. **$$–$$$**

City Star Pansion [185 E6] (8 rooms) Onešćukova 32; 036 580 080; e info@citystar.ba; w citystar.ba. Across the street from Motel Emen, & with the same ownership, is an equally stylish boutique *pansion*. The beautiful natural-stone interior captures the soul of Mostar, & is rendered even lovelier by the modern, minimal, yet comfortable interior design & furnishings. A lovely private terrace overlooking the narrow part of river, blossoming greenery, & the interior walls of old town Mostar, add a special touch. Guests can walk downstairs to dine at the same excellent restaurant connected to Motel Emen, see below. **$$**

City Hotel [184 A1] (66 rooms, 14 apts) Vukovarska bb; 036 349 090; **e** info@city-hotel.ba; **w** city-hotel.ba. Located by the bus station in West Mostar, this relatively new, modern & fully equipped hotel has a large capacity for groups. It is in very close proximity to a spa & wellness centre with a wide range of treatments available. **$$**

Hotel Mostar [184 C3] (97 rooms, 6 apts) Kneza Domagoja bb, Mostar; 036 446 500; **e** recepcija@hotelmostar.ba; **w** hotelmostar.ba. Hotel Mostar has gone through yet another facelift. This time it has emerged as a proper 4-star hotel. There are jacuzzi & Finnish sauna facilities, as well as a Turkish bath & a modern fitness room. The rooms are very comfy with modern natural décor. It is only a 15-min walk to the old town, & a 10-min walk to the bus & train station. **$$**

Motel Emen [185 E6] (6 rooms) Onešćukova 32; 036 581 120; **e** info@motel-emen.com; **w** motel-emen.com. Another newer addition to the old town's boutique-lodging selection, Emen has to be amongst the best. Having lived & worked in Switzerland, the owners have got just about everything right. The rooms are spacious with the utmost attention paid to décor & style. Many think the restaurant is the best in the old town (see opposite), & it offers a mix of local & international cuisine. The pizzas smell & taste delicious. Rooms are frequently fully booked, so make reservations well in advance. They have a guest-only terrace for breakfasts, sunbathing or just relaxing. **$$**

Villa Eden [185 G5] (30 rooms) Konak 18; 036 555 390; **e** info@vilaeden.com; **w** vilaeden.com. Because Eden is located on the outskirts of the city, this pleasant Herzegovina Villa has exceptional views of Mostar. The rooms are very comfy & most have spacious balconies to enjoy early morning coffee or an evening drink. The family restaurant uses fresh Herzegovinian products in preparing their traditional cuisine. The homemade wine isn't too bad either. **$$**

Budget

Pansion Botticelli [185 E6] (5 rooms) Muje Bjelavca 6; **m** 063 272 024; **e** info@villabotticelli.com; **w** villabotticelli.com. Family-owned B&B on the Radobolja River not far from the Old Bridge in the old town. It has well-designed rooms with lovely terraces & décor. **$–$$**

Pansion Cardak [185 E6] (3 rooms) Jusovina 3; 036 578 249; **e** info@pansion-cardak.com; **w** pansion-cardak.com. This small family-owned B&B is on a quiet street on the old town's west bank. The rooms are simple but cramped, each en suite. The common kitchen is cosy & has much more of a family-stay feel to it than most B&Bs in Mostar. The couple that run it are kind & attentive. **$–$$**

Pansion Kriva ćuprija [185 E6] (10 rooms, 4 apts) Onešćukova 23; 036 360 360; **e** info@hotel-mostar.ba; **w** hotel-mostar.ba. Perfectly located in the old town just 100m from the Old Bridge, this pension has upgraded its services since opening in 1998. The restaurant serves good local food as well as classic international dishes. **$–$$**

Pansion Most [185 D5] (8 rooms) Adema Buća 100; 036 552 528; **w** pansionmost.dzaba.com. This private house is conveniently located in Cernica not far from the Old Bridge. It's simple & clean & is a good spot for budget travellers & backpackers. **$–$$**

Backpackers Mostar [184 F4] (8 rooms) Braće Fejića 67; **m** 063 199 019; **e** backpackersmostar@gmail.com; **w** backpackersmostar.com. The hostel is oddly split between 2 buildings with a kitchen, bathroom & AC in each room. They organise daily tours around Herzegovina, inc the old towns of Blagaj & Počitelj, as well as Kravica Waterfalls near Ljubuški. They also offer walking tours with local guides. The hostel is 500m from the Old Bridge. **$**

Hostel Downtown [185 F7] (5 rooms) Maršala Tita 165; **m** 063 481 842; **e** house.mostar@gmail.com; **f** mostar.downtown.hostel. Downtown is a small hostel in the heart of the city. Modern & funky, it was designed to support the needs & tastes of contemporary travellers. There is free Wi-Fi & lockers for your bags. They can arrange bike or car rental. **$**

Hostel Miran [184 E2] (15 rooms) Pere Lažetića 13; **m** 061 823 555; **e** meskic_mo@hotmail.com; **w** hostelmiranmostar.com. Hostel Miran is a 2-min walk from the bus/train station & a 10-min walk from the Old Bridge. It is a quiet & friendly place with large rooms. They can organise tours around the area & offer a special war tour around Mostar. **$**

Pansion Rose [185 F8] (8 rooms) Bulevar bb; 036 578 300; **e** info@pansion-rose.ba;

w pansion-rose.ba. A great, inexpensive place just off the main boulevard in Donje Mahala. Comfy & clean rooms with bathroom, shower & TV. The hosts go out of their way to make your stay as comfortable as possible. It is a short walk to the Old Bridge. They also have private parking & internet connection for 1KM/hr. $

River Camp Half Island [185 G8] Buna bb; 036 836 159; e halfislandbuna@gmail.com; w camping-buna.com; Apr–Oct. Half Island is a camping site situated on the bank of Buna River. They provide all necessary amenities for camping, including spots for tents, trailers or campers, power supply, WC, showers, washing rooms, kitchen with fridge, stove & sink, Wi-Fi, grill, bike rentals, & a swimming area with a dock. You can fish for freshwater trout in the river, so if you're an angler, pack your fishing rod. Pets are also welcome. There is a bus stop close by for transport to Mostar. The owners of the camp also rent a house nearby for around 80KM per night, which sleeps up to 4 people. Although from the outside, the house isn't much, the interior is decorated in cosy traditional style, & there is a lovely terrace with barbecue capacities under the shade of a fig tree along the river bank. $

WHERE TO EAT AND DRINK Mostar has always been known for its fine local cuisine. Unfortunately, there is not a cuisine guide in any form to direct hungry guests to the best restaurants in town. With tourism on the rise in Mostar, several tourist restaurants have popped up as well, where the food may not be as good as in some other places. Mostar is no exception to the café culture that dominates Bosnia and Herzegovina. If you're only prepared for a coffee or a refreshing drink, all restaurants will gladly serve you. If you ask for a menu the tempting traditional meals and good-value prices may convince you to stay a bit longer. You won't find many particularly international venues in your choice of restaurants, though there are more options and variety than there were even just a few years ago. Traditional menus of 'just off the mountainside' meats and cheeses from Herzegovina are always popular with visitors, and Dalmatian-style foods, especially sea fish, have long been a local favourite in this inland Mediterranean city. Like most places in Herzegovina you'll also be able to find a good pizza or an Italian dish of some sort. Salads are not the elaborate Western type, but you can bet that the vegetables are home grown and very tasty. Herzegovina's ancient tradition of winemaking makes high-quality local wines very affordable: a good bottle of white (Žilavka) or red (Blatina or Vranac) wine shouldn't cost more than 35KM. It would be impossible to list all the good restaurants in town. You are encouraged to wander and snoop around for yourself; I've yet to come across a 'bad' restaurant in Mostar.

Above average

Restoran Picerija Megi [184 A2] Kralja Tomislava 29, Avenija; 036 321 911; e info@megi.ba; w megi.ba; 07.00–23.00 daily. Megi is a great family-owned restaurant that is most frequented by locals. Aside from a tasty Italian menu, the seafood and steaks are the house speciality. They pride themselves on mouth-watering cakes as well, so leave room for dessert. $$–$$$

Prestige [184 B1] Kardinala Stepnica bb; 036 445 585; e info@restoran-prestige.com; w restoran-prestige.com; 09.00–23.00 daily. Located in Mepas shopping mall on Mostar's west bank, Prestige represents a new culinary idea in BiH. It follows in the footsteps of the 5-star Mepas Hotel in the same shopping complex. It has a large, spacious & modern interior. The cuisine is a melange of international & local dishes, with a diverse choice of fresh seafood & traditional meat dishes. $$

Restoran Emen [185 E6] Onešćukova 32; 036 581 120; e info@motel-emen.com; w motel-emen.com; 08.00–23.00 daily. The restaurant, part of the Motel Emen (see opposite), is the best choice for lunch or dinner in the old town. The owners previously lived in Switzerland, bringing home the quality and taste with them. Dining outside or in, the service is excellent, & the local & international menu – not extensive but high quality – has something for everyone. The vibe of the restaurant differs from the others in old town, & has its own unpretentious style. It is usually difficult to find excellent pasta in restaurants around the country, but the artichoke pasta is very good. The trout & potatoes are prepared with care. $$

Romanca [185 G8] Konjusi bb; 036 350 331; e romanca@hercegovinavino.ba; w hercegovinavino.com/hr/romanca; 09.00–23.00 daily. This restaurant is located 10km from the city centre, in the heart of the Konjusi vineyard. The house wine is made from the grapes that surround the restaurant. It is a nice combination of casual dining with class. They have a good selection of Herzegovinian & Croatian wines, & serve excellent veal, lamb & fish dishes. $$

Food House [185 E6] Rade Bitange 12; m 061 209 388; 08.00–23.00 daily; f foodhousemostar. Located away from the noise but still in the city centre, this eatery has been getting rave reviews from travellers. Food House offers Bosnian home-style food, coupled with the classic selection of pizza, pastas, risotto, fish, grilled meat & desserts. Beer prices are laughable. Good value all the way around. $–$$

Radobolje Restaurant [185 B5] Kraljice Katarine 11a; 036 831 741; w radobolja.ba; 07.00–23.00 daily. Finding it may be your greatest challenge but when you do, you won't be disappointed. It's best to take a taxi, which should cost no more than 7–8KM from anywhere in the city centre. Situated at the source of the Radobolja River, it's a wonderfully refreshing spot for trout, Dalmatian specialities & good-quality *pršut* or ham. $–$$

Mid range

Hindin Han [185 F6] Jusovina bb; m 061 153 924; 11.00–midnight daily. You can't go wrong at this authentic traditional restaurant. Han specialises in locally made cheeses, meats & wines. The wine menu runs from 10–30KM per bottle of exclusively domestic products. $$

Restoran Goranci [185 A5] Goranci, Pod Jelom; 036 381 167; m 063 311 487; e info@konobagoranci.com; w konobagoranci.com; 08.00–23.00 daily. If you have the time, visit Restoran Goranci, which is located 12km north of Mostar. Sitting at 700m above sea level, this traditional restaurant is perched in a beautiful mountain setting. After a hearty meal of veal or lamb, or just a platter of *pršut*, cheese, fritters & domestic wine, you can hop on the mountain bike or hiking trail. The restaurant offers bike rentals & good information about the 13km path. $$

Restoran Udovice [185 B6] Sretnice bb, Krusevo; 036 486 389; e restoran@udovice.ba; w udovice.ba; 07.00–23.00 daily. Sretnice is a small settlement off the Mostar–Čitluk road. It is not too far from Mostar & well worth the short drive for one of Herzegovina's most popular restaurants. The grilled meats & local cheeses make it a popular destination for Mostarians. $$

Šadrvan [185 F6] Jusovina 11; m 061 891 189; e restoran_sadrvan@hotmail.com; w restoransadrvan.ba; 08.00–23.00 daily. Šadrvan means 'fountain' in the local language. It appropriately has an Ottoman-style fountain in its front garden. This restaurant serves the standard traditional & Dalmatian dishes, with a similar wine menu as the others. Šadrvan does serve vegetarian food. You may find seasonal live music as well. $$

Taurus [185 E6] Kriva ćuprija 4; 11.00–23.00 daily. Traditional restaurant near the Kriva ćuprija. They serve American-size portions of local, Italian & Dalmatian dishes. They're also big on fish, offering calamari, shark, trout & eel, to name just a few. The rustic décor & fireplace make it a great place for dinner, or the small terrace on the Radobolje is a great spot for lunch. $$

Cheap & cheerful

ABC [184 E4] Braće Fejića 45; 036 551 624; 09.00–23.00 daily. Has always been known as the best sweet shop in town. They've expanded their horizons, though, & built a very nice & inexpensive restaurant. Much of the menu is obviously aimed at foreign guests, offering a good selection of salads (real salads, not just cabbage & tomato), European dishes & of course the local favourites. $–$$

Babilon [185 F6] Taphana bb; 08.00–23.00 daily. This must be named after the Babylon-like walls of the old town. The multi-terraced restaurant has one of the best views of the Old Bridge & the powerful Neretva racing below it. Grapevines draped above keep it cool, even on the hottest days. The food is good & the servings are large. $–$$

Picerija Roma [184 A2] Stjepana Radića 21; 036 324 422; 07.00–23.00 daily. Simple & simply delicious. Great pizzas are good value for a light lunch or a chilled & inexpensive evening out. $–$$

Grill & Sandwich Bar Jimm [184 A3] StaroVelezovo; m 063 440 033; f jimmmostar; 08.00–midnight daily. Jimm has pretty much got it all. If you're wandering around town looking for some cheap but good eats, this very well might be your place. They serve hamburgers, pizza, salads, soups, crispy fries & 17 (yes, 17) different types of freshly prepared sandwiches. $

National Restaurant Tima-Irma [185 E6] Onešćukova bb; m 062 958 539; e info@cevabdzinica-tima.com; w cevabdzinica-tima.com; 08.00–midnight daily. This family business started before the war 30 years ago. It is one of the best quick-eat lunch restaurants in town. They obviously serve *cevapi* (meat sausages), as well as other traditional Bosnian 'fast food.' $

CAFÉS

Caffe Academia [184 A4] Kralja Petra Krešimira IV bb; m 063 483 428; 06.30–23.00 daily. Quiet café near the Herceg Stjepan Kosača cultural centre. The short espressos are the best in town. Staying honest to its name, Academia attracts a more intellectual crowd with students & artists gathering for a very academic activity – drinking one's potion of choice.

☆ **Kariola Club** [184 B3] Nikole Šubića Zrinskog bb; 08.00–22.00 daily. A popular café with the local Mostar crowd on the west bank. They serve excellent coffee & attract a wide range of clients depending on the hour of the day. Located near the park, it's a favourite spot for coffee lovers of all ages to congregate by day. The vibe changes as the younger crowd takes over for drinking & socialising at night.

ENTERTAINMENT AND NIGHTLIFE

Bars/nightclubs

Oscar [185 E6] Onešćukova bb; summer 19.00–02.00 daily. This exceptionally comfortable lounge bar is meant for you to do exactly that – lounge. Sip a smooth cocktail or a freshly squeezed juice on the cool terraces along the Radobolja River in the heart of Mostar's old town. It's only open in the summer & is a hopping spot with the 20- & 30-somethings.

Sky Bar [184 E3] Biosphere Centre, Braće Fejića bb; 036 512 257; summer 08.00–23.00 daily. Located on the roof of the Biosphere Centre, it has some of the best views in town. It's a perfect place for a coffee by day or something harder at night. Sky Bar usually attracts the 30-something crowd but is frequented by both younger & older generations. There is a DJ throughout the summer.

Beer ti&ja [184 C1] Kneza Višeslava bb; m 063 009 495; f beertiijaa; 06.30–midnight daily. Located behind the Mepas shopping mall, this relaxed pub is far from the crowds yet within walking distance from old town. A rotating selection of more than 50 beers are available, including craft beers from a variety of places around the world & also several local ones. The bar serves its own microbrew, Cooltura, in a variety of styles including APA and wheat.

Black Dog Pub [185 E6] Jusovina 5; m 061 175 120; w blackdog-pub.com; summer 09.00–midnight; winter 14.00–midnight. Located in old town, this classic-style pub owned by an American expat has an impressive selection of global beers, including microbrews from the area such as Oldbridž (from Mostar), Livanjsko (from Livno) and Lovac (from Široki Brijeg). The pub is vibrant & often has live music. It has a summer garden.

☆ **Ali-Baba Lounge** [185 F6] Kujundžiluk; f alibabamostar; summer 08.00–23.00 daily. Ali-Baba Lounge is a café by day & lounge by night. It is quickly turning into one of Mostar's favourite summertime dance halls. With a high-tech sound system & a natural acoustic den to match it (it is literally located inside of a cave), the dance club pumps out some serious sounds. Bar staff serve an impressive collection of alcoholic concoctions.

☆ **Under the Bridge** [185 F6] Under the Old Bridge; summer dusk–02.00 Fri–Sun. This open-air club is a popular summertime arena for dancing & drinking under the Stari most. Always with a live DJ, it manages to pull in loyal groupies & tourists alike. The cool Neretva & continual DJs' breeze under the clear Mostar sky make it an understandably popular party scene.

SHOPPING Shopping in Mostar is oriented around the tourist economy. Several cobblestone streets in the heart of the old town, to the immediate left and right of the

Old Bridge, are crammed with shops selling a wide array of souvenirs, ranging from kitschy to authentic, hand-crafted items. Many of the shops sell Turkish-inspired styles, and indeed a lot of those items are imported from Turkey. You may want to browse all the streets before deciding on what to buy, and bargaining might be a possibility – try it. Along these streets you can also find antiques from ex-Yugoslavia. Most of these shops are open from early morning until late evening. Some do close down during the winter, but even then you will find quite a selection to choose from.

For grocery shopping, try **Bingo** [184 B1] (*Kneza Višeslava;* 🕘 *07.00–22.00 Mon–Sat; 07.00–19.00 Sun*) and **Konzum** [184 A1] (*Bleiburških žrtava 33;* 🕘 *07.00–21.00 Mon–Sat; 07.00–14.00 Sun*).

Leroy Bar & Wine Shop [184 C1] Vokića i Lorkovića 91; **m** 063 282 798; 🕘 08.00–21.00 Mon–Fri. Herzegovina is known for its unique, delicious wines, so it would not be a bad idea to try a variety of them & pick up a bottle or a few. This bar & wine shop in one makes that convenient while in Herzegovina's largest town. There are over 250 bottles of regional & world wines to choose from. Located 2 blocks away from Mepas Mall.

Mepas Mall [184 B1] Ulica Kardinala Stepinca; ☎036 445 577; **w** mepas-mall.com; 🕘 09.00–21.00 Mon–Sat, 11.00–21.00 Sun; This is the largest shopping centre in Mostar & in all of Herzegovina. It's a huge complex: there are international chains, a large Konzum grocery store, a bio shop, a cinema & more. It is within a 10–20-min walk from most of the major tourist sites. Plenty of parking is available, & the first hour is free.

OTHER PRACTICALITIES There are innumerable ATMs on every street in and around the Old Bridge area.

Hospital

Dr Safet Mujić Hospital [184 F4] (Mostar Clinical Hospital) Kralja Tvrtka bb; ☎036 336 500; **e** ravnateljstvo@kb-mostar.org; **w** skbm.ba

Pharmacy

✚ **Europharm** [184 D3] Mostarskog bataljona bb; ☎036 580 280; 🕘 varies depending on the month, usually 07.30–midnight, sometimes 24 hrs. Mostar currently does not have one designated 24-hour pharmacy: there are several in the city that take turns staying open around the clock. Europharm has the longest consistent working hours.

Post office

✉ **Hrvatska pošta** [184 E3] Tvrtka Miloša 🕘 07.00–20.00 Mon–Sat; 09.00–noon Sun

Emergencies

Police station [184 D4] Brune Bušića; ☎036 383 111

WHAT TO SEE AND DO It's safe to say that the Unesco World Heritage Site of the Stari most (Old Bridge) has always been the main attraction in Mostar. The old town is very compact and is ideal for a walking tour, and most of the main tourist sights can be seen in one day. As there are as many cafés in Mostar as there are pubs in London, it's never difficult to find a cool spot to take a break from the hot Herzegovina sun. The old town has an enticing quality, particularly on the Neretva, which encourages you to sit for hours and just soak up the sights and sounds. Unlike in most tourist places in the world, café and restaurant owners in Mostar will never ask you to leave, even if you've been sipping a Turkish coffee for 2 hours.

Mostar is situated in one of the most beautiful valleys on the Balkan peninsula. There are many excursions for all types of tourists.

A walking tour through Mostar (For a marked route of tour see *Mostar* map, pages 184–5.) If you're looking for a guided tour of Mostar, it's best to find the tourist information centre on the west bank of the old town, very near to the Stari most. On the east side at the top of Kujundžiluk is Fortuna Tours (page 186) and they offer guided tours in most European languages. Mostar is small enough for those wanting to wander alone or follow this plan.

The east bank of the Old Bridge seems to be the most logical starting point. You'll know you've reached the old town when the streets have turned to old cobblestone or smooth marble stone.

No matter how many times one does it, crossing the **Stari most** always seems to be an exciting experience. This single-arch stone bridge is an exact replica of the original that stood for over 400 years, and that was designed by Hajrudin, a student of the great Turkish architect Sinan. The **Halebija** and **Tara towers** have always housed the guardians of the bridge and during Ottoman times were storehouses for ammunition. Crossing from the west bank to the east you'll also be symbolically crossing the ancient crossroads of where East and West actually met. Just to the right is a free photo gallery of how Mostar looked during and just after the siege. It's a stark reminder of the horrors that tortured this town in 1993. Beyond the photo gallery to the right is the main entrance to the **Stari most Museum** (page 197), which is housed in the Tara Tower. Upstairs are a few exhibitions with excellent views of the bridge on top. The stairs down to the right lead to the underbelly of the Old Bridge and provide a fascinating peek at how the old structure was built. At the end of a labyrinth is a small viewing room with a UNESCO film by Bosnian filmmaker Jasmila Žbanić about the reconstruction of the Old Bridge. When you exit the museum, turn right up the stairs and to the right is the oldest mosque in Mostar, the **Cejvan-ćehaj Mosque**, built in 1552. Later a *madrasa* (Islamic school) was built in the same compound.

Doubling back down the stairs you come to the ancient trading street of **Kujundžiluk**. This is the best place in town to find authentic paintings and copper or bronze engravings of the Stari most, pomegranates – the natural symbol of Herzegovina – or the famed *stećci* (medieval tombstones). Carpet-makers, coppersmiths and antique collectors all continue to pass on the tradition of *stari zanati* (old crafts) from father to son. You will find craftsmen working in their shops, not just for show but also as a way of traditional life that refuses to die in these parts. Kujundžiluk heads slightly uphill and here is the best photo opportunity to catch the awesome grace and beauty of the Stari most.

At the top of the hill the old town continues to the left, and is lined with yet more shops. Here you'll find carpet-makers and boutiques that sell the traditional attire of Herzegovina. These shops are rare and if you're a collector or just interested in the old-style wear of Herzegovina your best bet is probably here. To the left through a small archway is the **Koski Mehmed-Pasha Mosque** (page 196) that was built in 1617. It is open to visitors and is free of charge. Feel free to walk down to the *šadrvan* (fountain) and have a cool drink of water. Visitors may enter the mosque and take photos free of charge. Although it isn't always required, it is customary to remove one's shoes before entering. Women are not required to cover themselves as this mosque was especially designed to show Mostar's many guests the beauty of Ottoman Islamic architecture. The paintings inside are typical of Ottoman design and the detailed woodwork of the doors is an Ottoman trademark. The 'altar' with steps is for the *efendija* (Muslim cleric) to lead prayers or to address his congregation. Islam, however, does not follow sermon-type worship. The faithful are obliged to pray on their own, five times a day. For those willing to bear the dizzy spiral to the top, the minaret is also open to the public and is accessible from inside the mosque. The view speaks for itself! Carrying on to the left after leaving the mosque is the **Tepa Market**. This has been a busy marketplace since Ottoman times. It now sells mostly fresh produce grown in Herzegovina. When in season, the figs and pomegranates can't be beaten. Be sure to look for local honey produced in sunny villages all over Herzegovina. A large jar costs around 15–20KM.

Now head north on Brače Fejića (Fejića Street), the nightclub and café district. It's quite tiny, but in the evenings you'll be forced to choose between the sound systems that blare from each club – all within 100m of each other. For those looking for more peace and quiet, the **Bišćevića House** (*see opposite,* ☎ *036 550 677;* 🕘 *Apr–Nov 08.30–18.30 Mon–Fri; Dec–Mar, private tours only, by appointment; admission 4KM*) is just a bit further up to the left on Bišćevića Street. This 17th-century Turkish House rests (some parts on long pillars of over 5m long) on the eastern banks of the Neretva. There is a conversation or gathering room (*divanhan*) preserved in authentic Turkish style. Throughout the house are original household objects, and the courtyard is a fine example of the Ottoman style. Back on Fejića Street, and still heading north, you'll soon reach the **Karađoz-begova Mosque**. This is the most important and significant of all sacred Islamic architecture in Herzegovina. The mosque was heavily damaged during the war and its minaret completely destroyed by tank and artillery rounds from the Croatian forces. The mosque was completed in 1557. Its designer was Kodža Mimara Sinan, a great Turkish architect, and the work was probably carried out by local and Dalmatian stonemasons. The interior is marked with typical Ottoman characteristics but has lost much of its detailed paintings from water damage after its destruction. It opened to visitors again relatively recently, after being under construction for a long time. Continuing your stroll north on Fejića, there are more cafés and the ABC sweet shop and restaurant. This is a favourite local hangout for good ice cream, and is a great place to sit and people-watch.

At the next main intersection on Fejića head west towards the river. Trg Musala (Musala Square) is one of the main ones in town. Tito had his villa built right next to the famous **Hotel Neretva** here. Both were destroyed in the war. The **music school** and **public baths** are also located in the square. Both of these buildings are built in pseudo-Moorish style and were constructed during Austro-Hungarian times. The public baths are open to all for a swim or just a quick peek inside. A park has been built and is usually crowded with locals. There are, of course, several cafés within a 50m radius of the square. Take your pick if you've fallen into the groove of the local café culture. Hotel Bristol is just across Musala Bridge (most locals will call it Tito Bridge) and it has a great terrace for observing the white-water rapids of the Neretva.

After passing the Hotel Bristol on the west bank take the first right. This will be Šantića Street. Alexander Šantić was a famous poet who fell in love with a Muslim woman named Emina. Being a Christian he was not permitted to marry her and, although he was willing to convert to Islam to win her love, her family would not allow it. One of the most famous *sevdalinkas* (traditional love songs) was written in her honour. This street was the dividing line between the Croatian and Bosnian forces and saw some of the most intensive fighting of the whole war. Šantića Street soon becomes Buća Street, which is part of the administrative centre of Mostar. This area was largely created during the Austro-Hungarian rule at the turn of the 20th century. Returning the way you came and heading straight on will take you towards the old town through the *mahala* of **Cernica**. At the end of Buća Street is the Centre for Culture. Take a left there and that will take you directly back to the old town. There is a city map on the corner in front of the Hotel Ruža.

THE MYTH OF THE NEW ORTHODOX CHURCH

The Serbian priest had gone to the *beg* (local ruler in Turkish times) to ask permission to build a new church. It was often customary, especially for non-Muslims, to offer the *beg* some sort of gift. The *beg* already had something in mind and asked for the priest's daughter. When the priest refused, his request for the church was rejected and he was sent away. The priest, however, would not give up. He returned, insisting that he be allowed to build a church. The old church was no longer big enough to suit the growing Orthodox community and it was imperative that he be granted permission for both the land and the church. The *beg* again questioned the priest about his lovely daughter, but the priest would hear nothing of it. Again, he was sent away without the blessing of the *beg*. After returning yet once more the annoyed *beg* conceded – but under one condition. The land to be given by the authorities would be no larger than the wool jumper worn by the priest. The priest left discouraged and angry but as he walked home a brilliant idea struck him. He rushed back to his home and completely dismantled his jumper. He was a large man and the jumper consisted of dozens of metres of wool when it was all laid out. The priest brought this jumble of yarn to the *beg* and calculated that if he spread the entire contents of the yarn from his jumper it would cover an area large enough to build a new church on. The *beg* was so tickled by the priest's ingenious gesture that with a chuckle he granted the hard-headed priest permission to build the church.

Strolling back into the old town you'll find the oldest single-arch stone bridge in Mostar, the **Kriva ćuprija**, built in 1558 by the Turkish architect Cejvan Kethoda. From this point on you are back in the heart of the old town. Quaint souvenir shops and galleries line the narrow streets as you near the Old Bridge. Just before you reach it will be a small alleyway to the left. In this complex is the **Hammam and Tabhana Turkish Baths**. These were heavily damaged during the war but the courtyard and terrace is now a favourite gathering place for the young and old, sitting to enjoy a coffee or a meal on the terraced walls that offer one of the best views of the Stari most. The Turkish Baths, recognisable by their six domes, were built in the 16th century.

Bišćevića House [184 E4] (*Bišćevića bb;* ☎ *036 550 677;* ⏲ *Apr–Nov 08.30–18.30, Mon–Fri; Dec–Mar, private tours only, by appointment; admission 4KM*) Built on a quiet side street that leads down to the Neretva River, this 17th-century Turkish house, which is partially supported by 5m-long pillars, is one of three well-preserved Ottoman homes to visit in Mostar. The home is still owned by the Bišćević family, who proudly give guided tours. The main attraction is the large gathering room, or *divanhan*, which was designated for men to talk business. It is preserved in original Turkish style.

Herceg Stjepan Kosača Croatian Cultural Centre [184 B4] (*Trg hrvatskih velikana bb;* ☎ *036 314 605;* **e** *kosaca@kosaca.info;* **w** *kosaca-mostar.com;* ⏲ *08.00–15.00 Mon–Fri*). This centre, once called the Mostar Cultural Centre is, like many Yugoslav-era buildings in Herzegovina, built with an interesting blend of beautiful stone and awkward socialist-style interior. It hosts a wide array of impressive events, films, concerts, plays and countless other exhibitions throughout the year.

Museum of Herzegovina [185 F5] (*Bajatova 4;* ☎ *036 551 602;* **e** *info@muzejhercegovine.com;* **w** *muzejhercegovine.com;* ⌚ *Apr–Nov 10.00–18.00 Mon–Sat; entrance fee 5KM, students 3KM*). The museum allows researchers and students access to archives and documentary files (including films). It was founded in 1950 to promote the archaeological, ethnographic, literary and cultural history of Herzegovina.

Kajtaz House [185 G7] (*Gaše Ilica 21;* **m** *061 339 897,* ⌚ *Apr–Oct Mon–Fri 10.00–16.00*) A bit off the central circuit of the old town is this best-preserved Turkish-style house in Herzegovina, a UNESCO World Heritage Site, and now protected by law as the finest example of an Ottoman home. Fortuna Tours near the Old Bridge can arrange a tour guide, or you can wander up to the house yourself. The host does not speak English, but she will gladly walk you through the old-style kitchen with all of its original and functional furniture and equipment. The garden terrace, shadowed by Hum Mountain to the west, has plenty of seats to sit back and enjoy the hostess's homemade juice from roses – it is absolutely amazing and nearly impossible to find anywhere else. The upstairs floor is laid out in typical Turkish fashion. There are separate sleeping rooms for the women, all with bathing areas within the room. The women also had a large sitting room where they would receive guests and entertain. The men were situated on the southern side of the house, but the man of the house had free range to visit his many wives. The wooden wardrobes and large chests are carved with intricate oriental designs. In the open foyer upstairs, you can try on a set of traditional attire (men's and women's) – a great photo opportunity. The fact that the house is still lived in adds to its charm.

Koski Mehmed-Pasha Mosque [185 F5] (*Mala Tepa bb;* ⌚ *summer 08.00–18.00 daily; entrance fee 2KM*) Mostar is unique in that it has opened many of its most precious and historical mosques to be visited and viewed by tourists. This one was built in 1617 and although heavily damaged during the last war, it has been fully restored. Visitors are permitted to enter the mosque, and even climb the minaret for a phenomenal view of the Stari most. You must take your shoes off before entering a mosque. As this mosque is open for visitors, it is not required that women wear a headscarf. On the same premises you will find a *madrasa* (Islamic school), whichh was built in the 17th century.

Muslibegović House [184 F4] (*Osmana Đikića 41;* ☎ *036 551 379;* **w** *muslibegovichouse.com;* ⌚ *09.00–18.00 daily; entrance fee 4KM*) Arguably the finest example of Ottoman architecture in BiH, the Muslibegović House is one of Mostar's premiere attractions. The house itself is an exquisite model of 17th-century Ottoman architecture. The original house was built in the 16th century but it was later expanded and upgraded. The owners have adopted the Spanish model of national monument homes and opened the house as a boutique bed and breakfast (page 187). The museum visit is a 20-minute tour of the middle part of the house (the other parts house the guests) with interesting historical facts and anecdotes. The true experience, however, is to spend the night and live like a *beg* for an evening.

Pavarotti Music Centre [185 G7] (*Marsala Tita 179;* ☎ *036 550 750;* ⌚ *07.00–22.00 daily*) The British charity War Child was very active in Mostar during and after the war. They managed to gather many famous singers, including Bono and Pavarotti, to not only make an album to raise funds for innocent victims of war but to help build a music centre. It gives the people of Mostar, particularly the younger generation, an opportunity to learn, create and play music with modern equipment and facilities. There is also a café in the main lobby that exhibits local art. Foreigners often visit to drink a coffee and have a chat with local musicians and artists.

Stari most Museum [185 F6] (*Stari most bb; ⏲ summer 10.00–18.00 daily; entrance fee 2KM*) The museum is housed on the east bank in the Tara Tower. Although the history and architecture of the Old Bridge are fascinating, the museum barely manages to adequately present the cultural and historical significance of Stari most. The views and perspectives of the bridge and town are worth the entrance fee. Downstairs is literally the underbelly of the Stari most. Although it's very cool to walk through the underlying foundation of the bridge, there isn't much to stir the imagination. At the end of the tour there is a small room showing the UNESCO documentary on the reconstruction of the bridge, directed by Jasmila Žbanić, the 2006 Berlin Film Festival Golden Bear winner.

Churches One of most beautiful religious structures in Mostar was the **new Serbian Orthodox church**, but the war unfortunately erased this fine example of Byzantine architecture. The remains of the **old Orthodox church** [185 G5], located on the same grounds, are still an interesting place to visit, as is the old cemetery next to it. A new church is being reconstructed, and is close to completion [185 G5]. It is located on the east bank of the city on the M-17 overlooking the city. The folk tale behind the construction of the church is outlined in the box on page 195.

There are two Catholic churches in Mostar. The newer and more modern one does not necessarily represent a tourist attraction. The **old Catholic church** [185 D6], which was renovated, is nearly impossible to miss. A steeple of over 30m dominates the skyline just west of the bulevar that runs through the middle of town. The church was heavily damaged during the war.

Other sites and sights You may notice that on top of the hill (*hum*) in the centre of town a **large cross** [184 A6] has been erected. Although this is common in the Italian countryside it is a fairly new practice in Herzegovina. Whilst Međugorje is viewed by most as a holy site, the cross above Mostar is considered by many as a very provocative landmark. During the war, from the exact spot where the 35m cross has been erected, the Croatian forces pummelled east Mostar with artillery and anti-aircraft fire. Because of the no-fly zone enforced by NATO during the war there were no planes to fire at so the anti-aircraft weapons were fired at civilians. It is a painful reminder to many citizens of Mostar of not only the brutal war that divided the city but the deep rifts in relations between the ethnic groups today. On a lighter note, the **bishop's residence** in Mostar marks not only the long Catholic traditions of the region but also the Viennese architecture that greatly added to the town's charm. Somewhat bulky and markedly socialist, the **Partisan Memorial Cemetery** [184 A3] (*off K P Krešimira IV St on Bijeli Brijeg*) commemorates the fallen communists. This part of town is covered with lots of greenery and is also a pleasant place for a stroll with a great view of the city.

EXCURSIONS FROM MOSTAR

Herzegovina is a relatively compact region and most destinations are within an hour's drive of Mostar. Listed here are the closest, and the off-the-beaten-track ones. Keep in mind that the bus schedules listed are subject to change.

WINE COUNTRY

Herzegovina's rocky and sometimes harsh landscape is relieved not only by its emerald-coloured rivers, but also by the many green vineyards dotting the countryside. Increasing numbers of visitors are attracted to Herzegovina's 'Wine Route' (*vinska cesta*), where numerous wineries are located in relatively close proximity to one another.

Prior to the war, when Bosnia and Herzegovina was part of the former Yugoslavia, wine-production was structured slightly differently than it is today. In Yugoslavia, robust state-owned industries produced wine for local consumption and for export. People say that the quality of the wine varied from year to year and bottle to bottle, depending on a number of factors. Individual producers were allowed to grow their own grapes and make wine within a designated limit, but were not supposed to bottle it and sell it for private commercial purposes. In the past two decades – since the end of socialism – things have changed. While large local industries still produce wine (most of it not high quality), the number of small- and medium-sized wineries are on the rise, with variety increasing, and marketing getting more sophisticated, every year. Many say that the last two decades have also witnessed a noticeable increase in the quality of the wine available on the market. While there are already a number of exceptional wines coming out of Herzegovina, time will almost certainly lead to even better and more varieties of wine and wine production methods in the future. It's not easy to be a small winery in Bosnia-Herzegovina today, as the nation's market for fine wine is still developing as the export market for the country's wine grows.

The indigenous grapes of Herzegovina are Žilavka and Blatina. They are responsible for Herzegovina's visibility on the global wine map, and represent the core of wine-production in the area. Special varietals of Žilavka and Blatina are also available. Varieties such as Vranac, Trnjak, Merlot, Chardonnay, Cabernet Sauvignon, and many others are also grown. The wines of Herzegovina tend to be affordable. While there are a range of prices just like anywhere else in the world, it is not difficult to find an excellent bottle of Herzegovinian wine for 20–30KM.

The local tourism board has attempted to link all the wineries together along a designated Wine Route. More information, including a map, can be found on an interactive website: **w** vinskacesta.ba/en. Signage along the route could be improved, but does exist. Travelling slowly along the Wine Route is a pleasurable, and only slightly roundabout, way to pass through Herzegovina to the nearby Croatian seaside.

There are too many wines and wineries to list comprehensively. The wineries below are some of the best in Herzegovina, and all are accessible from the Wine Route.

WINE TASTING CELLARS OF HERZEGOVINA

Međugorje and Čitluk

AG Cellars Put Kovačici 18, Međugorje; 036 651 392; **m** 063 405 966; **e** info@ag-travel.org; **w** ag-travel.org. The AG wine cellar was founded in the mid 19th century. They produce several variations of Blatina & Žilavka, with the Carska Blatina barrique ranking as one of the better wines in Herzegovina. The medium-sized tasting facility can seat up to 50 people. The winery is connected to a travel agency, AG Travel Međugorje, which offers other services in Herzegovina.

Andrija Wines Paoča, Čitluk; 036 644 102; **m** 063 322 162; **e** podrumiandrija95@gmail.com; podrumiandrijapaoca. Andrija wines are synonymous with the town of Čitluk. Their vineyards are located on the sunny Paoča plateau, not far from the Shrine of the Queen of Peace in Međugorje. They produce quality

Žilavka & Blatina wines, as well as barrique varieties of both. The family cellar can host up to 60 guests, & a new, larger wine-tasting facility has been built in Paoča.

Brkić Wines Kralja Tvrtka 9, Čitluk; ☎ 036 644 466; m 063 320 205; e info@brkic.ba; w brkic.ba. The first modern cellar was founded in Herzegovina by the Brkić family in 1979. They have long prided themselves in natural, organic wine production. Their Žilavka & Blatina wines are not only unique but also known as one of the most full-bodied wines in the entire area. Mjesečar, or Sleepwalker, is Brkić's most famous wine, & they also produce an impressive collection of brandies. For eco-wine lovers, a visit to this vineyard is a must.

Buntić Winery Miletina, Međugorje; m 063 377 073; e vinarija.buntic@gmail.com; w vinarija-buntic.com. Buntić wines have gained in both quality & popularity in recent years. Besides the high quality Žilavka white & red Blatina, they produce a rosé, several different brandies & Blatina barrique. Their wines & brandies can be found in most specialty wine shops in the country or one can try them all at wine-tasting facilities in Međugorje.

Marijanović Vineyards Služanj bb, Čitluk; m 063 177 198, 063 313 953; e info@marijanovic.ba; w marijanovic.ba. This family-owned & -operated vineyard is located in Služanj, a quaint village situated not far from Čitluk & Međugorje. The Marijanovićs have always produced quality Žilavka & Blatina &, as of late, have been working at mastering the French Syrah & Cabernet Sauvignon grapes. Well-versed sommeliers walk you through the entire process of making their delicious wines. They make a rare & enticing quince brandy.

Mostar

Vilinka Cellar Sretnice bb, Mostar; ☎ 036 486 444; m 063 427 411; e info@vilinka.ba; w vilinka.ba. This relatively new small vineyard was planted in 2006. It is owned & operated by one of Herzegovina's youngest winemakers, Velimir Eres. His wines have won numerous medals at regional wine fairs. The Vilinka winery makes Žilavka, Blatina, Blatina barrique & others. Its cellar has a wine-tasting room with a capacity of 40. A terrace with a mountain view will be completed soon. The Blatina Barrique and X-Line Cuvee White are their outstanding wines.

Ljubuški

Keža Winery Kralja Zvonimira, Ljubuški; m 063 372 773; e info@pki-gmbh.de; w z-keza.com. Keža wines are conspicuously labeled with a big Ž. Their vineyards are spread over 25ha of fertile land in the village of Studenci. This area best suits the indigenous varieties of Žilavka & Blatina. Keža's wine can now be found in exclusive restaurants throughout BiH. If you'd like to try it out on the spot, they have a small tasting room.

Nuić Vineyards Crnopod bb, Ljubuški; ☎ 039 849 515; m 063 655 572; e info@vinogradinuic.com; w vinogradinuic.com. Although the Nuić family has been in the winegrowing business for quite some time, the Nuić Vineyards company was established in 2004. They planted 190,000 vines, primarily Žilavka & Blatina, on 35ha of prime grape-growing land in the village of Crnopod. The Blatina barrique is superb & ranks among Herzegovina's top Blatina wines. They have modern tasting facilities. For travellers on a budget, Nuić also offers some good bottles for a bargain – as low as 8KM in local shops. In general, buying wines priced lower than 10KM in BiH is not advisable, but this is a notable exception.

Trebinje

Anđelić Wines [221 B1] Gorica bb, Trebinje; ☎ 059 259 222; m 065 940 055; e milica@podrum-andjelic.com; w podrum-andjelic.com. The Anđelić family have produced fine wines for many decades & now make about 150,000 litres per year. The cellar has a small shop & reception area. The storage cellar below is a striking space of over 200m^2, dug right into the rock face. This provides the ideal conditions for the wine to mature naturally. Anđelić's wines have won regional awards for both their excellent taste & high quality.

Tvrdoš Wine Tvrdoš bb, Trebinje; ☎ 059 246 810; e tpodrumi@teol.net; w tvrdos.com. Around 2005, the Orthodox monks from Tvrdoš Monastery began to revitalise the 70ha of Vranac grapes grown in the Trebinje Fields. They have since planted 60ha of top-quality grapes in Popovo Polje.

WINE COUNTRY continued

The Vranac red wines are amongst the best produced in southeast Europe, and the Žilavka & Cabernet Sauvignon are also top notch. The monastery alone is worth a visit, & after a winding drive to its rural location 8km outside of Trebinje, a glass of great wine doesn't hurt either.

Vukoje Cellars 1982 Gallery & restaurant: [221 A2] Hrupjela 28, Trebinje; cellar: Mirna 28, Trebinje; 059 270 370; m 065 517 099; e podrum-vukoje@teol.net; w podrumivukoje1982.com. This is one of BiH's most famous wine producers. The vineyard relies on modern technology, with a controlled fermentation process & traditional settling in oak 'barrique' barrels in an underground cellar. The fine wines produced at Vukoje have been recipients of gold medals for quality in Paris, Geneva, Milan & Brussels. For wine lovers, the wine gallery & restaurant offers a spectacular panoramic view of the city, mountains & the vineyards, & there are tours of the facilities & the cellar.

BLAGAJ/BUNA The source of the Buna River is near the town of Blagaj. Both the spring and Blagaj itself are worth visiting. This can either be a full-day trip or just a lunch visit to the splendid fish-farm restaurant (see opposite). To get to Blagaj take bus 10 from Mostar's eastern station at 07.45, 11.00, 18.40, 14.00, 18.00 or 22.00 Mon–Fri; 8.00, 10.30, noon, 17.00, 19.00, 22.00 Sat; 06.30, 08.00, 10.30, noon, 15.30, 19.30, 22.00 Sun and holidays. This natural and cultural oasis definitely should not be missed – human remains have been found in Blagaj that date back 12,000 years, and the caves above the Buna Springs have long protected human settlements.

Where to stay

Hotel Ada (31 rooms) Branilaca Bosne bb, Blagaj; m 062 545 948. Located right on the Buna River (Buna Springs), 10km from Mostar. **$$–$$$**

Motel Kolo (8 rooms, 6 apts) Buna bb; 036 480 205; e info@motel-kolo.com; w motel-kolo.com. Motel Kolo has both modest motel rooms & new apts located in the quiet settlement of Buna along the Buna River. The rooms are basic, en suite with river views. The apts have all the facilities & a bit more space, but lack the river view. **$$**

Vila Ivankovic (11 rooms) Buna bb, Buna; 036 480 832; e info@vila-ivankovic.com; w vila-ivankovic.com. This is a classy establishment in the settlement of Buna. It's a great place to stay to beat the summer heat & only a short distance from Mostar. The rooms are excellent, with sat TV, minibar & AC. The terrace bar & restaurant are also top quality & a favourite spot for locals. **$$**

Villa Velagic Pansion (5 rooms) Velagićevina bb, Blagaj; m 061 707 088; e villavelagic@gmail.com; w villavelagic.com. This traditionally preserved house was a famous Ottoman compound, built in the late 18th century. It is under state protection as a historic & cultural monument, and is located in one of the oldest parts of Blagaj, just below the dramatic cliffs of the Buna Springs. **$$**

Mali Wimbledon Blagaj bb; 036 572 582; e ibrozalihic@hotmail.com; entrance fee 2KM. This is the region's largest camping facility. More than 7,000m^2 of land holds up to 40 large c/vans with all the hook-ups, including electricity, water, kitchen & toilet facilities. They also have 4 dbl rooms in the family house available to rent. The reason for the name is that Mali Wimbledon is home to the only professional grass court in the country. This perfectly manicured tennis facility is a magnet for those looking for a quiet but active vacation. Camper/van fees range from 15–30KM per night. **$**

River Camp Aganović Blagaj bb; m 061 169 495; e rcaganovac@yahoo.com; w camping-blagaj.com. Located directly on the banks of the Buna River near the town centre, this laid-back camping facility is a popular spot for both backpackers & family campers. They have the complete spectrum of camping services: toilets, hot showers, electricity hook-ups for c/vans, & kitchen facilities. The management is very helpful & has created the most relaxed atmosphere in town. From the site it is possible to fish & rent canoes or bikes. Facilities cost between 10–20KM for tent use. **$**

Where to eat and drink

Restoran Kolo Buna bb; 036 480 205; w motel-kolo.com; 08.00–23.00 daily. Restoran Kolo has a gorgeous island terrace in the middle of the Buna River. It's a perfect place for cooling down & having a leisurely lunch. If the Buna inspires you to stay overnight, there are several lovely places along the Buna River to stay (see opposite). $$–$$$

Ribliji restoran Mlinica Vrelo Bune; 036 572 999; e info@mlinica.com; w mlinica.com; 08.00–23.00 daily. Just a short walk from the *tekija* (see below) is Riblji restoran Mlinica. Here you can hand pick your choice of fresh trout from the cold waters of the Buna. The food is excellent, including traditional meat dishes as well as the fish. With wine, a hearty meal will cost around 20KM or less. $

What to see and do Atop the high cliffs is the **fortress of Herceg Stjepan** who ruled Hum (present-day Herzegovina) in the Middle Ages. This fort was originally an Illyrian tribe settlement that was later reinforced by the Roman invaders, further fortified by the ruling Bosnian state, and significantly expanded with the arrival of the Turks. The fort is accessible by a winding trail that takes 45–60 minutes to walk. It has not been conserved but many of its high walls are intact and it is a fascinating place for its view of the **Neretva Valley**, and is an ideal picnic spot. The trail is not marked but is not difficult to find, and there are no guides or entrance fees to the fort.

Back in the town is one of the most mystical destinations in all of BiH. When the Ottomans arrived, the sultan immediately ordered a dervish *tekija* (house/monastery) to be built. The ***tekija*** (*Blagaj bb; 036 572 551;* e *info@blagajtekija.ba;* w *blagajtekija.ba; daily; entrance fee 2KM; you must wear trousers to enter and women are given a shawl to cover their heads*) was built at the source of the River Buna; as one of the largest water sources in Europe it boasts an average flow of 40,000 litres per minute – larger than the source of the Danube River. This *tekija* was built in the 1500s for the dervish cults at the base of a 200m cliff wall. It now serves food, cold drinks, and Turkish tea and coffee in a beautiful garden overlooking the Buna source. To get there, drive through the tiny town centre of Blagaj to the large car park – parking costs 2–4KM depending on the time of year and can get quite crowded in the summer. Follow the other visitors down the hill, past the wooden stalls selling interesting handmade souvenirs and Islamic music. In about 500m, the *tekija* will appear in front of you. Buses will also drop you off near the car park. The tour of the *tekija* is self-guided and is most interesting for its woodwork and well-preserved old-style sitting and prayer rooms. The *tekija* has recently become a very popular tourist destination with busloads of travellers from Turkey arriving regularly, and its original peaceful and laid-back ambience is best experienced off-season. There is also a small trail across the wooden footbridge that leads almost directly to the cave where the Buna exits and which is a great place to capture the whole *tekija* house for a photograph. Blagaj's old town is worth taking a walk through. Away from the crowds around the *tekija*, this lazy Herzegovinian town moves at a slow pace and many of its old structures are reminiscent of Turkish days.

The famous **Velagić house** (*Velagićevina;* m *061 273 459; 10.00–19.00 daily*) was built in 1776 and is perhaps the most beautiful example of Ottoman stone masonry. In the vicinity are also old flour mills that the strong Buna powered. Here are three other things to do/see here for the more outdoor-minded travellers.

Bunica Canoe Safari (*Blagaj bb;* m *061 760 548;* e *info@blagaj-city.com;* w *blagaj-city.com; May–Oct 09.00–19.00 daily; entrance fee 24KM*) The lads from Blagaj have an impressive selection of equipment, from new canoes and safety gear, to a new transport van to begin the Bunica canoe safari. They offer several canoe and rafting trips, but this is certainly the highlight of their multi-trip repertoire. The

3-hour journey along the peaceful and cool Bunica River is a perfect novice outing for a relaxing day in nature or to entertain the kids. The trip includes all safety gear and transport to the launch site.

Eko centar Blagaj (*Galčići bb;* **m** *061 529 005;* **e** *office@novival.info;* **w** *novival.info;* ⌚ *09.00–19.00 Mon–Fri; entrance fee 1KM*) In an attempt to reintroduce the griffon vulture, which disappeared from the limestone cliffs that dominate southern Blagaj, the youth NGO Novi Val took it upon themselves to seek help and try to bring back this large, gracious and intimidating bird. With help from Spanish

CYCLAMEN GARDEN CLIMBING CENTRE *Massimo Moratti*

In Donja Drežnica is a place where history and adventure come together. Located at the very beginning of the Drežnica valley, Cyclamen Garden is the name given to this area by the first climbers when they saw the area covered with cyclamens.

On the Mostar–Sarajevo road, following the signs for Drežnica, cross the bridge and, immediately after the bridge, take the first road on the right-hand side and follow it for around 150m until you reach a right turn, with some space to park. Here is the entrance to the climbing centre.

An impressive rock pillar, named 'Kuk', 40m high and slightly leaning towards the lake, is the distinctive natural landmark of the climbing centre. The pillar sticks out from the terraced meadows, which follow the natural ridge of Drežnica. An artificial lake at the bottom, crossed by an arched railway bridge, gives a special touch to an idyllic setting. It is possible to camp here, after paying a small fee to the owner of the land.

HISTORICAL DETAIL If the rock pillar is the most distinctive natural feature, the Mastan Bubanjic inscription on the rock face, properly marked by a sign, is the reason why this area is interesting not only for climbers. Dating back to the 14th century, the inscription, in the Bosnian Cyrillic script, tells the story of the Mastan Bubanjic, a local notable who lived in the area between 1356 and 1366 with his sons. The inscription with the surrounding landscape was declared a National Monument by the Bosnian authorities.

THE CLIMBING Today, Drežnica is the most developed climbing area in BiH thanks to the work of local and international climbers. At the end of 1997, Edin Durmo of the Extreme Sports Club Scorpio in Zenica, with the help of Roberto Ferrante, an Italian colonel in the peacekeeping forces, and a few more local and international climbers, started bolting the first routes. The results are evident: the centre now offers more than 70 climbing routes divided into ten sectors. The rock is excellent, very solid white and grey limestone, giving a great variety of climbing styles, mostly single pitches. The Kuk is the sector with the most spectacular and difficult routes, one of which, 'Mostarska Lasta' (Mostar's swallow, dedicated to a famous Mostar bridge diver), reaches the peak of the Kuk after a series of overhangs and roofs.

Besides the Kuk, numerous sectors spread across the valley, on both sides of the asphalt road; the 'Stit' (shield) and the school sector 'Skolski' are not to be missed. The protections have been enhanced and new routes added. Climbing is possible throughout the year, although it might be hot during the summer.

counterparts, two griffon vultures have been brought to a holding pen at the Eco Centre near the *tekija*. This is part of the long process of releasing the male and female pair into the wild. In the meantime, they can be viewed at the Eco Centre, which is a modest complex, set in natural surroundings. There are also donkeys, a special breed of local sheepdogs and a place for refreshment. Camping and use of a climbing wall nearby are also possibilities, but contact the centre in advance.

Fida Sports Centre (*Blagaj bb;* **m** *062 545 948;* ⌚ *summer 08.00–21.00 daily; entrance fee 2KM*) Fida is a sports complex just next to Hotel Ada (page 200). The owners of Ada have expanded their accommodation offer to include sports-and-recreational tourism. Just a stone's throw from the Hotel Ada, the sports centre has a large swimming pool, well-groomed tennis courts and a football pitch. Accompanying all this is a café-bar with darts, billiards and a handful of video games. It's a perfect place to visit for those looking for a more active holiday.

POČITELJ A great half-day trip on your way to the coast or to Hutovo Blato, this quaint oriental-style town is located about a half-hour drive from Mostar, less than 30km south on the M-17 road towards the Adriatic. This unique settlement was heavily damaged during the war but its reconstruction has returned the town to its former glory, and it is now listed as a UNESCO World Heritage Site. Besides its stunning oriental architecture and Ottoman feel, it also hosted the longest-operating art colony in southeast Europe. It reopened in 2003 after ten years of inactivity due to the war. Artists from around the world have gathered here to paint the likes of the shiny red pomegranates and figs that grow in abundance on the hills of Počitelj.

Dadži-Alija Mosque has been reconstructed as well as the **Sisman-Ibrahimpasha's Madrasa** and the **Gavran Kapetanović House**, all of which are open to visitors. The most striking object in Počitelj is the **Sahat Kula**, a silo-shaped fort that towers from the top of the hill above the town. It housed watchmen and military to guard against possible invasion from the Neretva Valley. The old town was once completely encircled by a protective wall. It, too, is open, but there are no markings to point you in the right direction through the maze of winding stone steps.

If you'd like to stay in Počitelj, the art colony offers accommodation during the summer months, but is sometimes booked with groups of artists so it's not always a reliable place to stay. Along the river is a guesthouse called **Aurora Apartments** (**m** *061 622 051;* **e** *apartments-aurora@live.com;* **w** *apartmentsaurora.wordpress.com*). Coming from Mostar as you enter Počitelj turn right just after the INA petrol station. The street is a narrow one between two houses. After 300m or so on the left will be a green fence and a duplex apartment behind it. It's an exceptionally peaceful place to stay and enjoy the river and views of the surrounding hills. The apartments have kitchens, bathrooms, air conditioning and, most importantly, great terraces.

PODVELEŽJE Amongst the rich tourist destinations of Herzegovina this is one of the least-known gems. The Podveležje Plateau rests in between the towering peaks of **Velež mountain** and the city of Mostar. For centuries it has been home to highland shepherds and a traditional way of life. The landscape is harsh arid karst, dotted with small forests of beech and oak trees. Podveležje has even more sunny days than Mostar. Situated at 700m above sea level, it makes a pleasant escape during hot weather. Bus 16 goes to Podveležje from Mostar at 06.45, 10.45, 13.00, 15.30, 19.30 Monday to Friday, and at 15.30 and 19.30 on Saturdays. There is no Sunday bus service in this direction.

The small village of **Smajkići** is an ideal base for walking, mountain biking, medicinal herb picking, and challenging treks to Velež's highest peak at 1,980m. Here one can witness many of the old methods of traditional life, including sheep-shearing; milk, cheese and butter production; honey making; meat drying and wool sewing. It is a modest and undeveloped place, but quiet and far from the crowds of tourists in Mostar. There are miles of asphalted roads across the plateau with almost no traffic. Smajkići is located approximately 18km off the main road to Nevesinje from Mostar and is marked with signs starting from the turn-off to Blagaj on the M-17. Much of the journey is uphill along winding roads, and can take 45 minutes to reach by car.

Where to stay and eat

Eco-motel Sunce (8 rooms, 22 beds) Smajkići; 036 560 082; e info@sunce-podvelez.com; restaurant 09.00–varies. The restaurant ($) at the eco-motel Sunce serves traditional, organic Herzegovinian meals in one of the most peaceful places in the region. The motel is family owned & operated, & truly offers a remarkable mountain experience, only 20 minutes from Mostar. The friendly owner can arrange walks, hikes, biking (*3KM/hr*), & herb picking on the spot, & local guides can take you to Velež's peaks. Do try the house specialities of grilled lamb, pitta baked under the *sać* (see *Eating and drinking*, page 80), & homemade soup. Sunce serves many domestic Herzegovinian wines; the author recommends Žilavka white! Natural juices & homemade spirits are also available. The honey & jam served with home-baked bread at breakfast is worth the bargain price of 45KM for accommodation, breakfast, lunch & dinner. The sunsets will leave a lasting impression. **$**

DREŽNICA The settlement of Drežnica sits humbly under the massive rock faces of **Čabulja and Čvrsnica mountains**. Only 20km north of Mostar, it is easily accessed just off the M-17 towards Sarajevo. The **River Drežanka** cuts through the deep valley and 12 canyons feed it along its 18km of stunning terrain. It is an ideal car ride for the picturesque views and awe-inspiring canyons. The deeper you travel into the canyon, the further back in time you feel you've gone. The tiny villages that dot the mountainside are remnants of Old World Europe and a traditional way of life. With the exception of Pansion Teatar there is no 'tourism' *per se* in Drežnica. This guarantees you, at the very least, an authentic experience not seen even by most Bosnians and Herzegovinians. It is one of those off-the-beaten-track places that have been made accessible by recent road building, but no-one other than the locals is quite aware of it yet.

Pansion Teatar is located less than a kilometre after you cross the bridge towards Drežnica. This modest bed and breakfast is owned by an older actress from Mostar, Hatidza. The establishment serves good food and has an excellent swimming area on the lake. Accommodation is rather simple, but clean and good value. It is child friendly and there's a children's swimming pool. There are hiking trails throughout the canyon but very few are marked. Solo hiking is not recommended in this area due to the harsh terrain and the danger of falling rocks. Much of the canyon is loose limestone that can create hazards in areas unknown to hikers.

DIVA GRABOVICA For hikers and nature lovers, just a glimpse of this valley will tempt you to extend your trip. Diva Grabovica is the natural boundary between the Mediterranean and continental climates. Its position has produced an ecosystem unlike any other found in Bosnia and Herzegovina. In this tiny village, there are no more than ten homes. Like needles in a haystack, they sit in the green valley surrounded by a great wall of limestone rock that towers 2,000m above. This is the heart of the Via Dinarica White Trail in Herzegovina. Hidden in the dense beech forests at **Tise** is the hunting lodge built for King Karađorđević during the time of the Kingdom of Serbs, Croats and Slovenes. The king trekked up the mountain by horse, and this was apparently his favourite hunting spot. Tito also came to Diva Grabovica when it was a hunting preserve teeming with mouflons, chamois, bear and wolves. The war took a heavy toll on the wildlife here, and it is no longer a legal hunting zone. The long silences in the valley are often broken by the squawks of eagles and falcons nesting in the cliffs.

About a 90-minute trek up towards Hajdučka Vrata is Žlijeb. The mountain hut here was damaged during the war, or more like looted, but it still provides primitive shelter if you'd like to camp out. At the end of the valley, after a solid two-hour hike, is the largest rock face on the Balkan peninsula. **Veliki Kuk** dominates the skyline with over 1,000m of pure rock. It is climbable but few have done it. A guide and good safety gear are recommended. There are shorter routes marked for novice or average climbers that are challenging and fun. The small shelter, called **Bivak**, was built by a climbing club in Sarajevo. It comfortably sleeps six. On the ridge below Veliki Kuk is a small picnic area with a magnificent view of neighbouring Prenj Mountain. In the village itself, divided by a small ridge, one can find organic honey produced by the local villagers. A one-litre jar costs 10KM. The footpaths that circle around the village are well maintained, both by goats and their keepers, and are ideal for an easy stroll or if you have small children. The valley of Diva Grabovica is safe from mines, as the closest mines to this area are a good 4- or 5-hour hike straight up the mountain. If you'd like to explore and embark on a long adventure it is advisable to find a guide. Green Visions (page 89) offer guided hikes to Diva Grabovica.

MEĐUGORJE

The story of Međugorje is well known to most Catholics. Ever since 1981, when six teenagers reported that they had seen an apparition of the Blessed Virgin Mary, Queen of Peace, in the hills between here and the village of Bijakovići, this sleepy Herzegovinian town has become the second-largest Catholic pilgrimage site in the world. There has been much controversy over the legitimacy of the visions, so much so that the Pope has not recognised it as an official pilgrimage site. Nonetheless millions of the faithful from all over the world visit this sacred spot, and according to many accounts, miracles are a regular occurrence. Međugorje is undoubtedly the tourism hotspot of Bosnia and Herzegovina. It has the best tourism infrastructure in the country with excellent restaurants, accommodation, travel agencies and information. It is linked to the Croatian coast by 10km of highway. Although day trips and other packages are offered for the area's guests, paying homage to the Virgin Mary is the main activity in Međugorje.

GETTING THERE If there is anywhere in Herzegovina that you can reach day or night it is most certainly Međugorje. There are half a dozen daily buses to Međugorje from Mostar starting at 06.30 and running until at least 19.00. Dubrovnik, Split, Makarska and Zagreb have regular buses to Međugorje, with Split and Dubrovnik being the most frequent routes. There is now a 10km section of highway linking Međugorje with the coastal highway in Croatia.

TOUR OPERATORS

Global Bijakovići bb, Međugorje bb; ☎ 036 651 489/501; e ok@global-medjugorje.com; w global-medjugorje.com. Organises trips to Međugorje, also comfortable transport from the airports in Split, Dubrovnik, Mostar & Sarajevo to Međugorje. In Međugorje, the agency offers accommodation in private pensions, situated near the St James Church. They will organise a number of meetings with visionaries & priests from the parish of Međugorje, as well as the visit to Apparition Hill & Krizevac Mountain (Cross Mountain).

Globtour Međugorje bb; 036 651 393/593/693; e globtour@globtour.com; w globtour.com; 08.00–16.00 Mon–Fri, 08.00–13.00 Sat. Organises bus trips to Međugorje, the Croatian coast, & many other destinations.

Goya Tours Bijakovići bb; 036 651 700/650 061; e oli@goyatours.com; w goyatours.com. 08.00–16.00 Mon–Fri, 08.00–13.00 Sat. This agency offers secure & comfortable transport from Dubrovnik, Split & Sarajevo airports to Mostar & Međugorje, accommodation in private pensions next to the famous church, excursions to some of the most famous areas of Herzegovina & to Adriatic coastal cities, experienced guide services, meetings with Madonna viewers, souvenirs, exchange office & car-rental services.

Grace Travel Bijakovići bb; 036 651 311; e office@grace-medjugorje.com; w grace-medjugorje.com; 08.00–16.00 Mon–Fri.

Paddy Travel Pape Ivana Pavla II 46; 036 650 482; e paddy@tel.net.ba; w paddy-travel.info; 08.00–16.00 Mon–Fri. An Irish-Herzegovinian venture that deals with accommodation & bus charters from Ireland & the UK.

WHERE TO STAY There are literally too many options to even attempt to put them all in this guide. Owing to high demand and mainly Western guests, the accommodation standard in Međugorje and Bijakovići is very high. Feel free to knock on any door advertising rooms; this method is cheaper than going through a travel agency. Most places will give discounts to groups, but it is always good to make contact ahead of time to be sure. I've listed just a few of the better places, although almost every house provides good-quality private accommodation. In Bijakovići, you can find accommodation in many of the traditional stone homes, which have a more authentic feel. There are three websites that offer the most comprehensive accommodation information: www.gomedjugorje.com, w tripadvisor.com and w pilgrimreservations.com (search 'Međugorje'). They offer detailed descriptions of accommodation from small apartment rentals to large hotels.

Hotels

Herceg Etno Selo (28 rooms, 3 apts) Tromeda bb; 036 653 400; e info@etno-herceg.com; w etno-herceg.com. If you're visiting Međugorje or the surrounding area this is the place you should treat yourself to. The ethno village is the best example of natural & environmentally friendly architecture. The oak furnishings & natural mattresses make for an exceptionally relaxing stay. The restaurant is first class & the service is a model for how things should be done in BiH. On the premises are several small boutiques selling organic honey & tea, artwork & ceramics. There is a playground for children & a small petting zoo. **$$–$$$**

Hotel Palace (19 rooms, 4 apts) Bijakovići bb; 036 651 061; w medjugorjepalace.com. Hotel Palace is in the immediate vicinity of the Church of the Queen of Peace. All sides of the hotel have wonderful views of the most famous sites of Međugorje: Apparition Hill, Krizevac Mountain & the St James Church, located 200m from the hotel. Offers rooms with shower, toilet, hairdryer, AC, phone, & apts for 3–4 people. **$$–$$$**

Hotel Pax (70 rooms) Bijakovići bb; 036 651 604; e info@paxcordis.com; w paxcordis.com. Quite a pleasant hotel located just 300m from the Church of St Jacob & 1km from Apparition Hill. All rooms have bathroom & central heating. The restaurant seats over 300. **$$**

Hotel Ruža (40 rooms) Bijakovići bb; 036 651 822/643 118; e hotel-ruza@tel.net.ba; w hotelmedjugorje.net/index.php/hr. Hotel Ruža has spacious rooms, each with AC, a bath & balcony. The restaurant & the snack bar have AC, with a capacity of 100 people. **$$**

Hotel Annamaria (52 rooms, 4 apts) Bijakovići bb; 036 651 512; e info@hotelanamaria.com; w hotelannamaria.com. The apts are all equipped with bathroom, minibar, phone & TV. Every room also has bathroom, phone & TV. The restaurant offers various Herzegovinian & international culinary specialities, as well as a large choice of quality wines & excellent service. **$–$$**

Hotel Internacional (30 rooms) Pape Ivana Pavla II 14; 036 651 440; e hotelinternational.medjugorje@gmail.com; w medjugorje-international.com. The hotel is located by St James Church & a winery associated with it is in Bijakovići near the vineyards. It is best to ask at the hotel for information about visiting the winery. **$–$$**

Hotel San (25 rooms, 2 apts) Službanj bb; 036 650 463; w hotel-san.com. Only 1km away from the centre of Međugorje, this hotel has a swimming pool, aperitif bar & restaurant. Languages: English & German. $–$$

Hotel Marben (25 rooms, 1 apt) Pape Ivana Pavla II bb; 036 650 910; e marben@tel.net.ba; www.tel.net.ba/marben. The bathrooms of 4 of the rooms are adapted for people with disabilities. All accommodation is AC. Conference room. Situated in the centre, 150m from the church. $

B&Bs/Pensions

Pansion Ante (10 rooms) Bijakovići bb; 036 651 489; e ok@global-medjugorje.com; w global-medjugorje.com. Ante is around 500m from the Church of St James. $

Pansion Begušić (15 rooms) Bijakovići bb; 036 651 620; e ok@global-medjugorje.com; w global-medjugorje.com. Around 500m from the Church of St James. $

Pansion Bevanda (28 rooms) Bijakovići bb; 036 651 442; e info@medjugorje-bevanda.com. Café-bar, rooms with AC; close to the church. $

Pansion Ero (30 rooms) Kardinala Stepinca 49; m 063 323 350; e zdenka.sivric@tel.net.ba; w medjugorje.ba. 200m from St Jacob's Church, with room for 65. There is also a restaurant & a coffee bar attached to it. $

Pansion Mir (20 rooms) Međugorje bb; 036 334 839; e filip.kozina@tel.net.ba. $

Pansion Toni (20 rooms) Put za Križevac bb; 036 651 238; e tonisego@tel.net.ba. Near the main route to Cross Mountain. $

Pansion Zemo (26 rooms) Sibrići bb; 036 651 878; m 063 651 878; e jakov-sivric@tel.net.ba; www.tel.net.ba/medjugorje-pansion.kamp. Just 300m from the centre of Međugorje & the Church of St James. $

WHERE TO EAT AND DRINK There are plenty of good restaurants in Međugorje and Bijakovići. Most hotels, as above, have restaurants with good menus in at least three languages (and always English).

Garden Club and Restaurant Bijakovići bb; 036 650 49; e info@clubgardens.com; w clubgardens.com; 08.00–midnight daily. This is a good spot to keep on the radar. After praying & feeling the spirit, visit this oasis with modern décor & a wonderful terrace. The menu is varied & you'll find everything from seafood & grilled meats to pizzas. As the name implies, there is a club here as well. This is a nice place to tilt one back after elbowing past pilgrims all day. $$$

Herceg Etno Selo Tromeđa bb; 036 653 400; w etno-herceg.com; 07.00–23.00 daily. Hands down one of the best traditional restaurants in the country. They have an impressive international menu & are in a very rustic setting. $$$

Restaurant Ethno House Šurmanci bb; 036 650 312; m 063 753 000; e etno_kuca@yahoo.com; f etno.kuca.14; 08.00–23.00 Mon–Sat, noon–23.00 Sun. This is a great place to enjoy tasty Dalmatian-Mediterranean food & a pleasant atmosphere. Fresh fish is brought in from the Croatian coast daily & the meats are free range from the hills of Herzegovina. It is located on the way to the famous apparition hill in Međugorje, towards the village of Šurmanci. The authentic Herzegovina interior, using lots of stone, keeps things cool during hot summers. A cosy, stone fireplace contributes to the warmth of the place in the cooler months. A good selection of local wines & liqueurs, & sometimes live music, add to the good time. $$–$$$

Restoran La Casa Krstine 65; 036 650 390; e la.casa@sport-centar.info; 07.00–midnight daily. If you're looking for a modern, sleek & warm atmosphere with good, beautifully presented food & a wide selection of drinks, La Casa is it. Part of a hotel, La Casa serves meals all day, & is a noted destination for both locals & tourists. $$–$$$

Colombo Međugorje bb; 036 651 601; e colombo.medjugorje@yahoo.com; 08.00–23.30 daily. This local favourite restaurant is just to the right of the main church downtown, & is owned by a very nice gentleman from Mostar named Krešo. Colombo have gone out of their way to give you the best of both worlds – they serve many dishes that are close to home for Western guests, & also offer a good selection of traditional dishes for those looking for a more local flavour. $$

Viktor's Pape Ivana Plavla II bb; 036 650 958; e viktorsmedjugorje@yahoo.com; 08.00–23.00

Mon–Sat; noon–23.00 Sun. A must-visit for some good eating. They speak excellent English, the menu is in 9 languages, & you will always get fast & friendly service. Their local wine list is also quite good. $$

Irish Centre Dr Franje Tudjmana 29; 036 651 518; 07.00–23.00 daily. This restaurant caters to the large numbers of Irish tourists visiting Međugorje each year. If you need a delicious scone or an Irish-style meal, this is one of the only places in BiH where you can find them. They offer breakfast, lunch, dinner, & a pub. $$

SHOPPING Međugorje has no big, shiny, modern shopping centres. For one of those, visit nearby Mostar. However, being one of the main tourist destinations in BiH, this town is a place you can browse to your heart's content for both well-made traditional crafts and cheap, imported kitsch souvenirs. The majority of tourist shops here cater to the religiously minded, which is no wonder given the fact that most travellers visit Međugorje as part of a pilgrimage. Holy water, statues of the Blessed Virgin Mary, rosaries, and other items are in great abundance everywhere you turn. You can find something unique or spiritually-themed to buy on nearly every street

THE TWO QUEENS OF HERZEGOVINA

Josipa Andrijanić

Famed author Ivo Andrić once said 'Žilavka is full of laughter while Blatina is full of sweet transgression'. Wine, like art, is open to interpretation, so there's no guarantee that every person will react this way. What is certain, however, is that the former is white and the latter is a red grape variety. There is no doubt that each is utterly different to the eye and palate, yet they are inseparable and permanently connected by history and climate.

As the viticulture trend continues to grow internationally – with indigenous grapes taking centre stage – it also seems a sure bet that Herzegovina's wine will soon be in the spotlight. The reasons are obvious to those who watch burgeoning wine regions with an eye for marketing and a corkscrew at the ready. Herzegovina has a Mediterranean climate which provides loads of sun, hot summers and mild winters. The vines have a close proximity to the sea, and they grow in diverse topsoil. The overall combination creates a perfect environment for growing grapes and producing high quality wines.

ŽILAVKA Legend has it that Žilavka – a dry wine with 12–14% alcohol content – was named after the fine veins (*žilice*) visible through the transparent grape skin at the time of maturity. Some say the name comes from its tough, sinewy skin or *žilava*. Elders have rolled the theories into one, claiming this variety is all of these things. The amalgamation creates a full-bodied taste and a seductive aroma. The reasons for Žilavka's success, though, aren't due to its moniker. They are due to this sturdy grape's resistance to disease and drought. It also thrives in the harsh sun, making it the most commonly planted variety here. Simply put, Žilavka found an ideal substratum in Herzegovina's karst. (Traditionally, its wine production has always included a small percentage – about 15% – of Beno, Krkošija, and a few other indigenous varieties.)

Interestingly, although wine-producing varieties aren't usually sought-after table grapes, the mature, golden-yellow Žilavka is extraordinarily tasty. The reason is its harmonious ratio of sugar content and acid.

As every wine reflects its creator, every cellar offers its own type of Žilavka. The common denominator among the grapes is the crystal clear, greenish yellow – and at times golden – colour. The grape's specific aroma, well-balanced acidity and alcohol content have made it the most favourable of all sorts in Herzegovina.

and nook in Međugorje. For a grocery store, visit **Konzum** (*Lišnjačine; 07.00–21.00 daily*). Many establishments in Međugorje will not take cards, so bring cash.

PRACTICALITIES

Health Clinic

Malteška pomoć Gospin trg 4; 036 650 201; 09.00–14.30 & 15.30–21.00 daily. This emergency health clinic is run by the German division of the Order of Malta. It is staffed by both local & German personnel.

Pharmacy

Ljekarna Zvjezdana Pehar Međugorje bb – centar; 036 651 841. Međugorje does not have one designated 24-hour pharmacy. This one has the longest consistent working hours.

Police

Police station Međugorje bb; 036 651 652

Post office

Hrvatska Pošta Međugorje bb; 07.00–16.00 Mon–Fri; 07.00–noon Sat

Bank

$ Sparkasse Bank Tromeđa bb. ATM.

BLATINA Grown under favourable conditions, the Blatina grape produces high yields. If stressed by rains during the fertilisation period, flowers may abscise from the crop – that's why Blatina is sarcastically called *praznobačva* (empty barrel) and *zlorod* (evil crop). It requires a large amount of sun, as does Žilavka; but, unlike Žilavka, Blatina demands a considerable amount of water. Therefore, it prefers moist soils and gives its best results in valleys of the Neretva, Trebižat, and Trebišnjica rivers. Blatina – a dry and robust red wine with 12–13.5% alcohol content – is a grape that bears large, uneven, dark purple berries on sizeable, loose clusters. It is considered to be a quality varietal which, from well-chosen localities and given expert vinification, produces wines of high quality. It has an easily recognisable aroma, full and harmonious in flavour. When grown in a climate blessed by the sun, the wine has a satisfactory acid concentration.

Although technologies have changed, mostly wooden oak barrels are used with Blatina. Producers here have traditionally used Slavonian, American, and French barrels but a recent trend toward using handmade casks from the small village of Prusac in central Bosnia has made the wine even more BiH-sufficient.

INSIDER TIPS Many still remember, with nostalgia, how popular Žilavka was in 1970s and 1980s. This persistent queen is making a major comeback and new technologies have enabled a great number of interesting and superior versions. Žilavka Vukoje – the Trebinje wine cellar produces it from grapes grown in the former Imperial vineyards – has a complex aroma, a particular crispness, and is reminiscent of the past. Čitluk's Kameno Vino has become synonymous with quality. The Andrija family wine cellars, and their Žilavka Barrique, were the first to show how well Žilavka matures in wooden barrels. Josip Brkić's Greda and Mjesečar, aged *sur lie*, highlight the variety's incredible potential.

There are many versions of Blatina on the market. The one from the Prskalo family cellar is fresh, fragrant and vigorous. Josip Brkić's Plava Greda is a multi-layered Blatina with enhanced complexity. Blatina barrique from Andrija is both strong and tender. The Blatina barrique from the Nuić cellars epitomises the grape's full potential. An explosion of aroma and taste make this wine unique and special. Gentille wines from Grude are perhaps the best of them all.

WHAT TO SEE AND DO As mentioned above, in 1981 six teenagers were playing together in the hills between **Međugorje** and **Bijakovići**. It was on this barren hillside that the Virgin Mary allegedly appeared and spoke to them. When the children told their parents, their first reaction was, of course, scepticism. The apparitions, however, did not cease. She appeared again and again, and soon made believers even out of the most vocal of critics. Since then it is estimated that more than 15 million people have visited this tiny place. The Virgin Mary is still said to appear every day but only to one of the teenagers. A blue cross marks the bare mountain, now called **Apparition Hill**, where the children first saw her. A well-worn footpath on **Cross Mountain**, lined with Stations of the Cross, has been trekked by visitors from every corner of the globe. Many make the trek barefoot. The large cross planted on top of the hill is said to have been built to celebrate the 1,900th anniversary of the death of Christ, but it is more likely that it was built in 1934 to keep away the plague that had devastated several areas in the region.

The village of Međugorje has become quite commercialised. The capacity to receive tens of thousands of guests at any given moment has turned the once dead main street into a souvenir-shop bazaar. Every few metres there are shops selling crosses, rosaries, statues, pictures, posters, jewellery – you name it, it's there. It is easy to find internet connections, good information, guides in most European languages, and probably the best general service in the country. With that much practice, they've got it down pat. The main church, **St James's**, is in the middle of town. Whether or not there is a Mass on, the square around the church is bound to have people sitting, praying and contemplating. There will be something going on every Catholic holiday and saint's day. Just up the road is the even smaller village of **Bijakovići**. Despite the massive influx of tourists and pilgrims, it has managed to retain much of its original old Herzegovina style.

The tradition of **winemaking** here goes back much further than the apparition. Brkic wine from Čitluk has won numerous international awards. Tours of the cellars are possible. Red or white, you can't go wrong with Brkic. Čitluk is known for its good-quality Žilavka and Blatina grapes. The road leading to Čitluk is lined on both sides with rolling hills of vineyards. Aside from its winemaking tradition, Čitluk has also been an ideal place for growing **tobacco**. If you have a car, take any of the small side roads through the countryside; seeing the tobacco drying in front of old-style traditional homes, and the local villagers working the vineyards, is a glance of how things have been for centuries.

Although the main focus of tourism is in Međugorje itself, Čitluk is an excellent place for a visit to one of the many wine cellars.

Brkić Kralja Tvrtka 9, Čitluk; ☎ 036 644 466; **e** info@ brkic.ba; **w** brkic.ba. In 1979 the Brkić family founded a modern cellar, the first private one in BiH. The business idea of the Brkić cellar is to produce wine in the most natural way possible. In accordance with this, new production technologies have been applied (the *sur lie* & Australian red methods), aiming to gain the best possible drop with the least possible treatment on the grapes, must & wine. See also above.

Žarko Stojić-Matić Donji Hamziči, Ćitluk; ☎ 036 652 023. Stojić has been growing grapes & turning them into wine for decades, as well as producing natural brandies & liqueurs. In the beginning, the grape production was small-scale, on small plots of land, & wine was made & kept in small taverns. Several years ago, he was among the first in Herzegovina to plant a vineyard with Cabernet Sauvignon & Chardonnay varieties, out of which he creates wines of great quality.

Martin Buntić Miletina, Međugorje; 036 651 138; e vinarija-buntic@gmail.com; w vinarija-buntic.com. This family-run winery has been producing wine for hundreds of years, but quanities have increased dramatically in the last hundred years. They produce the high-quality Žilavka & Blatina, other products like Loza (grapevine brandy), rosé & Blatina barrique. See also, page 199.

LJUBUŠKI

Ljubuški is another ancient settlement in the vast rocky hills of western Herzegovina. The ruling family of the medieval Bosnian state expanded their reign to this region. The remains of the **old fort** jut out of the hill overlooking the **Trebižat river valley**. Both the Illyrians and the Romans settled the lands along the Trebižat before the Slavs settled in this part of the world. It is a small town of less than 30,000 people and can be easily seen in a couple hours on foot. The oldest museum in Bosnia and Herzegovina, existing since 1884, is at the **Humac Franciscan Monastery** (built in 1869), just outside the town. The quaint **Humac Museum** hosts one of the finest collections of ancient relics, all found in the vicinity of the monastery. The oldest script ever found in the territory of BiH was the Humska Ploća; this stone-carved slate, written in Glagolitic, is said to date back to the 10th century. The museum has a significant collection of relics from the Roman settlements including jewellery, weapons, helmets and hand-carved tombstones, many of the excavated items coming from the ruins of a Roman military camp, **Bigeste**, near the monastery.

The highlight of this region is the crystal-clear water of the Trebižat River and southeast of Ljubuški are the **Kravica Waterfalls**. Stretching over 100m across and tumbling down 25m, Kravica is one of the largest waterfalls in Herzegovina, and the most impressive. They have a natural pool dug out at the base of the falls by the constant rush of water. It is a favourite local swimming spot with picnic area, restaurants, cafés and even a place to pitch a tent. Bring a camera when you visit; seeing something as stunning as that is not an everyday occasion. During the summer months, it can be quite crowded and noisy – it's a place where many people gather to beat the heat, and the restaurants are in close proximity to the waterfall and swimming areas.

The village of **Vitina** is a bit off the beaten path to the north of Ljubuški. The source of the **River Vrioštice** has a great traditional restaurant called **Vrilo Vrioštice** (*039 840 088*) and is a good way to beat the summer heat. **Kočuša Waterfall** is a mini version of Kravica in Veljači just a few minutes outside Vitina. It's a bit tricky to find but well worth it if you're into waterfalls. Heading out from Ljubuški towards Grude, make a left just after Vitina towards Vrgorac and Makarska. Take the first fork to the right to Dole and continue on until you reach a football pitch. Turn right at the football pitch and the waterfall will be to the left. Just before the falls is **Konoba Kocusa** (**$$**). This is a 120-year-old working watermill that doubles as a restaurant/bar. It's a great place for a few drinks overlooking the cool Trebižat.

Ljubuški and the surrounding area are also famous for winemaking, the best being Nuić and Gangaš. Motel Most (page 212) is a favourite spot along the river for an excellent meal.

GETTING THERE AND AWAY

By bus Ljubuški is well connected to both Sarajevo and Croatia. A daily bus from Sarajevo to Split stops in Ljubuški. Buses from Zagreb to Čapljina, Dubrovnik to

Vinkovci, and Sarajevo to Grude, all stop at Ljubuški bus station (*Zvonimirova 1; 039 831 120*).

By car Ljubuški is 35km from Mostar, going via Čitluk. From Sarajevo, it will take a little over 2½ hours to drive 169km on the M-17 highway. From Dubrovnik, it's 131km driving on the main coastal road.

WHERE TO STAY AND EAT

Hotel Hum (8 rooms) Nikole Kordića bb; 039 839 400; **e** info@hotelhum.com; **w** hotelhum.com. A more business-type hotel in the middle of town. The rooms are modern with AC, sat TV & minibar. **$$–$$$**

Motel Most (12 rooms) Teskera 1; 039 838 288; **e** info@motel-most.com; **w** motel-most.com. Most has been a family-run motel for more than 60 years. The modest rooms have AC, minibar, TV & are all en suite. They have tennis courts & a playground. You can rent mountain bikes or canoes on the premises. The food & service are both excellent. **$–$$**

ŠIROKI BRIJEG

The **Franciscan monastery** on top of the hill here is open to guests and often receives visitors from Međugorje. The natural surroundings and rich water sources once again defy logic and paint this arid valley green. **Mostarsko Blato** is the large flood basin to the east of Široki Brijeg. In the rainy season this lush valley floods as the **Listica River** breaks its banks. The little villages dotting the valley are still preserved in the old style and the traditional **old mills** used over the centuries to grind wheat into flour can still be seen at the source of the Listica River. The old Franciscan church at **Čerigaj** is one of the few remaining Catholic structures in this part of Herzegovina. The best way of finding an interesting spot in or around Široki Brijeg is to follow the water to its source; life and leisure in these parts are completely dependent on it.

GETTING THERE AND AWAY Široki Brijeg is very well connected to both Mostar and Međugorje. Regular buses depart daily from both locations.

WHERE TO STAY AND EAT

Hotel Park Trg Ante Starčevića 4; 039 700 500; **e** info@ hotelpark.ba; **w** hotelpark.ba. Right in the centre of town, Hotel Park is a lovely hotel, with a very good restaurant (see below) & café. All rooms are en suite & have AC, minibar, internet, sat TV & offer room service. **$$$**

Restoran Domano in Hotel Park, Trg Ante Starčevića 4; 039 700 500; **e** info@restoran-domano.com; **w** restoran-domano.com; 07.00–midnight daily. This higher end restaurant stands out as one of the better places to eat in Herzegovina. They serve traditional, international & Mediterranean cuisine. Fish & seafood is supplied every day from the Adriatic coast while the meat is carefully selected & local. The wine list hosts the best of the region as well as fine Croatian wines. **$$–$$$**

Restoran Borak Vrelo Put za Borak bb; 039 705 701; **w** borak.ba; 08.00–midnight daily. This is a great spot for a cool lunch. They have a classic Mediterranean menu, specialising in grilled meats of all kinds. **$$**

GRUDE

Grude is yet another oasis in the harsh landscape of western Herzegovina. The town is small and not as touristic as much of the rest of Herzegovina, but if you're exploring the area or driving through, it is a good place to rest and take a stroll. The Trebižat River has given life to this town in similar ways to Ljubuški.

In the green valley along the Trebižat, tobacco and grapes are grown in large quantities. And Grude is no exception to Herzegovina's winemaking traditions, either. **Ravlića Caves** near the springs of the Trebižat have yielded evidence that human life has existed here since Neolithic times. The old mills and waterfalls at **Peć Mlini** offer just another way to get a feel for how it used to be. Krenica Lake north of Grude can be found on most maps and is a pleasant place to get away to, for a picnic or a swim.

As border crossings in this area are generally simple, it is worth a crossing to **Imotski** in Croatia for a quick excursion to **Modro** and **Crveno lakes**. Crveno Lake is no less than a natural phenomenon – it sits in a 296m-deep natural crater. Karst sinkholes in this region are not uncommon but this is truly a sight to see.

GETTING THERE AND AWAY

By bus There is a direct, daily line from Sarajevo to Grude. Buses on the Sarajevo–Split, Dubrovnik–Vinkovci and Zagreb–Neum routes all stop at Grude bus station (*Hrvatskih branitelja bb; 039 661 264*).

By car Grude is 50km from Mostar going via Široki Brijeg. From Sarajevo, it's 163km on the M-17/E73 route. It is 19km from the Croatian border town of Imotski and 104km from Split.

WHERE TO STAY AND EAT

Marica Gaj (10 rooms) Ružići bb; **m** 063 437 099; **e** info@agroturizam-hercegovina.com; **w** agroturizam-hercegovina.com. Just a few hundred metres from Motel Kiwi, this restored stone home offers quality village accommodation. The rooms are rustic but sensibly comfortable. This family-owned & operated establishment has a wine cellar, traditional restaurant, which serves good meals, & conference room, & offers walking, horse riding & mountain biking around the arid hills of western Herzegovina. **$$**

Motel Kiwi (27 rooms) Ružići 289; 039 674 079; **e** info@motelkiwi.com; **w** motelkiwi.com. The motel is 3.5km outside of town, on the main road to Međugorje (35km), 25km from Ljubuški and 52km from Mostar. There is also an on-site restaurant. Kiwi has its own shuttle service for nearby destinations, upon request. **$–$$**

ČAPLJINA

Čapljina is centrally located, with Mostar to the north and the Adriatic Sea to the south. It can be comfortably covered on foot in an hour or two, depending on how many stops you want to make. Međugorje and Ljubuški are less than 20km to the west, and Stolac is less than half an hour's drive to the east. This town on the west bank of the Neretva River may now have only about 28,000 inhabitants, but it was once the home to what is thought to have been the largest Roman military camp in the valley: **Mogorjelo** was built at the end of the 3rd century and two basilicas were added sometime in the 5th century. It makes for an interesting excursion while on your way to a **canoe safari** (**m** *063 323 515*) on the Trebižat River. The launching spot for the canoes is a bit hard to find but the **Villa Rustica** next to (or actually a part of) Mogorjelo can provide contact information on how to get there. The canoe safari is a 5-hour journey down the Trebižat River southeast of Kravica Waterfalls. The canoeing aspect is not difficult and is even suitable for children. Expect your arms to be a bit sore afterwards, but the river is calm with only a few small (and fun) cascades to conquer. The water is cold and refreshing if you do happen to fall in. Midway through the journey, you'll stop for a barbecue lunch prepared by your guide's team. The food is great and they cater for vegetarians.

The ancient Turkish town of **Počitelj** is only 5km upriver on the Neretva. You won't find another place like it in the country; it's more than worth the visit (page 203). Towards the border with Croatia is the ancient settlement of **Gabela**. It is mentioned for the first time in the second half of the 15th century and is believed by many to have been a significant settlement long before that.

GETTING THERE AND AWAY Čapljina is located on the west side of the Neretva River, only 12km from the Croatian border crossing at Doljani on the main M-17 road. It is also a stop on the rail route from Sarajevo to Ploče (Croatian coast). Čapljina can be reached from both Mostar and Sarajevo via daily buses, with several from both east and west Mostar running to Čapljina. Čapljina is approximately 30km from Mostar and 170km from Sarajevo.

By train The train from Ploče, Croatia, to Sarajevo stops in Čapljina. The train station (*Trg bana Josipa Jelačića bb; ☎ 036 808 798*) is in a fairly central location, making arrival in Čapljina slightly easier than in other small towns on the route.

By bus Given that Čapljina is on the M-17, it is a more frequently visited station compared to others in the wider region. Čapljina station (*Hrvatskih branitelja bb; ☎ 036 806 676*) is well connected to Mostar and Ploče, as well as with all other towns in western Herzegovina. There are also daily buses to Čapljina from Sarajevo.

By car Čapljina is conveniently located 30km from the Adriatic coast and about that same distance from Mostar. Situated on the west bank of the Neretva River, just off the M-17 road from Metković to Sarajevo, the town is easily accessible and perfect for a day trip by car.

WHERE TO STAY

Hotel Mogorjelo Kraljice Katarine bb; ☎ 036 810 815; e mogorjelo@makarthoteli.com; w hotelmogorjelo.com. Čapljina received its first high-end hotel in the last decade with the addition of Hotel Mogorjelo on the Neretva River, just off the Franjo Tuđman bridge. With 40 rooms & a handful of 5-star apts, it offers the best accommodation in the wider region. **$$$**

WHAT TO SEE AND DO

Hutovo Blato Bird Reserve (*Karaotok bb, Višići, 5km from Čapljina, clearly marked on the M-17; ☎ 036 814 716; e info@hutovo-blato.ba; w hutovo-blato.ba; ⌚ 07.00–15.00 Mon–Fri; entrance fee adults 2KM, children & students 1KM, visitors with disabilities free*) This excellent bird reserve is the largest of its kind in southeast Europe. One of the many natural phenomena found in the Herzegovina landscape, Hutovo Blato is home to more than 240 types of migratory birds, and dozens of other species make their permanent home in this sub-Mediterranean wetland surrounding **Deransko Lake**. It is estimated that over 10,000 birds flock to the lake at any one time. This marshland is created by the underground aquifer system of the **Krupa River**. It is fed from the limestone massif of **Ostrvo** that divides the **Deransko** and **Svitavsko lakes**. The park offers *barco* (boat) rides with a professional biologist guide. It also has a restaurant/café and a renovated motel. The wildlife area provides a unique oasis amongst the harsh, arid karst of western Herzegovina. Teeming with freshwater fish (trout, carp, sunfish, grey mullet, eel), wild ducks, geese, coots, hawks, herons, pheasants and wild boars, it accommodates birdwatchers, nature lovers and families with children. The International Council for Bird Protection has placed Hutovo Blato on the list of important bird habitats. January and February are the best months for bird lovers to witness the largest gathering of our feathered friends in southern Europe, as these are the main months for bird migration towards northern Africa. The cost of the photo safari is 100KM – they only rent the whole boat at one fixed rate, so if there are other guests, the costs will be split. The *barcos* hold a maximum of 15 people.

Getting there and away Hutovo Blato is located on the east side of the Neretva River in the municipality of Čapljina, just off the M-17. There are several road signs indicating the turn-off, which is less than 1km from the traffic-light road junction to Čapljina and Stolac coming from the east. There are no buses running to Hutovo Blato, but a 5km taxi ride from Čapljina will cost 6–10KM.

Where to stay and eat

Hotel Park Karaotok bb, Višići; 036 814 990; e park@makarthoteli.com; w hotelmogorjelo.com/hr/o_hotelu/karaotok. This hotel offers accommodation in the park as well as a café, picnic area & restaurant with local specialities. The hotel has recently had a face-lift with complete renovation of the entire premises. It's an ideal place for a quiet overnight stay, or for birdwatchers to spend a bit more time recording their sightings. **$$**

NEUM

Bosnia and Herzegovina is proud to have its own little slice of the Adriatic, even if it is only a 24km strip. The **Adriatic Sea** from Split to Dubrovnik is crystal clear and simply gorgeous, Neum included. The closed bay here, shielded by **Pelješac Peninsula**, is protected from many of the strong winds of the open sea. Most of the town was built during Yugoslav times as an isolated retreat for the communist elite. Although Neum can't compete with the likes of Dubrovnik, Ston and Makarska and is rather limited, it does offer good value for a seaside holiday. Some of the infrastructure is still run-down and even incomplete but year by year the tourist offer at Neum improves. During the summer months, it is quite crowded. This is not the place to go looking for a peaceful cove or empty beach.

Its face has drastically changed since communist days, with the construction of Dalmatian stone homes and more modern architecture. The large hotels from the socialist era appear awkward in the serene setting of the Adriatic, and the newer concrete buildings lack an aesthetic touch. Tourists have been coming in larger numbers each year though. One will find room and board in Neum for up to 20% less than in its Croatian coastal counterparts, which is one of the reasons why many Bosnian families vacation here.

GETTING THERE AND AROUND It may seem confusing when you look at the map of Neum, and note its position relative to Croatia: the only land connection Neum has to Bosnia and Herzegovina is through the hinterland towards Hutovo where a narrow two-lane road winds through the hills. To go to Neum via the main coastal road you must first enter Croatia (at the **Metković** border crossing if coming from Mostar), then re-enter BiH after the tourist settlement of **Klek**. Neum is 8km from the border crossing. Some 22km later and you'll be crossing back into Croatia heading towards Dubrovnik. It may sound baffling, or at the very least impractical, but the border control will usually wave you through, especially during the high season.

WHERE TO STAY The large hotels are like cities within themselves, offering almost everything you might need within each hotel compound. The pensions and bed and breakfasts around town are of equal quality and certainly provide more privacy.

Hotels

Grand Hotel Neum (380 rooms) Zagrebačka 2; 036 880 222; e prodaja@hotel-neum.com; w hotel-neum.com. Previously operating as the Hotel Neum, the Grand Hotel Neum is the largest hotel in the Neum Riviera. It has been recently renovated to rid itself of the look & feel of socialist design, & is now one of the better hotels on BiH's only stretch of coast. Aside from direct access to the beach via elevators, they have a modern wellness & spa centre, & swimming pools (both indoor & out). They organise a vast array of excursions, inc Dubrovnik, Korčula, Mljet, Hutovo Blato, Vjetrenica, Sarajevo, Kotor, Mostar & Međugorje. The rooms are perfectly fine, all with the standard AC, satellite TV, & mini-bar. But most importantly, all rooms have a sea view. **$$–$$$**

Hotel Jadran (28 rooms) Magistrala bb; 036 885 900; e info@hotel-jadran-neum.com; w hotel-jadran-neum.com. Located just next to the main road, this small hotel avoids the summer crowds found on the beach. They have comfortable & spacious rooms with good views of the sea, a seafood restaurant, small market, indoor pool, & a fitness & sauna centre. As it is quite a hike back up to the hotel from the beach, they organise transport to & from the beaches. **$$–$$$**

Hotel Luna (18 rooms, 6 apts) Zagrebačka 49a; 036 885 030; e info@hotel-luna.ba; w hotel-luna.ba. Several minutes on foot from the beach, with bar & restaurant in hotel. **$$–$$$**

Hotel Stella (85 rooms) Ruđera Boškovića bb; 036 880 050; e info@stella-neum.com; w stella-neum.com. Stella has a great panoramic view of the bay, easy access to the beach & a beautiful terrace restaurant. The rooms are pleasant & have AC, phone & sat TV. The restaurant, as is the norm in Neum, serves Dalmatian & local specialities, & has a great local wine list. **$$**

Hotel Sunce (193 rooms, 9 apts) Kralja Tomislava bb; 036 880 033–5; e info@hotel-sunce.com; w hotel-sunce.com. Right on the beach in the centre of Neum with a capacity of 400, it offers sgl & dbl rooms as well as apts. There is a dentist, hairdresser, boutique, billiards & aperitif bar on the premises. In addition, there is a restaurant, tavern, beer & wine cellar, pastry shop & pizzeria. **$$**

Hotel Zenit (169 rooms, 5 apts) Rudera Boškovića 3; 036 880 144; w hotel-zenit.com. The most spacious hotel with a 340-bed capacity & a large beach on the premises. The rooms are simple but suffice if you plan on being at the beach all day. There is an indoor swimming pool, sauna, playground, tennis courts & a small bowling alley. Excursions by boat or coach can be organised to other seaside towns & to the hinterland. **$$**

Villa Matić Zagrebačka bb; 036 880 153; e kotakt@hotelvillamatic.com; w hotelvillamatic.com. **$$**

Hotel Posejdon (15 rooms, 10 apts) Primorska 61 b; 036 885 112; e posejdon@tel.net.ba; w posejdon-neum.com. **$**

Private rooms

Vila Nova Prmorska 7; 036 885 220; e nova@villa-nova.info; w villa-nova.info. This is one of the finest small pensions directly on the beach. The rooms all have AC & there is a restaurant here. **$$**

Motel More Jadranska turistička magistrala bb; 036 880 677. Featuring an open-air terrace & a number of rooms with sea views. **$–$$**

Aparthotel Adria Zagrebačka 2a; 036 880 401; e hotel.adria@tel.net.ba; w hotel-adria.biz. The rooms are clean & comfortable, but basic. Some overlook the water. **$**

Vila Barbara Prmorska 7a; 036 880 026; e info@villa-barbara.ba; w villa-barbara.ba. Next door to the Nova & offering similar accommodation. **$**

WHERE TO EAT AND DRINK All of the hotels have restaurants, and most of the package deals include full board. If you want to get out and go for a meal in a more intimate and authentic setting, there are many excellent restaurants with Dalmatian and Herzegovinian specialities on the menu. Or if you just want a pizza and to look at a football match on the television, Neum has several local 'dives' too.

Porat Prmorska 140a; **m** 063 868 034; **e** info@hotel-porat.ba; **w** hotel-porat.ba/index.php/ponuda/restoran; 06.00–23.00 daily. The Porat restaurant is located in the hotel right on the water front. They serve great seafood, with oysters being a specialty, & have a good regional wine selection. All of the fish is locally caught, & in comparison to Croatia, the price is right for fresh seafood. $$

Restoran Bonaca Kralja Tomislava bb; 036 880 182; 08.00–23.00 daily. A classy restaurant with good seafood dishes & Dalmatian wine. $–$$

Restoran Laguna Kralja Tomislava 26; 036 880 812; lagunaneum; 08.00–midnight daily. An inexpensive place for a good pizza & a chilled atmosphere. $–$$

SHOPPING As a seaside tourist destination, there are souvenir shops all along the waterfront, many of which stock water shoes, inexpensive snorkelling gear, inflatable rafts, swimsuits, towels, and other things one might need for seaside fun. Otherwise, there is not much shopping to be done in Neum. For a grocery store, visit **Bingo,** located on road M-17, number 3 (*07.00–22.00 Mon–Sat; 07.00–18.00 Sun*), or **Konzum** on the main road M2/E65 (07.00–20.00 Mon–Sat).

PRACTICALITIES

Police

Police station Kralja Tomislava 54; 036 880 192

Bank

$ **Intesa Sanpaolo Bank** Zagrebačka 2; 033 497 657; ATM 24 hours

Health clinic

Dom Zdravlja Neum Zagrebačka bb; 036 880 094

Post office

Hrvatskih velikana 2; 07.00–21.00 Mon–Sat

Pharmacy

Ljekarna Neum Zagrebačka; 036 880 193

WHAT TO SEE AND DO Neum is a holiday resort town. There is not much on the cultural 'to do' list, but there is plenty of fun and sun to be had. Besides swimming and sunbathing, there are boats for rent at several places on the beach, and from Neum, you can jump on the excursion boats that travel up and down the Adriatic coastline. **Watersports** are generally cheaper here than in Croatia. Scuba-diving gear, parasailing equipment, boats and jet skis can be rented on the beach, and the bay is perfect for a fun day on the water. Four of the major hotels can arrange watersport rentals from the beachside outlets. **Dubrovnik** is only an hour's drive from Neum, and the peninsula of Pelješac is a stone's throw away. From **Orebić** on Pelješac you can catch a ferry to the beautiful island of Korčula. In the hinterland behind Neum is the village of **Hutovo** and the ancient ruins of **Hadžibegova Kula Fortress**, used by the Turks to defend their western front. The holy site of **Svetište Kraljica mira** is a shrine to the Queen of Peace in **Hrasno**. It has mostly local significance but those who have come on a pilgrimage often pay a visit to this tiny hinterland shrine. Hutovo Blato, Ljubuški and Međugorje are all within an hour's drive of Neum for day trips. Mostar is just a bit further away.

STOLAC

Stolac has long been the place for tracing Herzegovina's ancient history. This quaint, sunny southern town of striking Ottoman architecture is a true playground for those intrigued by anthropology, archaeology and history. The area has been settled for at least 15,000 years, as evinced by the markings in **Badanj Cave**, which experts have dated to 16 000–12 000BC. The town itself saw significant damage from the war. After a short siege by the Bosnian Serb army in 1992 and continued shelling into 1993, the Croat–Bosniak alliance fell apart and the Croatian Defence Council (HVO) expelled and/or imprisoned most of the Muslim inhabitants. Shortly afterwards they levelled most of the town's Ottoman heritage, and many Muslim homes.

Stolac has made a comeback, however, and much of its oriental flavour has been restored. The town has a sleepy, Mediterranean air to it and is lined with cafés along the crystal-clear **Bregava River**. The Bregava is a favourite spot for youths to swim and dive, and you will often find most of the town near the water during the hot and dry summers. The central area enjoys lush trees and foliage, with unique pines darting into the skyline near the ancient old town fortress of **Vidoška** (built in the 14th century). The Bregava has made Stolac and the surrounding region (called **Dubrava**) one of the most fertile areas in the country. Vegetables and fruit from here seem to taste just that bit better.

In the nearby village of **Domanovići**, red and white Doman wines and a sparkling wine are produced from the harvests of the local vineyards. Doman is a great inexpensive wine; it can be found in the shops for 5–6KM a bottle. Most people in the area make their living from agriculture as the industries that once thrived in Stolac have been out of operation since the early 1990s. Maybe the most remarkable aspect of this tiny town is its cultural heritage. At the northern entrance is the country's oldest necropolis, **Radimlja**. There are 122 medieval tombstones marked with unique carvings made by 13th–15th-century Slavic members of the Bosnian Church. The famous poet Mak Dizdar wonderfully captures the imagination through his portrayal of the medieval Bosnian Church and the so-called Bogomils in his poetry and prose. No other town in Bosnia and Herzegovina has produced such a rich array of intellectuals, artists, poets and leaders. Strolling through town to the sound of the rushing Bregava and the many songbirds, it is easy to imagine the inspiration felt by Stolac's many generations of extraordinary personalities.

Not far from Stolac is the oldest remaining human settlement in Bosnia and Herzegovina. The Daorsi tribe is said to have lived in these parts over 4,000 years ago. Remnants of Hellenistic art and design have suggested that at least some elements of the Hellenistic civilisation reached this far north. Near the small village of **Ošanići** is the 'Herzegovina Stonehenge'. Massive cyclopean walls are hidden in the thorny brush above Stolac and the Bregava. It may be difficult to find, but it's worth a visit to admire the ingenuity that creating a structure of this magnitude in the 4th century BC must have required! The **Church of Sts Peter and Paul**, from the year 1500, remains intact despite most sacred buildings in and around Stolac being destroyed. Although much of the oriental architecture and Islamic structures were also destroyed, several trademark Ottoman bridges remain. The **Inat ćuprija** (bridge) was built in the mid-17th century and still stands in the middle of town; the **Podgradska ćuprija** was built over half a century before the Inat Bridge; and the construction of the **Begovska ćuprija** was finished at the beginning of the 19th century.

GETTING THERE AND AWAY Stolac is located less than 30km south of Mostar. However, the back roads leading to Stolac (via Buna) are not always clear, so it's a safer bet to travel via Čapljina and head south at the road junction with the only set of traffic lights on the M-17 from Mostar to the coast. Buses run daily from Mostar and Čapljina to Stolac. If one is arriving from the Dubrovnik or Trebinje area, the main road north (and the only one) from Trebinje goes through Ljubinje and leads directly into Stolac.

WHERE TO STAY, EAT AND DRINK

Motel Vila Ragusa (14 rooms) Kralja Tomislava bb; 036 853 700. Vila Ragusa is Stolac's sole accommodation provider. Although there may be a handful of locals willing to rent out a room, nothing is organised or advertised. For an overnight in Stolac, this is probably your only choice. They have decent rooms & a large restaurant that is often used for conferences & weddings. The rooms are basic, clean & comfortable. They are all en suite & have AC & TV. The restaurant terrace is located on the Bregava River, a perfect place to enjoy homemade travarica: a brandy with medicinal herbs. **$–$$**

Restoran Behar Podgrad bb; m 061 490 166 08.00–23.00 daily. This family-run establishment is Stolac's best eatery. Located at the entrance of town, just before the petrol station, it's hard to miss. The back terrace hovers over the cool Bregava waters & is shaded by neighbouring pine trees. The veal dishes are the cook's speciality. They serve a wide range of grilled meats that all come with tasty French fries. **$$**

Caffe bar Nota Banovinska bb; m 063 159 514; notastolac; 07.00–midnight daily. The concrete terrace & plastic chairs may not be this café's best attribute, but the good coffee & views of the Bregava Falls compensate for their lack of attention to details. Located in the far end of the old part of town, Nota is a no-frills café where many flock to simply enjoy the pleasant natural surroundings & the spray of the cascading Bregava waters.

Slastičarna Čaršija Centar bb; m 063 159 514; 07.00–midnight daily. The most popular café in Stolac's old town is located directly across from the large mosque in the main town square. The café has been restored to its original form after being razed during the war. It doesn't serve alcohol but does have the town's best selection of cakes, & good, strong coffee. The front terrace is a favourite gathering spot & is usually packed in the morning & evening. The residents of Stolac spend the summer afternoons in siesta mode.

WHAT TO SEE AND DO

Badanj Cave Archaeologists were amazed when they accidentally discovered the cave carvings – later dated to about 16000BC. Although the cave itself is rather small and the engravings hard to decipher, there are only a few similar discoveries in the whole of Europe. An agricultural co-op beautified the access to the cave. An impressive walking trail, hand railings and a nice picnic area rest below the rock face above the calm Bregava River. Bring a picnic lunch, as it will be only you and Mother Nature.

Daorson No other community in Bosnia and Herzegovina has more physical evidence of its ancient history than Stolac. On the hilltop plateau flanking the east entrance to Stolac, the ruins of the ancient Daorsi tribe can be found. It is believed this area used to be the northern frontier of the Hellenistic civilisation more than 4,000 years ago. The cyclopean walls, with stones many metres in diameter and weighing more than 14 tonnes, are known as the Herzegovina Stonehenge. They might not be too far off. Located near the small village of Ošanići, a new cement road has been paved all the way to the location. From the plateau, the road is marked with a handful of signs; the key is to find the right turn-off from Stolac itself (the first right coming from Stolac centre). The large walls are the remains of a complex believed to have been a sacred energy centre of the Daorsi.

Radimlja Necropolis The necropolis is home to Bosnia and Herzegovina's largest urban collection of medieval tombstones, called *stećci*, UNESCO listed since 2016. There are 122 of these enormous, limestone tombstones said to date from around the 13th–15th century. It is believed the Slavic worshippers of the then extant

Bosnian Church actually carved their own epitaphs during their lifetime. The necropolis is located 3km before the entrance to Stolac from the Mostar direction. There is an entrance fee of 4KM.

Vidoška This 14th-century fortification was impressively constructed on a sloping hilltop in the middle of Stolac and was utilised by Bosnian royalty. The Ottoman invaders later expanded it, but by the 18th century it had lost most of its strategic significance. Today the fortress goes relatively unnoticed, although the EU approved a million euros for its reconstruction. As with most things in Stolac, the reconstruction has become a political issue and the project never started. It is free to visit and wander. Be careful of loose stones.

TREBINJE

Trebinje is the southernmost city in BiH, boasting 260 sunny days per year. With its mild Mediterranean climate, the crystal-clear **Trebišnjica River,** and unique architecture, it ranks among the most beautiful towns in Herzegovina.

Trebinje is located under **Leotar Mountain**, 28km from Dubrovnik, whose influence – its architects were very involved in its construction – is felt and seen throughout town. Unlike many other Bosnian and Herzegovinian cities, streets in Trebinje are wide and spacious. They are paved with white stone. Even the ancient walls around the old city are unique, with an additional line of stones – or 'rib' – serving as extra protection, similar to that of Dubrovnik's wall construction.

Trebinje has a rich history. It was first mentioned in the 10th century under the name of Tribunia. In the Middle Ages, during the Byzantine era, Trebinje's development began; most of the city, though, was constructed during the Ottoman and Austro-Hungarian period. Mehmed Paša Sokolović built the beautiful **Arslanagića Bridge** in the 16th century. With the arrival of the Austro-Hungarians in 1877, many government buildings, hospitals and schools were built. The former Austrian military barracks in the old town serve as the Museum of Herzegovina. Sitting high above the city, **Crkvina Hill** has a new Orthodox church with some of the best views of Trebinje. One of the most charming marketplaces in all of BiH is Trebinje's central square. Every Saturday the square is packed with local vendors from the surrounding area selling the finest domestic cheeses, wines, spirits, fruits and vegetables. Superb-quality honey production has become a trademark of the Trebinje region. Not far from there is the main park, dedicated to **Jovan Dučić** (page 227). It is urban Trebinje's largest green space and is dotted with various monuments to the town's famous people and events.

Trebinje suffered very little physical damage during the war in the 1990s, and therefore has a different feeling from many other towns in BiH. Because it is so far from everything else in the country, it has its own character. The influence of the nearby coast is palpable, as is the Mediterranean spirit; the central square is packed with cafés and people sitting outside enjoying coffee at their leisure.

North of Trebinje, towards Ljubinje and Stolac, is the vast and incredibly fertile **Popovo Polje.** In its northern part, near the town of Ravno, are the **Vjetrenica Caves,** which have more than 6,300m of underground canals and 200 different animal species – it is purported to be the most biologically diverse cave system on earth. The caves were closed when the supporting infrastructure was destroyed during the war but have been reopened. Very near the cave entrance is the quaint, Orthodox **Zavala Monastery**, which has an impressive collection of faded frescoes. To the east of town is the stunning **Lastva Lake** area, ideal for kayaking or canoeing.

Towards the southern border with Montenegro is **Petrovo Polje,** home to a cluster of old world villages and Hercegovina's only female Serbian Orthodox monastery. The monastery of **Duzi** is believed to be one of the most beautiful and authentic-looking old-world Orthodox Monasteries.

Herzegovina, and the Trebinje area especially, was always known for its wines. The winemaking tradition dates to Roman times – old Roman wine barrels were recently excavated in the Trebinje region. The **Žilavka** wine variety – from the nearby Lastva area – was served at the Habsburg court. Today, there are countless cellars in and around Trebinje; **Vukoje, Anđelić, Tvrdoš** and **Anđušić** are some of

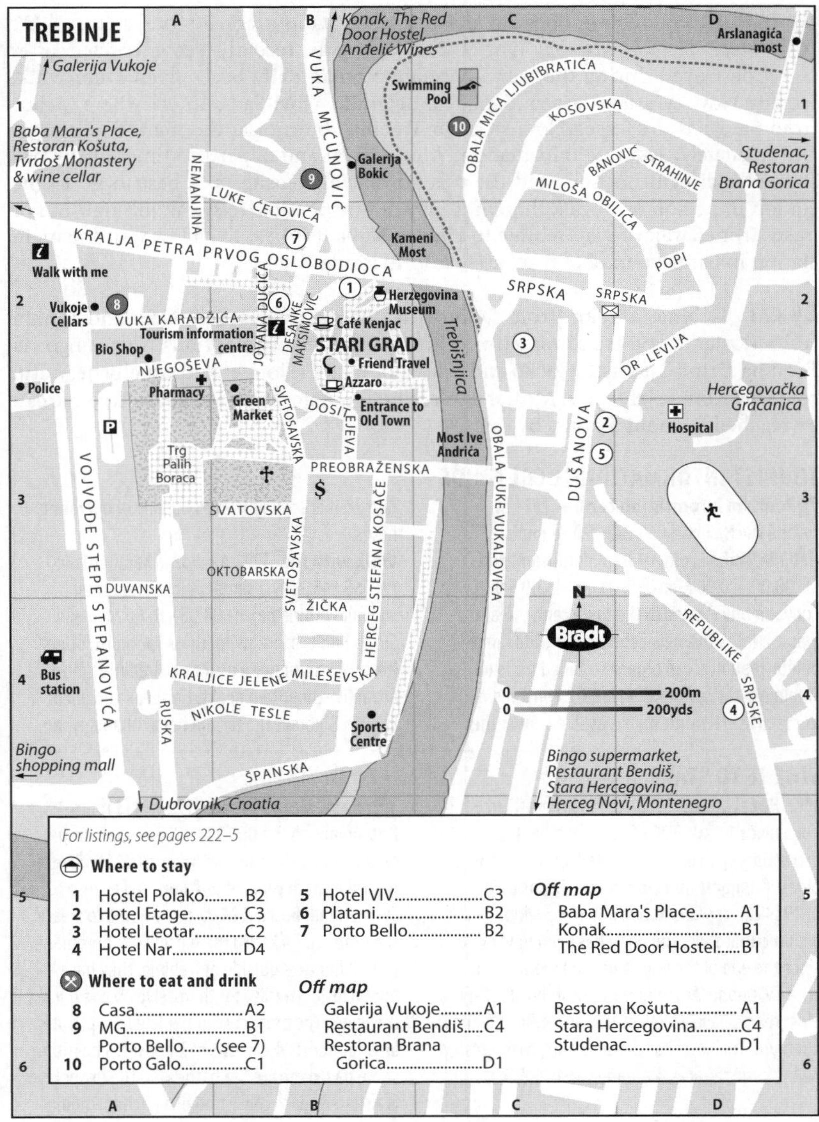

the best. In the **Tvrdoš Monastery** (4km from the city) monks have been making fantastic wine for centuries. The monastery – and its wine shop – is open to the public daily 09.00–19.00.

GETTING THERE AND AWAY

By plane There are three airports close to Trebinje. Dubrovnik's Ćilipi airport is only 40km away. Further down the Adriatic coast in Montenegro is Tivat airport, which is just over 60km from Trebinje, whilst Montenegro's capital city Podgorica is 120km and a 2-hour drive away.

By train/bus Trebinje does not have a train station, and its bus station [221 A4] (*Stepe Stepanovića bb;* ☎ *059 240 003*) was recently reconstructed after being destroyed during the war. There are regular, daily buses from Dubrovnik, Herceg-Novi, Mostar, Eastern Sarajevo, Belgrade, Novi Sad and elsewhere. A bus from Sarajevo to Herceg Novi stops in Trebinje, but not at the main bus station. Unfortunately, accurate information about arrival and departure times at the bus station is difficult to find, and there is no official website. It is best to go to the station in person or to call, though it may not be possible to speak in English. For buses from Sarajevo via Trebinje to Herzeg Novi, it is best to call or visit the main station in Sarajevo to obtain accurate information.

By car Trebinje is 28km from Dubrovnik, 40km from Herceg Novi and 158km from Mostar. If you are coming from Sarajevo there are two options. You can go via Brod na Drini, Tjentište, Gacko and Bileća, or take the longer and equally beautiful route via Konjic, Jablanica, Mostar, Stolac and Ljubinje. From Sarajevo, Trebinje can be reached in about 5 hours by car.

TOURIST INFORMATION/LOCAL GUIDE

Tourism information centre [221 B2] Jovana Dučića bb; ☎ 059 273 120; e tourist_trebinje@yahoo.com; w trebinjeturizam.com; ⏲ 08.00–20.00 Mon–Fri, 09.00–15.00 Sat. Conveniently located in the town centre near the Platani Hotel, this new centre has a wide range of information & can organise guided tours to Trebinje & the surrounding area. A convenient, interactive electronic map is available near the door, & it is accessible even outside of operating hours.

Walk with me [221 A2] Vožda Karađorđa 9; m 065 645 224; e sindakunic@yahoo.com; w walkwithme.ba; ⏲ 08.00–16.00 Mon–Fri. Siniša Kunić, a local wilderness specialist, offers hiking & camping excursions to Trebinje's most attractive mountain peaks. He speaks excellent English & knows the terrain better than anyone.

WHERE TO STAY

Hotel Leotar [221 C2] (80 rooms) Luke Vukalovića 1; ☎ 059 261 086; e hotelleotar.marketing@paleol.net; w hotelleotar.com.The oldest & biggest hotel in Trebinje. It was built in 1954 & is representative of Herzegovina's architectural style. The hotel has been renovated since the end of the war, & now all rooms come with TV, phone, AC, minibar, deposit box & Wi-Fi. Most rooms have a view of Trebišnjica River & the old town. The hotel has 2 restaurants, a congress hall, 3 large terraces & garage space. **$$$**

Baba Mara's Place [221 A1] (3 rooms) Dobromani bb; m 066 873 192; e ivankarmp@gmail.com; w airbnb.com/rooms/6411668. After returning from years of self-imposed exile in Switzerland, Bosko & Mara came home to create their dream. Tucked in the hillside of Dobromani, just 20 minutes outside of Trebinje, they have built a little paradise for themselves & a few lucky travellers. The property's upper level is a private area for guests & consists of 2 houses, a beautiful stone paved terrace & a bathroom. The lower level is a shared space consisting of a kitchen, dining area, an organic pool & another bathroom. It is a typical old-world Mediterranean village, with traditional stone houses, perfectly preserved nature & more sights, sounds, & aromas than one could imagine. The comfortable & tastefully decorated homes provide a perfect place to unplug. They intentionally have no internet or television. It is located 2km from the main road connecting Dubrovnik – Mostar – Sarajevo, & is equally far from the only other restaurant in the surrounding area. **$$–$$$**

Hotel Etage [221 C3] (40 rooms) Dušanova bb; 059 261 443; w etagehotel.com. Hotel Etage opened in 2006 on Trebinje's main street. It has 40 rooms with colourful walls & modern furnishings. All rooms have a phone, AC & TV. The hotel has a 2-storey underground garage with video surveillance, a restaurant & a café with a big outdoor terrace. **$$**

Hotel Nar [221 D4] (32 rooms, 1 apt) Republike Srpske 35; 059 226 600; e info@hotel-nar.com; w hotel-nar.com. Nar was designed by the famous Sarajevo architect Zec. Besides well-equipped, comfortable rooms, the hotel has a wine bar & restaurant serving traditional Herzegovinian dishes & drinks. For quiet evenings, there is a café bar on the roof. **$$**

Hotel VIV [221 C3] (15 rooms) Dušanova 11; 059 273 500; e hotelviv@gmail.com; w hotelviv-trebinje.com. Located on Trebinje's main street – on the way to Dubrovnik & Herceg Novi, & 100m from the old town. The rooms are clean & comfortable with AC & free internet access. The balconies overlook the main street. The hotel has a café & offers laundry & ironing services. **$$**

Konak [221 B1] (20 rooms) Mosko bb; 059 481 288; m 065 520 297. About 10km from Trebinje, on the way to Dubrovnik. Rooms are not luxurious, but they are clean & comfortable with tasteful decorations. The motel also has a restaurant & a big wedding salon, which seats 300 people. Of interest to tourists: the property's stone house, decorated in authentic Herzegovina style, which is open to visitors. **$$**

Platani Hotel [221 B2] (30 rooms, 2 apts) Cvjetni trg 1; 059 274 050; e hotel.platani@gmail.com; w hotel-platani-trebinje.com. Located in the centre of town & on the main square next to the old town, surrounded by huge sycamore trees, or *platani* (hence the name). The beautiful stone building, with red wooden shutters, was constructed at the beginning of the 20th century. The interior was renovated in 2002. Across the street from Platani is Platani II . . . a new version of the hotel with luxurious rooms, which have TV, AC & Wi-Fi. The hotel has a restaurant, café & a gorgeous terrace, where patrons can drink beneath the trees. Run by the same group & reservations can be made at the above contact information. Platani II is roomier & a tad nicer than Platani I. **$$**

Porto Bello [221 B2] (6 apts) Stari grad bb; m 065 580 571; e portobelloinfo@yahoo.com; w portobello-trebinje.com. Motel located in the old town. They have luxurious & spacious apts with French beds & on request they'll add additional beds. All the apts have cable TV, AC, internet access & fridge. Unlike most spots in the old town, this one has its own parking space. Downstairs there is an outstanding restaurant serving a wide array of local & international dishes (page 224). **$$**

Hostel Polako [221 B2] (4 rooms) Svetozara Ćorovića 8; m 066 380 722; e hostelpolako@gmail.com; w hostelpolakotrebinje.com. Hostel Polako in Trebinje is run by two backpackers from America & Poland. Their main goal is to create a social atmosphere where you can meet & hang out with other travellers. As any backpacker knows, breakfast is an important part of the deal. They make fresh, homemade breakfast as part of the offer. The hostel offers Wi-Fi & free coffee/tea, free bed linen & towels, as well as a laundry service. It is a very chill place to be. **$**

The Red Door Hostel [221 B1] (5 rooms) Nikšićki put 17; m 066 652 219; e contact@thereddoor-trebinje.com; w thereddoor-trebinje.com. The Red Door Hostel is the perfect accommodation for backpackers or travel groups visiting Trebinje. It is situated in Gorica, a quiet part of town, only 1.5km from the beautiful old town. They have double & multi-bed rooms that can be arranged according to your needs. The rooms are large, bright & spacious with modern interiors. **$**

WHERE TO EAT AND DRINK

Galerija Vukoje [221 A1] Hrupjela br. 28; 059 270-374; e podrum-vukoje@teol.net; w podrumivukoje1982.com; 09.00–midnight. This wine gallery & restaurant, connected with the Vukoje wine cellar listed on page 228 is not to be missed. The menu is crafted to perfection, offering a wide range of expertly prepared local & international dishes, with a contemporary twist. Vegetarian dishes are available. The wine list is extensive. Set on a hill with a view of the entire city & the mountains of nearby Montenegro, one can see almost to the Croatian coast. Multiple levels of diversely arranged terraces, ringed with Mediterranean plants & flowers, including a full-blown rooftop garden with wooden tables, make this a perfect place to impress a date. The top-level terrace has couches & is perfect for an after-dinner party with a large group of friends. The modern architecture has an upmarket touch, particularly the interior dining area, with its dramatic staircases & floor to ceiling flow of water. The prices are affordable considering the ambiance, quality of food, professionalism of the staff, & variety of wines. Tourists from Dubrovnik come to Trebinje for one evening just to go to this place. There is capacity for up to 300 people, & private parking is available. **$$–$$$**

Restoran Brana Gorica [221 D1] Melentija Petrovića 68; 059 280 007; **e** restoranbg@yahoo.com; **w** vinskacesta.ba/bs/content/brana-gorica; 07.30–23.00 daily. In a completely renovated space Brana Gorica offers delicious snacks & sips of wine, blending bohemian tradition & culinary delight. Ask the waiters to recommend the best food & drinks. **$$–$$$**

Restoran Košuta [221 A1] Vinogradi bb; **m** 065 669 667; 08.00–23.00 daily. Located just a bit out of town on the road towards Bileća to the northeast. Owned & operated by the Vukoje family, one of the most famous wine producers in Herzegovina. They serve excellent local cuisine & have a generous menu of international dishes as well. The wine list is, of course, highlighted by the family's locally produced wine. **$$–$$$**

Porto Bello [221 B2] Stari grad bb; **m** 065 580 571; **e** portobelloinfo@yahoo.com; **w** portobello-trebinje.com. This restaurant is part of a motel located in the old town. The restaurant on the first floor is excellent, and boasts an open-plan kitchen & a shaded terrace set in stone walls to conquer the summer heat. The interior is made of natural wood & stone. The menu is extensive & well-curated. The hearty fish stew & very fresh Serbian salad (*srpska salata*) are both excellent. There is a fireplace for cosy winter evenings. **$$**

Restaurant Bendiš [221 C4] Grab bb; **m** 065 363 586, 065 536 820; 07.00–23.00 daily. In this authentic Herzegovinian house, built in 1872, Bendiš offers the many traditional recipes that have been passed down through their family for centuries. Located just 12km from Trebinje, on the main road to Herceg Novi, this restaurant offers an authentically rustic dining experience. All spirits are made locally, as are the hams, cheese and other delicacies. **$$**

Restoran MG [221 B2] Majke Jugovića 11; 059 260 877; restoranmg.trebinje; 08.00–23.00 daily. As you walk from the old town towards the Herzegovina Museum, you'll see a big MG sign in one of the alley streets on your left. MG might not look like much from the outside, but the food is excellent. They have all kinds of fish dishes (eel included) & steaks. The speciality of the house is the MG plate: an assortment of meat & it's more than enough for 2 people. The wine list is extensive & mainly focused on Herzegovinian wines. **$$**

Stara Hercegovina [221 C4] Tuli bb; **m** 065 669 707; **e** restoranstarahercegovina@yahoo.com; **w** starahercegovina.com; 10.00–23.00 daily. Some 5km from Trebinje, on the way to Herceg Novi. It is built to remind one of old (*stara*) Herzegovina. The building is made of white stone, characteristic for the area. Inside, many old utensils & tools are on display. As you walk in, the first thing you will notice is a huge tree in the middle of the room. The restaurant was built around it. A rustic fireplace, the wooden floors, & the chairs & tables give it its old-house look. The food is mouth-watering. They have all kinds of steaks & fish. The top choice is the veal under the *sač* (page 80). It comes with baked potatoes & their wonderful, fresh bread. **$$**

Studenac [221 D1] Milentija Perovića bb; 059 281 581; **w** motelstudenac.com; 08.00–23.00 daily. If you are looking for fresh trout, there is no better place than Studenac. It's located on the crystal-clear, cold Trebišnjica River & behind the Arslanagića Bridge. During hot summer days, the best choice is to sit outside. They have a fish pond & you can pick your own trout. Also, make sure to try their homemade bread. **$$**

Casa [221 A2] Vuka Karadžića 19; 059 270 610; 06.30–23.00 Mon–Sat, 07.00–23.00 Sun. One of the most charming places in Trebinje. This recently renovated café/pizzeria is a favourite spot for Trebinje's young & hip crowd. Inside, it is cheerfully decorated with funky furniture & colourful walls. Behind the building, there is a gorgeous terrace. Numerous pots are filled with blooming flowers & everything is painted in bright colours. Grab a quick lunch here – they offer sandwiches, pastas & pancakes – & chat with the extremely nice & hospitable owner. $–$$

Porto Galo [221 C1] Obala Mića Ljubibratića 5; m 066 851 493; Jun–Sep 08.00–midnight Sun–Thu, 08.00–01.00 Sat–Sun; Oct–May 08.00–23.00 daily. Having moved back to Trebinje from Portugal with her husband, the owner has found a unique niche for herself by opening the first Portuguese restaurant in the country. The food here has much more of a Mediterranean flavour, with lots of spices & marinades being the trademark of her dishes. One thing it does have in common with local cuisine is that the menu is largely based on meat. The food is somewhere between high quality fast food & a proper meal. The plate of small, local fried fish (*girice*) is a seasonal speciality. Refreshing cocktails, inc sangria, are served. There is an enormous, breezy terrace overlooking the river & a park with a walking path. It a refreshing place to escape the heat & enjoy the kindness of the owner & her husband. The prices are shockingly low, with small plates starting at 2KM. $

OLD TOWN BARS AND CAFÉS The compact area referred to as Old Town (*Stari grad*) Trebinje may be surrounded by old walls, but it is full of many youthful bars and cafés. From venues with a club-like atmosphere to options offering a relaxing drink on the terrace or street-side tables, there is something for everyone. It is fun just to stroll around these streets on a warm evening, and observe the positive vibes of people out enjoying themselves. Most of the streets in this small area are referred to as 'Stari grad'. No map is necessary: if you walk around for five minutes, you are sure to find all the places listed.

For those looking to party, when entering the old town from the direction of the central square, you will immediately come across a number of kitschy bars pumping loud music, where it is possible that dancing will break out later in the evening depending on the mood.

Azzaro [221 B2] Stari grad bb; m 065 753 896; 08.00–23.00 Mon–Sat, 10.00–23.00 Sun. Always full of people, this is one of the more lively pubs in the area & has a large outdoor seating area as well as a cosy wooden interior, which is comfortable in winter. The bar plays alternative & ex-Yugoslav rock music, & the walls are decorated with postcards from all over the world. Their herbal brandy is a deep golden colour & tastes very fresh.

Kenjac [221 B2] Stari grad bb; 08.00–23.00 daily. An endearing establishment, votive candles burn softly on tables set under tall spruce trees in the garden, & a pop-art vibe defines the interior. In addition to alcoholic beverages such as wine, beer & spirits, Kenjac serves milkshakes & natural juices.

PRACTICALITIES

Police

Police station [221 A2] Vojvode Stepe Stepanovića 20; 059 279 100

Hospital

General Hospital [221 D3] Dr Levija 2; 059 223 755

Pharmacy

Apoteka Stari Platan [221 A2] Njegoševa 2; 059 260 086; 09.00–23.00 daily. Trebinje currently does not have one designated 24-hr pharmacy. This has the longest consistent working hours.

Bank

$ **Addiko Bank** [221 B3] Preobraženska 2. ATM.

Travel agency

Friend Travel [221 B2] Stari grad 132; ☎ 059 226 198; **e** friendtravel@teol.net; **w** friendtravel.net; ⌚ 08.00–17.00 Mon–Sat. This agency can help arrange adventure tours – sporting trips in the surrounding area, including river rafting.

SHOPPING For hand-crafted goods and souvenirs, visit the series of small souvenir shops at the entrance to the old town [221 B2] (*Stari grad bb;* ⌚ *late morning to early evening daily*). For a grocery store, try **Bingo** [221 A4] (*Kolubarska bb,* ⌚ *08.00–22.00 Mon–Sat; 09.00–19.00 Sun*). **Bio Shop** is a decently stocked shop with organic food and other products [221 A2] (*Njegoševa bb;* **m** *065 753 638;* ⌚ *09.00–19.00 Mon–Sat*). Other than that, plus the wine cellars as listed below, Trebinje is not a place with notable shopping options. However, it does have a couple of unique establishments.

Galerija Bokić [221 B1] Vuka Mićunovića 8; ☎ 059 483 803; **m** 065 803 538; **w** galerijabokic.com; ⌚ 08.00–20.00 daily; free admission. This privately owned art gallery is a must-see. In fact, you literally cannot miss it when walking through Trebinje: set on its own by the banks of the river, the oddly-shaped building is somehow wavy despite being made of stone, & is decorated with elaborate carvings & varying textures. The slightly alien structure sticks out & is completely different from anything around it. That's because it was designed & built by a prolific local artist who might be considered an eccentric genius. Now in his 80s, Milivoje Bokić is still active. He has held exhibitions all around the world. He worked on this building for 18 years, & built parts of the façade & interior by hand. He lives on the ground floor. The other floors serve as an art gallery & were recently opened to the public. There is a small lounge in the gallery, where you can order a coffee, beer, or glass of wine.

Green market [221 B2] ⌚ approximately 07.00–02.00 daily. The green market in the central square of Trebinje is considered by many to be the best in the country. In addition to fresh & inexpensive fruit & veg (including local figs, oranges, lemons & pomegranates, when they are in season), the market is staffed with vendors selling homemade products like cheese, *rakija* (brandy), dried herbs, tea, olive oil & honey. Eggs & dried meat, such as prosciutto, may also be available. While most of the stalls are authentic small farmers, who often use semi-organic methods of production, a few stalls in the market sell imported produce. Three of Herzegovina's most unique foodstuffs can be found at this green market: *škripavac* cheese, sack cheese & the Poljak bean. It is worth it just to walk through the market & observe the interactions & look at the daily offerings. Get there early – the best products go fast. There are at least five cafés adjacent to the market, so it's a good opportunity to combine this excursion with a coffee in the morning sun.

WHAT TO SEE AND DO

Anđelić Wine Cellar [221 B1] (*Gorica bb;* ☎ *059 259 222;* **e** *dragan@podrum-andjelic.com;* **w** *podrum-andjelic.com*) Trebinje is famous for its wine production. There are several wine cellars in the area and Anđelić is one of the best. In their family cellar, there are six kinds of white, red and rosé. They have Blatina and Žilavka. This family produces around 150,000 litres of wine annually.

Arslanagić Bridge [221 D1] A Trebinje calling card, the bridge was built in 1537, by the order of Grand Vizier Mehmed Paša Sokolović, who also built the famous bridge in Višegrad. The bridge was flooded in 1965 when hydro-electric facilities were built on the Trebišnjica River. It was then dissembled, stone by stone, and left on a nearby field where it was abandoned for several years. In 1970, the bridge was

THE LEGEND OF KONJIC

Long before the town of Konjic was established as a settlement, there was a small village tucked in the deep valley of Prenj Mountain near Boračko Lake. In this village lived a widow with her two children. One evening a lone traveller appeared in the village, tired and dirty from his journey. He asked several villagers for some food, drink and a place to sleep but, wary of foreigners, they turned him down. He eventually came to the door of the widow and she kindly let him in. As they were eating supper this mysterious vagabond told the widow of an imminent danger that would destroy the village. He warned her to leave at once, at first light, in order to save herself and the children. 'I have come as a messenger, and your fellow villagers have all turned me away.' He instructed her to gather her belongings and take her children on horses over the large mountain to the northwest. The man told her when her horse stopped and dug his hoof into the ground three times, this was the place she would be safe and should make her new home. When the woman awoke the next morning the stranger was gone. She didn't know what to believe. She spoke to her neighbours and they laughed at her. She was frightened for her children and wanted to save her neighbours from the impending doom but they would not be convinced. The woman gathered her things and saddled her horses. The journey over the mountain took several days until she reached an open valley near a river. Her little horse bucked and jumped. Bowing to the ground the horse dug his hoof into the ground three times. At that moment a large roar rolled down through the valley and the earth shook. It was here that she settled with her children as the man had instructed her. The little horse had led them to safety and a new life. The settlement of Konjic, meaning 'little horse', began on this day.

moved to a new location, and each stone was numbered and transported. Two years later the bridge was assembled on its present location. There is some controversy regarding the name of the bridge. At its previous location, there was a village called Arslanagići, and for decades the bridge was taken care of by members of the Arslanagići family. It is now referred to as both Perovic and Arslanagić Bridge. Either way, it will leave no visitor indifferent to its beauty.

Hercegovačka Gračanica [221 D2] (*Crkvina hill, behind the town centre*) This Orthodox church was built as a copy of the Gračanica monastery in Kosovo as requested by Trebinje's famous writer Jovan Dučić. His remains were brought back from the United States, where he had passed away, and laid next to the church. There is a small souvenir shop and a large open plateau for pleasant walks and excellent photographing opportunities of Trebinje's panorama.

Herzegovina Museum [221 B2] (*Stari grad 59;* ☎ *059 271 061;* **e** *info@muzejhercegovine.org;* **w** *muzejhercegovine.org;* 🕘 *08.00–18.00 Mon–Fri; entrance fee 2KM*) The museum is located in the old Austrian military compound. Once a high school, in 1989 it was turned into a museum. It has 1,000m^2 of exhibition space with more than a thousand exhibits. Visitors can see an archaeological collection with prehistoric artefacts, an ethnographic collection from the 16th century, and numerous paintings and sculptures from the best-known regional artists. Guides and curators speak English and will be happy to give you a tour.

Tvrdoš Orthodox Monastery and wine cellar [221 A1] (*Tvrdoš hill, 4km west of Trebinje;* ☎ *059 270 370;* ⏲ *08.00–19.00 Mon–Sat;* **w** *tvrdos.com*) The 14th-century monastery is built on the foundations of the old medieval church. It was severely damaged in 1694 – in battles between Turks and Venetians – when the entire inventory of the monastery was moved to Savina Monastery in Herceg Novi, where it still remains. Today, Tvrdoš is the Episcopal residency, and it is known for the excellent red wine produced by its monks.

Vukoje Cellars 1982 [221 A1] (*Hrupjela 28;* **m** *065 517 099;* **e** *podrum-vukoje@teol.net;* **w** *podrumivukoje1982.com;* ⏲ *09.00–18.00 Mon–Sat, 09.00–14.00 Sun*) Vukoje is amongst the most acclaimed wine producers in Bosnia and Herzegovina. It has won countless international awards for both its light and fruity Žilavka white and robust Vranac red wines. The cellar is open to visitors and can seat up to 60 guests. The Vukoje family also own and operate the excellent **Restoran Košuta**, near the cellar (page 224).

KONJIC

Konjic is an exciting place not because it has a hopping downtown district (it's really quite dead), but rather because of the wilderness adventures happening left, right and centre. The Neretva River running through town and Prenj Mountain hovering behind dominate Konjic. It is possible to wade (or even briefly bathe, at your own risk) in the cold water: many locals do it, and there is a 'beach' of sorts on the riverbanks in the town. One of the best things to see here (and shop around in) are the family-owned woodcarving shops. From massive hutches to intricately designed small boxes, Konjic has long been known for its wood craftsmen. **Braća Nikšić** (*Varda 2;* ☎ *036 725 239;* **w** *bracaniksic.com;* ⏲ *08.00–16.00*) is one of the few firms left that continue to pass on the family trade from father to son. The first craft shop was opened by the Nikšić family in 1935, although they had been craftsmen long before that. Their work is mainly done in walnut, and you can order almost anything you like. There are also a number of small museums.

The real adventure, however, awaits you over the mountain top near **Boračko Lake**. Follow the signs for 'rafting' up the long and winding mountain road. It takes about half an hour to travel up and over the mountain. Boračko's glacier lake is snuggled in between **Prenj, Bjelašnica** and **Visočica mountains**. It is open to the public for camping, swimming and barbecues, and a few of the locals have opened bed and breakfasts along the shores. It costs 2KM per person to get into the lake area; the best spot is across the lake by the restaurant where you will find a great freshwater stream and plenty of shade. But that's not the adventure I'm talking about. About 5km away, the main road will start to run along the banks of the Neretva again. This whole area is marked as campgrounds for the rafting companies that guide white-water rafting trips down the Neretva Canyon. It's an all-day adventure, and there are many rafting outfits to choose from. Some have better gear than others but they all provide you with breakfast and lunch (lunch is usually a barbecue somewhere deep in the canyon) included in the price. The price is more or less standard and foreigners pay 100KM per person. Some operators give group discounts.

The rafting companies working in the Konjic area are:

Europe Rafting Kolonija 16, Konjic; **m** 061 817 209; **e** samir.krivic@icloud.com; **w** europerafting.com; ⏲ 08.00–16.00 Mon–Fri. One of 2 rafting agencies that have international certification on the Neretva River. They serve b/fast at the Restaurant Stari Mlin in Konjic along the Neretva, before transporting you for the ride. Europe Rafting has a campground called Tin. Lunch is prepared either in the wilderness or back at the restaurant when the trip is over – your choice! 80KM pp.

HITko Rafting Glavatičevo, Konjic; ☎036 739 221; **m** 061 175 326; **e** hitko@hitkorafting.com; **w** hitkorafting.com. This company, near Ban Vir, offers rafting & kayaking with good gear & guides. They also have a beautiful log cabin along the eastern banks of the river & a set of 5 traditional huts. Working time varies.

Rafting Tours Salihamidzic Džajići bb; **m** 070 213 080; **e**; salihamidzic@ambasadaneretva.com; **w** ambasadaneretva.com. A smaller outfit with good boats & skippers who are internationally certified. They have a very nice place in Džajići with excellent food after a long day on the river.

Tajo-Raft Konjic Glavatičevo bb; ☎036 739 236; **m** 061 204 260; **e** tajoraft@bih.net.ba; **w** tajoraft.com

GETTING THERE AND AWAY

By train The Zagreb–Sarajevo–Ploče line goes through Konjic station (*Željeznička bb; ☎036 726 060*) once per day, though currently the train does not run all the way to Croatia but may again in the future.

By bus There is no official bus station in Konjic to call or buy tickets. Most buses coming from Sarajevo to Mostar or Jablanica will stop at the city's main department store on Kolonija bb.

By car Coming from Sarajevo, it takes around an hour to drive the 64km to Konjic. You will go via Hadžići, Tarčin and Bradina. When exiting Sarajevo, follow the signs to Mostar. From Mostar it is 74km on the M-17 going through Jablanica and Ostrožac. A highway is being built from Sarajevo to the Adriatic coast via Konjic, but currently only covers about a third of the distance, saving about 20 minutes of driving.

WHERE TO STAY

Hotel Oaza (33 rooms) Maršala Tita 59; ☎036 726 772; **e** info@hoteloazakonjic.com; **w** hoteloazakonjic.com. Oaza is situated 100m from the Old Konjic Bridge in the town centre. All rooms have AC, TV, Wi-Fi, safe & a minibar. There's also a free room with a kitchenette & washing machine, as well as a VIP saloon. Be sure to indulge in some sweets from the pastry shop within the hotel that has been trading for more than 65 years. **$$**

Motel Konak (22 rooms) Stari grad bb; ☎036 735 550; **w** hotelkonak.ba. Located on the Neretva riverbank, right next to the Old Bridge. Rooms are comfy & elegantly furnished in dark wood with red curtains. All rooms have a TV, AC, phone, minibar & free internet access. Possibly the best thing about it is that some rooms have balconies overlooking the Neretva River & the Old Bridge. Leave the windows open & you can listen to the river. Downstairs there is an excellent restaurant. **$$**

Boračko Lake Apartments (4 rooms, 5 apartments) Boračko jezero bb; **m** 062 115 015; **e** info@borackojezero.com; **w** borackojezero.com. The most luxurious accommodation on the lake. Just 100m from the Prenj beach, all rooms & apts are modernly decorated in light colours & outfitted with chic wooden furniture. Each unit has a TV, & most importantly, a balcony with a lake view. Prices are up to 20% lower in the winter. Its restaurant serves excellent trout. **$–$$**

Eco Village Boračko Jezero (106 beds) Prkanj 1; ☎033 200 249; **e** ekoselo-bih@ekoselo-bih.com; **w** ekoselo-bih.com. Eco Village is located on the shores of Boracko Lake 18km from Konjic. They have their own private access to the lake. The complex has a large capacity for several types of clients. There is the rustic, small wooden huts that sleep 2, a pair of log cabins that can sleep up to 8 people, & 5 larger log cabins that have 12 beds each. There is a restaurant & café bar on the premises, as well as volleyball & football pitches. Camping with tents or camper vans is also possible, with water & electric hook-ups available. It's an exceptionally pleasant place to relax in the shade & when it gets too hot, you can jump in the cool semi-glacier lake. **$–$$**

Hostel Džajića Buk (15 rooms) Plaža Džajićabuk bb; 036 724 162; e dzajick@bih.net.ba; w neretvarafting.ba. Neretva Rafting organises rafting on the Neretva River & offers accommodation in Hostel Džajića Buk, located 5km from Konjic, for their guests. The location alone is well worth booking a trip with them for, tucked in the serene part of the canyon on the banks of the river. Rooms are very basic, with not much of the standard amenities, but make up for it with comfort & gracious hospitality. **$–$$**

Konoba (6 rooms) Boračko jezero bb; m 062 609 630. This family-operated place is located just across from the Prenj beach. The rooms are simple, but clean & comfy. They have a restaurant offering a variety of grilled dishes. **$–$$**

Pansion Borašnica (12 rooms, 34 bungalows) Boračko jezero bb; 036 739 513. Still the lake's main accommodation, the pension offers slightly antiquated rooms, but its main strength is a beautiful terrace overlooking the lake. The bungalows are almost on the beach, which belongs to Borašnica. At night, DJs play house music & the beach becomes a club. **$–$$**

Vila Sunce (15 rooms) Boračko jezero bb; m 061 498 480; e info@vila-sunce.com; w vila-sunce.com. Vila Sunce is located 300m from the 1st beach on Boračko Lake, just above Šištica River. It has spectacular views of Prenj Mountain from the main outdoor sitting area. The English-speaking staff are exceptionally friendly & open to conversing with guests while preparing food & drink in the outside dining area. They can organise single-day trips of your liking, whether it be rafting, hiking, fishing or cycling. The rooms are basic but quite comfortable, & are all en suite. The kitchen & large terrace are shared. **$**

WHERE TO EAT AND DRINK

Han Donje Polje bb; m 061 227 587; 06.00–23.00 daily. Located behind the Old Bridge, towards the Prenj Mountain, & on the road for Boračko Lake, Han is hard to miss. It looks like a modern villa. The wooden terrace wraps around the entire building. Inside, everything is modern, chic & ideal for power lunches. Order any kind of pizza, pitta or steak; their Vienna steak is excellent. Leave room for dessert because they have Bosnian specialities: *baklava* & *tufahija*. **$$**

Konak Stari čaršija bb; 036 735 550; 06.00–23.00 daily. Located in the old town & on the Neretva riverbank overlooking the Old Bridge. This elegant restaurant is one of the best places to eat in town. The interior is decorated in dark wood with special old Bosnian accents: antique furniture, *sećije* (Bosnian benches) & old pots & pans. But, during warm spring & summer days, the best place to be is on the huge terrace, where you can enjoy the sounds of the river. The food is excellent, too. They offer all kinds of steaks, grilled-meat dishes & traditional meals such as stuffed peppers or beans with meat. Try their Konak steak. **$$**

Neretva Trg državnosti bb; 036 730 747; 07.00–midnight daily. Neretva is one of the older & more traditional restaurants in town. It's located, logically, on Neretva's riverbank, close to the city's green market. The interior is furnished basically, & has a beautiful terrace overlooking both bridges in Konjic. For years, this restaurant has been known for veal under the *sač* & excellent trout. **$$**

Novalića kula Maršala Tita bb; 036 727 170; 07.00–23.00 daily. Konjic's old town has an impressive 4-storey structure built as an old-style clock tower, traditionally called *sahatkula*. On the top floor is the Bosnian room where one can enjoy a steak dinner while looking over the Old Konjic Bridge that spans the Neretva River. The food is good. The views are magnificent. **$$**

Orahovica Orahovica bb; 036 721 580; 08.00–midnight daily. A little outside of Konjic on the main road to Jablanica, it's a big stone-&-wood building sitting right across from the petrol station. The restaurant has a great reputation amongst Konjičani, who gladly take the short drive from the town to enjoy great food & an even better view. The huge terrace is built directly above the dark-green water, & it's hard to imagine a better place to take a break from your trip. They offer a wide variety of food, but are known for veal under the *sač*, pitta or their speciality, Orahovica steak. Upstairs, there are several rooms for rent. $$

Restoran Pećina Čelebići bb; m 062 757 925; 08.00–21.00 daily. Situated in the village of Čelebići at the foot of Prenj Mountain, just 10km from Konjic, this restaurant is unique in that half of it is located in a cave along the Baštica River. Herzegovina is known for its intense heat. Well, no worries about that from this spot! With the river & cave acting as a double air conditioner, it's a wonderfully pleasant place for lunch. They serve homemade polenta that is milled in the area, & the trout comes from their private fishery on the premises. $$

Miki Aščinica Maršala Tita bb; 07.00–23.00 daily. For a quick & cheap meal, stop at Miki's pitta place right next to the Old Bridge. The spot is small & no-frills, but the food is tasty. They offer all kinds of pizzas & Bosnian pies made under the *sač*. The pies are filled with meat, cheese or potato. $–$$

Restoran Vidikovac Musala bb; 036 831 534; e restoranvidikovac.konjic@gmail.com; w restoran-vidikovac.com; 08.00–23.00 daily. The greatest advantage of this restaurant is the astonishing view of Konjic, the Neretva River & the surrounding hills. If you want a more romantic atmosphere, the restaurant offers private tables, with candlelit dinner to watch the sunset. The food is mainly traditional & uses local ingredients. $–$$

WHAT TO SEE AND DO **Tito's Bunker** (*Hadžića polje; m 061 918 324, 061 072 027; e info@visitkonjic.com; by appointment only, via the phone number or email of the agency listed here; entrance fee varies, usually 10KM; large group tours can be arranged upon request*) might be considered one of the most fascinating attractions in the area, and some say it is one of the most unique museums in all of the former Yugoslavia. This 6,500m^2 underground bunker was one of the most expensive structures in Yugoslavia. Designed with the purpose of withstanding nuclear war and sheltering Yugoslav government officials, army generals, and Tito himself and his family, its location, and very existence, were a secret in Yugoslavia. It is located in the mountains, 10–15 minutes above the old town of Konjic by car, and is difficult to find because it was intentionally hidden. The entrance is concealed behind what seems to be the garage door of an ordinary house. It is accessible by car only, unless you are a super-hiker. Arranging a taxi ride in Konjic may be possible, and will cost 10–20KM (*try Mehić Taxi; m 062 987 747*). Since you will have to call in advance to make a reservation anyway, it is best to ask at that time for directions and advice on finding the place, or ask to have transport arranged. The bunker was only made available to private tours and the public within the last few years, and is still surprisingly under-visited considering its value. Once per year, usually in the early summer, the bunker is open to all as part of an impressive contemporary art festival (*w bijenale.ba*).

The **Regional Museum** (*Stara čaršija bb; 036 727 080; 09.00–16.30 daily; admission 4KM*) is a modest, yet interesting, museum in Konjic offering artefacts from the areas's past, and providing a glimpse into the way people lived through the ages. There are rotating exhibitions. The guide at this museum can also take you down the street to an adjacent museum, the **House of Zuko Džumhur.** Džumhur was an important cult literary figure and artist in Yugoslavia. His home, built in traditional Ottoman style with a lovely garden, has been turned into a museum. One can browse his works, including his famous caricatures of powerful people, and look at the rooms and traditional furnishings from his childhood. The opening hours and contact information are the same as the Regional Museum, but entrance must be arranged at the front desk of the Regional Museum. If it is a slow day, it is very likely you will get a free guided tour of the house. The entrance fee is included in the price for the Regional Museum.

AROUND KONJIC

The isolated string of mountain communities in the highlands of **Visočica** and southern **Bjelašnica** are among the most beautiful in the country. On Visoćica Mountain the inhabitants of the many villages of **Bijelemići** continue to live in the traditional way. Relying mostly on large sheep flocks and small farms, their lifestyles have changed very little here over the centuries. The villages are well connected, and gravel roads travel far into the high mountains near the peak of Visoćica (**Mount Džamija** at 1,967m). This central peak offers staggering views of **Treskavica**, **Zelengora**, **Prenj** and **Bjelašnica mountains** (all over 2,000m) and **Velež** (1,969m). Across the rugged canyon of **Rakitnica** is the village of **Dubočani** on the Bjelašnica mountain side. It is said that the villagers were the last of the followers of the Bosnian Church to convert to Islam after the Turks had conquered Herzegovina. There are great hiking trails on Čepa ridge towards **Vis** and **Ostro** peaks. The view of the Rakitnica Canyon from this point has been described as one of the most beautiful in southeast Europe. You can also try your hand at mini-rafting, an improvised form of rafting in tight canyon areas where regular rafts cannot pass. The rafts themselves are usually reinforced children's rafts. Travelling the entire length of the canyon (26km) takes several days. All of these mountain destinations are part of the Via Dinarica White Trail and can be found on **w** viadinarica.com.

JABLANICA

In the Alps in Austria or Switzerland a place like Jablanica would be a mountain resort town. Instead, here, it remains a tiny town with little or no developed mountain tourism. But things are changing. Nestled on a terraced plateau below the intimidating peaks of **Prenj** and **Čvrsnica mountains**, Jablanica teeters between the Mediterranean and continental climates.

The **Neretva River** carves its way through the centre, dividing the massive mountain ranges. It was at Jablanica that the Partisans won an unlikely victory in World War II, in the **Battle of the Neretva**. The bridge that the Partisans downed and cleverly escaped over with 4,000 wounded still hangs from the high cliffs as a reminder of one of their greatest victories. The **War Museum**, which exhibits pictures and tells the story of the famous battle, is just next to the bridge, and an old German bunker on the east side of the river has now been converted into a restaurant and café.

Apart from this famous battle, Jablanica is known for *jagnjetina* (roast lamb). On the main road south of town are the trademark restaurants that have made Jablanica a place at which most locals, and those passing through, have spent some time. There are more than ten such restaurants, each selling the exact same thing, that make a killing providing hungry guests with grilled lamb. This old tradition of roasting sheep over an open fire has brought new meaning to the word 'rest stop'. Most restaurants will be filled day and night, and all bus routes heading south to Mostar or north to Sarajevo will certainly stop for a taste of this mouth-watering delicacy. They do, of course, sell other types of food but the craze is definitely the lamb by the kilo. If you are having trouble choosing which to stop at, **Zdrava Voda** (**$$**), meaning healthy water, is certainly one of the nicest, as is **Restoran Jablanica** (**$$**). There is only one hotel in town, the **Hotel Jablanica** (☎ *036 753 136;* **$$**), located in the centre of the town on the main road.

North of Jablanica through the **Lendava Tunnel** is where the **Jablaničko Lake** system begins. This area has developed a tourism niche on the lake. There are several good restaurants – my particular favourite is **Restoran San San** (🕘 *08.00–23.00 daily;* **$$**) – and the entire length of the lake is lined with pensions, hotels, private rooms and campgrounds. The lake itself has some of the best fishing in the country, as proved by the locals standing on the side of the road selling their 'catches of the day' – large carp, trout, bass, and a few other fish whose names I haven't been able to translate. Jablaničko Lake is safe for swimming, but don't expect to find lifeguards or any other safety mechanisms in case of an emergency. The limited **campgrounds** are mainly for primitive camping. **Kamp-Plaza Miris Ljeta** in **Ostrožac** has camping facilities on the 'beach' of the lake (**m** *062 716 161*). There are no hook-ups for electricity or water. There is access for campers and places to pitch a tent, but they are usually quite crowded with local people. Private rooms are easy to find and signs are posted along the road. Unless you don't care what you pay, you should bargain for the price of the room – a room with a bathroom and shower shouldn't cost more than 25KM per night. A bit further north in the town of Čelebići is a fantastic restaurant built into the side of a cave. **Restaurant Pećina** (**$$**) (page 231) is situated along a small river that cascades next to the dining terrace. Do visit.

If you're a hiker, it's hard not to gaze up at the massive peaks of Prenj (facing Jablanica) and imagine what the view would be like from the top. It's a bit complicated to find your way up there by yourself, and trails are not well marked so it is advisable to contact the mountain association or an ecotourism outfit to guide you up. The trek to **Milanova Koliba** (Milan's mountain hut) takes 3 to 5 hours. From that saddle between **Cetine** and **Izgorila Gruda** peaks, the hike to the top is a little more than an hour away. The view is heavenly! For an easier time on Prenj there is a drivable route from **Bijeli Canyon** off the M-17 south. A long and winding gravel road takes you up to **Glogovo Heights** where you'll drive past highland shepherds and the endangered (and endemic) **Munika black pines**. There is a mountain hut there that is often left open for mountaineers. Again, hiking in such a large region that is mined in some remote areas is not wise. Find a guide; you'll be glad you did.

The road from Jablanica following the **River Doljanka** towards Doljani leads to another magnificent hiking area on Čvrsnica Mountain. There is a new gravel road that climbs to the base of the high plateau of **Plasa**. This road, unfortunately, was built for the illegal exploitation of the rich forests on this side of the mountain. Uncontrolled logging in this part of the country is a major environmental concern. Once on Plasa, there is a tiny hut used by hikers and hunters. The drill with these improvised huts is that you are free to enter and sleep if there is no-one else there, but you are expected to clean up and leave the hut as you found it. Leftover food like sugar, tea or conserves should always be left behind for the next guest. The hike across Plasa leads to high peaks around **Velinac** (2,118m) and **Strmac**, with **Diva Grabovica** (200m) deep in the valley below. The view on to Pestibrdo is awe-inspiring and you may find yourself sitting there for a while just contemplating.

GETTING THERE AND AWAY

By train Jablanica used to be easily reachable by train from either Sarajevo or Croatia. The Sarajevo–Ploče train stopped at Jablanica station. This line has been suspended until further notice (it now runs to/from Sarajevo–Konjic only), but may be reinstated at any time (*Željeznička bb;* ☎ *036 752 798*).

By bus There are several buses daily from Sarajevo to Mostar, stopping in Jablanica (*Željeznička bb;* ☎ *036 752 243*). A Zenica–Dubrovnik bus stops here, too. Almost all buses from Mostar or Međugorje to Konjic or Sarajevo stop in Jablanica.

By car Coming from Sarajevo it will take you around an hour and a half to drive 86km on the M-17 to Jablanica. It is possible to drive 23km of the road on a highway, saving about 20 minutes of driving time. Eventually, the highway is supposed to go all the way to Konjic, and beyond – down to the coast. From Mostar it is 53km. Jablanica is 363km from Zagreb, Croatia, and 384km from Belgrade, Serbia.

PROZOR AND RAMSKO LAKE

Prozor and Ramsko Lake are the northernmost points in Herzegovina. Catholics and Muslims mostly inhabit this area. Ramsko Lake is home to Sit Island, where the **House of Peace** at the **Franciscan monastery Rama-Ščit** welcomes guests who are looking for peace and quiet, a bit of counselling or just a day of fishing on the lake (*036 780 740;* **e** *samostan@rama.co.ba*; **w** *rama.co.ba*). It is run by the monks who live there all year round. The monastery was the base for the Partisans during World War II, where they prepared their counter-offensive for the Battle of the Neretva.

The area is lush and green and offers great fishing and boating, walking and hiking, and an interesting look at village life in the surrounding hills. If you're looking for peace and quiet, look no more – Ramsko Lake will meet your needs. There isn't a 'tourist offer' to speak of, but foreign guests are not uncommon, particularly at the monastery. The local villagers are very kind and getting off into the hills you'll find fascinating Catholic villages where women still dress in traditional attire and practise the ancient ritual of tattooing crosses on their hands, arms and even foreheads.

The town of Prozor, to the east of Ramsko Lake, is a small mountain settlement with not much more to do than walk around and check out life in a small town. The Muslim population, expelled during the war, has returned in large numbers, bringing the town back to life a bit. Some of the Muslim villages around Prozor are as equally fascinating as the Catholic ones. Just down the road from Prozor is the village of **Duge** (meaning 'rainbow'). It is worth taking a walk through the village. Duge is blessed with an immense water supply and a powerful waterfall called **Duge Falls**. It has this name because of its unique position in relation to the sun. As the water plummets over 30m to the rocks below the mist mixes with the rays of the sun and almost always creates a rainbow. The locals are fighting against a local businessman who wants to build a small dam near the waterfall that would not only ruin the falls, but also the entire ambience of the village. If you have a vehicle and a decent map look for the villages of **Šćipe, Kute** and **Here**. Šćipe is the furthest away but situated in the magical highlands between **Bitovnja** and **Vranica mountains**. The locals are very friendly and the hilly terrain above the village is great for walking, mushroom picking and finding countless medicinal herbs.

WEST BOSNIA

West Bosnia has strong political and cultural ties with western Herzegovina. For this reason, we've tagged it on to the Herzegovina section, but many locations will be shown on the map on pages 280–1. Although this area is not a geographical part of Herzegovina, many of its residents consider themselves part of the Herzegovina community. The entire area falls under the Federation Canton of Herceg-Bosna and has a majority Croatian Catholic population. Livno is the cultural and political centre of this vast area. West Bosnia has a very low population density, and long open valleys and unpopulated mountains and hills cover most of the region. The Herceg-Bosna Canton is ideal for long bike rides, paragliding, caving, walking and hiking, as well as the many watersports available on Buško and Blidinje lakes.

The musical traditions of the region are unique. It is here that the *ganga* and Bećarac styles, coupled with the hand-carved *gusle*, cry out and tell of the hardships and resistance of the *hajduks,* who opposed Turkish rule. There is even a village in the Blidinje Nature Park that declared itself independent from Bosnia and Herzegovina, calling itself the Hajdučka Republika or Republic of the Rebels. They created their own seal, don't pay taxes and have their own passports.

The staff at the **Tourist Information** centre (*Trg Kralja Tomislava bb; 034 201 104; 08.00–16.00 Mon–Fri*) speak English and can direct you to attractions and lodging.

LIVNO Prince Mutimir's **Povelja Charter** from 28 September 892 is celebrated as the birthday of the town of Livno. However, as in many areas in Bosnia and Herzegovina, archaeological research in and around Livno has uncovered human settlements from more than 4,000 years ago. Many of these finds are located at **Duman**, a large karst cave that is the source of the **River Bistrica**. This source greatly resembles the one found in Blagaj where the Buna River originates. On the high, steep cliffs of **Teber** there are also the same type of caves as seen in Blagaj. It is thought that the indigenous Illyrian tribes built the first fortifications atop the cliffs, and the Romans, Slavs and Turks later reinforced them. The great rush of water from the caves made it an ideal location for powering mills. The Ottomans later built a lovely stone arched bridge over the Duma.

The town itself is an interesting blend of Dalmatian, Ottoman and socialist structures. Apart from some good restaurants and cafés, the only thing worth seeing inside the town is the **Franciscan Museum and Gorica Gallery** (*Gorička bb; 034 200 922;* **e** *info@fmgg-livno.com;* **w** *fmgg-livno.com; 09.00–15.00 Mon–Sat*). Gorica certainly ranks among the country's best Franciscan galleries and has a permanent exhibition of the works of Gabriel Jurkić. Jurkić was one of the most famous painters in the history of Bosnia and Herzegovina; his work can also be seen at the National Gallery in Sarajevo. The museum traces the history of the church and its followers in fine Franciscan fashion. The **Franciscan Monastery** (*Gorička cesta bb; 034 200 311*) is in the same compound, but separated from the museum and gallery. It is a beautiful and interesting place to visit.

Livno has a long-standing custom of producing a fabulous hard yellow cheese called **Livanjski Sir**. You don't have to go to Livno to get it, but if you do at least you'll know you're getting the real McCoy. It goes marvelously well with a fine bottle of Herzegovina red wine and some local *pršut* (dry-cured ham). There are quite a few restaurants in town serving the local cuisine. For adventurous types, the countryside around Livno is famous for its wild horses. Ask around – someone may be able to help point you in their direction.

Getting there and away

By bus There are daily buses from Mostar and Split to Livno (*Želimira Županа bb; 034 201 706*). Livno is also a transit stop for some traffic from Sarajevo and central Bosnia, namely Vitez and Travnik, going to Split via Bugojno, Kupres, Livno and Kamensko, along the M16.

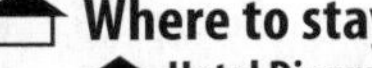

Where to stay

Hotel Dinara (60 rooms) Trg branitelja bb; 034 201 054. Situated in the heart of Livno, the Dinara has been renovated with modern facilities. **$$**

Hotel Park (30 rooms, 10 apts) Kneza Mutimira 56; 034 202 149; **e** hotel.park.livno@gmail.com; **w** hotelpark-livno.ba. By far the best choice. The entire hotel has been renovated with modern facilities. Each room has sat TV, but only the apts have a minibar (they also come with a mini-kitchen). There are a few apts with small jacuzzis in the bathrooms. For your entertainment, there is an excellent pool/billiards hall, & within the hotel complex is the Night Flight disco. The restaurant serves international & traditional dishes. **$$**

Pansion San Domobranska 3; 034 202 018. A simpler & cheaper alternative. The rooms are nice & clean with TV & plenty of hot water. **$**

Where to eat and drink

Restoran M&B Zagrebačka 22; 034 202 280, 08.00–23.00. The name may be uninspiring but the food & service are good. Prices are about average for BiH, anywhere from 8KM to 12KM for a main course. With wine, you can expect to spend 50KM for 2 people. **$–$$**

Pivnica Kneza Mutimira 14; 034 205 071; 08.00–23.00 daily. This is a European-style beer hall serving local beers including dark & light Livanjsko pivo, from Livno itself. The pub fare for lunch & dinner is decent. **$**

TOMISLAVGRAD There is not much to attract tourists to Tomislavgrad, southeast of Livno. The most appealing aspect of this sleepy town of a few thousand is its natural surroundings. The largest storage lake in Europe, **Lake Buško**, whose surface covers 57km^2, borders the town. For anglers there are more fish than one can handle. Carp catches of 10kg are not uncommon! The wind from the long valleys of **Livanjsko** and **Duvanjsko Fields** provides optimum conditions for parasailing. Water skiing, rowing and canoeing are among the watersports that the tourism association here is developing. There is an annual canoeing and kayaking competition held in August for central European countries – it has generated great popularity with the locals. You can camp along the banks of the lake, and there are a few wooded areas that are good for setting up camp. The entire area is completely clear of mines. Tomislavgrad is also the gatekeeper to **Blidinje Nature Park** (see below). The entrance to the park is marked from the outskirts of town towards **Lipa**. Don't let the dirt track confuse you; good gravel roads connect a large portion of the park. Regular buses to Tomislavgrad travel from Livno and Mostar. There are no buses that travel through Blidinje. **Eco Village Grabovica** [map, pages 280–1] (*Grabovica bb, Prisoje; 034 366 851, 034 366 020;* **e** *info@ecoselograbovica.com;* **w** *ecoselograbovica.com;* **$$**) is located on Buško Lake near the border with Croatia, where the Bosnian Alpine and Dalmatian-Mediterranean climates intersect at an altitude of 700m. This is a higher-end facility, and certainly one of the best in the country. The Eco Village is surrounded by mountains, making summer nights fresh and comfortable for sleeping during the hottest parts of the year. The tasteful combination of wood, stone and ceramic mosaic gives the apartments an archaic look, but all are equipped with modern amenities. The Eco Village restaurant serves homemade eco food inspired by rich regional traditions, such as *meze* with smoked meat, cheese, bread and beignets, roasted veal and lamb *ispod saca*, a variety of grilled dishes, and many soups and stews. This child-friendly establishment also has a small petting zoo with domestic and wild animals such as rabbits, deer, peacocks and hogs. However, the main animal attraction is the Equestrian Club, suitable for riders of all ages (one class with instructor costs 25KM). The facility can organise long-distance horseback riding, mountain biking and hiking, as it is on the new Via Dinarica mega-trail that connects the Dinaric Alps mountain chain throughout the region.

BLIDINJE NATURE PARK (*JP Park prirode Blidinje, Masna Luka, Posušje; 039 718 514/5;* **e** *info@blidinje.net;* **w** *blidinje.net; all year; no entrance fee*) We've included a map of the park (page 238), as it can be a rather confusing experience trying to make head or tail of the dirt tracks that seem to go in every direction, and with few or no signposts. There are many access roads to the park, but it's best to stick to the three main roads via **Rakitno** northeast from **Posušje**, **Lipa** from **Tomislavgrad**, and due west from **Jablanica** via **Doljani**.

The open and barren valley leading into the park is a result of the past two ice ages. The melting glaciers from Čvrsnica created this massive valley between the **Čvrsnica** and **Vran mountains**. **Blidinje Lake** is the direct result of a glacial retreat located at an altitude of 1,184m in the valley below. This runway for ice, water and debris did not, however, manage to stop a wide range of life forms from prospering here. To contrast some of the rocky and seemingly lifeless slopes are thick forests of pine, including the endemic white bark pine at **Masna Luka** called *Pinus leuco dermis*. Three types of wild thyme and dozens of wildflowers cover the valley and mountainsides in the spring and summer. The 3–5km valley, situated at an elevation ranging from 1,150–1,300m, is dotted with the trademark *stećci* tombstones from medieval times. It is not clear how long human settlements have existed here, but research began when Blidinje received nature park status. Traces of Illyrian graves and Roman roads indicate that Blidinje has been settled for at least 2,500 years. The large necropolis at **Dugo Polje** indicates that the waves of Slavs that came in the 7th century also made this area their home.

The park is set in long sweeping valleys. To the north and southeast are the 2,000m+ peaks of Vran and Čvrsnica. **Pločna** on Čvrsnica is the highest peak in Herzegovina at 2,228m. This is a main hub for the Via Dinarica White Trail and an important trail head towards Central Herzegovina high mountains and the Dinara Mountain range that BiH shares with neighbouring Croatia. The peak is unfortunately a military installation and is out of bounds to hikers. The park itself is free of mines, with well-marked trails. It's best to visit the motel by the ski-lifts at **Risovac** for information. They will also have information about the park, its history and the **Franciscan monastery** that is located within the park and open to visitors.

Croatian people believe that Blidinje is a gift from God. There are few things in this country that aren't politicised, and these include the wonders of nature. The park's ever-so-tiny population is Croatian. Houses here are traditional shepherd homes with straw roofs that are mainly used during the spring and summer seasons. Winter is harsh and cold in these parts. The **ski centre** at Risovac (*Masna Luka 29, Posušje;* *039 718 514;* e *info@blidinje.biz;* w *blidinje.biz*) opens in winter. There is the small **Motel Risovac** nearby that sleeps 40 (*Zelenike bb;* *039 718 580;* f *motelrisovac;* **$–$$**). The ski resort also features a restaurant, **Staza**, which is open year-round (*Risovac bb;* *039 718 515;* f *restoran.Staza.Blidinje;* *08.00–23.00 daily*). Risovac is a popular ski destination for folks from Mostar and Split, as well as the local population from Livno and Tomislavgrad. There are four slopes.

Where to stay and eat *Map, page 238.*

Hotel Hajdučke Vrleti (25 rooms) Vran planina bb, Rakitno; 039 718 522; e info@hajduckevrleti-blidinje.com; w hajduckevrleti-blidinje.com. This is a facility with very nice, albeit simple rooms. The traditional restaurant is excellent. **$–$$**

KUPRES [map, pages 280–1] The highest settlement in west Bosnia, northeast of Livno, is home to the country's most rugged inhabitants. By rugged, I mean that the people of Kupres live a challenging lifestyle closely tied to nature and the elements. At 1,200m above sea level, Kupres is covered in snow for at least five months of the year. The long and bare valley of **Kupreško Polje** creates harsh winter conditions. It also makes Kupres a main winter recreation centre in western Bosnia. **Hotel Adria Ski** (page 239) is the main centre for skiing in the area, along with **Risovac** in

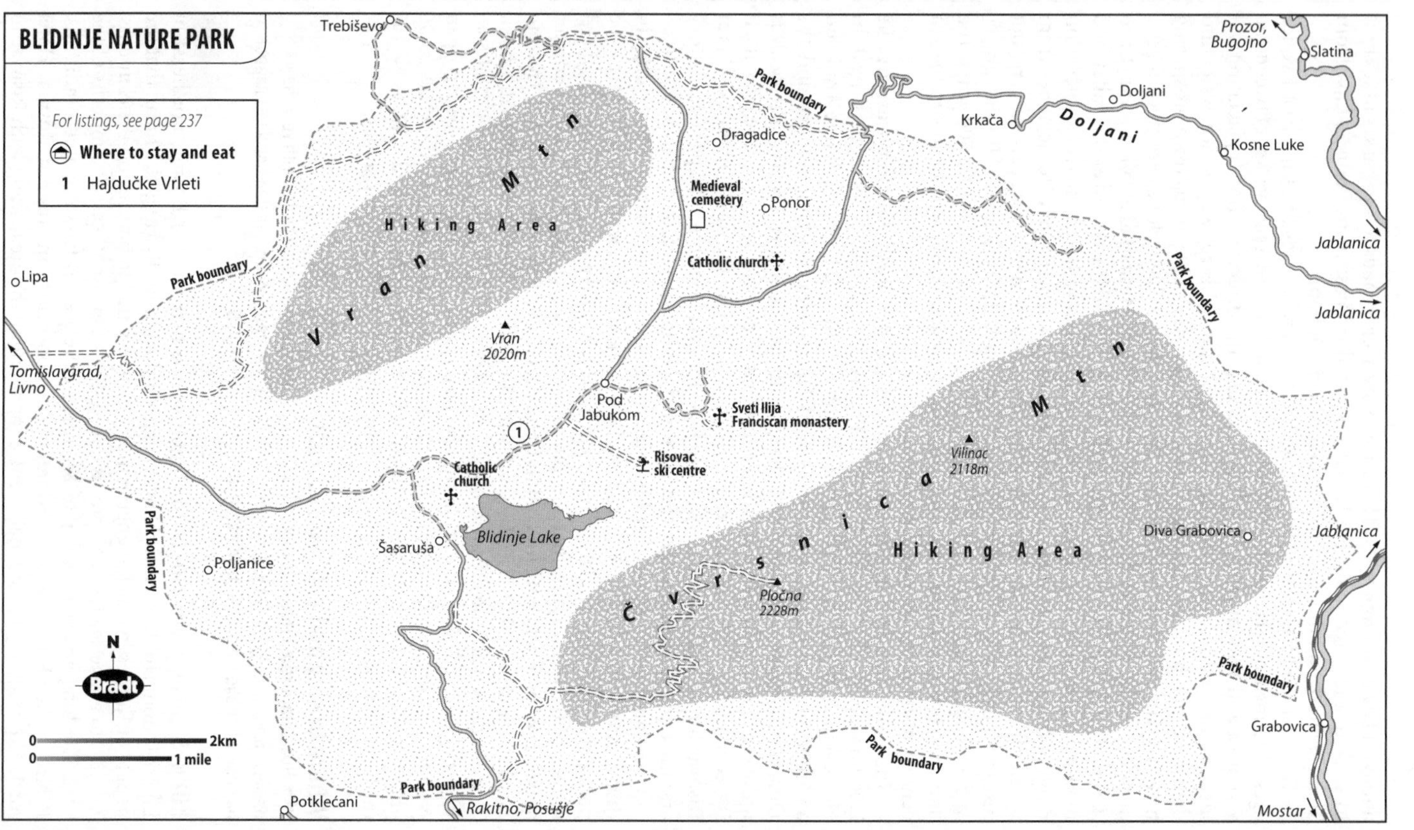
BLIDINJE NATURE PARK
For listings, see page 237
Where to stay and eat
1 Hajdučke Vrleti
Trebiševo
Lipa
Tomislavgrad, Livno
Park boundary
Vran Mtn
Hiking Area
Vran 2020m
Dragadice
Medieval cemetery
Ponor
Catholic church
Pod Jabukom
Sveti Ilija Franciscan monastery
Risovac ski centre
Catholic church
Blidinje Lake
Šasaruša
Poljanice
Potklećani
Rakitno, Posušje
Krkača
Doljani
Doljani
Kosne Luke
Prozor, Bugojno
Slatina
Jablanica
Jablanica
Jablanica
Čvrsnica Mtn
Hiking Area
Vilinac 2118m
Pločna 2228m
Diva Grabovica
Grabovica
Mostar
N
Bradt
0 2km
0 1 mile

Blidinje Park (pages 236–7). The hotel has been renovated to attract guests from the Dalmatian coast looking for a nearby ski vacation. The ski-lift runs right out of the back of the hotel. The slopes aren't steep or super fast, but the opportunity to ski in the middle of nowhere is, for some, very appealing.

A very rich aspect of Bosnian Croat culture has emerged in this tiny town between Bugojno and Livno. Many of the traditions that are performed only at folk shows in other places are regularly practised here. The old methods of farming are celebrated each May on the first Sunday with the *Strljanica* competition. Expansive fields of long grass are hacked down with traditional sickles to see who is the most skilled in quick cutting. It may seem funny but try it out and you will see not only the skill needed but also the tremendous back and forearm strength that the 'sport' requires. Kupres is known throughout the country for this annual event. Horse races, an almost forgotten rural event, also happen each year in the fields of Kupres. The traditional Ganga and Bećarac song of the *hajduks* can often be heard echoing through the valley.

Owing to the high altitude, many of the local residents cannot rely on farming for a living, although they often partake in sheep farming. Most folks from in and around Kupres will attest to the great grilled lamb and sheep's cheese prepared in the traditional Kupres way. If you have the opportunity to eat with a local family, don't pass it up.

Getting there and away Kupres is a transit town from central Bosnia to Livno and the Adriatic coast. Daily buses to and from Vitez and Travnik stop in Kupres if requested.

Where to stay and eat

Hotel Adria Ski [map, pages 280–1] (25+ rooms) Čajuša bb; 034 275 100; e info@adriaski.net; w adriaski.net. This is an old-school hotel that has received a much-needed face-lift. The facilities are decent & conveniently located next to the ski-lifts. **$$**

Apartments Rebrina Zagrebačka 4; 052 816 122; m 098 324 633. This is a small pension in the centre of Kupres. It still maintains a natural setting & offers horse riding & walking in this beautiful & wild area. **$**

Pansion Kraljica Splitska 1; 034 274 568; 034 351 070; e pansion.kraljica@gmail.com. Just 3km from the ski centre, with modern facilities. It's a very comfy place, in the centre of Kupres, with a homely feel to it. **$**

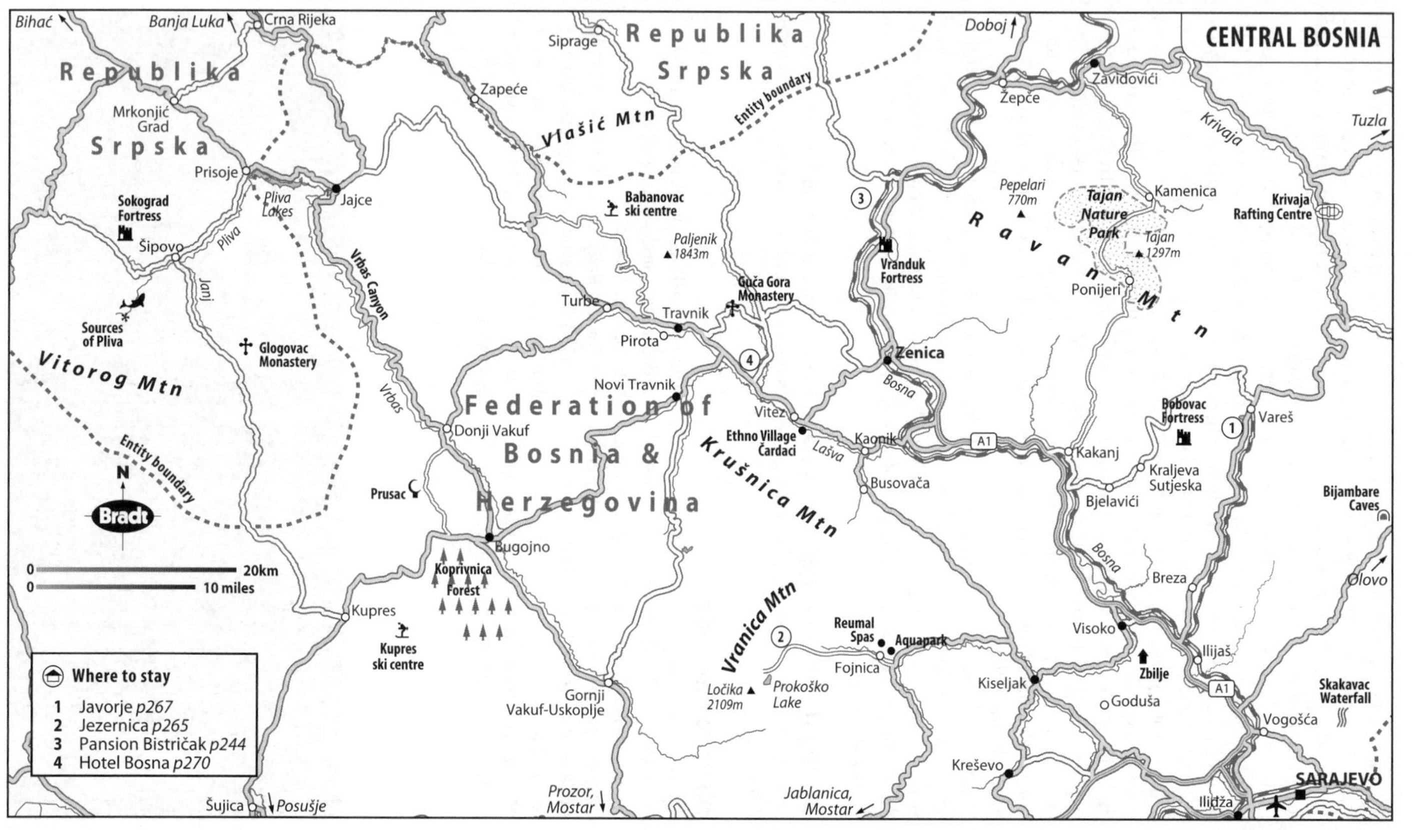
CENTRAL BOSNIA
Bihać
Banja Luka
Crna Rijeka
Siprage
Republika Srpska
Doboj
Tuzla
Republika Srpska
Mrkonjić Grad
Zapeće
Vlašić Mtn
Entity boundary
Žepče
Zavidovići
Krivaja
Prisoje
Jajce
Pliva Lakes
Sokograd Fortress
Šipovo
Pliva
Janj
Babanovac ski centre
Paljenik 1843m
Pepelari 770m
Tajan Nature Park
Tajan 1297m
Kamenica
Krivaja Rafting Centre
Ravan Mtn
Vranduk Fortress
Ponijeri
Vrbas Canyon
Sources of Pliva
Glogovac Monastery
Turbe
Travnik
Pirota
Guča Gora Monastery
Zenica
Vitorog Mtn
Vrbas
Novi Travnik
Federation of Bosnia & Herzegovina
Bosna
Vitez
Ethno Village Čardaci
Lašva
Kaonik
A1
Kakanj
Bobovac Fortress
Vareš
Donji Vakuf
Entity boundary
N
Bradt
Prusac
Krušnica Mtn
Busovača
Kraljeva Sutjeska
Bjelavići
Bijambare Caves
Bugojno
0 20km
0 10 miles
Koprivnica Forest
Bosna
Breza
Olovo
Kupres
Kupres ski centre
Vranica Mtn
Reumal Spas
Aquapark
Fojnica
Visoko
Ilijaš
Zbilje
Where to stay
1 Javorje p267
2 Jezernica p265
3 Pansion Bistričak p244
4 Hotel Bosna p270
Gornji Vakuf-Uskoplje
Ločika 2109m
Prokoško Lake
Kiseljak
Goduša
A1
Skakavac Waterfall
Vogošća
Kreševo
SARAJEVO
Šujica
Posušje
Prozor, Mostar
Jablanica, Mostar
Ilidža

Central Bosnia

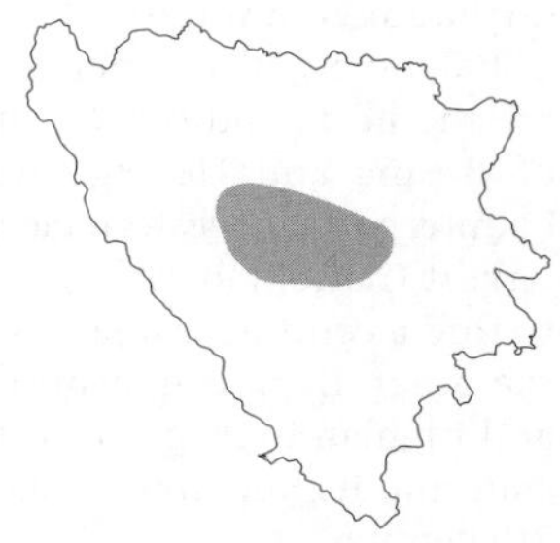

Central Bosnia has a long and remarkable history. The delicate and fascinating melange of Western and Eastern cultures marks the true character of the region. This tiny kingdom, with its fortresses perched atop lush, green, rolling hills, offers a warm and hospitable experience in the heart of Bosnia's cultural heritage.

Despite the dire political and economic situation in this region, life in central Bosnia has taken great strides since the conflict. Ordinary people for the most part get along and economic and community ties are steadily being re-established. It is quite clear that one community cannot survive without the other and that the similarities in language, culture, traditions and ways of life will overcome the few differences. For the outsider it is probably impossible to see the divides in some communities and even more difficult to understand why they exist. As the birthplace of the Bosnian state, this region plays a major role in the cultural, natural and historical heritage of past and present-day Bosnia and Herzegovina. A major highway is being constructed in BiH and most of it cuts through this region, which will surely make exploring central Bosnia much easier than before.

HISTORY

The central part of Bosnia and Herzegovina was the seat of the Bosnian state in medieval times. Known as the **Bosna Srebrena** (Silver Bosna) region it was the political, cultural and religious heart of Bosnia. All the Bosnian kings resided in central Bosnia, from Bobovac and Kraljeva Sutjeska to the castle at Jajce that fell to the Turks in 1528. The unique 'heretic' Bosnian Church was the spiritual backbone of the small Slav communities that dotted the lush and green countryside until the 14th century. By 1340 the Franciscans had established their first order in Bosnia, and in a very short space of time Catholicism spread and monasteries in Kraljeva Sutjeska, Visoko, Kreševo and Fojnica were built.

With the arrival of the Turks in the mid 15th century, Ottoman and oriental culture asserted its influence in places like Travnik, Visoko, Donji Vakuf and Jajce. Travnik became not only the main city in central Bosnia, but also the centre of the Ottoman Empire's establishment in Bosnia and Herzegovina. *Mahalas* (neighbourhoods/quarters) sprang up in many towns, and the spread of Islam had a major impact on life in Bosnia. Small settlements developed into towns and cities, and the once isolated mountain communities became more interconnected. The Lašva Valley was a main trading route from Dalmatia, Serbia and beyond. Travnik, once heralded as the European Istanbul, soon became known for its magnificent oriental architecture and bustling trade centres.

Of all the ethnically mixed communities in Bosnia, this region, in particular, maintained a balance of Catholic and Muslim inhabitants (with a much smaller

Orthodox community). The Catholics view themselves as the only continual line of defenders of the ancient Christian Bosnian state. The Bosnian Franciscans are the heart and soul of this sentiment and remain loyal to the preservation of Bosnia and Herzegovina's sovereignty, unlike many of their Franciscan counterparts in western Herzegovina. The parish of Srebrena Bosna remains the largest Catholic parish in Bosnia. In short, it would be difficult or impossible to find a central Bosnia town or community that hasn't intimately meshed with the other. Exploring central Bosnia's ancient fortresses, monasteries, mosques and highland villages is a journey into the very heart of the original Bosnian state and its long line of Slavic ancestors that have settled these lands since the 7th century.

GETTING THERE AND AWAY

With a highly efficient bus system, both public and private, every destination in central Bosnia has daily buses from any of the main centres, namely Zenica, Travnik, Kiseljak, Vitez and Bugojno (see **w** centrotrans.com). Daily buses from Zagreb and Bihać travel via Jajce, Donji Vakuf, Travnik and Vitez to Sarajevo. The only city in central Bosnia on the train route is Zenica, where trains stop on the route between Sarajevo and Zagreb, also joining up with Banja Luka. With the exception of Kreševo, Kraljeva Sutjeska, Fojnica and Vranica Mountain, all towns in the guide are located on **main roads** and are clearly marked on any map of Bosnia and Herzegovina. Zenica and other towns are located on a newly constructed highway linked to Sarajevo, making central Bosnia more accessible than ever before.

SUGGESTED ITINERARIES

THREE-DAY EXCURSION

Day 1 Visit Visoko's old town and walk up Visočica Hill to the ruins of the royal fortress; visit Goduša village and the handicraft exhibition – traditional lunch there. Short drive to and overnight in Kraljeva Sutjeska.

Day 2 Morning hike to Bobovac Fortress, return to Kraljeva Sutjeska for lunch. Afternoon tour of the town, including Dusper House, mosque and Franciscan monastery. Travel to and overnight in Travnik.

Day 3 City tour of Travnik, including old fortress and Ivo Andrić House. Lunch at Plava Voda. Return to Sarajevo.

THREE-DAY EXCURSION

Day 1 Visit Vranduk Fortress on the River Bosna. Walk through village and picnic lunch in the fortress courtyard. Travel to and overnight in Travnik.

DAY 2 City tour of Travnik. Lunch at Plava Voda. Afternoon visit to Guča Gora Monastery or Mount Vlašić. Dinner at Ivo Andrić House. Travel to Donji Vakuf and overnight in Hotel Vrbas.

Day 3 Travel to Prusac. Village tour of Prusac, fortress, mosque and handicraft workshops. Lunch in Prusac. Afternoon walk to pilgrimage site in forest. Return to Sarajevo.

FIVE-DAY EXCURSION

Day 1 Visit Visoko's old town and walk up Visočica Hill to the ruins of the royal fortress; visit Goduša village and the handicraft exhibition – traditional lunch there. Short drive to and overnight in Kraljeva Sutjeska.

Day 2 Morning hike to Bobovac Fortress, return to Kraljeva Sutjeska for lunch. Afternoon tour of the town, including Dusper House, mosque and Franciscan monastery. One more night in Kraljeva Sutjeska.

Day 3 Visit Vranduk Fortress on the River Bosna. Walk through village and picnic lunch in the fortress courtyard. Travel to and overnight in Travnik.

Day 4 City tour of Travnik. Lunch at Plava Voda. Afternoon visit to Guča Gora Monastery or Mount Vlašić. Dinner at Ivo Andrić House. Travel to Donje Vakuf and overnight in Hotel Vrbas.

Day 5 Travel to Prusac. Village tour of Prusac, fortress, mosque and handicraft workshops. Lunch in Prusac. Afternoon walk to pilgrimage site in forest. Return to Sarajevo.

ZENICA

Zenica is the largest and most industrial town in central Bosnia. It is the political, administrative and cultural centre of the **Zenica-Doboj Canton**. There is more to Zenica than the rather intrusive industrial zone that dominates the city's image. Mostly known for its massive steel industry, the city grew significantly during Tito's Yugoslavia as many apartment blocks were erected to house the growing mining communities. The city's pre-war population has slightly diminished, but at the last count there were approximately 120,000 people in Zenica, making it the fourth-largest city in the country. Peeling back the socialist layer of crude architecture and bulky industry reveals the old Zenica and the true heart of the city – a quaint downtown district with mosques, churches of Catholic and Orthodox denomination and a Jewish synagogue.

I can't say that Zenica is a town you *must* see while visiting Bosnia and Herzegovina. Its industrial look and noticeable pollution from the steel factory awkwardly located near the city centre do tend to put foreign visitors off, but for those of you who opt to take a closer look, you will certainly find something worthwhile.

GETTING THERE Zenica is located just 70km northwest of Sarajevo along the M-17 and is a main transit route for both trains and buses. The bus and railway stations are at the same location. All of central Bosnia and the northeast is covered by a very efficient public and private bus system. The railway station is along the main Sarajevo–Zagreb route, with one train daily to Zenica from Sarajevo (7.5KM/12KM) leaving at 10.21. From Zenica, there is also one daily train to and from Zagreb (departs from Zenica at 11.45). Sarajevo, Tuzla and Mostar have frequent, daily buses to Zenica. A new highway (A1) now connects Sarajevo with Zenica, making the trip less than 1 hour by car or a little over an hour by bus. Not all buses travel on the highway, so make sure you check the timetable before purchasing a ticket, otherwise the trip can take up to 3 hours. A one-way ticket costs around 8KM, and return fare is about 11KM.

Zenica Bus Station Bulevar Kralja Tvrtka; 032 241 253

Zenica Train Station Stanični trg; 032 404 911

TOURIST INFORMATION AND LOCAL TOUR OPERATORS The **Tourism Board of the Zenica-Doboj Canton**, located in the centre of Zenica (*Maršala Tita; 032 441 050;* **e** *info@zedoturizam.ba;* **w** *zedoturizam.ba*), is not an information centre as such, but they can offer some advice in English, particularly about accommodation.

Bisstours Nikole Tesle 4; 032 246 306; **e** bbabic@biss-tours.ba; **w** biss-tours.ba. Among the offers of this travel agency is a 9-day tour through BiH (Sarajevo–Zenica–Tešanj–Travnik–Bihać–Mostar), as well as programmes of religious tourism (Međugorje visit).

Extreme Sports Club Scorpio Nurije Pozderca 11; **m** 061 608 130; **e** info@scorpio.ba; **w** scorpio.ba. Offers a wide variety of sports: rock climbing, mountain biking, paragliding, canyoning, hiking, ski touring & ice climbing.

WHERE TO STAY

Hotel Dubrovnik (34 rooms) Školska 10; 032 202 700; **w** hoteldubrovnik.ba. Excellent rooms, décor, service, location & amenities make Dubrovnik one of the best places to stay in town. Luckily the past few years have seen some welcome additions to the town's accommodation offerings. Dubrovnik is a top-notch hotel with all the amenities to make it an exceptionally comfortable & affordable 4-star hotel. The restaurant, wine bar & microbrewery make the drinking & dining experience there second to none in Zenica. **$$$$**

Pansion Fontana (17 rooms, 5 apts) Zacarina 17; **m** 061 176 686; **e** info@pansion-fontana.ba or fontana@zenica.ba; www.pansion-fontana.ba. In the centre of town. Offers B&B accommodation. **$$–$$$**

Hotel Dom Penzionera (60 rooms, 12 apts) 1 Zeničke brigade 1d; 032 424 284; **e** info@visitmycountry.net. The original plan for Dom Penzionera was for it to be a retirement home. When that plan fell through, it was converted into one of the nicer hotels in town. The rooms are spacious & have modern fittings. **$$**

Hotel Internacional (59 rooms, 4 apts) Bulevar Kulina bana 29; 032 240 150; **e** hotel.internacional@bih.net.ba; **w** hinternacional.com.ba. The Internacional is the best of 3 socialist-era hotels on the same road. **$$**

Hotel Zenica (85 rooms) Kamberovića Polje bb; 032 209 600; **w** hotelzenica.ba. A comfortable, standard international-style hotel with a swimming pool, sauna, free Wi-Fi, pastry shop, 2 restaurants, lovely garden & in walking distance from the centre. **$$**

Pansion Bistričak [map, page 240] (34 rooms, 2 apts) Bistričak 16a, Nemila; 032 678 584; **w** hinternacional.com.ba/bistricak.html. Located at the Bistričak picnic place. It is some 25km away from Zenica at an altitude of 432m. **$**

WHERE TO EAT AND DRINK

Traditional restaurants and pizzerias are what you'll mostly find in Zenica.

Restoran Dubrovnik Školska 10; 032 202 700; 07.00–23.30 Mon–Sat. Inspired by the cuisine of Dubrovnik, this is Zenica's only sea-fish-speciality restaurant. Try the baked squid with a fine wine from their impressive list. This restaurant falls under the domain of Hotel Dubrovnik's wings. **$$–$$$**

Salčinović M Tarabara 8; 032 285 867; 07.00–23.00 daily. This family-owned & operated restaurant is one in a small chain the Salčinović family have opened in Zenica. They are known for their grilled meat & fish dishes. **$$**

Trubadur Hotel Dubrovnik, Školska 10; 032 202 700; 19.00–midnight daily. Trubadur is arguably the city's best & most luxurious restaurant. The cuisine is largely Mediterranean & French. The service, wine & dessert are as good as the main menu. **$$**

Miris Dunja Sarajevska 53; **m** 061 402 134; 07.00–23.00 Mon–Sat. A classic Zenica dining destination, this traditional restaurant with a tasteful ethno décor serves the best of BiH's classic cuisine. Try the *klepe*, *sogan dolma* or *bamija* – best enjoyed in the large summer garden, which seats more than 75. $–$$

Restaurant Fontana Krivače St, Zacarina 17; 032 462 999; e restoran_fontana@yahoo.com; 08.00–22.00 daily. It is somewhat off the beaten track, with an attractive *mahala* ambience. The food is fantastic, & the terrace along the stream is on the sunny south side. They also have a few rooms with modern facilities. $–$$

Restaurant Kod Kasima Dr Abdulaha Aska Borića St, next to Gatto (see below). One of 3 restaurants that the proprietor Kasim has opened. They serve traditional Bosnian meat dishes, mainly lamb & beef, in many tasty forms. $–$$

Beslić Travnička cesta 45; 032 406 871; 10.00–22.00 daily. Known as the BBQ man, Vahid Beslić knows his meat. With baked veal, mixed-meat platters & his locally famous *ćevapi* with *kajmak*, Beslić is a carnivore's heaven. $

Ladjana Londza bb; 032 405 859; 08.00–19.00 daily. A perfect quick-&-easy lunch spot for pitta, Ladjana makes all types of fresh baked versions, including spinach, cheese, minced meat & potato pie. $

ENTERTAINMENT AND NIGHTLIFE

Da Vinci's Pub Branilaca Bosne 2; e jezz-lion@hotmail.com; DaVincisPubZenica; 07.00–23.00 Sun–Thu, 07.00–midnight Fri–Sat. Popular among the younger crowds because of live music and/or DJs on weekends, this place can get packed & smoky. You can drink well, & experience the real Zenica.

The Gatto-Club Dr Abdulaha Aska Borića St. A microbrewery that has live local rock music every w/end. It is the best bar in town. The beer & music are great, although like most good bars in Bosnia, it's very smoky.

Pivnica Libertas Školska 10; 032 202 731; 07.00–23.30 Mon–Sat. Part of Hotel Dubrovnik, this is a relaxed pub to enjoy light or dark beer, & occasionally hear live music.

OTHER PRACTICALITIES If you're looking to shop for more than basics, it is better to go to nearby Sarajevo where options are plentiful.

Hospital

Cantonal Hospital of Zenica Crkvice 67; 032 405 133

Pharmacy

Mr Weiss Apoteka Adolfa Golbergera 6; 032 401 007; 24 hours

Police station

Trg Bosne i Hercegovine 1; 032 449 249

Bank

$ **Sparkasse Bank** Maršala Tita br 9. ATM.

Post Office

Masarykova 46; 032 466 110; 07.00–20.00 Mon–Fri, 07.00–15.00 Sat

Taxi

Zenica Taxi m 061 414 614; w zenicataxi.com

WHAT TO SEE AND DO The most attractive part of town is known as *stara čaršija*, meaning the old quarter. This has been the main gathering place for locals since Ottoman times. In the square between Serdarevića and Maršala Tita streets are the **Čaršijska Džamija**, **Madrasa**, **Hadžimazića House** and the **Austrian fountain**. The Hadžimazića House (*09.00–16.30 Mon–Fri*) is similar to the Svrzina kuća in Sarajevo (page 139): an old *beg* family house that has been preserved in its original form. The entire square is lined with cafés and competes with the **Kamberovića Polje** walkway across the Bosna River as the most popular pedestrian area in town. The **synagogue** on Jevrejska Street has been converted into the **City Museum and Art Gallery** (*Jevrejska 1; 032 209 511; 08.00–20.00 Mon–Sat; entrance free*). It is a very basic 'museum' of the old synagogue with a hall for local art exhibitions.

THE IRON FOOTBALL TEAM

What guidebook would be complete without at least a touch of sports history? And, of course, that would be about football. Central Bosnia is home to only one Premier League team, and that is Čelik from Zenica. Zenica is known for several things; one of them is fanatical Čelik fans. Most opposing teams dread playing in Bilino Polje, the team's home stadium, as the home team is hard to beat there. The ground is unique in Bosnia in that there is no athletics track around the perimeter, so fans are close up to the pitch. Here's a short history of Čelik and their famous stadium.

NK Čelik (Nogometni Klub Čelik) are the powerhouse team of football in central Bosnia. The name Čelik means 'Iron', which is meant to symbolise the strength and power of the club – but it more likely stems from the fact that Zenica has a massive iron ore and steel industry. Don't try to convince Čelik fans of that, though. During Yugoslav times, Čelik was almost always in the Yugoslav Premier League. With that structure defunct, Čelik is now in the Football Association of Bosnia and Herzegovina and is a member of its Premier League. The club has won three Premier League titles in the past but has begun to slip, and what seems to be holding them together as a Premier League team is the uncompromising number of supporters at every NK Čelik home match. They have by far the highest attendance levels and the BiH national side has even begun to play its home matches away from Sarajevo to lure opponents into Čelik's den. Win or lose, you don't want to be an opposition supporter at Bilino Polje.

- Home stadium: Bilino Polje (18,000 capacity), Zenica
- Team strip: black and dark red
- Address: Bulevar Kulina bana 28E, Zenica, Bosnia and Herzegovina

On the side of town where Branilaca Bosne and Dr Abdulaha Aska Borića streets meet are the **Svetog Ilije Catholic Church** and school. Behind Branilaca Bosne on Travnička cesta is the **old Orthodox church**. I've never found it open but nevertheless the architecture is admirable, even from only the outside. Along the **Kočeva Stream**, not far from the church is the **Sučića Mlin**, an old family mill that is still functional.

As with all Bosnian towns there are also several *izletište* in proximity to Zenica. *Izletište* is a difficult word to translate, the best phrase being 'recreation area'. The most visited one is at **Bistričak**, about 30km north of Zenica. You'll find Zeničani (people from Zenica) along the clear Ograjina River preparing a *roštilj* (barbecue), playing volleyball and football, and enjoying the sunny fields. There is a small but very popular bed and breakfast named after the recreation area with a massive terrace that seats 100 people.

Mountains The surrounding mountains of **Lisac**, **Pepelari**, **Vepar**, **Zmajevac** and **Smetovi** have nice hiking areas. The **Smetovi Mountaineering Hostel** (contact Scorpio Extreme Sports Club, see below) is generally known as the lungs of Zenica. During the heyday of the steel industry, Smetovi was a welcome escape from the air pollution. Now it serves a similar purpose, although the air pollution in Zenica has been reduced to almost nil. There are well-marked trails, a restaurant, great walking paths and even a mini ski-lift for beginners.

Scorpio Extreme Sports Club (*Smetovi bb (Recreation Centre) & Nurije Pozderca 11 (Office);* **m** *061 608 130;* **e** *scorpioze@yahoo.com;* **w** *scorpio.ba*) organises hiking, biking, alpine climbing and paragliding on and around Smetovi. The club's organiser, Edin Durmo, also arranges high alpine climbs in Herzegovina and tour skiing on Vlašić Mountain. Scorpio also has a recreation centre and mountain lodge on Smetovi, where you can take paragliding lessons or just chill out in the comfy lodge.

One of the numerous benefits of the socialist period was the number of large recreation areas that were built for workers. The health workers' association had a lovely mountain hut built for them on **Pepelari Mountain** at 770m. Located a good 48km from Zenica, it has long been a popular holiday spot for those seeking the peace and quiet of the pine forests and rolling hills. For some reason, the mountain lodge even has satellite television. The lodge can receive about 40 guests and also has two special suites that can be rented (*032 679 056;* **$**).

Tajan-Lisac Mountain Hostel (*032 281 250;* **$**) is my personal favourite. It is run by the Tajan Mountain Association and is the only lodge that is not accessible by vehicle. There are big open fields surrounded by large beech trees and the two-part lodge is perched 1,000m above sea level on a ridge that overlooks the surrounding mountains. It's a great getaway and is only 12km from Zenica. The phone may or may not be answered by an English-speaking person. Better to contact the tourism board or the local tour operators that work in the area (page 252). Directions for this remote hostel are available from the Mountain Association (*Bulevar kralja Tvrtka 13, Zenica*).

VRANDUK *Enes Škrgo*

Vranduk holds significant importance in the region's history. It is a nest-like settlement with a fortress, built on an insurmountable cliff over the fast-flowing River Bosna. The history of the fortress is also the history of Vranduk. A long series of sieges and attacks, but also the wise decisions of famous military commanders like Eugene of Savoy to bypass the fort, caused various calamities for the inhabitants of the sleepy little village below. Yet anyone who has ever stood at the foot of the fortress or walked along its battlements has been impressed by the scenery and extraordinary experience that make Vranduk a part of the Bosnian 'Valley of Fortresses'. Every traveller, soldier, spy, priest and artist has been fascinated by that exciting touch of unusual nature and the architectural ingenuity of Bosnian architects and masons. Below are several extracts taken from travel books and journals, which speak of this old fortress and settlement.

> Vranduk and its surroundings are certainly the crown of all beauties of God's nature in the proud land of Bosnia. It is with excitement that anyone who has passed here at least once remembers and mentions this magnificent area, the magical passage and the divine God's nature that has strewed its dark mountain pearls around this place.
>
> *Baron Rudolf Maldini Wildenhainski*

> A winding road led up the steep slope of the mountain. Looking from its top, the Vranduk passage appeared deep in the valley, all covered with woods, and from that distance it seemed to have been veiled in velvet.
>
> *George Arbuthnot, English lieutenant, 1861*

> The goal of our trip was Vranduk, a small village situated above one of the turns of the river of Bosna, one of the most interesting places in the whole country. The station is located on the right, and the village on the left riverbank, and the only way to reach it

is by a log-canoe. The boatman, an important person, requested us to sit on the bottom of that primitive boat and he ferried us across the swollen river, turbid from the rain like the Tiber. It was along a narrow path that we then clambered to the top of the hill, where there stood the wooden houses of Vranduk, closely built and looking like groups of swallow nests. The place seemed to be completely deserted since all men had gone to tend flocks in the hills, and the few women that we saw hid their faces and ran away as we approached. There was no place where we could get some food or drinks. Yet, a crowd of children quickly realised that we wanted to tour the place, so one of them ran away and brought the key to the old fortress, a wonderful old ruin whose interior had turned into a park full of trees. We immediately realised what an important strategic position Vranduk used to have in the past, which has given it the name of 'the Gate of Bosnia'.

William Miller, historian

The Bosna River is the third-longest river in Bosnia and Herzegovina, and is considered one of the country's three major internal rivers, along with the Neretva and Vrbas. It flows for 271km (168 miles) before emptying into the Sava in the north of the country. There are a couple of theories about the origins of its name. One has it that in Roman times the river was called the Basana, and historians think this is the origin of the word *Bosnia*. The other claims that *bosana* is an Indo-European word for water and that Bosnia received its name because of the abundance of it.

The River Bosna also makes up the Bosna river valley, one of the country's industrial centres and home to close on a million people. For this guide, it is useful to know that the settlements of Visoko, Zenica and Vranduk are all in the Bosna river valley. The river's biggest tributaries are the Željeznica, Miljacka, Fojnica, Lašva, Gostović, Krivaja, Usora and Spreča rivers. The river originates at the Vrelo Bosne (*vrelo* means 'source') on the outskirts of Sarajevo at the base of Mount Igman. The spring is one of Sarajevo's most visited natural landmarks and tourist attractions. From there it flows north until it feeds into the River Sava.

GETTING THERE Vranduk is easily reachable from Zenica and Sarajevo. There are regular buses between Zenica and Vranduk and most buses travelling north on the M-17 towards Doboj will stop at Vranduk upon request. The train station in Zenica, 12km north of Vranduk, is accessible from Zagreb and Banja Luka to the north, and Sarajevo and Mostar from the south. Signs along the main highway clearly indicate Vranduk's approach. You know you're there if you reach a stretch of two long tunnels on the main M-17 highway.

TOURIST INFORMATION The **Tourism Board of the Zenica-Doboj Canton** (*Maršala Tita 73;* *032 441 050;* **e** *info@zedoturizam.ba;* **w** *zedoturizam.ba/index.php/bs/*) is located in the centre of Zenica. Although it is not an information centre as such, they can offer some general advice in English, particularly about accommodation.

WHERE TO STAY There is not a great deal of private accommodation available in Vranduk itself. Staying in nearby Zenica (page 244) or up the road a bit at Nemila, at the Bistričak pension (page 244), are good options.

Royal Village Kotromanićevo Šešlije bb; 053 282 835; **e** kotromanicevo.recepcija@yahoo.com; **w** kotromanicevo.com/etno-village.html. This traditional-style Bosnian home has been renovated into a fully equipped, modern pension, & is conveniently located just along the M-17 highway. It has Wi-Fi, AC, a restaurant, a sand volleyball court in the summer & other comforts. **$**

WHERE TO EAT AND DRINK The small **café** at the entrance to the fort serves a wide range of soft drinks and small local dishes of pitta filled with potato, spinach, cheese or beef. A local traditional lunch can also be organised with the museum staff inside the fortress. The fortress courtyard makes an ideal spot for a picnic lunch – it's a wonderful experience. For more restaurants see the Zenica section, pages 244–5.

WHAT TO SEE AND DO Despite its small size, Vranduk is an excellent place for a half-day excursion. The layout of the town is an interesting experience in itself, and is a great place for wandering around as there is little or no traffic within the town. The fort is one of the best-restored medieval structures in all of Bosnia and Herzegovina. It has a very good small café at its entrance, and within the fort there is a unique opportunity to see the exhibitions of artefacts from excavations and objects saved from the local community. Besides the exhibitions, there is also a chance to see the local women practising traditional handicrafts. There are often workshops for small children to engage in art, drawing and working with the traditional tools used to weave carpets and clothes.

You can just stroll around the ancient walls with spectacular views of the Bosna River or the forest-covered hills surrounding it. For another great scenic viewpoint, ask a local to point you to the trailhead that will take you across the river and up to the next village – from here you can take the classic Vranduk photograph of the walled fortress protruding out towards the windy Bosna River. The walk takes about 30–40 minutes as a round trip. If you don't fancy a hike, a simple walk around the town is highly recommended.

KRALJEVA SUTJESKA

Since the Middle Ages, the centre of life in this tiny town has been the Franciscan church. Closely tied in importance to Visoko, Kraljeva Sutjeska and the citadel at Bobovac was once the seat of two Bosnian kings, Tomaš and Tvrtko, of the Kotromanić dynasty. The last Bosnian queen, St Katarina, is mourned today by the local townswomen who still wear black scarves as part of the traditional dress (see box, page 251). Kraljeva Sutjeska was a proper royal settlement. The castle was located next to the present-day monastery, whilst Bobovac Fortress was hidden in a valley in case of invasion from either the north or southeast. Today, Kraljeva Sutjeska is a quiet, small, tourist place, located in the Kakanj municipality just north of Sarajevo. The 50km ride from Sarajevo takes a little over an hour. Although this place holds great historical significance for BiH, it may seem a bit neglected. Many of the town's residents have left to pursue better economic opportunities, and despite the plethora of places to see and things to do here, it may seem like a bit of a ghost town to some during parts of the year.

HISTORY Kraljeva Sutjeska's Franciscan monastery and church would be an architectural and spiritual gem in any European town. The monastery was built in the first half of the 14th century. The first writings about it were by the Franciscan writer Bartolo Pisanski in 1385. The original monastery was probably destroyed in 1463, the same year that the Turkish army destroyed the royal residence and sacked Bobovac.

After the Ottoman conquest of BiH, the monastery was mentioned in Turkish records from the year 1469, meaning that it must have been rebuilt in that short time span. After 50 years of relatively harmonious co-existence, this monastery and many others in the territory of Bosnia was violently destroyed in 1524. Permission to rebuild took many years and the Franciscans were forbidden to use any long-lasting building materials such as brick or stone. This made the monastery vulnerable to fire, and it burned down several times over the next few centuries.

Indeed, in 1658 it went up in flames, which took all its valuables including its meticulous archives and library. A new one was rebuilt in 1664, but due to the Vienna wars throughout the 17th century, the Franciscans were forced to abandon the monastery and live in village huts. As the political situation eased, the Franciscans returned in 1704. After a long period of relative harmony, the monastery was renovated in 1821 and expanded in 1833. During this entire time the Franciscan monks were not only the keepers of the monastery, but of the Catholic faith in the heart of central Bosnia. Islam spread in many of the larger areas, and the Orthodox Church enjoyed prosperity as most of the Byzantine Empire fell under Ottoman jurisdiction. The Catholics, seen as allies to the Austro-Hungarian enemy, did not fare as well. In times of political unrest, the Franciscans would often dress in regular clothes and would be referred to by the locals as *ujak* (uncle). This signified their status and they were well taken care of by the local communities.

Life for the local community very much centred around two things: working the land, and the Church. This was the nexus of a disappearing culture and it seemed like the residents of Kraljeva Sutjeska were somehow aware of this. They were key in preserving the rich cultural heritage not only of the Bosnian kingdom, but also of the original Franciscan Church in Bosnia. Despite times of intense political pressure, the local Catholics in Kraljeva Sutjeska generally had good relations with their Muslim neighbours.

In 1889, after the total collapse of the Ottomans in the territory of Bosnia and Herzegovina, the monastery was completely rebuilt. By 1892 the community of Kraljeva Sutjeska had a new, rather larger monastery under Austro-Hungarian rule. This new structure is the present-day monastery at Kraljeva Sutjeska. In 1914 a water system was introduced, and by 1920 a small hydro-electric dam was built on the Trstionica stream to provide electricity for the first time.

Today's church, as part of the monastery complex, is of a basilica type with neo-Renaissance influence. It was built from 1906–08 by the architect Josip Vancaš. The interior was painted by Marko Antonini in 1908, with the central painting of the Baptism of Christ on the River Jordan. The church was dedicated to St John the Baptist. It is believed that in the crypt lie the 15th-century remains of one of the last Bosnian kings. In 1988, a bronze statue of the Bosnian Queen Katarina was created by Zagreb sculptor Josip Marinović. At the entrance to the monastery complex is a beautiful mosaic with the kingdom's shield.

King Tvrtko Kotromanić (1338–91) was an important native ruler of medieval Bosnia, who transformed the country from an autonomous banate into an independent kingdom. Tvrtko was the son of Vladislav Kotromanić and Jelena Šubić, and was a descendant of the founder of Serbia's Nemanjić dynasty. At the age of 15, Tvrtko became Ban of Bosnia in 1353 when his uncle, Ban Stjepan Kotromanić, died.

During the first part of his reign as *ban*, he had to contend with incursions, revolts and confiscation of Bosnian territory by Hungary. In 1366, in the midst of a political chess match, he was forced to seek refuge in the Hungarian court when a de facto coup d'état by a group of Bosnian nobles placed his brother Vuk on the throne. He was restored as *ban* the following year with the assistance of King Louis I of Hungary.

Tvrtko later assisted Prince Lazar Hrebljanović of neighbouring Serbia in consolidating his control of the Serbian territories to the east. As a gesture of appreciation, Tvrtko was able to expand his own territory to include parts of

QUEEN KATARINA

Queen Katarina of the medieval Bosnian state is definitely the most famous woman in Bosnian history. She left deep traces in the history of this nation through her tragic destiny. She came to the area in 1446 by her marriage to King Stjepan Tomaš, and lived for 17 years between Bobovac Fortress and Kraljeva Sutjeska. She was captured with the fall of Bobovac in 1463 and is believed to have fled in exile to Rome. It was reported that her children were taken to Istanbul, where her son converted to Islam, became a janissary and was later a major figure in the Ottoman administration.

She is said to have had a great love for the area and its people. Legend has it that she suffered for her homeland until the day she died and had always yearned to return to her beloved Kraljeva Sutjeska. That sense of love and pride has been passed down from generation to generation, as the women of Kraljeva Sutjeska continue to wear black scarves in mourning and respect for the exiled queen. Even today, more than 500 years after her death, every 25 October is celebrated with a traditional Mass in the monastery and the church in the name of Queen Katarina.

Zahumlje (present-day Herzegovina), Zeta (Montenegro) and parts of Serbia to the immediate east of today's Bosnian border.

Tvrtko had himself crowned King of Serbia, Bosnia and Primorje (seaboard) at Mileševo in 1377. Although he had declared himself King of Serbia after the death of his kinsman Stefan Uroš V of Serbia, he held only limited parts of western Serbia and made no serious attempts to extend his kingdom further east into Serb lands. He maintained his alliance with Prince Lazar, and sent an army, headed by Vlatko Vuković, to fight alongside Lazar at the Battle of Kosovo Polje in June 1389.

Tvrtko continued to expand his kingdom to the south and west. His predecessor, Ban Stjepan Kotromanić, had added part of the Dalmatian coastline between Ragusa and Split to the Bosnian kingdom, and Tvrtko expanded northwards and southwards along the coast, from south of Zara to the Bay of Kotor, with the exception of Ragusa (Dubrovnik), which remained independent. He established the port of Novi (modern Herceg Novi on the Bay of Kotor), and in the last few years of his reign also called himself King of Croatia and Dalmatia.

Tvrtko died in 1391, and by the end of his reign the medieval Bosnian state had reached its greatest power and territorial extent. He married Dorteja (Dorothy) of Vidin, a Bulgarian princess, and had a daughter, Katarina, and a son, Ostoja Kotromanić, who succeeded him as king upon his death. His illegitimate son was Tvrtko II, who was later crowned King of Bosnia.

During the times of the Bosnian–Serb war of 1350, the Serbian tsar Stefan Dušan tried to conquer Bobovac but was met with strong resistance. In September 1407, the Hungarian army managed to conquer Bobovac and kept army units there with the intention of returning King Ostoja, who was temporarily overthrown, to the throne. King Stjepan Tomašević, the last of the Bosnian kings, was force to flee to the castle at Jajce because of Ottoman attacks. Jajce eventually fell in 1528 and the last king was beheaded by the Ottoman sultan.

There are no accurate surviving records relating to the battle for Bobovac. It is thought that the battle lasted only three days and the mighty Ottoman army overwhelmed the fortress with cannon, which the Bosnians had never seen before. Other versions suggest that Bobovac was betrayed by Tsar Radak, who was promised rich rewards by the Ottomans but was later killed by them. King Stjepan believed the fortress would hold out against a traditional attack for years. The new type of firepower brought by the Turks gave the army no time to seek backup from abroad. When news that Bobovac had fallen so quickly reached the other towns, many simply gave up, knowing they were no match for the sultan's army. The Ottomans largely destroyed Bobovac but, because of its strategic and military importance, they rebuilt parts of it for their army units. They remained stationed there until 1626, when the Ottoman army made large gains in the north of Bosnia and left Bobovac for newer frontiers, including Prusac near Donji Vakuf.

GETTING THERE If you have your **own vehicle**, turn off into Kakanj before the flyover when coming on the M-17 from Sarajevo. Follow the road and turn right under the railway bridge. Continue without turning for another 15 minutes, then pass again under a railway bridge and turn immediately right. Stay on this road until you see the sign for Kraljeva Sutjeska. The road is well marked with signs from Kakanj all the way to Kraljeva Sutjeska. An alternative route is to get off at the Kakanj exit on highway A1 which stretches between Sarajevo and Zenica, and follow the signs to Kraljeva Sutjeska.

Buses from Sarajevo to Kakanj depart every day at 06:00, 08:00, 08:30, 09:30, 11:30, 12:30, 13:30, and 15:30. The price of a ticket one way is 9.40KM and a return ticket is 13.20KM. There is also a bus line from Kakanj to Kraljeva Sutjeska, a distance of 12km. Buses run five times per day.

From the **taxi** stand in Kakanj you can get to Kraljeva Sutjeska for about 10KM per person.

TOURIST INFORMATION AND LOCAL TOUR OPERATORS The **tourist information office** (*7 Kraljice Katarine St;* ☎ *032 552 160;* e *kontakt@visit-ks.info*) is located at the bus station. There are clear signs leading you to the desk. Here you will also find great handmade souvenirs mainly made by local women. These handicrafts are part of a cultural heritage project implemented by the Mozaik Foundation and the local NGO Curia Bani. They not only support local women but are also great gifts for friends or family. The staff speak English and German. The **Tourism Association of Zenica-Doboj Canton** (*73 Marsala Tita St;* ☎ *032 441 050;* e *info@zedoturizam.ba;* w *zedoturizam.ba*) is in the premises of the department store Bosanka.

Eki Tours Safvet bega Basagica bb, Zavidovići; ☎ 032 878 300; e eki_tours@hotmail.com; w ekitours.com.ba. This English-speaking agency offers 3- & 4-day tours of central Bosnia & historical monuments in the region.

Franjevački Samostan Kraljeva Sutjeska; ☎ 032 771 700; e samostan@kraljeva-sutjeska.com; w kraljeva-sutjeska.com

Green Visions Trg Barcelona 9, Sarajevo; ☎ 033 717 290; ⏲ 09.00–17.00 Mon–Fri; e sarajevo@greenvisions.ba; w greenvisions.ba. Green Visions offers year-round day trips to Kraljeva Sutjeska in co-operation with the Katarina agency in Kraljeva Sutjeska. During the season (May–Sep), it has guaranteed weekly trips from Sarajevo including guide, transport & lunch every Wed.

Mountaineering Club Bobovac Osmana Dzafica, Kakanj; ☎ 032 553 045; e pdbobovac@kakanj.net. The club manages the mountaineering lodge Bocica on Ravan Mountain, which is located at 920m, about 30km from Zenica & 10km from Kraljeva Sutjeska. The lodge is surrounded by deciduous & evergreen forest ideal for camping, hiking & walking.

Tourist Agency 'Katarina' Kraljice Katarine, Kraljeva Sutjeska; ☎ 032 779 091; m 061 433 470; e agencijakatarina@yahoo.com; f Turisticka-Agencija-Katarina-201898446510817. This agency is on the main road into Kraljeva Sutjeska on the left-hand side. They can arrange a full range of tours, inc a guided tour of the town & the monastery, a walk or drive to the ancient fortress of Bobovac & a great traditional lunch.

WHERE TO STAY The best accommodation experience hereabouts is private, offered in Kraljeva Sutjeska itself. Local bed and breakfasts are a great way to truly experience the heart and soul of this special community. The tourist information centre (see opposite) offers a wide range of private homestays. The following establishments are at Kakanj:

Hotel Premium Željeznička bb, Kakanj; 032 771 900; w bhtour.ba/premium-hotel. In the centre of Kakanj town, about 30km from Zenica & 12km from Kraljeva Sutjeska. There is a restaurant & summer garden with lots of green space around. **$–$$**

Motel Tiron 311 Lahke brigade bb, Kakanj; 032 557 280; e info@moteltiron.com; w moteltiron.com. On the Sarajevo–Zenica M-17, about 1km from the centre of Kakanj, 30km from Zenica & 12km from Kraljeva Sutjeska. Offers comfortable accommodation in spacious rooms or apartments, a restaurant, bar & Wi-Fi. **$–$$**

Pansion Kameni dvorac Čatici bb, Kakanj; 032 775 144. On the Sarajevo–Zenica M-17 about 30km from Zenica & 12km from Kraljeva Sutjeska. A modest motel-style boarding house above a restaurant, near the M-17 highway, offers basic yet comfortable facilities. A tennis court is on the premises. **$**

WHERE TO EAT AND DRINK The one restaurant in Kraljeva Sutjeska doesn't operate on a regular basis but the information centre is a good place to find out where one can get a meal in town. One of the best places to eat (and one of the only ones) in Kraljeva Sutjeska is at the home of Josip and Katarina. This couple runs the **Tourist Agency 'Katarina'** (see opposite) in town and cook the best homemade meals around.

WHAT TO SEE AND DO Arriving in **Kraljeva Sutjeska** can often feel like stepping through a time warp. The filthy streams and dust-covered roofs of Kakanj disappear as you near this tiny, ancient village. The houses are well kept, the gardens are in perfect shape, and the reflection of the sun off the water is caused by the white stones and not the usual discarded tin can. You'll find that a few of the older women still dress in traditional attire, but as time goes by, one encounters this less frequently. Most people are farmers, but you'll find the odd carpenter or shop owner hammering away or selling their wares. The village was a bustling one of almost 12,000 before the war, but now has a population of just over 2,000. Times have changed indeed, but the charm hasn't faded.

It's always good to start at the **tourist information centre** (see opposite). Here you will get the best information on what to see and how to see it. They are very helpful and friendly and can arrange a guide if you wish. There are also promotional materials available as well as the local handicrafts made by the women of Kraljeva Sutjeska. The **tourist agency 'Katarina'** (see opposite) is just a few doors down and offers a full range of services, including guided tours and homemade lunches. If you want to wander on your own, feel free. The *čaršija* (old town) that runs through the centre is tiny and at times a tad sleepy, but very pleasant nonetheless. You will have to use a guide if you want to visit the town's main sights. These include the **Franciscan monastery** (page 254), the **old Dusper House** and the **old mosque**. **Bobovac**, the medieval citadel tucked in the hills of the next valley, can be reached by car or by foot. It is not easy to find, so a guide is again recommended.

Dusper House (m *061 433 470 (Josip)*) in the village is the oldest house in central Bosnia, dating back to the early 18th century. The house has a very particular type of architecture and it is doubtful that anything of this sort exists anywhere else in Bosnia and Herzegovina. There are two covered porches, a large living area, a brick stove and an open fireplace used for cooking and heating. It has also preserved a large amount of kitchenware and utensils, as well as the original old furniture sets. The house is built mostly of wood and the roof is made of wooden shingles, and has been designated a protected national monument; it is the first site in Kakanj municipality under protection of the state. Despite this status, however, its expensive renovation and restoration was funded by the Croatian government.

The **old mosque** in Kraljeva Sutjeska is proclaimed to be one of the oldest in the country. It was apparently built in just three days after the fall of Bobovac and the king's residence in Kraljeva Sutjeska. Due more to its age and location than its design and significance, the mosque is also listed by the Institute for Protection of Cultural, Historical and Natural Heritage of BiH. There is a keeper who will gladly show you in and tell you tales of the mosque. It is easy to find her through Katarina tourist agency, as they have an agreement with her about showing the mosque to groups.

One of the most striking characteristics of mosques are the spiral stairs leading to the tops of minarets. Legend has it that the sultan, after sacking the town, was visiting sites to decide where the mosque would be built. He stood looking at the present-day site with a walking stick in hand. When he looked down an ant was spiralling up to the top of his stick, much as the stairs of a mosque do inside the minaret. He watched with interest until the ant reached his hand, took the act as a sign of God and ordered the mosque to be built on that spot!

Franciscan monastery (*032 779 015/291; by request or Wed, Fri & Sat 08.00–16.00; entrance free but donation appreciated*) A visit to Kraljeva Sutjeska without seeing the monastery wouldn't be complete. It is a complex so large that it far exceeds the requirements of the six monks now residing in the town.

The church Designed in the Venetian style, the high-vaulted ceilings are now cracking in places as a result of some flaws in the original design. What is assumed to be the oldest organ in the country was previously hidden in the monastery and is now displayed in the church. A massive statue paying tribute to Queen Katarina dominates the east side of the church. Even on the hottest summer days the church is often chilly. The energy inside is quite humbling, as is listening to the monks tell tales of the trials and tribulations of the Catholics during Ottoman times. The monks at Kraljeva Sutjeska are reasonably objective in their depiction of history and do a fair job of separating historical fact from folklore.

The museum The museum houses a limited collection of art, documents and artefacts gathered or discovered at Bobovac or brought back by monks travelling the Christian world. The paintings are mostly from local artists, dating as far back as the 17th century. The collection is quite impressive for a small three-room museum tucked away in the hills of central Bosnia. A cross from 7th-century Syria is displayed among a collection of elaborate crosses from Germany, Venice and Rome. The old chapel bell was recovered when Bosnia was annexed by Austria. Church bells were illegal during Turkish times and were hidden by the monks. When the bishop was ordered out of Bosnia, only the Franciscans were permitted to stay. They went to great lengths to hide and protect the sacred objects that the priests left behind. Robes, crosses and altarpieces from the old church in Vareš are also exhibited in the museum.

The oldest and probably the most valuable painting in the monastery is *The Gift of Christ the King who Fell before the Cross*, which is believed to date from the 15th century. There are two other paintings from the domestic artist Stjepan Dragojlović. He lived from the 16th–17th century in Kraljeva Sutjeska and had

HANDICRAFTS

The women of Kraljeva Sutjeska are no strangers to preserving ancient traditions. They are famous for wearing their traditional attire with a black scarf, which signifies the mourning for Queen Katarina who was sent into exile over 500 years ago. Perhaps this is where their flair for tradition comes from. The women's forum 'Alternativa', based in Kakanj, is an organisation dedicated to preserving the classic handicrafts and patterns from ancient Bosnia. The movement not only contributes to the preservation of traditional embroidery but also strengthens community development and provides small incomes to many families.

Sutjeska's embroidery is copied from original samples of traditional attire and *urneks*. *Urneks* are linen pieces containing traditional motifs that date as far back as the days of Queen Katarina in the mid-15th century. The crafts are also created from patterns of the Ottoman period, with a very rich oriental touch to design and colour. Aside from embroidered linens, the women make beautiful shirts, wall hangings, baskets and other authentic goods.

When visiting small communities, remember to always try to give something back. Buying handmade, local goods not only supports these women and their families but also preserves ancient trades that are dying out or have died out in most of Europe. The tourism information centre in Kraljeva Sutjeska (page 252) has a wonderful selection of these handicrafts that make great souvenirs or gifts for family or friends.

You can also contact the **Women's Forum Alternative** (*309 Brdske Brigade P4, Kakanj;* *032 556 288;* e alternative@bih.net.ba; w *nvo-alternative.org*).

been art-educated in Venice. His first painting is *Raspeće* (1597) and the second *Bezgrešno začeće* (1621). Each painting is a self-portrait. There are also various 17th-century Venetian paintings including *The Head of Christ with Thorned Crown*, a Baroque work that remained unknown until 1988. There is also a highly valued painting of *Queen Katarina* from Italy and *Madonna with Christ and St Anthony*.

The library The library, for me, is a much more interesting visit, its books and documents illustrating a colourful past. The largest collection of *incunabula* (books printed before 1500) is housed here, and there are 31 books written before the 15th century. This accounts for over half of all the incunabula in Bosnia and Herzegovina. There are volumes and volumes of philosophy, theology, chemistry and history written in Italian, Latin, German, French and the local language, totalling over 11,000 books in all. The books were mainly collected from local boys who went to the West to be educated and brought back Catholic teachings. The first Bible to be translated into the local Bosančica language also has an introduction to the local alphabet so the illiterate villagers could learn to read and write.

Another room is dedicated to miniature models of the village's old architecture, traditional dress and ways of life. The role of the *ujak* (uncles), as monks were called so as not to attract the attention of the Turkish officials, was key to the spiritual survival of the villagers. The Franciscans documented births, deaths, marriages and migrations from the area when there was little or no public record-keeping. These records show the increase or decrease of the Catholic population, including the plagues that hit many Croatian areas. The original permits to rebuild the monastery issued by both the sultan and the local vizier from Visoko are displayed. These two documents cost more than the actual construction of the monastery. Perhaps the most important of all the Ottoman documents regarding the monastery was the *Ahdnama* issued by Sultan Mehmed II El Fatiha in 1463, which declares that the monks are to be left alone and treated well by all, including his subjects from the Ottoman army. This document was used for centuries to protect the rights of the Franciscan monks who were often persecuted for their religious beliefs and practices.

Towards the end of the library are the diverse collections of all the monks who ever passed through here. An enormous Bible was printed in order for several monks to read at the same time over each other's shoulders. Printed material for Catholics was often difficult to come by. The monastery was also the final resting place for the monks who served the Srebrena Bosna parish. They would come here for their final days and leave all their belongings to the monastery. Their legacy is a fascinating collection of books.

Bobovac Bobovac is considered part of Kraljeva Sutjeska. The ancient town of Kraljeva Sutjeska became more and more difficult to defend due to its position in the valley. The fortress of Bobovac, a 5km walk from Kraljeva Sutjeska, was situated on a high ridge above the Bukovica River and was strategically easier to defend. The citadel is close to the villages of Mijakovici and Dragovici in the Vareš municipality. You can reach Bobovac from two sides, either from Kraljeva Sutjeska or from Vareš. Access from Kraljeva Sutjeska is much easier and closer. Bobovac has an upper section with a square tower (ruins of the tower still exist), and a lower section most probably inhabited by the peasants during conflicts.

It was there that a walled city was built and the inhabitants of Kraljeva Sutjeska lived either when under attack or in the years before the final invasion by the Turks, when they moved there permanently. The royal family is known to have retreated here from the Ottoman invasion, and it is from here that King Stjepan left to fight his last battle against the Ottoman army, and from where Queen Katarina and her children set off on their journey to Dubrovnik. The fortified town had quarters for the noble family on the western end, while the central and lowest part

BOBOVAC FORTRESS

Bobovac is perhaps the most important fortress from the medieval Bosnian state, built on the steep, sloping rock faces on the south side of Dragovici and Mijakovici mountains. The fortress is lined on either side by the Bukovica River (*bukva* is 'beech tree' in the local language and the river runs through a thick forest of beautiful beech).

Bobovac was built by Stjepan Kotromanić II, in the first half of the 14th century. It was the residence of Bosnia's aristocracy from that period until Bosnia lost its independence to the invading Ottomans. Bobovac is first mentioned in documents from 1349. The strategic location of Bobovac Fortress was perfect for defensive purposes and was used as an administrative and military base by the Bosnian kings during its final years. Kraljeva Sutjeska itself was not fortified and served as a residence in times of peace and as the administrative and political centre of the Kotromanić dynasty. The king's crown, originally from Mile in Visoko, was hidden in Bobovac. There was a mausoleum built there by King Ostoja as a royal burial ground for three Bosnian kings: Stjepan Ostoja, Tvrtko II Kotromanić and Stjepan Tomaš.

of the ridge housed the townspeople. The church, stables and military barracks were situated on the upper eastern hill overlooking the entire fortress and the surrounding mountains.

Bobovac is not accessible by car. Getting there is a pleasant 45-minute walk along the **Bukovica river** through thick beech forests. In the summer months, the trail is lined with blackberries and fresh mint growing near the water. The only fully intact structure remaining at Bobovac is the mausoleum that Queen Katarina had built following the death of Tvrtko. His remains were removed during the last conflict and taken to an undisclosed location. Some of the outer walls and part of the stables can be seen on the high ridge behind the mausoleum and the king's quarters are slowly crumbling away. The view from this little nest in the valley is quite remarkable. If possible, go to the monastery first and take a tour with one of the Franciscans. The old drawings of Bobovac will help create a much clearer picture of how things looked in 13th- and 14th-century Bosnia. Bobovac is an open-air fortress and is always open to the public. (See also box, Bobovac fortress, opposite.)

VISOKO

Much has been stirring in the past several years in and around Visoko, about 30km northwest of Sarajevo (map, pages 148–9). Its economy, like many others, collapsed after the conflict of the early 1990s. New political boundaries for the first time set Visoko out of the Sarajevo district, which didn't do much to improve its social and economic problems. Its leather industry and the famous Vispak – a food producer and packager – have come back to life and have created many jobs. Tourism was a distant thought just a few years back but now with several projects under way to preserve the ancient handicrafts and ruins of the old Bosnian kingdom, it seems as if the tide is turning. Well known for its handicrafts, particularly its leathersmithing, these old skills are starting to return to the former capital of the medieval Bosnian state.

The discovery of the Valley of the Bosnian Pyramids (page 263), though highly controversial, has already made an impact on Visoko, and will probably continue to impact both this town and the entire country – once again bringing Visoko back into the limelight, and perhaps bringing back some of its lost glory. Even if many people and experts question the legitimacy of the pyramids, some local organisations and individuals are still struggling for their recognition, and have used the opportunity to attract tourists and volunteer archaeologists to Visoko on an ongoing basis. Visiting the Valley of the Pyramids is a personal choice which can be made out of genuine curiosity, or interest in the kitsch appeal of the semi-spiritual tourism industry that has sprung up around them. One will find in Visoko that there isn't a tourism industry to speak of. But there are fascinating cultural monuments to discover and the ingenuity of the craftspeople to admire in the tiny shops in the old town or in the surrounding villages. Visoko is a place to go with a purpose – to see the old trade of leather sandal-making or the infamous wooden filter pipes (*čibuk*) that this town is so well known for, or to walk up Visočica Hill and imagine the ancient civilisations that may have settled there and soak in the controversy surrounding the Valley of the Pyramids.

HISTORY Visoko municipality is host to more protected cultural heritage monuments than any other in Bosnia and Herzegovina. The first traces of this settlement date back to the Neolithic period. Not much is known about the Neolithic tribes but research has uncovered that there were significant settlements throughout the area, including Sarajevo's famous Butmir Neolithic settlement. The indigenous Illyrian tribes that dominated this region for perhaps thousands of years left little trace in the Visoko area, but there are findings from the Roman era when the Illyrians were forcefully integrated into the Roman Empire.

Due to its convenient geographic and economic conditions the Visoko basin developed into the main political, economic and cultural centre of the medieval Bosnia state. This was the case, not only under the rule of Bosnian *bans*, but also well into the reign of the Bosnian kings, and remained so up to the Turkish invasion in the 15th century. Visoko reached the peak of its development during the late Middle Ages. It was here that foreign envoys were received and state assemblies of the Bosnian kingdom held. Alongside the royalty there were the chief houses and university centre of the Bosnian Church. Visoko, from this time on, was an important trading centre and attracted a considerable colony of merchants from Ragusa (present-day Dubrovnik). The entire area, open to Ragusans by the request of the Bosnian aristocracy, flourished as Bosnia and Ragusa enhanced its trade and improved its gold- and silver-mining techniques.

PRESENT-DAY VISOKO The economy and demographic structure of the town changed quite a bit as a result of the war. Many factories had been damaged or destroyed, and the reconstruction process has been slow. Visoko is home, however, to several steadily growing industries. The leather company KTK is still Bosnia's leading producer of leather goods, and Vispak is one of BiH's best food-processing companies. They are especially famous for coffee and tea. The textile industry has made a slight comeback but still struggles as BiH finds it difficult to compete in today's free-market system. Most economic activities in Visoko are based on small and medium-sized enterprises, with most of its residents living a very modest lifestyle. Regardless of the economic woes, Visoko, like most other Bosnian towns, still has a thriving café culture that is most welcoming in the warmer months.

GETTING THERE Finding the way to Visoko is much less of a challenge than more off-the-beaten-track destinations around Sarajevo. Visoko is a mere 30km from the capital and is connected to the highway. **Buses** go several times a day from Sarajevo to Visoko and take around 30 minutes. By **car**, it is only a 20-minute drive. The train that travels from Sarajevo to Zenica does not stop in Visoko.

TOURIST INFORMATION There is no official tourist information centre here. However, the town museum (*Ulica Alija Izetbegovića; 032 736 267*) is perhaps best equipped to deal with requests and provide promotional material and directions to the local attractions. It has many brochures and helpful hints on how to get around Visoko and more importantly the impressive sites that are in the surrounding area. The museum is in the centre of town, across from the municipality building, just opposite where the Fojnica River flows into the Bosna River. There is also the **Zenica Doboj-Canton Tourism Association** (*032 441 050;* **e** *info@zedoturizam.ba;* **w** *zedoturizam.ba*).

WHERE TO STAY

Hotel Piramida Sunca (28 rooms) Musala 1; 032 731 450; **e** info@hotelpiramidasunca.com; hotelpiramidasunca.com. Inspired by the thought of the pyramid theory coming true, the Pyramid Motel, as it is commonly referred to, was built a few years after Semir Osmanagić's discovery (page 263). This 3-star hotel can accommodate larger groups; it has modern facilities & the amenities that usually accompany them. The restaurant has a perfect view of Visočica Hill (the pyramid) & serves a wide variety of national & international dishes. **$$**

Hotel Centar Braće Zečević 3/A (17 rooms, 1 apt); 032 730 020; w hotelcentar.ba. Hotel Centar has new en-suite rooms & apts available just behind the restaurant. The apts are simply, but nicely, decorated. They all have internet, central heating, AC, cable TV & a massage bath. **$–$$**

Hotel Džale (15 rooms, 2 apts) Muhasinovići bb; 032 742 111; e info@hotel.dzale.com; w hotel-dzale.com. Each room has cable TV & AC, & the apts are fitted with jacuzzis. The rooms are decorated in various themes, which can be spot on or lean to the kitsch side. The staff speak English & German. **$**

Motel San Remo (12 rooms) Bistua Nuova 4A; 032 421 326; e info@motel-sanmarino.com; w motel-sanmarino.com. There are a few bright spots about San Remo. The staff are friendly & helpful. The rooms are always clean & tidy. The design & layout of the place may not exactly inspire but there's a lot to say for authentic, local experiences. Behind the tasteless décor of the restaurant is actually good food. The rooms, which aren't too far off design-wise from the rest of the motel, are comfortable nonetheless. **$**

Pansion La Pam (8 rooms) Donje Moštre; 032 740 180; e porca-doo@hotmail.com. This small pension is located just off the highway on the old stretch of the M-17. They have a handful of basic rooms with TVs & AC in each. The layout of the rooms is simple & slightly bare. La Pam is better known for its restaurant, which serves BBQ meat dishes & local meat specialities. Don't be discouraged if you're looking for a place to stay & see a full car park, thinking they have no vacancies. They are most likely restaurant guests. **$**

WHERE TO EAT AND DRINK As in most tiny towns in Bosnia and Herzegovina the cuisine is rather simple and local. Visoko has several good restaurants and other places to eat in the centre of town. The main traditional meals of veal, Bosnian stew, *ćevapi* and *burek* are never hard to find. Other dishes may include Italian food.

Bonaca Branilaca 51; m 062 278 097; noon–21.30 daily. Bonaca is yet another self-proclaimed 'exclusive' restaurant. Although the décor may leave a bit to be desired, one certainly cannot complain about the quality of the food & service. Alongside the classic Bosnian dishes, which are always meat-heavy, they specialise in Dalmatian seafood cuisine. They order fresh fish from the Adriatic on a regular basis & pride themselves on the specialities of Hvar Island off the Croatian coast. Most of their wine is locally produced in Herzegovina, with most selections coming from Stolac & Čitluk. **$$**

Avlija Braće Zečevića 3/A; 032 730 820; 07.00–22.00 daily. They pride themselves on attracting all generations to enjoy their traditional Bosnian cuisine at Avlija. It's true, the young & old both gather here for the pleasant atmosphere & tasty, home-cooked meals. The prices are also very reasonable & the servings are generous. Try the *sogan dolma* or *klepe* dishes that are a welcome change from the meat-only dishes found in most restaurants. **$–$$**

Konoba Lacy Patriotske lige 5; 032 738 527; 08.00–23.00 daily. A nice spot in the centre of town with a mix of ethno & traditional style; it's much nicer to eat on a terrace & people-watch while enjoying your meal. The menu is not horribly creative, serving the classic Bosnian meal dishes of veal, various schnitzels & grilled meats. The grilled dishes are good, but try to avoid the fried dishes, as they tend to be a bit greasy. **$–$$**

Verdi Branilaca 61; 032 738 129; e info@pizzeriaverdi.co.ba; w pizzeriaverdi.ba; 06.30–23.00. Definitely one of Visoko's nicer places for lunch or dinner, Verdi serves a wide variety of local & international dishes. You can grab a quick pizza, baked in a stone oven, or indulge in their rich selection of trout, chicken & beef dishes. There is also a good wine selection. **$–$$**

Ćevabdžinica Ihtijarević Čaršijska 40; 032 737 136; 07.00–20.00 daily. The perfect place for quality fast food. *Ćevapi* is a good way to go for a tasty lunch that is cheap, quick & yet still gives you a quality meal. Ihtijarević uses fresh meat supplied locally, & cooks on an open fire of locally produced wood charcoal. This is the recipe for success with

MEDIEVAL BOSNIAN STATE

Visoko was named after the medieval town of Visoki, once located on the prominent Visočica Hill. The name Visoko is mentioned for the first time in 1355, in a charter issued to the merchants of Dubrovnik (Ragusa) by King Tvrtko I. However, the oldest manuscript in Bosančica (the ancient Bosnian language similar to Cyrillic and Glagolitic) was the Charter of Ban Kulin from 1189, which was apparently written in Mile near Visoko. Archaeological explorations in Mile have located the grave sites of two Bosnian rulers – Stjepan II Kotromanić and King Tvrtko Kotromanić.

Ban Kulin (1163–1204) was a powerful Bosnian *ban* who ruled from 1180 to 1204. He first ruled as a vassal of the Byzantine Empire and then of the Kingdom of Hungary. Ban Kulin was brought to power by the Byzantine emperor Manuel I Comnenus. He had a son, Stjepan, who succeeded him as Bosnian *ban*.

Kulin was brought to Bosnia at the age of three by the Byzantine emperor who took the country from the Hungarians. In 1180, at the age of 17, Manuel I Comnenus placed Kulin as his vassal.

Ban Kulin's rule is often thought of as Bosnia's 'golden age', and he is generally remembered as a hero in Bosnian national folklore. Bosnia lived through a mostly peaceful era throughout his rule. In 1183, he led his troops against the forces of Hungary that had attacked the Byzantine Empire, together with the Serbs led by the Duke of All Serbia, Stefan Nemanja. In Kulin's time, the term Bosnia encompassed roughly the lands of Vrhbosna, Usora, Soli, the Lower Edges and Rama, which is approximately equivalent to most of modern Bosnia.

The heretic Bosnian Church spread greatly during his reign. He was reported to the Pope for his heretical practices and supporting the Bosnian Church. The Pope wrote to King Emeric of Hungary ordering him to either make Kulin get rid of the 'heretics' or dispose of him. Kulin subsequently organised a congress in 1203 in Bilino Polje, which the Pope's emissaries attended. He officially declared his allegiance to the Catholic Church and asserted that he was none other than a true pious Catholic. Most believe that his declaration was simply a tactical move, as the Bosnian Church continued to flourish after his death in 1204. His policy was not successfully continued by his heir, Stjepan.

THE KULIN CHARTER Perhaps what made him so famous though was writing the first document of the medieval Bosnian state. The Charter of Kulin is a symbolic 'birth certificate' of Bosnian statehood, as it is the first written document that speaks of Bosnian borders (between the rivers Drina, Sava and Una), and of the elements of the Bosnian state: its ruler, throne and political organisation. The charter was a trade agreement between Bosnia and the Republic of Ragusa. Bosnia and Ragusa have held close political and trading ties since then. The charter is held in a museum in Moscow and the many attempts to retrieve this precious document have been unsuccessful.

ćevapi, which is often served with pitta bread (*somun*), freshly diced onions & a yoghurt drink. Some like to add *kajmak*, which is a buttery cheese topping. $

Gurman Mule Hodžića 15; m 066 887 789; 07.00–21.00 daily. This *aščinica* very much resembles a cafeteria-like set-up. The only difference is that *aščinicas* prepare traditional dishes with fresh ingredients every day. It's a good place to find a few vegetarian dishes, even if it's just a mixed vegetable dish or mashed potatoes. Most go for the ready meals of *sitni cevap*, green beans & beef, & stuffed onions. Gurman is reasonably priced & a full meal with a drink shouldn't cost more than 8KM. $

WHAT TO SEE AND DO Visoko is not yet a town that caters for tourists. Although there is plenty to see and do, if you are an independent traveller expect to have to hunt around to find what you may be looking for. Visoko's *čaršija* (old town) is a good start. It's an enjoyable place to roam and check out the local leathersmiths and a few of the other specialised *zanati* (handicrafts). This is a great place to window shop and sit and have a coffee. Store owners tend to be very laid-back and don't mind at all if you enter to watch the old trades being performed right there in the shop.

Perhaps the best source of information is the Visoko **Zavičajni muzej**, or the town museum (pages 272–3). The museum itself has an interesting collection from the medieval Bosnian state. Most of the relics are from Mile, Biskupici and Mostre, which were the seats of the kingdom. There are ancient documents and artefacts from that era as well as pieces of the old fortress of Visoki.

A visit to Visoko wouldn't be complete without visiting the important medieval sites. Visoki, the ancient site of the medieval fortress, is located on the top of Visočica Hill. This 'hill' is claimed by some to be a pyramid, though this remains controversial. For believers or sceptics, it's still an amazing thing to visit the site of a medieval fortress that was built on top of the 'pyramid' (page 263). There is an asphalt road to the top from the rear side and the roads are well marked. The site has a plaque describing what you are looking at, which is basically the ruins of what was once a rather large fortress.

Mile, also now known as Arnautović, is also an important place, if not the most important place in terms of medieval Bosnia. Mile is where the state councils met and held meetings. Many decorated graves of the royalty were found and are still preserved there. Buried there was Stjepan II Kotromanić of the Kotromanić dynasty and the first Bosnian king, Tvrtko. Mile was also the place where the kings were crowned, as was Tvrtko in 1377. There are still significant remains of St Kuzme and Damjana churches, which were first mentioned in 1244. The Franciscan

LEATHER PRODUCTION IN VISOKO

The old production methods of Visoko's *tabaka* (leatherworks), with the well-known *tabhana*, or leathersmiths, have been a tradition since the onset of Ottoman rule. The traditional way of making leather was upheld even during the Austro-Hungarian period. It wasn't until after World War I that modern methods were applied to producing goods from leather like shoes, sandals and mats. This was the first time that leather production was mechanised and leathersmith workshops were equipped with new machines to make the process tremendously easier. In 1929, the first school for leathersmiths was opened to educate skilled labour in this growing industry. This was the main school in the whole of former Yugoslavia and students came from each of the six republics to learn the trade. The long history of leather-making has made Visoko the largest centre for leather trade in the wider region.

Today, there are small movements within the leathersmith community that are trying to bring back the old methods of leather-making, particularly for the traditional *opanci* or sandals. Regardless of whether the techniques are old or new, the tradition of leather-making is the true hallmark of Visoko.

headquarters was located here from around 1340 and the archives of the medieval Bosnian state were found as well.

The famous Ban Kulin's carved slate from 1193 was found in Biskupić, along with the remains of an old church and tombstones. Where the Ban Kulin Charter was written, however, still remains a mystery. Nearby is the location of Mostre where it is believed that one of the oldest universities in Europe was founded. It is said that theology, medicine, cosmology, ethics and other subjects were taught. In 1323 and 1381, Ban Stjepan and King Tvrtko issued charters from Mostre to other regional kings and leaders, which clearly points to the great significance of this location. Although in many of these places not much remains, it isn't difficult to imagine how this area became the valley of the kings.

Aside from its rich cultural heritage, Visoko is located in the beautiful valley of the Bosna and Fojnica rivers. The natural surroundings offer a wide range of possibilities for outdoor-lovers. One such place is the mountain lodge Zbilje owned by the Mountaineer Association Visočica, which is located at 645m above sea level on the Fojnica River. Not far from Visoko, this easily accessible lodge is a great place for a day hike or even to spend a day or two wandering the hillsides. The Mountaineer Association (see below) can also prepare traditional meals and provide guide services.

Further specialist information can also be obtained from Extreme Sport Club Eko Viking.

Extreme Sport Club Eko Viking Alije Izetbegovića 2, Visoko; **m** 061 160 755; **e** kikif@bih.net.ba. Organises rafting on Fojnica River, hiking, skiing, mountain biking, paragliding, climbing, etc. Rafting 1 day (inc equipment & 2 meals) on Fojnica River, 50KM.

Mountaineer Association Visočica [map, page 240] Zbilje bb 71300, Visoko; **m** 061 417 755. Owns a mountain lodge on Zbilje Mountain, 2km from Visoko. It organises hiking excursions to Mt Visočica. Mountain lodge accommodation 8KM pp.

HANDICRAFTS IN GODUŠA AND LIJEŠEVE VILLAGES

An extension of Visoko Museum (crafts) has been built in the small village of Goduša. There is a small exhibition of the old *zanati* of hand-carved wooden pipes called *čibuk*. Another unique trade is the *česljar*, which is comb-making from bull horns. It is said that this trade is even older than the craft of *čibuk*-making. The exhibition has old tools on display and offers the opportunity to see the ancient trade being practised by the local villagers who have preserved this tradition since Ottoman times. They also make exquisite chess sets and produce copper *ibriks* – beautiful oriental water pots that were used during Ottoman times to collect drinking water. In the village of Liješeve the local craftsmen are famous for clay pottery. These craftsmen are called *grnčari*. Many of the traditional Bosnian dishes are specially prepared in clay pots and bowls that are made only in Visoko. One can find these lovely handmade crafts both in the village and in souvenir shops in Visoko. It is important to note that these ancient trades are rarely practised in modern-day Europe. The movement to preserve this way of life is protecting the cultural heritage of the small communities that have passed on these traditions throughout the generations. One should always have in mind that by supporting local communities and buying local handicrafts you help localise economies and protect a rare cultural heritage.

The Bosnian pyramids: a continuing mystery or a hoax? In April 2005 during a visit to Visoko, Semir Osmanagić, a Bosnian researcher based in Houston, noticed two geometrically symmetrical elevations: Visočica Hill (now called the Bosnian pyramid of the Sun) and Plješevica Hill (named Bosnian pyramid of the Moon). Even though there was significant tree cover on the hills it was evident that both of them shared characteristics of pyramids. The shapes and angles that Osmanagić had studied in Central and South America and Egypt gave him no doubt that he was looking at pyramids. This unbelievable hypothesis quickly created a stir and quite a lot of scepticism. But after several geological excavations he concluded that the formations were not natural in form.

Semir Osmanagić's work entailed intensive research in the Maya world, visiting dozens of the ancient sites in the jungles and tourist centres of Central America. He also worked at pyramid sites in Peru and studied pre-Illyrian civilisations in Herzegovina and Dalmatia. During one of the probing digs, a clear structure of the walls of a pyramid emerged. Stone tiles created a massive set of stairs that climbed 220m and smoothed, treated stone tiles were found at access points to the plateau. Although many have remained sceptical, and in recent years most experts, including the The European Association of Archaeologists, have refuted the pyramid theory based on scientific evidence, Osmanagić still has no doubts that he has ventured upon the greatest discovery in modern European history.

While the current expert consensus is that the theory is false, Osmanagić persists in his interpretation and continues to tell his story, which attracts tourists to Visoko. Gazing up at the two hills after hearing such claims while witnessing the procession of tourists who believe in them (some even claim that the rocks inside the 'pyramids' have healing power) does tend to make one wonder about their true nature. If nothing else, the history of the controversy, and the spectacle created by it, may be interesting to travellers. Entering the 'pyramids' with a short guided tour is possible and can be arranged on site during the day – but one should keep the history of the controversy in mind when listening to the tour guide. Healing and meditation visits for those who believe in the spiritual power of the site can be arranged in advance, though one should undertake them with full awareness of the issues mentioned here and decide for oneself.

KREŠEVO

Famed for his Christian writings and as a master of the Slavic language, Father Grga Martić has been recorded in history, particularly Franciscan history, as one of Bosnia's greatest writers. He taught and wrote in the remote valley tucked below Bitovnja and Lopata mountains in the tiny town of Kreševo. The **Franciscan monastery** there has been serving its community for centuries, and the Catholic traditions here are very strong. The monastery has organised a rustic museum, library and gallery (☎ *030 806 075;* 🕘 *09.00–noon & 15.00–17.00 Mon–Sat*), and as in most Franciscan monasteries in Bosnia and Herzegovina, the monks are very welcoming to visitors.

With no more than a few thousand inhabitants, Kreševo medieval village settlement expanded with the arrival of German blacksmiths. In several areas of Bosnia, small German and Ragusan (present-day Dubrovnik) mining communities were established. The noble families of the Bosnian state were keen to exploit the plentiful resources of gold and silver but they didn't have the skills to do so. The craft was passed on from these migrant miners and can be found today in the old town.

Kreševo is known for its old Bosnian architecture. The walls are made of clay and straw plaster, and the roof tiles are specially treated cherry-wood shingles. The village of Vranići just a few kilometres from Kreševo is home to the finest example of this old type of building. It's a great place to visit and one of a handful of places that hasn't suffered from the destruction of war.

If you do pay Kreševo a visit, then there is an unwritten rule that every traveller must stop at **Restaurant Banja** (*Banjska 13; 030 806 820; 08.00–23.00;* **e** *restoranbanja@yahoo.com*). The food and service are great, but the real attraction is the mysterious spring that flows from a hidden cave next to the restaurant. It creates a natural swimming pool of mineral water in which you are free to take a dip. Some swear it has healing powers. I found it, at the very least, wonderfully refreshing. **Restaurant Ribnjak** (*Vrela bb; 030 806 670; 08.00–23.00*) grills fresh trout plucked from its own fish pond. If you like trout, you'll love this place.

Kreševo is located off the main road from Sarajevo to Kiseljak. It is less than an hour's drive from the capital through some picturesque and winding roads.

FOJNICA

It is thought the Illyrians had major settlements here, and upon the Roman conquest the city rapidly gained importance for its rich gold deposits. The gold was often mined from the three rivers flowing down from the surrounding mountains of Vranica, Bitovnja and Šit. The rivers Gvozdanka and Jezernica flow into the Fojnica River, which is a main tributary of the River Bosna. Handicrafts and trade were well established even before the arrival of the Turks in the old-name towns of Kozograd, Zvonigrad and Kasteli. Fojnica as a town was first mentioned in 1365. Towards the late 15th century, after the invasion of the Turks, Fojnica recorded 329 families. In the same period Mostar, a city now 20 times the size of Fojnica, recorded only 19 dwellings.

The Catholic traditions of Srebrena Bosna (the Silver Bosnia) are best represented in Fojnica and Kraljeva Sutjeska. The **Holy Spirit Franciscan Museum** (see opposite) *Mon–Fri*), located in a hilltop monastery, holds over 17,000 volumes of books, records and documents, and the second-largest collection of incunabula (books printed before 1500) in Bosnia and Herzegovina. One of its treasured manuscripts is the *Fojnicki grovnik* ('Fojnica Book of Arms') depicting the medieval coats of arms of Bosnian noble families, and the *Ahdnama*, an Ottoman-era documents.

Fojnica also has an important place in the history of the Bosnian state – Kozograd, just above Fojnica (a possible hiking trip), is the place where the last Bosnian queen Katarina rested before she finally left Bosnia for Dubrovnik, fleeing the Ottoman invaders. The legend has it that Queen Katarina and her protectors managed to fool the Ottomans by riding their horses backwards, which allowed them to establish a safe distance and thus evade capture.

Fojnica is also home to one of the 19 spas that operate in the country. While I do not doubt the high quality and medicinal benefits of the mineral waters here, the accommodation and food are generally not up to Western standards.

Fojnica is located 60km northwest of Sarajevo via Kiseljak, tucked below the peaks of Vranica Mountain that dominates much of central Bosnia.

WHERE TO STAY

Aqua Reumal (60 apts) Banjska 3; 030 547 600; **e** recepcija@aquareumal.ba; **w** aquareumal.ba. Aqua Reumal organise apartment rental throughout the year. The apts are nice duplexes with kitchens, dining rooms & bathrooms downstairs & bedrooms up. They are more comfortable & modern than Reumal Fojnica & are within walking distance of the restaurants, Aqua Park & spa centre. **$$**

Recreational Centre Brusnica (16 rooms) Poljane; 030 630 200; e rc.brusnica@gmail.com; w brusnica.ba. Great mountain accommodation with all the comforts one could ask for. Sgls, dbls & apts available. The apts have jacuzzis & small kitchens. No need for AC that high, but the heating works well. **$$**

Reumal Fojnica (120 rooms) Banjska 1; 030 838 800; e rezervacije@reumal.ba; w reumal.ba. Reumal represents a touch of the old school. The accommodation here is very decent, always clean, but slightly outdated. Most people who stay here are either doing physical rehabilitation or are visiting the spas on a package deal. **$$**

Jezernica [map, page 240] (6 rooms) Vranica Mountain; m 061 189 153; w jezernica.ba. Jezernica is a mountain lodge halfway up the mountain towards Prokoško Lake. It is easy to access this location as the roads to this point are still decent. This renovated lodge sleeps 37. There are dbl rooms as well as dormitory-style accommodation. The rooms & facilities are clean, neat & well organised. The restaurant serves good traditional food & has a nice fireplace room for chilly nights. Overnight stay c10KM. **$**

WHERE TO EAT AND DRINK

Aqua Reumal Banjska 3; 030 547 500; e recepcija@aquareumal.ba; w aquareumal.ba; 07.00–23.00 daily. Within the complex of the new apts & Aqua Park there is a café & a restaurant. The latter serves both national & international cuisine. The food & service are probably the best in Fojnica town. The décor is an eye-easing yellow with a small ethno section towards the back. **$$**

Restoran Brusnica Poljane; 030 630 200; e rc.brusnica@gmail.com; w brusnica.ba; 07.00–23.00 daily. Most are surprised when they climb the 11km of gravel road & reach Brusnica. The restaurant serves largely national dishes, including several pork specialities. Much of the food is grown & produced locally. The cheeses & meats are all locally produced & of very high quality. **$$**

Restoran Central Mehmeda Spahe bb; 030 831 710; 07.00–23.00 daily. Located in the town centre this is Fojnica's non-spa location. Central is just that, centrally situated on the road towards the spas. They serve excellent meat dishes, try the veal medallion or grilled meat dish. **$–$$**

WHAT TO SEE AND DO

Aqua Park Fojnica (*Banjska 3; 030 547 500; e recepcija@aquareumal.ba; w aquareumal.ba*) This pool complex covers more than 12,000m² of wet and wild fun. Located just behind the Reumal Fojnica, this large fun park is the latest addition to Fojnica's spa offerings. The facilities are modern and safe. It's a great place for a day trip with the kids. During winter months the pools are only open to Aqua Remural hotel guests, but are open to everyone during the summer.

Holy Spirit Franciscan Monastery Fojnica (*Fra Andjela Zvizdovica 1; 030 832 081; 9.00–noon & 13.30–16.30 Tue–Sat; e samostan.fojnica@gmail.com; w fojnica-samostan.com*) Overlooking the town of Fojnica, this hilltop monastery is home to approximately 17,000 volumes of books, records and documents. Next to Kraljeva Sutjeska library, the Holy Spirit Monastery holds the second-largest collection of pre-1500 books in Bosnia and Herzegovina. The museum also exhibits one of the most valued Ottoman era documents, the *Ahdnama*. This document, written in Arabic, is one of the most important orders issued by Sultan Mehmed II to the Catholic communities of Bosnia and Herzegovina. The 16th-century decree allowed Christians, at least in principle, to freely practise their Christian beliefs.

Prokoško Lake About an hour's drive through the mountains from Fojnica, this popular hiking and weekend location is certainly a highlight of all the mountain ranges in central Bosnia. It offers exceptional hiking and it's easily doable by novice hikers. There are several places to eat, and accommodation is available on a regular basis in several of the *katunis* (shepherds' huts) turned bed and breakfasts. It may be possible to reserve a hut in advance by calling m 063 369 089 or visiting w koli.ba/bs. The other huts don't advertise well, so just ask around.

Vranica Mountain This is another one of these places in Bosnia and Herzegovina of which visitors ask, 'Why isn't this a national park?' Vranica Mountain is central Bosnia's highest mountain at 2,112m. Like most of the ranges in the central part of the country, the slopes gently climb to great heights, leaving much of the mountain accessible even by car. Vranica is located in between Gornji Vakuf and Fojnica. The easiest and most common access is from the eastern slopes near Fojnica.

There is an 11km gravel road to the heart of Vranica at Prokoško Lake from the town of Fojnica. Be sure to keep an eye out for the signs and ask a local if you doubt whether you are heading in the right direction or not. Before the lake is the **Jezernice mountain lodge** (page 265). Set in a pristine forest along the cascading waters of the Fojnica, this is one of the best spots on the mountain for a peaceful stay. There is no phone number or address, but it is the only lodge on the only road leading up to Prokoško from Fojnica. Ask any local if you don't feel comfortable finding your way.

Prokoško Lake is another half-hour drive away. Famed for its endemic triton salamander, there have been a growing number of local scientists and ecologists calling for its protection. The salamanders are gradually becoming an endangered species as the lake continues to shrink in size. The lake is also home to a large trout population that continues to thrive in these high mountain conditions. The lake formed as a result of melting glaciers from the high peaks of Vranica. As the glaciers continued to melt they carved out the mountain stream of Borovnica that flows into Fojnica River in the valley below. The excess water collected in a karst sinkhole. As the glaciers retreated Borovnica River was reduced to a stream and the lake took on the form seen today.

For centuries, highlanders have used Prokoško Lake as a summer shepherd settlement. The famous *katunis* dot the countryside around the lake. *Katunis* are known for their wood shingles and steep roofs designed to keep the snow from accumulating. The interiors are usually rather primitive due to the fact that they were mainly used for summer grazing and most of the time was spent outdoors. Town dwellers soon caught on to the wonders of Prokoško Lake and began building weekend huts in the vicinity. Luckily the small valley at 1,635m will not allow for much more development and Prokoško will maintain its traditional look. The highlanders are very friendly, and walking up to someone's hut is actually expected. They will, of course, treat you with the great hospitality that most highlanders bestow on foreign guests. While you are guaranteed success if you go fishing in the lake, please remember to limit your catch so as not to adversely affect the trout population.

Vranica is a paradise for hikers and walkers. The landscape above the lake is rather bare, which makes it much easier to keep one's bearings. The hike to **Močika Peak** (2,108m) takes about an hour from Prokoško. Central Herzegovina opens up from the top and the views of Čvrsnica, Prenj and Bjelašnica are amazing. You'll more than likely come across a flock of sheep, as well as many of the shepherds who gravitate to the sunny slopes of Ločika. Bears, wolves, boars, deer, martens and the occasional chamois inhabit this mountain's pristine landscape. The deep valleys to the northwest are covered in thick forests and much of the wildlife seeks shelter there. Situated at 1,427m, the fishing society has a mountain hut and hatchery to the northeast. Both of these places are accessible by car on gravel roads.

VAREŠ

This tiny mining town is situated in the centre of the middle Bosnian mountain massif of the **Kapija**, **Stijene**, **Zvijezda** and **Perun** mountains. It is located approximately 20km from the exit ramp of the M-17 roadway for Breza and Vareš travelling north from Sarajevo. The newer part of town is centred on the mining industry, whereas the old town is the site of the ancient **Oglavić Church**, the early Christian basilica in **Dabravine**, and the old Illyrian city on Zvijezda Mountain to the east. The Catholic church was built here after the first Franciscan order was established in the area in 1340. Artefacts from Vareš can be viewed at the **Kraljeva Sutjeska Monastery Museum** (pages 254–5). **Karići Mosque** is a fine example of Ottoman architecture and design.

For those of you unable to resist the tempting pine-covered mountains surrounding Vareš, there are excellent hiking and walking areas on Perun Mountain. The mountain lodge **Javorje** [map, page 240] is situated at 1,427m and is perfect terrain for easy hiking. It has a restaurant that serves traditional highland food and some national dishes, and a fairly large dormitory that sleeps up to 30.

The remains of the medieval fortress in the royal town of **Bobovac** (**w** *bobovac.org*) are easily accessible from Vareš via well-maintained gravel roads. Bobovac (pages 256–7) had a primarily defensive and strategic role for the Bosnian monarchs until the death of Stjepan Tomašević in 1463. Bobovac is positioned so that it is surrounded by deep canyons on three sides, with road access from Kraljeva or from Vareš. The neighbouring villages, the protectors of Bobovac in olden times, will welcome visitors with traditional homemade dishes and produce. Archaeological excavations of Bobovac were carried out in 1959–67 and the finds can be seen at the National Museum in Sarajevo.

OLOVO

Olovo, a mining town located 40km to the northeast of Sarajevo, means 'lead' in the local language. This ore-rich area has been mined for centuries. Its most valued natural resource, however, is the thermal wells with temperatures of 36°C. The spa **Aquaterm** (*Branilaca bb;* **** *032 829 600;* **w** *aquaterm.olovo.ba*) is well known for its healing powers to treat joint and muscle problems, cardiovascular and nervous system diseases, or just a tired body. Throughout history, Olovo has been known for its diverse belief systems. The Bosnian Church obviously left its mark in this mountain town. The holy site of **Gospa Olovska** from the 14th century has been visited by Muslims since the early Ottoman days. The belief that miracles have occurred in this church has drawn people of all religions to seek help or simply peace of mind.

Olovo sits in a bowl completely surrounded by lush green forest of mainly pine trees. Three rivers cross in Olovo, the largest being the **Krivaja River** that flows to Zavidovići, and there are several spots for great kayaking and fishing. Olovo to the east and southeast was a front-line town: be careful not to wander into the forest on those sides. By the Krivaja River it is perfectly safe for a walk, kayaking trip, fishing or a picnic. On the main road coming from Sarajevo is the **Restoran Panorama** (**m** *061 713 798;* **e** *panorama@bih.net.ba;* **w** *panorama-olovo.com;* ⌚ *5.30–22.30 daily;* **$**), obviously named for its great view. The food is just as good and they have a small bed and breakfast with ten beds (**$**). If you plan to stay the night after a long day of kayaking or waiting on a miracle from the Mother of God Church, **Motel Onix** (*Tuzlanska-Olovska luka bb;* ☎ *035 550 205;* e *info@moteloniks.com;* **$**) offers simple, clean and inexpensive accommodation.

BIJAMBARA CAVES Not far from Olovo are the Bijambara Caves, located less than an hour from Sarajevo, on the main road to Tuzla via Olovo in the municipality of Ilijaš. These caves were first recorded in the early 1900s during the Austro-Hungarian period, but it is assumed that they have been used for centuries. The whole area around the caves is referred to as Bijambare, and as of 2003 is a protected landscape. Nestled within thick pine forests, the five caves meander more than 300m into the belly of the mountain, but only one is accessible to visitors.

Getting there and away The easiest way to get to Bijambare is by car via the M-18 road from Sarajevo towards Tuzla. The caves are located about 40km from Sarajevo, 31km after the suburb of Vogošća. Parking is available on site and is included in the ticket price. Getting there by bus is also not impossible, though perhaps trickier to figure out if one does not speak the local language. Many buses (approximately one every hour) from Sarajevo going to Tuzla will stop within easy walking distance of the caves. The best thing to do is to ask at the bus station for a timetable and tell the bus driver where you want to get off.

What to see and do The cave open to the public has a paved walkway, and is 500m long. It consists of four chambers ornamented with fascinating stalagmites and stalactites. One cavern is named the 'music hall' for its rich acoustic effects. In another cave, artefacts have been found indicating human presence in the Stone Age. Those tools and weapons are now housed in the National Museum in Sarajevo. It is thought the cave system is only a fraction of what remains to be discovered. Entrance to the caves costs 2KM, and children under 7 get in for free. Nearby is an **Information Centre** with a restaurant (☎ *033 201 112;* e *harita.colakovic@zppks.ba*). The cave is advertised as being open to visitors for guided tours every day at 11.00, 13.00, 15.00, 17.00, though it is wise to call/email in advance to confirm, to be on the safe side. Trips can also be organised through the tourist information centre in Sarajevo (page 114), Green Visions (page 89), or the Bijambare Mountaineer Association (☎ *033 401 017*). In the area around the caves is a **mountain lodge** that sleeps 50 and serves homemade meals throughout the year (☎ *033 401 017*).

The general Bijambare area has a playground for kids, and a **miniature train** ride. There are also several marked **walking trails**. One trail extends up to 3km through level, open meadows and thick pine forests. A longer 3km hiking trail is a bit more challenging. It travels uphill and finishes at the mountain lodge. There is a picnic area at the lodge, and a smaller area on the ledge of the upper cave with a magnificent view of the surrounding area, just above the tree line.

TRAVNIK

Travnik sits as the hub of central Bosnia, located in the heart of the Lašva Valley, only 80km (a 1½ hour drive) northwest from Sarajevo. Since its days as the former residence of the early Ottoman rulers of Bosnia and Herzegovina, Travnik has been a sort of cultural powerhouse in central Bosnia. It is the political and administrative centre of the Central Bosnia Canton. The city is situated in the narrow valley of the Lašva River and bordered by Vlašić Mountain to the north and Mount Vilenica to the south. Wherever you wander in Travnik you will find traces of a rich culture and an eventful history. In its glory days Travnik was the number-one city in the Ottoman Empire and has managed to preserve its medieval character well. The arrival of the Turks meant that mosques, *madrasas* (schools) and *mahalas* (quarters) were constructed. The town's road and water systems were built, the medieval fortress was further fortified and a mini-city was built within its high stone walls. Travellers to this area from the 16th–19th century remarked that Travnik was the most oriental-looking town in Bosnia and it therefore received the honour of being called the European Istanbul. A large fire in 1903, however, reduced much of the city to ashes leaving only a few of the many *mahalas* intact.

The ancient fortress managed to survive the fire, and this imposing structure that for centuries defended the city from invaders still dominates the horizon, along with the many minarets that sprout up from all over the city. The fortress is open to guests – the only question is when. Try your luck and climb the stone steps leading to the main entrance. There may be a gatekeeper to let you in but equally there may not be. The walk up is lovely and the old quarters around the fortress have some very impressive traditional homes. Apart from being the administrative headquarters for Ottoman rule in Bosnia, Travnik is best known as an ancient trading place. The markets were always filled with visitors and traders from Dubrovnik, Serbia and other Ottoman territories. Just as Mostar and Sarajevo's *čaršijas* developed into craftsmen's quarters, so too did the old town of Travnik.

Travnik is the birthplace of Ivo Andrić, who won the Nobel Prize in literature for his novel *The Bridge on the Drina*. He also wrote *Travnik Chronicles*, which portrayed the author's view of life in Travnik during Ottoman rule. The **Ivo Andrić House** is now a museum and a restaurant, although it has been said that the museum is not the actual house in which he was born. The restaurant, built as an old-style Bosnian room with the walls covered in local art, is one of the most atmospheric places in town.

GETTING THERE AND AWAY

By road The M-5 highway is a very busy road that runs through Travnik and connects it with other centres; it also connects Sarajevo and Banja Luka. To get to Travnik you can use the regional road (R413) that runs from Banja Luka through Skender Vakuf and Vlašić to Travnik. Towns near Travnik connect to the new highway, the A1. To get to Vlašić Mountain you can use the old Vlašićka road, starting your way from the settlement of Kalibunar, and the road (R413) that branches off at the eastern entrance to Turbe.

The valley of the Bila River, known as the Bila area, is connected by an asphalt road, which branches off from the M-5 highway in Bila. It is also possible to get to Travnik through the village of Guča Gora, which is on a road that runs to Zenica.

In winter all roads in the municipality of Travnik are passable. Normally the main road leading to Vlašić is better maintained than the town centre. In winter people are sometimes advised to avoid driving along the hilly parts and streets in the town.

The main roads that run through the Central Bosnia Canton are:

- E761 Bihać–Bosanski Petrovac–Jajce–Travnik–Sarajevo–Mostar
- E661 Banja Luka–Jajce–Travnik–Sarajevo–Mostar
- E73 Slavonski Brod–Doboj–Zenica–Travnik–Donji Vakuf–Livno
- A1 Doboj–Zenica–Sarajevo–Mostar–Čapljina

By train The nearest railway station is in Zenica (*032 201 535*), 60km away from Travnik (a 40–45-minute drive).

By bus The bus station is located on the Lašva Valley road (E761) that cuts through the centre of Travnik. Buses run regularly to and from Travnik for Zenica and Sarajevo as well as to the northwest toward Donji Vakuf and Bugojno. As it is on the major bus routes, most traffic through the Lašva Valley stops in Travnik.

GETTING AROUND Walking around is certainly the best bet in Travnik. It's a small town with the most interesting things to see and do in the old town. If you are keen on going up to Vlašić Mountain it's best to drive or hire a taxi from the taxi stand in the old town near the Coloured Mosque.

TOURIST INFORMATION/TOUR OPERATOR

Tourist information centre Travnik, Bosanska 75 (opposite the clock tower & Haji Alibey Mosque); 030 511 588; e info@tzsbk.com; w tzsbk.com; 08.00–16.00 Mon–Fri. Staff members speak English & German.

San Tours Travel Agency Bosanska 135; 032 511 910; e santours@bih.net.ba

WHERE TO STAY

Motel Aba (6 rooms, 1 apt) Šumeće 166; 032 511 462; e motel@aba.ba; w aba.ba/motel. This is a very comfortable hotel near the Plava Voda. The rooms are simple but its proximity to the old town is quite convenient. The only disadvantage is that several rooms face the highway. **$$**

Hotel Bosna [map, page 240] (12 rooms) Donje Putićevo bb, Nova Bila; 030 708 150 or 030 707 777; w motel-bosna.com. This hotel is between Vitez & Travnik. The rooms are pleasant & the service good. It is a local favourite & has a good menu, including decent meals for vegetarians. **$–$$**

Motel Bajra (15 rooms) Dolac on Lašva; 030 547 400; w bajra.ba. Has modern décor & a decent restaurant. About 2km from the town centre on the main highway coming into Travnik from the east. It's not ideal for peace & quiet but is certainly one of the nicest places in town. **$**

Motel Konzul (7 rooms, 1 apt) Pirota; m 061 376 243. Located in a detached settlement of Pirota, at the family estate of the renowned Hafizadić family. They named their motel Konzul because they believed that their family house had once been the Austrian Consulate. **$**

Pansion Onix (7 rooms) Žitarnica; 032 512 182. B&B-type place which is family owned & operated. The rooms are basic but pleasant, though they are situated close to the highway. **$**

WHERE TO EAT AND DRINK You should not leave Travnik without tasting at least one of these local favourites. The famous Travnik (Vlašić) cheese, the unique *ćevapi* (small rolls of grilled minced meat), trout, roasted lamb, *tirit* pie (with chicken meat and crumble made of flour, egg yolk and butter), *sogan dolma* (stuffed onions), *tufahija* (baked apple stuffed with walnuts), the aphrodisiacal pear *jeribasma*, and Lutvo's and Hamdi-bey's coffee at Lutvina Kahva.

Divan Zenjak 13; 030 511 492; 08.00–23.00 Mon–Fri. Located in the museum complex of Ivo Andrić's Birth House. It is decorated in a traditional Bosnian way to blend in with the house itself. After visiting the museum, feel free to sit in the house courtyard & enjoy one of the many dishes they offer. If you are really hungry, go for the filled *uštipak* (Bosnian version of salty doughnut). It comes with cheese or meat. **$$**

Lovac Bosanska 63; 030 512 774; 07.00–22.00 daily. On Travnik's main drag, this restaurant does not look impressive from the outside, but has some of the best food in town. From the basic comforts of sturdy wooden chairs &

tables, order a speciality of the house, the hunter's steak with Travnik cheese & mushrooms, for instance. For the more adventurous, there is fried veal brain. $$

Ćevabdžinica Hari Žitarnica bb; 030 511 727; 08.00–20.00 daily. This is one busy & crowded place with small tables & chairs & waiters desperately working to serve all the hungry guests. The restaurant has been around for 16 years. It is one of the most popular *ćevapi* joints in town. $

Konoba Plava Voda Šumeće bb; m 061 798 040; e plavavodakonoba@gmail.com; f konobaplavavoda; 07.00–23.00 daily. Located across from Lutvina Kahva, this might be the best place to eat in the Plava Voda area. Their stream trout is a speciality you should not miss. Try with a carafe of the excellent house wine. The combination of taste & efficient service with the old-Bosnian-style interior (wooden, rustic chairs & tables) will make the experience even better. $

Lutvina Kahva Šumeće bb; m 061 154 520; 07.00–22.00 daily. This is definitely the most popular spot in town, especially if you want to try real Travnički *ćevapi*. Located next to the water source Šumeće, or Plava Voda (Blue Waters), it is a magnet for tourists. Beside its famous *ćevapi*, Lutvina Kahva is famous for something else as well: this is the place where Prince Rudolph had a coffee before the Mayerling tragedy in 1889. This place is still known as Rudolph's café. Also, it is the place where Andrić's *Travnik Chronicles* begins & ends. Unfortunately, today there is nothing to remind us of its famous history. $

Vlašićka kuća Turbe bb; 030 530 360; 07.00–22.00 daily. This restaurant is located in Turbe, where the road branches off to Vlašić. Its extraordinary architecture makes it hard to miss. Their excellent cheese is the reason to make a stop. It looks like a modern villa made completely out of brick & wood. If you have already had enough of Travnik (Vlašić) cheese at this point, there are plenty of other delicious meals to pick from the menu. $

Egipat Sweet Shop Bosanska 71; m 062 875 541; 07.00–23.00 daily. Located on the main street, this is probably the oldest sweet shop in Travnik. It is a busy place with a nice outdoor terrace & a very friendly staff. Inside, you can choose from a number of cakes. They are most famous for their homemade ice cream & have used the same recipe for almost 100 years.

Saher Sweet Shop Donja Čaršija 193; 030 511 659; 07.00–23.00 daily. Old, traditional sweet shop close to the Coloured Mosque (Šarena Džamija). It's been around for years & made its reputation by making the best *saher* cake in town. They also serve all sorts of tasty pitta (*burek* – meat; *zeljanica* – spinach; *krompiruša* – potato; *sirnica* – cheese).

WHAT TO SEE AND DO *Enes Škrgo*

Perhaps the best place to start and finish a tour of Travnik is at the **Plava Voda** (*030 540 055*). Plava Voda (Blue Waters), also known as Šumeće, is the heart of this ancient town. Restaurants and cafés line the crystal-clear stream that runs through the middle of this favourite gathering spot. On hot summer days the cold mountain spring cools the area, making it an ideal spot for lunch and a drink. It's a pleasant walk with a paved footpath following the stream up to its spring. Feel free to indulge in the fresh water; it is healthy and perfectly safe. The folks from Travnik, and in fact the whole region, claim to have the best *ćevapi* in the country. Freshwater trout is also a local speciality, as is *tucana kafa* (hand-ground coffee) from **Lutvina Kahva**. From here you can make your way up to the old town fortress or head across the main road to Šarena Mosque. Either way, it's a good idea to finish your visit of Travnik at this famous site.

The **old town** (*10.00–18.00 daily; entrance 1KM*) is the fortress that dominates the Travnik skyline. The fortification, which was built in the late 14th or early 15th century, hides a mystery about its architect. Archaeological studies about its building style suggest that King Tvrtko II Kotromanić may have been the architect of the fortress. After the royal escutcheon was replaced by the victorious flags of Sultan Mehmed II on 3 June 1463, the Ottoman Turks pulled down the royal palace built of wood and erected a mosque, naming it after Sultan the Conqueror. Only the minaret of the mosque has been preserved to the present day; the mosque, being in a state of disrepair, disappeared in the period between the two world wars. They also pulled down the fortification reinforcements such as the tower, cistern and defensive walls. The secret passage from the fortress to the Šumeće water sources was filled up over time.

In the late 20th century, the five old defensive walls began to crack. In an attempt to preserve the old town, the Zavičajni Museum of Travnik, in co-operation with the Mozaik Foundation, set up a summer stage and amphitheatre. Thanks to the European Commission, much of the fortress has been restored and its crumbling walls saved from further decline. There is now a shop in the old town that sells traditional souvenirs of Travnik and handicrafts made by the local craftsmen. Travnik is the only city in Bosnia and Herzegovina to have two **clock towers**. In the 18th century the viziers of Travnik erected 20m-tall towers to show the time on all four sides of Donja and Gornja *čaršija* (old town). The tower clock at Musala was constructed first. Its exterior part has been restored but the timing mechanisms are apparently in dire need of repair. The **sun clock** in Travnik is the only one of its kind in BiH. Some technical studies have shown that this clock is very accurate owing to the careful calculations of the astronomical experts from Ottoman times.

It's hard to miss the **Sulejmanija/Šarena Mosque** (Coloured Mosque). With its bright colours and unusual intricate artistic details on the outside walls, it is one of the most beautiful mosques in the Balkans. The old wooden doors are equally impressive and if the door is open and it is not prayer time you are welcome to enter. Remember to take your shoes off and if you are a woman to cover your head with a scarf or shawl. Muslims here are very tolerant of foreigners, so don't feel ashamed if you have to be reminded of the customs. The mosque is a unique example of Islamic architecture: its exterior is decorated with floral ornaments (motifs of grapevines, grapes and cypress flowers), which is unusual for an Islamic place of worship. The minaret is on the western instead of the eastern side. The ground floor accommodates a *bezistan* (bazaar complex) with small trades and craft shops, whose rent money was used for the maintenance of the mosque. The building itself is a mixture of secular and religious architectural elements. It is believed that some hairs from the beard of the prophet Muhammad, given to Sulejman-pasha Skopljak as a high military award, are kept in the building.

It was built in the early 16th century by Gazi-agha. Almost nothing is known about him, but you can see his grave next to the building. From 1757 the building was called Ćamilija, after having been renovated by Ćamil Ahmed-pasha. It was renamed Sulejmanija in 1815 after the vizier Sulejman-pasha Skopljak. It still remains a mystery how the mosque escaped destruction in the fire of 1903 that destroyed all the surrounding buildings.

The **Jeni Mosque**, which dates back to 1549, is the oldest-preserved mosque in Travnik. It has the Turkish name *Jeni*, which means 'new'. There is a belief that it was once the Catholic church of St Catherine. Jeni Mosque is also a *tekke* of the Kadiri and Bedevi dervish orders. The old graveyard with the vizier's *turbe* of Abdul-pasha Defterdarija is situated next to the mosque.

Southeast along the Lašva River from the Šarena Džamija is one of the few remaining old-style Bosnian *mahalas*. These neighbourhoods of old homes, built with steep roofs due to heavy snow, are fine examples of the traditional architectural style. In the centre of town is the **Zavičajni Museum** (☎ *030 518 140; Mehmedpaše Kukavice 1;* **e** *muzej.travnik@bih.net.ba;* **w** *muzejtravnik.ba;* ⌚ *9.00–15.00 Mon–Fri; 10.00–14.00 Sat & Sun; entrance 2.50KM*). Although it is by no means up to Western standards, for history buffs or interested folks there are enough noteworthy artfacts about Travnik to make it a worthwhile visit. The **Memorial Museum – Birth House of Ivo Andrić** (*Zenjak 13;* ☎ *030 501 477;* **e** *zavicajni.muzej@bih.net.ba;* **w** *muzejtravnik.ba/rodna-kuca-ive-andrica; permanent exhibition* ⌚ *09.00–15.00 Mon–Fri, 10.00–14.00 Sat & Sun; entrance 2.50KM*) is located in the Travnik *mahala* of Zenjak and was opened as a memorial museum on 30 August 1974. On 13 March 1975, the day of the famous writer's death, it was renamed the Ivo Andrić Memorial Museum. It is the only museum of its kind in Bosnia, dedicated to the only winner of the Nobel Prize in literature from the former Yugoslavia. It includes a study, the *Travnik Chronicles* room, a library and an interesting photo collection. The curator offers explanations in the local language and English and will be glad to recommend interesting places. Just down the road is the **Hafizadić House**, an ivy-clad house that once belonged to the Austrian consulate. After escaping the unsuccessful revolution in Hungary in 1848, a Hungarian physician, Dr Gabor Galantay, built the first European-style urban house of the era. At that time the consulates in Sarajevo had been closed. The house is owned by the renowned family Hafizadić, whose female descendants wrote using Bosančica, the ancient Bosnian script, until the end of the 20th century. Dr Sulejman Hafizadić was the first physician from Travnik to be educated in Vienna and Istanbul.

Elči-Ibrahim pasha's *madrasa*, which dates from 1706, was built in the neo-Moorish style. The town's first library was established in it after Ibrahim-pasha donated 103 manuscript books. A memorial tablet, as a reminder of that event, stands by the entrance. The tablet was unveiled on 15 October 1972 by Ivo Andrić, on his last visit to his birth town. The space of the madrasa is architecturally arranged to create an unusual experience of quietness and light. There is still a professor resident in the madrasa, who will be glad to explain to groups of visitors about the background and organisation of one of the oldest schools in Bosnia.

Very near to the centre of Travnik is the Catholic village of **Guča Gora**. It is one of the oldest villages around Travnik and even today it represents a place where efforts have been made to preserve the traditional culture and customs. It is assumed that it was named after the famous medieval tradesmen of the Dubrovnik Gučetić family. The village was first mentioned in 1425, in a charter granted by the Hungarian King Sigismund, in which he rewarded the aristocrat Vuk from that village for his efforts in battles against the Turks. The Franciscan monastery dominates the village. The founder of the monastery was Father Marijan Šunjić, known as a linguist who spoke 13 languages and was educated in Italy by the esteemed philologist Mezzofanti. He was appointed a bishop and was buried within the monastery. Kind and humble friars will gladly interpret for you the history of the monastery and show you the artistic and historical collections relating the cultural heritage of the Travnik area. An authentic folklore group named Sloga is very active. They perform characteristic dances in traditional folk costumes and amazing traditional songs that are not taught at any music academy. You may notice the characteristic custom of tattooing. The women have tattoos on their arms, representing both pagan and Christian symbols. They are considered the most beautiful traditional tattoos in central Bosnia.

Not far from Guča Gora is the central Bosnian town of **Vitez**. It is more known for its shopping centres than anything else, but it does hold one of central Bosnia's best kept secrets. **Ethno Village Čardaci** (*Poslovni centar 96, Zona II, Vitez;* ☎ *030 718 718;* **e** *info@cardaci.ba;* **w** *cardaci.ba;* ⌚ *07.00–22.00 daily*) is located just outside the town of Vitez, about an hour's drive from Sarajevo. This rustic complex includes accommodation facilities, a restaurant, water park, beer house & fishery. Accommodation is available in small, rustically equipped ethno houses named after the Old Slavic Gods or a recently opened motel (*12 rooms, 1 apt;* **$–$$**). The Lašva River flows through the centre of the village. Just across a small wooden foot bridge is the restaurant named Kod Mlina (*030 712 739;* 08.00–23.00 daily; **$–$$**). They specialise in traditional (mainly meat) dishes, or freshly grilled fish supplied to the restaurant from a fishpond located within the complex. The beer house, Kod Crnog Mačka, is a popular night spot. Some of the local folk music sounds better after a few rakija's (locally distilled brandy), wine and beer, but it's a good spot to have a few drinks and grab dinner with local live music. The water park is just a hop, skip and a jump away. It offers four swimming pools with varying depths, a cocktail bar, fast food, volleyball, football and badminton sand fields, as well as a number of sandy beaches.

VLAŠIĆ MOUNTAIN

The tradition of living in high, isolated areas is a trademark of the peoples who first settled in BiH. Vlašić was not only home to old Illyrian highlanders and the followers of the medieval Bosnian Church, but also to a large shepherd community that continues to live off the fertile lands across the vast plateaus of Vlašić Mountain. The life of the highlanders was markedly affected by the conflict in the early 1990s, and many of them were forced to abandon the lifestyles that they and their ancestors had enjoyed for centuries. Much of that life has returned to Vlašić, however, and the highlanders have resumed their age-old customs of sheep-raising and cheese production.

GETTING THERE The revitalisation of many of the villages has also brought back many domestic tourists to the ski resort and mountain lodges that were popular holiday spots before the war. Babanovac ski area is only 28km from Travnik and a good road keeps it accessible all year round. Only 2km west of Travnik, before the town of Turbe, is the turn-off for Vlašić. The climb will take 15–20 minutes before you reach the first plateau. After driving another 4–5km the only turn-off to the right (which is well marked) leads to Babanovac. There aren't many roads on Vlašić, so it's pretty hard to make a wrong turn. There is also a bus (*Mon–Sat*) from Travnik to Vlašić (Babanovac) at 10.00 and 15.00. The bus departs from Babanovac at 11.35 and 16.00. A one-way ticket is 4.00KM. On Sundays, there is only one bus (10.00 from Travnik, returning at 16.00 from Babanovac). Vlašić is located 95 km from Sarajevo, and can be reached by car via M-5 to Travnik. Several daily buses also connect Sarajevo to Travnik.

WHERE TO STAY

Hotel Blanca (38 rooms) Babanovac bb; 030 519 900; **e** recepcija@blanca-resort.com; **w** blanca-resort.com. Blanca is a 4-star boutique hotel in the mountains. This is by far the nicest & fanciest of the accommodation facilities on Vlašić Mountain. All the spacious rooms are equipped with Wi-Fi, AC, minibar & sat TV. The beautiful spa centre is complete with Turkish bath, sauna, jacuzzi, full massage & pedicure services & a fitness centre. The resort overlooks the ski area. **$$$**

Eko-Fis Vlašić (23 apts & 14 cabins) Babanovac bb; 030 294 528; **e** eko-fis@fis.ba; **w** eko-fisvlasic.ba. Eko-Fis is a tourist village offering modern, comfortable accommodation in small, medium & large apts, or houses/cabins designed in natural styles. It also offers numerous recreational facilities such as a paintball park, an adrenaline park, kids' playground, sports, a spa with a pool, etc. There is a restaurant with good, affordable meals, a vast menu & a bar. In terms of lodging, food, or activities, there's something for everyone's taste & budget. Located 1km from the Babanovac ski area. **$–$$$**

Hotel Pahuljica (32 rooms) Babanovac bb; 030 540 022; **e** info@pahuljica.com; **w** pahuljica.com. All rooms are comfortable &

each has a minibar, TV & phone. The hotel also has a wellness & spa centre, a restaurant, a ski bar & a conference room. During the summer, there is an anti-stress w/end offer for about 169KM pp & includes a 2-night stay, 2 40-minute massages of your choice, & you have unlimited use of the hotel's fitness facilities, pool & recreation area. **$$**

Villa Ugar (20 rooms) Babanovac bb; 030 540 140; **e** info@villa-ugar.ba; **w** villa-ugar.ba. All rooms are equipped with TV & minibar. They are nicely furnished with modern, wooden furniture & colourful bedding. You can rent a snowmobile here. **$$**

WHERE TO EAT AND DRINK

Restoran Mt Blanc Babanovac bb; 030 519 900; **e** recepcija@blanca-resort.com; **w** blanca-resort.com; 07.00–23.00 daily. Besides the comfort & aesthetics of dining in Mt Blanc, the food, service & wine list are as good as the hotel where it's located. Serving an impressive menu of local, international & Dalmatian cuisine this is Mt Vlašić's best dining experience. **$$–$$$**

Restoran Pahuljica Šišava bb; 030 540 022; **e** info@pahuljica.com; **w** pahuljica.com; winter 07.00–midnight; summer 07.00–23.00 daily. Hotel Pahuljica, although not as fancy as its competitor Hotel Blanca, is Vlašić's most established hotel & restaurant. With a heavier slant on Bosnian national dishes, the menu has plenty of international cuisine to satisfy all tastes. The service is friendly & prompt. **$$**

Ćevabžinica Hari Babanovac bb; **m** 061 171 270; 07.00–23.00 daily. For good Travnički *ćevapi* on Vlašić, this is a place to go. Furnished completely in wood, it is always crowded but the organised & efficient staff keep things under control. There is also a Hari in Travnik. That *ćevabžinica* has nearly 20 years of tradition. At the Hari on Vlašić, you can also rent rooms (**$**). **$**

WHAT TO SEE AND DO Vlašić Mountain is the second-highest mountain in central Bosnia after Vranica Mountain near Fojnica. Its highest peak, **Paljenik** at 1,943m, is not like the steep and sometimes treacherous peaks of the Dinaric chain in Herzegovina. Vlašić is known for its mild and easily accessed highlands. The road infrastructure is excellent and most places can be reached by 4x4. The mountain is often used as a short cut from Travnik to Banja Luka.

During peaceful times Vlašić Mountain was the pride and joy of Travnik. During the war, however, it placed Travnik directly in the artillery gunners' sights. In a massive offensive in the winter of 1995, the Bosnian army climbed and conquered the frozen and snow-covered peaks in one of the most dramatic victories of the war.

Skiing on Vlašić doesn't compare to the Olympic-quality skiing available on Jahorina or Bjelašnica, but it certainly provides an attractive alternative and the capacity of the ski area of **Babanovac** is, in fact, larger than on Bjelašnica Mountain. There are also 15km of cross-country ski trails and the ski jumps (the biggest at 90m) were used during the **International Vlašić Cup Contest** that was integrated into the European Cup. A daily ski pass costs 27KM. Snowboarders, too, have found a new playground and many clubs set up camp all winter to board. The snowboarding club is located at Babanovac (*030 511 696;* **m** *061 826 570;* **e** *boardout@hotmail.com*). Ski and board rental is possible at **Babanovac Ski Centre**. Visit **w** vlasic.ba/en for more information about conditions and options on Vlašić.

Hiking on Vlašić is a different story. The curse of the beautiful mountain regions of Bosnia and Herzegovina is that they are also of the utmost strategic importance during wars, and the side that holds the highlands will do all they can to keep them. Old-style warfare called for minefields and Vlašić has no shortage of them. The trails to **Devečani mountain lodge** at 1,760m are safe for walking and totally free of mines. The ski area at Babanovac is also clear of the evil aftermath of war. Other areas, however, are risky and best trekked only with a guide. The dense pine forests and soft, rolling hills on the high plateau are perfect walking, biking and hiking terrain. For the free spirits who love to wander through the mountains, I share in your frustration, but it is best to call an ecotourism group. Scorpio Extreme Sports Club from Zenica organise hiking and biking trips (pages 246–7).

Don't leave Vlašić without buying some Vlašićki *sir*, or cheese. Foreign markets have just got wind of this heavenly, white and salty cheese, and the organic and traditional way of preparing it only adds to the appreciation of this local delicacy.

PRUSAC

To the north of Bugojno near the village of Prusac is the largest Muslim pilgrimage site in Europe. Every June thousands of Muslims gather at the holy site at Ajvatovica. This has been Europe's largest Muslim pilgrimage ever since a believer prayed for a long drought to end. Legend has it that during this prayer a large rock face split and water flowed from a resulting crevice. Prusac went untouched during the war, despite the fact that heavy fighting took place in every direction around the small village. The traditional architecture is almost as beautiful as the green hills that roll on as far as the eye can see. Holy spots always seem to have a different energy to them and unlike many other sacred places, Prusac has yet to be commercialised. On an ordinary day one cannot find much of anything going on except people going about their ordinary lives. It's a tiny place where people simply live the way they always have, and come June they wait for the thousands of visitors with open arms. There are daily buses from Bugojno and Donji Vakuf to Prusac. There won't be signs in English or even many trail markers, but you can wander around and then join the locals in a café for a coffee. The turn-off for this little village is in between the towns of Donji Vakuf and Bugojno on the 16 road (as seen on most maps).

WHERE TO STAY AND EAT There is no public place in Prusac where you can eat. In two or three cafés you can have coffee and soft drinks. As tourism further develops expect to see more bed and breakfasts and private accommodation available. The tourism information office (*Novo Naselje bb;* ☎ *030 205 500;* e *prusac@bosnae.ba*) at the entrance to Prusac will have up-to-date information.

Hotel Vrbas (60 rooms) Trg Ibrahim-bega Malkoca 1, Donji Vakuf; ☎ 030 203 100. Located in the centre of Donji Vakuf, about 12km from Bugojno & 6km from Prusac. The staff speak English & German. **$–$$**

WHAT TO SEE AND DO

Old town Prusac has a fortress which dates back to ancient, Illyrian, classical, imperial and Turkish times. The castle is the most dominating structure in Prusac and really is a must-see. It was built on a natural elevation on a cliff that made it unconquerable by any army. There are small caves and pits there that probably served as secret escape passages from the fortress. Citadels, bastions and wells were subsequently added in a different architectural style. Watchtowers and loopholes on the walls 6–10m high and 2.4m wide are still visible. A ditch at the gate once had a drawbridge that used chains to go up and down at night.

Clock tower The Prusac clock tower stands on one of the most dominating locations in Prusac, next to the fortress, close to the polygonal tower, in what used to be a ditch, below the town's pen. It was built in the 18th century, along with clock

LEGEND OF DEDO AJVAZ

The legend of Dedo Ajvaz tells of a great drought that threatened the existence of the small community of Prusac. There was barely enough water for the villagers, let alone for the livestock they depended on for their survival. An old grandfather, Dedo Ajvaz, decided to pray for water. He prayed for 40 days and on the 40th day a large rock near the village began to tremble. The powerful trembling continued and soon the massive rock split in half. From the gap created by the split, water began to flow. News of the miracle spread fast and Muslims and Christians alike came to see for themselves the new spring and the large gorge created by the quake. From that spot water, now venerated at Ajvatovica, continues to flow from beneath the earth and Muslims come here to give thanks.

towers in various other Bosnian towns, so this also shows the Turkish measurement of time. The clock tower is 10m high and rests on a rectangular base with sides 4m long and 80cm wide. At the top it narrows somewhat into a double roof with an open space. It is believed in Prusac that the clock mechanism was built by a craftsman from Gornji Vakuf. The bell in the tower is among the smaller high-pitched ones and is supposed to represent war booty. Note the four interesting cast reliefs that show the crucified Jesus, the Virgin Mary with the baby Jesus, John the Baptist and an unknown archbishop.

Traditional trades and handicrafts It appears that every merchant in central Bosnia has known about the skills of the Prusac craftsmen ever since the time of first barters. Especially in the time of the sultanate, handicrafts in Prusac were a part of both family and community tradition. Until the beginning of war in 1992, there were 15 coopers in Prusac; these are the families in which the secrets of the trade are passed down from one generation to another. Their barrels were mostly produced for Dalmatian winegrowers. Today, there are only a few coopers left in Prusac. Most of them work out of their garages along the village's main road. Feel free to wander and enter any open workshop that you see along the road. These experienced craftsmen will gladly take a break from their hard work to explain to visitors how the fir, juniper and beech timber has to be carefully selected from the Prusac woods and patiently dried, what the names of old tools are and how to use them, and that a huge amount of knowledge and skill is necessary in order to make a barrel as well as a simple wooden wine pitcher. These coopers can sell you wonderful wooden souvenirs at affordable prices.

BOSNIA ONLINE

7

Northwest Bosnia

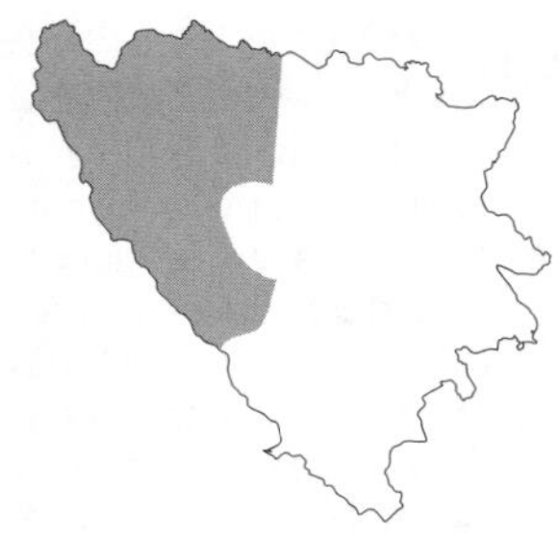

The translation of Krajina is 'frontier'. *Kraj* literally means 'end'. It was this 'end' of the Turkish front that was for centuries the frontier land against the Austro-Hungarian Empire. The Croatian Krajina, just over the border to the west, was at one time crucial to the Ottoman conquest and was used by the Ottomans as a defence line. As the empire began to decline the frontier slipped back into Bosnia where the entire northwest part of the country became known as the Bosanska Krajina (the Bosnian Frontier). It was the policy of the Ottoman administration to settle this land with janissaries, soldiers and their families. As administrators in the empire, Muslims were given incentives such as large tracts of land to resettle in the Krajina. Serbs and Vlachs were also given land to settle in order to defend these areas. The Vlachs in particular were sought after by the Turkish army for their fierce fighting skills. Many Catholics fled or converted during Ottoman times but a significant minority of Croats still inhabit present-day Krajina. The current boundaries between the Federation and Republika Srpska are more political, and for all practical purposes should not affect your travels.

What is most striking about the Krajina is not its political divide, but rather the beautiful interconnected rivers and the lush, green countryside. The sheer quantity of crystal-clear rivers in this region is phenomenal. The Vrbas, Una, Sana, Sanica and Unac rivers are only a few of the pure water sources that flow into the Sava River. The Bosnian Krajina's greatest tourist attractions all revolve around its natural resources. In just about any place in the Krajina there are beautiful places to hike, walk, bike, fish or just enjoy a lazy day in the great outdoors. Although there are no tourist cities like Mostar or Sarajevo to visit, Banja Luka and Bihać are regional centres with things to see and do. But chances are you will spend no more than a day in the city before you find yourself rafting on the Una, or relaxing in the thermal spas at Slatina.

BANJA LUKA

It is fair to call Banja Luka – the administrative capital of the Republika Srpska – an underrated city. Most visitors to Bosnia and Herzegovina don't come here. That is starting to change. Geographically, it is perfect. It is the centre of a rectangle, which includes Sarajevo, the Adriatic Sea, Zagreb in Croatia, and Belgrade in Serbia.

From a tourism standpoint, it is also pretty special. Nestled in green hills, it is full of culture, restaurants and good lodging options. The relaxed feeling one has here comes from the Vrbas River, which is gentle as it putters through town but flexes its muscles just a short distance away. The region is world famous as a rafting haven.

Historically, Banja Luka was on the Roman trade route from Salona to Servitium and also held a strategic spot near the border of Rome's Pannonia and Dalmatia provinces. The Romans built a fortress here to protect this position (along with its healing water springs). They were quite aware of the importance of this locale, where the Dinaric Alps met the Pannonian Plain at 164m above sea level. After the Romans, the Slavs moved in during the 7th century AD.

As a border town, Banja Luka has often found itself at historical crossroads. In the Ottoman era, it was damaged time and again during battles against Habsburg armies. In the 19th century the Austro-Hungarians absorbed the ancient town and gave it more modern touches, connecting it to the rest of the empire. Even though both World War II and a major earthquake in 1969 had devastating effects on the town, it grew by leaps and bounds in the 20th century. To put it in perspective, at the end of the 19th century Banja Luka had around 15,000 residents. Today it claims about 200,000 and is by far the largest city in the northern part of the country and second only to Sarajevo for all of Bosnia and Herzegovina.

Banja Luka has a thriving nightlife and is well known for both its club scene and its live music festivals, namely Demofest. It also has a strong art component, and for the most part all exhibitions, like those at the Contemporary Art Museum, are free of charge. Loaded with lots of leafy parks – so one doesn't feel trapped in an urban jungle – Banja Luka also has a distinctly young vibe, which is fuelled by its university.

For many, the town is and will always be synonymous with rafting. Banja Luka and the Vrbas River hosted the 2005 European Rafting Championship and the 2009 World Rafting Championship. Every year more tour companies and more sophisticated tourism packages are on offer.

GETTING THERE AND AWAY Getting to Banja Luka is fairly easy. The city is the main hub of western Republika Srpska and the second largest city in BiH. Dozens of **buses** leave Banja Luka daily to most destinations in the Republika Srpska and to the main destinations in the Federation, including Sarajevo (*5 hours; approximately 30KM one way, 45KM return, several buses per day*). There are also frequent daily buses to Zagreb, Croatia (*3 hours; approximately 30KM one way, 50KM return*). From Zagreb, there are countless daily buses, trains, and flights to and from a wide variety of international destinations, and even more routes connecting to the Croatian coast, some within just 2 hours. Daily buses run to and from Belgrade, Serbia (*5–7 hours; approximately 40KM one way, 65KM return*). A daily bus also runs to and from Vienna, Austria (*8–9 hours; 70KM one way, 128KM return*). Other European destinations are reachable by bus from Banja Luka. The city is quite well-connected with most cities and small towns in the Republika Srpska, as people often travel daily to the administrative capital.

By **car**, Banja Luka is about 2¼ hours from the charming Croatian capital city of Zagreb – a large part of the route is via the E70 highway. Getting to BiH's largest city, Sarajevo, by car will take longer – about 3–4 hours, though part of that route is via a newly built highway which is still being extended. Belgrade, the capital of Serbia and a bustling metropolis with exciting nightlife, is also reachable by car in about 4 hours.

Daily **trains**, from both Zagreb and Sarajevo, stop in Banja Luka. However, this is one of the most time-consuming routes to either destination (*travel time: 5 hours in either direction*). The train from either destination costs approximately 30–35KM one way, and 50–55KM return. With buses more frequent and of equal or lesser cost, the train is not necessarily the best option, though you might find it more interesting.

By **air**, the only destination currently accessible from Banja Luka is Belgrade, Serbia.

TOURIST INFORMATION The **Tourist Organisation of Banja Luka** (*Kralja Petra I Karađorđevića 87;* ☎ *051 490 308;* **e** *tobl@teol.net;* **w** *banjaluka-tourism.com*) office is the place to go for info about hotels, restaurants, shopping, nightclubbing,

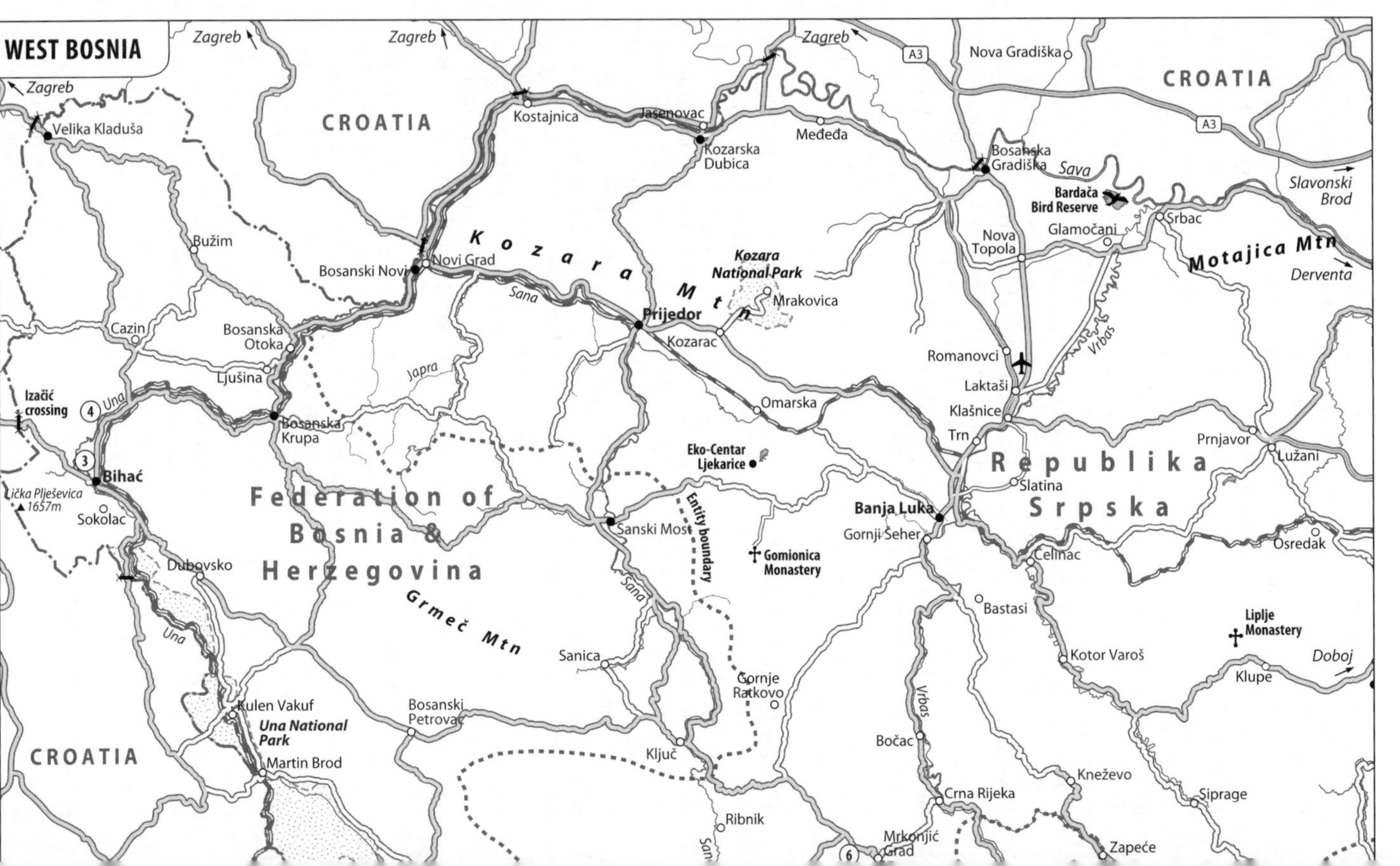
WEST BOSNIA
Zagreb
Zagreb
Zagreb
Zagreb
CROATIA
CROATIA
CROATIA
A3
Nova Gradiška
Slavonski Brod
Derventa
Doboj
Velika Kladuša
Kostajnica
Jasenovac
Kozarska Dubica
Međeđa
Bosanska Gradiška
Sava
Bardača Bird Reserve
Srbac
Glamočani
Nova Topola
Motajica Mtn
Kozara Mtn
Kozara National Park
Mrakovica
Bužim
Bosanski Novi
Novi Grad
Sana
Prijedor
Kozarac
Romanovci
Vrbas
Laktaši
Klašnice
Trn
Prnjavor
Lužani
Cazin
Bosanska Otoka
Ljušina
Japra
Omarska
Izačić crossing
Una
Bosanska Krupa
Bihać
Lička Plješevica 1657m
Sokolac
Eko-Centar Ljekarice
Republika Srpska
Slatina
Federation of Bosnia & Herzegovina
Sanski Most
Entity boundary
Banja Luka
Gornji Šeher
Osredak
Gomionica Monastery
Čelinac
Dubovsko
Grmeč Mtn
Bastasi
Liplje Monastery
Kotor Varoš
Klupe
Sanica
Gornje Ratkovo
Kulen Vakuf
Una National Park
Martin Brod
Bosanski Petrovac
Ključ
Bočac
Kneževo
Crna Rijeka
Šiprage
Ribnik
Mrkonjić Grad
Zapeće

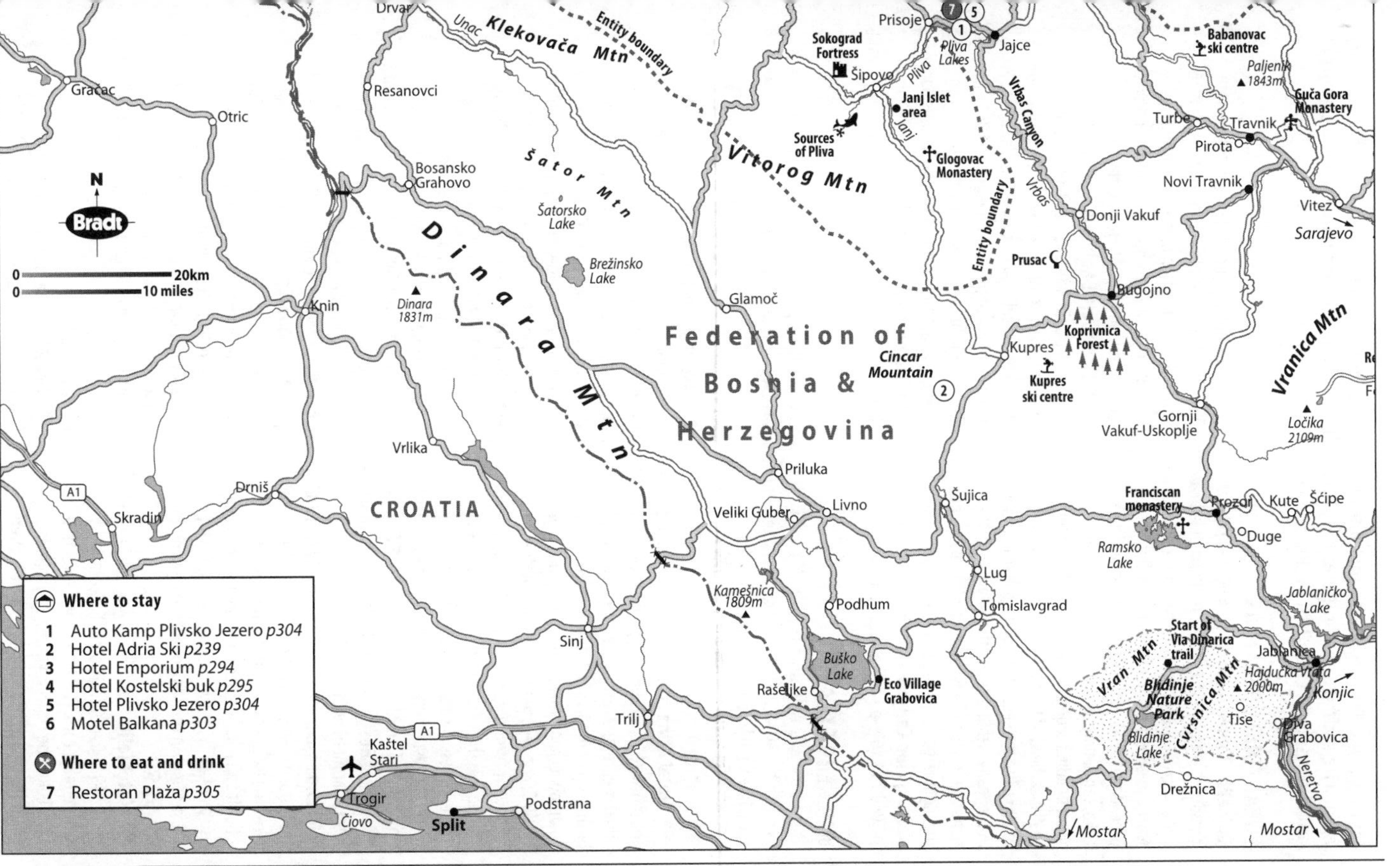
Where to stay
1 Auto Kamp Plivsko Jezero p304
2 Hotel Adria Ski p239
3 Hotel Emporium p294
4 Hotel Kostelski buk p295
5 Hotel Plivsko Jezero p304
6 Motel Balkana p303
Where to eat and drink
7 Restoran Plaža p305
N
Bradt
0 20km
0 10 miles
Federation of Bosnia & Herzegovina
CROATIA
Dinara Mtn
Dinara 1831m
Šator Mtn
Šatorsko Lake
Brežinsko Lake
Klekovača Mtn
Entity boundary
Vitorog Mtn
Vranica Mtn
Ločika 2109m
Cincar Mountain
Kamešnica 1809m
Vran Mtn
Cvrsnica Mtn
Hajducka Vrata 2000m
Blidinje Nature Park
Blidinje Lake
Start of Via Dinarica trail
Ramsko Lake
Franciscan monastery
Jablaničko Lake
Buško Lake
Eco Village Grabovica
Koprivnica Forest
Kupres ski centre
Babanovac ski centre
Paljenik 1843m
Guča Gora Monastery
Sokograd Fortress
Sources of Pliva
Janj Islet area
Glogovac Monastery
Pliva Lakes
Vrbas Canyon
Prusac
Drvar
Unac
Prisoje
Šipovo
Pliva
Janj
Jajce
Vrbas
Turbe
Travnik
Pirota
Novi Travnik
Vitez
Sarajevo
Donji Vakuf
Bugojno
Kupres
Gornji Vakuf-Uskoplje
Prozor
Kute
Šćipe
Duge
Jablanica
Konjic
Tise
Diva Grabovica
Neretva
Drežnica
Mostar
Šujica
Lug
Tomislavgrad
Podhum
Livno
Priluka
Veliki Guber
Glamoč
Rašeljke
Trilj
Sinj
Gračac
Otric
Resanovci
Bosansko Grahovo
Knin
Vrlika
Drniš
Skradin
A1
Kaštel Stari
Trogir
Čiovo
Split
Podstrana

sightseeing, day trips, and just about anything else you have in mind while in the area. The staff are as competent and friendly as you'll find anywhere in the country and they speak a handful of languages.

LOCAL TOUR OPERATORS

Guideline Tourist Agency [284 B1] Kralja Petra I Karađorđevića; 051 212 600; e info@guidelinebl.com; w guidelinebl.com. This contact is key for at least 2 reasons. First, the folks at Guideline, which is headquartered on the Vrbas 11km from Banja Luka, can handle all your rafting, hiking, biking, team building & guiding needs. This is the group that spearheaded the World Rafting Championship in 2009. But the second reason to keep this contact at the ready is that they are the only agency that handles this type of adventure tourism. Ask about the night rafting – a unique offering.

Rafting Club Canyon [284 B2] Karanovac; m 066 714 169; e kanjon@teol.net; w raftingklubkanjon.com. Located 11km south from Banja Luka next to the main road, the M16. This is also the location of the eco-rafting centre. They offer rafting adventures on the Vrbas River & hiking & biking trips throughout the region.

Zepter Passport Banja Luka [285 E3] Veselina Masleše 8/I; 051 213 394; e info@zepterpassport.com; w zepterpassport.com. One of the best travel agencies that organises tours & guides in the Krajina & in other areas of BiH. They also arrange hunting & fishing trips. Zepter can arrange permits, gear/gun rental & customs papers if the hunters would like to take their spoils with them.

WHERE TO STAY

Banja Luka's role as a regional centre has spurred rapid growth in good hotels. Most are in the 50–120KM range, and appear to compete on the basis of style, service and facilities rather than price.

Upmarket

Hotel Atina [284 D3] (20 rooms) Slobodana Kokanovića 5; 051 961 100; e recepcija@atinahotel.com; w atinahotel.com. Close to the business part of town but still removed from the downtown chaos. All rooms are equipped with TV, Wi-Fi & a deposit box. Elegantly outfitted with mahogany furniture, many rooms have balconies overlooking the Vrbas River. The hotel has a spa centre (fitness, jacuzzi, sauna) & its own parking space. The restaurant downstairs is excellent: try the scampi in red sauce (*škampi na buzaru*). **$$–$$$**

Hotel Bosna [285 E3] (300 rooms) Kralja Petra I Karađorđevića 97; 051 215 775; e info@hotelbosna.com; w hotelbosna.com. Built in 1885, this is the oldest & largest hotel in town. The rooms here are also spacious with all the standard extras – but it's all a little older. Compared with the nicer & newer hotels in town, rooms here are overpriced. B/fast comes in the form of a large open buffet. **$$–$$$**

Hotel Talija [285 E3] (53 rooms) Srpska 9; 051 349 200; e info@hoteltalija.com; w hoteltalija.com. This is the only 5-star hotel in Banja Luka. The city has waited 20 years since the end of the war to add a 5-star to its repertoire. Although it may not be obvious from the outside, the interior has superior design. Aside from the aesthetics, the deluxe rooms are large & exceptionally comfortable. The swimming pool, sauna & fitness centre are all top notch. The staff is knowledgeable & friendly. The hotel also offers garage parking & airport transfers. **$$–$$$**

Olimpus [285 E3] (13 apts) Ivana Franje Jukića 7; 051 211 230; e olimpus@olimpus-apartmani.com; w olimpus-apartmani.com. A hotel apartment complex in downtown Banja Luka. This is the only place in town that rents apts to foreign guests. If you plan to be in town for some time & want to cook for yourself, the apts come with a complete kitchen. **$$–$$$**

Hotel Vidović [285 E3] (50 rooms) Ivana Franje Juića; 051 245 800; e info@hotelvidovic.com; w hotelvidovic.com. Vidović is just one street from the main pedestrian street. Its rooms are elegantly decorated & all come with a TV, minibar, phone & internet access. The hotel has its own cafeteria, as well as a restaurant & car park. **$$**

Mid range

Hotel Fortuna [285 H3] (20 rooms) Rakovačkih rudara 12; 051 358 640/1; e info@

wellnessfortuna.com; w wellnessfortuna.com. Part of a much bigger wellness complex. Located 2km from the city centre, this spa complex has a hotel, 3 pools, a wine bar, a cocktail bar & a restaurant. The rooms are comfy. The hotel pool, sauna & fitness centre are included in the price of the stay. **$$–$$$**

Alas [285 E1] (6 rooms) Braće Mažar i majke Marije 48; 051 212 602; e info@restoran-motel-banjaluka.com; w restoran-motel-banjaluka.com. Located on a side street just a 10min walk from the centre & above the best seafood restaurant in town, this hotel – which opened in 2007 – has no-frills rooms with internet, free use of phone (for calls in the area) & AC. B/fast comes with the price. **$$**

Hotel Cezar [285 H5] (20 rooms) Mladena Stojanovića 123; 051 326 400; e info@hotel-cezar.com; w hotel-cezar.com. Close to the government building & Mladen Stojanović Pk. It has sgl rooms (all with French beds), dbls & apts. All rooms are modernly decorated & have Wi-Fi, AC & minibar. The hotel has its own parking space, a restaurant with places for 40 people & a bar. **$$**

Hotel Jelena [285 G1] (58 rooms) Jovana Dučića 25; 051 329 200; e recepcija@hotel-jelenabl.com; w hotel-jelenabl.com. The rooms at this modern hotel have lots of natural light, which complements its décor. All rooms have AC, mini-bar & cable TVs. The restaurant is a great plus to the overall experience. **$$**

Hotel Palas [284 D2] (69 rooms, 3 apts) Ul Petra I Karađorđevića 60; 051 223 040; e info@hotelpalasbl.com; w hotelpalasbl.com. Palas, built in 1933, is one of the oldest hotels in Banja Luka & it is the standard. It is located on the city square (Trg Krajine) & across from Mladen Stojanović Pk. Even though it is in the centre of town, it still has its own parking garage. The hotel has rooms with modern wooden furniture & colourful rugs. All rooms have TV, minibar & Wi-Fi. The downstairs restaurant-café Harizma serves excellent food. **$$**

Hotel Vila Vrbas [284 C2] (20 rooms, 3 apts) Braće Potkonjaka 1; 051 433 840; e info@hotelvillavrbas.com; w hotelvilavrbas.com. This riverside hotel has dbl & sgl rooms & apts with parquet floors & tasteful, dark wood furniture. The clean & spacious apts come with big beds, TVs & Wi-Fi. **$$**

Motel Dragana [284 B1] (12 rooms) Vojvode Uroša Drenovića 129; 051 413 050; e moteldragana@hotmail.com. This comfortable & pleasant hotel is located a bit outside of the city centre along the banks of the Vrbas River. The rooms all have AC, TV & minibar. They are tastefully decorated, & most have nice views of the river. The terrace is a perfect spot to relax & enjoy the cool breeze the Vrbas brings with its currents. **$$**

Budget

Hostel Balkan [285 E1] (3 rooms) Braće Mažara i majke Marije 41; m 065 588 889; e hostelbalkanbl@gmail.com; w hostelbalkan.com. Hostel Balkan is situated in the historical main street of Banja Luka only a 5-min walk from both the city centre & the old Kastel fortress. Rooms are dorm style but very clean & cosy. There's a small bar in the lobby area. **$**

Hostel Banja Luka [285 H5] (4 rooms) Srpskih Ustanika 26; m 066 477 803; e info@hostelbanjaluka.com; w hostelbanjaluka.com. This hostel is a bit out of town but conveniently located next to the bus station if you arrive late or need to depart early. They have limited capacity so it's best to call to make reservations before your arrival. The rooms are simple & clean with shared bathrooms. **$–$$**

Hostel Cuba [284 D1] (42 rooms) Đure Jakšića 18; m 065 284 820; e hostelcubabl@gmail.com; w hostelcubabl.com. Banja Luka's largest hostel has much to offer. They have sgl, dbl, shared & luxury rooms available for any type of traveller. The rooms are all well-designed, clean & built for comfort. There are 2 sitting rooms, 2 kitchens & a large dining room to make sure no one is bumping into each other. It's a very laid-back place, with darts & billiards available for guests. They can also organise trips, guides, rent-a-car or airport transfers. **$**

Hostel Havana [285 G3] (12 rooms) I Krajiškog korpusa bb; m 066 134 001; e hostelhavana3@gmail.com; w draganradic.wix.com/hostel-havana. This hostel caters to both tourist & business travellers. They offer en-suite private rooms at very good value, as well as dormitory-style rooms, also en suite. The downtown location is perfect for getting around by foot. **$**

Hostel Monaco Dreams [285 H3] (6 rooms) Njegoševa 34; m 066 723 725; e hostelmonaco.dreams@gmail.com; w hostelmonacodreams.net. A small but very pleasant hostel in Banja Luka's city centre. There is a shared living room with a fireplace, as well as a kitchen & dining room. They offer both private & dormitory accommodation. **$**

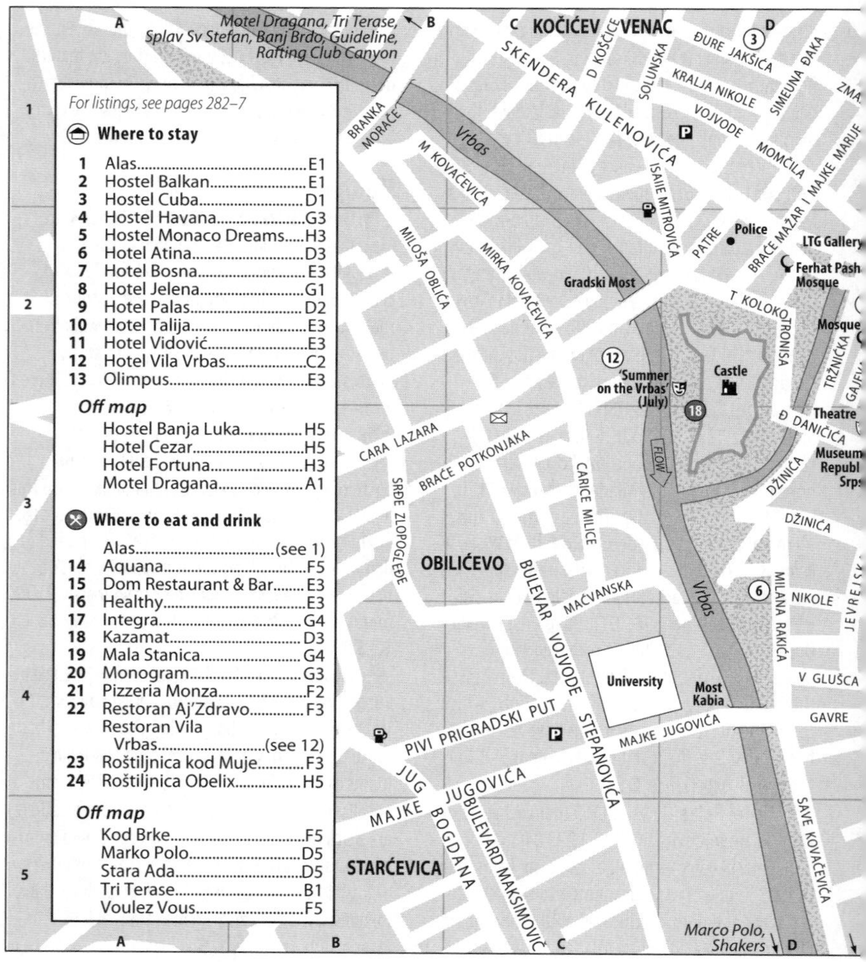

WHERE TO EAT AND DRINK

Dom Restaurant & Bar [285 E3] Bana Milosavljevića 8; 051 218 300; DOMrestaurantbar; 07.30–midnight. If you're looking for a taste of Russia & other Far Eastern Slavic cuisine, this is one of the only places in the country to find it. There are also Mediterranean & continental dishes. Located in the centre of Banja Luka on a peaceful street, the ambiance is modern & casually elegant. Service is very professional. There is a good wine & cocktail list, & live music/DJ on some evenings. **$$–$$$**

Integra [285 G4] Trg Republike Srpske 8; 051 337 430; **e** info@restoranintegra.com; **w** restoranintegra.com; 7.30–midnight Mon–Thu, 07.30–01.00 Fri, 08.00–01.00 Sat, 08.00–midnight Sun. Situated in the business centre building on the 14th floor, there are excellent views of the city. Integra has more of a business atmosphere with classic décor & more formal dining settings. The food is good, but not as good as the views. There is a lounge bar & VIP saloon. **$$–$$$**

Monogram [285 G3] Svetozara Markovića 5J; 051 260 162; **m** 066 661 661; **e** monogram@igmin-group.com; **w** monogramrakije.com/restoran; 07.00–23.00 daily. This family restaurant serves traditional Serbian food in a very hedonistic environment. The chef has won a

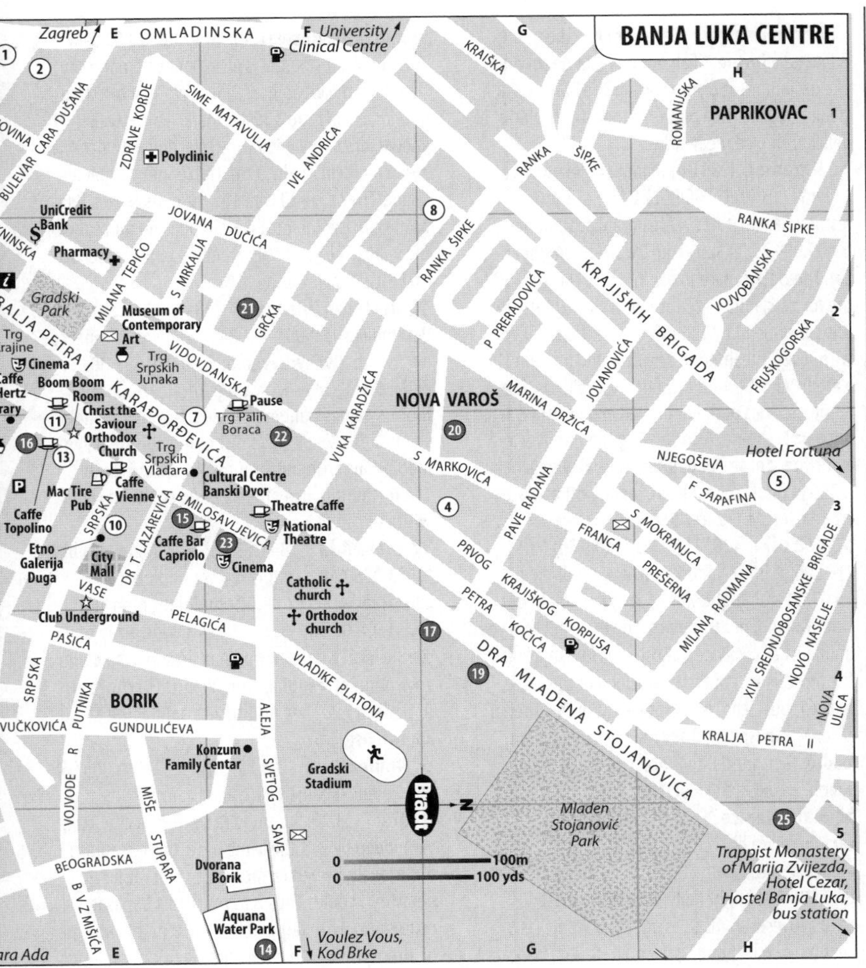

handful of awards at international competitions & gastronomic festivals. He takes great pride not only in the taste of his food, but the aesthetics as well. The desserts rank among the best in town. The Mediterranean dishes are Monogram's signature. Try the *dunje* (quince) *rakija* as an aperitif. **$$–$$$**

Alas [285 E1] Braće Mažar i majke Marije 48; 051 212 602; e info@restoran-motel-banjaluka.com; w restoran-motel-banjaluka.com; 08.00–23.00 daily. The place to go for fish, Alas specialises in both sea & river types: trout, perch & plenty of first-class Adriatic white varieties. The octopus risotto is mouth-watering. The terrace is big & has a stone fireplace for grilling. Inside, the dining room has a formal, tavern feel with brick walls, antique furniture & red-white-checked tablecloths. The mood is perfect to order one of the many bottles of red & white wines on the menu. The restaurant is located on the edge of the centre so just ask if you get lost as everyone knows this place. **$$**

Aquana [285 F5] Aleja Svetog Save 80; 051 231 419; e restoran-aquana@aquana.ba; w aquana.ba/vodeni-park/restoran-aquana; 07.00–23.00 daily. Located at the attractive aqua park (page 289), the restaurant has a uniquely Mediterranean feel. With white décor & loads of natural light, it is one of Banja Luka's most pleasant dining experiences, complete with a VIP room for meetings or special groups. The menu is loaded with great fish options & large servings of excellent meat dishes such as the Banja Luka steak or Gurmanska plata – a monstrous platter of delicious mixed meat. $$

Kazamat [284 D3] Teodora Kolokotronisa 1 (Tvrđava Kastel); 051 224 460; e info@restorankazamat.net; w restorankazamat.net; 09.00–23.00 Sun–Thu, 09.00–midnight Fri–Sat. The classic place to eat in town. Located inside the fortress, it has a terrace with views of the river & is surrounded by beautiful flower boxes filled with roses. The interior, as you would imagine, has a medieval vibe with arched, brick ceilings. The menu includes pork fillet rolled in pancetta & filled peppers & cheese. Also serves grilled trout & an assortment of seafood. International wine labels – 300 in total – come from, among other places, Croatia, Italy & France. $$

Kod Brke [285 F5] Ulica Srpska 36; 051 216 006; e info@kodbrke.pizza; w kodbrke.pizza; 07.00–midnight Mon–Sat; noon–midnight Sun. Walking into this place, you may feel that you could just as easily be in Boston as in Banja Luka. The hipster-ness of the title & logo of the place, 'at the moustache', is also apparent in the interior décor & atmosphere. They mainly serve Italian food, & their speciality is pizza on thick, bready dough, baked in a skillet. $$

Mala Stanica [285 G4] Kralja Petra I Karađorđevića bb; 051 326 730; e malastanica3@gmail.com; w malastanica.com; 07.00–midnight daily. One of the most exclusive restaurants in town, Mala Stanica is a can't miss. Mala Stanica, or small station, is located in the old train station constructed in 1891. The building is a protected cultural site. After valet-parking your car, go through an open garden & past the 120-year-old well. Inside, the ground floor is dominated by a huge bar with 12m of actual railway track integrated into it. Upstairs (a non-smoking area), you can relax in comfortable red leather chairs. While waiting for food, check out the numerous photos & details from the 19th century. Oh yeah, the food is extraordinary. The beef carpaccio is divine, but the best dish on the menu is the chocolate soufflé. In addition, the wine list has over 100 varieties from all over the world. $$

Marko Polo [284 D5] Stepe Stepanovića 185a; 051 238 040; e info@restoranmarcopolo.com; w restoranmarcopolo.com; 07.00–23.00 daily. This popular restaurant is just 10mins from the city centre, on the Vrbas River. They have an interesting interior mix of retro & rustic. Marko Polo is well known for its very good wine selection, international menu & exceptionally comfortable summer garden dining. They have 30 wines by the glass & over 100 bottle labels from most wine-producing countries in the world. The good-value menu & excellent service make it a local favourite. $$

Restoran Vila Vrbas [284 C2] Braće Potkonjaka 1; 051 433 840; e vilavrbas@inecco.net; w hotelvilavrbas.com; 07.00–23.00 daily. On the river with a big interior dining room & tables hanging above the water & under shady trees, Vila Vrbas's dishes include steak, veal medallions with mushrooms, & roasted lamb. The restaurant also offers a good choice of red & white wines. $$

Stara Ada [284 D5] Veljka Mlađenovića bb; 051 456 444; e kontakt@staraada.ba; w staraada.ba; 08.00–midnight Mon–Fri; 08.00–02.00 Sat–Sun. Serves a wide array of classic local & international dishes in a spacious environment, ranging from Viennese schnitzel to pork chops. They also have a solid wine & aperitif list. $$

Voulez Vous [285 F5] Srpska 101; m 066 068 066; e vulevubanjaluka@gmail.com; 07.00–23.00. Surrounded by the big city park, yet hidden by it at the same time, this restaurant has a lovely garden terrace perfect for romantic getaways. Voulez Vous is as much of a bar as it is a restaurant, with frequent live DJs, a nightclub type of atmosphere with neon lights & chic décor. Good food & drink selection. $$

Pizzeria Monza [285 F2] Grčka 11; 051 214 030; 07.00–23.00 daily. Good offer of pizzas & other domestic/international specialities. Monza is a popular local pizzeria with modern décor & a relaxing atmosphere. $–$$

Roštiljnica Obelix [285 H5] Pete Kozarske brigade 9; 051 315 100; e info@obelixbl.com; w obelixbl.com; 08.00–23.00 daily. If it's meat you're seeking, look no further. Inspired by the elements of Gaelic villages, Barbeque Obelix is an ideal location to try out the famous Banja Luka *ćevapi* & other types of grilled meats. They use all locally produced, high-quality meat from a butcher with a 40-year-long tradition in the Banja Luka area. Although one of Sarajevo's claims to fame is *ćevapi*, some argue that Banja Luka *ćevapi* take the crown. You decide. $–$$

Tri Terase [285 B1] Karanovac bb; **m** 065 006 333; **e** triterase@gmail.com; **w** triterase.com; 10.00–03.00. Located on the bank of the Vrbas River, this restaurant is spread over 3 large terraces. It's a favourite summer spot when the weather is warm. Locals also come to swim & sip cocktails on the 'beach.' They offer a wide range of food including crêpes, classic fast food, Greek & Mediterranean cuisine, pizza, sandwiches, & a handful of vegetarian meals. The food is nothing to write home about, but not bad either. It is very popular with the locals as a hang-out spot for drinks & good value meals. $–$$

Healthy [285 E3] Jevrejska bb; **m** 066 424 139; 08.00–20.00 Mon–Fri, 08.00–16.00 Sat. It does live up to its name – healthy, good value, quick meals. This small restaurant is almost always full but it's worth the wait. $

Restoran Aj'Zdravo [285 F3] Vidovdanska 6; 051 211 544; **e** restoran.ajzdravo@yahoo.com; **w** ajzdravo.com; 07.00–23.00 Mon–Sat. Banja Luka just added another top restaurant to its growing list of good eateries. Embellished with a creative interior made from reclaimed wood, the organic ingredients & innovative recipes (such as homemade kale chips or avocado-lime cake) makes Aj'Zdravo one of the better places for a good value, healthy meal in Banja Luka. $

Roštiljnica kod Muje [285 F3] Braće Mažar i majke Marije 24; 051 319 912; **e** kontakt@cevabdzinicakodmuje.com; 07.00–23.00 daily. No Bosnian town would be complete without its *ćevapi*. Although Sarajevo & Travnik both boast the best *ćevapi* in BiH, Banja Luka *ćevapi* are certainly in the running for the top spot. Kod Muje is a classic & very busy grilled-meat establishment for quick, easy & good-value meals. They have been in business since 1923. A visit to Banja Luka just wouldn't be complete without a taste of Kod Muje. $

CAFÉS/BARS/CLUBS

Caffe Bar Capriolo [285 F3] Bana Milosavljevića 14; 051 346 840/2; 07.00–23.00 daily. When you walk all the way down the main pedestrian street & pass book & jewellery stands, you will find yourself in a street lined with cafés. If you want quick refreshment & something sweet, Capriolo is the best choice. Doubling as a sweet shop, it serves all kinds of Italian cakes. A decade of experience guarantees their homemade ice cream is top quality. Relax on their huge patio. If you're hungry, grab a sandwich.

Caffe Hertz [285 E2] Jevrejska 1; 051 217 500; 07.00–midnight Sun–Thu, 07.00–01.00 Fri–Sat. This small place, just to the right of where Veselina Masleše starts, is crowded any time of day. Here, you can see a young crowd exchanging the latest gossip, businessmen taking a break from work, or retirees reading newspapers. Outside, the little terrace is packed with wicker chairs & cute colourful tables. Inside, there are marble floors & black leather bar stools.

Caffe Topolino [285 E3] Bana Franje Jukića 9; 051 314 493; 07.00–midnight Sun–Thu, 07.00–01.00 Fri/Sat. Next to the shopping centre Vidović, Topolino has been in this spot for 22 years. It has a tropical look outside with wicker chairs & colourful sunshades. The interior has funky walls painted blue & grey. They play good rock & pop music & the friendly staff make this a locals' favourite.

Café Vienne [285 E3] Veselina Masleše 30a; 051 215 444; 07.00–midnight Sun–Thu, 07.00–02.00 Fri/Sat. Vienne's terrace is so close to Ramazzoti's that they seem like one. You can easily get confused about which café you're in. But inside, Vienne has its own personality. Decorated to remind you of the Austrian capital, there are pictures & details of it all over the walls. The music here is loud, but they never play turbo folk. Every once in while, a DJ'ed party will turn this café into a nightclub.

Mr Black & Mr Brown [285 E3] Kralja Petra Karađorđevića 97; 051 215 775; 07.00–midnight Sun–Thu, 07.00–01.00 Fri–Sat. These are terrace cafés integrated into Hotel Bosna. The huge patio, full of wicker chairs & tables, sits across the street from Christ the Saviour church downtown. The trees of Mladen Stojanović Pk provide the perfect shade as you sip your drink & enjoy the view. During the day, the place is packed with business people taking coffee breaks. At night, this is a starting point for Banja Luka nightlife.

Pause [285 F2] Vidovdanska bb; 07.00–midnight daily. By day or night, this is probably one of the hipper bars/cafés in town. It caters to a young, alternative crowd, & offers a wide range of drinks, inc regional craft brews. Try a cold one from the gourmet Serbian microbrewery Kabinet.

Splav Sv Stefan [284 B1] Obala Vrbasa bb; 09.00–23.00 Sun–Thu, 09.00–midnight Fri–Sat. This spot is directly on the river – actually on the river. A *splav* is a raft. From here you are within arm's reach of kayakers & fishermen. For the most part this café is a big, wooden-decked terrace. There is a boathouse-esque interior as well. Regardless of where one sits, though, expect draught beer, wine, juices & coffee . . . best enjoyed with a nice river breeze at sunset.

Theatre Caffe [285 F3] Kralja Petra I Karađorđevića 78; 07.00–23.00 daily. In the tradition of drama scenes worldwide, this café is next to the National Theatre & is filled with actors during the day & patrons at night. Paintings of different theatrical scenes hang from the walls of this wide-open space with lots of windows – & thus light – which opens out on to a terrace with wicker furniture & views of a flower-filled park. Beer, wine, juice &, of course, coffee are on offer.

Shakers [284 D5] Stepe Stepanovića 185; m 066 234 104; 08.00–23.00 daily. With more than 100 concoctions, this is a real 'house of cocktails' & maybe the best in the region. Owned & managed by professional bartenders, it has every mixture you've heard of, & some you never have & likely won't again. If you want a quick rush, try Liquid Cocaine. Good thing that the black, velvet sofas are wide & comfy, because standing up afterwards might be a challenge. The bar in the city closes at 23.00, but they have their satellite bar in Kanjon Rafting Club, where the party goes all night long.

Mac Tire Pub [285 E3] Srpska 2–4; 051 221 444; 08.00–01.00 Sun–Thu, 08.00–02.00 Fri–Sat. This Irish-style pub will make you feel at home: cosy interior with wood detailing, frequent live music performances, especially jazz, soul & funk, & a great selection of local & imported beers, whisky, & hearty food.

☆ **Boom Boom Room** [285 E3] Veselina Masleše 15; m 065 510 816; 07.00–02.00 Tue–Thu, 19.00–03.00 Fri–Sat. On the main Banja Luka street. Pass through huge double black doors & follow a bright red hallway down into a dungeon. Now, you are in a real disco haven. Different-sized disco balls hang from the ceilings. Pink walls with glass bubbles contrast with black leather booths. Boom Boom Room easily accommodates 350 people & with 3KM Coronas on Fri, it's packed. Cocktails are free for ladies on Thu. DJ Igor plays disco, house & funk except on Wed, when ex-Yugo rock music thumps.

☆ **Club Cabaret** [284 D2] Kralja Petra I Karađorđevića 60; 21.00–04.00 Thu–Sat. In the same building as the Hotel Palas. Many will tell you that this is the best place to dance in the city. Their motto is 'We own the night'. DJs mix in house & pop at this swanky club with seductive red lighting. Patrons – an all-ages crowd – slurp cocktails under disco balls & mirrored ceilings. Entrance is free.

☆ **Pastir** [284 B1] Karanovac bb; 051 466 411; m 066 714 171; 08.00–midnight; club 08.00–03.00 daily. This spot could fit into several classifications. This is the locale for one of the Vrbas's main rafting launches. It is a wonderful café with a 100m-long terrace of wooden decking hanging over the river & a relaxed atmosphere all day long. There's a beach where the bronzed & bikini-clad gather. It is a great restaurant (technically called Pastir, after the owner) that pays attention to details & combines casual fare – *ćevapi* & grilled trout – with fine cutlery & top service. At night though, this place is all club. DJs crank out dance tunes: disco, techno & house. What's more, the cocktails are as good as you'll ever taste.

☆ **Club Underground** [285 E3] Vase Pelagića 10; 21.00–02.00 Sun–Thu, 21.00–03.00 Fri–Sat. The first thing you will notice about this place is the huge London Underground sign & their slogan 'We love them all, we serve them all'. To make sure you'll be loved & served as promised, go down the lobby filled with red & silver tiles. The downstairs is dominated by a central bar with dancing podiums all around it. They play commercial music, & most of the time it's turbo folk. Occasionally, they organise go-go-dancer parties.

SHOPPING Shopping options in Banja Luka are solid if you are looking for basics and a bit more. There are several decent shopping centres offering various types of goods. **Konzum Family Centar** [285 F4] (*Aleja Svetog Save 69; ⌚ 07.30–22.00 Mon–Sat, 08.00–16.00 Sun*) is currently the largest mall in Banja Luka, and includes a large grocery store and 40 shops and boutiques, including some global brands. **City Mall** [285 E3] (*Vase Pelagića bb*), a mega shopping complex with more international brands, is currently under construction and will probably be completed by 2018. For original souvenirs, there are several locally owned shops scattered around town. For example, **Etno Gallery Duga** [285 E3] (*Srpska 14; 051 315 882; ⌚ 09.00–20.00 Mon–Fri, 09.00–17.00 Sat*) offers a variety of creative handmade and tradition-inspired items. For Serbian Orthodox-inspired gifts, try **Riznica Bookstore and Gallery** [285 E3] (*Ivana Franje Jukića bb; 051 211 802; ⌚ 08.00–20.00 Mon–Fri, 08.00–15.00 Sat*). It is always preferable to support small local businesses when possible, because that directly boosts the seriously struggling local economy.

OTHER PRACTICALITIES

Hospital

University Clinical Centre of the Republic of Srpska [285 F1] Dvanaest beba; 051 342 100; **w** kc-bl.com

Pharmacy

Prvi Maj [285 E2] Milana Tepića 17; 051 223 540; **e** ap.1maj@mojaapoteka.net; ⌚ 24 hours

Police station

[284 D2] Kralja Petra I Karađorđevića 5; 051 337 201

Bank

$ UniCredit Bank [285 E2] Marije Bursać 7; ⌚ 08.00–19.00 Mon–Sat. ATM

Post office

Main Post Office [285 F5] Aleja Svetog Save 19; 051 211 219; ⌚ 07.00–20.00 Mon–Fri, 07.00–16.00 Sat

Taxi

Patrol Taxi 051 229 500; **w** patroltaxi.com

WHAT TO SEE AND DO True to its role as the Republika Srpska's main city, Banja Luka is loaded with museums, galleries, churches and, generally, plenty of cultural venues. Visitors here will not find themselves at a loss for things to do.

Aquana Water Park [285 F5] (*Aleja Svetog Save 80; 051 228 400; **e** info@aquana.ba; **w** aquana.ba/vodeni-park; ⌚ May–Sep 09.00–19.00 Mon–Fri, 09.00–19.00 Sat–Sun; entrance fee 5KM*) Aquana Water Park is Banja Luka's main water and urban attraction. This large complex comes complete with Olympic pool, self-service restaurant, café-bar and a great full-service restaurant (pages 285–6). The water is kept at a constant 28°C.

Banj brdo [284 A1] (*South side of the city*) This is – if one had to classify it – a picnic area. But in reality it serves a multitude of purposes for locals and tourists alike. At 403m above sea level, it is a perfect 30-minute hike. From there, walkers are afforded great views of Banja Luka. It is also a park with a World War II sculpture by acclaimed sculptor Antun Augustiničić.

Christ the Saviour Orthodox Church [285 E3] (*Kralja Petra I Karađorđevića*) It's impossible to miss this golden-domed church, as it sits right in the middle of town along the main street and next to the promenade. The original was constructed in 1929 and destroyed during World War II.

Ferhat Pasha Mosque [284 D2] (*Kralja Petra I Karađorđevića*) The largest and most central mosque in Banja Luka is also known as the Ferhadija Mosque.

CALENDAR OF ANNUAL CULTURAL EVENTS

Name of event	Organiser	Date
International Festival Banja Luka Choir Gathering	SPCD Jedinstvo, Banja Luka	April–May
Banja Luka Theatre Festival	'Teatar Fest' Narodno pozoriste RS	May
The Month of Rock Music	Hard Rock Radio	June
Banja Luka Summer Games	Srpski Kulturni Centar	August
Folklore Days	Banja Luka Kulturno-umjetnicka drustva	July–August, every Thursday
Summer on the Vrbas	Sport Council of the town assembly Banja Luka	July

The original 16th-century structure was a beautiful example of classical Ottoman architecture, and was a UNESCO-protected site. However, it was destroyed during the most recent war. The mosque was reconstructed and re-opened in May 2016. Remnants of the original mosque remain, and the new building is completed on the foundations that survived the destruction. Its post-war reconstruction as a place of worship and a cultural landmark has deep symbolic value.

Cultural Centre Banski Dvor [285 E3] (*Trg srpskih vladara 2;* ☎ *051 305 336;* 🕘 *08.00–22.00 Mon–Sat, 09.00–13.00 Sun; entrance free*) Built in 1931–32, this public building has a lathered-in-marble, national-theatre atmosphere. It was originally constructed for the region's *ban* (governor) and his court. Today it has a continually rotating series of exhibitions including paintings and book events. There are regular concerts held in the building's parquet-floored hall.

Kastel [284 D2] (*Left bank of the Vrbas*) The castle is the most important site in town and the one that reverberates with the most historic resonance. The fortress has been the headquarters of every group moving through this strategically located town. The walls are 16th century and Turkish but the foundations are Roman. Today, an assortment of performances and festivals take advantage of the Kastel's summer stage.

LTG galerija [284 D2] (*Kralja Petra I Karađorđevića 109;* ☎ *051 221 221;* **m** *065 538 994;* **e** *info@ltggalerija.com;* **w** *ltggalerija.com;* 🕘 *13.00–20.00 Mon–Fri, 10.00–15.00 Sat; entrance free*) This gallery hosts some of the more complex exhibitions. Alongside its exhibition space for contemporary art shows the gallery also organises cultural events and sells the works of well-known artists.

Museum of Contemporary Art [285 E2] (*Trg srpskih junaka 2;* ☎ *051 215 364;* **e** *muzejsurs@gmail.com;* **w** *msurs.net;* 🕘 *10.00–22.00 daily; entrance free*) There were 27 exhibitions here last year. Paintings, sculpture, photography and graphics are among the pieces shown in the building, which was once the old railway station. This is a great place to see established and young artists' work.

Museum of Republika Srpska [285 E3] (*Đure Daničića 1;* ☎ *051 215 973;* **w** *muzejrs.com;* 🕘 *08.00–20.00 daily; entrance fee 1KM*) Established in 1930, the museum moved into its present location – next to the library and children's theatre – in 1982. The collection includes some 30,000 pieces in the areas of archaeology, ethnography, art, science and history. Tools, traditional costumes, jewellery and a very graphic exhibition describing the horrors of World War II can be found in the museum's 3,700 square metres. Of special interest are the rooms containing pieces of Banja Luka memorabilia from the early 20th century. Pocket watches, silver hairbrushes and evening gowns provide an insight into the town during the Kingdom of Yugoslavia.

National Theatre [285 F3] (*Kralja Petra I Karađorđevića 78;* ☎ *051 317 996;* **w** *np.rs.ba;* ⌚ *variable hours; entrance fee 6KM*) The theatre puts on four premieres and 10–15 different musicals, dramas and comedies per season, which lasts from September to July. Shows start, typically, at 20.00.

Trappist Monastery of Marija Zuijezda [285 H5] (*Slatinska 1;* ☎ *051 300 951;* **e** *zupnik@trapisti-banjaluka.org;* **w** *trapisti-banjaluka.org;* ⌚ *by appointment; entrance free*) Just a few minutes from Banja Luka, this was once a massive estate that has been whittled down over the years. The monastery was established in Banja Luka in 1869 and the old church of the monastery was built between 1874 and 1875. Apart from the liturgical objects made of precious metals dating from the 19th and 20th centuries, the collection of the monastery includes two precious paintings – the *Crucifixion* and *St Filomena*, both Venetian works from the 16th century. Like most monasteries it too has a collection of old printed books, among which is a collection of writings by St Augustine, printed in Basel in 1493. The monks – two of them – are friendly and make visitors a priority. This is also a good place to purchase magnificent cheese, which is made on the premises and costs 35KM for a wheel.

AROUND BANJA LUKA *Bočac* is a 15th-century medieval town situated on the left bank of the Vrbas River, halfway between Banja Luka and Jajce. There have been several initiatives to create eco-centres to preserve its natural beauty and clean the river of build-up from the hydro-electric dam. Although there is no accommodation yet there is a zoo and a restaurant in Bočac. It has been placed on the list of national monuments by the government of Republika Srpska. If you're up for a wander, the road leading south out of Banja Luka through the Vrbas Canyon will take you there. It's in quite a beautiful setting but little is organised for the tourist.

Gomionica Monastery (*in the village of Kmecani, 42km west of Banja Luka*) is one of the finest examples of eastern Orthodox monasteries in northern Bosnia. It also has a church on the grounds dedicated to Vavedenje Bogorodice by Bronzani Mejdan, dated 1536. There are several frescoes preserved in similar, but less striking, style than those in the Orthodox monasteries in the Carpathian Mountains in Romania, and a great number of valuable icons and old manuscripts. One can also find an interesting collection of old printed books (all in Cyrillic), as well as other precious objects of crafts used for the liturgy.

Above the grounds of **Krupa na VrbasuMonastery of St Ilija** is the **medieval fortress** of Greben town situated in the Vrbas Canyon. It is believed that the original church was built within the ancient town but with most of the fortress in ruins and little archaeological work completed it has not been confirmed. In the 15th century, the feudal family Vojsalić, successors of Hrvoje Vukčić Hrvatinić, took care of maintenance of the monastery below the Greben Grad. The Church of St Ilija in Krupa on the Vrbas was rebuilt by Sava Kosanović in 1889 shortly after the fall of the Ottoman Empire.

Romanovci is a small wooden church located near the town of Gradiška to the northeast of Banja Luka. It is dedicated to St Nikola by the villagers of Romanovci on the eastern slopes of Kozara Mountain, 20km south of Gradiška. It was built in the first half of the 18th century and is one of the few remaining wooden Orthodox structures in the country.

Bardača Bird Reserve The Bardača wetlands is a series of 11 lakes situated between the rivers Vrbas and Sava, northeast of Banja Luka near the town of **Srbac**. This 670ha reserve is home to over 180 types of birds. I find it a fascinating place for birdwatching; most find it a fun place for bird hunting and, unlike Hutovo Blato in Herzegovina, where hunting is forbidden, this 'reserve' is open for fishing and hunting. It is not an official bird reserve as of yet so there are no public authorities to contact for information. Zepter Passport in Banja Luka (page 282) can give information about the reserve or you can go to **Bardača Sports and Recreation Centre** on site. They have a mediocre hotel with a decent restaurant and a massive swimming pool. Several buses per day go to Srbac from Banja Luka and Bosanska Gradiška.

Slatina spas Slatina is a small town 13km to the northeast of Banja Luka. Not much goes on aside from the 43°C water that flows from the earth at **Banja Slatina** (*Slatinska 11;* ☎ *058 788 054;* **w** *slatina.antireuma.com*). This region is extremely rich in medicinal thermal mineral water. There are four such spas in the Krajina alone. The **Dr Miroslav Zotović Institute for Rehabilitation** specialises in treating rheumatic and degenerative disorders. The facilities may not meet the luxurious standards of the West, but the water quality for the price is a true bargain. Most spas in BiH are 20% the cost of Western spas.

The **Slateks Hotel** (☎ *051 587 040;* **$$**) has also tapped into the warm waters of Slatina and built a nice hotel complex with thermal baths. It is worth a night or two if you are in the region for a while. There are several buses a day to Slatina from Banja Luka. A taxi ride from Banja Luka will cost around 20KM. By car it is only a 20-minute drive.

Kozara National Park (☎ *052 211 169;* **e** *info@npkozara.com;* **w** *npkozara.com*) Kozara was proclaimed a protected national forest in 1967. Situated between the rivers **Una**, **Sava**, **Sana** and **Vrbas**, northwest of Banja Luka, these 34km² of dense forest and hilly meadows have earned it the nickname 'Green Beauty of Krajina'. Kozara is a popular hunting ground, with a large area of the park open to regulated hunting of deer, pheasants, foxes, boars, wild hares and ducks.

A smaller part of the park is designated for nature lovers. Walking, hiking, biking and herb picking are among the many activities in Kozara. Hiking to **Lisina**, the highest point of the park at 938m, offers a wide panoramic view of this part of the Krajina. The park is unquestionably a lovely nature reserve, but the underfunded park management has not been able to put a more concrete programme together. Even basic information is hard to come by, and there are no bike rentals or walking maps with recorded distances.

For the winter months there are mini ski-lifts and ski rental available at the park. There is a motel and restaurant in the national park complex.

Eko-Centar Ljekarice (☎ *052 333 267;* **e** *j.lekanic@mediaproline.net*) This is an interesting experiment on the halfway mark between **Banja Luka** and **Prijedor**. Armed with only a beautiful piece of property, a few visionaries had the idea of creating an eco-centre in the **Omarska** area. They have built a 30-acre park complete with walking paths, ten ponds/lakes for fishing and swimming, and a health-food restaurant. The dense hardwood forests cover a good part of the centre and there are walking trails through them. The wild game is protected, as hunting is not permitted. **Lončari** has campground facilities, and is perfect for backpackers looking for a safe and inexpensive place to camp out while travelling through or towards Bihać or Banja Luka. Many buses travel through the outskirts of Omarska via Prijedor and Banja Luka. There are a few daily buses from both those places that stop in Omarska.

BIHAĆ

Bihać is mentioned in 1260, in a document of King Bela IV. It is widely accepted, however, that the area was settled at least from Illyrian and Roman times. Bihać has certainly been at the forefront of the gateway between East and West. It was these far northwest frontier lands that also drew the line between the Ottomans and the Austro-Hungarians. Those days are long gone, however, and life in Bihać now tackles more pressing contemporary issues. Before the conflict in the early 1990s, Bihać and the entire region was fairly wealthy compared with country standards, but the war devastated the economy in this area. A large number of Krajinans have at some time worked in Germany or Austria and many of them still have family working and living abroad, so it's not surprising that numerous goods to be found on the shelves are German and Austrian products. The Germans operate a Meggle milk factory in Bihać, and the development of tourism is a key component of the strategic development plan for the entire region, and in particular Bihać.

GETTING THERE AND AWAY Bihać is a good 5- or 6-hour **bus** ride from Sarajevo and several daily buses ply the route. Be sure to check bus routes from Zagreb and Sarajevo too; some routes travel through Bihać, and some travel via Slavonski Brod in Croatia, and cross much further east. Ask specifically if those buses travel the Bihać–Jajce–Travnik–Sarajevo route. Plitvice National Park is just across the border and many tour buses and tourists come through the Izačić border crossing. Bihać bus station links all the cities and towns in the upper region of the Krajina. Daily buses go to Bosanski Petrovac, Bosanska Krupa, Sanski Most, Cazin, Bužim, Velika Kladuša and Ključ several times a day. There are daily buses to Zagreb and Karlovac in Croatia and to Sarajevo, and all the stops *en route*.

By **car** the best access from Croatia is the Izačić crossing. From the southeast there is only one major road leading to Bihać – the Sarajevo–Travnik–Jajce route. You can't miss it on a map.

The train from Banja Luka does not go through this northwest pocket of Krajina.

TOURIST INFORMATION For general tourist information there is the **Bihać Tourist Information Centre** (*037 322 079;* e *turizamb@bih.net.ba*), which is mainly responsible for Bihać and the immediate area. The **Una-Sana Canton Tourism Association** (*037 222 777*) covers the whole territory of the Federation part of the Krajina.

LOCAL TOUR OPERATORS There are two professional rafting operators working out of Bihać. **Una Kiro Rafting** (*Golubić bb; 037 361 110;* e *extreme@una-kiro-rafting.com;* w *una-kiro-rafting.com*) has the only international certified rafting skippers. They have a great team of young professionals and offer a wide range of services from hiking and biking, to fishing and private accommodation. They also have a great boarding house for their guests. **Sport Bijeli** (*Klokot – Pecikovići bb; 037*

380 222; **e** *raftbeli@bih.net.ba;* **w** *una-rafting.ba*) is equipped with modern gear and their skippers are very good. What I like most about Bijeli is that it doesn't just end after rafting. The entire tour with traditional food, camping and playing music is a wonderful experience. They can organise fishing trips (a licence in this canton costs 50KM/day) at Klokot River and by the stunning falls at Martin Brod near Kulen Vakuf. Take advantage of their local knowledge.

The mountains of Plješevica and Grmeč are rich in wild animals and very convenient for hiking. It is wise to hike with a guide if you are unfamiliar with the area. Bihać was an enclave surrounded by Serbian forces and there are several minefields in the mountains around the city. The **Aero Klub** from Bihać (*037 333 652;* **e** *aeroklub-bihac@hotmail.com;* **w** *aeroclub-bihac.com*) can organise some high flying above the Una with small plane rides from Bihać's mini airport.

WHERE TO STAY There are several options for accommodation while staying in Bihać. If you've come for the rafting adventure of your life, then check with the rafting operators as they often have their own bed and breakfasts or have an arrangement with someone providing inexpensive places to stay. Bed and breakfasts greatly outnumber the hotels.

Hotel Opal Exclusive (26 rooms) Krupska bb; 037 224 183; **e** info@hotelopal.ba; **w** hotelopal.ba. Perhaps the best all-round place to stay in town. Its great location & service are matched by large, comfy rooms with nice views of the Una River. The rooms are en suite & have all the amenities for a more than pleasant stay. **$$–$$$**

Avlija Motel (7 rooms, 2 apts) Trg maršala Tita 7; **m** 061 021 021; **f** AvlijaBihac. There is a boutique atmosphere inside this motel, which is sited just off the main pedestrianised avenue. The rooms & apts are big, with nice furniture, TV, Wi-Fi & views of the town centre. B/fast is included in the price. **$$**

Hotel Ada (78 rooms) Orljani bb; 037 318 100; **e** info@aduna.ba. The rooms have sat TV & phone. The gardens have neatly trimmed lawns & landscaped flowerbeds. The receptionist doesn't speak English, but if you know a few words of German, that'll help. **$$**

Hotel Ada S-Bihać (53 rooms) Husrefa Redžića 1; **m** 062 818 814; **e** info@hotelbihac.com; **w** hotel_ada.tripod.com. A great budget-minded spot, Hotel Ada S is on the other side of the river from the town centre but in the middle of the party scene, including the Ada S disco & the Papaya Club. For younger folks who want to party all night & then crash, this is the spot. The rooms are simple but clean & have Wi-Fi. B/fast is included but it seems unlikely that anyone will be up to eat it. **$$**

Hotel Emporium [map, pages 280–1] (28 rooms) Dr Irfana Ljubijankića 90; 037 316 600; **e** info@emporium.ba; **w** emporium.ba. Bihać is located pretty much half-way between the Una & Plitvica Lakes National Parks. For that reason the Emporium offers weekend trips to visit both of these places with transport, guides, accommodation & half-board meals all covered in the price. They can also offer rafting tours on the Una River with an experienced & professional outfitter. The rooms have everything a 4-star hotel should offer – comfort, space, design & great service. **$$**

Hotel Paviljon (13 rooms) Aleja Alije Izetbegovića bb; 037 224 194; **e** info@hotel-paviljon.com; **w** hotelpaviljon.ba. Yet another example of this town's wide range of lodging options, the 3-star Paviljon is boutique-ish in all the right ways. The rooms have flat-screen TVs, French beds, balconies, tiled bathrooms & Wi-Fi. Half have views of the park & the others look over the river. The whole package sits above one of the best cafés in town. **$$**

New Sanatron Motel (8 rooms, 4 apts) Kulskaobala bb; 052 751 653; **e** info@newsanatron.com. Situated at the mouth of the Una River, New Sanatron Motel can boast beautiful views of both the river & the centre of town. The hotel has modern rooms & facilities with Wi-Fi, cleaning services, cable TV & friendly staff. There is also a log cabin on the edge of the forest, just a few kilometres away. It can accommodate up to

5. It's perfect for a self-catering family or friends outing. The house has a large garden & BBQ. **$$**

Una Aqua Centre – 5 Island Camp (2 apts) Račić bb; **m** 061 604 313; **e** info@una-aqua.com; **w** una-aqua.com. Una Aqua Rafting has 2 weekend houses that can accommodate between 4 &10 people. They also have camping facilities. The 5 Island Camp is on the banks of the Una River; describing the river will do little justice but it is exceptional in every way. Accommodation is usually earmarked for rafting or cycling clients, but rooms are available for those just looking for some R&R on the river. The centre promotes sustainable tourism, & organises activities such as rafting, cycling & hiking. There's a 3D model of the camp on the website. **$$**

Villa Una (12 rooms) Bihaćkihbranilaca 20; **m** 061 459 520; **e** info@villa-una.com; **w** villa-una.com. This hotel has clean, comfortable & quiet rooms, & friendly staff. Not all rooms have balconies so do request a room with one. It is a pleasant & straightforward 10min walk from Villa Una to the centre. Traditional Bosnian b/fast inc. **$$**

Hotel Kostelski buk [map, pages 280–1] (50 rooms) Kostela bb; 037 302 340; **m** 061 105 133; **e** info@kostelski-buk.com; **w** kostelski-buk.com. Sited 4km north of Bihać in the direction of Cazin, this is one of the nicest & most atmospheric hotels in the area. This 4-star, which sits next to waterfalls, has a VIP lounge & an excellent restaurant. **$–$$**

Hotel Park (68 rooms) V Korpusa 3; 037 226 394; **e** info@aduna.ba; **w** aduna.ba. First opened in 1960, Park is one of the elder hotel statesmen in town. Not to worry. Its 4 floors & 68 rooms have been renovated, & while there is still an antiquated feel about the place, the staff are friendly & the location – in the central park, logically – can't be beaten. There is a great b/fast buffet that comes with the price. **$–$$**

Hotel Sedra Ostrožac na Uni bb; 037 532 106; **e** info@hotelsedra.ba; **w** hotelsedra.ba. A large complex sitting right on the banks of the Una River. It's a local favourite & many families will go & spend w/ends there. They are famous for their traditional local cuisine. The rooms are good but not great, & the service is definitely up to par. **$–$$**

Pansion Saraj (20 beds) Kulen Vakuf; **m** 066 483 935, 061 798 232; **e** info@pansionsaraj.com; **w** pansionsaraj.com. Located in the small town of Kulen Vakuf on the Una River, 46km from the city of Bihać. It is only 100m away from the beautiful banks of the river, surrounded by lush green nature. This B&B offers modern & fashionably equipped rooms with a total of 20 beds (2 apts). They have a restaurant that serves largely traditional cuisine. Saraj also has its own beach along the river. There are biking & hiking trailheads just minutes from here. **$–$$**

Pansion Edo Hanovi 6; 037 310 537. Just 5mins from the centre, close to the bus station & on the Una, Edo might take the prize for best budget option. At any rate, it is a good spot to have on your list. The dbls, trpls & apts are simple but adequate & have a homely feel. **$**

WHERE TO EAT AND DRINK The many good eateries, most of them along the Una, are the second-best way to enjoy the river. The very best, of course, are on the river itself. If you're a vegetarian you might want to find a pizzeria, and **Caffe Bar picerija Bondeno** on Bosanska bb in the centre of town has good pizzas for 6–8KM, as does **Pizzeria Bistro** on the same road.

In addition to those listed below, restaurants **Čardak na Uni** (*502 Viteška brigada bb; 037 331 822;* **$$**) and **River Una** (*Džemala Bijedića 12;* **$$**) offer casual dining with excellent traditional food. The fresh trout is usually priced around 10KM. Both are located right on the river, and Čardak offers horse and carriage rides along the river and through the park in town. Also on Džemala Bijedića is the classy **Unski biser Restaurant** (*037 333 732;* **$$**). I wouldn't classify it as fine dining but it is a step up from the other more casual spots.

Belvedere Trg slobode 8; 037 222 157; Belvedererestoran; 24 hrs. This Italian restaurant is located in the old part of town. They mainly do pizzas, pastas & salads. There is often live music on weekends but some weekends it can be a bit folky. They can cater for large groups. **$$**

Hajdučkačesma Dubovsko bb; 037 290 038; **e** info@hajducka-cesma.com; **w** hajducka-cesma.com; ⌚ 08.00–23.00. There is no lack of fresh water supply in the Bihać area. The Rebels Fountain, as it translates, was built next to a natural water spring discovered in the 19th century. It has a traditional/rustic interior & serves traditional cuisine. $$

Restoran Kostelski Buk Kostela bb; 037 302 340; ⌚ 07.00–23.00 daily. A bit out of town on the main road to Cazin is this classic restaurant, which is a popular meeting place for lunch & dinner. Although it rests right on the main road, you'll hardly be able to tell from your table overlooking the Una River that a road is anywhere near. They serve mainly traditional meals, which means meat dishes of lamb & beef. $$

Restoran Sunce Bosanska 1; 037 310 487; e info@aduna.ba; ⌚ 24 hours. Located on the bank of the Una River in the cascade area. It can only be reached by crossing a small footbridge. It has the capacity to receive up to 230 guests. The menu has a wide range of traditional & international dishes, but the local fish from the Una are superb. $$

Gradska kafana Paviljon Bihačkih branilaca bb; ⌚ 08.00–03.25 daily. Another regularly frequented local spot. $

La Mamma Ul bosanske nezavisnosti bb; 037 227 031; ⌚ 08.00–23.00 daily. Italian food is pretty popular in Bihać. Although it is not comparable to a true Italian dining experience, the cosy interior, lovely summer garden, pizza, friendly service & good food make it worth the visit. $

ENTERTAINMENT AND NIGHTLIFE

Cafés/bars/clubs

Avlija Caffe Trg maršala Tita 7; 037 220 882; ⌚ 24 hrs. On the ground floor of the motel with the same name, this café has a long terrace with an ornate wrought-iron door. Covered by red parasols, patrons sit in padded wicker chairs atop tile & brick floors. Inside, around the flagstone bar, leather stools & old black-&-whites of Bihać set the mood. This is a great place to warm up for an evening out. Avlija serves beer, wine & an assortment of teas & coffee.

Caffe Bar Bondenon Bosanska 6; 037 222 603; ⌚ 07.00–midnight daily. This is one of the most hopping cafés among those lined along the main promenade through town. It has a little something for everyone, with a café, restaurant, pizzeria & a wonderful patio, which sits near the main mosque & faces the city's gallery. They serve all the required beers & wines, but they also concoct fruit shakes: banana, kiwi & strawberry.

Caffe RB Bosanska 13; ⌚ 07.00–22.00 daily. Caffe RB is a locals' spot. The pub interior has pea-green booths & chairs, & waiters dispense a handful of whisky varieties, beers & wines to regulars mainly. But maybe the best reason to come here is to relax on the patch of terrace filled with wicker chairs, which sits right on the main pedestrian promenade.

Gradska pivnica Bosanske državnosti bb; 037 223 784; ⌚ 07.00–23.00 Sun–Thu, 07.00–midnight Fri/Sat. Gradska pivnica, or city brewery, is a stunning place to enjoy a cold beer & mix with the urban crowd. They serve pub food ($$), too! The inside is dominated by a huge wooden bar & benches that fit perfectly with the stone wall interior. Of course, they have all kinds of beer – draught & bottled. Outside, the terrace looks like a picnic area with seating right next to the water. Live music – rock & funk – performances are organised on w/ends.

Kaffe-Bar Flash Art Gazihusref-begova bb; ⌚ 07.00–23.00 daily. An arty & all-ages crowd fills this café dominated by a long outdoor terrace under the Kapetanova Kula. You can't miss the place. Look for the giant Flash Art sign. Though outside is the place to be, the inside is also worth a look. Iconic images of Marilyn Monroe, Muhammad Ali & James Dean are paired, interestingly, with pictures of a woman in a thong & a group of gangster rappers. Besides coffee, there is alcohol. Beer choices include local Preminger & Stella Artois.

☆ **Bistro** Bihačkih branilaca 2; ⌚ 07.00–01.00 daily. Bistro is a huge summer beer garden on the Una, & you will see it the moment you cross the city bridge. It easily accommodates 500 people & on w/ends it's packed. There are always DJs here playing mostly turbo folk. Wed is reserved for cocktail parties & on Thu it is Heineken night. Almost every w/end, professional dancers heat up the proceedings.

☆ **Papaya** Husrefa Redžića 1; ⌚ 08.00–23.00 Sun–Thu, 08.00–01.00 Fri–Sat. Papaya is another summer-garden café across the street from Bistro. This one, though, has a singular personality. It was created to mimic Papaya bar on the Zrće beach in Croatia, & with its tropical look, it somewhat succeeds. DJs play house, funk & techno. No turbo folk is allowed.

☆ **Santos** Darivalaca krvi bb; ⌚ 07.00–03.00 Wed, Fri & Sat. Owned by the same person as Papaya, this is its winter version. The club is located 10mins from downtown, towards the city's hospital. It is divided into 2 levels, with spiral stairs between. The place is dark, with black bar tables & metal bar stools. They have live music with many regional rock, funk & house bands performing. This is the favourite gathering spot for the more alternative, urban crowd.

WHAT TO SEE AND DO Close to town is **Sokolac**, a perfectly preserved fortification built by the Austrians in the 14th century. Christianity and Islam met and often clashed here. The present-day **Fathija Mosque** was once the **Church of St Anton**. The *stećci* in the town square mark the presence of the heretic Bosnian Church in these parts. The square is dominated by the **Kapetanova Tower** (used as a lookout), the **Zvonik church** and an Ottoman **turbe**, proving the multi-ethnic flavour this community has maintained. The **Town Gallery** (*Bosanska 15;* ☎ *037 223 083;* **e** *gradskagalerija@bih.net.ba;* ⌚ *Mon–Fri and some w/ends in summer; entrance free*) has very nice exhibits of local artists' work. The **Pounja Museum** on the same street is a tiny museum with many Illyrian, Roman, Austrian and Ottoman artefacts discovered in the area.

If you ask the folks from Bihać what there is to see of their town they may eventually murmur something about their history, but the first answer will be the Una. The **Una River** is treated as a member of the family and one might say that the people of Bihać have the strongest collective ecological consciousness in the country. The full length of the river, beginning in the **Croatian Krajina** and entering the **Sava at Jasenovac**, is 207km. It is the fourth-largest river in Bosnia and Herzegovina with a volume of 270m^3 per second. But locals won't tell you that. They will tell you about the crystal-blue waters that have dug deep limestone canyons, the fertile valleys fed by its water, their favourite swimming holes as kids, and, without exception, the thrill of white-water rafting on the mighty Una. The legend behind the river's name goes back to Roman times when a legionnaire had his first glance at the sparkling waters and uttered 'Una, solo una' – the only one – suggesting he had never seen anything like it in his life. You might feel the same.

Rafting on the Una is becoming a national pastime. The annual international **Una Regatta** has increased so much in popularity that places in the 3-day competition are booked months in advance. It's a fabulous experience, and if you've come to Bosnia and Herzegovina or you're passing through Croatia by Plitvice National Park on your way to Dalmatia, trust me, it's more than worth a stop. There are at least four different raft runs on the Una River, from 2 hours of easy rafting to 6 hours of up to class VI rapids. The most attractive, interesting and exciting part of the river is the **Strbački Buk–Lahovo** run. This 15km route is a IV–V-class run that conquers the kind of waterfalls you've only seen in movies.

Una National Park (*Bosanska 1;* ☎ *037 221 528;* **e** *info@nationalpark-una.ba;* **w** *nationalpark-una.ba;* ⌚ *all year; admission 12KM*) Until recently, Bosnia and Herzegovina was scraping the bottom of the barrel with regard to protecting natural resources. It had the smallest percentage of protected territory in Europe with a mere 0.6% of its area marked as environmentally important. The tables have started to turn, however, with a new addition to Bosnia and Herzegovina's national park system. A large swath of the Una River Valley – in the far northwest corner of the country – was declared a national park in 2008.

For many, the term national park might hint to ranger stations, entrance fees, tourist information, and a developed infrastructure to guide nature enthusiasts. Una

National Park defies that logic. With the exception of a makeshift sign, most would never know they've entered a national park. But what the government has failed to do, Mother Nature has handled. The park's territory is amongst the finest and most pristine wilderness areas in Bosnia's northwest. It just comes in raw format.

The park is obviously centred on the Una River. All area whitewater rafting adventures start within the park boundaries. The two settlements inside the park, Kulen Vakuf and Martin Brod, are where a large majority of the infrastructure lies. A handful of B&Bs, cafés, raft launches, and restaurants are the extent of the park's human touches. The falls at Martin Brod and Štrbački Buk rank among the best waterfalls in southeastern Europe, and the colour and purity of the Una River is breathtaking. This aquatic lifeline is completely engulfed in a deep-green forest of vegetation, including many rare and endemic species. The park is on the Green Trail of the Via Dinarica (**w** *viadinarica.com*), and is connected with hiking trails all the way to Sarajevo and west into Croatia.

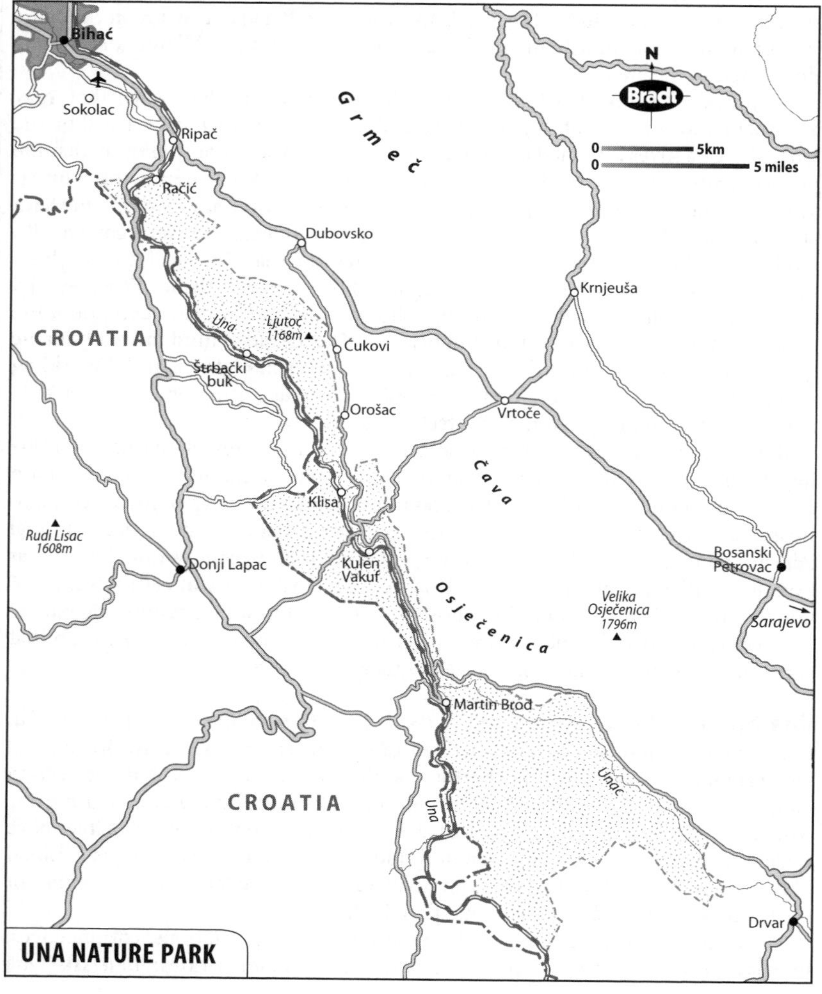

UNA NATURE PARK

A recent EU-funded tourism development project and strong support from the local government have helped sort out some of the organisational kinks of the national park. Scenic viewpoints, wildlife-observation towers, mountain-bike rentals, information packages, lodge refurbishments, and trail-and-road markings have all been constructed.

In the neighbourhood of the Una National park is the **Rural Household Čardaklije** (*Vrtoče bb;* **m** *066 810 000, 066 809 859;* **e** *cardaklije.vrtoce@gmail.com, cardaklijesd@hotmail.com;* **w** *cardaklije.vrtoce.com;* ⌚ *07.00–22.00 daily;* **$$**).This idyllic rural tourist household certainly ranks high on the authentic-meets-rustic scale. Čardaklije is located in Vrtoče village on the highland plateau between Bihać and Bosanski Petrovac, 12km from the Una National Park and 70km from the Plitvice Lakes National Park in Croatia. Brothers Zoran and Zdravko Radosevic had the idea of melding the authentic lives of their ancestors, who have lived there for centuries, with a uniquely original tourist facility. Čardaklije is best known as a place to unplug and enjoy fine traditional meals and drinks in a peaceful atmosphere away from the city and modern life. Most of the food is produced locally and is, by default, organic. The restaurant is in the main building within the complex, a guesthouse built in a traditional architectural style, with décor that is typical of rural Bosnian homes. On the ground floor is a tavern and upstairs is the restaurant with a capacity of 75 seats. Elsewhere on the property, under the shade of an old oak tree, is where they prepare meat and milk products, processed in the traditional way. The house also has a bakery and kitchen where bread and pastries are prepared from different types of flour and organic cereals. *Vesela kuća* (happy house) provides visitors with a chance to become acquainted with the original technology of *rakija* production; if you're driving, you may want to book a room after sipping some of the local firewater. The *vanjsko ognjište* (open campfire) is a magnet for mingling as well as to enjoy the sights and sounds as the Radosevic brothers prepare traditional meat dishes over an open fire. The modest educational and environmental centre is perfect for those interested in the traditional production methods of pomegranate and plum jam, berry juice and various types of organic tea. Accommodation is basic, but more than suitable for a comfortable stay in typical village houses with apartments of four and six beds. I highly recommend a visit if you're in the neighbourhood.

Bosanska Krupa About 33km from Bihać, on the banks of the **Una** and **Krušnica rivers**, is the little town of Bosanska Krupa. The area is well known for its characteristic watermills and the fishing houses built on stilts. The town centre was built around the ruins of a Middle Ages town called **Psata** at the end of the 19th century. Much of the old town is intact, and in typical Bosnian fashion a Catholic church and an Orthodox church stand side by side with a mosque. The most attractive part of town is the rivers and the source of the Krušnica. It's a paradise for anglers and walkers. Fishing is second only to rafting and canoeing in Krupa. Large carp and trout can be found in both rivers, but the Krušnica River seems to be the place for bigger catches. Krušnica spring is home to a diverse world of fish with carp, trout, grayling, pike and chub. The local fishing association can guide visiting anglers to the hotspots and arrange for a licence.

There was once an artists' colony here, and many works are displayed in the **Town Gallery**. Most of the paintings capture the old-style bridges, and the unique little islands with natural beaches in the middle of the river. These islands are ideal for camping and bonfires. Even on the hottest days the river always makes the evenings cool and sometimes chilly. Some 22km of the rafting routes go through Krupa in the **Una Canyon** to **Ostrožac**. Fishing competitions are also held in this part of the canyon.

Where to stay and eat Accommodation in the **Hotel Stari Grad Ilma** (*44 rooms; Trg Alije Izetbegovića bb; 037 471 061;* **$**) is not bad but outdated, being yet another large concrete hotel. **Hotel Eki** (*12 rooms; Medumostovi bb; 037 473 001;* **$**) is a beautiful building right on the riverbank of the Una. The rooms are small but are equipped with modern furniture and facilities. The restaurant and bar serve excellent food and drink. **Bistro Una** at Ljušina bb (*037 477 471*) is a good spot that serves local specialities. Besides the standard meat dishes, they offer a wide array of fresh grilled fish.

Cazin About 26km from Bihać, in a quiet valley surrounded by a picturesque hilly landscape, lies the settlement of Cazin. Although small in size, Cazin has played a significant role in the country's history. Since the 14th century, it has been a strategic point for the foreign powers that lusted for the land of Bosnia and Herzegovina. The medieval remains of Ostrožac, Radetina Tower, Stijena and Trzač give the town a special atmosphere. The most beautiful and impressive is **Ostrožac Castle**, which was built in a neo-Gothic style. Ostrožac is one of the main attractions in **Una Sana Canton**. It was here that the Austro-Hungarian Empire set up camp to defend its frontier and from time to time launch offensives against its Turkish foes. Ostrožac was eventually captured by the Turks, but it was one of the last frontier territories to be conquered. Cazin nowadays has a majority Bosniak population.

The old town, or *čaršija*, is the heart of the town with a lovely little brook cutting through the middle. A good portion of the Una Regatta travels through the outskirts of Cazin.

Where to stay and eat

Hostel Rez Cazin (12 rooms) Puškari bb; m 063 793 883. Basic, clean & newly constructed, this place offers shared or private rooms, a terrace, restaurant, AC & free Wi-Fi. Bear in mind it is located right next to a petrol station. **$**

Restoran Šadrvan K Ljubijankica 1; 037 514 156. On the road from Cazin towards Krupa. **$$**

Restoran Unski smaragdi Srbljani bb; 037 531 190. Just across the river from Hotel Sedra, Unski smaragdi has the best food in town. The service is great & the atmosphere inside & out gets my vote. **$$**

Sanski most Much of the tourism in the Una Sana Canton seems to revolve around Bihać and the Una River. Although Sanski most, which is about 100km from Bihać, is a town on five rivers with rich thermal mineral springs, it has practically no tourism industry to speak of. The **Banja Ilidža** is famous locally for its healing waters, but has not developed at a regional level.

I think it's fair to say that there probably has never been a drought in Krajina, and Sanski most has rivers coming at it from every direction. Not far from the town centre is the source of the **Dabar River**, which swells from an enormous cave. The **Blihi River** tumbles 72m creating a beautiful waterfall. The prehistoric remains of ceramic pottery from nearby Hrustovačka Caves have been dated to the Neolithic era. The **Hamza-begova Mosque**, dated 1557, was built on the place where Sultan Mehmed Fatih first prayed after conquering the town in 1463.

Sanski most is reachable by buses from the Republika Srpska and the Federation. Buses travel daily from Ključ and Bihać. Local buses from nearby Prijedor operate several times per day, and Banja Luka also has a Sanski most route via Prijedor.

Tourist information centre Trg Oslobodilaca bb; 037 684 112; m 061 815 293; 07.30–16.00 Mon–Fri. Established in 2011, & located in the centre of Sanski most. The TIC can provide any & all information on tourism attractions in & around the town, including how to get to some of the harder-to-find places like Blihe Waterfall & Hrustovačka Cave.

Velika Kladuša The Velika Kladuša municipality is the northwesternmost location in Bosnia and Herzegovina and sits right on the border with Croatia. The moderate continental climate and rich unspoiled forests are said to be ideal for hunting and fishing. The area was one of the wealthiest towns in BiH during Yugoslav days, when the large AgroKomerc company, run by Fikret Abdić, was one of the most successful in the country. During the war Kladuša was an enclave within an enclave. The townspeople, mainly Bosniak, backed the business and political leader Abdić, who sought to keep hold of his successful enterprise. He formed his own military units and, backed by the Serbs, held a front line against the surrounded Muslim population of the Bihać enclave. In the offensives of 1995, after NATO air strikes and the Storm Offensive by the Croatian army, the rebels from Kladuša also fell. Velika Kladuša is now part of the Federation and one of the nine municipalities of the Una Sana Canton.

The oldest written document about the town dates back to 1280. The remains of the ancient towns of **Podzvizd**, **Vrnograc**, **Todorovo** and the old part of Velika Kladuša are remnants of centuries of Western influence in the area. The rivers **Glinica**, **Kladušnica** and **Grbarska** are well known as quality fishing areas.

One of the ancient forts in the old town has been converted into a hotel. The nine-room **Hotel Stari Grad** (*Zagrad bb;* m *061 448 155;* **$$**) is the only hotel in the region that is a combination of the old castles and authentic Bosnian-style architecture.

At the entrance to town, from the Bihać direction, you can't miss the large thermal swimming pool in **Mala Kladuša**. This thermal spring is rich in minerals and open to the public.

PLIVA RIVER REGION *John Snyder*

The Pliva River region is located in the north central part of Bosnia and Herzegovina. The area is dominated by several major rivers such as the Pliva, Vrbas and Janj. For many hundreds of years this region was the ultimate stronghold of the Bosnian kingdom. The castle in Jajce was the fortress of the last Bosnian king. The three largest communities in the Pliva River watershed include Šipovo, Jezero, and Jajce. The town of Šipovo is located near the source of the Pliva River, the village of Jezero is located near the Pliva Lakes, and Jajce is located where the Pliva River flows into the Vrbas River. This intersection is the site of a spectacular waterfall that is 15m in height.

The Pliva River plays a vital role in the environmental and economic development of this region of Bosnia. It is the single most important environmental feature because it provides water to sustain human and wildlife populations, a natural transport corridor through the mountains, the best available sites for human settlement, support for agricultural production and hydro-energy resources, and a diverse supply of outdoor recreation resources. The Pliva River provides the natural connection between the three towns of Jajce, Jezero and Šipovo.

The pure, spring-fed waters in the rivers and lakes of the Pliva River region have provided superb **fishing** opportunities for decades. The Pliva River has a well-deserved reputation as one of Europe's best fly-fishing rivers. The middle and lower segments of the Pliva, and the other four large rivers in the region, provide excellent fishing opportunities for all types of anglers. Enormous fish have been caught in the Pliva Lakes from both the shore and from boats. The rivers and lakes in the Pliva River region have a diversity of large and healthy fish species that are caught by the sports angler. Passive to very active fishing techniques may be employed in this region. The sports angler may pursue streamside fishing by either spin casting or fly fishing or considerably more leisurely boat fishing in the lakes.

All of these quality waters are easily accessible from an excellent paved road system that runs alongside the rivers and lakes.

The prize fish species near the source of the Pliva River is the grayling. The brown trout is also native to the Pliva River and this wary fish provides the angler with both challenges and action. The midsection of the river has California and brook trout, as well as browns.

Lake trout, carp, catfish and California trout can be caught in the Pliva Lakes. The largest lake trout caught in these waters was 24kg. Sport fishing from either the shore or from boats is very popular.

BOATING AND KAYAKING ON THE PLIVA Travelling along the Pliva by kayak offers you a wonderful glimpse of the natural beauty and wildlife of the river and lakes. The **kayak** experience also allows the individual to actively participate in a centuries-old mode of travel. The pace of travel is established by means of a compromise between the desires of the paddler and the natural conditions of the region. Given the length of the river and the size of the lakes, the opportunity to explore a large region of Bosnia is exceptional. **Eko Pliva** (☎ *033 654 100;* e *eko.pliva@gmail.com*) provides a kayaking experience on the Pliva. They assess the kayaker's skill and experience level, equipment needs and familiarity with local conditions. Based on this, the kayaker is then provided with the appropriate basic training, equipment, information and potentially with a guide. The kayaks available for tourists include two- and four-seater boats, and you can also hire floats, paddles, spray skirts, float bags and helmets.

For those seeking boating recreation, there are **canoes** and **pedal boats** available for hire. Safety equipment and appropriate instruction are provided for visitors desiring to use these boats. Pedal boats may be hired at the rate of 2KM per hour for a maximum of ten hours' use.

The Pliva is a magnet for paddlers, and it attracts kayakers from all over the world. Easy access from the paved road that runs parallel to the river and lakes contributes to its appeal. The largely protected waters of the Pliva Lakes make them a good place for less experienced paddlers to sharpen their skills.

Paddlers can find a range of conditions to suit them within the region. White-water conditions may be found in the upper reaches of the Pliva and these are particularly rigorous during the spring run-off. Placid segments of the river provide leisurely paddling while the lake offers an enormous body of water for pleasurable paddling or testing one's competitive skills.

Wildlife viewing from kayaks and boats can be an especially pleasurable activity. All of the kayaking experiences in the Pliva River Valley may be witnessed by wild bears, wolves and deer that frequent the shores of the river. Swans, ducks, loons, geese and many other species of birds can be seen. These animals should be respected, especially during the time that they are raising their young. But there is no danger to the tourist viewing these animals from the boats.

Kayakers and boaters should be aware of the cold temperatures of the river and lakes. Appropriate clothing and personal flotation devices are essential for the water conditions of the Pliva.

The islands in the Great Pliva Lake have attractive picnic sites. Kayakers and boaters may travel for as long as they wish and then enjoy natural settings for picnics. Comfortable rest stops may be found within a leisurely one-hour paddle from the kayak club.

Half-day and full-day recreation opportunities are available. The paddling time for the recreational kayaker or boater from the kayak club to the end of the lake is only 2 hours. Paddling around the entire perimeter of the Great Pliva Lake is a very pleasurable activity that can be experienced for the entire day.

The beach of the Small Pliva Lake is occasionally used for **concerts**. A schedule of these events is available from Eko Pliva (see opposite), the Plivsko Jezero Motel (*Mile bb, Jajce;* *030 654 090;* e *plivsko.jezero@tel.net.ba;* **$$**) or the Plaza Restaurant next door (**$$**).

WHERE TO STAY AND EAT

Association of private accommodation providers 050 212 505; e ekopliva@gmail.com. Some 30 Šipovo families have turned their houses into private accommodation centres for international visitors & have already hosted thousands of them. **$$**

Ribnik Villas (4 villas & 1 bungalow) Ribnik bb; 050 430 111; e info@ribnikflyfish.com; w ribnikflyfish.com. This complex has villas all named after the best fly-fishing rivers in the northwest. All of the villas comfortably sleep 6. They are completely outfitted with modern décor, internet, a fitness room, DVD players, large kitchens, 3 bathrooms & their own small wine cellar. The complex also has a restaurant that serves impeccable food if you're not up for cooking in your villa. **$$**

Oaza Mira – Eco Centre Sanica (4 apts) Željeznička 24, 79285 Sanica; 052 236 005, 037 671 462; m 062 472 864; e jadrankozolak@yahoo.com; w oazamirasanica.com.ba. The 'Oasis of Peace' apts have a 20-bed total capacity, each one equipped with a kitchenette, TV & sat TV, bathroom & a spacious terrace. Besides an outdoor pool & BBQ area, the café & restaurant serves local & international cuisine. The food is prepared exclusively on the grill & *sač* (mainly veal & lamb dishes). They offer a wide range of trips to attractive locations such as Strbački Buk, Martin Brod, Unac, Ribnik, Šipovo, Pliva Lakes, Hrustovačka Cave & Blihe Waterfalls. **$–$$**

Tourist Centre & Motel Balkana [Map, pages 280–1] (40 rooms) Turistiki centar Balkana bb, Mrkonjić Grad; 050 212 505; w hotelbalkana.com/smjestaj. The motel is located on the regional Bihać–Sarajevo road, 4km away from the centre of Mrkonjić Grad & 25km from Jajce. It is situated on a lovely lake with great walking paths & a play area for children. The restaurant serves good traditional food. **$–$$**

Camp Zelenkovac (8 rooms) Podrašnica; 050 278 649; e zelenkovac@blic.net; w zelenkovac.org. An off-the-beaten-track eco-lodge where many young travellers go for an inexpensive & friendly nature break. It is past Mrkonjić Grad heading north towards Bihać & is a great stopover for backpackers. **$**

Etno Centre Vrtoce (4 rooms) Bosanski Petrovac; 037 887 007/452; e centarzaocuvanjesela@hotmail.com. A beautiful ethno-village along the road that connects the Pliva & Una river regions. The village, reconstructed according to traditional architecture, is a testament to the old ways of life in the Krajina highland region. Traditional food & crafts are available on site. Staff speak English & Spanish. **$**

JAJCE The time will soon come when this town realises its tourist potential. Still living under poor economic conditions since the war ended, Jajce's only success story has been an aluminium tyre-rim factory that makes millions in profits. The rest of the town seems caught in a strange time warp. Jajce changed hands several times during the war and in the last offensives by the Bosnian Croat and Muslim armies the Serbs lost the city and retreated to Banja Luka before all three sides were called to the Dayton peace talks. Jajce has had its fair share of battles. It was the last fortress to fall to the Turkish invasions, holding out until 1528. The town also changed hands several times before the independent Bosnian state was finally conquered. In 1943, Jajce hosted the second session of the Anti-Fascist Council of the National Liberation of Yugoslavia (AVNOJ), which paved the way for Bosnia and Herzegovina to enter the Federal Republic of Yugoslavia. Jajce was captured by the Bosnian Croat Army (HVO) in 1995 and since then has remained a largely Catholic enclave. Bosniaks and Serbs have begun to return in small numbers.

The brighter side of Jajce is the spectacular medieval citadel set on top of the hill in the middle of town. Hugging the old fortress are beautiful Ottoman-style homes, and rushing below them are two spectacular 27m waterfalls on the Pliva River. No other town in Bosnia and Herzegovina can boast so many cultural layers and such numerous architectural styles in a place so small. The 3rd-century sacred temple dedicated to the god **Mithras,** from Roman times, sits side by side with the most valued example of medieval architecture in the old steeple of **St Luke's Church**. Beneath the church are the **catacombs,** where high priests and the nobility were buried. The **Esma Sultan Mosque**, the most prestigious in the region, was destroyed during the past war. These sites are open to the public, the only problem once again being that there is no information office, website or many signs around town to point you in the right direction. The town may seem a bit dead at first, but after a good wander around the citadel and through the old part of town things just seem to come to life.

The outskirts of town are blessed with an abundance of water, which is probably what made it so attractive and practical as a settlement in earlier times. The **Vrbas** and **Pliva rivers** have been a favourite fishing and swimming hole since the hydro-electric dam was built in the 1970s, creating the large artificial lake. The **Vrbas Canyon** is an amazing drive if you're heading to **Banja Luka**. In the other direction up the Pliva River is the greatest collection of **old mills** in the country. In the wide areas of the Pliva, you can find many mills that were built during Ottoman times. In the past families would gather here to work, grind wheat, wash clothes and collect water. Most of the mills are still in decent shape, and some remain in use.

Where to stay

Hotel Stari Grad (12 rooms) Svetog Luke 3; 030 654 006; **e** starigrad@jajcetours.com; **w** jajcetours.com. This hotel is certainly the best in the region. The location is fantastic, the rooms are comfortable with modern facilities, & the food & service are top quality. It's a great deal for the price! **$$**

Hotel Turist 98 (50 rooms) Kraljice Katarine 1, Jajce; 030 658 151; **e** utd.turist98@tel.net.ba; **w** hotel-turist98.com. A renovated socialist-era hotel. The rooms are simple, but clean. It is conveniently located just off the main road towards the lakes in the centre of Jajce. **$$**

Hotel Plivsko Jezero [map, pages 280–1] (12 rooms) Mile bb; 030 654 090; **e** plivsko.jezero@tel.net.ba. This small hotel is situated right on the banks of Pliva Lakes – perfect for those looking for a nice, natural setting & interested in partaking in some of the many activities on the lake. They have kayak & canoe rentals here as well as bike rentals for the long trail along some parts of the lake. The restaurant is quite good & the hotel rooms are modern, clean & comfy. Child friendly. **$$**

Jajce Youth Hostel (15 rooms) StjepanTomašević 11; **m** 063 262 168; **e** jajceyh@gmail.com; **w** jajce-youth-hostel.com. A basic, clean, no-frills youth hostel with both private & mixed rooms. Bathrooms are shared. B/fast is available at extra charge. There is a shared kitchen & free Wi-Fi. **$**

Auto Kamp Plivsko Jezero [map, pages 280–1] Svetog Luke 3; 030 654 006; **e** booking@jajcetours.com; **w** jajcetours.com; mid April–30 Sep. The camping facilities on the lake are owned & operated by the Hotel Stari Grad. With 33,000m^2 of grounds just off the lake, modern facilities, tennis courts, bungalows, restaurant & café, & views to die for, Auto Kamp is among the best camping spots in the country. The campgrounds have wheelchair access, laundry facilities, & space for 600 campers. From 19KM/€10.

Where to eat and drink

Konoba Slapovi Jajce Plivskih jezera bb; 030 654 027; **e** info@visitjajce.com; 09.00–21.00 daily. The food here is certainly good. But the main pull to this eatery is because of the astonishing views of the waterfalls from almost every table. It's a very relaxing place for a meal or a drink. There is nothing out of the ordinary about the cuisine, but it certainly warrants a visit. $$

Panorama Mile bb; 030 647 170; 07.00–23.00 daily. At first glance it may not look like a great roadside stop. At second glance, you won't want to leave. Panorama is one of the best restaurants in Jajce (located just north of the town). Excellent service, great grilled fish & meats, & quite possibly the best view of the Pliva Lakes make this a worthwhile choice. It's a must-do dining experience if one is staying in Jajce for a few days. It's also a convenient stop if just travelling through town. $$

Hotel Stari Grad Svetog Luke 3; 030 654 006; e starigrad@jajcetours.com; w jajcetours.com; 10.00–22.00 daily. The place to spice it up while in Jajce. $$

Restoran kod Asima Sadije Softića bb; m 063 351 985; 08.00–23.00 daily. Asim's place is a characteristic example of traditional Ottoman architecture. It is located near the Old Fortress Gate. Despite it being a favourite local eatery, there seems to be the tradition of telling stories about Jajce's history. Better go with a local to translate the interesting folklore. $$

Restoran Šadrvan Vinac bb; 030 273 151; 08.00–22.00. Located just outside town, this restaurant is encircled by beautiful nature. Šadrvan serves primarily domestic dishes, which include lamb & veal specialities. It is a popular choice for weekend lunches, or a hearty meal after a long hiking tour. $$

Restoran Una Hrvoja Vukčića Hrvatinića bb; m 061 686 534; 08.00–23.00 daily. Another favourite among the locals, located on the main strip in the old part of town. They serve local cuisine, priding themselves on their veal dishes. It's a good place to see & be seen since it's on the main promenade, just before the arches of the old town. $$

Restoran Plaža [map, pages 280–1] Plivska Jezera bb; 030 647 200; 08.00–22.00 daily. Located 5km north of Jajce, directly on the Pliva Lakes next to the Hotel Plivsko Jezero. As one would expect, the lake fish are the best meals on the menu. The restaurant serves an array of grilled meats & national dishes. The lakeside terrace gives you an on-the-lake dining experience … & also keeps it cool in the summertime. $–$$

Pite ispod sača kod Hamde Skela bb; m 063 293 371; 08.00–22.00. Most locals seem to agree that the pies made here are among the best in the town. The reason to go to Hamde's is obviously for the delicious pies, but they also serve a tasty baked potato & beef dish as well. Everything is prepared in the traditional manner '*ispod saća*' (page 80). $

Pizzeria Megi Dea Hrvoja Vukčića Hrvatinića bb; 030 657 944; 10.00–23.00 daily. Good pizza. Good service. Good atmosphere. It's, well, a good place to eat. The décor is modern & natural. Megi Dea, not to be confused with its neighbour Pizzeria Dea, is a popular place & is usually quite busy. A large pizza & a drink cost around 10KM.$

What to see and do

Avnoj Museum (*2 Zasjedanja Avnoj-a; 030 657 998; 08.00–18.00 daily; entrance 1KM*) Jajce was a key city in the creation of the second Yugoslavia during World War II. It was here, in November 1943, that Tito and the anti-fascist Partisans' council from Croatia, Slovenia, Serbia, Bosnia and Herzegovina, Montenegro, and Macedonia declared Yugoslavia a federal, socialist people's state (page 303). The museum is a tribute holding an array of various Partisan documents, weapons, photographs and other exhibits.

Čaršijska džamija/Esma Sultana Mosque (*In the heart of the trading quarters of Jajce's old town, between the Travnik and Banja Luka arched gates*) This mosque is the most significant Islamic structure in present-day Jajce. It was completely destroyed during the last war in 1993 and has only restored its exterior. The inside is still not completed. The mosque grounds are open for visitors but access to the interior is usually limited due to reconstruction.

Catacombs/Underground Church Believed to have been built in the early 15th century by order of Duke Hrvoje Vukčić, this is the only catacomb ever found in Bosnia and Herzegovina. Jajce took on great importance towards the end of the Bosnian kingdom era. The catacombs are located within the city walls but do not keep regular operating hours. It is best to jump on a town tour where the guide has already arranged for the catacombs to be open.

St Mary's Church/Mehmed II Mosque St Mary's Church dates from the early to mid 1400s and was the place where a Papal council crowned the last Bosnian king, Stjepan Tomašević, in 1461. The large bell tower, named after St Luke, is the most visible and intact part of the ancient complex. It is the only medieval bell tower remaining on the continental Balkan peninsula. When the Ottomans overran Bosnia in 1528, the church was converted to a mosque. After several fires the church/mosque was put out of commission by the mid 19th century. It is located in the old town.

Crkva Sv Ive Krstitelja/St John the Baptist Church (*Podmilačje, about 10km from Jajce*) One of the region's most charming Catholic churches. Unlike St Mary's, St John the Baptist Church was not touched by the invading Ottomans. The church served its community until 1993, when it was razed to the ground. It has been completely renovated after the war – in its original style – and is a popular attraction for visitors. The church is open for visitors and there is no admission fee.

Hram boga Mitre/Temple of the God Mithra (*Centre of town*) Estimated to have been built in the 4th century AD, the temple for the deity of sun and light is the only one of its kind in Bosnia and Herzegovina. Although the cult of the invincible sun was widespread throughout the Roman Empire and the Romans had settled in the territory of present-day Bosnia and Herzegovina from the 1st century, no other traces of this cult have been found elsewhere. The temple itself still bears visible carvings to their deity as well a handful of statues from that era. The Mithras temple is open to visitors but, as with many attractions in Jajce, it doesn't keep regular hours. There is no entrance fee.

Jajce Fortress (🕘 *Summer 09.00–19.00 daily; winter 09.00–16.00 daily; admission 2KM*) This medieval fortification crowns the hilltop settlement of the old town. Built sometime in the 13th century, the fortress eventually became the Bosnian royal residence in the early 15th century. A stone-carved shield on the fortress walls indicates that in 1421 Jajce became the seat of the kingdom that lasted between Tvrtko II and King Tomašević's rule. The walled fortress is open for visitors and the wall walks provide phenomenal views of the surrounding area.

Pliva Waterfall Locals claim this waterfall is amongst the 12 most beautiful in the world. It's on the official site of the tourism association. Who has actually ranked it 12th is never mentioned. The important thing here is that this waterfall is most definitely stunning and it gives Jajce its most unique brand. In the centre of the town, it cascades 21m into the Vrbas River. The best view for a photograph is from the bridge at the southwestern entrance to Jajce from the Donji Vakuf direction.

Pliva Watermills Situated between the big and small part of the Pliva Lakes, these mills were a symbol of great wealth and power in medieval Bosnia. Wheat was milled for flour here for centuries. The unwritten rule was that one was never to pay for usage of the mills with money, but it was expected that a tenth of the product be left for the owner. The watermills are in such a beautiful and pristine setting that it would be a shame to visit Jajce and not take the 5km trip to see them. Several of the mills have been restored and are functional. The entire complex has been declared a national monument.

ŠIPOVO

It's fair to say **Šipovo** was a no-man's-land for a very long time. After exchanging hands on several occasions during the last war and eventually being part of a big territory swap in peace negotiations, Šipovo has seen some ups and downs. But things are changing.

Following an ecotourism development project funded by the Japanese International Co-operation Agency, the community has mobilised to cash in on the many gifts Mother Nature bestowed on them. Šipovo is a sleepy town, sandwiched between the great and barren valleys of western Bosnia and the towns of **Jajce** and **Mrkonjić Grad** to the east. Many in Šipovo are small-scale agriculturists. The soil is fertile and rich, and the vast quantities of fresh water create an ideal microclimate for successful farming. The countryside is dotted with quaint villages, lakes and rolling hills. It is also dominated by the high peaks of **Vitorog Mountain** to the west, and the gushing sources of **Pliva** and **Janj rivers**.

Šipovo is a nature lover's destination. With the exception of **Sokograd Fortress** and **Glogovac Monastery**, there is not much to speak of in terms of cultural and historical sites … that's what neighbour Jajce is for. The easiest area to access is the **Pljeva** region just 6km southwest of Šipovo. This is where you'll find **Olić** and **Đol** lakes, the largest cluster of bed and breakfast accommodations, the source of the Pliva River and one of the region's most popular fly-fishing destinations. A bit further from Šipovo is the **Janj Islet** area. There are a handful of bed and breakfasts here. Nature does all the rest.

It should be noted that although there are many attractive and beautiful things to see in and around Šipovo, tourism activities are not organised in a user-friendly way. If you'd like to just wander and explore, Šipovo is still a good place to do so.

WHERE TO STAY

LTG Tourist Complex (8 bungalows) Pljeva bb; 050 320 000; e info@plivaflyfish.com; w plivaflyfish.com. Not far from the Pliva Springs are bungalows, each with a capacity of 6–8 persons. They are decked out with comfortable, modern furniture but maintain a traditional & rustic aesthetic. The bungalows are intended mostly for fly fishermen but are by no means limited to them. The area is ideal for light walks, bike riding or just relaxing in the natural surroundings of Šipovo's outskirts. There is also a small restaurant/bar on the premises, & they can organise fishing licenses for their clients. **$$**

WHERE TO EAT AND DRINK

Ladna Voda Čifluk bb; 050 371 610; e office@sipovo-tourism.com; 07.00–23.00 daily. On the main road out of Šipovo in the Kupres direction. This somewhat remote area is located in a beautiful natural setting along the river. The restaurant serves exceptional food, with speciality dishes like baked lamb & pork, *sač*-cooked veal, & grilled trout & grayling. The interior is decorated in an ethno style, with the large outside terraces outfitted with wooden tables & benches. **$$**

Ribnjak Dedo Sime Šolaje bb; m 065 435 284; 07.00–22.00 daily. Found on the road north out of Šipovo towards Pljeva, Ribnjak Dedo serves the trout it farms in the Pliva. Dedo is an old man who was seriously wounded during the war. He returned to his devastated house to start a small fish farm. Over the years his business has grown enough to open up a modest restaurant that serves excellent trout dishes. **$$**

Ribolovačka priča Srpskih boraca bb; m 066 808 322; 07.00–23.00 daily. In the middle of town. Although it tends to be slightly dark inside, the terrace is a very pleasant place for one of their excellent dishes. The fishermen's story, as the restaurant name translates in English, obviously focuses on fish. They also serve excellent smoked ham & Vojvodina *ćevapi*. Aside from the grilled trout & grayling dishes, they make a mean steak. **$$**

Atina Tavern Srpskih branilaca 4; 050 371 259; 07.00–23.00 daily. Centrally located in Šipovo, Atina Tavern was inspired by Greek cooking. That doesn't mean you'll get a good Greek salad or *spanakopita* here, but the veal & steaks are prepared the Greek way. They also serve good local fish, mainly farmed in the Pliva River. **$–$$**

Mlinčić Mujdžići bb; 050 373 520; 08.00–22.00 daily. On the Janj River, this tiny restaurant is the only choice near the Janj Islets. The dishes are national in style, with a focus on grilled meats & fish. The local spirits are homemade, strong & oh so good. **$–$$**

WHAT TO SEE AND DO

Janj's Islets Part of the Janj River, this 1km-long and 300m-wide section of the river splits and forms a series of small islets. It is one of the more popular recreation spots for locals and is ideal for walking, picnicking or to just unplug and enjoy a day in nature. There is a good gravel road that leads to this part of the river.

Glogovac Monastery Many of the isolated Orthodox monasteries in Bosnia and Herzegovina maintain a medieval style. There are several somewhat confusing legends about Glogovac. It is said, for instance, that when permission had been sought from the Ottoman vizier to build the church he, to the surprise of the community, reluctantly granted it but ordered the church to be built so the church bells could not be heard. This story is repeated in many places around Bosnia and Herzegovina. The confusing aspect of this story: the church was built in 1886, eight years after the Austro-Hungarians gained control from the Ottomans.

Pliva sources The beauty of the astounding Pliva River is best understood at its sources. The three major sources are about 7km from Šipovo towards the settlement of Pljeva. Here the riverside is dotted with old mills and traditional-style homes, untouched by time and war. All three sources are accessible. There are no facilities around the sources but they make ideal spots for a picnic.

River Janj The river is special for many reasons. The main tributary to the Pliva River, its pure, crystal-clear water and remoteness make it a peaceful oasis. The old-growth forests of Janj are in this river valley. The Glogovac Monastery was built here. Sited 13km to the south of Šipovo, Janj has long been among the most popular destinations for visitors and locals alike.

Sokograd Fortress Perhaps the most important medieval heritage site in the area, the remains of the Sokograd Fortress are located 6km northwest of Šipovo. The fortress is first mentioned in 1363 when Tvrtko defeated a surprised Hungarian army. It was an important stronghold until the collapse of the Bosnian kingdom. The Ottomans utilised it as a guard post until 1833 when their guards permanently retreated from the area. Since that time the fortress has been abandoned and has fallen into disrepair. The fortress is accessible and there are several road signs once you near the fortress in the village of Barači.

Sokol's Cave This cave is found just opposite the Sokograd Fortress in the Sokočnica river valley, 575m above sea level with caverns and trails leading in over 100m. The remains of ceramics and utensils clearly indicate it was used, and perhaps lived in, during medieval times. The cave is gated and access is possible during the summer tourist season only with a guide provided on site. Entrance fee is 2KM.

Vitorog Mountain This is the highest peak in the Šipovo region. Just under the 2,000m mark, it flanks Šipovo's entire western side. The Vitorog Mountain Association (*Braće Jugović 2, Šipovo;* **m** *065 591 171*) is quite active and through the tourism association one can arrange a hiking excursion. An EU-funded project should help with making it easier for independent travellers to enjoy Šipovo's nature without the necessity of a guide.

SEND US YOUR SNAPS!

We'd love to follow your adventures using our *Bosnia* guide – why not send us your photos and stories via Twitter (@BradtGuides) and Instagram (@bradtguides) using the hashtag #bosnia. Alternatively, you can upload your photos directly to the gallery on the Bosnia destination page via our website (*www.bradtguides.com/bosnia*).

8

Northeast Bosnia

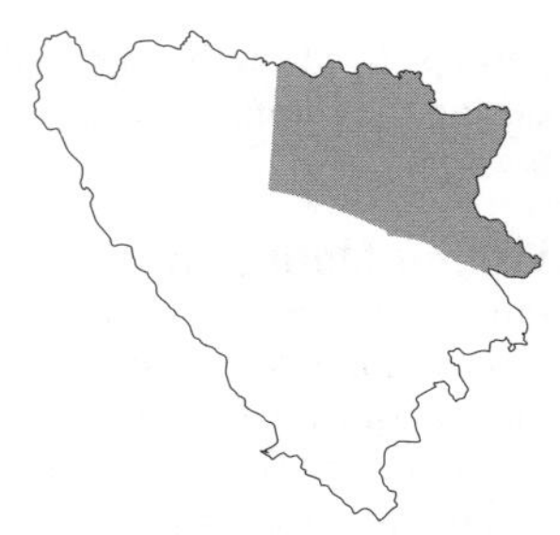

The northeast corner of Bosnia and Herzegovina is the industrial backbone of the country. Don't let that deter you as there are still dozens of places to see and visit, and as in any other part of BiH you don't have to go very far to find an isolated mountain, a cool stream or a thick green forest. The areas along the Sava River to the extreme northeast are the most fertile regions in the country. Agriculture in the entire northeast pocket is the number-one industry and employer, with over 50% of its territory used for agricultural purposes. Around the central city of Tuzla is the heart of the country's industry. Tuzla was named during Ottoman times after its salt mines. Large coal deposits are mined here to fuel the thermo-electric plants, creating the largest energy potential in Bosnia and Herzegovina. The five plants also create the worst air pollution in the region. To be honest, this city does not possess the kind of tourism attractions that most other parts of the country do. Nonetheless this does not detract from the rich natural, cultural and historical heritage of the northeast region.

Konjuh, Majevica and Ozren criss-cross the middle section of the northeast and create large natural boundaries between the mountain hill climates and the long flatlands of Semberija in the extreme north of the region. Majevica and Ozren saw quite a lot of fighting during the war so hiking solo is not a good idea. The local mountain associations are very active and have several mountain huts. If you are truly keen on a hike, it will take some perseverance on your behalf to locate an English-speaking member. If your sign-language skills are good, local hikers are always glad to take a guest along with them and will show you the ropes.

The most confusing aspect of this corner of the world is not how to avoid intimidating socialist smokestacks, but rather how to ascertain which entity, canton or district you may be in at any given time. It seems odd that the part of the country with the largest multi-ethnic population should be carved up into so many little pieces.

The central region of the northeast belongs to or falls under Tuzla and Zenica-Doboj cantons in the Federation. Due west of Tuzla at Doboj is the beginning of western Republika Srpska. To the east is also Republika Srpska and to the north is the semi-autonomous district of Brčko. Confused yet? To the west of the small corridor that Brčko creates are the two little 'islands' of the Posavina Canton, at Orašje and Odžak on the Croatian border. It would take days to make head or tail of all this, so I'll do my best to put it in layman's terms.

During the war the entire eastern border of Bosnia and Herzegovina fell quickly and easily to the Serbs. They marched south and west from Bijeljina and Zvornik to secure the border with Serbia and Montenegro to the south, and the northern border of Slavonia with Croatia. This strategy would unite the Serbs in Slavonia and the Croatian Krajina to the west, and in eastern BiH with Montenegro in the far south. The most challenging part of this was getting past Brčko. Brčko was and is a key city (hence its current district status, not belonging to either the Federation or the Republika). Brčko got pounded from both sides. The Croats fought from the north and the Bosnian–Croat alliance fought from the south to keep the Brčko corridor from being the supply route for the Serb-captured lands to the west. And this is the simple version.

When the Dayton Peace Accords were signed, the future of Brčko was 'to be decided later'. This basically meant that the parties could not agree and as it threatened the entire peace process all sides decided to give it the status of district. The people of Odžak and Orašje along the Croatian border and just across the Sava from Croatia managed to hold on to their little towns with great help from the Croatian army.

The isolated 'finger' of Usora, Tešanj and Maglaj is part of the Zenica-Doboj Canton. Tuzla, Gradačac and as far as Čelić near Brčko, are part of the Tuzla Canton. In a nutshell the northeast is divided into the Brčko district, Tuzla Canton of the Federation, Zenica-Doboj Canton of the Federation, Posavina Canton of the Federation, and the eastern and western parts of Republika Srpska.

TUZLA

Situated on the southeast slopes of the Majevica Mountain, the city of Tuzla occupies the central area of northeast Bosnia. The elevation of the town is 239m above sea level, and it stretches across an area of approximately 15km^2. The city's population is about 100,000, but the greater municipal area has over 170,000 inhabitants. Tuzla claims to be the economic, scientific, cultural, educational, health and tourist centre of northeast Bosnia, basically taking credit for most things that go on in the northeast, and to some extent this is true.

Tuzla is the home of major industrial, commercial and construction companies such as coal mine Kleka, chemical complex Sodaso, production commercial complex PTK, industrial construction company Tehnograd, and the thermo-electric power station Termoelektrana.

HISTORY The area of Tuzla's saltwater springs has been inhabited from the Neolithic age to the present day. The settlement of Tuzla has always been closely tied to its salt resources. The oldest written records, left behind by the Greeks, prove that even they knew of the region. In his historic writings from AD950, the Byzantine historian and tsar Constantine Porfirogenet mentions the existence of Tuzla's saltwater springs and the settlements surrounding them. Tuzla received its name – after its abundant mineral resource – much later. The present-day name is derived from the Turkish word *tuz,* meaning 'salt'. The first document recording the exploitation of Tuzla's saltwater springs dates from 1548. Salt was produced here all year round and salt wells were located on the present-day Salt Square. The daily salt production in Donja and Gornja Tuzla was approximately 500kg. With the arrival of the Turks that number increased fivefold.

The region was in constant contact with the Turks by 1460. In 1474, the occupation was complete. Within the Bosnian *vilayet*, Tuzla was under the administrative government of the Zvornik Sanjak. It was granted the status of *kadžiluk* first in Gornja Tuzla, which was later relocated to Tuzla proper around the middle of the 17th century.

The importance of the settlement greatly increased under Turkish rule. Owing to vast reforms in the Turkish administration starting in the 17th century, a freer development of the town economy occurred. With the introduction of modern

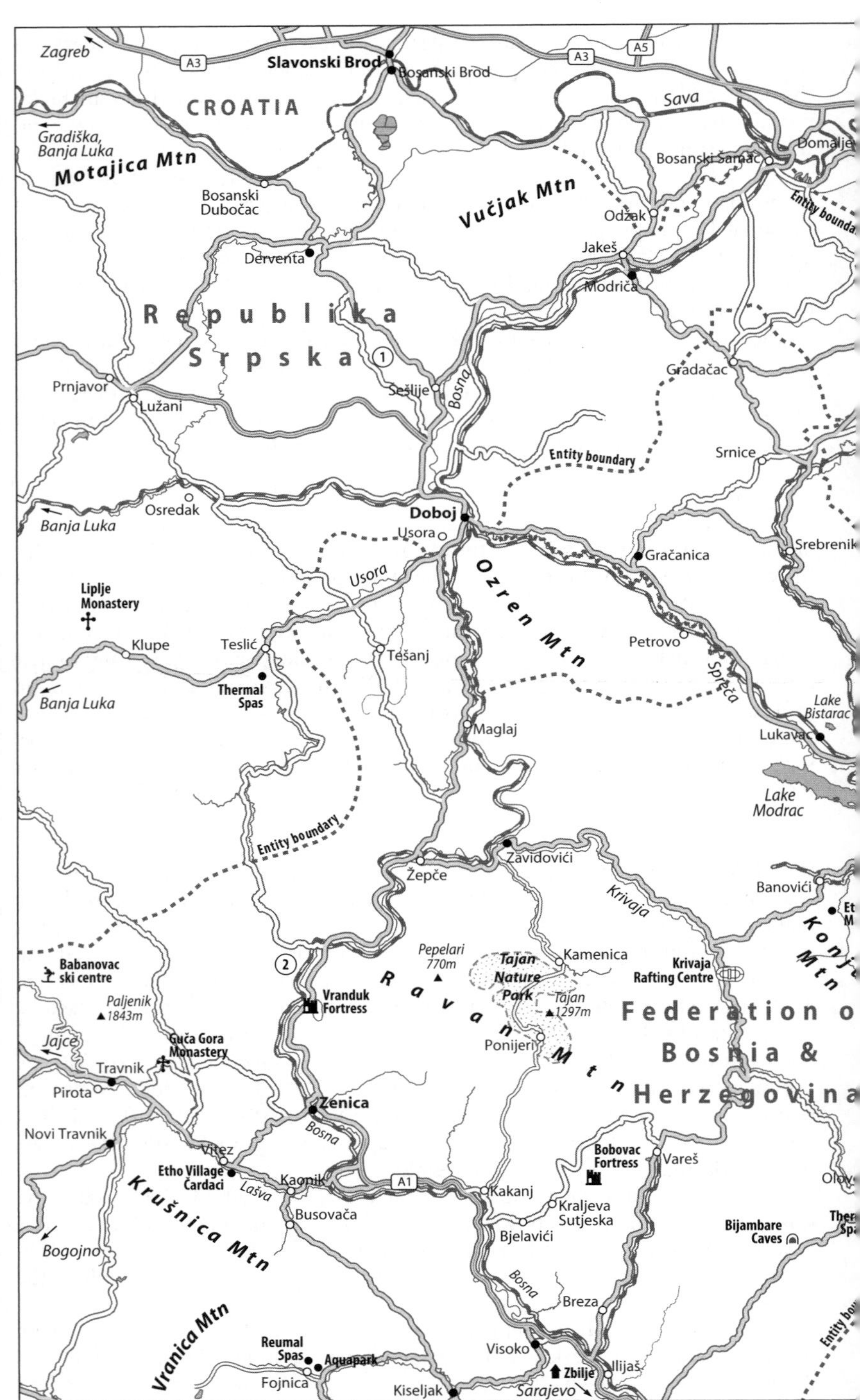
Zagreb
A3
Slavonski Brod
Bosanski Brod
A3
A5
CROATIA
Sava
Gradiška, Banja Luka
Motajica Mtn
Bosanski Dubočac
Vučjak Mtn
Bosanski Šamac
Domaljevac
Odžak
Entity boundary
Jakeš
Modriča
Derventa
Republika Srpska
1
Gradačac
Prnjavor
Lužani
Šešlije
Bosna
Entity boundary
Srnice
Osredak
Banja Luka
Doboj
Usora
Gračanica
Srebrenik
Usora
Ozren Mtn
Liplje Monastery
Klupe
Teslić
Tešanj
Petrovo
Thermal Spas
Banja Luka
Spreča
Lake Bistarac
Maglaj
Lukavac
Lake Modrac
Entity boundary
Zavidovići
Žepče
Krivaja
Banovići
Konjuh Mtn
Pepelari 770m
Babanovac ski centre
2
Tajan Nature Park
Kamenica
Krivaja Rafting Centre
Vranduk Fortress
Ravan Mtn
Paljenik 1843m
Tajan 1297m
Federation of Bosnia & Herzegovina
Jajce
Guča Gora Monastery
Ponijeri
Travnik
Pirota
Zenica
Novi Travnik
Bosna
Vitez
Bobovac Fortress
Vareš
Etho Village Čardaci
Kaonik
A1
Lašva
Kakanj
Kruśnica Mtn
Kraljeva Sutjeska
Busovača
Bjelavići
Bijambare Caves
Bogojno
Bosna
Breza
Vranica Mtn
Entity boundary
Reumal Spas
Aquapark
Visoko
Zbilje
Ilijaš
Fojnica
Kiseljak
Sarajevo

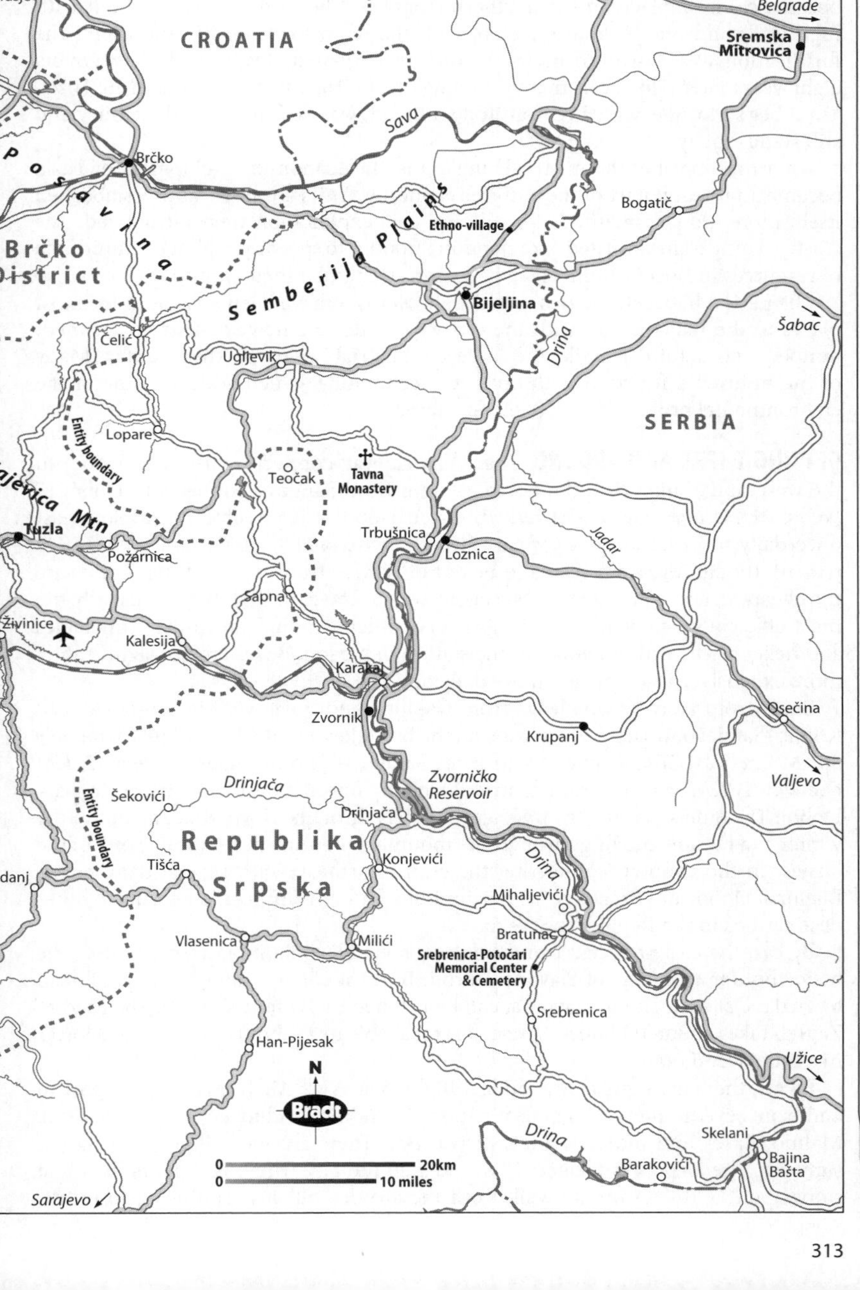

NORTHEASTERN BOSNIA
Where to stay
1 Kotromanicevo Royal Village p248
2 Pansion Bistričak p244
Vinkovci
Županja
A3
Orašje
CROATIA
Novi Sad, Belgrade
Sremska Mitrovica
Sava
Brčko
Posavina
Brčko District
Semberija Plains
Ethno-village
Bogatič
Bijeljina
Drina
Šabac
Čelić
Ugljevik
Lopare
Entity boundary
SERBIA
Teočak
Tavna Monastery
Majevica Mtn
Tuzla
Požarnica
Trbušnica
Loznica
Jadar
Sapna
Živinice
Kalesija
Karakaj
Zvornik
Krupanj
Osečina
Valjevo
Zvorničko Reservoir
Drinjača
Šekovići
Drinjača
Republika Srpska
Konjevići
Tišća
Mihaljevići
Bratunac
Vlasenica
Milići
Srebrenica-Potočari Memorial Center & Cemetery
Srebrenica
Han-Pijesak
Užice
N
Bradt
Skelani
Drina
Bajina Bašta
Barakovići
0 20km
0 10 miles
Sarajevo

crafts, Tuzla developed into the administrative centre of the Zvornik *sandžak* and became an important communications, military, trade and cultural centre in northeast Bosnia. Towards the end of Turkish rule, Tuzla had approximately 5,000 inhabitants, making it one of the largest towns in Bosnia and Herzegovina.

In the early 18th century, a rectangular fortification was built in the town centre. Tensions with the Austrians had been significantly raised, and raids and battles became commonplace on the northern frontiers. The fortification was built with high walls and one lookout on each, with the main tower within the walls. The fortification was destroyed in 1870, and the Turks left Bosnia and Herzegovina eight years later. However, many buildings from Turkish times remain in Tuzla. Turalibeg's Mosque, with a typical stone minaret, was built in the 16th century and still stands today.

After the arrival of the Austro-Hungarians, the economic development of Tuzla became an integral part of the empire's economy. As its administration established itself, more modern methods for salt and coal exploitation were introduced. The Austro-Hungarians invested a tremendous amount to speedily exploit the multitude of resources in Bosnia and Herzegovina and strengthen their empire.

The period between the two world wars seems to have been a vacuum for most places in the Balkans, but with the victory of Tito, the new socialist government jumped into action to build the largest industrial region in the country. Many of the industries function with outdated technology, which adds to some of the environmental problems that Tuzla now faces.

GETTING THERE AND AROUND There is a **railway** connecting Tuzla to Doboj to the west, and Vinkovci to the north. A train from Sarajevo connects to Doboj (*3 hours, 21KM one way, 34KM return*). From Doboj it is possible to travel at least once daily to Tuzla and vice versa (*1½hrs, approximately 10KM one way, 17KM return*), though the train seems to be out of service from time to time. Trains are the cheapest, and sometimes most scenic, way to travel in BiH, but not usually the most efficient or convenient. It is also very difficult to find up-to-date timetables and ticket prices without going to the station in person. Buses are not significantly more expensive, and there are more daily options.

Buses from Herzegovina leave from Čapljina and travel via Mostar–Jablanica–Konjic–Sarajevo to Tuzla. From Mostar, the bus takes about 6 hours (*approximately 36KM one-way, 50KM return*) and from Sarajevo 3 hours (*approximately 21KM one way, 28KM return*). From central Bosnia by bus, the best route is via Zenica–Doboj. The quickest route from Sarajevo travels through Olovo-Kladanj, but in the winter can be slow moving through the mountains. Tuzla's bus station is one of the busiest in the country, connecting the entire northeast with several daily buses. Bijeljina, Doboj and Brčko are also major hubs for bus transport, especially to other destinations in the Republika Srpska.

By **car**, the easiest access from the west is via Slavonia in eastern Croatia. The major border crossings of Slavonski Brod, Bosanski Šamac and Županija all lead to Tuzla. Osijek, a city in Slavonia, can be reached in 3¼ hours by car. The road to Zagreb takes about 4½ hours. Sarajevo is reachable in 2½ hours or less, and Mostar in a little over 5 hours.

By **air,** there are regular low-budget flights via Wizz Air from Tuzla Airport to and from several international destinations including Eindhoven, Frankfurt, Oslo, Malmo, Basel, and more (**w** *tuzla-airport.ba*). There are more flights during the summer. The airport is located 15km outside the city. There is a public bus that stops about a 10–15-minute walk from the airport, but it is confusing to locate.

It is better to take a taxi. A taxi to or from the city centre will be around 15–20KM. It is possible to get a shuttle or taxi transfer from Tuzla airport to Sarajevo, or take a bus from the central bus station. The journey can take between 2 and 5 hours, depending on the mode of transport. Wizz Air offers a shuttle service (**w** *wizzairporttransfer.com*) several times a day (timetable varies) to and from Sarajevo (44KM single, 88KM return). The journey takes about 2 hours in one direction. A reservation must be booked at least 24 hours in advance.

TOURIST INFORMATION AND TOUR OPERATOR I'm reluctant to say this, but still must warn you that receptive tourism for international tourists hasn't really taken off here yet. The demand is low, and most of the tourism in this region is local/domestic. This undoubtedly adds to its authenticity, but it doesn't make it easy for the foreign guest. However, that is slowly changing, especially with the addition of regular international flights flying in and out of Tuzla Airport.

Tuzla Canton Tourism Association Soni Trg bb; ☎035 228 800; **e** turisticka.zajednica@bih.net.ba; **w** tourism-tk.ba. Helpful for accommodation, for what to see around town & regional information. They have decent local maps, which are always useful if you have to get around on your own.

Hit Tours Hadžibakirbega Tuzlića bb; ☎035 258 311; **e** agencija@hit-tours.ba; **w** hit-tours.ba; ⏲ 09.00–05.00 Mon–Fri, 09.00–15.00 Sat

WHERE TO STAY

Golden Star Hotel (8 rooms) Jevrejska ulica 5; ☎035 258 100; **e** info@goldenstarhotel.ba; **w** goldenstarhotel.ba. This is a nice hotel in downtown Tuzla. The rooms are clean & modern, with all the general amenities one would expect, mini-bar, TV, AC, Wi-Fi. Golden Star serves an excellent buffet breakfast & staff are very friendly & helpful. **$$**

Hotel Antalija Tuzla (3 rooms) Soni trg; **m** 063 391 836; **e** antalyatuzla@gmail.com; **w** antalyatuzla.weebly.com. The initial idea of Antalija was to open a restaurant. They did that & it immediately became one of the best restaurants in town. They've expanded on that idea & have built a small, but higher end, hotel that has only 3 rooms. The rooms are fantastic, with superb design & comfort. It is the best value hotel in Tuzla. **$$**

Hotel Senad od Bosne (27 rooms, 1 apt) Magistralni put bb; ☎035 561 222; **e** info@hotelsenandodbosne.com; **w** hotelsenadodbosne.com. Right on Lake Modrac, the hotel has sgl, dbl & trpl options as well as the apt. They are all outfitted with homely wooden furniture. There's a honeymoon suite for those with a hankering for some romance. The complex is a great choice for business gatherings or for something a little special. The restaurant serves local specialities. **$$**

Hotel Tuzla (120 rooms) Zavnobih-a 13; ☎035 369 600; **e** info@hoteltuzla.com; **w** hoteltuzla.ba. Centrally located & with a capacity of 330, this is one of the largest & most sensible hotels in the country. Though something of a throwback to the socialist era, it is really quite nice, with an indoor swimming pool & saunas, restaurants, a disco & cafés. The rooms are modern with chic designs & wooden headboards. A perfect spot for business visitors. **$$**

Motel Royal (10 rooms) Bosne srebrene 105-a; ☎035 315 666; **e** info@royalmotel.ba; **w** royalmotel.ba. On a larger road & just a few mins' walk from the centre, the motel has modern & spacious rooms with comfy beds. Each has a TV & internet access. This is the town's most strategically placed motel for Tuzla's bus & railway stations. **$$**

Pansion Centar (5 rooms) Trg Stara Tržnica 8; **m** 061 149 291; **e** pansioncentar@hotmail.com; **w** pansioncentar.com. Pansion Centar is located just as its name purports, in the central Salt Square. The rooms are simple, modern & clean. Each room is en suite & has AC, heating, free Wi-Fi & a TV. Although the rooms are basic, the location is good as is the price. **$$**

Pansion Miris Dunja 88 (20 rooms) Goli Brijeg 8; ☎035 296 453; **m** 062 137 029; **e** info@mirisdunja88.ba; **w** mirisdunja88.ba. A good example of the solid – but less expensive – places starting to open in town. A 5-min walk to the Korzo & town centre, this establishment with a total of 60 beds has small but clean & modern rooms. Bathrooms are small but, again, nice & clean. The staff speak a bit of English. B/fast inc. **$$**

Tehnograd Hotel (72 rooms) Goste Lazerevića bb; 035 226 396; **e** info@hotel-tehnograd.com; **w** hotel-tehnograd.com. Tehnograd is ranked among the top 40 hotels in the country according to Priceline Group, despite its 3-star category. The rooms are comfortable & spacious, but what sets it apart is that staff go out of their way to organise your trip in & around Tuzla. The hotel is popular with businessmen/women visiting, as well as with the locals on the weekend for the live music. That may be their weakest point, the music is often turbo-folkish. **$$**

Pansion Diskrecija (8 rooms) Husinska-Partizanske Čete 103; 035 380 422; **m** 061 728 007; **e** diskrecija@bih.net.ba; **w** diskrecija.com.ba. Though it's located at Tuzla's entrance & close to the large coal plant, don't be discouraged. The rooms are simple but nice, & the whole place gives off the sense of being in a forest hideaway. The property has a leafy garden, a playground for the little ones & a restaurant. Plus, the price is right & the staff are friendly. **$**

Pansion Kipovi (10 rooms) Franjevačka 10; **m** 062 389 478; **e** pansionkipovi@gmail.com; **w** pansionkipovi.com. An easy place to miss near the river & just up the street from the Franciscan monastery, Kipovi (or 'statues' – so named because of the ones standing atop the nearby bridge) has simple & dorm-like rooms with sgl beds framed by either cheerful pink or yellow walls. Key here: everything is clean, convenient & AC. **$**

WHERE TO EAT AND DRINK

Restaurants

Baltazar Džafer Mahala 29; 035 257 461; 09.00–22.30 Mon–Thu, 09.00–23.30 Fri–Sat, closed Sun. Some refer to Baltazar as the best restaurant in Tuzla owing to the fact that it has the largest selection of meals & wines on offer. If we're talking volume, then they certainly win. They serve more than 13 kinds of soups, 45 types of cheese, 30 types of cold/warm appetizers as well as 12 sorts of fish & meat daily. Additionally, there are around 700 wine varieties in their wine list. I'm not sure I believe that they have 700 wines in stock, but I'll give them an A for effort. The food is quite good by the way. **$$–$$$**

Big Hilton Bosnesrebrene bb; 030 281 588. For a pretty decent restaurant with a creative menu, they make it a bit hard to find. Aside from the lack of info (no web or email), the restaurant, located in a business building, manages to serve up tasty meals for all pallets, including vegetarian. **$$-$$$**

Antalya Solni trg bb; **m** 063 391 836; **e** antalyatuzla@gmail.com; **w** antalyatuzla.weebly.com/restoran.html; 10.00–23.00. Part of the tiny 3-room hotel of the same name, this modern-looking restaurant is located in the heart of Tuzla, with a view of Salt Square. The restaurant has a modest elegance to it, & the food is always fresh. **$$**

Heartland Kazan Mahala 10; 035 255 111; 08.00–midnight daily. Nominally a pizzeria & a café, Heartland is much nicer than that. Sited on a street parallel to Korzo & just a skip from the National Theatre, the interior is 2 floors & awash in dark wood & pub-ish libation adverts – like the framed Jack Daniels mirror. There's a wood-fired oven if you are in the market for a pizza, but there are also big salads, pastas & even omelettes for b/fast. This is a pleasant place to enjoy an afternoon beer on the front, covered terrace. **$$**

Ljetna Bašta Pannonica Lake; 035 246 711; **w** panonika.ba; 08.00–20.00 daily. Mainly a grill serving hamburgers & the like, this spot is on Pannonica Lake's grounds & looks over its waterfalls. Patrons can also sip ice-cold beer & an assortment of spirits on a big wooden patio that spreads out over 3 levels. **$$**

Ontario Lake Bistarac; 035 553 349; **m** 061 724 110; 07.00–23.00 daily. Between Lukavac & Tuzla, this is the restaurant serving Camp Ontario on Lake Bistarac. But, don't let the word camp fool you. This is a wonderful restaurant with a large – & open – interior & a multi-tiered terrace . . . all with front-row seats for views of the lake. This is to say nothing of the food. The fish is fresh, of course, & there are also rib-sticking soups, veal steaks & even pizza. **$$**

Pivnica Taverna Maršala Tita 163; 035 300 110; **e** pivara@pivaratuzla.ba; www.pivaratuzla.ba/PivnicaTaverna; 07.00–23.30 daily. Located in the basement of the old Tuzla brewery, this Austro Hungarian-era building is the perfect venue for a brew pub. The restaurant began working only a few years ago, but the owners managed to keep its original 1884 look. It's one of Tuzla's favourite drinking holes, especially during the summer. The menu is surprisingly diverse & the locally brewed beer (Tuzlanski pilsner) is among the best of the country's larger breweries. $$

Vinoteka Madeira Zavnobih-a 13; 035 369 607; w hoteltuzla.ba; noon–midnight daily. In the basement of Hotel Tuzla, this is a fairly swanky place with reasonable prices. The speciality of the house is sea fish ... a little strange considering how far inland it is. Nevertheless, first-class seafood is well priced at about 15KM for a main course. The interior is decorated with hundreds of wine bottles hanging from the ceiling & corks filling the walls. Naturally there's a long list of whites & reds to choose from. $$

Restoran Behar Maršala Tita 34; 035 260 392; 07.00–23.00 daily. On a strip of cafés & restaurants less than a 10-min walk from the city centre, Behar serves traditional dishes like *sarma* (minced meat wrapped in cabbage) & *ćevapi*, but also stuffed chicken, veal chops (10KM) & salads. There's a healthy choice of beer like Stella Artois & Tuzlansko on draught, & a sophisticated wine menu, including coastal Croatian reds. $–$$

Sezam Pivnica Korzo Turalibegova 22; 035 257 123; 07.00–midnight daily. It won't take long before you start to notice the word Sezam everywhere. This restaurant chain includes kiosk-type stands, national restaurants & a big multi-room, multi-terrace complex overlooking the clay tennis courts by the Pannonica Lake. The constant across these establishments is solid grub, which mostly leans toward grilled meat & pizzas. There is, of course, plenty in the way of liquid refreshment choices offered as well. $–$$

Aščinica Bujrum Stupine B11; m 062 560 588; 08.00–16.00; 'Bujrum' means 'Please, come in, you are welcome'. The name says it all. This no-frills; Aščinica has excellent local cuisine with an exceptionally welcoming staff. It is located a bit far from the centre, but it can be reached from there with an inexpensive & easy taxi ride. $

Fast food Salso Alije Izetbegovića bb; m 061 720 309; 07.00–23.00. Typical fast food with a standard quick-bite type of menu. Quick & easy if you're on the run or looking for a cheap & cheery meal. $

Sofra Sonitrg bb; 035 961 666; 08.00–18.00 daily. This restaurant serves mainly simple but tasty traditional dishes like *ćevapi*, *maslenica*, or sweets like *tulumba*. There is outside summer seating. For a quick & good value meal, Sofra is a good choice. $

ENTERTAINMENT AND NIGHTLIFE

Cafés/bars/clubs

Caffe Bar Barok Trg Slobode 10; m 061 187 251; 07.00–23.00 daily. On the beautifully renovated Trg Slobode (Freedom Square) at the end of Korzo, this is slick in a modern & tasteful way: there's Wi-Fi (like all of the city centre), track lighting, artwork, leather high stools & solid, wrought-iron tables. Outside customers sit under big, white parasols on a terrace that lets out on to the square & next to the enormous fountain ... perfect during the summer.

Press Klub Patriotske Lige 4; 07.00–23.00 daily; f SetnjomDoZdravlja. To be sure, Press Klub's leafy terrace café has a lovely location – overlooking Tuzla's central park. It also has a secluded vibe. But potentially the best part of the café is the fact that it sits next to the Konjuh Mountaineer Klub's office. After a cup of coffee, rap on the door to learn about hiking in the area.

Žuta Kuća Kazandžijska 8; 035 257 107; 09.00–22.30 daily. A handy – & cheap – place to keep in your back pocket, it has pizzas, hamburgers, sandwiches, salads, ice cream & other desserts all served in, yes, a *žuta kuća*, or yellow house. There are 2 terraces. One spills out on to Korzo, Tuzla's main pedestrian drag. There are 2 floors inside & plenty of space to snuggle with a date.

Caffe Autor Klosterska bb; 035 257 525; 08.00–23.00 daily. Right around the corner from artist Ismet Mujezinović's house & gallery, this long-time cornerstone serves pizzas & pub fare in a dining room framed by artwork & posters of the famous painter. There are also multiple terraces, where regulars sip on one of a bevy of beers, wine, or harder combinations.

Caffe Bar Sydney Turalibegova 50; m 061 501 087; 06.00–midnight daily. The waiting staff & signs spell this place – a foundation stone in the Tuzla café scene – Sidnej. Menus & some signs spell it like the Australian town it's named after: Sydney. Regardless, you'll have no trouble finding the spot. Truly boho, this watering hole sits at the rear of the National Theatre & is a favourite among actors & drama regulars, who sit on the expansive back terrace shaded by trees, which sprout from the brick patio between street lamps & green tables & a for-effect-only wading pool. Coffee drinks are on the menu, of course, but also a variety of beers, liquors & wine.

Caffe Friends Pozorišna; m 061 633 419; 07.00–23:00 daily. Take a walk from Korzo to the National Theatre & you'll see Friends on your left. A tiny café with red leather chairs & a bar full of spirits is doubled in size by an outdoor terrace. There's a sociable vibe here with folks speaking between tables & all within earshot of the river. Beer drinkers can choose between beers like Stella, Laško & local Tuzlansko on draught.

Caffe Sloboda Soni trg 10; m 062 580 819; w caffesloboda.ba; 08.00–23.00 daily. An easy-going crowd comes here to lounge on the terrace & get ready for the night out. Grooves are reggae & world beats during the day & DJs spin at night. It targets a mixed-aged crowd, & serves a wide array of draught beer, wine & cocktails.

St James Irish Pub Muse Ćazima Ćatića 3; m 061 298 141; 16.00–01.00 Sun–Wed, 16.00–02.00 Thu–Sat. This Irish-inspired pub is a popular place to enjoy a variety of beers (inc Guinness) & substantial portions of good bar food. It's cosy, & there is sometimes live music.

☆ **Club Plaža** Prokosovići bb; 035 561 450; 08.00–03.00 Fri–Sat; 08.00–midnight Sun. This is the classic disco & live-music venue on Lake Modrac. You'll notice posters all over the area advertising upcoming mid-level stars, who play on the elevated stage in this big hall, surrounded by windows & looking out to the water. Part of the building is dedicated to serving pizzas. Entrance is usually free. Music tends towards turbo-folk & popular romantica acts.

☆ **Diskoteka Roma** Hadžibakirbega Tuzlića; m 061 716 170; f cafeclubroma; 08.00–01.00 Sun–Thu, 08.00–03.00 Fri–Sat. As the name implies, this place is a little something of everything. Folks relax on the terrace by day, & by night they crowd inside the huge, multi-floored, decadent interior with overstuffed armchairs, dark wooden mouldings, paintings of Rome & TVs. This is a turbo-folk hotspot & expect only the heavy thumps of that Serbian art form here. There are DJs on Sat nights & decent-sized crowds all w/end long.

OTHER PRACTICALITIES

Hospital

University Clinical Centre Trnovac bb; 035 303 190; w ukctuzla.ba

Pharmacy

Gradske Apoteke Albina i Franje Herljevića 3; 035 280 784; 24 hours

Police station

Turalibegova bb; 035 270 555

Bank

$ **Sparkasse Bank** Slatina 5. ATM.

Post Office

Main Post Office Aleja Alije Izetbegovića 29; 035 308 144; 07.00–20.00 Mon–Fri, 07.00–15.00 Sat

Taxi

Tuzla Taxi 035 360 725
Slatina Taxi m 061 657 029

WHAT TO SEE AND DO The downside is that Tuzla once actually had more in the way of museums. The upside is that what still exists is, for the most part, within walking distance from the city centre – making it easy to check out attractions like the International Portrait Gallery or the National Theatre and then walk back to your new favourite café. The lack of town sights also makes Tuzla a more likely regional, day-trip headquarters candidate because the museum-esque options can easily be seen within a day.

Franciscan Monastery and Parish of St Peter and Paul (*Franjevačka 26; 035 266 314; w fst.ba*) This funky and angular monastery survived the war and sits on the edge of the old town near the Jala River and on the other side of town from its Orthodox counterpart. There's a library and an art gallery inside. The point should be made that the Franciscan monastery gets a mention here because of its singularity and as an example of Tuzla's general spirit of tolerance.

International Portrait Gallery (*Druge tuzlanske brigade 13;* ☎ *035 252 002;* **m** *061 185 733;* **e** *galerijaportretatuzla@gmail.com;* **w** *galerijaportreta.ba;* ⏲ *08.00–15.00 Mon–Fri, 09.00–13.00 Sat*) The gallery, which dates back to 1964, makes a fine diversion to a day spent on the streets, mountains and lakes around Tuzla. Inside is a collection of 19th- and 20th-century contemporary portrait artists.

Ismet Mujezinović Gallery (*Klosterska 19;* ☎ *035 252 002;* **w** *galerijaportreta.ba/atelje.htm;* ⏲ *08.00–15.00 Mon–Fri, 09.00–13.00 Sat*) A branch of the International Portrait Gallery, this one is dedicated to famous local painter Ismet Mujezinović and actually resides in his former atelier. Founded in 1982, the building holds eight decades of watercolours, drawings and paintings.

Kapija This 'gate' is actually more of a building, lime green and Austro-Hungarian in its form. It resides squarely in the middle of the pedestrian-only Korzo, which is the old town's main artery, and acts as its living room. Towards the end of the war, when most thought the fighting might finally be over, an artillery round fell here killing more than 70 young people on National Youth Day. Today there is a monument on the Kapija dedicated to their memory.

Lake Modrac and Lake Bistarac To the west of town and near the town of Lukavac, these two artificial lakes – lined with beaches – attract big crowds in the summer. By far the larger is Modrac (a taxi boat costs 20KM for half an hour), which is surrounded by restaurants, cafés, hotels, bed and breakfasts and discos. The smaller Lake Bistarac, also known as Ontario, caters to a loyal following, which comes for the more homely atmosphere, fishing and reasonable rates for bungalows and camping.

National Theatre (*Pozorišna 4;* ☎ *035 251 646;* **e** *nptz@nptz.ba;* **w** *nptz.ba*). Tuzla has a long theatre tradition. The first theatre in Tuzla was built in 1898. Today's incarnation, located between Korzo and the river, is six decades old and provides visitors plenty of opportunity to take in a show. The theatre season is a long one – extending from August or September, and lasting until June or July. During that time between five and ten performances circulate … everything from locally written plays to Shakespeare. Tickets typically run in the 5KM range.

Old town The old town is a living museum piece and it's worth taking time just to walk along its streets. Chief among them is the pedestrian-only promenade Korzo, where visitors and citizens alike revel in Tuzla's university-town vibe and lounge in one of the many cafés that line its stone paving. Unfortunately, another reason to spend time in the old town is because, literally, it is slipping away. Underground erosion due to years of salt excavation has caused sinkholes as deep as 10m. Many famous streets, squares and neighbourhoods of old Tuzla have disappeared. The good news is that in recent years the downtown area has been renovated. The most obvious example of this is the reconstruction of the expansive and beautiful Trg Slobode (Freedom Square).

Gazi Turali Beg Mosque (*Turalibegova*) Turali Beg, the founder of the mosque and many other monuments around the city, is generally considered to be one of the most important figures in the early urban development of Tuzla. Built between 1548 and 1572, the architecture of the mosque is unique: it was originally built of stone with a wooden roof and a single-space planning basis. It is best known for its dome-shaped vault – a rare feature in the architecture of Bosnian mosques. Sinking soil led to serious damage to the structure. It was reconstructed and reopened to the public in 2014. The new building has a more contemporary look, but still retains some of the special features of the original. It is not a glamorous mosque, but is an important piece of the city's history and diversity. It was declared a national monument in 2005.

Orthodox Church (*Đorđa Mihajlovića 3; ☎ 055 222 300; ⏲ 08.00–14.00 daily*) This beautiful, green onion-domed church sits between the old town and the local Pannonica Lake. A testament to the city itself, this building was left undamaged during the last war. Like the Franciscan monastery and Gazi Turali Beg Mosque, the Orthodox church gets mention here because of its singularity and as an example of Tuzla's general spirit of tolerance.

Pannonica Lake (*Šetalište Slana Banja bb; ☎ 035 246 711;* **w** *panonika.ba; ⏲ 08.00–20.00 daily*) This facility is part kitsch and part necessity. The kitsch part is the cascading waterfalls and, somehow, the concept of having artificial lakes in the centre of town generally. Having said that, kitsch is trumped by the necessity part: it gets hot here in the summer and this urban body of water gives families a walking-distance activity and a place to cool down. There are actually two lakes here as well as an archaeological park, a restaurant, grill, café and a curious outdoor gym. The best part: after chilling in the salty – it was created near the saltwater wells – lakes under the old salt excavating derricks, it is just a five-minute walk to the old town. An example of how popular this place is: it was visited by 100,000 people in less than two months when it first opened.

Etno Avlija Mačkovac (*Hrvatska brana bb, Banovići;* **m** *061 146 800;* **e** etnoavlija@hotmail.com; **f** etnoavlijamackovac) is 5km from Banovići towards the base of Mount Konjuh along the River Oskova. Although Banovići may not be on anyone's must-see destinations in Bosnia, both Konjuh Mountain and the Mačkovac ethno house are well worth the visit if one is in the area. It is a holiday resort mostly frequented by locals and diaspora visiting friends and family over the holidays. There are great walking and hiking paths in the area. There is a very strong tradition of nature walks that end with a hearty meal. This is the perfect place to do just that. The founder, Refik Halilović, makes and sells souvenirs such as wooden musical instruments, wall clocks, clay and copper dishes, and baking bells. The funds raised from these sales go to the care and expansion of Mačkovac, which represents an important cultural monument in the area.

BIJELJINA

In the vast flat plains that stretch from Hungary deep into Serbia is the far northeast corner of Bosnia and Herzegovina. Bijeljina is the pivotal city in this subregion, with all roads leading here. Like most places in the Semberija plains along the Sava and Drina rivers, Bijeljina is blessed with rich, fertile soil. The largest industry, by far, is agriculture.

The abrupt change in landscape around Bijeljina was created 30 million years ago when the area was part of the **Pannonian Sea** (Paratetis). The erosion during the following Ice Ages left a marine-lake sediment that has made **Semberija** so fertile.

In terms of human history, this area has long been settled due to its easy access and the steady migration of peoples across the great plains.

The **Museum Semberija** in Bijeljina has an interesting collection of archaeological finds from the area, including many ancient farming tools used to till the land from the earliest of times.

Bijeljina has a different feel from many places in Bosnia. The houses and gardens resemble those in Hungary and Serbia. The parks and pedestrianised areas around town are neatly arranged with fences and well-kept lawns. The oriental character has been largely erased from the area. A significant Muslim minority was driven from the town at the onset of the war. All the mosques in the town, including **Atik Mosque** dating from well before 1566, were destroyed. The Serbian tradition of rebellion is very strong and many of the rebellions against the Turks and Austrians manifested themselves here. The town was largely destroyed in 1876 by the Austrians trying to suppress the Serbian uprisings. The **Tavna Orthodox Monastery**, from the 15th century, is in the middle of town. It's quite tiny, as most Orthodox monasteries are, but the interior is very detailed and beautiful.

The swimming and fishing areas in the vicinity of the **Drina River** are pleasant, and the area enjoys a mild climate: Bijeljina has 1,800 hours of sun per year.

The **Ethno Village** here is perhaps the finest in Bosnia and Herzegovina and is an ideal spot for a fun family outing (page 322). Bijeljina is a convenient access route to Novi Sad and Belgrade in Serbia. The border crossing is fairly large by Bosnian standards, and the highway across the border makes it a quick jaunt to both places.

WHERE TO STAY

Hotel Pirg – Ethno Village Stanišić (30 rooms) Pavlovića put; 055 350 306; e hotelpirg@etno-selo.com; w etno-selo.com. The hotel in Ethno Village Stanišić (page 322) is nothing short of a marvel. The rooms sprawl across a modern castle. Through the windows – looking on to the bridges & lakes of the compound – one is soothed by the sound of bubbling fountains. Sturdy wooden tables, chairs, beds & bureaus reinforce the medieval theme, which is only broken by the flat-screen TVs in the rooms & infinity pool in the spa & jacuzzi area. **$$–$$$**

Hotel Drina (37 rooms) Kneza Miloša 1; 055 416-900; e info@hoteldrina.com; w hoteldrina.com. A renovated Yugo throwback, Hotel Drina is a well-priced hotel with some contemporary rooms, apartments & suites. You will have everything you need: comfortable beds, TVs, a wine bar, a restaurant, clean lodgings, & a spa & wellness centre. A 60-min massage starts at 40KM. **$$**

Hotel Šico (18 rooms) Jovana Dučića 3; 055 210 952; e hotelsico@teol.net. In a square near the Sveti Vasilije Ostroški Monastery, the 3-star Hotel Šico opened in 1997. It has parking, Wi-Fi, & b/fast comes with the price. The rooms are spacious & modern with flat-screen TVs & minimalist wooden furniture, & have views overlooking the nearby belfry. **$$**

Motel Despotović (20 rooms) Cara Uroša 52; 055 245 200. Owned by the same family that has a pizzeria in the centre of town, this property is fairly bare bones, but is clean & offers an alternative to the more expensive lodging options. **$$**

Spa Dvorovi (45 rooms) Karađorđeva bb; 055 350 626; e banjadvorovih@teol.net. Like most spas in the country, Dvorovi has more of a socialist approach to service & accommodation. Although there has been some renovation & a service upgrade, the spa mainly serves local clientele. **$$**

WHERE TO EAT AND DRINK

Konoba Stanišić Pavlovića put 32; 055 351 651; w etno-selo.com; 07.00–midnight daily. Part of a 5-ha 'ethno village' (page 322), made to recall days of yore, it is one of the more frequented places in the area (it's a few km outside the town). It has a very wide choice of local food in an inimitable atmosphere, warmed by the wooden interior & fireplace, or cooler on the outdoor terrace in summer. **$$**

Pet Jezera Ulica Kralija Dragutina bb; 055 424 500; 07.00–23.00 daily. This restaurant's nautical theme, outdoor pools, view on the waterfront & tasty fish dishes on the menu fit the name of the place, which means 'Five Lakes'. It is cosy & colourful, with much more than fish to choose from, including traditional barbecue fare. There is sometimes live music. $$

Restoran Drina Amajlije bb; 055 480 004; 08.00–22.00 daily. This traditional restaurant is part of the Amajlija recreation area near the Drina river. It has a great outdoor terrace & is a local favourite. $–$$

Semberski Salaš Pavlovića put bb, Dvorovi; 055 257 500; f SemberskiSalas; 07.00–23.00 daily. Located a few km northeast of Bijeljina, this popular restaurant can be pleasantly packed when the weather is good, & the playground & pool will appeal to families. It has a spacious dining hall & long wooden benches reminiscent of a German beer garden. The food is local & Central European. $–$$

WHAT TO SEE AND DO

Ethno Village Stanišić (*Etno Selo Stanišić, Pavlovića put bb;* **m** *066 902 712;* **e** *office@etno-selo.com;* **w** *etno-selo.com*) With examples of traditional architectural styles, and a whole host of attractions, it is hard to even know where to begin describing this excellent family-friendly place. In its attempt to have many different facilities, the village has become everything to everyone. It is estimated that around a million visitors a year come here. There's the 5-star Hotel Pirg (page 321), cabin-esque apartments, an open-air ethno museum-cum-village, tennis courts, a kids' playground, two restaurants, three lakes, a cocktail bar and a team full of employees making sure your every whim is catered for. There are also lovely walking trails around the complex and lakes. The wood-constructed objects are an interesting peek into BiH's past. There is also a hayride with horses for the children, and a fascinating Orthodox church replica within the village. It is situated 3km north from Bijeljina towards Pavlovica Bridge.

Museum of Semberija (*Karađorđeva 2; 055 205 603; 08.00–19.00 Mon–Fri, 08.00–13.00 Sat*) Located in the oldest building in Bijeljina (constructed in 1876), the museum was established in 1970 and has been in its present locale since 1978. It has four exhibition rooms. The archaeological collection resides on the bottom floor with pieces that range from the Neolithic period to medieval times and include Roman stones and weapons. Other exhibits include pieces from Bijeljina city culture, ethnographic articles and tools from traditional village life.

Tavna Orthodox Monastery (*Banjica; 055 552 455;* **w** *manastirtavna.rs.sr*) This 15th-century monastery – located south of Bijeljina – was mentioned as far back as the Ottoman tax documents from the early 16th century. The structure was bombed during World War II. Today, this beautiful, white-stoned, green onion-domed building is a big reason for visitors to come to Bijeljina and the area generally. The interior is breathtaking, is loaded with frescoes and awash in finely carved wood and gold.

Sveti Vasilije Ostroški Monastery (*Jovana Dučića 40; 055 222 300*) Right in the centre of town, this monastery-and-church complex is, by area standards, fairly new – built in 2001. Visitors are welcome to enter the intimate and ornate church or just relax in the meticulously manicured garden teeming with roses.

LOWER DRINA

The Lower Drina is nestled in a remote part of the Drina Valley that borders with neighbouring Serbia. The Drina River has, in many places, been converted into a series of lakes due to the construction of several hydro-electric dams in the 1970s. This in no way, however, detracts from the raw beauty of this area.

The Lower Drina mainly consists of three towns: **Srebrenica, Bratunac** and **Zvornik** – all having far-stretching infrastructure into the surrounding countryside with dozens of quaint villages. Although this area isn't particularly strong on tourism, it is as authentic and off-the-beaten-track as it gets. Thanks to several projects, including an Oxfam Italia tourism development programme, there are more and more tourism activities and private accommodation now available in the region. In all of these places it is best to first stop at the tourism information centres. It may otherwise be hard to navigate through these areas.

SREBRENICA It's hard to talk about this place in a guidebook. It's like writing about Krakow and Auschwitz in the same breath; somehow it just doesn't go. Srebrenica was declared a UN safe zone when French general Morillon promised that the United Nations would protect the besieged community from the surrounding Bosnian Serb army. A humanitarian convoy was supposed to bring food and supplies to the encircled enclave of Bosnian Muslims. The Bosnian Serb army would not allow the convoy through, but they did allow the general and an envoy of UN aid workers in to assess the situation in Srebrenica. When General Morillon arrived he was greeted by a cheering crowd; when he tried to leave his convoy was stopped by a human blockade. The civilians would not let the UN convoy out, fearing it was only a matter of time before they would die at the hands of the Serbian military.

Srebrenica was already overloaded with Muslim refugees who had fled or been expelled from the surrounding areas of Bratunac and Vlasenica. Most Muslims felt that if the UN did not take immediate action, the fate of the 50,000 refugees would be left in the hands of their enemies. After a long night General Morillon came to the window with a megaphone and announced that Srebrenica was now under the protection of the United Nations. This created a tremendous amount of heat within the UN, but nonetheless the United Nations Security Council passed a resolution declaring Srebrenica a safe haven.

The Serbs would abide by the resolution only if Bosnian government forces were disarmed, arguing that if the Bosniaks were under the protection of the United Nations they wouldn't need weapons. The UN agreed and disarmed the Bosnian government forces. Several years later, and as observed by the Dutch UN troops stationed there, Serbian forces began mounting at the borders of the enclave. It has been said that the Serbs did not fear reprisal from NATO or the UN, because indicted war criminal and Bosnian Serb general Ratko Mladić had apparently struck a deal with the new French commander, General Janvier, that the Serbs would leave the UN alone if no retaliatory action was taken against the Bosnian Serbs. Bosnian Serb troops rolled into Srebrenica without a fight. The Dutch 'peacekeepers', undermanned and poorly armed, simply watched as boys and men were separated from the women. NATO requested pinpoint airstrikes to stop the offensive, but General Janvier and UN Special Envoy to ex-Yugoslavia Akashi denied that request. They have never given an adequate answer as to why.

Most of the women were shipped to Tuzla on buses and the men and boys, numbering more than 8,000, simply disappeared. The people's worst nightmares came true. Some men fled through the mountains and were hunted down by Serbian troops. Many committed suicide as Serb forces closed the loop around them. Most, however, were systematically executed, some on the spot and many more driven to the town of Zvornik in order to avoid UN peacekeepers or Red

Cross workers. Mass graves are still being found today and the painful memory of the Srebrenica massacre remains fresh in the minds of many.

In 2003, the **Srebrenica-Potočari Memorial Centre & Cemetery** (also known as the **The Srebrenica Genocide Memorial**) (*Potočari bb;* ☎ *056 440 486, 056 440 082;* **e** *info@potocarimc.org;* **w** *potocarimc.org;* ⏲ *08.00–14.00 Mon–Fri*) was opened. Bill Clinton was the guest of honour and spoke at the opening ceremony. The cemetery is a resting place for those whose bodies have been found, and stone panels engraved with the names and birth year of each victim provide a common site of mourning for loved ones and others. The centre also has stirring exhibits that shed light on the stories of the victims and survivors. It is a beautiful and touching place, albeit deeply painful. Many aspects, including disturbing graffiti left by Dutch blue helmets who were present in Srebrenica, are chilling but important historical evidence of what happened there. This is a place one can go to pay respects to the victims, mourn, learn from the past, and reflect. Visitors should prepare for what might be a difficult and emotional journey. Alongside the Memorial Centre & Cemetery, daily life may be returning to normal in Srebrenica, but the women and children who survived will continue to live their lives without their brothers, fathers, husbands and friends.

Srebrenica is a sad place. I can't tell you of the beautiful dense forests that line the hillside or the numbers of bears and wolves that roam the wilderness to the southeast of town.

Despite Srebrenica's horrendous past, progress has been made with projects from Care International, the Dutch government and eight municipalities in the region to develop tourism in the Lower Drina river valley. They have started developing a wide range of regional packages, including bed and breakfasts in the rural areas in and around Srebrenica. Fishing and wildlife observation are also becoming popular activities in the area and more is being done to accommodate foreign guests to enjoy these offers. If you plan a trip to Srebrenica be sure to look into what might be available; the natural surroundings are amazing and it's a good way to give something back to a community that has lost so much.

Tourist Information

Tourist Information Centre Srebrenica Srebreničkog odreda bb; ☎ 056 440 072; **e** tours_srebrenica@yahoo.com; ⏲ 09.00–17.00 Mon–Fri. Located in the centre of town. This is the best & perhaps only recommendable nearby public stop for information on the Srebrenica-Potočari Memorial Centre & Cemetery. They can also advise on where to eat, & accommodation facilities in the wider region. The information desk has internet facilities on site.

Tourist Information Centre Zvornik Svetog Save 56; ☎ 056 210 184; **e** tooz@teol.net; **w** zvornikturizam.org; ⏲ 08.00–15.00 Mon–Fri. Located in downtown Zvornik. It has an information desk, PC, fax machine, scanner, copier & visitor seating. Offers information on tourism attractions in the region, accommodation facilities, local tourism products for purchasing & tasting & rent-a-guide services.

Where to stay

Glisic B&B (3 rooms) Petric, Srebrenica; ☎ 056 482 684; **e** nvodrina@yahoo.com. A few steps from the Drina River in the village of Petric. Glisic B&B boasts both a stunning view of the river & the fields of raspberries & strawberries just behind them. The family house & a separate wooden cottage are available for accommodation. They are a very child-friendly establishment, offering a kids' swimming pool, basketball court & football field. If one fancies an active/working holiday there are opportunities to participate in orchard & greenhouse work, raspberry planting & cooking with the family. **$**

Muminovic B&B (3 rooms) Barakovići, Srebrenica; **m** 065 857 565; **e** muminovic_drina@yahoo.com. In the village of Barakovići near

Srebrenica. It is surrounded by green rolling hills in a totally natural environment. They have 6 beds on offer, with shared kitchen & toilet facilities. There is also a small bungalow close by, just next to the Drina River, ideal for sport fishermen. $

Pansion Misirlije (4 rooms) Petriča bb; 056 445 295; e info@misirlije.ba; w misirlije.ba. This family-run establishment is located 800m from the town centre, 5km from the Potočari Memorial Centre, on the regional Srebrenica–Bajina Bašta road. Aside from good accommodation, Misirlije is even better known for its restaurant that serves both traditional & international cuisine. There is free parking & Wi-Fi. $

Where to eat and drink The best place to eat in Srebrenica itself is Misirlije; the other establishments listed below are not in Srebrenica but in the surrounding area.

Točak Restaurant Bratunac; m 065 437 497; 07.00–22.00 daily. Well known for a variety of meat dishes & its ethnic-style interior décor. Located just 3km from Bratunac (heading towards Skelani), it's an easy find along the main road. The food is traditionally prepared using old family recipes & organic products from the region. The homemade soups are truly excellent & the grilled meats & fish are good quality & good value. The average price per meal, including drinks, is around 19KM. $$

Lađarica Restaurant Mihaljevići bb, Bratunac; m 066 924 625, 065 899 400; 08.00–23.00 daily. In the village of Mihaljevići, 4km from downtown Bratunac, along the Drina River. Accommodates up to 60 indoors with a large summer terrace that doubles its capacity. Fish & meat specialities are top notch & the restaurant owners make their own marmalades & jams as well as fruit wines. The area around the restaurant is superb terrain for fly fishing, kayaking & walking. Paradise Beach is 2km from here. $–$$

Misirlije Petriča bb; 056 445 295; e info@misirlije.ba; w misirlije.ba; 07.00–23.00 daily. Part of the Pansion listed above, Misirlije is even better known for its restaurant that serves both traditional & international cuisine in generous portions. It is probably the most known restaurant in Srebrenica, and is located 5km from the Srebrenica-Potočari Memorial Centre & Cemetery. $–$$

Restoran Avala Zvornik; 056 210 001/231 131; e avalarestoran@spinter.net; 08.00–23.00 daily. Located in the heart of Zvornik, overlooking the Drina, Avala certainly ranks amongst the most favourite local spots. It's a cosy space with a welcoming atmosphere & professional service. The attractively flowered terraces are a perfect place to enjoy the views & tasty traditional food. $–$$

Etno restoran Šoja Vuka Karadžića 98, Zvornik; 056 211 021; e restoran.soja@yahoo.com; w restoransoja.com; 08.00–22.00 daily. Šoja has excellent food & a mishmash traditional atmosphere. It has a bit of everything, mixing traditionally woven carpets with more socialist era-style table settings. The garden seating is by far the most pleasant, but don't miss out on strolling through the interior to peek at some of the décor. The grilled meat dishes are superb & the portions large. $

EAST POSAVINA

Posavina is one of the few flatlands found in BiH, and it makes up a large part of BiH's northern border with Croatia. This area saw a considerable amount of fighting during the war and is still recovering from the devastation. This region has always been known for its rich agricultural lands but has recently begun to realise its tourism potential with an EU-funded tourism development project. Fishing and watersports on the Sava River are most certainly the highlights of tourism in East Posavina, but don't expect much in terms of tourism infrastructure or easy-to-find information.

BRČKO I've listed Brčko, not as a tourism destination but for practical purposes. Brčko has a special status within the Republic of Bosnia and Herzegovina: at the Dayton Peace Accords it was designated as a district. Brčko is the largest port town in BiH, about 30km north of Tuzla as the crow flies. Its strategic significance is its location on the **Sava River**, which is a tributary of the **Danube** and belongs to the **Black Sea basin**. For industrial towns like Tuzla and Zenica, Brčko is key for moving goods in and out of the country via rail and boat. For the Republika Srpska, it is the only land link between its eastern and western territories and Serbia. The district has always been the centre of the **Posavina region**. Its population of 90,000 works mainly in agriculture and the port transport industry. You can cross into Croatia from here as well but it is more practical to cross further west if you are heading towards Zagreb or Budapest. If you intend to go to Serbia, then Brčko is a good place to cross and catch the main Zagreb–Croatia motorway.

Orašje and **Odžak**, two small enclaves in the Posavina area that remained in Federation hands following Dayton, are key border points. If you've been travelling from western Europe and want to break for the night before heading south, there are several good hotels in Orašje, Odžak and Brčko. Besides its border towns, this rich agricultural area is interesting for many reasons. Life here largely revolves around the fertile fields along the Sava River and the river itself. Vast fields of corn, wheat and other staple products are a large source of food for both BiH and Croatia. The **Sava River**, though, is an interesting waterway. Aside from it being a major navigation alley to the Danube, there are dozens of hidden spots for **canoeing** and **high-quality fishing**. There are many fishing associations in the region that can organise competitions and outings. Posavina is also well known for its reed weaving. The strong reeds that grow along the Sava and its tributaries have been used for centuries as hard material for weaving beautiful baskets, chairs and even coffee tables. Be sure to visit a handicraft shop if you're in the area; they offer affordable, high-quality, practical gifts.

Where to stay

Grand Hotel Posavina (32 rooms) Trg Mladih 4; 049 220 111; e grand.bc@teol.net; w grand-hotel-posavina.com. Built in 1891, this was the first hotel in Brčko. It was destroyed during the war but was reconstructed in 2001. Today, the striped, 32-room building has again regained its prominence in the centre of town. **$$**

Hotel Jelena (20 rooms) Bulevar mira 3; 049 232 850; e recepcija@hotel-jelena.com; w hotel-jelena.com. Hotel Jelena has spacious rooms & is a solid choice when staying in the Posavina region. The rooms have internet. Sited in the centre of town & just a couple of mins from the Croatian border, Jelena has a restaurant & conference halls with space for hundreds. **$$**

Vila Cicibela (18 rooms) Vuka Karadžića 37; 049 231 810; e vila_cicibela@hotmail.com; w cicibela.com. Filled with exposed brick details all over, Cicibela is a beautiful hotel in the middle of town. Besides rooms & apts, the old-fashioned yellow building has a restaurant & a wine vault. **$$**

Grand Euro (40 rooms) Titova bb, Odžak; 031 762 900; e euro.odzak@tel.net.ba; w hotel-euro.info. In the centre of Odžak. It has Wi-Fi, TV, AC, a small gym, restaurant & café. **$–$$**

Hotel Evropa (150 beds) M.14.1; 049 301 244; e hotelevropa@elispanic.net. Approx 3km from the centre of Brčko. **$**

Hotel Leo (12 rooms) Ugljara zaobilaznica bb, Orašje; 031 713 605. In the centre of Orašje. **$**

Pansion MD (8 rooms) Brka 123; 049 500 161. 6km from the centre of Brčko. **$**

Where to eat and drink

Osteria Restaurant & Wine Bar Bulevar Mira 4; 049 232 321; 08.00–23.00 daily. Located in the centre of Brčko, Osteria crosses fine dining with traditional dishes. True to the name, the restaurant – with mosaics on the walls, wood-plank floors, arched-brick ceilings – takes pride in a wine list with around 50 wines from France, Spain, Croatia, Serbia, Italy, Argentina, Chile & Australia. On Sat one can expect folkloric musicians roaming & playing between the tables. Started in

2005, the eatery serves steak, trout, pork chops & a slew of salads. $$

✕ **Azzurro** Trg Mira bb; 049 217 866; 07.00–23.00 Mon–Fri, 07.00–midnight Sat–Sun. Something for everyone here. Azzurro is a pizzeria, sweet shop & fast-food restaurant. The interior is expansive & has a soda-parlour feel. Outside, the terrace looks on to the main street. During the summer this is a perfect place to have a tea & a piece of *baklava*. $–$$

✕ **Balkan Pub** Branislava Nušića; 07.00–midnight daily. If you're looking for a beer, wine, refreshing cocktail, or *rakija* in a lively atmosphere, this is one of a few happening bars in town. $

SREBRENIK

Srebrenik is only 36km from Tuzla in the small river valley of Tinja. Most famous for its old fort above the endless plains of Posavina, this medieval town makes for an interesting visit. The villages in the surrounding areas have a storybook appearance, with quaint, well-maintained homes and beautiful gardens with orchards of apple, plum and pear. The clear streams that run from the hills to the encroaching plains paint the fields bright green in the springtime. The old fort is interesting but is also a quick visit. Unless there is a local with a *gusle* playing traditional songs and *sevdalinka*, which is not unrealistic, the fort and walking around take up only an hour of your time. In August and September, there is an art festival called **Open Town of Art**, where artists from all over the country set up art colonies around the area to exchange ideas, meet and paint the lovely landscapes of the towns and villages around the Tinja.

GRADAČAC

This is certainly one of the places to see when you visit the northeast of Bosnia. On the **River Gradišnica**, between the mountains of **Majevica** and **Trebava**, lies this beautiful town, some 25km north of Srebrenik. It is first mentioned as Gračac, and later as Gradačac after the arrival of the Turks.

This town holds great historical significance for Bosnians. Husein-kapetan Gradaščević was a ruling *beg* during Ottoman times. He was a warrior and a leader and was highly respected and feared throughout the region. Gradaščević posed a real threat to Ottoman authority and this gave him great bargaining power for more autonomy, self-rule and land rights. There are several versions of history, but the common one is that he and his army were able to defend the territories of the northeastern frontier when the Turks could not. He was greatly feared by the Turks, and when the rebellious 'Dragon of Bosnia' (as he was called) decided to tackle the Turks, he marched his army all the way to Kosovo to confront them in 1831. The Dragon's army defeated the Turks and further destabilised the empire's hold on Bosnia. This rebellious spirit proved contagious among the local *pashas* and ruling families, and sparked many more rebellions. Gradaščević was later betrayed and forced to flee across the Sava to Austria. The numerous buildings bearing his name attest to his role in the history of the town. The **Gradaščević family house** was built in 1786 and today is a private museum. The town is recognisable by the **tower of Husein-kapetan Gradaščević** that was built in 1821. The large complex was damaged in the last war but has been renovated in its original form. The old part of town has a cultural centre, museum, gallery and library, all named after him. Underneath the city gate there is a mosque of Husein, which was built in 1826, and is characterised by its high and narrow minarets. In this same period a four-level **Sahat clock tower,** 22m high, was built. The town in general has very much preserved its oriental character.

WHERE TO STAY

Hotel Gradina (4 rooms) Gradačac Tower (Gradačačka Kula); 035 816 625. Like the structure itself, the dbl rooms in the tower have a hearty, wooden, medieval feel. Having said that, you won't feel like you've drifted back hundreds of years in comfort by staying here. They are comfy, clean & big with expansive views of the valley & town. This is a wonderful spot to get into a historic mood. It is also a short walk into the centre for cafés & more modern fun. **$$**

Motel Konak (12 rooms) HK Gradaščevića 92; **m** 035 817 367; **e** info@motel-konak.com; **w** motel-konak.com. This 3-star motel sits in the middle of the social district. Many of the town's cafés & shops surround it. Consequently, this is also where the 20-somethings cruise the streets at the w/ends. Upstairs are bright, spacious & sparse rooms. Downstairs, the ice cream parlour stays bopping all day & evening with families & schoolkids. **$$**

WHERE TO EAT AND DRINK

Restoran Gradina Gradačac Tower (Gradačačka Kula); 035 816 625; 07.00–23.00 daily. Tower-top views & good food make this the best place to eat in town. The main restaurant is located in the top of the famous city tower & affords diners with a full panorama of the town & wider area. Dishes include mixed grill, veal, delicious soups & a fresh homemade *baklava*. **$$**

San Remo Pizzeria Trg heroja 29; **m** 061 677 820; 08.00–23.00 Mon–Sat, 15.00–23.00 Sun. Not a lot of mystery here with what's on the menu. But, the pizza is tasty & there are a few other choices for those pizza-ed out: lasagna, salads & beefsteak. San Remo is a family restaurant & popular. The 2 floors inside – filled with soda-shop booths – stay busy. From the front terrace, diners can watch sporting events that are periodically projected on a big wall across the yard. **$$**

Kapija Bosna Hadžiefendijina bb; 06.30–15.00 Mon–Sat, 07.00–13.00 Sun. A lunchtime restaurant only – Kapija Bosna serves traditional, grilled dishes, so *ćevapi* is, of course, a given. What's more, the food is good. But, the real beauty of this place is 2-fold. First, it is at the bottom of the hill & easy to find after investigating the tower. Second, it has a terrace that straddles a canal. The picturesque patio is flanked by pretty flower boxes bursting with purple & pink pansies. **$**

Caffe Bar Cinema HK Gradaščevića bb; **m** 061 724 132; 18.30–midnight daily. After walking down the hill from the tower above town, Cinema is a civilised way to relax. Overlooking Gradačac's main & central park – with monuments to the heroes of World War II & the war of the 1990s – this relaxed watering hole serves cold draught beer, coffee & assorted spirits. **$**

GRAČANICA

Gračanica is located about 50km west of Tuzla in the lower valley of the River Spreča along the main highway to Doboj. It is said that this town was formed in the Middle Ages, in the period when the town of Soko above the Sokoluša brook was built. From 1580 Gračanica began to develop into a regional and cultural urban centre for the dozens of rural settlements in the surrounding countryside. Agriculture is the main industry in the region, and several factories produce natural juices, jams and preserved vegetables that have attracted even foreign markets.

The old town is a typical *čaršija*. The attractive old homes and craft shops line the old quarter, which is highlighted by the Ahmed-pasha or Čaršija Mosque, built in 1595. The massive 27m *Sahat* clock tower was built at the end of the 16th century. It was renovated after a fire in 1812, and again in 1952. In 1889, the *madrasa* was built, and it is interesting to note that at this time the Austrians had established themselves as the new occupiers and the Muslim Turks were long gone.

DOBOJ

Doboj is at a pivotal point on the rivers Usora and Bosna, about 25km west of Gračanica. There was intense fighting in the area during the war, and Doboj now falls under the jurisdiction of Republika Srpska. To the immediate south and east, however, is the Federation. In order to pass from Maglaj in the south to Tuzla in the east, one has to travel through Doboj, and for a quick minute or two, change entities.

Although life here has been traced back to the Stone Age, the first recorded settlement dates to the 1st century AD when the Romans conquered these territories and built the Kastrum and the small settlement of Kanube. The **Kastrum** is now the main fortress in the centre of the town and was added to by the Bosnian aristocracy and the Turks when they arrived in Doboj in the 16th century. The Turks lost the main fortress in both the 17th and 18th centuries. Eugene of Savoy marched the Austrian army right down this valley all the way to Sarajevo.

Much of the fort is intact and looks down on the town centre from its hilltop position. This is most certainly the highlight of Doboj. The town has a large displaced population of Serbs. The minority populations have returned but in very small numbers, and Doboj doesn't seem to have recuperated from its war days. It is a town you have to go through to get to most places in the northeast, yet very few people stop here.

WHERE TO STAY

Hotel Integra (16 rooms, 2 apts) Vidovdanska bb; 053 224 264; e info@hotelintegra.com; w hotelintegra.com. Opened in 2005, the 3-star Integra is, to a great degree, the only show in town. It is equipped with a conference room that doubles as a banquet hall for wedding receptions. Each room/apt has Wi-Fi, a minibar, cable TV & a svelte wooden bureau. Apts have bathtubs. Importantly, all rooms are non-smoking. In the marble-laden lobby, laptops are available for patrons. **$$**

Kotromanicevo Royal Village (6 bungalows) Vojvode Misica 32; 053 282 835; e kotromanicevo.resort@yahoo.com; w kotromanicevo.com. Equipped with modest but exceptionally comfortable traditional Bosnian bungalows, this is an impressive replica made in honour of the ancient royal family. Accommodation is both affordable & convenient, set back from the main road in a quiet natural setting along a stream. **$–$$**

WHERE TO EAT AND DRINK

Etno Restoran Čarda Bare bb; m 065 537 616; 07.00–23.00 daily. Čarda is a great place to enjoy fresh fish & relax on the banks of the Bosna River. It is most pleasant in the summer, with a lovely terrace. The restaurant serves great trout & steaks. The interior is more formal but equally cosy. **$$**

Hotel Integra Restaurant Vidovdanska bb; 053 224 274; 06.00–23.00 daily. Located within the Hotel Integra, this à la carte restaurant serves pork chops, beef tartar, fish (sea & river), veal & the omnipresent meat plate, among other offerings, to go with a long list of wines. The interior is plush with marble & dark wood, & has a country-club feel. Diners, who should make reservations at the w/ends, can also take meals on the terrace. **$$**

Kotromanicevo Royal Village Vojvode Misica 32; 053 282 835; e kotromanicevo.resort@yahoo.com; w kotromanicevo.com; 08.00–22.00 daily. The best restaurant 'in town'. Located around 20km from Doboj on the main road towards Derventa, this ethno-style restaurant serves a tasty menu of traditional Bosnian food with large portions in a cosy & pleasant rustic environment. It's the perfect place for a stopover if travelling in northern Bosnia. **$$**

Pizzeria Grazia Vidovdanska 22; 053 228 297; 07.00–23.00 daily. It is hard to fully describe the sturdiness of this restaurant's interior. Imagine a battleship, cross it with a safe, & then add a medieval fortress. Everything is made of solid, handcrafted wood & wrapped in wrought iron. The dining room is flanked by wooden casks filled with the house wine they serve. They also have a bevy of beers, &, of course, the menu is full of pizza ... real Italian pizza. Don't even think of asking for ketchup here. You'll be asked to leave. The house pizza comes topped with veal or pork. If the interior is too secure for you, the terrace, which is adorned with streetlamps, is a little more open. **$$**

City Café Restaurant Cara Dušana 37; 053 221 371; 07.00–23.00 Mon–Sat, 10.00–23.00 Sun. This restaurant in the centre has a sophisticated pub atmosphere. Plush red carpets cover 2 floors with little dining nooks around every corner. There are old pictures & a hotchpotch collection of art prints. On the terrace, wicker chairs face the tree-lined avenue. The menu includes veal soup, chicken pasta & the City Steak: pork-filled & served with bacon. Also on offer: trout & salads. **$–$$**

TESLIĆ

Teslić is a tiny town in the **Usora River valley** about 20km southwest of Doboj. Since Roman times the thermal springs here have brought settlers and travellers to the area. This is another classic example of high-quality thermal mineral waters in an ex-Yugoslav setting. The land around the **Banja Vrućica** or 'Hot Spas' (*053 431 270;* **e** *banjavrucica@com;* **w** *banja-vrucica.com*) is full of lovely soft rolling hills that are excellent for walking. The accommodation varies. **Hotel Kardial** (*196 rooms; 053 421 200;* **$$–$$$**) has been renovated into a large, four-star, very modern, chic hotel with a wellness centre, pool, bowling alley, gym, excellent bar and many other services. **Hotel Hercegovina** (*69 rooms; 053 431 415;* **$–$$**) was also renovated recently. While not as fancy as Kardial, it has a clean and contemporary design, is comfortable and offers all the necessities that a modern hotel would, along with physical rehabilitation facilities. **Hotel Posavina** (*136 rooms; 053 430 345;* **$–$$**) is mediocre with largely socialist décor but it is not uncomfortable, and it does offer Wi-Fi. The rooms are clean and simple with few or no extras. Just out the back there is also access to the natural springs that are used in the rehabilitation centre for rheumatism, heart disease and circulation problems. The water quality at the spa and hotels is unquestionable. It remains to this day a popular spot for locals. While they are beginning to attract foreign tourists, they are still far from crowded, which is perhaps why the prices remain so affordable.

Through the mountains towards Banja Luka is a stunning Orthodox monastery from the 14th century. **Liplje Monastery**'s (*Liplje bb; 053 441 022*) architecture makes it, in my opinion, one of the most beautiful sacred places in Bosnia and Herzegovina. It is open to visitors but with no specific time schedules. In Teslić town, the local **Orthodox Art Gallery and Museum** (*Svetog Save 60; 053 736 363*) is certainly a worthwhile visit. You may find reasonably priced gifts and handmade souvenirs that are distinctly Byzantine in style.

TEŠANJ

Many Bosnians didn't even know much about this town until two rather significant events occurred. First, Tešanj's Oaza mineral water won a gold medal at the Berkeley Springs Mineral Water Contest in the United States. Rumour has it that even President Bill Clinton drank Oaza in the White House. This event was a great source of local pride and national envy. Secondly, Pjer Žalica's film, *Gori Vatra* ('Fuse') was set in Tešanj. The film won the Sarajevo Film Festival Grand Prize in 2003, and was nominated for the Oscars. This finally put Tešanj in the limelight.

Just to the northeast of Teslić the old town is dominated by the well-preserved fortress that overlooks the whole city. The fortress is a result of the many different layers of civilisation that have made Bosnia and Herzegovina their home. The uncle of King Stjepan Tomašević, Radoje Krstić, was 'given' the town of Tešanj by his nephew in 1461. Tešanj became the seat of the kingdom where the noble Krstić family lived and reigned until 1476. It was not long, however, before the Ottomans dethroned everyone, and Tešanj was no exception. The main Ottoman figure in the early days of Tešanj's new rule was Gazi Ferhad *beg*. His most significant contribution was the building of the **Ferhadija Mosque**, which still stands in the old town and dates back to the early 16th century. The old **Eminagić House** is the oldest house in Tešanj, and is said to have been built at the end of the 17th century.

The fort is open to visitors but it doesn't have information boards to tell you more about the place. The entire town is walkable and is a lovely, quiet place for a day visit. You don't have to buy a bottle of mineral water in Tešanj; you can go directly to the public source called **Tešanjski Kiseljak** and drink your fill. Around the spring is a local picnic area and swimming pool. The **Usora River** is a much better angling spot than the **Bosna River**. The Bosna tends to be rather polluted and wading in the river or eating fish out of it is probably not wise.

WHERE TO STAY

Hotel AA [16 rooms] Husein Kapetana Gradaščevića bb, Jelah; 032 663 609; w hotelaa.ba. Situated in Jelah, about 4km northwest of Tešanj. **$$**

WHERE TO EAT AND DRINK The traditional restaurants in Tešanj are very good and rather inexpensive, and there are several excellent *aščinice*. An *aščinica* is a cafeteria-like eatery with a wide range of local dishes (including some for vegetarians). You'll find grilled mushrooms, mashed potatoes, fried okra and almost every national dish noted in *Eating and drinking*, pages 79–84. Two of the noteworthy ones are: **Aščinica Hotić** (*Krndija bb; 032 942 777; 07.00–21.00 Mon–Sat;* **$**) and **Aščinica Saračević** (*Maršala Tita bb; 032 650 328; 07.00–21.00 Mon–Sat;* **$**). By the old mosque is **Kahva** (*Trg Gazi Ferhad bega, 032 650 455; 07.00–18.00 daily;* **$**), a restaurant run by the Islamic community of Tešanj. It has quite a different atmosphere from a regular Bosnian restaurant and the food is excellent. Most towns with a Muslim majority don't serve pork as Islamic law forbids it, so definitely don't ask for pork at Kahva.

MAGLAJ

I have visited this town many times over the years, and have always been impressed by the **Old Fortress** in the old town. Many towns in this region have hilltop fortresses built by the Romans, Hungarians or Turks, but there has always been something special about Maglaj. Maglaj means 'fog', and the wide valley along this part of the **Bosna River** has mystic fog frequently rolling in, especially in the early morning hours.

Kuršumlija Mosque in the old town near the fortress is a beautiful example of Ottoman architecture. It was built in 1560 by Kalavun Jusuf Pasha. I don't know why one always finds pictures of a socialist building or an empty pool in tourist brochures about Maglaj; there really is so much more. The town is rich in apple and pear orchards, particularly along the river. If you get a chance, climb up to the tower, where the view of the valley is magnificent. It's an easy walking town and a nice day trip from Tuzla or Zenica.

 **WHERE TO STAY AND EAT** The **Motel Chicago** (m *061 376 924;* **$$**) has a great traditional restaurant with stews, grilled lamb and dish-baked *ispod sača*. It's right on the M-17 highway from Zenica to Doboj that runs through Maglaj, but the rooms are nice and the service is friendly. **Hotel Galeb** (**$$**) is in town on Sulejman Omerovića bb and not as busy as Chicago. On Aleja ljiljana Street in downtown Maglaj are most of the best cafés, restaurants and sweet shops. Check out **Izletište Borik** (**$$**) there. **Sweet shop Carigrad** (**$**) on Aleja Ljiljana 10 has great cakes, and **Caffe Bar Check Point** (**$**) is a local favourite.

ZAVIDOVIĆI

The town of Zavidovići doesn't offer much for the visitor. It is located 15km east of the main road from Zenica to Doboj. The turn-off is through the town of Žepče. The town is home to Krivaja Wood Industries, which sells a considerable amount of wood and furniture to American and European markets. They take full advantage of the 41,000ha of forest that covers the municipality. On the outskirts of town to the east is the beautiful valley of the Krivaja River. This long valley stretches all the way to Olovo. The Krivaja and Gostović valleys are wonderful fishing spots and have several long runs of rapids for kayaking. There is a mountain lodge on the highest point in the area on Tajan, about 32km from town. Scorpio Extreme Sports Club from Zenica organises kayaking in this wild region (pages 246–7).

 **WHERE TO STAY AND EAT** With over 100 weekend houses, **Kamenica** is only about 17km from Zavidovići and connected with Tajan Nature Park (see opposite). It is located on the banks of Gostović River at around 400m above sea level. Despite its low elevation a real mountain climate dominates the region. The current accommodation capacity is around 31 beds located in two different hunting lodges: Trbušnica (*11 beds*) and Old Kamenica (*20 beds*). Some cosy bungalows for rent have recently been added, and plans are in development to increase the capacity of this resort further. Dining, telephone and information services can be received in the restaurant, a former mountain hut, which is located just above the waterfall on the River Gostović.

Just 1km from Kamenica, also on the banks of the River Gostović, the Tourism Association of Zavidovići built a sport-recreation centre called 'Luke'. This place is ideal for camping and you can pitch a tent here. There are a lot of facilities for basketball, beach volleyball and football. Next to those there is a playground with equipment for young children. There is also a mountain-biking trail that is being used for competition every year in May.

Ponijeri is a weekend place with a much larger accommodation capacity than Kamenica. At over 1,100m above sea level it makes for an ideal mountain getaway. Accommodation is not luxurious but comfortable and relatively cheap. A bed typically goes for about 20KM. **Ski Center Ponijeri** (*R456, Vukanovići*) offers very accessible slopes, which are enhancing the tourism appeal of this beautiful place. The slopes are about 1,000m long, and ski lifts work in the winter from 10.00–16.00. Lift passes are extremely affordable: 10KM for half-day, 15KM for a full day. Instructors are available upon request, for a fee, of course (w *kscekakanj.ba/ski-centar-ponijeri*). On Ponijeri there are around 400 weekend houses, one restaurant and two buildings with 85 beds in total. There is also the option to rent a house. The main guesthouse (m *061 769 649;* f *Pansion-Ponijeri-174961829196719;* **$**), which is rustic but clean, offers beds in dormitory-syle rooms plus breakfast for 20KM a night per person.

Hotel Kristal Maršala Tita bb; 032 879 774; e kristal@krivajamobel.com. An old building, with basic, socialist-style rooms. Wi-Fi & a parking garage, which is free for hotel guests. **$–$$**

Hotel Marić Donje Ravne bb; 032 881 440; w mariczepce.com. This motel is in Žepče, on the M-17 Zenica–Doboj road, about 12km from Zavidovići. Very basic but comfortable. The higher-priced rooms are more spacious; some offer bigger beds & bathtubs with a water massage function. **$**

Restoran Kamenica Kamenica, Zavidovići bb; 032 851 215; RestoranKamenica; 08.00–22.00 daily. A mountain-lodge style restaurant in a beautiful rural setting, with hearty, filling food. They also offer accommodation in modest but modern & cosy apartments with Wi-Fi, from 30–50KM per night per room. **$**

WHAT TO SEE AND DO

Tajan Nature Park (*032 851 090;* e *info@tajan.ba;* w *www.tajan.ba*) This park was acknowledged as a protected area in 2010. A wonderful grassroots movement from environmental groups, mountain associations, caving clubs and nature lovers from the Zavidovići area has put a tremendous amount of energy into making this beautiful little corner of northern Bosnia a protected one. The mountains in this area aren't like the towering peaks of the central Dinaric Alps. Nonetheless, the thick conifer forests and endless tracks of hills and forest provide nature lovers with a wide range of activities. As of 2017, much progress has been made but some things are still developing, so there might still be a few hitches organisation-wise. However, it should be mentioned that the knowledge and passion that have gone into the ecotourism development of this area are extraordinary and should be an example for the rest of the country.

Canyons One of the most beautiful canyons in the northern part of BiH is **Mašica Canyon**. It was shaped by water cutting through Triassic limestone with the help of tectonic forces. The water divided the limestone massif into two faces, Mašica and Middle Rock. The lowest depth is about 350m. During heavy rainfalls when the canyon is unable to hold all the water, the beautiful brook of Suvodol is formed. The floor of the canyon in some parts is only 3m wide. Those parts were once even tighter, but because of forest exploitation some parts have been widened. The **Mašićka rock face** reaches to 250m on the right bank of the Mašica Canyon. It is an ideal place for free climbing and offers some fun and challenging routes for climbers. At the base of the rock face are many small caves, fun for leisurely exploration – but only in the summer. These caves are often inhabited by bears during the winter.

Duboke Tajašnice Canyon, through which flows a crystal-clear brook, has not been explored by many. It falls very steep from the peaks of Tajana, creating a lot of waterfalls. There are some plans for collecting the water of the brook and adding it to the **Suha Canyon**. The characteristic of this canyon is that during summertime there is almost no water due to the underground aquifer systems in the area, hence the name Suha, meaning dry. Suha Canyon serves as a travel communication network between Kamenica and Ponijere. At the end of the canyon is the Suha source. Along the entire length of the canyon there are many cave formations as well as archaeological and palaeontological finds.

Caves The region beside the peaks of Tajan Mountain and the upper flow of the Suha is scattered with caves and pits. It's estimated that there are over a hundred caves in the Tajan area. Cavers have been exploring this area since the 1980s and there is an active caving club in Zavidovići.

The **Atom Pit** is found on the northeast face of Tajan Mountain between magma and limestone rocks, which give it not only its remarkable size but also its unique characteristics. This pit is actually a sinkhole that collects water and feeds the source of the Suha River. Full exploration has yet to be completed due to its size and difficult access, but the depth was measured to be 170m and length about 1km, which makes it the longest and deepest cave formation in the Zenica-Doboj Canton.

Lukina Cave is located at the base of a vertical rock face at Middle Rock. The entire 200m length is lined with deposits of crystalline calcium carbonate of varying colours ranging from white to dark red. Remains of the extinct cave bear (*Ursus spelaeus*), which are over 15,000 years old, have been found in Lukina. The cave is accessible for even amateur cavers.

The **Youth Pit** entrance is on a plateau of Rapte Mountain. It is 114m deep with its lowest room 70m long and 30m high.

The **Middle Rock Cave**, found in May 2004, is situated close to Lukina Cave. It has lots of large caverns and domed rooms with beautiful cave decorations.

The **Atom Caving Club** is a group of local activists and adventurists who have helped establish the park. For more contact information it may be better to get in touch with Green Visions in Sarajevo (page 89) who will provide information or organise a trip for you.

Flora and fauna The Tajan area is a dynamic ecosystem and is home to several endemic plants. The most significant of these is *Gregersen mljecika* (*Euphorbia gregersenii*, family Euphorbiaceas). This type of plant is protected and is now on the international red list of endangered plants. Ivy about 30cm in diameter (*Hedera helix*) grows at the very entrance to Lukina Cave. In Tajan there is also an endemic Bosnian lily (*Lilium bosnaiacum*) which has for centuries been the symbol of the Bosnian state. The fauna within the region is rich in wild animals due to the thick forests that cover the entire park. In this region animals such as bears, wolves, foxes, deer, rabbits, wild cats, wild boars and grouse can be found. There are also many cave species of insects and spiders that live in the underground region of the park. The caves mentioned above all house bats, which are seriously endangered in Europe, as well as black bears. The brooks and streams are rich in fish, mainly trout and shellfish. Research has uncovered palaeontological findings dating back over 15,000 years, including remains of the cave hyena, red deer (*Cervus elaphus*), as well as the cave bear.

Activities The upper flow of the Gostović River has perfect conditions for **fly fishing** several types of trout. Alpine conditions in the park offer a lot of possibilities for **climbing** fans. The routes are easy and fun for climbers of all ages. There is no organisation in the area that can provide the full gear so if you're up for a climb, you'll have to carry your own equipment. The rock faces of Duboke Tajašnice, Suhe, Rujnice, Ljevičkog stone, Mašice and Middle Rock are all doable, but the small climbing community there has only developed two routes: Ljevički Stone (45m) and the Rock Face in Rujnice (15m). Pioneers can set the stage on the other more difficult routes. **Mountain biking** in Tajan Nature Park (page 333) is excellent. Owing largely to forestry roads, a large system of bike trails has been developed. Every year in May the hiking association organises a mountain-biking competition. The Park offers guides for hire. There is a great selection of lodging in private or shared cabins, and equipment rental is available for a number of activities, including mountaineering, biking, and caving.

Appendix 1

LANGUAGE

PRONUNCIATION

Latin		Cyrillic
A, a	A,a	as in father
B, b	B, b	as in bats
C, c	Ц, ц	as in Betsy
Č, č	Ч, ч	as in culture
Ć, ć	Ћ, ћ	as in cheese
D, d	Д, д	as in doctor
Dž, dž	Џ, џ	as in jam
Đ, đ	Ђ, ђ	as in judge
E, e	E, e	as in pet
F, f	Ф, ф	as in free
G, g	Г, г	as in goat
H, h	X, x	as in hat
I, i	И, и	as in feet
J, j	J, j	as in yet
K, k	К, к	as in kept
L, l	Л, л	as in leg
Lj, lj	Љ, љ	as in million
M, m	М, м	as in mother
N, n	Н, н	as in no
Nj, nj	Њ, њ	as in onion
O, o	O, o	as in hot
P, p	П, п	as in pie
R, r	P, p	as in rabbit (but rolled)
S, s	C, c	as in sand
Š, š	Ш, ш	as in shovel
T, t	Т, т	as in too
U, u	У, у	as in look
V, v	В, в	as in very
Z, z	З, з	as in zoo
Ž, ž	Ж, ж	as in treasure

GREETINGS

Good morning	*Dobro jutro*	Hello/Goodbye	*Ćao*
Good afternoon	*Dobar dan*	What is your name?	*Kako se zoveš?*
Good evening	*Dobra večer*	How are you?	*Kako si?*
Good night	*Laku noć*	I am well	*Dobro sam*

BASIC PHRASES

please	*molim vas*
thank you	*hvala*
you're welcome	*nema na čemu* (reply to thank you)
there is no	*nema*
excuse me	*oprostite/izvinite*
give me	*dajte mi*
I like to	*želim*
I would like	*želio bih*
how?	*kako?*
how much/many?	*koliko?*
how much (cost)?	*koliko košta?*
too much	*previše*
what?	*šta?*
what's this (called)?	*kako se kaže?*
who?	*ko?*
when?	*kada?*
where?	*gdje?*
from where?	*odakle?*
do you know?	*znate li?*
I don't know	*ne znam*
I don't understand	*ne razumijem*
good	*dobrar/dobra/dobro* (m/f/n)

NUMBERS

one	*jedan*
two	*dva*
three	*tri*
four	*četiri*
five	*pet*
six	*šest*
seven	*sedam*
eight	*osam*
nine	*devet*
ten	*deset*
eleven	*jedanaest*
twelve	*dvanaest*
twenty	*dvadeset*
thirty-one	*trideset i jedan*
one hundred	*stotina*
one thousand	*hiljada*

FOOD AND DRINK

baked	*pečeno*
bean	*grah*
beef	*govedina/junetina*
beer	*pivo*
boiled	*kuhano*
bon appetit	*prijatno*
brandy	*loza*
bread	*hljeb/kruh*
breakfast	*doručak*
cabbage	*kupus/zelja*
cake	*kolač/torta*
cheese	*sir*
chicken	*piletina*
chips, French fries	*pomfrit*
coffee	*kafa/kahva*
cucumber	*krastavac*
dinner	*večera*
drink (noun)	*piće*
drink (verb)	*piti*
eggs	*jaja*
fish	*riba*
fried	*prženo*
fruit	*voće*
grilled	*sa roštilja*
homemade	*domaće*
juice	*đus/sok*
lamb	*jagnjetina/janjetina*
lemon	*limun*
lunch	*ručak*
meat	*meso*
milk	*mlijeko*
onion	*luk*
orange	*naranča/narandža*
pasta	*tjestinina*
peaches	*breskve*
pears	*kruške*
plums	*šljive*
pork	*svinjetina*
potato	*krompir*
restaurant	*restoran*
rice	*riža*
salt	*so*
soup	*supa*
spirit	*rakija*
sugar	*šećer*
tea	*čaj*
to eat	*jesti*
tomato	*paradajz*
veal	*teletina*
vegetables	*povrće*
water	*voda*
wine	*vino*

For a description of some local dishes, see pages 79–81.

SHOPPING

bank *banka*
bookshop *knjižara*
chemist *apoteka*
market *tržnica*
money *pare/novac*
postcard *razglednica*
post office *pošta*
shop *prodavaonica/trgovina*
toilet paper *toalet papir*

GETTING AROUND

ahead/behind *naprijed/iza*
departure/arrival *polazak/dolazak/*
bus *autobus*
bus station *autobusna stanica*
car/taxi *auto/taxi*
east/west *istok/zapad*
entrance/exit *ulaz/izlaz*
here/there *ovdje/tamo*
hill/mountain *brdo/planina*
left/right *lijevo/desno*
near/far *blizu/daleko*
north/south *sjever/jug*
open/closed *otvoreno/zatvoreno*
petrol *benzin*
petrol station *benzinska pumpa*
plane/airport *avion/aerodrom*
road/bridge *cesta/most*
straight on *pravo*
train *voz*
train station *željeznička stanica*
under/over *ispod/iznad*
up/down *gore/dole*
village/town *selo/grad*
waterfall *vodopad*

TIME

hour/minute *sat/minuta*
week/day *sedmica/dan*
year/month *godina/mjesec*
now *sada*
soon *uskoro*
today/tomorrow *danas/sutra*
yesterday *jučer*
morning *jutro*
afternoon *poslijepodne*
evening/night *večer/noć*
Monday *ponedeljak*
Tuesday *utorak*
Wednesday *srijeda*
Thursday *četvrtak*
Friday *petak*
Saturday *subota*
Sunday *nedelja*
spring *proljeće*
summer *ljeto*
autumn *jesen*
winter *zima*

OTHER USEFUL WORDS

a little *malo*
a lot *puno*
after *poslije*
bathroom *kupatilo*
bed *krevet*
before *prije*
buildings *zgrade*
child *dijete*
church *crkva*
cold *hladno*
currency *valuta*
dry *suho*
embassy *ambasada*
enough *dosta*
film *film*
hospital *bolnica*
hot/warm *vruće/toplo*
hotel *hotel*
house *kuća*
hut *koliba*
key *ključ*
lake *jezero*
large *veliko*
lorry *kamion*
mosque *džamija*
never *nikad*
night *noć*
nightclub *diskoteka*

nothing	*ništa*	small	*malo*
police	*policija*	street	*ulica*
rain	*kiša*	to swim	*plivati*
river	*rijeka*	tourist office	*turistički ured*
room	*soba*	you	*Vi/ti*
sea	*more*		

HEALTH WORDS AND PHRASES

dentist	*zubar*
doctor	*doktor*
fever	*groznica*
ill	*bolestan*
to hurt	*boljeti*
I need a doctor	*Trebam doktora*
Please call an ambulance	*Molim Vas, pozovite hitnu pomoć*
I'm feeling dizzy	*Vrti mi se*
I ate something bad	*Pojeo (m)/Pojela (f) sam nešto loše*
I don't feel well	*Ne osjećam se dobro*
I have a headache	*Boli me glava*
My stomach hurts	*Boli me želudac*
I am allergic to penicillin	*Alergičan (m)/Alergična (f) sam na pencilin*
Where is the pharmacy	*Gdje je apoteka*
I forgot my prescription	*Zaboravio (m)/Zaboravila (f) sam svoj recept*

Appendix 2

FURTHER INFORMATION

BOOKS

History/politics

Bringa, Tone *Being Muslim the Bosnian Way: Identity and Community in a Central Bosnian Village* Princeton University Press 1995

Glenny, Misha *The Balkans 1804–1999: Nationalism, War and the Great Powers* Granta Books, 2000 (2nd ed)

Gutman, Roy *Witness to Genocide* Element Books, 1993

Holbrook, Richard *To End a War* Modern Library, 1999

Lovrenović, Ivan *Bosnia: A Cultural History* Saqi Books, 2001

Maas, Peter *Love Thy Neighbour* Papermac, 1996

Malcolm, Noel *Bosnia: A Short History* New York University Press, 1994

Ramet, Sabrina P *Balkan Babel: The Disintegration of Yugoslavia from the Death of Tito to the Fall of Milosević* Westview Press, 2002

Sacco, Joe *Safe Area Goražde: The War in Eastern Bosnia, 1992–1995*, Fantagraphics Books, 2001

Simms, Brendon *Unfinest Hour: Britain and the Destruction of Bosnia* Penguin, 2003

Literature from Bosnia and Herzegovina *(published in English)*

Andrić, Ivo *Bridge over the Drina: Travnik Chronicles* (sometimes referred to as the 'Bosnian Chronicle') Harvill Press, 1995, Travnik Chronicles

Hemon, Alexander *Question of Bruno* Picador, 2001

Hemon, Alexander *Nowhere Man* Picador, 2003

Filipović, Zlata *Zlata's Diary* Penguin, *1993*

Jergović, Miljenko *Sarajevo Marlboro* Archipelago Books, 2004

Selimović, Meša *Death and the Dervish* Northwestern University Press, 1996

Other Bradt guides for nearby destinations:

Abraham, Rudolf and Evans, Thammy, *Croatia: Istria* (2nd edition) Bradt Travel Guides, 2017

Evans, Thammy *Macedonia* (5th edition) Bradt Travel Guides, 2015

Gloyer, Gillian *Albania* (5th edition) Bradt Travel Guides, 2015

Kay, Annie *Bulgaria* (2nd edition) Bradt Travel Guides, 2015

Letcher, Piers and Abraham, Rudolf *Croatia* (6th edition) Bradt Travel Guides, 2016

Mitchell, Laurence *Serbia* (5th edition) Bradt Travel Guides, 2017

Rellie, Annalisa *Montenegro* (5th edition) Bradt Travel Guides, 2015

Warrander, Gail and Knaus, Verena *Kosovo* (3rd edition) Bradt Travel Guides, 2017

WEBSITES The web is, perhaps needless to say, ubiquitous today in Bosnia and Herzegovina. Wi-Fi is cheap and affordable, and like everywhere else, social media is extremely popular.

Most of the younger generation has a smartphone. However, in terms of finding reliable websites and accurate information on the internet, it becomes more noticeable that the way the internet is used in BiH is different from Western Europe. Most sites are, logically, in the local language. There are quite a few good and helpful websites in English that can be used for tourist or general information. Some of them simply offer a different angle as to what is going on in the country. When checking these sites you'll find some better than others, but nonetheless they all have a value to those looking to get to know Bosnia and Herzegovina a little bit better. Increasingly, people, companies and organizations in BiH are using Facebook as a platform for their service or product instead of a website. If you can't find a website for something, do give Facebook a try before giving up.

Tourism

W **banjaluka-tourism.com** Comprehensive website of the tourism association of Banja Luka. Has up-to-date schedules for cultural events and exhibitions as well as what to do and where.
W **bhtourism.ba** The official tourism website of the country. Its content is good but offers more general information rather than concrete data. It's certainly amongst the best tourism sites coming out of BiH.
W **city.ba** Current news on cultural events in Sarajevo.
W **discoverbosnia.com** A good guide to discovering some of the hidden jewels of Bosnia's tourism destinations.
W **exploringbh.com** Good tourism site covering the whole of the country, with some quirky tour suggestions.
W **greenvisions.ba** BiH's leading ecotourism group. This site offers detailed information on Bosnia and Herzegovina, tourism, culture and nature in English and French.
W **hercegovina.ba** A site created by the Herzegovina Neretva Canton Tourism Association, representing only the Federation area of this Herzegovina canton.
W **sarajevo-tourism.com** Tourism Association of Sarajevo Canton; a good site for general tourist information.
W **sarajevo.ba** A site about the city of Sarajevo: what there is to see and what's happening in the fastest-changing city in Europe.
W **sarajevo.travel** A very detailed website covering Sarajevo's sights along with entertainment and tourist offers. Has a complete monthly calendar of events.
W **thebosniaguy.com** The author's blog on various subjects regarding Bosnia and Herzegovina and his experiences in the Balkans.
W **viadinarica.com** A website dedicated to mountain and adventure tourism that features hiking and biking trails, and all the service provisions needed for a Dinaric Alps outdoor adventure. Great map content!
W **visitmycountry.net/bosnia_herzegovina** One of the most comprehensive websites on tourism information for BiH.

Government

W **sarajevo.usembassy.gov** The American Embassy in BiH is very active. The site will give US citizens all the information they need while travelling as an American here.
W **britishcouncil.org/bih.htm** The British Council supports many cultural and educational activities. They are very up-to-date on the culture scene in BiH.
W **fzs.ba** The Federal Bureau of Statistics may post statistics but don't count on all of them being correct. Accurate information, as I found out when writing this book, is very difficult to come by.
W **komorabih.ba** Website of the Chambers of Foreign Commerce. The information provided is good and has many links to other informative websites in the country.

W ohr.int The Office of the High Representative in BiH is the international governing body in the country. There are many updates on the economy, human rights, reform, and general information about who is who and what's going on in Bosnia and Herzegovina.

General

W balkaninsight.com A reliable site in English for news, culture and blogs for BiH and the wider Balkan region

W balkanvibe.com A travel site for the Western Balkans, including BiH. Provides links to a variety of tour operators.

W balkanist.net A culturally focused site that provides a lot of fascinating alternative cultural information.

W bhmac.org Official site of the Mine Action Centre. It's not to scare you; it's meant to inform you.

W bosnia.org.uk The Bosnian Institute site that is a tremendous source of inside information and links to many local sites. **W ekoakcija.com** News about environmental issues and initiatives in Bosnia and Herzegovina.

W rtvfbih.ba Official site of Bosnia and Herzegovina national television.

W sarajevo-airport.ba Flight schedules and other miscellaneous information about coming and going to Sarajevo are available on this site.

W unsa.ba The University of Sarajevo gives a little insight into what programmes are available, what people are learning and what students in this part of the world are all about.

NOTES

Index

Entries in **bold** indicate main entries; those in *italics* indicate maps. BiH refers to Bosnia and Herzegovina.

INDEX OF ADVERTISERS